MUSEU

COM
MUN
ISM

MUSEUMS OF COMMUNISM

NEW MEMORY SITES IN CENTRAL AND EASTERN EUROPE

EDITED BY STEPHEN M. NORRIS

INDIANA UNIVERSITY PRESS

This book is a publication of

Indiana University Press
Office of Scholarly Publishing
Herman B Wells Library 350
1320 East 10th Street
Bloomington, Indiana 47405 USA

iupress.indiana.edu

© 2020 by Indiana University Press

All rights reserved

No part of this book may be reproduced or utilized in any form or by any means, electronic or mechanical, including photocopying and recording, or by any information storage and retrieval system, without permission in writing from the publisher. The paper used in this publication meets the minimum requirements of the American National Standard for Information Sciences—Permanence of Paper for Printed Library Materials, ANSI Z39.48–1992.

Manufactured in the United States of America

Cataloging information is available from the Library of Congress.

ISBN 978-0-253-05030-4 (hardback)
ISBN 978-0-253-05032-8 (paperback)
ISBN 978-0-253-05031-1 (web PDF)

1 2 3 4 5 25 24 23 22 21 20

CONTENTS

From Communist Museums to Museums
of Communism: An Introduction / *Stephen M. Norris*   1

   EXHIBIT A: *Hall of Genocide, Occupation, and Terror*   18

1. Sovereign Pain: Liberation and Suffering in the
   Museum of Occupations and Freedom Fights in
   Lithuania / *Neringa Klumbytė*   22
2. Visualizing Revisionism: Europeanized Anticommunism
   at the House of Terror Museum in Budapest /
   Máté Zombory   46
3. Inside L'viv's Lonsky Prison: Capturing Ukrainian
   Memory after Communism / *Stephen M. Norris*   78
4. Remembering the Gulag in Post-Soviet Kazakhstan /
   Steven A. Barnes   106
5. Riga's Cheka House: From a Soviet Place of Terror to a
   Latvian Site of Remembrance? / *Katja Wezel*   136

   EXHIBIT B: *Hall of National Tragedies*   156

6. Sensing the Uprising: The Warsaw Uprising Museum
   and the Emotions of the Past / *Stephen M. Norris*   162
7. Enforcing National Memory, Remembering Famine's
   Victims: The National Museum "Holodomor Victims
   Memorial" / *Daria Mattingly*   188

   EXHIBIT C: *Hall of Everyday Life*   214

8. The Czech Museum of Communism: What National
   Narrative for the Past? / *Muriel Blaive*   218
9. Stasiland or Spreewald Pickles? The Battle over the GDR
   in Berlin's DDR Museum / *Stephen M. Norris*   244

EXHIBIT D: *Hall of Russian Memory*   270

10. Commemorating and Forgetting Soviet Repression: Moscow's State Museum of GULAG History / *Jeffrey Hardy*   274

11. The Butovskii Shooting Range: History of an Unfinished Museum / *Julie Fedor and Tomas Sniegon*   304

12. The Museum of Soviet Arcade Games: Nostalgia for a Socialist Childhood / *Roman Abramov*   344

EXHIBIT E: *Rotating Exhibits*   370

13. A Museum of a Museum? Fused and Parallel Historical Narratives in the Joseph Stalin State Museum / *Katrine Bendtsen Gotfredsen*   374

14. Between Occupations and Freedoms: Memory, Narrative, and Practice at Vabamu in Tallinn, Estonia / *A. Lorraine Weekes*   400

Index   425

MUSEUMS OF
COMMUNISM

From Communist Museums to Museums of Communism

An Introduction

STEPHEN M. NORRIS

In his 1986 novel, *The Suitcase*, Sergei Dovlatov opens with a description of his emigration from the Soviet Union. Although the state allotted him three suitcases to pack his belongings, Dovlatov needed only one. Upon arrival in the United States, he places his suitcase inside his closet. It sits for four years before his son rediscovers it. Dovlatov takes it out, opens it, and gazes at the eight items he brought with him. He shuts the suitcase, notes that it contained "all I had acquired in thirty-six years." The contents represented "my lost, precious, only life."[1] At that moment, however, Dovlatov writes, "memories engulfed me." "They must have been hidden in the folds of those pathetic rags," he notes. The rest of his novel consists of how he acquired the eight objects and how they act as mnemonic devices to the past. Through his socks, boots, suit, belt, shirt, winter hat, and gloves, Dovlatov remembers his former life in the country he has left. In the end, ruminating on his own revived memories and the items that inspired them, he concludes, "there's a reason that every book, even one that isn't very serious, is shaped like a suitcase."[2]

The Suitcase serves as a useful metaphor to open the present book. In the pages that follow, you will travel and take virtual tours of fourteen museums and memorial sites that dot the central and eastern European landscape. Each site of memory attempts to wrestle with the communist era and, in doing so, offer visitors a vivid chance to understand it and to draw lessons from it. From Warsaw to Moscow, Tallinn to Gori, Kyiv to L'viv, museums of communism contain objects that attempt to remember the communist era. Visiting them—in this case virtually—is a visit into the important ways postcommunist states have fashioned meaning out of the recent past. Much like Dovlatov's description, the new museums that seek to interpret the communist era contain items that had been stored away in closets and attics. The objects form the collections of the new museums in hopes of awakening old memories.

Before we travel to present-day places and view them, however, let's take another journey and travel back to the Moscow of the not-too-distant past. Like just about all travelers, we would visit a museum or two. A visit to the Soviet capital before 1991 would allow us to visit still-popular sites such as the Kremlin and the Tretyakov Gallery. We might also see two now-defunct museums. Between 1924 and 1991, however, the Central Lenin Museum and the Museum of the Revolution acted as vital historical-memory-propaganda centers, narrating the history of the world's first socialist state and its leader.

We might start with a trip to the Central Lenin Museum, founded in May 1924 just after the leader's death and located adjacent to the State History Museum on Red Square (see fig. 0.1). Inside, we could walk through its halls and exhibit spaces to learn about Lenin's life, his habits, his role in bringing about revolution, his work to build the Soviet state, and the model he provides to everyone. The Lenin Museum represented what we might now call a "communist museum" at its finest (or its worst, depending on your view of these things). It was a didactic site designed with one specific narrative in mind: Lenin's world-historical significance. A trip to the Central Lenin Museum would bring you face-to-face with all sorts of Leniniana. Lenin's clothes. His walking stick. Drafts of his important writings. His Party card, placed lovingly on red velvet. A replica of his Kremlin desk in Room 13, complete with signage stating, "The furniture is unpretentious" and his working day "began very early and lasted late into the night. Here, in his study, he worked on plans for socialist construction and directed the country's defense efforts during the Civil War and foreign intervention."[3]

One of the museum's central tasks, as a guidebook stated, was "to bring him close to us."[4] A second purpose that percolated throughout its halls was, of course, to demonstrate how "no other man in history has had so much influence on the life of entire nations and on the course of events throughout the world." "Millions of people," the guidebook stated, "pronounce his name with love and reverence."[5] Lenin lived, lives, will live, the Central Lenin Museum loudly declared, echoing Mayakovsky's famous dictum.[6] His life and work, the museum made clear, is inextricably linked to the building of the world's first socialist state; thus, the museum becomes both a hagiographical showcase of the first leader and a beacon announcing the importance of the Soviet Union he founded. By the late 1980s, the museum boasted that more than 55 million people from more than one hundred countries had absorbed its contents. After our visit, we would no doubt be inspired to stroll over and see the embalmed remains of the socialist saint. We might also pick up a guidebook or some postcards and pack them in our suitcase for the return home.

The Museum is not only for excursions. It also arranges classes in history and scientific communism for high-school students. Nine-year-olds come here on Lenin's birthday to enroll in the USSR Young Pioneer Organisation named after him.

Figure 00.01 A virtual trip to a defunct museum. From a Soviet-Era guidebook to the Central Lenin Museum. From *The Central Lenin Museum: A Guide* (Moscow: Raduga, 1986)

The museum mapped out Lenin's impact in stark, clear, visual terms. The back of one guidebook (for sale in the museum store for 1 ruble, 30 kopeks, in 1986) featured a map of "Lenin Memorial Places," broken down into places where the great man lived, worked, or visited as well as other V. I. Lenin state museums, memorial houses, and apartments. Dots mapped out the former category in locations across the continent; the state museums, however, existed only inside the Iron Curtain (with one exception: Paris). If the building and the artifacts it showed off helped to narrate the sort of didactic history that defined communist museums, the map told a related story: this approach to museology (and, more broadly, to history) was the only one permissible in the Soviet empire and only on display in this geographical space.

The Central Lenin Museum formed part of the broader Lenin cult, which, as Nina Tumarkin has noted, helped to make Lenin "awesome and yet accessible, available to anyone who wished to brave the long queues that inevitably formed before the mausoleum." Lenin thus became "a modern mixture of saint, tsar, and revolutionary martyr."[7] In the first edition of her book (1983), Tumarkin could talk about the "enduring success of the Lenin cult as a stabilizing and legitimizing force in Soviet political life."[8] The Party engaged in strenuous efforts to propagate Lenin and Leninism as the basis for all understanding of the Soviet experience after 1924, an approach reflected quite clearly in the museum. Ultimately the cult and a visit to the museum became ritual, mostly aimed at the young. In 1983 Tumarkin wrote that "few people come simply to visit Lenin museums except in organized groups on guided tours. Packs of schoolchildren, for example, trot through the Central Lenin Museum in Moscow, stopping to listen to the guide intone tired praises of young Ulianov's excellent study habits, as they all gaze at a reproduction of the honor-roll certificate from the Simbirsk gimnazium with Ulianov's name on it."[9]

Our second museum stop in our time-travel trip takes us to the Museum of Revolution. Located in the former English Club a short walk up Gorky Street (now Tverskaya once more) from the Lenin Museum and also founded in May 1924, the Museum of Revolution featured the same sort of approach as its brother building down the street.[10] The museum, as a 1974 *Pravda* article celebrating its half-century anniversary declared, inspired a "generation of fighters" willing to defend communism.[11] A 1929 book on the museum explicitly noted that "the exhibits in our museum are not academic, but political"; it was not a space dedicated to exploring the history of revolutionary activities in Russia, from Pugachev to the Decembrists to 1905. Instead, it was a site where "we consider our past in relation to the present, where we look for the roots of our contemporary era in the past and hand down the lessons from the past to the present for our future fight for world revolution."[12] Its exhibits showcased the heroic struggle to bring about the socialist motherland, the preeminent role of the Bolshevik Party, and the significance of the Great October Revolution (after 1945, the Great Patriotic War was added to the displays).

Taken together, and including all their sister sites elsewhere in the communist world, the Lenin Museum and Museum of Revolution established hegemonic versions of "communist museums." They formed part of what might be best termed the "Soviet memory project" that in turn created a "settled past"; that is, a state-led campaign to fashion the "right" historical line, bringing it into line with Marxist-Leninist thought, and using the past to inspire future generations. The two museums acted as foundational sites for the foundation myth of Soviet history, which stressed Lenin's political authority and the historic significance of the October Revolution.¹³ Anatoly Khazanov has noted that Soviet history museums functioned mostly to propagandize and "had to present history in a way that would legitimate communist rule and reinforce its authority."¹⁴ Communist museums had to create the historical canon to create ideological stability; the "most privileged position" in this effort was occupied by "museums directly connected to the Central Committee of the Communist Party."¹⁵

These communist museums served the traditional function of museums as "storehouses of memory." In this sense, to return to Dovlatov's suitcase, museums put on display objects that acted as mnemonic devices. As Susan Crane has described it, a museum, "like an archive, holds the material manifestations of cultural and scientific production as records," as well as the "articulated memories removed from the mental world and literally placed in the physical world." Museums thus function as storehouses, as the "repository of memory, [the] location of the collections that form the basis of cultural or national identity, of scientific knowledge and aesthetic value."¹⁶ Modern museums are sites where subjectivities and objectivities collide, providing meeting space between the personal and public, individual and institutional, subjective and objective, and create new, "highly energized relationships between museums and memory."¹⁷ Museums "deliberately forge memories in physical form to prevent the natural erosion of memory, both personal and collective."¹⁸

Communist museums such as the Central Lenin Museum and the Museum of Revolution certainly functioned as storehouses of memory in this broad context; they also served as central mediating sites where the Party could work on building new Soviet subjects and Soviet subjectivities. Becoming closer to Lenin and closer to revolutionary history as a means of learning the right "lessons" for present-day battles required you to work on your "self" in an effort to transform yourself into the New Soviet Person the state hoped to create.¹⁹ In this aim, too, the communist museum grew from nineteenth-century roots. As Katia Dianina has noted, Moscow's State History Museum, which opened in 1872, operated as a way to "lay a foundation for national consciousness."²⁰ Visitors to the museum could learn about Russian imperial civilization as the apex of all the civilizations that had been built throughout time in the Eurasian landscape (the Soviet-era version of the State History Museum made the same claim). Communist museums of history built on this preexisting structure (literally): the Central Lenin Museum occupied the building next door.

These functions established a precedent adopted elsewhere: Chang-tai Hung has illustrated how the Museum of the Chinese Revolution explicitly borrowed from the Soviet model.²¹ So too did the Museum für Deutsche Geschichte (MfDG) in Berlin. In the words of H. Glenn Penny III, the MfDG "provided a power base for Marxist-Leninist historians, acted as a central organ for history in the GDR, and set the tone for both academic research and popular education concerning German history."[22] Its permanent exhibition "portrayed the history of the Germans as an ongoing struggle between progressive forces—workers, revolutionaries, the common people—against the forces of reaction—capitalists, imperialists, fascists."[23] The humanistic traditions of German culture, the museum narrated, found their highest expression in the GDR, which also (naturally) represented the triumph of this struggle.

Similar claims could be made of just about every communist museum. Yet Penny notes another important issue with the MfDG that can also be applied to Moscow's museums: their objects, exhibits, and displays changed over time, keeping up with the changing political conditions.[24] Adam Jolles has characterized the communist-era museum through its nickname: "talking museums [*samogovoriashchie muzei*]," which reflected their didactic, preachy, exhibition style meant to "speak" to everyone who visited and to "tell" them about the narrative offered inside.[25] The talking points, however, shifted over the history of the Soviet experiment. A 1939 guidebook to the Lenin Museum, for example, contains no mention of Trotsky or even older Bolsheviks;[26] instead, the museum and its publications played up the role of Stalin as Lenin's "most trusted adviser" and "logical" heir. After Nikita Khrushchev denounced Stalin's cult of personality in his 1956 "Secret Speech," museum displays and museum guidebooks had to change again. Communist museums, it would be clear on our time travels, just like communist-era history lessons in general, were not reliable sources of information about the past.

The collapse of the Soviet system made the communist museum obsolete. The events of 1989 to 1991 in part resulted from Mikhail Gorbachev's decisions to look back more critically at the foundational events of the Soviet Union, including the Lenin cult and the October Revolution.[27] As more and more historians, journalists, and citizens examined the past, the mythic foundations on which the Soviet Union rested began to crumble. The Central Lenin Museum closed in 1992. The Museum of the Revolution went through a renovation and renamed itself the State Central Museum of Contemporary History.

The abandoned Lenin Museum and rebranded history museum no longer serve as beacons to the rest of the world, nor do they offer a dominant paradigm to be copied elsewhere. No one gets close to Lenin in order to build a new self these days. Instead, new, independent nation-states have formed out of former Soviet Republics and Warsaw Pact member states. Each of these new nations has tried to create historical narratives and build new museums and new memorial sites dedicated to "their" pasts.[28] This museum-building boom has taken place during a worldwide memory boom. Europe in particular, Sharon Macdonald has recently written, has "become a memoryland," a place "obsessed with the disappearance of collective memory and its preservation," so much so that we might be able to speak of a "European memory complex."[29] Macdonald sees a general pattern that encompasses all the memorylands of Europe, even while acknowledging regional and national variations. In her work, she pays significant attention to the ways that the past is being told, felt (through affect, materiality, embodiment, place), sold (commodification), and musealized and reviews transcultural and cosmopolitan forms of memory.

We should understand the creation of new museums in central and eastern Europe as part of the general trends Macdonald discusses, but we should also be attuned to the ways that what we now can call "museums of communism"—that is, museums that seek to narrate the communist pasts—overturn the dominant narratives offered in the Lenin Museum and Museum of Revolution even though they mostly retain their didactic interpretations and efforts to mold memories. These new museums of communism, fourteen of which you can tour in subsequent chapters, do not turn to the artifacts and paraphernalia housed in communist museums for their historical narratives; instead, they mostly turn to the memories, stories, and viewpoints that were whispered or talked about quietly over kitchen tables throughout the former communist world. In a sense, these new museums are important moments in and monuments to the politics of transition away from communism. The basis of the museums of communism, in short, is the history left out of the communist museums. To get a sense for how this process of remembrance informed the new museums of communism, let's recall Dovlatov's suitcase once more.

The suitcase did not contain just tangible items, as Dovlatov recounts, it contained long-suppressed and long-forgotten memories. Once opened, Dovlatov could touch his former belongings and reclaim his former life. The museums of communism might be understood similarly: they are larger versions of the suitcase, opening up the storehouses of memories that had been kept in the back of the closet for decades. We can find similar suitcases and guides to interpreting them in two other novels. Our first docent is Slavenka Drakulić and her novel, *A Guided Tour through the Museum of Communism*. Drakulić treats the experience of communism itself as a museum. She starts by stating that many Europeans tend to think that the stories from the recent past are not true. She assures us "it all really happened." She goes on: "I came to the conclusion that we did not have 'too much history,' as it is often said about this part of the world. Rather, we had too much memory and too many myths. And, in my life experience, this is a dangerous combination that has often resulted in ideology and manipulation leading to conflict and terrible suffering.[30]

Her "guided tour" takes the form of fables, with stops in eight countries. It begins in Prague's Museum of Communism and with a mouse that walks through it. The mouse tells us that communism should be remembered, but that it "is not so much about exhibits, about *seeing*. It is about how one lived in those times, or more to the point, how one survived them."[31] At the same time, the mouse warns us against memories of communism that claim "we were all victims," for "most of us complied in order not just to survive . . . but just to live better," even if few "really collaborated."[32] The mouse wants a museum of ugly things, banal things, shortages, shades of gray, a place that reveals what you cannot see: "fear, complicity, and the hypocrisy of life under communism."[33]

Our second guide to the new museums of communism is Oksana Zabuzhko. In her sprawling, 750-page historical novel, *The Museum of Abandoned Secrets*, Zabuzhko suggests, like Drakulić, that the basis for postcommunist memory resides in pent-up frustrations and hidden secrets. The plot centers on one woman's chance encounter with a photograph of Ukrainian insurgents during World War II, a group that includes her grandfather, and her subsequent explorations into Ukrainian memory and history across the violent century (she finds the photograph in a suitcase). In Ukraine, these hidden memories mostly concern the war and its lingering traumas. Children fought about the war's meanings in playgrounds, but, as Zabuzhko's narrator recollects, "for our parents, the war was still alive, not something fixed in books, and the families' accumulated memories diverged way too far from what we were supposed to memorize, resulting in a nearly chemical incompatibility, words and memories bubbling and bursting, finally depositing the textbook in the clear and despised category of 'Bullshit!'"[34]

It's significant that both novelists use museums as their central metaphors even though only the mouse fable actually takes place in one. It's equally significant that both authors see postcommunist narratives as stemming from grievances nurtured under communism. In both novels, the museum is a mental construct and it by and large refers to the sort of communist museums cited earlier; places that, as Zabuzhko's narrator recounts, were often thought of as "bullshit." In place of communist museums, family stories, fables, personal artifacts, and accounts of survival served as "true" sources about the past. These suitcases full of memories—as Zabuzhko describes them—often took the form of "victim stories" or "personal myths"—as Drakulić calls them. When the Soviet state collapsed and, with it, the versions of history packaged in its museums, these suitcases of fables served as the basis for the new museums of communism.[35]

Drakulić correctly identified the dominant tendency that has characterized the new museums. As we will see in subsequent chapters, many museums of communism narrate the recent past through the prism of victimhood, a stance that suggests all residents of a new nation suffered at the hands of the Soviets (mostly Russians). The past on display in these new museums of communism, in other words, is still a foreign country, to borrow Tony Judt's memorable phrase.[36]

Many of the museums you will tour in this volume vie for the unofficial position of "most victimized nation of the twentieth century," narrating their wartime and Soviet pasts through the lens of suffering and experiences the rest of the world has ignored. In taking this stance, the new museums do not include much space for fear, for issues of complicity, and for the hypocrisy of life under communism (as Drakulić called for).

Our starting point for evaluating the museums of communism will be the communist museums cited at the outset of this introduction: clearly the Central Lenin Museum and Museum of the Revolution did not allow for exhibits on any "shades of gray" that Drakulić referred to. The ways that Soviet-era museums ignored the experiences of millions of its citizens, particularly the harm done to them under Stalinism, serves as the foundational impetus for many of the museums to be examined herein. Because of this, a "double victimization" narrative dominates many of them. The notion that Stalinist crimes have not been studied or understood as much as Nazi ones pervades the region (and there's some justification in thinking so). The politicization of this view, however, particularly by far-right groups or political parties such as Poland's Law and Justice Party, has led to campaigns that advocate a view that Nazi crimes and Stalinist crimes are equal. The logical conclusion to this thinking is that nations such as Lithuania, Latvia, Estonia, and Poland suffered through two genocides and that ethnic Lithuanians, Latvians, Estonians, and Poles therefore suffered more than Jews. An even more dangerous conclusion to this line of remembrance holds that the peoples who suffered doubly can be seen only as victims, not victimizers. Antony Polonsky has termed this thinking "the suffering Olympics."[37] Many of the memory games in this competition have come in the form of museums, especially the museums of occupations in the Baltic republics. The point of the suffering narrative on display in these museums is simple yet misleading: heroes cannot also be villains, victims cannot be victimizers.

The new museums of communism therefore frequently function as sites to shift attention away from more problematic issues of collaboration and war crimes committed by the very groups identified as victims. In several of the cases explored in our chapters, this sidestepping of guilt and atonement comes at the behest of new institutes of national history and memory, which are themselves creations of new political regimes working to build usable pasts. Throughout the former communist world, museums and the histories they enshrine are meant to cultivate a sense of patriotism among young people. Focusing on victimizers or crimes of the past tends to be viewed by the museum officials and officials working in the institutes of memory (as well as politicians) as histories that cannot be usable for a new nation to build new citizens. In Poland, to take an important example, many young people have embraced antiestablishment, xenophobic, and

Eurosceptic discourses to the extent that one scholar believes Poland has a particular problem with "youth nationalism."[38] The major institution responsible for this politicization is the Institute of National Remembrance (IPN).[39] It is, as Tom Junes describes, "the largest historical research institute in the country, has a wide network of publishing houses, incorporates archives, it has a prosecutor's branch to investigate historical crimes against the nation, has around two thousand employees, and its budget eclipses that of all the other historical research institutes combined." The IPN, he concludes, is "unrivalled not only in Poland, but in the region."[40]

The IPN, which was established in 1998, became more politicized under the Law and Justice Party, for the leaders changed its legal role and selected historians to run the IPN who advocated Law and Justice's vision of the past. Junes describes this vision as one that "aims to educate the country's youth in a 'correct and patriotic' fashion, which includes emphasizing the victimization of the Polish nation and the glorification of new 'heroes'—such as the so-called 'damned soldiers' who fought the communist regime in a guerilla war immediately after the Second World War but whose actions also include anti-Semitic excesses and murderous crimes against other ethnic groups."[41] The IPN's activities have also fueled a phenomenon of "consuming patriotism, which has substituted [for] historical consciousness among the younger generation." Its operations have led the scholar Dariusz Stola to question whether it's really an institute of remembrance or an Orwellian ministry of memory.[42]

We could say similar things about similar institutes in other postcommunist states. Ukraine's Institute of National Memory, as Jared McBride has noted, has overseen a whitewashing of nationalist activities during World War II. Led by Volodymyr Viatrovych from 2014 to 2019, the institute engaged in "memory manipulation."[43] The problem is that these institutes, their leaders, their historians, and their political patrons all see their work as "real history," as "patriotic," and as righting wrongs inflicted under communism.[44] These conflicts over history and memory mean that the museums tasked with becoming a storehouse of the memories of grievances under communism become the front lines in the battles over understanding the recent past: enshrining national myths or suppressed memories as "history" ensures a certain degree of permanence to the version of history narrated inside a museum's halls and exhibit spaces.[45]

Communist regimes, a recent scholarly collection reminds us, "effectively whitewashed their own people's anti-Semitism and collaboration with the Nazis." At the same time, local populations in eastern and central Europe experienced imprisonment, exile, and violence at the hands of communist regimes, meaning that "memories of the long decades of Communist rule overshadow the shorter and more distant time of German domination."[46] As a result, Igor Torbakov has written, the past two decades "have witnessed an escalation of memory wars in which Russia has largely found itself on the defensive, its official historical narrative being vigorously assaulted by a number of the newly independent ex-Soviet states."[47] Torbakov provides two powerful examples of this sentiment: occupation museums and institutes of national memory, citing Latvia's, Estonia's, and Georgia's museums and Polish and Ukrainian institutes. Torbakov contextualizes these sites within the searches for usable pasts and new national identities after 1989–91, but he is also critical of the nationalization of history these memory sites have codified.

The memory landscape of postcommunist central and eastern Europe is defensive, argumentative, and still in flux. It has been carved out of bitter memories from living under communism, heroic myths and memories of resistance, and the settling of historical scores. To a certain extent, the new museums of communism see their work as necessary, an attempt to come out from under the shadows cast by the Soviet version of history and to gain recognition for horrific events that had long been ignored. In an extensive study of postsocialist memory, Alexander Etkind, Uilleam Blacker, and Julie Fedor analyze these divided memories, the postcolonial and postsocialist categories of these memories, and the battles over them.[48] Certain "knots" of memory in the region have remained untied: the revolutionary experience of 1917, the world wars, Soviet rule (both direct and indirect), and independence. The state of eastern European memory, they conclude, is "uneven, contested, invariably rich" and may be best conceptualized as "postsocialist, postcatastrophic," and, in some cases, "postcolonial."[49] They see eastern European memory as different from the western for two reasons: first, the central focus is not on the Holocaust and Nazis; and, second, the forms of memory are not set "in stone," in museums and memorials, but in memoirs, novels, films, and debates.[50] When museums and memorials do exist, they too are fluid and troubling, producing an overall "tortured and warped memory" (a conclusion Etkind has reached in his influential book, *Warped Mourning*).[51]

With our initial visit complete, let's turn to tours through the new museums of communism. This volume is arranged thematically: readers might best imagine their virtual tour as if they are walking through a series of exhibits. The first, permanent, exhibit space is taken up by spaces and objects that narrate stories of suffering, genocide, occupation, and terror. This part of our tour will take you to Vilnius, Budapest, L'viv, Kazakhstan, and Riga, where new museums seek to remember collective traumas. Our second exhibit space is a hall of national tragedies, where museums in Poland and Ukraine focus on a specific tragedy as the foundation for new nations. The Hall of Everyday Life, another permanent exhibit space, offers an alternative understanding to the communist period, one where Prague and Berlin will be our stops. This hall features private museums that focus on ordinary life, a museum strategy that many critics believe trivializes the communist past by evoking nostalgia. The fourth section takes us into the Hall of Russian Memory in order to see how Russians—so frequently cast as the victimizer in our other museums—have established new museums and memorials after 1991. As you will discover, Moscow's memory sites have their own versions of victimhood, heroes, and a nostalgic everyday. Finally, our last section takes us to the traveling exhibitions, here understood metaphorically through two case studies on the Stalin Museum in Georgia and the Occupation Museum in Tallinn, the second of which changed its name and narrative focus in 2017. The former site has had to wrestle with the competing legacies of Gori's most (in)famous son, becoming a "museum within a museum," while the latter's organizers have decided to change its focus away from trauma and victimhood to something else. This last hall reminds us that, much like the communist-era museums, postcommunist museums continue to evolve too. Taken together, the fourteen stops and five halls, like Dovlatov's suitcase, attempt to engulf the visitor with memories.

NOTES

1. Sergei Dovlatov, *The Suitcase*, translated by Antonia Bouis (Berkeley, CA: Counterpoint, 2011), 7.
2. Ibid., 129.
3. *Tsentral'nyi muzei V. I. Lenina: putevoditel'* (Moscow: Raduga, 1988), 96.
4. Ibid., 7.
5. Ibid.
6. Quoted in Nina Tumarkin, *Lenin Lives! The Lenin Cult in Soviet Russia* (Cambridge, MA: Harvard University Press, 1983), 236. The line was popularized in the Soviet Union even though Mayakovsky, in the longer version of the poem, warned people not to "traffic in Lenin."
7. Ibid., 196.
8. Ibid., 200.
9. Ibid., 266.
10. Its cousin in Leningrad, then Petrograd, was founded in 1919 in the Winter Palace itself before being moved to the Kseshenskaia mansion in 1955 and renamed the Museum of Political History. The same sort of historical/propagandistic approach defined it.
11. F. Krotov, "Zaveshchano pokoleniiami bortsov," *Pravda*, May 31, 1974, 3.
12. S. I. Mitskevich, "Piatiletie muzeia revoliuttsii soiuza SSR i blizhaishie perspektivy ego raboty," in *Muzei revoliuttsii Soiuza SSR* (Moscow, 1929), 6.
13. Frederick Corney has written the best account of a particular version of this project; namely, how the Bolsheviks established the storming of the Winter Palace in October 1917 as the defining moment of the Revolution. See his *Telling October:*

Memory and the Making of the Bolshevik Revolution (Ithaca, NY: Cornell University Press, 2004). For more on the Bolshevik use of history and memory, see Evgeny Dobrenko, *Stalinist Cinema and the Production of History: Museum of Revolution* (New Haven, CT: Yale University Press, 2008), and Thomas Sherlock, *Historical Narratives in the Soviet Union and Post-Soviet Russia: Destroying the Settled Past, Creating an Uncertain Future* (New York: Palgrave Macmillan, 2007). The term "settled past" comes from Sherlock.

14. Anatoly Khazanov, "Selecting the Past: The Politics of Memory in Moscow's History Museums," *City and Society* 12, no. 2 (2000): 37.

15. Ibid., 37–38.

16. Ibid., 4.

17. Ibid., 7.

18. Ibid., 9.

19. For an excellent overview and commentary of the Soviet subject and subjectivities debate, see Choi Chatterjee and Karen Petrone, "Models of Self and Subjectivity: The Soviet Case in Historical Perspective," *Slavic Review* 67, no. 4 (2008): 967–86.

20. Katia Dianina, "The Return of History: Museum, Heritage, and National Identity in Imperial Russia," *Journal of Eurasian Studies* 1, no. 2 (2010): 111–18.

21. Chang-Tai Hung, "The Red Line: Creating a Museum of the Chinese Revolution," *China Quarterly* 184 (December 2005): 914–33.

22. H. Glenn Penny III, "The Museum für Deutsche Geschichte and German National Identity," *Central European History* 28, no. 3 (1995): 347.

23. Ibid.

24. Museums changing with the political winds are not just a phenomenon within the communist world. For a US analog, one that traces Smithsonian exhibits during the Cold War and decolonization, see Claire Wintle, "Decolonizing the Smithsonian: Museums as Microcosm of Political Encounter," *American Historical Review* 121, no 5 (2016): 1492–520.

25. Adam Jolles, "Stalin's Talking Museums," *Oxford Art Journal* 28, no. 3 (2005): 430–55.

26. *Lenin: Compiled from Material in the Central Lenin Museum, Moscow* (Moscow: State Publishing House of Political Literature, 1939).

27. See, among others, Sherlock, *Historical Narratives*.

28. As Jared McBride has written, using the July 1943 Malyn massacre of Jews as a case study, funding a cogent narrative about contentious events is nearly impossible: as he counts, fifteen separate accounts of the massacre exist within four broad "discursive landscapes" (Soviet, Polish, Czech, and Ukrainian). See his "Contesting the Malyn Massacre: The Legacy of Inter-ethnic Violence and the Second World War in Eastern Europe," *Carl Beck Papers* 2405 (2016): 1–78.

29. Sharon Macdonald, *Memorylands: Heritage and Identity in Europe Today* (New York: Routledge, 2013), 1.

30. Slavenka Drakulić, *A Guided Tour through the Museum of Communism: Fables from a Mouse, a Parrot, a Bear, a Cat, a Mole, a Pig, a Dog, and a Raven* (New York: Penguin, 2011), xiii.

31. Ibid., 6.

32. Ibid., 7–8.

33. Ibid., 24–25.

34. Oksana Zabuzhko, *The Museum of Abandoned Secrets*, trans. Nina Shevchuk-Murray (Las Vegas: Amazon Crossing, 2012), 43.

35. Simona Mitroiu, writing about Romania after communism, refers to this as "recuperative memory" and delves into oral testimonies, autobiographies, fiction, and films as the basis for this postcommunist memory process ("Recuperative Memory in Romanian Post-Communist Society," *Nationalities Papers* 44, no. 5 [2016]: 751–71).

36. Tony Judt, "The Past Is Another Country: Myth and Memory in Postwar Europe," *Daedalus* 121, no. 4 (1992): 83–118. See also Zuzanna Bogumił, Joanna Wawrzyniak, Tim Buchen, Christian Ganzer, and Maria Senina, *The Enemy on Display: The Second World War in Eastern European Museums* (New York: Berghahn, 2015). The book analyzes three city museums in Saint Petersburg, Warsaw, and Dresden and how their war displays use the enemy to tighten community relationships. In his magnificent book *Postwar*, Judt expanded on his earlier essay and the notion that European memory tends to shift blame onto another country. In doing so, Judt becomes a useful guide to our fifteen museums and the historical interpretations offered in them. He reminds us that memory about the Holocaust, "the very definition and guarantee of the continent's restored humanity" (804), was not always there. Most in Europe after 1945 wanted to forget about the nastier aspects of the war (the so-called Vichy syndrome); Primo Levi's book about his experiences in the camps did not initially find a publisher, and then was published in small run. "There was nothing 'usable' about the Holocaust" (809), Judt astutely noted. Reading Judt's analysis is a useful reminder: it takes time to remember horrific pasts, as well as the work of committed historians, writers, artists, and government officials. The communist forgetting of the Holocaust created particular problems in that part of Europe and gave rise to the notion of "comparative victimhood." Judt dissects this idea succinctly and powerfully: "For Poles, it was difficult to survive under German occupation, but in principle you could. For Jews it was possible to survive under German occupation, but in principle you could not" (823). Tony Judt, *Postwar: A History of Europe since 1945* (New York: Penguin, 2006).

37. Quoted in Roger Cohen, "The Suffering Olympics," *New York Times*, January 30, 2012, http://www.nytimes.com/2012/01/31/opinion/the-suffering-olympics.html.

38. Tom Junes, "The Rise of 'Youth Nationalism' in Poland," *Open Democracy*, July 26, 2016, https://www.opendemocracy.net/can-europe-make-it/tom-junes/rise-of-youth-nationalism-in-poland.

39. The Institute's webpage is: https://ipn.gov.pl/pl.

40. Junes, "The Rise of 'Youth Nationalism' in Poland."

41. Ibid.

42. Dariusz Stola, "Poland's Institute of National Remembrance: A Ministry of Memory?," in *The Convolutions of Historical Politics*, ed. Alexei Miller and Masha Lipman (Budapest: Central European University Press, 2012), 45–58.

43. Jared McBride, "Ukrainian Holocaust Perpetrators Are Being Honored in Place of Their Victims," *Tablet*, July 20, 2016, http://www.tabletmag.com/jewish-news-and-politics/208439/holocaust-perpetrators-honored.

44. For an inkling of these battles and the stakes at play over memory in Ukraine, see Jared McBride's excellent review essay, "Who's Afraid of Ukrainian Nationalism?," *Kritika* 17, no. 3 (2016): 647–63. McBride reviews three recent books, including one by Volodymyr Viatrovych, which he characterizes as "a myopic, poorly researched apology for Ukrainian nationalist violence" (657).

45. These institutes also prepare laws and lobby for their passing. To take another Ukrainian example: In 2015 the Institute of National Memory helped to prepare the four laws that passed the parliament on April 9. Referred to as the "decommunization laws" and passed without public or parliamentary debate, the first law (2558) now established the criminality of both the Nazi and Soviet states and forbids denying them as such. A second (2538-1), and by far the most contentious, officially recognized Ukrainian nationalist groups as "fighters for Ukraine's independence in the twentieth century." What this meant is that Stepan Bandera's Organization of Ukrainian Nationalists and the Ukrainian Insurgent Army both received this honor; legally, no Ukrainian can engage in "public display of disrespectful attitudes" toward these freedom fighters, nor can he or she deny the "legitimacy of the struggle for Ukraine's independence in the twentieth century." A third law, on commemorating the victory over Nazism in World War II, contained a contentious provision that outlawed "falsification" of this event, and the fourth allowed archival access to the records of repressive bodies of the "totalitarian regime from 1917 to 1991." Critics, as Oxana Shevel has written, immediately pointed out that the laws effectively stifled debate over the past by introducing legal punishments for what could be termed a "wrong" opinion about the communist era. Laws advocated by one memory institute may anger another: the Ukrainian laws have produced frictions in Poland, where the Organization of Ukrainian Nationalists and Ukrainian Insurgent Army are remembered for massacres of Poles living in Volyn. See Oxana Shevel, "The Battle for Historical Memory in Postrevolutionary Ukraine," *Current History* (October 2016): 260–61. See also Emily Channell-Justice, "Ukraine's Long Road to 'Decommunization,'" *Anthropology News* 56, no. 5 (July 2015): 5.

46. Daniel Chirot, Gi-Wook Shin, and Daniel Sneider, eds., Introduction to *Confronting Memories of World War II: European and Asian Legacies* (Seattle: University of Washington Press, 2014), 6–7.

47. Igor Torbakov, "Divisive Historical Memories: Russia and Eastern Europe," in Chirot et al., *Confronting Memories*, 235.

48. Alexander Etkind, Uilleam Blacker, and Julie Fedor, eds., *Memory and Theory in Eastern Europe* (New York: Palgrave Macmillan, 2013).

49. Ibid., 2.

50. Ibid., 5. We might fruitfully compare other postsocialist memory cultures to Japan's. In her work, Akiko Hashimoto analyzes what she calls the "cultural trauma" of defeat that has characterized Japanese remembrance issues since 1945. As she describes it, "multiple memories of war and defeat with different moral frames coexist and vie for legitimacy" (4). These multiple memories include debates over how much weight should be given to commemorating heroes, victims, and perpetrators as well as an ongoing sense in Japan that "Western" memory cultures stressing a straightforward "coming to terms with the past" are not so easily applied to Japan. See her *Long Defeat: Cultural Trauma, Memory, and Identity in Japan* (Oxford: Oxford University Press, 2015).

51. Alexander Etkind, *Warped Mourning: Stories of the Undead in the Land of the Unburied* (Stanford, CA: Stanford University Press, 2013). It is also worth citing another volume that helped to inform the present one: Michael Bernhard and Jan Kubik's *Twenty Years after Communism: The Politics of Memory and Commemoration* (Oxford: Oxford University Press, 2014), which, as its title suggests, deals with "the explosion of the politics of memory triggered by the twentieth anniversary of the fall of state socialism in Eastern Europe" (2). Featuring twelve case studies written by political scientists, Bernhard and Kubik's volume aims to bring memory into the realm of comparative politics, testing out the political processes that lead to commemorations and memory efforts. As the editors state, "the way people remember state socialism is closely intertwined with the manner they envision historical justice" (3). The collection is therefore about developing "a novel theoretical framework for understanding the importance of memory for politics on a general level" (4) and through case studies (Russia being left out deliberately). The contributors focus on "mnemonic actors" (that is, political forces specifically invested in a specific interpretation of the past) and "mnemonic regimes" (dominant forms of remembrance in a political system) before developing a political-science framework of variables and choices in memory regimes.

STEPHEN M. NORRIS is Walter E. Havighurst Professor of Russian History and Director of the Havighurst Center for Russian and Post-Soviet Studies at Miami University (Ohio). He is author of two books on Russian cultural history, including *Blockbuster History in the New Russia: Movies, Memory, Patriotism* (2012), and editor of five books on Russian history and culture, including *Russia's People of Empire: Life Stories from Eurasia, 1500 to the Present* (with Willard Sunderland, 2012). He is currently writing a biography of the Soviet political caricaturist Boris Efimov.

Figure A.01. Halls of Terror, sites of violence. Museum of Occupations and Freedom Fights, Vilnius. *Photograph by Stephen M. Norris*

HALL OF GENOCIDE, OCCUPATION, AND TERROR

In his magisterial history of postwar Europe, the late Tony Judt concludes that "the politics of aggrieved memories—however much these differed in detail and even contradicted one another—constituted the last remaining bond between the former Soviet heartland and its imperial holdings."[1] The hegemony of Soviet historical narratives, which stressed that the Red Army had liberated the countries of Eastern and Central Europe and which tended to ignore the murder of the Jewish population of Europe, ensured that many people who lived in these countries would nurse grudges about the past. Soviet occupation and the communist systems that Moscow helped to establish meant that Eastern and Central Europeans predominately viewed the historical views offered from the Kremlin as another form of occupation. When the communist systems collapsed across the region between 1989 and 1991, Judt writes, it "brought in its wake a torrent of bitter memories."[2]

Such recollections formed the basis of new national histories and, with them, the foundational narratives of new museums dedicated to commemorating the past sufferings and losses under communism. The new museums that opened in the 1990s and 2000s attempted to explain how "ordinary" Lithuanians, Latvians, Estonians, Hungarians, and Poles (and others) had been doubly victimized, first under Nazism and then under Communism. These narratives of suffering focused on the dominant national groups of new nations and constituted a sort of unofficial competition over which group suffered the most. Although the impulse to commemorate the violence under communism is understandable, as we shall see in the chapters that make up this section, the new museums that set the aggrieved memories in stone have proven to be problematic.

The photograph at the start of this section is one I took in 2016 at the Museum of Genocide Victims in Vilnius, Lithuania (the museum changed its name in 2018 to the Museum of Occupations and Freedom Fights after criticisms that the original name ignored the Nazi genocide). It is an image of death. It is a photograph of the basement floor in the building that once served as the headquarters of the Soviet security services. In its bowels, the very place where I snapped this photograph, members of that organization imprisoned, tortured, and executed political prisoners. What you see in this photograph are shoes discovered in post-1991 excavations now encased in glass, as well as another, blown-up photograph of skeletons from these political murders. Other objects that once belonged to the dead are also displayed in this room.

The Museum of Occupations and Freedom Fights is a site where the unburied are now buried and where the unremembered of the Communist Era are now remembered. It is a place where a new nation, or more properly, a renewed nation—Lithuania—is reconstituted around past trauma. The building that housed the *Komitet Gosudarstvennoy Bezopasnosti* (KGB; Committee for State Security) in Lithuania became the site around which alternative interpretations of Soviet "liberation" formed, a focal point for the "aggrieved memories" I have referred to. This was a place of occupation, of violence, of victimhood.

As we will see in this section, similar sites have proliferated across the region. The Budapest House of Terror's basement contains rooms where executions took place. The records of rejected appeals for clemency are displayed on the walls. Loudspeakers read the names of "martyrs" and the staircases contain a photograph gallery of victimizers: the "yes-men and stooges" of the Fascist and Communist systems in Hungary.[3] Lonsky Prison in L'viv, Ukraine, has cells where political executions took place. Its courtyard also witnessed horrifying violence now commemorated as a foundational struggle for the new Ukraine. The Karlag Museum in Kazakhstan contains torture cells complete with graphic reconstructions of the death that occurred in them. The Corner House in Riga, Latvia, also functioned as the Soviet security service's headquarters in that city. Its displays are reminiscent of the other sites.

These places function as "memorial museums" in the way Paul Williams has identified: places that add a moral framework—in these cases national suffering under occupying regimes—to the narration of gruesome histories.[4] Visitors are asked not just to read about atrocities but to *feel* something. The sites, explored here through locations in Hungary, Lithuania, Ukraine, Kazakhstan, and Latvia, are powerful ones. The organizers of the museums, often working with government officials and local scholars, carefully selected the objects, displays, and spaces and presented them to evoke emotions, to draw the visitor into the horrors once meted out inside the building. In doing so, they capture a particular postcommunist form of "thanatourism," or "death tourism"; that is, sites built for visitors that are predicated on death and on trauma. They have overlapping functions: educational, mourning, healing, nation building, political, activist.[5] Like other sites in this subgenre, the purpose of postcommunist memorial museums is to offer finality, to perform funeral rites, to remember the dead, but to do so in a fashion that evokes feeling—even outrage—and that contributes to the foundation of a new or revived nationhood.

The sites in this section's chapters are the most common form of the new museum of communism. They use spaces once known for violence to build a national narrative of suffering around them. Many pay nominal attention to other occupations, but the main focus is the Soviet one. Thus, the recent past on display in these museums becomes an act of remembrance and an act of defiance, blaming the suffering that once occurred within on another country.

NOTES

1. Tony Judt, *Postwar: A History of Europe since 1945* (New York: Penguin, 2005), 825.

2. Ibid., 824.

3. See the museum's website: http://www.terrorhaza.hu/en/allando-kiallitas/basement/staircase-gallery-of-victimisers.

4. Paul Williams, *Memorial Museums: The Global Rush to Commemorate Atrocities* (New York: Berg, 2007), 8.

5. See Brigitte Sion, ed., *Death Tourism: Disaster Sites as Recreational Landscape* (London: Seagull, 2014), 3.

Figure 1.1. Museum of Occupations and Freedom Fights, Vilnius, founded 1992. http://genocid.lt/muziejus/en/. *Photograph by Stephen M. Norris*

ONE

Sovereign Pain

Liberation and Suffering in the Museum of Occupations and Freedom Fights in Lithuania

NERINGA KLUMBYTĖ

"Your suffering liberated us."
—Algirdas Bakūnas[1]

If not for golden summers,
The skies of rye flowers
We wouldn't come here
Where days are gray.
Where is the dusty train
It takes us far away...
Oh dear mother, I recall
The meadows green.
The summers pass in a rush
The hopes like flowers bloom
The tears we quietly brush
At the grave of our youth.
If not for golden summers,
The skies of rye flowers
We wouldn't come here
Where days are gray.[2]

The beautiful sounds of this song touch me deeply as I film the Day of Occupation and Genocide commemorating seventy-five years of Lithuania's occupation taking place at Victim Street in front of the Museum of Genocide Victims in Vilnius on June 15, 2015 (see fig. 1.1).[3] On June 15, 1940, the Soviet Army moved into the territory of Lithuania, then a sovereign state. At the commemoration, Lithuanian president Dalia Grybauskaitė reminded everyone about contemporary

Figure 1.2. President Dalia Grybauskaitė (in front of the flag) and the government delegation walking to the Museum of Genocide Victims square to commemorate the Day of Occupation and Genocide and the Day of Mourning and Hope.
Photograph by Neringa Klumbytė, June 15, 2015

threats from Russia as well as the importance of memory: "It's important that everyone who can testify, does testify, with memories, truth, and facts. We were occupied. Nobody can erase this word from our memory, from our understanding of history. It also means these facts oblige us to defend our state every day, not only from outside threats, but also from internal betrayal"[4] (fig. 1.2). After a few other speeches by the government officials, poet and writer Vladas Kalvaitis, a former political prisoner and a deportee, stood up, interrupted the event, and pointed to the windows of the Museum of Genocide Victims. Kalvaitis was tortured there, in the former prison of the People's Commissariat of Internal Affairs (NKVD). Speeches, songs, and flowers for those who died for Lithuania's freedom followed and then the sounds of the song "If Not for Golden Summers." It was so powerful, beautiful, and sorrowful. Some of the audience joined in singing. I heard an older lady sob behind my back. I turned around, she wiped her eyes. Was she imprisoned here, too?

The museum building, in front of which the commemorations of Lithuania's occupation take place every year, has a long history under different political regimes. In 1899 it was built as a courthouse of the Vilnius province of the Russian empire. In 1899, some passersby must have recalled the hanging of revolutionaries from the 1863 uprising in the square facing the building. As years passed, this building hosted government institutions of the Russian empire, the German empire, the Republic of Lithuania, the Bolshevik government, Poland, the Soviet Union, Nazi Germany, again the Soviet Union, and again Lithuania—at least nine different governments in a little more than a hundred years. In the Soviet period, the building housed the People's Commissariat of Internal Affairs (NKVD), the People's Commissariat of State Security (NKGB), the Ministry for State Security (MGB), and the Committee of State Security (KGB). In post-1991 Lithuania, the building has again served as a courthouse; it also hosts the Research Center for Resistance and Genocide of Lithuania's population, the KGB archives, a small chapel for "Lithuania's genocide victims," and the Museum of Genocide Victims. The Museum of Genocide Victims was renamed to the Museum of Occupations and Freedom Fights on May 2, 2018.

The building and the space around it have now been dedicated as a memorial site. A plaque on the building recalls Soviet and Nazi eras of terror and oppression: "During the occupations of the 20th century, the following repressive bodies operated in this building: the Gestapo and the KGB. The genocide of the population was planned here. Citizens of Lithuania were imprisoned, interrogated, tortured, and killed."[5] The names of many victims who perished in the prison are engraved on the building's walls. There is a plaque on the pavement for partisan Petras Vizbaras Vapsva, who died in 1953 after jumping out the third floor window to escape interrogation. During commemoration events, candles are lit at the building walls and at the monuments nearby (fig. 1.3). The museum webpage states that "For the Lithuanian nation this building is a symbol of the 50-year-long Soviet occupation, [and] therefore it is of special importance that here the museum is founded to remind the present generation and to tell the future generations about the years 1940–1991, difficult and tragic for Lithuania and its people."[6]

The name and mission statements of the museum label Soviet terror genocide. Order No. 1230/236 of October 14, 1992, signed by the Lithuanian Culture and Education Ministry and the Union of Political Prisoners and Deportees, established the museum to commemorate the "victims of the Soviet Union genocide."[7] The museum's aim is to "gather, research and propagate historical documentary material that reflects the physical and spiritual forms of genocide performed by the Soviet occupiers against the Lithuanian inhabitants, demonstrates the methods and extent of resistance to the occupying regime, and commemorates genocide victims and freedom fighters."[8]

Figure 1.3. The monument *Victims of Soviet Occupation*, behind which commemorations of the Day of Mourning and Hope and the Day of Occupation and Genocide take place. Erected on June 14, 1994. Photograph by Neringa Klumbytė, June 14, 2009

The museum has been criticized for the use of the term *genocide* to refer to Soviet terror as well as for the "double genocide" approach, that is, the recognition of both, the Holocaust and Soviet terror as genocides.[9] Critics of the double genocide approach argue that labeling other histories of terror as genocides undermines the singular significance of the Holocaust.[10] In the case of Lithuania, focus on the Soviet genocide also threatens to overshadow discussions of Lithuanian-Nazi collaboration during the Nazi period (1941–44), during which 195,196, or more than 95 percent, of Lithuanian Jews were killed, more than 80 percent of whom were killed in Lithuania.[11] The double genocide approach instituted in the museum has a legal basis. According to the Lithuanian Criminal Code Article 99, genocide refers not only to national, ethnic, racial, and religious groups as in the United Nations Convention but also to social and political groups.[12] The double genocide approach has been accepted by the Prague Declaration of 2008 *On European Conscience and Communism*, initiated and signed by Central and Eastern European state representatives, including Lithuania's.

The museum's exhibitions represent an "excessive focus on the victimization and heroizing of titular ethnic groups" at the expense of other groups' suffering in which the titular ethnic groups were involved.[13] In the Museum of Genocide Victims, the suffering of Lithuanian political prisoners and deportees is at the center of the exhibition, with only one prison cell devoted to the Holocaust and one prison cell to the genocide of the Roma. The history of founding the museum partially accounts for institutionalization of the approach to titular ethnic groups. The Museum of Genocide Victims was established by political prisoners and deportees.[14] Their memories, even if partial and fragmented as all memories are, and their experiences, even if not necessarily representative of a large part of population, are integral to the narrative on Soviet history in the museum.

This chapter focuses on the Museum of Genocide Victims as a political institution, which advances a history of a nation's liberation from the Soviet Union through anti-Soviet resistance and the suffering of the Lithuanian people. I explore how this history is articulated through material and textual artifacts of the past. This history identifies various aspects of Soviet terror in Lithuania during and after World War II: (1) torture and execution of political prisoners, (2) violent suppression of the armed anti-Soviet resistance, and (3) forced deportations of political prisoners and civilians to the Gulag, a system of prisons and forced labor camps in Siberia. I argue that the museum creates an affective ideology of sovereignty by reclaiming victims of violence as sovereign subjects and by projecting forms of affective subjectification onto visitors. The narrative of terror, resistance, and suffering historicizes and institutionalizes post-1991 sovereignty. The officially supported political history of the Russian Federation denies Eastern European and Baltic perspectives of Soviet genocide and calls it "historical revisionism," "rewriting of history," or "questioning of the outcomes of World War II."[15] The museum's narrative is a political statement directed at the Russian Federation as well as a claim for recognition aimed at the international audience.

The museum's narrative reflects broader memory politics in Lithuania going back to Sąjūdis, the Reform Movement of Lithuania during Perestroika that transformed into the liberation movement from the Soviet Union.[16] It was during the secession movement that idioms depicting deportations and Gulag as terror emerged. Moreover, as argued by Alvydas Nikžentaitis, the discourse of a loss of independence during World War II and a heroic struggle for its restoration has constituted the major historical plot line in the public space in the post-Soviet period.[17] The Lithuanian armed resistance after World War II has become a symbol of a heroic resistance against the Soviets.[18] The dissident movement throughout Soviet times, the publishing of the illegal Catholic Chronicles in 1972–89, the self-immolation of high school student Romas Kalanta in 1972, the founding of Sąjūdis in 1988, and the death of civilians in 1991 have constituted the heroic resistance story leading to sovereignty, all themes covered in the museum.[19] Many important days in the Lithuanian calendar of events are devoted to the commemoration of tragic events during World War II and Soviet times.[20] Rasa Čepaitienė argues that these observances reflect the formation of memory focused on

"Soviet times as dramatic and the time of suffering and injustice."[21] Public discussions of Lithuanian history are always ongoing; and the government has reacted with some controversial laws in response to growing geopolitical insecurity.[22] In 2010 the Lithuanian Parliament accepted the Criminal Code Article 170–2, which criminalized public approval of crimes committed by the Soviet Union or Nazi Germany against the Lithuanian Republic or its residents, as well as denial or gross diminishing of such crimes.[23]

Although all ideologies are *affective*, I use the term *affective ideology* to emphasize the affective side of the political process, that is legitimating sovereignty through deeply emotional experiences such as suffering through torture or forced exile.[24] I use a very broad definition of suffering as a response to a termination of a flow in life, a stoppage, a blockade, which brings about distress and emotional or physical pain.[25] In Lithuanian "suffering" is translated as *kančia*, or *kentėjimas*, but it can also mean "patience" and "pain." *Kančia* is related to *kankinys*, a martyr, which may have a religious or political meaning. Political prisoners, tortured by the NKVD, the NKGB, or the KGB, are invoked as martyrs in commemorative events. Some Lithuanian scholars call the studies of deportations to Siberia "martyrology."[26] In political prisoners' and deportees' memoirs and recollections of World War II and the post–World War II era, suffering can cover a variety of physical and emotional experiences, whether physical torture, being displaced from home, or poverty in Siberia.[27]

The museum's affective ideology of sovereignty is articulated through representations of the tragic events of World War II and the post–World War II era and the tragic fates of anti-Soviet resistance fighters, deportees, and dissidents. The first exhibit in this museum was opened in 1992 in the basement of the building where the prison was located. The guides were political prisoners who had been imprisoned there.[28] In 2016 the museum exhibitions included (1) the NKVD and NKGB (MGB, KGB) prison museum in the basement, where political prisoners were imprisoned, tortured, and killed, with an exhibition on the Holocaust in Lithuania; (2) the first-floor exhibition about the occupation and Sovietization of Lithuania and the Lithuanian armed resistance in 1944–53; (3) the second-floor exhibition on Lithuanian people in Gulag in 1944–56, on deportations in 1944–53, and on KGB activities in 1954–91. There is also an exhibition of the 1954–91 civil resistance to the Soviet rule.[29]

Founded as a museum-prison in the former NKVD, NKGB, Gestapo, MGB, and KGB prison, the museum has evolved into an institution covering other aspects of the Soviet period and has expanded its exhibitions to spaces outside the prison. The Memorial Complex of the Tuskulėnai Peace Park, where many political prisoners were executed, was annexed to the museum in 2008. The museum's exhibition on occupation, Sovietization, and anti-Soviet resistance was added in 2004, the exhibition on the KGB in 2006, the exhibition on civil resistance in 2006 and 2007, and the Holocaust exhibition in 2011. Historical documents testify that the prison has a rich history of Gestapo violence and terror and incarceration of people of different ethnicities. But the museum predominantly focuses on Soviet terror, especially in the years of 1940–41 and 1944–48.[30]

In the following sections, I take three tours through the museum by exploring its exhibitions and presentations of Soviet history. The three tours build a progressive narrative of terror and suffering: torture and complete annihilation of people in prison and execution cells; heroic resistance by partisans and its violent suppression; and forced exile and grueling lives in Gulag prisons and labor camps. These exhibitions reinscribe victims as sovereign subjects by incorporating them into the narrative of the anti-Soviet resistance that led to liberation. They also project affective subjectification by shocking visitors, appealing to their compassion for victims, and giving them memories of the tragic past.

TOUR 1: BASEMENT PRISON: TERROR

After purchasing tickets, visitors first descend into the former NKVD, NKGB, Gestapo, MGB, and KGB prison in the basement. During the first three years of the second Soviet occupation (1944–47), 767 people were shot in this prison and later buried in the Tuskulėnai estate territory in Vilnius.[31] From the end of 1944 to the beginning of the 1960s, more than 1,000 people were killed in the execution cell. One-third of them were participants in the anti-Soviet resistance movement.[32] After 1950, people killed in this prison were buried within a twenty- to thirty-kilometer radius in various places around Vilnius.[33] In 1953 Lavrentiy Beria issued a law forbidding torture. According to the historian Ričardas Padvaiskas, "in Vilnius they do not necessarily follow Moscow laws precisely ... in 1956 they tortured Ramanauskas Vanagas," one of the leaders of the Lithuanian anti-Soviet armed resistance, whose portrait hangs on the wall in one of the prison cells.[34]

The unpleasant sound of a heavy metal door takes the visitor back many years. Cell bars; old, small, dusty windows; peeling paint; worn wooden floors; and metal beds speak of the unbearable conditions in which prisoners spent their days. In one cell, fifteen to twenty people were incarcerated; until 1947 there was no furniture, and detainees slept on a cement floor. In the 1960s and 1970s, when the anti-Soviet armed resistance was finally suppressed, cells held only one to three people, and they had beds with blankets and a closet for personal items.[35]

In the basement prison there are several special cells. Prisoners were incarcerated in the punishment cell if they did not collaborate in the investigation.

In it, prisoners received three hundred grams of bread and half a liter of warm water per day. Clad only in their underwear and barefoot, they could not meet with visitors, write letters, or go outside. In the water cell, prisoners stood in cold water or ice in winter. They could stand on a small, elevated part of the floor if they kept their balance and stayed awake.[36] The cell with padded walls did not transmit any sound, screams, or laments. It was used for those who resisted or were psychologically unstable.

People imprisoned in the basement in the postwar period remembered terror, tortures, and unbearable conditions: "[we were] without air, food, lice attacked unbearably and I hit myself from one wall to another and called St. Mary and all saints so all this could end, because I could not bear it any longer" (Janina Jalinskaitė-Kluonienė); "They interrogated at night and did not let you sleep during the day.... After two weeks, you stop thinking, you don't know what you are saying or doing" (Juozas Burneika); "They kicked me, hit me, he did anything he wanted" (Ona Trakimienė).[37]

The most terrifying cell in the prison is the one where executions took place. The installation has a glass floor through which one can see prisoners' things, such as an old comb, shoes, or buttons. In this cell they executed prisoners mostly by shooting them in the back of the head. In addition to shooting, many had other blunt injuries to the skull or stabbing injuries to the head with a four-sided bayonet (*keturbriaunis durtuvas*). The blood ran through a drain, and it was washed from the floor to prepare the cell for another execution. The walls of this cell still have bullet marks. The television screen shows ongoing executions from Andrzej Wajda's 2007 film *Katyn*, and you repeatedly hear shots fired. On your way back, on the right, there is a small prison yard, and you can breathe in some fresh air. Prisoners were brought here for walks. It makes you wonder how a small patch of the sky looked to prisoners many years ago.

Back in the prison cells, you will encounter photographs of prison inmates: the leaders of the Lithuania's Fight for Freedom Movement (Lietuvos Laisvės Kovos Sąjūdis), including general Jonas Žemaitis, who in 2009 was posthumously recognized as the president of Lithuania for the years 1949–54; the photographs of the repressed clergy of the Lithuanian Catholic Church; and other fighters for religious and human rights imprisoned in the 1960s and 1970s. But the collage of mutilated faces and bodies of men and women partisans on the prison wall stands out as unbearably graphic evidence of Soviet terror. The photographs are from well-known public displays in town market squares of the captured, tortured, and shot partisans (see fig. 1.4). Soviet authorities used these tactics to terrify the population and identify families of the victims. Family members tried not to show that they recognized their sons, husbands, daughters, or other relatives so they would not be interrogated and deported to Gulag.[38]

Figure 1.4. A collage with dead partisans publicly displayed in towns in the basement prison in the Museum of Genocide Victims. *Photograph by Neringa Klumbytė, July 10, 2015*

The basement prison engages visitors through sensory articulations of death, torture, and executions. Images of mutilated bodies and piles of bones; photographs of prisoners before and after imprisonment or of deformed skulls and the prisoners they had belonged to; and examples of various types of torture equipment constitute material and biographical evidence of the Soviet history of terror. Political prisoners are associated with the regime of pre–World War II sovereign Lithuania and its active defense after Lithuania's incorporation into the Soviet Union. Their resistance subsumed various forms of opposition, from peaceful opposition by priests to armed resistance.

TOUR 2: THE FIRST FLOOR: LIVES FOR FREEDOM

The first-floor exhibition introduces the occupation and Sovietization of Lithuania and the Lithuanian armed resistance after World War II. Between 1944 and 1954, the armed underground consisted of 76,762 people.[39] More than twenty thousand partisan fighters died between 1944 and 1958; an additional seven

Figure 1.5. An installation on partisan publishing. "At least 54 files of periodicals and 18 non-periodical publications were published in Lithuania during the time of the partisan war" (the description on partisan publishing, the Museum of Genocide Victims). *Photograph by Neringa Klumbytė, July 10, 2015*

hundred had died in 1941.[40] The majority of partisans died before their twenty-second birthday.[41] Resistance against the Soviet Army lasted until the spring of 1953, when the last partisan bases were destroyed and presidium chairman Jonas Žemaitis of Lithuania's Fight for Freedom Movement was captured.[42] The last known trial of a partisan leader was held in Kėdainiai on May 6–8, 1963.[43] The partisan underground press and military political documents emphasized that resistance against Soviet occupation was "the great fight for the liberation of the nation" (see fig. 1.5).[44]

The museum first floor takes visitors through several rooms with wallpapers of partisans in the forest. They were known as forest brothers. Smiling faces of partisans in the beginning of the exhibition speak of youthful times when the hope of freedom was still alive. The majority of them were young men and women. Letters, uniforms, rifles, typewriters, and anti-resistance newspapers, pamphlets, and documents tell a story of an organized resistance and life in the woods. Anti-Soviet resistance would not have been possible without support of local people, who provided food, clothing, and shelter. The exhibition includes photographs of farmers who supported partisans at great risk as well as partisan liaisons.

The museum reclaims partisans and liaisons as sovereign subjects by placing them in a narrative of Lithuania's sovereignty in a variety of ways. The maps of Lithuania illustrate post–World War II resistance and emphasize territoriality and sovereignty. The uniforms of the Lithuanian Army and images of Lithuanian partisans taking an oath or writing a letter about Lithuania's freedom build a narrative of partisans as freedom fighters. In a photograph of a partisans' grave, women in national costumes decorate it with flowers and religious and Lithuanian state symbols. There are also symbols of Lithuanian statehood in the exhibit, such as a little sculpture of *Vytis*, a knight on a horse—a Lithuanian emblem. *Istrebiteli* [local NKVD paramilitary units] used it as a shooting target in the Varėna region.

Other rooms display photographs and documents on suppression of the armed resistance. A 1963 film that depicts episodes in the post–World War II suppression of the partisan resistance is screened in one room. A few installations display instruments used for torturing partisans who were caught and imprisoned, some of them tortured in the basement prison of this museum.

This exhibition sharply contrasts with Soviet versions of the postwar history of Lithuania, which depicted civil war and class struggle. Soviet official history presents partisans as "bandits" who terrorized the local population. Various crimes were attributed to partisans and many partisans were punished according to Article 58 for antirevolutionary actions, such as betrayal of homeland or armed resistance.[45] Moreover, current Russian Federation government officials and the Russian media use the rhetoric of "fascists" and "Nazi collaborators" to oppose and redefine the Baltic glorification of postwar resistance fighters. After the annexation of Crimea and the war in Eastern Ukraine, the Lithuanian history on the postwar resistance is part of the NATO narrative on postwar Baltic resistance as well.[46]

TOUR 3: THE SECOND FLOOR: THE EXILED NATION

The second-floor exhibition focuses on people of Lithuania in the Gulag in 1944–56, on deportations in 1944–53, and KGB activities in 1954–91. Among the most brutal of the early mass deportations were the deportations of June 14, 1941, now commemorated by a national holiday called the Day of Mourning and Hope. On June 14–18, 1941, eighteen thousand people were deported; many men were separated from their families and transported to Gulag camps.[47] Among those deported to labor camps and deportation sites in Siberia in 1941 and the postwar years there were at least 50,000 women and 39,000 children.[48] After the war many partisan families were deported as an antiresistance measure; people who helped partisans were also a target of the state repressive apparatus. In all Lithuanian Communist Party (b) Central Committee documents on deportations, the importance of forced deportation of partisan families and their supporters is emphasized as one of the major conditions to eliminate armed resistance.[49] Between 1945 and 1953 there were thirty-four other mass deportations of Lithuanian citizens to the depths of the Soviet Union.[50] In 1945–53, 106,000–108,000 people, or 29,230 families, were deported according to LSSR MGB-KGB (the Ministry of State Security—Committee of State Security) data.[51]

The Gulag exhibition introduces visitors to Gulag prisoners, ranging from Lithuanian presidents and government officials to unnamed people. The photographs of prisoners, their clothing and shoes, self-made bread rosaries, prayer books, and their letters and postcards speak of extremely harsh conditions as well as of Gulag prisoners' hopes and dignity. The description of the Gulag exhibition states that "when the Soviet Union occupied Lithuania, it immediately started physical and spiritual annihilation of the nation based on communist ideology principles." Twenty to twenty-five thousand people died in Gulag and labor camps; "They rest in the graves already destroyed by time."[52]

Photographs of the 1944–53 deportations of civilians and families elaborate on the previous themes of terror, annihilation of the nation, and the suffering of innocent people. The exhibition tells us that "Entire families, parents, grandparents, children, newborn babies and the sick, were secretly, usually in the dead of night, carried away in cattle cars."[53] Children especially amplify the suffering you envision and mobilize your empathy: Why did innocent, weak, and helpless children have to experience this terror? Five thousand deported children died: "One of the most terrifying pages of the deportation history of Lithuanians," states the museum exhibition guide.[54] The first years for many families were tragic: "Children

Figure 1.6. Lithuanian deportee children in a day care in the Irkutsk region, 1948. Photograph in the exhibition on exile. *Photograph by Neringa Klumbytė, July 10, 2015*

were the first to get sick and die because of lack of food, epidemics, unsanitary conditions, lack of medical help."[55] There is a photograph with a father in front of a little coffin of his newborn son, another with sled full of firewood exhibiting a child worker. Captions of other photographs speak of children's longing for the homeland, the longing passed to them by their parents since many children were born in Siberia: "Let us [go] to the homeland" and "Little children wish to return to the homeland." An image of a beautiful young girl in a school uniform has a caption "Happy childhood in Lithuania" in contrast to the childhood in Siberia, which is represented through hardships and children's suffering.

A photograph installation labeled "Life Goes On" takes you into celebrations of Christmas and Easter, weddings, baptisms, and funerals. This section tells a story of survival and resistance despite all the hardships: "Lithuanian deportees and prisoners, despite hard work, shortages, severe climate, and hostile attitudes of the state and often of the local population, which regarded them as "socially dangerous," did everything to survive, raise their children, preserve their customs and language and historic self-awareness, and cherish Christian values in their everyday life" (see fig. 1.6).[56]

The story of life in Siberia is mediated by symbols of death. The exhibition on exile in Siberia is populated with many crosses, presenting Siberia as a land of death. One room exhibits crosses on the walls and features photographs of crosses hanging from ceilings. Like the lives and deaths of political prisoners or partisans, the exiled people's biographies are incorporated into the sovereignty narrative. The deaths in exile are added to prisoner and partisan deaths as sacrifices for the nation. The exhibition on deportations introduces deportations as "one of the most brutal of the Soviet regime's means against the local population."[57] State emblems and Lithuanian flag colors on personal things and images of political borders of Lithuania on installations invoke Lithuania's sovereignty.

The narrative on Soviet terror is developed further in exhibitions on other aspects of Soviet history: the criminal NKVD, NKGB, MGB, and KGB activities throughout the Soviet period, the Lithuanian civil resistance until the late 1980s, the nationalist movement in the late 1980s and early 1990s, and the regaining of sovereignty in 1990. These exhibitions end the museum's powerful affective narrative about Soviet terror, resistance, and suffering. The exhibition ends with civil resistance and Lithuania's liberation movement in the late 1980s and early 1990s, connecting terror and suffering with liberation.

CONCLUSIONS

One of the installations at the Museum of Genocide Victims (currently Museum of Occupations and Freedom Fights) summarizes the losses of citizens of Lithuania during the Soviet and Nazi occupation period from June 15, 1940, when the Soviet Army entered Lithuania, to 1990 when Lithuania proclaimed independence. During the Soviet occupation of Lithuania, 200,000 were arrested, interrogated, and imprisoned; 132,000 were deported; 20,000–25,000 perished in Gulag and prisons; 28,000 died in exile; and 21,500 partisans and their supporters were killed. Based on incomplete archival data, historian Arvydas Anušauskas estimates that no fewer than 456,000 people in Lithuania were Soviet "genocide and terror victims and experienced violence."[58] These numbers translate into "every third adult Lithuanian or every second man, every eighth woman, and every fifteenth child."[59] The installation states that during the Nazi occupation there were 29,000 imprisoned and deported to concentration camps; 240,000 (200,000 of whom were Jews) killed; and 60,000 deported to Germany for forced labor.[60] In Lithuania the total population loss during World War II and post-World War II due to Soviet and Nazi occupation, emigration, and war was 1.058 m people out of 2.5 m inhabitants in 1945.[61]

The lost lives during the Soviet occupation constitute sovereign subjects reclaimed by the museum exhibitions through affective ideology of sovereignty. According to Katherine Verdery, the dead are good political symbols because they cannot speak for themselves; they are ambiguous, multivocal and polysemic and, therefore, open to different readings.[62] In the case of partisans and deportees, many of their life résumés are short and their participation in the anti-Soviet resistance and commitment to Lithuania's freedom is not always well-documented, but their biographies are read in the context of the museum's narrative on liberation and Lithuania's sovereignty. Moreover, in the case of deportees, their experiences are diverse: some deported in 1948 or 1949 experienced none of the atrocities inflicted on those deported in 1941, and some admit to not having suffered at all.[63] But through ascription of certain emotional experiences, they are all integrated into the story on suffering of Lithuanian deportees. Images of tortured bodies of partisans, piles of bones of the executed, deformed skulls, tiny skeletons of deportee children, faces of the dead and of the alive, full of fear, distress or pain in their eyes, not only testify, they also standardize the Soviet period experience as suffering. Moreover, the museum's affective ideology of sovereignty produces a particular form of affective subjectification projected onto visitors through which they can exist politically by identifying with the victims and their biographies of suffering.

The museum does not ignore historical facts, and its exhibitions are based on archival research and data as well as political prisoners' and deportees' accounts. You can still meet some of these firsthand witnesses, like former political prisoner and nun Nijolė Sadūnaitė, a human rights activist, who guides tours in the corridors of the museum.[64] But the museum tells the history from a position of the primarily titular victimized group, and it is their intent to testify and transfer this memory rather than search for multiple voices and reconciliation. In Lithuania, the threat to sovereignty after the Russia-Ukraine conflict in 2014 and the war in Eastern Ukraine is a constant focus in geopolitical discourse, scholarly debates, and media coverage. In official speeches and the media, "blood" and "sacrifice" are routinely used to legitimate sovereignty.[65] Affective ideologies create solidarities[66] that are enacted in many contexts and in multiple institutions, including the museum.

Affective ideologies of sovereignty are integrated into history narratives not only in small states with a history of terror like Lithuania. In Russia, the World War II ideology is an important identity narrative,[67] "the foundational myth of a post-Soviet Russia."[68] On May 9, Victory against Nazi Germany Day, hundreds of thousands of people in Russian cities carry placards with portraits of family members who took part in World War II. On May 9, 2015, the seventieth anniversary of the victory over the Nazi regime, Russian president Vladimir Putin led more than 500,000 people through Red Square in Moscow holding a portrait of his father in a Soviet Navy uniform.[69] This event was deeply touching to many participants and was proclaimed by some to be beyond politics.[70] Like commemorations of occupation in Lithuania, this event celebrated life, recognized people's sacrifice, and created affective solidarities. Participants' painful family histories were sanctified as part of their country's history, pride, and honor. Examining the complexities of commemoration of victims in Lithuania and Russia reveals how paradoxical affective ideologies are: they condemn terror that causes suffering, express compassion to the suffering people, and legitimate suffering as a path to sovereignty.

NOTES

1. Algirdas Bakūnas, *Auksinės sielos žmonės* (Vilnius: Danielius, 2004), 21. The author of these lines writes about his friend Petras, who was in Karaganda Gulag camps: "He lost health and came back very sick. He died before Independence.... Your sentence was not in vain, twenty-five years you were imprisoned in Karaganda camps, your suffering liberated us. We straightened up. We withstood communism. The occupants."

2. The excerpt of the partisan song "If not for golden summers" from the compact disc *Už Laisvę, Tėvynę ir Tave: Gražiausios Lietuvos partizanų dainos* (2007) [For freedom, homeland, and you: the best Lithuanian partisan songs]. My translation. Various versions of this song and music in Lithuanian are available at http://dainutekstai.lt/r2964/aidas-giniotis-jei-ne-auksines-vasaros-partizanu-daina.html, accessed June 16, 2016.

3. In this chapter I use the old name of the museum since the research was completed when the museum was still called the Museum of Genocide Victims. The museum is also known to people by its unofficial names, the KGB museum or the Genocide museum. The annual commemorations described in the beginning of this chapter usually take place on June 14, the Day of Mourning and Hope, the day of the first mass deportations. The Day of Occupation is June 15.

4. Excerpt from President Dalia Grybauskaitė's speech at the seventy-fifth commemoration of Lithuania's occupation and of the Day of Mourning and Hope, recorded by the author. The event took place on June 15, 2015, at the Museum of Genocide Victims, Vilnius. Grybauskaitė did not mention Russia, but "our neighbors."

5. The front (north) side of the building. Vilnius. October, 2016.

6. The Museum of Genocide Victims webpage http://genocid.lt/muziejus/en/695/c/, accessed October 30, 2016. Monuments to Lithuania's freedom and Lithuania's freedom fighters and deportees have been among the most common expressions of public commemoration in the post-Soviet period and have been erected in many cities and towns in Lithuania. See Rūta Trimonienė, *Paminklai Lietuvos sovietinio genocido aukoms ir rezistencijos dalyviams atminti (1941–1953, 1988–2006)* (MA thesis, Vilnius University, 2006), https://epublications.vu.lt/object/elaba:2153128/.

7. Museum of Genocide Victims, "On the Establishment of the Museum of Victims of Genocide in Lithuania," http://genocid.lt/muziejus/en/, accessed January 22,

2020. Since 1997 the museum has been part of the Genocide and Resistance Research Center of Lithuania.

8. "Activities" tab of the Genocide and Resistance Research Center of Lithuania, http://genocid.lt/muziejus/en/708/c/, accessed July 26, 2015.

9. See, for example, "Holokausto ekspozicija bandoma spręsti istorinį 'nesusipratimą,'" *BNS news*, December 17, 2010, at https://www.delfi.lt/news/daily/lithuania/holokausto-ekspozicija-bandoma-spresti-istorini-nesusipratima.d?id=39811239.

10. In response to criticism about double genocide approach, on September 6, 2017, the government institutions and nongovernmental organizations agreed to change the name of the museum into "Museum of Occupations and Fights for Freedom." The old name was replaced on May 2, 2018. See "Po ilgų diskusijų sutarta pervadinti Genocido aukų muziejų," *BNS News*, September 8, 2017, https://www.delfi.lt/news/daily/lithuania/po-ilgu-diskusiju-sutarta-pervadinti-genocido-auku-muzieju.d?id=75703131.

11. See Arvydas Anušauskas et al., *Lietuva 1940–1990: okupuotos Lietuvos istorija* (Vilnius: Lietuvos gyventojų genocido ir rezistencijos tyrimo centras, 2005), 222.

12. See the 1992 legal act "Regarding Responsibility for the Genocide of Lithuanian Citizens" and amendments at https://www.e-tar.lt/portal/lt/legalAct/TAR.83DF9659EC0D. The English version of the Article 99 Genocide is available at https://www.legislationline.org/download/id/8272/file/Lithuania_CC_2000_am2017_en.pdf, accessed April 13, 2020. For a discussion of Lithuanian and international articles on genocide, see Justinas Žilinskas, "'Genocidas'—sąvokos traktuotė Lietuvoje ir užsienyje," last updated January 30, 2004, http://genocid.lt/Leidyba/10/justinas.htm. On the use of the term *Soviet genocide* in Lithuanian historiography since 1944, see Arvydas Anušauskas, "'Genocido' sąvoka Lietuvos istorijoje," Lithuanian Center for Genocide and Resistance Research, last updated January 30, 2004, http://genocid.lt/Leidyba/10/arvydas.htm. Anušauskas compares Soviet terror with Nazi terror and claims that Soviet terror in its scope and violence almost exceeded Nazi terror (Arvydas Anušauskas, "Sovietinis genocidas buvo baisesnis už nacių terorą," *TV3 News Lithuania*, March 16, 2012, http://www.tv3.lt/naujiena/587312/a-anusauskas-sovietinis-genocidas-buvo-baisesnis-uz-naciu-terora). For a detailed analysis of Soviet terror, see Anušauskas, *Teroras 1940–1958 m.* (Vilnius: Versus aureus, 2012). For a different opinion in Lithuania on the Holocaust as the only genocide in the history of humanity, see Leonidas Donskis, "Sąvokų infliacija ir diskusijų kriminalizacija," *Online Daily Bernardinai.lt*, November 7, 2008, http://www.bernardinai.lt/straipsnis/2008-11-07-leonidas-donskis-savoku-infliacija-ir-diskusiju-kriminalizacija/29372.

13. Eglė Rindzevičiūtė, "The Overflow of Secrets: The Disclosure of Soviet Repression in Museums as an Excess," *Current Anthropology* 56 (2015), https://www.journals.uchicago.edu/doi/full/10.1086/683297?mobileUi=0&.

14. The Holocaust is represented in other museums, including the Vilna Gaon Jewish State Museum, funded by the government.

15. See Концепция внешней политики Российской Федерации, July 15, 2008, http://kremlin.ru/acts/news/785. For a discussion of Lithuania's and Russia's politics of history, see Neringa Klumbytė, "Bipolinės istorinio teisingumo struktūros ir politinė atskirtis: Lietuvos rusakalbių prisiminimai apie Antrąjį pasaulinį karą Lietuvos ir Rusijos istorijos politikos kontekste" (Bipolar structures of historical justice and political exclusion: Lithuanian Russian memories of World War II in the context of the politics of history in Lithuania and Russia), *Sociologija. Mintis ir Veiksmas* no. 2 (2017): 136–67.

16. On memories of the post–World War II era in Lithuania, see Dovilė Budrytė, "From Partisan Warfare to Memory Battlefields: Two Women's Stories about the Second World War and Its Aftermath in Lithuania," *Gender and History* 28, no. 3 (2016): 754–74; Violeta Davoliūtė and Tomas Balkelis, eds., *Maps of Memory: Trauma, Identity and Exile in Deportation Memoirs from the Baltic States* (Vilnius: Institute of Lithuanian Literature and Folklore, 2012); and Davoliūtė, *The Making and Breaking of Soviet Lithuania: Memory and Identity in the Wake of War* (London: Routledge, 2013).

17. Alvydas Nikžentaitis, "Atminties ir istorijos politika Lietuvoje," in *Atminties daugiasluoksniškumas: miestas, valstybė, regionas*, ed. Alvydas Nikžentaitis (Vilnius: Lietuvos istorijos institutas, 2013), 517–38.

18. Ibid., 531. See also Rasa Čepaitienė, "Nacionalinis pasakojimas versus lokalios istorijos: "Kultūrinės atminties raiška Lietuvos provincijoje" (The national narrative versus local histories: the expression of the cultural memory in the Lithuanian provinces), in *Daugiasluoksnė atmintis: miestas, valstybė, regionas* (Multidimensional memory: city, state, region), ed. Alvydas Nikžentaitis (Vilnius: Lietuvos Istorijos Institutas Press, 2013), 229–66.

19. See Nikžentaitis, "Atminties ir istorijos politika Lietuvoje."

20. Twelve out of forty-four days in the 2006 Lithuanian memorable day calendar are devoted to commemorating tragic events from World War II and the Soviet era.

21. Čepaitienė, "Nacionalinis pasakojimas versus lokalios istorijos," 249.

22. See Klumbytė, "Bipolinės istorinio teisingumo struktūros ir politinė atskirtis."

23. Lithuanian Criminal Code, Article 170-2, http://www.infolex.lt/ta/66150:str170-2, accessed July 23, 2016. The article has the qualification that endorsement has to be carried out "publicly and in a threatening, offensive or insulting manner, or it results in disturbance of public order" (cited in Žilinskas 2012: 321). It introduces a safeguard to balance freedom of expression. For a discussion of this law from a legal perspective, see Justinas Žilinskas, "Introduction of 'Crime of Denial' in the Lithuanian Criminal Law and First Instances of Its Application," *Jurisprudencija/Jurisprudence* 19, no. 1 (2012): 315–29, https://www.mruni.eu/upload/iblock/205/017_zilinskas.pdf.

24. As argued by Eglė Rindzevičiūtė ("Hegemony or Legitimacy? Assembling Soviet Deportations in Lithuanian Museums," in *Maps of Memory: Trauma, Identity and*

Exile in Deportation Memoirs from the Baltic States, ed. Violeta Davoliūtė and Tomas Balkelis, 153–77 [Vilnius: Institute of Lithuanian Literature and Folklore, 2012]), in the case of the narratives about deportations in Lithuanian state museums, they are not hegemonic and driven by some coherent state policy. Stories about Soviet deportations, according to Rindzevičiūtė (156) are legitimate: they are features in presidential speeches, government programs, and museum mission statements. The Museum of Genocide Victims, however, assembled its collection relating to the deportations almost exclusively through private donations, according to its staff (166). According to Rindzevičiūtė, there is no consensus or a government strategy behind any particular museum display (177). For renewed significance of historical justice narratives after 2014, see Klumbytė, Neringa "Sovereign Uncertainty and the Dangers to Liberalism at the Baltic Frontier." *Slavic Review* 78, no. 2 (2019): 336–47.

25. In English, "suffering" *is* often connected to physical pain or a medical condition (the term *suffering* in English means "pain that is caused by injury, illness, loss, etc.: physical, mental, or emotional pain" [Merriam-Webster.com, accessed January 23, 2020, https://www.merriam-webster.com/dictionary/suffering]).

26. The term *martyrology* has been used by some scholars, intellectuals, and politicians. See, for example, Egidijus Aleksandravičius, "Prie kančios ir stiprybės šaltinio," in *Sibire ... tremtinių žeme. Dienoraštis 1942–1956,* ed. Onutė Alksninytė-Garbštienė (Vilnius: Lietuvos Rašytojų Sąjungos, 1993), and "Iš praeities," 150, introduction to the first official publication of Dalia Grinkevičiūtė's memoirs, *Lietuviai prie Laptevų jūros: Pergalė* 8 (1988): 151–65.

27. Neringa Klumbytė, *Sovereign Pain: Affective Politics, Memory, and Soviet Terror in Lithuania,* paper delivered at the American Anthropological Association Annual Meeting, Denver, November 2015.

28. Interview with Ričardas Padvaiskas, "Laisvės kryžkelės: Genocido aukų muziejus," *bernardinai.lt,* October 13, 2008, http://www.bernardinai.lt/straipsnis/2008-10-13-laisves-kryzkeles-genocido-auku-muziejus/3567.

29. The History tab on the museum website, http://genocid.lt/muziejus/lt/563/c/, accessed October 30, 2016.

30. The walls of Cell 3 bear inscriptions left by inmates between 1942 and 1944 when the Gestapo worked in the building. Most of them are in Polish. (Interview with Eugenijus Peikštenis, the director of the Museum of Genocide Victims, "Laisvės kryžkelės: Genocido aukų muziejus," October 13, 2008, http://www.bernardinai.lt/straipsnis/2008-10-13-laisves-kryzkeles-genocido-auku-muziejus/3567.)

31. Peikštenis, in Antanaitis, "Laisvės kryžkelės."

32. Data from the execution chamber exhibition, July 10, 2015. Also cited at http://genocid.lt/muziejus/lt/243/a/, accessed April 12, 2020.

33. Peikštenis, in Antanaitis, "Laisvės kryžkelės."

34. Padvaiskas, in Antanaitis, "Laisvės kryžkelės."

35. Data from the exhibition at the Museum of Occupations and Freedom Fights, July 10, 2015.

36. A water cell was used from 1945 and through the 1950s (KBG Prison tab on the museum website, http://genocid.lt/muziejus/lt/128/a/, accessed May 15, 2016).

37. See the testimonies "Laisvės kryžkelės: KGB kalėjimas ir jo istorija," https://www.youtube.com/watch?v=7tn_hqPjgrs, accessed October 30, 2016.

38. Anušauskas, *Teroras*, 167.

39. Report No. 4.1 by LSSR MVD unit 4, 2nd department chair Martusevičius, about the 1944–45 killed and arrested members of the armed resistance, LYA. F.K-1. Ap.3. B.530. P.38, cited in Vytautas Tininis, *The Crimes of the Communist Regime in Lithuania in 1944–1953: The Role of the Political Bodies, Their Local Subdivisions, Collaborationists of the Soviet Union in Committing Crimes in 1944–1953*, vol. 2, *A Historical Study and a Set of Documents in Facsimile* (Vilnius, 2003), 7.

40. Anušauskas, *Teroras*, 279. The NKGB-MGB statistics on how many people were captured, killed, and legalized are not accurate; in their reports, the numbers were increased or diminished in order to align with Moscow's expectations (Tininis, *Crimes of the Communist Regime*, 7). According to Lithuanian Soviet Socialist Republic KGB data, in 1944–54 "38,141 member of the armed underground were liquidated, out of which 20,138 killed, 18,003 arrested and imprisoned"; 38,621 members were underground and later became legal. For a discussion of different data see Tininis, *Crimes of the Communist Regime*, 7.

41. Dalia Kuodytė and Algis Kašėta, *Laisvės kovos 1944–1953 metais: A collection of documents* (Kaunas, Lith.: Jakšto, 1996), 12.

42. Anušauskas et al., *Lietuva 1940–1990*, 316.

43. Stanley V. Vardys, "Soviet Social Engineering in Lithuania: An Appraisal," in *Lithuania under the Soviets: Portrait of a Nation, 1940–1965*, ed. Stanley V. Vardys (New York: Praeger, 1965), 249.

44. See, e.g., "Lietuvos Laisvės Kovos Sąjūdžio Tarybos Prezidiumo kreipimasis į sąjūdžio dalyvius ir į visus krašto gyventojus" in *Laisvės kovos 1944–1953 metais*, ed. Kuodytė and Kašėta, 315.

45. On research of partisan crimes as crimes against humanity in Lithuania, see a review by Rimantas Jokimaitis: "Lietuvos partizanų kovų vaizdai 'Kitos mėnulio pusės' šviesai pašvietus," *Literatūra ir menas* no. 3267 (January 15, 2010), http://eia.libis.lt:8080/archyvas/viesas/20110731191449/http://www.culture.lt/lmenas/?leid_id=3267&kas=straipsnis&st_id=15914. Pocius's responses to Jokimaitis: "Mindaugas Pocius: Apie kritiką be 'emocijų'" *Bernardinai.lt*, February 22, 2010, http://www.bernardinai.lt/straipsnis/2010-02-22-mindaugas-pocius-apie-kritika-be-emociju/40788; Violeta Davoliūtė's interview with Pocius about his book, "Kita mėnulio pusė—partizanų kova su koloborantais," *Lrytas.lt*, September 30, 2009, http://kultura.lrytas.lt/-12542487121253272586-kita-m%C4%97nulio-pus%C4%97-partizan%C5%B3-kova-su-kolaborantais.htm.

46. See the short video by NATO, "Forest Brothers—Fight for the Baltics." July 11, 2017, https://www.youtube.com/watch?v=h5rQFp7FF9c. In response to this video, Maria Zakharova, Russian Federation Foreign Affairs Ministry Director for

Information and Print Media, announced on her Facebook page that "forest brothers" was an organization "created by fascists," Facebook entry July 12, 2017, https://www.facebook.com/photo.php?fbid=10214029522081798&set=a.4365446944032&type=3&theater. See also Klumbytė, "Bipolinės istorinio teisingumo struktūros ir politinė atskirtis."

47. See Soviet state security people's deputy commissar Ivan Serov's instruction on deporting anti-Soviet elements from Lithuania, Latvia, and Estonia. The document was issued on May 19, 1941, or later and was published in Grunskis et al., *Lietuvos kovų ir kančių istorija*, vol. 1, *Lietuvos gyventojų trėmimai 1941, 1945–52* (Vilnius: Mokslo ir enciklopedijų leidykla, 1994), 14–20. Poles, Jews, Russians, and other nationalities constituted 7 percent of all prisoners and 4 percent of all deportees (Anušauskas, *Teroras*, 280). The museum exhibitions do not discuss deportation of other ethnic groups.

48. Arvydas Anušauskas et al., *Lietuva 1940–1990*, 302. The last deportees were released only in 1963. Some sixty thousand managed to return to Lithuania (see Lithuania's State Public Organization Archive document in Grunskis, Eugenijus, Kašauskienė, Valda, and Šadžius Henrikas, *Lietuvos kovų ir kančių istorija*, 425).

49. Tininis, *Crimes of the Communist Regime*, 13.

50. See Stephen C. Rowell, Reda Griškaitė, and Gediminas Rudis, *History of Lithuania* (Vilnius: Organization Committee Frankfurt, 2002).

51. The 1945–53 deportations were carried out by the Communist Party, government, and repressive structures (Tininis, *Crimes of the Communist Regime*, 17). From 1945 to 1948, deportations were carried out using the Soviet NKVD and MGB directives. From 1948, decisions about deportations were accepted by LCP (b) CC and LSSR MT. For a discussion of the data, see Tininis, *Crimes of the Communist Regime*, 10.

52. The Museum of Genocide Victims, Gulag exhibition description, July 10, 2015.

53. The Museum of Occupations and Freedom Fights, "Expositions: Deportations: 1944–1953," http://genocid.lt/muziejus/en/387/a/, accessed February 5, 2020.

54. Lietuvos gyventojų genocido ir rezistencijos tyrimo centras, *Museum of Genocide Victims Exhibition Guide* (Vilnius: Lietuvos gyventojų genocido ir rezistencijos tyrimo centras), 65. The death rates were especially high in the first years of deportation. According to Birutė Burauskaitė (2008), for example, in Igarka, half of all people and 71 percent of the children died in the first year of deportation in 1948–49. Every tenth child was less than one year old and more than half of the children who died were less than five years old. See Birutė Burauskaitė, "Lietuvos vaikai–1948-ųjų tremtiniai." *Genocidas ir Rezistencija* 2, 2008, http://www.genocid.lt/centras/lt/718/a//, accessed April 12, 2020.

55. The Museum of Genocide Victims, description of the exhibition on children, July 10, 2015.

56. The second floor of the Museum of Genocide Victims, description of installation 7 and 8, July 10, 2015.

57. The second floor of the Museum of Genocide Victims, July 10, 2015.

58. Anušauskas, *Teroras*, 280.

59. Ibid.

60. The installation numbers are approximate (The Museum of Genocide Victims, July 18, 2013).

61. Ibid., 279. According to 1970 data, eighty thousand people (twenty thousand Soviet prison and camp inmates and sixty thousand deportees) returned to Lithuania (Anušauskas et al., *Lietuva 1940–1990*, 418).

62. Katherine Verdery, *Political Lives of Dead Bodies: Reburial and Post-Socialist Change* (New York: Columbia University Press, 1999).

63. Dovilė Grickevičiūtė, *Kančia ir pilietiškumas lietuvių tremtinių pasakojimuose apie 1941–1953 metų tremtį* (MA thesis, Vytautas Magnus University, 2015).

64. Nijolė Sadūnaitė is a nun who was sentenced to imprisonment in Gulag in 1975 for publishing and distributing the secret Lithuanian Catholic Church Chronicles.

65. For example, in a Twitter post of President Dalia Grybauskaitė, "Our independence was gained through the blood and sacrifice of the Lithuanian people. No-one has the right to threaten it, and only we will decide our fate" ("Russian Prosecutor General's Office to examine legitimacy of Baltic States; Lithuania responds angrily," *Baltic Times*, June 30, 2015, http://www.baltictimes.com/russian_prosecutor _general_s_office_to_examine_legitimacy_of_baltic_states__lithuania _responds_angrily/).

66. Serguei A. Oushakine, *The Patriotism of Despair: Nation, War, and Loss in Russia* (Ithaca, NY: Cornell University Press, 2009).

67. See, for example, Geoffrey Hosking, "The Second World War and Russian National Consciousness," *Past and Present* 175, no. 1 (2002): 162–87; Stephen M. Norris, "Guiding Stars: The Comet-like Rise of the War Film in Putin's Russia; Recent World War II Films and Historical Memories," *Studies in Russian and Soviet Cinema* 1, no. 2 (2007): 163–89; and Samuel Greene, Maria Lipman, and Andrey Ryabov, "Engaging History: The Problems and Politics of Memory in Russia," in *Engaging History: The Problems and Politics of Memory in Russia and the Post-Socialist Space*, ed. Samuel A. Greene, Carnegie Moscow Center Working Papers no. 2 (Moscow: Carnegie Moscow Center, 2010).

68. Nikolay Koposov, *Memory Laws, Memory Wars* (Cambridge: Cambridge University Press, 2018), 248.

69. The number of participants was provided by "'Immortal Regiment' Marches through Streets of Russia," *NBC News*, May 9, 2015, http://www.nbcnews.com/news /world/immortal-regiment-marches-through-streets-russia-n356561.

70. According to anchor Vladimir Solovyev, "There were no loud announcements and no commotion" about President Putin's participation in the "Immortal Regiment." Why? "Because this is an amazing event at which politics moves into the background. It is a day when all are equal" (Stephen Ennis, "Putin's Russian Image

Change: Action Man to Mr Ordinary," *BBC News*, May 15, 2015, http://www.bbc.com/news/world-europe-32741458).

NERINGA KLUMBYTĖ is Associate Professor of Anthropology at Miami University. She has published on authoritarianism and political participation, political marketing in Lithuania, sovereignty and nationalism, electoral politics, humor and censorship, memories of World War II, and nostalgia for socialism. She is coeditor of *Soviet Society in the Era of Late Socialism, 1964–85* (2012), and one of the authors of *Social and Historical Justice in Lithuania* (2018).

Figure 2.1. House of Terror Museum, Budapest, founded 2002. http://www.terrorhaza.hu/hu. *Wikimedia Commons*

TWO

Visualizing Revisionism

Europeanized Anticommunism at the House of
Terror Museum in Budapest

MÁTÉ ZOMBORY

The House of Terror Museum in Budapest has already been the subject of several articles, and so it is not simply a rhetorical question whether one can still say something relevant in relation to the museum. This chapter aims to put the House of Terror Museum in a new light by applying a transnational framework of analysis. I consider the museum as an institutional attempt of historical revisionism, inscribed into the European debate on the historical legacy of the twentieth century, in particular the relation between the memory of Nazism and of Communism. The debate unfolded in a transnational space of memory politics, which emerged in the 1970s and received a boost after the end of the bipolar world system. In the post–Cold War context, the European Union (EU) gradually embraced the universalist memory of the Holocaust as a historical experience constitutive of European identity and prescribed its cultivation to the candidate states as a "soft" EU-membership criterion.[1] Thus, the postcommunist European memory debates were structured by the uniqueness claim of Holocaust memory, opposed to challenging claims of victimization and suffering.[2] In the unequal power relations constituted by European enlargement, candidate countries, which were unable to influence the criteria of accession, strove to accumulate symbolic resources to reflect their subjugated position. Together with the European policies, this tactic enormously increased the social value attributed to memory. By the end of the 1990s, national debates on recent history in the region mirrored the points of reference within the wider European context.

The House of Terror Museum was founded in 2002, at a time when adhering to Europeanized norms of historical consciousness formed a part of EU expansion. Unlike the first wave of memorial museums in the EU candidate countries, the creation of the House of Terror Museum was part of a state discourse aiming to internationally demonstrate the Europeanness of Hungary and at the same time to present communism both as an additional historical trauma, an "eastern experience" beside the Holocaust, and as a historical specificity unknown to the West.[3] The main features of the House of Terror Museum arise from the transnational political context: the question of communism is raised as a memory issue in relation to the Holocaust and is represented according the canonic model of global Holocaust memory. In the national context, the same strategy served to discredit political adversaries by implementing a new canon of historical memory.

The House of Terror attempted to revise history in both senses of the term. On the one hand, the House of Terror Museum tried to provide a new interpretation by pursuing a political and moral mission against the supposed misunderstanding, silencing, and so-called falsification of history.[4] In the international context of Hungary at the millennium, this mission made sense in the prevailing European memory discourse in relation to the universal conception of the Holocaust. The House of Terror Museum, by reclaiming the memory of communism, reappropriated the European norms of historical consciousness and provided a "Europeanized" version of anticommunism that differed considerably from the previously prevailing anticommunist nationalism of early post–Cold War Hungary. On the other hand, the House of Terror Museum strove to revise history in a visual sense; that is, through representing its interpretation of the past in the material space of exhibition. This study argues that the House of Terror visualized an already existing set of anticommunist arguments processed and distributed by the newly established scholarly infrastructure around the museum.

After a brief presentation of the Hungarian political imagery of the early 1990s, I discuss strategies of historical revisionism with regard to the House of Terror Museum in the following registers: historical argumentations of anticommunist antitotalitarianism, memorialization and ritual, exhibit conception, the visual-material exhibition, and certain techniques of representation applied by the museum. In the end, as we will see, the historical revisionism of the House of Terror Museum has been relatively successful, since it relied on the recently Europeanized norms of historical consciousness, particularly the representational repertoire of Holocaust memory. It has established a contentious interpretation of recent Hungarian history that privileges Hungarian suffering under "foreign" communism while attempting to equate suffering under communism with that of the Holocaust.

ANTICOMMUNISMS

In the early 1990s, the new political system in Hungary gained its legitimacy from the myth of national memory recovery after its decades-long communist suppression. Nationalism and communism were believed to be in antagonistic opposition. The conventional narrative about the changes in 1989 focused on the reinterpretation of the 1956 revolution, presented by the communist regime as counterrevolutionary, and culminated in the reburial of Imre Nagy and his fellow martyrs on June 16, 1989 (executed for their role in the revolution and buried in unmarked graves). Their proper burial in 1989 was frequently identified with the symbolic burial of communist legitimacy. Previously suppressed memory of the past, that is, of 1956, presented anew as a national uprising against communism, was equated with historical truth in strict opposition with the official lies of the system. In this political imagery, 1989 completed the 1956 revolution, which itself relied on the liberation in 1945 and the short-lived quasi-democracy before the communist takeover. Because the "true history" of the nation was supposed to have been silenced by the regime, the post-Stalinist period, named after the general secretary of the Hungarian Socialist Workers' Party, János Kádár (in position 1956–88), was easily equated with "tabooization" and amnesia—in opposition to which the 1990s and the democratic system could appear to be characterized by free speech and free remembering. Reclaiming national memory, with the accompanying reinterpretation of the past, was thus the main practice of producing historical truth and political legitimacy.

In the early postcommunist years, Hungary did not commemorate communism in the strict sense of the word; the new system's main symbolic and political objective was to introduce a clear break with the ancien régime. Political imagery instead focused on the idea of a return: to normality, to the nation, to truth, to Europe.[5] The state socialist period was bracketed as the dead end of history as the new political elite strove to symbolically continue history from the point at which it got onto the wrong track with the communist takeover and the repression of the 1956 uprising. In this national canon, cultural and political emphasis was put on the cultivation of the heroes of resistance who had fought against communist oppression and on the supposed return of Hungarians to Europe and to the West. NATO and EU membership was supposed to put a definitive end not only to the transitional situation created by the fall of the communist regime, but to the half-century-long harmful association with the "wrong side"; namely, the East. The essentially pro-European anticommunism of this period defined the former regime negatively: communism meant all that was opposite to the positive values attributed to the nation and to Europe.

The memory of the Holocaust had become legitimate in public discourses since 1989, but until the end of the decade it never served as the point of reference of the Hungarian national canon. References to fascism and communism did, however, play a role in political struggles: the conservative camp usually tried to assign culpability for communism to the postcommunist left, now composed of the liberals and the socialists (the heir of the state-party with no classic socialdemocratic value-system), while the left tended to accuse the conservatives of anti-Semitism and non-Europeanism ("barbarism"). In this typical constellation of public debates, the blame of historical continuity with communism clashed with the accusation of denying the Hungarians' part in the Holocaust. To leftistliberal circles, the modern and European Hungarian nation was not conceivable without "coming to terms with the past," especially with Hungarians' collaboration with the Nazis and their participation in the deportation of nearly a half million Jews from Hungary in 1944. The second half of the decade witnessed the conservatives' growing attempt to confront the prevailing Europe discourse, in which the Hungarian nation was perceived as being positioned as a perpetrator during the Holocaust. In order to restore national pride, they launched their fight against what they termed the "left-wing hegemony" in cultural matters in general and in interpretations of Hungary's past in particular.

It is not by chance, therefore, that the leading historical institution of this epoch, one established to deal with the social and political legacy of the recent past, the Institute for the History of the 1956 Hungarian Revolution, was created in 1989 the day after the reburial of Imre Nagy and his fellow martyrs.[6] In the beginning, it was financed from various sources and by individual governmental support until its formation as a public foundation in 1994. In 1998, when the first cabinet led by Viktor Orbán began its work, the parliament withdrew the budget submitted for the public foundation to run the 1956 Institute: in 1998 it received 60 million Hungarian forints from the national budget, but in 1999 it got only 6 million. The budgetary law for the year 1999 was modified by the parties in parliament in such a way that the 73 million forints initially assigned to the 1956 Institute was reduced by 67 million, and the 50 million subvention of another research institute, the Foundation of Political History, was completely withdrawn;[7] at the same time, exactly 117 million was put under the new title of "historical research on the 20th century."[8] In February 1999, the resolution of the government created the Public Foundation for the Research of Central and East European History and Society (Kelet-és Közép-európai Történelem és Társadalom Kutatásáért Közalapítvány, KKTTKK) and assigned 117 million forints to its functioning. The new institution's articles of association declare that "the public foundation, in order to realize its objectives, operates a museal institution at number 60 Andrássy Road, 6th district, Budapest."[9]

The shifts in Hungarian national canon are clearly visible in this symbolic calendar: the House of Terror Museum was opened at 60 Andrássy Road on February 24, 2002, the eve of the Day of the Victims of the Communist Dictatorships.[10] The parliament created this commemorative day on June 16, 2000, the anniversary of the reburial of the revolutionary prime minister of 1956. Gradually cultural emphasis on the recent past shifted from national heroism to victimization by communism. The process culminated in a number of symbolic decisions after 2010, when the second Orbán government formed with the support of a two-thirds majority in the parliament. The preamble of the new constitution of 2011, which was supposed to put a definitive end to the transitional and compromised postcommunist era, declared that on March 19, 1944, Hungary lost its sovereignty and regained it only on May 2, 1990, with the forming of the first parliament. In the new symbolic periodization, the 1956 revolution, together with the early postwar pluralistic quasi-democracy, faded away from the national canon, and the landmarks of 1945 and 1989 are reinterpreted. From liberation, 1945 transforms into occupation, and 1989 shifted from a revolution that completed the one begun in 1956 into an incomplete, semirevolution that failed to dispense justice to the communists. The recent past is presented as the suffering of the nation, victimized by alien communist domination; and a particular memory of communism is cultivated.

As the flagship of the struggle for a new national canon of recent history and memory, the House of Terror Museum played a crucial role in this transformation of historical consciousness. János M. Rainer, the director of the 1956 Institute, when he visited the new exhibition, saw the government's efforts in the "house of terror-phenomenon" to build a new historical canon that excludes the previous post-89 public discussions about the recent past.[11] The shift meant that not just political parties clashed during the long debates about the House of Terror Museum: these were two opposing anticommunist visions of recent history, both fundamentally defining the political life of Hungary's present.

THE ORIGINS OF ANTITOTALITARIANISM

What made the House of Terror Museum novel in a national context was that it attempted to revise the past not by providing breakthrough historical reinterpretations within the scholarly field but through a straightforward memory claim. That statement might be surprising when the majority of the KKTTKK board of trustees are professional historians.[12] Yet history writing associated with the new institutional infrastructure behind the House of Terror Museum played a peculiar role. Although the museum opened in 2002, its story had already begun in 1998, when the new government created the KKTTKK, whose organization, besides the "museal institution" at 60 Andrássy Road, includes the 20th Century Institute (created by government decision in May 1999), and the 21st Century Institute (founded by the government in September 2000). Both are research institutions for fostering scientific research and the distribution of historical knowledge. Not connected to the ministry responsible for higher education and research, this infrastructure was created separately from the ordinary scholarly field, under the Ministry of National Cultural Patrimony. If the government deprived two former research institutes of public support when establishing the new laboratories of knowledge production about recent history in 1998–2000, it did, however, allow the academic research infrastructure proper to remain intact; that is, the historical institute at the Hungarian Academy of Sciences and the universities' history departments. Not only was the new scholarly and public infrastructure parallel to the existing research institutions dealing with recent history, but it neither attached its activity to the related existing academic research nor did it take part in the ongoing academic debate on the relation between Nazism and communism.[13] Historian Mária Schmidt, a member of the board of trustees at the KKTTKK, director of the House of Terror Museum and of the two related research institutions, and adviser of Prime Minister Viktor Orbán from 1998 to 2002, justified the creation of the foundation in an interview as follows: "We would like to have the leftist opinion-monopoly finally broken, that there would also be place for different approaches and views in the market of ideas."[14]

Instead of directly confronting the domestic scholarly field of history, the activities of the KKTTKK relied heavily on European debates about the uniqueness of the Holocaust. Schmidt contended in several publications in the second half of the 1990s that communism, or more precisely, the memory of its horrors, had been forgotten in relation to that of the Holocaust.[15] Besides postulating a leftist hegemony on these historical matters, the director explicitly relied on the arguments of US journalist Anne Applebaum, a regular participant in events organized by the 20th Century Institute. According to one of those arguments, the complicity of Western intellectuals and political powers in allying with one totalitarian power to defeat another prevented confrontation with the war crimes committed by communist countries. Another key reference of Schmidt is Alain Besançon, who is a member of the international advisory board attached to the House of Terror Museum. In 1997, the French historian gave a lecture at the Institut de France in which he argued that victims of communism need the same recognition as those of the Holocaust and that Nazism and communism were equally criminal.[16] Besançon tried to assess in a related book the historical role of communism by using the model that Raul Hilberg had elaborated in *The Destruction of the European Jews* and introduced the idea of an opposition between the hypermnesia of Nazism and the amnesia of communism.[17] Schmidt and her institutions adopted the stance that their task should be accounting for the silence around the crimes of communism. An additional, powerful argument they made concerned the so-called "missed Nuremberg" for communism; that is, unless governments tried the criminals of communism, post–Eastern Bloc countries cannot successfully fulfill the transition to democracy. Schmidt, for example, discussed in detail an article of Applebaum's on the subject, arguing that the "missed historical justice, the denial of confronting the past weighs heavily on our public life. Suppressing common memory leads to collective amnesia and thus to identity crisis."[18]

Another important Western influence on the argumentative strategies of the House of Terror Museum was *The Black Book of Communism: Crimes, Terror, Repression*, particularly Stéphane Courtois's introduction. The French historian, who borrowed the equation of "genocide of race" and "genocide of class" from his German colleague Ernst Nolte,[19] made the highly contested estimation that communism had altogether 100 million victims. Without indicating the source or referring to the intense criticism it fostered, Schmidt borrowed the magical number of 100 million and reproduced the comparison made by Courtois that in relation to that, Nazism had "only" 25 million victims.[20] In May 2000, the 20th Century Institute organized an international conference on *The Black Book of Communism*, in which Courtois, Nicolas Werth, Jean-Louis Panné, and Andrzej Paczkowski participated as authors, together with Besançon, and published the conference material the same year.

Well before the opening of the House of Terror Museum, its preceding background institutions engaged in the task of distributing historical knowledge produced by various Western authors. With the support of the 20th Century Institute, such classics as Tony Judt's *A Grand Illusion? An Essay on Europe* (1996, translation in 2002) and Konrad Löw's *Das Rotbuch der kommunistischen Ideologie: Marx and Engels, Die Väter des Terrors* (1999, translation in 2003), prefaced by Courtois, appeared in Hungarian.[21] In 2003 the 20th Century Institute published Ernst Nolte's *Der Faschismus in seiner Epoche* (1963, translated into English in 1965),[22] and organized a public discussion about it in the presence of the author. The next day Nolte gave a lecture to the Hungarian public on the consequences of the West German historians' controversy in 1986–87, in which he played an eminent role by infamously claiming that the Nazi Final Solution, considered only in technical terms, can be considered as a reaction to the communist program of extermination. The 20th Century Institute also published the works of historians who are members of the international advisory board to the KKTTKA: Paul Johnson's *Modern Times: The World from the Twenties to the Nineties* in 2000,[23] Mart Laar's *Back to the Future* in 2002,[24] and *Judgement in Moscow*, the book by the influential Soviet dissident Vladimir Bukovsky, dealing with the question of the Nuremberg of communism, in 2009.[25]

Through this vast body of literature, a complete vocabulary and argumentative repertoire of anticommunist historical revisionism made its way into the Hungarian context. According to this discourse, unlike victims of Nazism, victims of communism are not recognized, their human dignity is not respected; this perceived inequality is morally unacceptable all the more because they were more numerous than the victims of Nazism. From the moral obligation of equal respect for the suffering of innocent victims follows the historically untenable thesis of the equal criminality of the two systems.[26] The silencing of the crimes of communism, the argument goes on, can be attributed to the inability of certain (leftist) contemporaries who are either blinded by the false promises of Marxism or by the moral compromise of allying with one evil to defeat another. If the Nuremberg trials of communism were unfortunately "missed" in 1989, today it is necessary to at least morally and publicly condemn communism and its perpetrators, in order to definitely put an end to their ongoing influence. As in the case of the memory of the Holocaust, it is a moral mission to make these crimes and their victims publicly recognized, and those who can show historical truth are only those who lived through communism: who were subjugated to its regime in Eastern Europe or to its ideology in the West (like Besançon, who had been member of the French Communist Party). In this discourse, communism and Nazism are juxtaposed by the quasi-scientific concept of totalitarianism, particularly its anticommunist version elaborated in the 1970s by leftist French intellectuals criticizing the politics of the French Communist Party.[27] Clearly visible in the emphasis put on "coming to terms with" the "difficult past" of communism, without which today's societies are not capable of fully build democracy, the anticommunist discourse of communism memory follows the model of Holocaust memory.[28] Historiography of this cause is characterized by the detachment of argument from empirical historical context. The shifting of reasoning to the abstract realm of ideas and ideologies enables practitioners of this school to relate historically and geographically distant phenomena, such as discussing past events and figures in the conceptual, political, and moral framework of the historian's present.[29] A result of this repositioning can be termed the return of cosmology in history (writing), that is, treating historical phenomena in a moralizing manner as manifestations of evil (it is interesting that good is lacking in the vocabulary).

Besides an accumulated pan-European discursive repertoire of reclaiming the memory of communism, the House of Terror Museum was aided by an international network of people who were in one way or another engaged in the creation of communism memory and its museal representation. Besides historians (Besançon, Johnson, Laar, or Michael Wolffson), the international advisory board to the KKTTKK included prestigious American and European experts (such as Norman Podhoretz), particularly Zbigniew Brzezinski, who contributed to the inauguration ceremony of the House of Terror Museum with a letter of support that was read at the assembly.[30] He is also member of the international advisory board of Directors of the Museum of the Occupation in Latvia and also, together with Alain Besançon, the honorary board to the SocLand Foundation, in charge of creating the museum of communism of Poland. In addition, eminent former dissidents are taking part in the work of the international advisory board, representatives of a strong moral engagement in anticommunism.[31] An important member of the international advisory board to the House of Terror Museum was human right activist Vladimir Bukovsky (1942–2019), who was also a member, together with Courtois, of the Scientific Council associated to the Sighet Memorial in Romania, and the Polish architect Czesłav Bielecki, the initiator of SocLand Foundation. Founded in 1999, Bielecki's foundation organized a temporary exhibition in Warsaw on communism, which, in conception and composition, shared several features with the House of Terror Museum—not surprising, since the 20th Century Institute co-organized the event.[32]

With such an influential network and a discursive repertoire in the background, by 2002 only the visual-material realization of the memory claim of communism remained. This task fell to the House of Terror Museum.

MONUMENT, MEMORIAL, MEMENTO

It is hard to find another institution dealing with the representation of the recent past that has triggered criticism as intensive as the House of Terror Museum has. The opening of the exhibition in February 2002 shocked many intellectuals, experts, and academics dealing with history, museography, aesthetics, and memory. Why the Hungarian intellectual field, mainly those associated to the postcommunist left, was seemingly so unprepared for the exhibition at the House of Terror Museum despite the preceding two-year-long activity of the public foundation behind it is a question that is hard to answer. Another, more important, one is how the House of Terror Museum could gain legitimacy in such a hostile intellectual environment. In this respect, the thesis developed here is that the actors connected with the new institution succeeded in both setting and controlling the context of the debate. Both in its exhibition and in the supporting discourses, the House of Terror Museum referred to the prevailing norms of European historical consciousness, precisely to the norms of Holocaust-memory. Most important, it justified itself by a memory claim: the need to give respect to the innocent victims of historical trauma. Few things remained uncontested during the debate about the House of Terror Museum: one was the need to commemorate the victims, another that all victims' dignity must be restored. The House of Terror Museum could set the debate in such a way that no one called into question the very existence of an institution dealing with the memory of the victims of twentieth-century totalitarian regimes. The most powerful argument in this respect was the site of the exhibition. The building at 60 Andrássy Road served as headquarters of the Hungarian pro-Nazi Arrow Cross Party, which on October 15, 1944, seized power and continued its war against Bolshevism even while fleeing toward Germany in January 1945. Later that month, the communist-led political police, eventually the state security forces of the one-party system (Államvédelmi Hatóság), settled in the building and functioned there until 1951 (integrated into the Ministry of the Interior, it ceased to exist as an autonomous organ in 1953 and was finally abolished in 1956). Later on, the building was used as an office by various commercial companies.

The creators of the museum aimed from the beginning to make the building a monument, and after having studied examples abroad, they decided to design it to shock passersby.[33] The black passe-partout framing of the building plays that role and provides a monumental function to the building. (See fig. 2.1.) According to architect Attila Ferenczfy Kovács, author of the visual concept of the House of Terror Museum, 60 Andrássy Road "as a museum is not anymore a building" but "a statue of a building form," the "statue of terror."[34] But 60 Andrássy Road was supposed to be much more than a mere monument. The opening ceremony was organized as a ritual, a tribute to respect the victims as participants were asked to bring and light a candle in the memory of the victims. The ritual constituted the monument as a site of mourning, a gesture continuously reinforced by the shrine at the entrance hall, where two marble plates stand, one black, one red, with the symbols of the Arrow Cross and five-pointed star are placed, with lit lampions and flowers placed in front (see fig. 2.2). In some of her several public claims in defense of her institution, Mária Schmidt interpreted the framing of the façade, casting the shadow of the word *terror* on the building, together with the symbols of the displayed political ideologies, as a "frame of mourning" and argued that the House of Terror is supposed to foster a common thinking about the last decades so that "finally the work of mourning begins, the necessity of which is so incontestably described by our Nobel-prize laureate, Imre Kertész, in relation to the Holocaust."[35]

The opening ceremony was celebrated by the prime minister, Viktor Orbán, who devoted his speech largely to the building: "This house is a memento. Living suffering.... We locked two dictatorships together within the walls of this house. They stem from different sources, but you can see, they get on well with each other. This is not coincidental. There's no need to evade our own responsibility, but our children need to know that both dictatorships were systems that would not have been able either to gain or maintain power in our country without the support of foreign armies."[36]

In a strict sense, the memorial function of the House of Terror Museum is about reminding later generations of the horrors of the past and thus reassuring the values of freedom and independence. The political context of the creation and the opening, however, together with the discourses about the uncompleted revolution in 1989 and the identification of the postcommunist left with the

Figure 2.2. The building as memorial: Andrassy Road. *Wikimedia Commons*

communists, easily inspire interpretations of the House of Terror Museum as a memento of the continual need to struggle against communism.

Objections that the House of Terror Museum reproduced political instrumentalization, formulated many times even before the opening, were easily put aside by references to the sacred nature of the site. To the criticism that the inauguration by Viktor Orbán one month before the general elections was part of the political campaign of the ruling conservative party, the general director replied that it had been created "in the memory of the suffering of a nation with the burden of history. We wanted to create a memorial to the victims," and those who project political issues to it "are incapable of paying tribute to the memory of the victims."[37] Another key counterargument against the accusation of political instrumentalization of the past was that the opponents are, under the pretense of professional criticism, mounting a political offensive against the House of Terror Museum.[38] At the same time, as will be shown later, the director in some cases did not let the criticisms go unchallenged and argued in favor of her institution as a historical museum.

In fact, an important layer of the controversy around the House of Terror Museum was the definition of the new institution. Is it monument, memorial, memento, or museum? Museologist István Ihász affirms that without classical museum functions—such as collection, registry, storage, conservation—it is hard to put the House of Terror Museum into a precise category of the continuum memorial-collection-exhibition site-museum.[39] For Sándor Radnóti, aesthete and literary historian, possible interpretations include "historical site of memory, site of traumatic communicative memories, monument, museumized site of memory, museum, postmodern museum of torture, architectural construction, vision and gesture of Attila Ferenczfy Kovács, performance and waxworks."[40] Following up on Radnóti's article, literary historian András Rényi observed that all attempts at scholarly criticisms, whether historical, aesthetic, or political, fail because the House of Terror Museum performs history instead of describing it, and thus it can be considered as a rhetorical gesture aiming at persuasion and justice.[41] In any case, the indeterminacy of social roles attributed to the site, particularly the tensions between the historical and the monumental function, provided the House of Terror Museum a considerable space for self-defense and avoiding criticism—while it succeeded in tracing out the discursive boundaries of the debate.

FALSIFYING HISTORY OR DISPLAYING THE TRUTH?

In what way could the promoters of the memory of communism control the debate on the Hungarian past triggered within the exhibition? Because the legitimacy of commemorating the victims of communist repression according to the principle that "one cannot make a difference between victim and victim" was uncontested,[42] criticism was restricted to the way the display expresses the relation between the memory of the Holocaust and that of communism. Positions in relation to the House of Terror Museum were structured in a pattern similar to that in other memory competitions generated by the uniqueness claim of the Holocaust: the challenger blames the other by the denial of historical truth, while the defender accuses the other by falsifying history through the relativization of the Holocaust. The Hungarian controversy, in different variations, concentrated on aspects of the question of balance in historical representation: periodization and responsibility.

The way the exhibition represents periods of post–World War II Hungarian history aroused vociferous criticism. Both the starting point and the endpoint of the historical narrative were questioned. The House of Terror Museum does not deal with the deportation of the Jews of the Hungarian countryside that took place after the German occupation and before the Arrow Cross takeover, under the legitimate Horthy regime. The omission was interpreted as falsifying the history of terror: either as downplaying the memory of the Holocaust[43] or as an attempt to display the Nazi dictatorship as an alibi for representing communism as the real horror of history.[44] Another critique focused on the way that the Arrow Cross rule is presented, for the site presents it as having no historical relation with the former regime and instead that it was sui generis.[45] The end of the display's historical narrative was similarly contested; mainly, that it does not differentiate between the Stalinist Rákosi-era (1948–53) and the "soft-dictatorship" of the Kádár-era (1956–89) by extending the historical display until the Soviet troops left Hungary in 1991, and thus representing a four-decade-long, homogeneous and continuously terroristic communist domination.[46] Intellectuals supporting the conception of the House of Terror Museum did not see any unbalance in the display and celebrated the brave and honest endeavor of finally putting communism in the same place within historical consciousness where it belongs, together with Nazism.[47] Stéphane Courtois, when asked by a national daily newspaper as a scientific expert of communism, justified the underrepresentation of the Holocaust in the House of Terror Museum by citing the historical fact that communists ruled the country much longer than the Nazis.[48]

The House of Terror Museum usually replied to attacks on periodization by emphasizing that the display is restricted to the history of the building (though, in fact, the Arrow Cross Party used parts of the house from 1937, and the communist state security left it in 1951). According to the director, the "Hungarian Holocaust cannot be squeezed, either as antecedent, or as addition, into the history of the house."[49] Another argument was that according to a governmental resolution in

1999, a museum for the victims of the Holocaust was under realization (eventually opened in 2004 as Holocaust Documentation and Memorial Center), which would be the "proper" site for commemorating the Jewish tragedy.[50] At the same time, the exhibition starts in fact with the troops of Nazi Germany marching in Hungary on March 19, 1944, and ends with footage on the Red Army leaving Hungary in June 19, 1991, even by some shots of the museum's opening. Though the director several times explained that the exhibition presents a historical framework of losing and regaining national sovereignty and, in reality, the display covers Hungarian history from the Arrow Cross takeover and until the end of reprisals of the 1956 revolution in 1963, it is really hard to resist the temptation to refer what one see at 60 Andrássy Road to the period between March 19, 1944, and the 1990s.

In fact, the debates over historical periodization unfolded around the question of who can be considered as the subject of the exhibition. The House of Terror Museum is quite ambiguous in this respect in that it openly asserts that it shows the history attached to the building of 60 Andrássy Road; in its mise-en-scène, however, it continuously refers to the whole Hungarian nation as the victim of communism. The display presents scenes, such as the ones on gulags, on forced deliveries, or on post-1956 emigration that are connected to the history of the building only in that they all form part of the same, larger, national history. The concept of an exhibition that is strictly bound to the history of the terror in the building, framed by the events of the Arrow Cross takeover and the departure of the Államvédelmi Hatóság from the building would have found supporters among otherwise critical experts.[51] The cause behind the House of Terror Museum (and also the Museum of Genocide Victims in Vilnius, for instance) becomes clearly visible in comparison with other memorial museums located in former headquarters of terror apparatuses, such as the "Runde Ecke" Memorial Museum (1990, Leipzig) or the Stasi Museum (1990, Berlin). Though they too may serve simultaneously as sites of memory and sites of mourning, their exhibitions show the functioning of the state security service in the German Democratic Republic and not of communism in general. As collection-based museums, they are also preoccupied by the knowledge of the past, which is legitimized by the authenticity of the site. By contrast, the House of Terror Museum does not seem to be interested in the history of the terror apparatuses that functioned in its building. Rather, it shows a mythic struggle between the nation and communism. This requires a strategy of rhetorical extension: the metonymic extension of the history of suffering at the site to the entire nation, and the metaphoric extension of terror of the state security service to communism per se. As a result of this double rhetorical shift, legitimized by the cultural value attributed to the memory of the victims, the House of Terror Museum performs a political allegory of national suffering by communism.

The other main target of critiques was the imbalance in the relation between victims and perpetrators. Many pointed out that the exhibition, by employing the theory of "double occupation" and the emphasis on lack of national sovereignty, represents the Hungarian nation solely as the victim of foreign oppression and thus denies Hungarian responsibility for the terror.[52] As an innocent victim, the nation only endures the terror exercised by foreign powers. As it was argued, this victimization narrative prevents an accurate account for how the two "systems" related to each other, especially that Hungarian communists fought the Nazi regime, and that it was actually the Red Army that put an end to Nazism in Hungary.[53] A reoccurring criticism was the lack of antifascist opposition to Nazism, which certainly would put communism in a different light.[54]

The problem of national responsibility was at the heart of the critique offered by historian Krisztián Ungváry, who contended that "falsifications of history with a political purpose" in the House of Terror Museum prevent the "objective confrontation with the past" and make bearing the responsibility for past misdeeds impossible.[55] "What kind of responsibility does he think of, anyway?"—asks Schmidt in her reply to Ungváry: "The Arrow Cross could only seize power as a result of the violent Nazi action; this happened at a time of foreign great power occupation, under foreign pressure and in foreign interests. The responsibility fell on the foreign occupiers and their servers.... In the 'Gallery of Perpetrators,' only photographs of Hungarians are hung out."[56]

Ungváry also criticized the exhibition for obscuring the criteria by which the victims were defined: it is not clear why especially those people are represented as victims. He points out, for example, that "the exhibition aiming to display the victims of communism" portrays as its first "martyrs" the principals responsible for the deportation of the Jews. These members of the Hungarian quisling government were convicted after the war by the national political tribunals. In the periodization imposed by the museum, the so-called coalition period (1945–48) dissolves into the extended and homogenized concept of communism between 1945 and 1990, which enables a presentation of war criminals, convicted by the postwar people's courts, as the innocent victims of communism. This strategy of obscure definition was criticized not only in respect of victims,[57] but also of perpetrators,[58] such as presenting a former antifascist resistant merely as a perpetrator.[59]

THEATER OF HISTORY

Scholarly criticism of imbalances in historical representation ran against the rocks not only because of the obscure definition of the period and the historical subject displayed, but also because those criticisms called the exhibition to account for something it did not really attempt. To put it simply, scholarly critiques showed how ahistorical the exhibition was despite the fact that its creators do not seem to have attempted to make a historical museum from the beginning. Rather, they formed a decontextualized and ahistorical space of comparison without preventing an interpretation of the display as historically referential. As Schmidt put it in an interview, "both dictatorships were an equally inhuman nightmare of a terrorist type":[60] in this light, Nazism and communism have little to do with historical reality, causality, or human relations. As irrational evils of a transcendent history, they occur as blows of fate irrespective of human interventions. At the same time, the display presents them as historical forces affecting the body of the nation. That the display enables both historical references and symbolic associations is clearly visible in how various actors have interpreted the way the House of Terror Museum relates the "two dictatorships." The hall called Changeroom is arranged as a changing room with lockers against the wall. In the middle, the uniform of the Arrow Cross and that of the communist secret police both stand, put against their backs on a turning stand. The arrangement recalls the historical event when the Hungarian Communist Party allowed party membership to former ordinary, non-office-holding Arrow Cross party members. While historians, reading referentially the scene and the objects, assess the scene as a falsification of history, since "no Arrow Cross member dressed up in the uniform of the political police,"[61] the historian-director in the same interview interprets the two uniforms as a "symbol of the dictatorships"[62] put in the center of a room whose conception "symbolizes the continuity of the dictatorships, as well as denoting that all strata of society 'changed clothes,' entering into a totally different world."[63] The historian, interpreting the installation as associative to historical reality, criticizes it as unfounded because actual scholarship does not know how many former Arrow Cross members had Communist Party cards.[64] Finally, the aesthete, who takes the changing-clothes scene as the script of the whole exhibition, contests the commonplace suggestion that "those were the same, or at least the same type, who realized the two sorts of terror."[65] In the exhibition space of symbolic-associative relations, historical reasoning appears as just another interpretation among many others. Critics of the ideology of continuous terror, and what is more, the suggestion that what happened in the building and thus in the country was nothing else than the thirsty revenge of Jewish communists[66] could be positioned as visitors seeing something that was actually not there. What is indeed not there is the history of "changing clothes": when, who, how many, and why former Arrow Cross members joined the communists.

In this space of simulacra, visual-material representations do not refer to past history but rather foster associations with iconic popular images of history. In the center of the scene called "Resettlement and Deportation," there is a huge black car behind black curtains. As the catalog explains, "The ZIM automobile on display is a frightening relic of the times: it evokes the infamous 'black car' used by the communist political police to pick up its victims, usually in the middle of the night."[67]

The infamous black car coming for you in the middle of the night—this image of terror, without any historical reasoning, remains in the sphere of commonplace representations of the communist regime. Objects put on display do not stand for their own history but symbolize free-floating ideas about the past. The ZIM car could, however, play an authentic role on its own terms in that Khrushchev himself owned it.[68] In the prison basement of the building, which was reconstructed according to testimonies of detainees,[69] each cell is thematized by photographs of persons presented as victims, irrespective of their connection to the site. One visits punishment cells, traditional cells, and an execution place after having listened to a witness's detailed description of a hanging that plays in the elevator. As András Mink admits, "The experience is shocking despite the fact that it is known: there were no executions at 60 Andrássy Road."[70]

In the reconstructed cellar labyrinth a gallows is exhibited, which was actually used until the abolishment of capital punishment (1990)—but not at the site, where there were no hangings.[71] What is more, one can also observe "six replica scaffolds" in the basement, in the room of the reprisals of the 1956 revolution.

Objects put on display include authentic ones linked to the history of the site, authentic ones with no connection to the building, replicas and reconstructions, and objects whose relevance is unclear. They all are put into relation to constitute a network of signs to evoke ideas and ideologies of history. This strategy of representation results necessarily in an obliteration of the boundaries between the types of objects on display and poor contextualization by way of few and "hidden" inscriptions or commentaries.[72] How to explain the ability of the exhibition to acquire legitimacy as a historical exhibition? Besides the fact that the museum publicly presents itself as a museum, the authenticity of the building (the "Real" object of the exhibition) is so strong that it, by the "spirit of the place," transfers to the objects put on display. Also, the symbolism of the exhibition evokes canonized and iconic images of history and terror, probably well known, thus commonly legitimate to the visitor.

Those who expected a proper historical exhibition at 60 Andrássy Road condemned the way in which "the museum turns into theater, tragedy into dramatized story, and scientific severity into a trivial commonplace performed by theatrical props."[73] The House of Terror Museum, together with apologetic commentators, tends to frame the same characteristic as innovative museography that breaks with the boring world of dusty vitrines. From this perspective, the lack of authentic objects is "sensationally counterbalanced by installation" that is easily consumable to the post-1989 generation, a primary target of the House of Terror Museum. Ihász also praised how the curators "put the objects, pictures, films, well known by the profession, all into a staggeringly installed context by applying theatrical and cinematic sign-systems used experimentally during the last decades." From this perspective, the essence of the mise-en-scène conception is to evoke the atmosphere of an epoch.[74] It is worth noting that Attila Ferenczfy Kovács, responsible for the visual concept of the House of Terror Museum, had important experiences in cinematographic representation, for he constructed the grotesque scenes of the banned film Álombrigád, directed by András Jeles in 1983. Ákos Kovács, the rock musician in charge of the music and sound effects of the exhibit, compared his task to composing the music for a movie. After having received the Officer's Cross of the Order of Merit of the Republic of Hungary for his contribution to bring the House of Terror Museum into being, he said in an interview that "The music, the special sound effects, such as the scenery- and theater-like elements, builds on associations. This might represent more accurately the period's stifling air than authenticity pretending to be precise."[75]

Important elements of the House of Terror Museum's self-image are its innovation, creativity, and interactivity, creating a modern, up-to-date, even unusual museography alien to the older generations of scholars. The House of Terror Museum would then subscribe to the trend in which "museums shift their emphasis from preservation and study to dramatic delivery" and, in order to deliver an experience to the audience, "exhibitions are becoming more public oriented, more theatrical, and more self-consciously rhetorical."[76] Putting experience on display has important consequences with respect to museology. Unlike objects, experiences are not collectible, not located in time and space. As Hilde Hein has noted, "Experiential reality is phenomenologically self-contained and divorced from both its causes and consequences. Whatever the stimulus and however great its intensity, no corroborating referent or vindication other than the fact of its presentation matters."[77]

The role of the historical museum tends to be that of a provider of circumstances in which the visitors can live through more-or-less subjective but genuine experiences about the past. Instead of delivering prestructured and static knowledge, "the museum provides the conditions under which certain types of experiences may be expected to take place."[78] Its status transforms accordingly into a platform in which the public can discover their real experiences in relation to the subject on display. The main instrument of this is interactivity. Such shifts in priorities of museography put the ethical responsibility of the museum in the forefront.

Though the House of Terror Museum seems to meet some features of this trend, it is contrary to it in several respects. First, it detaches objectivity from objects. Though it claims to collect objects as part of its activity, it primarily imitates collection by limiting it mainly to immaterial phenomena. In a sense, the House of Terror Museum subordinates objects and their authenticity to creative and many times arbitrary meaning attribution and uses them as symbolic elements of an installation. Second, it shares a conservative attitude in relation to museum practices. Its interactivity is strictly technical, limited to the use of audio effects, video screenings, and computerized access to information. Its relation to the exhibition—to the role of the museum—is authoritative in that it doesn't allow alternative interpretations, let alone different experiences according to the particularities of the audience. The House of Terror Museum, unlike "new museums," doesn't cooperate with the local population, or with the public at large. In short, it "valorizes the emotive over cognitive meaning"[79] while keeping the ordinary hierarchical and authoritative posture on exhibiting. The result is more similar to insisting on its own truth than providing conditions enabling one to discover one's own truth. The overall visiting experience that the exhibit allows thus resembles a filmic experience more than an exploration, even though the visitor can access digitalized information in playful ways.

"IT IS NOT I WHO AM CONCERNED WITH THE CREATION OF THE HOLOCAUST-MUSEUM"

So Mária Schmidt asserted in an interview and expressed her hope that the museum-plan of the Holocaust-museum will be finished soon so that one can finally commemorate the victims of the Hungarian Holocaust in a proper way.[80] Indeed, not being a Holocaust museum is an important element of the House of Terror Museum's self-image. It is true, as has been demonstrated here, in spite of the fact that it appropriates certain elements of the global holocaust discourse, such as legitimizing its existence by means of the "duty to memory" or by putting emphasis on the victim/perpetrator classification. But also the House of Terror Museum relies heavily on the canonic representational repertoire, the techniques and the iconography of Holocaust memory. In other words, the House of Terror Museum takes part in the "global Holocaust assemblage."[81] Three features seem to be significant in this respect: narrative enactment, the personalized vision of history, and a moral lesson as an organic part of the museum's public role.

Down into Inferno and Back

Narrative enactment of the exhibition is an essential museographic strategy of transmitting the educational moral lesson in memorial museums. Jeshajahu Weinberg, who oversaw the final design of the Holocaust Memorial Museum in Washington, DC, emphasized that narrative museums, unlike collection-based

Figure 2.3. The Gulag Room. *Wikimedia Commons*

ones, invite visitors to internalize the moral lessons of history through ensuring emotional involvement in the narrative plot.[82] In the case of the House of Terror Museum, narrative emplotment is connected to the site-specific nature of the exhibition. Visits start at the second floor, continue down to the basement, and end on the ground floor. This symbolic trajectory leads to the deepest darkness of history, and—according to the intentions of the creators—finishes in the sunlight as a revelation that the dark past is over and that Hungary is now a free country.[83] The itinerary is not only allegoric but abstract, detached from historical reality: there are several jumps in time and space. The themes of the trajectory are the following: second floor: "double occupation," Arrow Cross rule, gulag in the Soviet Union (see fig. 2.3), "Changeroom," the fifties, workday communism, Soviet advisers (this reports about the imposition of Soviet "methods and lifestyle on to Hungarian society"), and resistance. The first floor exhibits resettlement and deportation, the torture chamber, "Compulsory Deliveries" during the collectivization campaigns (without economic and political contextualization, depicted as the meaningless torture of peasantry by the malignant communists), the political police, the practice of arbitrary jurisprudence (confusing trials of various types from 1945 to 1956), the absurd and ridiculous propaganda from the 1950s, the aluminum room on the shining but valueless "Hungarian silver," religion and Cardinal József Mindszenty. From the first floor, by elevator visitors reach the basement: the reconstructed subterranean prison and cells. Here victims of whatever kind of terror and executions are presented; thematic internment, the 1956 revolution and the reprisals, emigration, and the 1980s to early 1990s in the room called Farewell are covered.[84]

Us and Them

An important feature of the Holocaust assemblage is the personalization of history; that is, presenting the past through individual stories and from the perspectives of the victims. Identification with the victims is supposed to foster emotional identification with those who suffered and thus to arouse moral engagement to fight against intolerance and anti-Semitism. Thus, a great deal of significance is attributed to photographs and video recordings of (former) victims, with the most famous examples being the Hall of Names at Yad Vashem or the Tower of Faces at the US Holocaust Memorial Museum in Washington, DC. Several commentators affirmed an affinity between global Holocaust museums and the House of Terror.[85] Yet there are significant differences. In the US Holocaust Memorial Museum the visitor can contemplate the collection of an entire population of a Lithuanian town through prewar photographs depicting everyday life; the collection is supposed to be the photographic embodiment of the life of the village, depicting the Jewish community before victimization; it is through the narrative trajectory of the exhibition that later the visitors are informed about the fate of the people represented in the Tower of Faces.[86] As with the identity card of a victim offered to visitors, victims at the US Holocaust Memorial Museum are enumerated and presented in the framework of their more-or-less detailed life stories. On the walls of the inner courtyard of the building, the House of Terror Museum presents the face of thirty-five hundred victims in a standardized way, using the mug shot photographs without any information about the persons and offering the possibility to browse the collection (see fig. 2.4). The history of the victims is left obscure, and the fiction of standardization coming from the display suggests that what is seen is a singular registry, in which the faces do not stand for themselves but "appear as documents, as evidence of the two terror regime's common archive."[87]

This architectural design constitutes a position in which it is hard to identify with the victims. Instead it more likely triggers moral indignation facing the immense loss of innocent life. It is the abstract concept of the nation that can establish a common framework, a sense of commonality with the standardized and serial representation of unknown victims. The basement also has a "Hall of Tears" with the "names of those who were executed for political reasons between 1945 and 1957."[88]

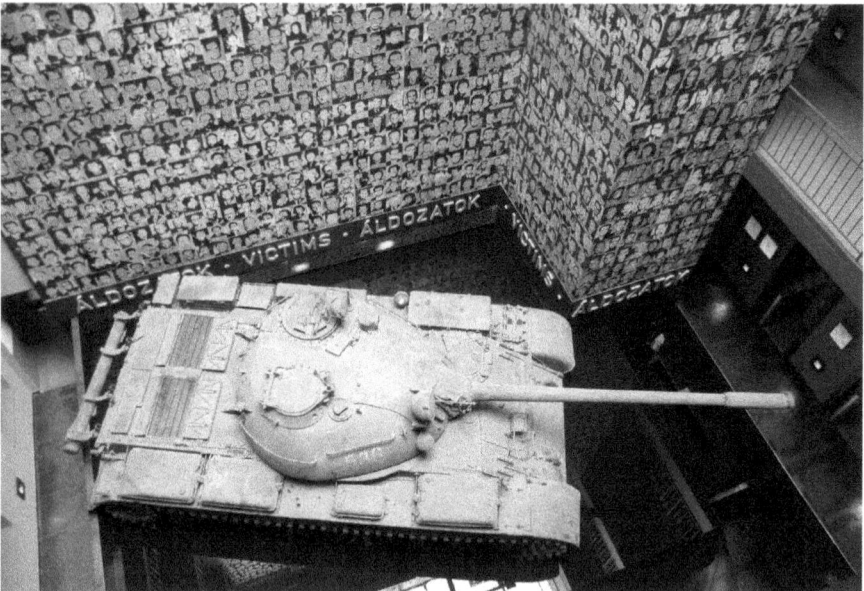

Figure 2.4. A T-54 tank before the Wall of Victims. *Wikimedia Commons*

Doing Justice

Like Holocaust museums, the House of Terror Museum shares the vocation of transmitting a moral lesson to the public, since it is positioned in the discourse about the "duty to remember" (Never again!) that is, the imperative of commemoration in order to avoid the repetition of past injustice. But the fight against the "past that never passes" has a judiciary dimension. The alleged public role attributed to the museum by its creators is grounded by the discourse on the missed opportunity to have a Nuremberg trial of the crimes of communism. The House of Terror Museum explicitly assumes the role of contributing to bring the perpetrators to justice. According to the initial plans, the research attached to the exhibition site aimed to continue and eventually finish the identification of all the victims and perpetrators of communism. Thus completing the "archive of communism." Yet the perpetrators are represented differently as the victims. Leaving the basement, on the way to the ground floor, the audience is led through the Gallery of Perpetrators. This scene displays the photographs, names, and birth and death dates of former members of the secret police between 1945 and 1956. The fact that many of the persons identified as perpetrators are still among the living (because only their date of birth is indicated), and that the identified circle of victimizers was supposed to continuously expand, points to the specific social and political role its creators attributed to the institution. The Nuremberg model is important also to make communist crimes recognized as war crimes or crimes against humanity that have no statutory limitation. Otherwise, only the possibility of moral condemnation remains. As the professional director of the House of Terror, one of its founders, stated to a journalist in 2002, the institution accuses and condemns all employees of the former secret police using the Nuremberg Trial as a model. Since the statute of limitations to try a perpetrator has passed, and judicial trials would not be possible in the context of present-day laws, he said, the task falls on historians to morally take revenge on the perpetrators.[89] Several critiques objected that—instead of taking the ethical responsibility for its own activity as a museum—the House of Terror Museum rather aims to foster judgment and resentment toward what is displayed.[90]

CONCLUSION—THE RELATIVE SUCCESS OF HISTORICAL REVISIONISM

Not only did an exceptionally intense criticism target the House of Terror during its first years, the museum also lost governmental support after the victory of the postcommunist left in the 2002 legislative elections. Though the new parliament cut the previous generous budget almost by half (from 330 million forints to 180 million) for the budgetary year of 2003, the House of Terror Museum was not forced to face austerity measures because the new prime minister, Péter Medgyessy, after the controversy about his former attachment to the communist state security services, partly (by 100 million) restored the missing amount from the budgetary provisions. Eventually also the plans of "equilibrating" the exhibition faded away and the House of Terror Museum has become a legitimate public institution that survived governmental changes and could continue its activity on more-or-less stable grounds.

The main reason for public legitimacy attributed to the House of Terror Museum was that the creators relied on a "Europeanized" discourse that reappropriated the European norms of historical consciousness in a country at the gates of the EU. The new anticommunist historical consciousness speaks the prevailing European language of memory when calling for "coming to terms with" the communist past in the same way that the West confronted Nazism. Never calling into question the cultural importance of the Holocaust, it "only" calls for an adjustment of historical memory. Though the House of Terror Museum's permanent exhibition at the time of its creation was accused of downplaying the memory of the Holocaust, the institution itself addressed the question in the following years. In 2004, the sixtieth anniversary of the Holocaust in Hungary, the House of Terror Museum had several temporary exhibitions on the subject: on children in the Holocaust, on Raoul Wallenberg, and on the "Hungarian tragedy" in 1944. It also organized several events in relation to the commemorative year, for example Claude Lanzmann's *Shoah* was projected in the House of Terror Museum as many times as there was an audience. Since 2007, the House of Terror Museum has organized an annual commemoration of the Holocaust at the building. After the heated debates around the opening of the permanent exhibition, politicians, intellectuals, and scholars associated with the left began to contribute to activities of the House of Terror Museum and the background research institutes.

During the controversy around the permanent exhibition, the House of Terror Museum could set and control the debate that also contributed to its legitimacy. Although, from the perspective of the uniqueness of the Holocaust, the claim of equal criminality of Nazism and communism was blasphemy, the juxtaposition of the two political systems impeded criticism because the refusal of the memory construction of communism would also have meant going against commemorating the Holocaust. Thus the necessity of the House of Terror Museum could not be called into question—only the relation it constructed between the memories of the two depicted political systems. Moreover, by commemorating communism in the representational framework of Holocaust memory as part of the double occupation, the House of Terror Museum avoids criticism by definitively refusing the way it interprets state socialism in Hungary.

The exhibition at the House of Terror Museum relies on an extended and already elaborated European anticommunist discourse about reclaiming the memory of communism in relation to the memory of the Holocaust. The museographical space and the installations reflect the abstract and mythic nature of this discourse. The site at 60 Andrássy Road, however, by relying on the "spirit of the place," not only could refer the meanings of the display to historical reality but also provide the whole exhibition with authenticity. The House of Terror Museum could successfully position itself as a sacred site of the dead, a memorial to the victims.

Yet this success story of historical revisionism has certain limitations. The House of Terror Museum is poorly embedded in the local cultural life of Budapest and Hungary. First, its creation was not at all participatory because it did not allow the direct social and cultural environment to influence either the conception or the strategies of exhibition (cooperation remained in the confines of collecting material by way of campaigns for donation). Second, the House of Terror Museum seems to be rather a touristic destination than a national institution, as declared by its representatives, of coming to terms with the past. In its first ten years of existence, half of the nearly 4 million visitors were foreigners (the House of Terror Museum is recommended in a prominent place by popular international touristic agencies);[91] the organized school class visits included, that additionally reduce the proportion of Hungarians who attend the institution by their own will and interest in historical and commemorative matters. Moreover, third, the House of Terror Museum's strategy of representation, the authoritative attitude toward the exhibition combined with the emphasis on meaning construction and transmitting emotions, makes doubtful the successful impact on historical knowledge of the visitors. It is thus not surprising that the permanent exhibition, according to a recent study with high school students, could affect only those young visitors who had already had a particular interest in the period displayed.[92]

The international embeddedness of the House of Terror Museum is also a relative success. As the Hungarian founding member of the Platform of European Memory and Conscience, aiming, according to their website, to "increase public awareness about European history and crimes committed by totalitarian regimes," the House of Terror Museum forms part of a supposedly pan-European initiative capable in principle of fundraising and influencing policies of historical consciousness. The impact of the platform is, however, limited mainly to East-Central European institutions sharing the agenda of criminalizing communism.[93]

ACKNOWLEDGEMENTS

This research project was supported by the Collegium de Lyon, where I was invited researcher during the academic year of 2015–16 and the National Research, Development and Innovation Office (NKFIH, PD 115736). I am grateful to the members of the Post-Communist Traditionalism research group at the Centre for Social Sciences, and to Raluca Grosescu for their insightful comments to earlier versions of this chapter.

NOTES

1. Claus Leggewie, "Equally Criminal? Totalitarian Experience and European Memory," *Tr@nsit Online*, April 27, 2010, http://www.iwm.at/read-listen-watch /transit-online/equally-criminal/.

2. Charles S. Maier, "A Surfeit of Memory? Reflections on History, Melancholy and Denial," *History and Memory* 5, no. 2 (1993): 136–52; Tzvetan Todorov, *Les abus de la mémoire* (Paris: Arléa, 1995); Jean-Michel Chaumont. *La concurrence des victimes: génocide, identité, reconnaissance* (Paris: La Découverte, 1997); Peter Novick. *The Holocaust in American Life* (Boston: Houghton Mifflin, 1999).

3. The first such institutions, such as the Museum of Genocide Victims, Vilnius, Lithuania (1992), the Museum of Occupations in Riga, Latvia (1993), and the Sighet Memorial for the Victims of Communism and the Resistance in Sighetul Marmatiei, Romania (1993), were initiated by anticommunist political diasporas consisting of former political prisoners, dissidents, and exiles. Fascinated by the cultural

importance attributed to the memory of the Holocaust that they were familiar with in the West, these early initiatives on communism memory strove to show to the world that communism was as horrible as Nazism, if not even worse. See in detail Máté Zombory, "The Birth of the Memory of Communism: Memorial Museums in Europe," *Journal of Nationalism and Ethnicity* 45, no. 6 (2017): 1028–46, doi:10.1080/00905992.2017.1339680.

4. On the concept of historical revisionism, see Enzo Traverso, *Le passé, mode d'emploi: histoire, mémoire, politique* (Paris: La Fabrique, 2005).

5. Mikko Lagerspetz, "Postsocialism as a Return: Notes on a Discursive Strategy," *East European Politics and Societies* 13, no. 2 (March 1, 1999): 377–90, doi:10.1177/0888325499013002019.

6. Ferenc Laczó and Máté Zombory, "Between Transnational Embeddedness and Relative Isolation: The Moderate Rise of Memory Studies in Hungary," *Acta Poloniae Historica* 106 (2012): 99–125, doi:http://dx.doi.org/10.12775/APH.2012.106.05.

7. The Foundation of Political History was created in 1990 by the Hungarian Socialist Party (the heir of the Communist Party) from the Institute of Party History.

8. See the budgetary law for the year of 1999: "1998. évi XC. törvény a Magyar Köztársaság 1999: évi költségvetéséről," http://net.jogtar.hu/jr/gen/hjegy_doc.cgi?docid=99800090.TV.

9. See points XI.1 and XV.1 of the institution's articles of association: http://www.nefmi.gov.hu/letolt/minisz/alapito_okirat/kozalap/alapito_okirat_kkeuropai_tort_tars_kutatas_kozalap.pdf.

10. The day in 1947 when the Soviet Red Army dragged away Béla Kovács, the general secretary of the majority Smallholders' Party in the 1945 parliament.

11. János M. Rainer, "A Terror Háza-jelenség," *Magyar Hírlap*, February 3, 2002.

12. The three members of the board of trustees of the public foundation maintaining the museum are historians: professor Mária Schmidt (Pázmány Páter Catholic University), professor László Tőkéczki (1951–2018) (Eötvös Loránd University), and professor Károly Kapronczay (Semmelweis University, Hungarian Academy of Sciences). The president of the board of trustees is László Balás-Piri (pharmacy technician), vice chairman of the Historical Justice Committee. Its vice president is political scientist László Gy. Tóth. Schmidt and Tóth were chief advisers of the first Orbán government, Tőkéczki was closely related to Orbán's party, Fidesz, and to its repositioning as a new national-conservative political force after 1994.

13. See Paul Gradvohl, "Historians and the Political Stakes of the Past in Hungary," in *Stalinism and Nazism: History and Memory Compared*, ed. Henry Rousso (Lincoln: University of Nebraska Press, 2004), 200–204.

14. Mária Schmidt, "'A nagy hazugságok százada van mögöttünk'," in *Egyazon mércével: a visszaperelt történelem* (Budapest: Hungarian University Press, 2003), 230.

15. Mária Schmidt, "Az elfelejtett kommunizmus," in *Egyazon mércével*, 17–19; Schmidt, "'Holocaustok' a huszadik században," in *Egyazon mércével*, 10–16.

16. Alain Besançon, *Le malheur du siècle: sur le communisme, le nazisme et l'unicité de la Shoah* (Paris: Fayard, 1998), 155–63.

17. Besançon, *Malheur du siècle*; Raul Hilberg, *The Destruction of the European Jews*, rev. and definitive ed. (New York: Holmes and Meier, 1985).

18. Anne Applebaum, "Absent History," *Prospect*, April 20, 1996, http://www.prospectmagazine.co.uk/features/absenthistory; Schmidt, "Az elmaradt igazságtétel—amerikai szemmel," in *Egyazon mércével*, 117.

19. Henry Rousso, *Stalinism and Nazism: History and Memory Compared* (Lincoln: University of Nebraska Press, 2004), 4.

20. Stéphane Courtois, "Les crimes du communism," in *Le livre noir du communisme: crimes, terreur et répression* (Paris: Laffont, 1997), 25; Mária Schmidt, "'Holocaustok' a huszadik században," in *Egyazon mércével*, 12.

21. Tony Judt, *Európa—A nagy ábránd?* (Budapest: XX. Század Intézet – Kairosz Kiadó, 2002); Konrad Löw, *A kommunista ideológia vörös könyve* (Budapest: XX. Század Intézet, 2003).

22. Ernst Nolte, *A fasizmus korszaka* (Budapest: XX. Század Intézet – Kairosz Kiadó, 2003).

23. Paul Johnson, *A modern kor—A huszadik század igazi arca* (Budapest: XX. Század Intézet – Kairosz Kiadó, 2000).

24. Mart Laar, *Vissza a jövőbe* (Budapest: XX. Század Intézet – Kairosz Kiadó, 2002).

25. Vlagyimir Bukovszkij, *A moszkvai per* (Budapest: XX. Század Intézet, 2009).

26. Rousso, *Stalinism and Nazism*.

27. Michael Scott Christofferson, *French Intellectuals against the Left: The Antitotalitarian Moment of the 1970's* (New York: Berghahn, 2004).

28. Donald Reid, "In Search of the Communist Syndrome: Opening the Black Book of the New Anti-Communism in France," *International History Review* 27, no. 2 (2005): 295–318.

29. See the work of François Furet, an emblematic figure of French historical revisionism (Christofferson, *French Intellectuals*, 229–66), who, as indicated in the *Black Book of Communism*, agreed to write the preface but died shortly before the publication.

30. Johnson—journalist, historian, author, adviser of Prime Minister Margaret Thatcher—is a conservative and anticommunism thinker. Schmidt summarized Johnson's book *Modern Times*, published in Hungarian by Schmidt's institute, which, in opposition to the leftist monopoly of opinion, establishes that the twentieth century was the century of lies (Schmidt, "'A nagy hazugságok százada van mögöttünk'," in *Egyazon mércével*, 230). Laar is historian and former prime minister of Estonia (1992–1994 and 1999–2002), who wrote an additional chapter, titled "Estonia and Communism," in the Estonian publication of *The Black Book of Communism* in 2002. Laar was cofounder of the Foundation for the Investigation of Communist Crimes in 2008. German historian Michael Wolffsohn is author of the book *Eternal Guilt?* (1988, 1993 in English), in which he argues against the interpretation of German-Jewish-Israeli relations in terms of the Holocaust (which in case of Germans means the sense of guilt for Nazism). Schmidt reviewed Wolffsohn's book *Die Deutschland*

Akte: Juden und Deutsche in Ost und West: Tatsachen und Legenden (1995), suggesting that even the early postunification neo-Nazi activities might be attributed to East German antifascist propaganda to discredit the Federal Republic with the Nazi stain and raising the rhetorical question why communist systems' anti-Semitism hasn't yet been acknowledged (Schmidt, "Az antifasiszta NDK. Adalékok a politikai megtévesztés történetéhez," in *Egyazon mércével*, 43–46). Further members of the international advisory board are Norman Podhoretz, a US neoconservative thinker and former editor-in-chief of *Commentary* magazine; Carlos Flores Juberías, a Spanish professor of constitutional law and expert on Eastern European democratization; Italian professor Leonardo Morlino, also an expert on Eastern European democratization; and US geostrategist, foreign relations expert, and politician Brzezinski is former national security adviser of US president Jimmy Carter and author of *Grand Failure: The Birth and Death of Communism in the Twentieth Century* (New York: Charles Scribner's Sons, 1989).

31. Hungarian engineer István Fehérváry was also member of the international advisory board until his death in 2014. Convicted to forced labor in 1949, released in 1956, he lived in political diaspora until his return to Hungary after the political changes. From 1990 he was president of the Community of Hungarian Political Prisoners between 1945 and 1956. Fehérváry is author of the books *Prison Universe in Hungary* (Börtönvilág Magyarországon [Budapest: Magyar Politikai Foglyok Szövetsége, 1978]) and *Soviet World in Hungary* (Szovjetvilág Magyarországon, München-Santa Fe: Nemzetőr-Pro Libertate Publishing House, 1984).

32. Czesław Bielecki, ed. *SocLand: Muzeum Komunizmu (w budowie)* [Museum of Communism (under construction)] (Warsaw: Volumen, 2003).

33. Noémi Sümegi, "Szabadon a Terror Házában," *Válasz.hu*, January 18, 2002, http://valasz.hu/itthon/szabadon-a-terror-hazaban-2742.

34. Quoted by Tamás Szőnyei, "Épül a Terror Háza: Árnyékvilág," *Magyar Narancs*, no. 3 (January 24, 2003), http://magyarnarancs.hu/belpol/epul_a_terror_haza_arnyekvilag-62550.

35. Mária Schmidt, "A Terror Háza Múzeum első éve," in *Egyazon mércével*, 185.

36. Viktor Orbán, "A terror házáról," in *20 év: beszédek, írások, interjúk, 1986–2006* (Budapest: Heti Válasz Lap- és Könyvkiadó, 2006), 284–85.

37. Schmidt, "A Terror Háza Múzeum," 179.

38. Noémi Sümegi, "Össztűz a Terror Házára," *Válasz.hu*, January 24, 2003, http://valasz.hu/reflektor/ossztuz-a-terror-hazara-6481.

39. István Ihász, "Gomb és kabát: A profán valóság bemutatásának kísérlete a Terror Háza Múzeumban," in *Történeti muzeológiai szemle, a magyar múzeumi történész társulat évkönyve 2* (Budapest: Magyar Múzeumi Történész Társulat, 2002), 97.

40. Sándor Radnóti, "Mi a Terror Háza?,"*Magyar Múzeumok* 9. évf. 2. sz.2003), 6–9.

41. András Rényi, "A retorika terrorja: A Terror Háza mint esztétikai probléma," *Élet és Irodalom* 47, no. 27 (August 7, 2003): 15–17.

42. Mária Schmidt, "Katarzist szeretnénk kiváltani," in *Egyazon mércével*, 240.

43. Péter György, "c.n.," *Beszélő* 8, no. 4 (April 2003), http://beszelo.c3.hu/node/12700; László Karsai and László Varga, "A horror háza." *Hetek*, March 5, 2002, http://www.hetek.hu/hatter/200205/a_horror_haza; Rainer, "A Terror Háza—jelenség"; László Varga, "Békévé oldja az emlékezés?" *Élet és Irodalom* 46, no. 8 (February 22, 2002).

44. András Mink, "Alibi terror—egy bemutatkozásra," *Népszabadság*, February 20, 2002.

45. András Mink, "Kommunizmus, Terror, Péter Gábor Ollója," *Beszélő* 7, no. 3 (2002), http://beszelo.c3.hu/cikkek/kommunizmus-terror-peter-gabor-olloja; Krisztián Ungváry, "A káosz háza," *Magyar Narancs* 14, no. 10 (July 3, 2002), http://magyarnarancs.hu/archivum_reszletes/2002/10; László Seres, "Andrássy út 60," *Élet És Irodalom* 46, no. 6 (February 8, 2002), https://www.es.hu/cikk/2003-01-03/seres-laszlo/andrassy-ut-60.html.

46. See "Beszélgetés Ormos Mária Történésszel," *Népszabadság*, May 25, 2002; Radnóti, "Mi a Terror Háza?"

47. Tamás Molnár, "Terror Háza: jelképek egyenlősége," *Magyar Nemzet*, January 22, 2002.

48. Stéphane Courtois, "Szükséges a történelmi tükör: Interjú Stéphane Courtois-val," *Magyar Nemzet*, March 27, 2003.

49. Schmidt, "A Terror Háza Múzeum," 192.

50. Zsolt Gréczy, "'A látottak közös emlékezetté válnak' Schmidt Mária leendő főigazagtó a Terror Házáról—Brzezinski a tanácsadó testületben," *Magyar Hírlap*, March 1, 2002; Schmidt, "A Terror Háza Múzeum."

51. Radnóti, "Mi a Terror Háza?"; Ungváry, "A káosz háza."

52. József Berta, "Az emlékezés vége," *Élet és Irodalom* 54, no. 33 (August 19, 2010), https://www.es.hu/cikk/2010-08-22/berta-jozsef/az-emlekezes-vege.html; Éva Kovács, "Az ironikus és a cinikus: A kommunizmus emlékezetéről," *Élet és Irodalom* 47, no. 35 (August 29, 2003); Mink, "Kommunizmus;" Krisztián Ungváry, "A pártmúzeum," *Népszabadság*, May 7, 2003, Weekend section.

53. Mink, "Alibi terror—egy bemutatkozásra."

54. Ungváry, "A káosz háza."

55. Ungváry, "A pártmúzeum."

56. Mária Schmidt, "Egy történ(elmietlen)ész kritikája," *Népszabadság*, September 8, 2003.

57. See also Karsai and Varga, "A horror háza."

58. Mink, "Kommunizmus"; Radnóti, "Mi a Terror Háza?"

59. Ungváry, "A káosz háza."

60. Schmidt, "Katarzist szeretnénk miváltani," in *Egyazon mércével*, 239.

61. Ungváry, "A pártmúzeum"; see also Karsai and Varga, "A horror háza."

62. Schmidt, "Egy történ(elmietlen)ész kritikája."

63. Mária Schmidt, ed., *Terror Háza, Andrássy út 60* (House of terror, Andrássy út 60) (Budapest: Public Endowment for Research in Central and East-European History and Society, 2003), 15.

64. Mink, "Kommunizmus."
65. Radnóti, "Mi a Terror Háza?"
66. See Seres, "Andrássy út 60."
67. Schmidt, *Terror Háza, Andrássy út 60*, 27.
68. Sümegi, "Össztűz a Terror Házára."
69. Ibid.
70. Mink, "Kommunizmus."
71. Rainer, "A Terror Háza-jelenség."
72. Zsófia Frazon and Zsolt K. Horváth, "A megsértett Magyarország: a Terror Háza mint tárgybemutatás, emlékmű és politikai rítus," *Regio—Kisebbség, Politika, Társadalom* 13, no. 4 (2002): 303–47.
73. Frazon and Horváth, "A Megsértett Magyarország," 324.
74. Ihász, "Gomb és kabát," 104.
75. Anita Élő, "Ákos keresztje," *Heti Válasz*, March 29, 2002, http://valasz.hu/itthon/akos-keresztje-3652.
76. Hilde S. Hein, *The Museum in Transition: A Philosophical Perspective* (Washington, DC: Smithsonian Books, 2000), 5.
77. Ibid., 8.
78. Ibid., 86.
79. Ibid., 79.
80. Schmidt, "'Katarzist szeretnénk kiváltani'," in *Egyazon mércével*, 241.
81. Sharon Macdonald, *Memorylands: Heritage and Identity in Europe Today* (London: Routledge, 2013).
82. Jeshajahu Weinberg, "A Narrative History Museum," *Curator* 37, no. 4 (December 1994): 231–39.
83. Schmidt, "Katarzist szeretnénk kiváltani."
84. See in detail the catalog of the exhibition, Schmidt, *Terror Háza, Andrássy út 60*.
85. Radnóti, "Mi a Terror Háza?"; Rényi, "A retorika terrorja"; Mink, "Kommunizmus," Ihász, "Gomb és kabát."
86. Edward Tabor Linenthal, *Preserving Memory: The Struggle to Create America's Holocaust Museum* (New York: Columbia University Press, 2001), 167–92.
87. Rényi, "A retorika terrorja."
88. Schmidt, *Terror Háza, Andrássy út 60*, 66.
89. Márton Gergely, "Magyar múltfeltárás: Terror Háza; Tettesek a falon," *Magyar Narancs*, no. 44 (January 11, 2002), http://magyarnarancs.hu/belpol/magyar_multfeltaras_terror_haza_tettesek_a_falon-61032.
90. Péter György, "A Terror Háza/a terror topográfiája (Budapest, Berlin)," *Élet és Irodalom* 54, no. 24 (June 18, 2010), http://archiv.magyarmuzeumok.hu/kiallitas/88_a_terror_haza__a_terror_topografiaja; Kovács, "Az ironikus és a cinikus."
91. Bálint Ablonczy, "Békévé oldja?," *válasz.hu*, March 19, 2012, http://valasz.hu/reflektor/bekeve-oldja-46948.

92. Domonkos Sik, "Memory Transmission and Political Socialization in Post-Socialist Hungary," *The Sociological Review* 63, no. 2_suppl (December 2015): 53–71.

93. Laure Neumayer, "Integrating the Central European Past into a Common Narrative: The Mobilizations around the 'Crimes of Communism' in the European Parliament," *Journal of Contemporary European Studies* 23, no. 3 (July 2015): 344–63, doi:10.1080/14782804.2014.1001825.

MÁTÉ ZOMBORY is a sociologist and research fellow at the Centre for Social Sciences at the Hungarian Academy of Sciences. He is author of *Maps of Remembrance: Space, Belonging, and the Politics of Memory* (2012) and is currently researching the historical sociological critique of normative memory regimes. His other research projects include the history of memory in Eastern Europe and the social theory of competitive victimization.

Figure 3.1. National Memorial-Museum to the Victims of Occupying Regimes, L'viv, founded 2009. http://www.lonckoho.lviv.ua/. *Photograph by Stephen M. Norris*

THREE

Inside L'viv's Lonsky Prison
Capturing Ukrainian Memory after Communism

STEPHEN M. NORRIS

On a hot summer day in July 2011, I visited the Lonsky Prison in L'viv, Ukraine (the official name of the site is the rather unwieldy National Memorial–Museum to the Victims of Occupying Regimes). At the time, I knew little about the site or its history. Once inside, the scorching day turned cold. The prison's faded paint, ominous displays, and horrific photographs disturbed me. After my visit, I decided to learn more about the site. Two aspects of Lonsky stood out to me on that day: the sense of death that pervaded the place, even though it had not been used as a prison for decades, and the inclusion of Stepan Bandera, the controversial Ukrainian nationalist, among the displays.

As I have subsequently understood, my unease was an appropriate response. Searching for a more concrete way to interpret the site, I discovered Annabel Jane Wharton's book, *Architectural Agents*. In it, Wharton uses the term *agent* in the sense chemists do and applies it to buildings; that is, nonhuman entities, spatial objects in particular, that "have an effect on their animate environments, independent of intension."[1] Buildings, she posits, can have lives and agency of their own, beyond what their builders intended. One of the ways buildings have agency is how they preserve their own sense of history. "The ethical lessons of a building," she writes, "are deeply historical."[2]

The Lonsky Prison and Museum Memorial has this kind of agency. Founded in 2009 and declared a national museum that same year, the museum's organizers speak about Lonsky in their mission statement as if it were a living entity: the prison is said to communicate through "language artifacts" that will help to convey its purpose to visitors. The main ideas the site communicates are to transmit stories about good triumphing over evil, that the struggle for Ukrainian independence involved sacrifice but that Ukrainians eventually won out, and that death and torture could not kill the spirit for freedom. The slogans the building shouts, according to the mission statement, are "Never Again!" and "For Freedom!"[3] The building tells a particular story, or, to be more precise, particular stories, that in turn preserve a sense of history. The history is a contentious, controversial one that articulates the ongoing politics of remembrance in Ukraine specifically and other postcommunist societies more generally. The former prison, as I discovered in 2011, produces feelings that convey the larger unease associated with remembering what happened inside in 1941.

A TOUR THROUGH THE LONSKY MUSEUM

When you approach the prison from L'viv's central square (it's a five-minute walk up Kopernyka Street), you are confronted with the first of several memorial plaques (see fig. 3.1): "To the memory of victims of the NKVD, Gestapo, and MGB, 1939–1953." Surrounding this plaque are others that memorialize individuals, including Maria Kyzymovych and Grygorii Goliash, both members of the Organization of Ukrainian Nationalists [OUN] who were arrested after World War II.

The prison's interior consists mostly of stark cells that testify to the punishments, deprivations, and tortures its inhabitants endured. Peering through the door slats provides a prison-guard view of the interiors of several cells (see fig. 3.2). One interior is decorated with propaganda prints, providing the worldview of the Soviet jailers who once controlled the prison. The sparse prison warden's office contains a few pieces of furniture, but overall it looks like the other cells. A portrait of Joseph Stalin hangs on the wall, a testament to one of the central messages the site narrates: this is a site that testifies mostly to Soviet oppression. The museum is meant to convey to visitors the feeling of confinement and foreboding within the former prison. It's as though a setting for an American horror movie was made real.

The walls and hallways of the prison tell a story of suffering and national resistance. Succinct displays narrate the story of the building, completed in 1889–90 and used as a prison from the early 1900s, and the story of its victims. The central years of this history lesson, however, are 1939 to 1941, when the building served as a prison for occupying Soviet forces. Throughout the halls, files of the People's Commissariat for Internal Affairs (Narodnyi Komissariat Vnutrennykh Del: NKVD) further provide the museum's central focus on these years. (See fig. 3.3.) The official title of the site declares it to be a "Memorial Museum of Occupation Regimes," but only one really matters.

Outside in the prison yard, a cross stands where NKVD guards murdered prisoners. On the day I visited, the museum guide talked about the June 1941

Figure 3.2. Inside a cell. *Photograph by Stephen M. Norris*

Figure 3.3. NKVD files on Lonsky's walls. *Photograph by Stephen M. Norris*

massacres here. As the Nazi armies advanced on L'viv, Soviet forces murdered the prison's inhabitants—mostly, as she narrated, Ukrainian nationalists. After these massacres, others would follow, this time at the hands of Nazi policemen. Lonsky Prison Museum witnessed hundreds, if not thousands, of executions. No wonder the effect is so chilling.

My visit in 2011 is the one most visitors experience. The building is frightening. The displays and guides tell appalling stories. The most significant one takes place in June and July 1941, when residents fell victim to the violence of two successive occupying powers. The building has a relatively simple, extremely tragic, story to tell about L'viv's experiences at war. Yet, as I began to discover in July 2011, the museum's is a highly selective, extremely contentious, version of the truth. The Lonsky Prison today also functions as a site where victims of political violence are commemorated, but also where victimizers become victims. My initial clue on that July day was the translated document on one display from the Nazis denouncing Stepan Bandera and his followers as dangerous elements. The rest of this chapter will seek to interpret this clue and to explain how the Lonsky Prison Museum performs two roles, as a site of memory promoting a national cult of the dead and as a site where memory gets laundered. Both roles mix truth and myth. Both help to provide the spirit that transforms the building into a living agent.

THE PRISON AND THE CULT OF NATIONAL DEATH

The site is pervaded by death. The Lonsky Prison attempts to memorialize the victims murdered in 1941 and, in doing so, offers a particularly post-Soviet version of the sacralization of death in the twentieth century.[4] The building does not help to create a cult of the soldier, as so many other war memorials do, but instead lays the foundation for a cult of the national victim murdered for the Ukrainian nation.

In her book on how buildings have their own agency, Wharton highlights murder as one aspect of how buildings convey historicity. "Buildings are rarely accused of murder," she notes, but the destruction of a site might make a building a victim.[5] Yet what if the building itself is a site of murder? In a sense, the site functions as a brick-and-mortar embodiment of the political violence that washed over the region in the 1930s and 1940s. Lonsky Prison, in short, is a building that tells the story of the bloodlands. And, as Timothy Snyder has written in his influential book about the subject, the very worst of this killing began in June 1941.[6]

The most important story the Lonsky Prison tells from this period occurred at the end of June 1941. It is partly a true story, partly one that covers up other truths: my point in this exploration is not so much to go over the history, which is still being argued over, but the way the event has been remembered and encoded at Lonsky and why this memory site takes the form it does.[7] John-Paul Himka has written that the museum "presents a one-sided, politically motivated version of what transpired on its site," an apt characterization of the story to be traced here.[8]

That month in that year saw the end of a two-year occupation by Soviet authorities and the beginning of an occupation of nearly four years by German authorities. After the Nazi armies invaded on June 22, the Soviet forces in western Ukraine began to retreat. Before doing so, NKVD agents murdered thousands of Ukrainians, mostly Ukrainian nationalists, but also Jews, Poles, and others. When the German forces reached the city on Monday, June 30, they were greeted with the smell of death: thousands of corpses littered the grounds of prisons and other sites, including the one on Lonsky Street.[9] The Germans ordered L'viv's Jews to bring out the bodies and exhume those that had been crudely buried and then lay them out for all to see.[10] Nazi soldiers filmed these events and took photographs. The arrangement of these corpses took place at the Zamarstyniv Street Prison, the Brygidki Prison, and the one on Lonsky.

As witnesses noted and as a growing number of scholars have corroborated, these acts of laying out the dead served as the trigger for a citywide pogrom. The dead in June 1941 were deemed to be Ukrainian nationalists; their murderers were deemed to be the Jews and Bolsheviks. That the corpses included other ethnic, national, and religious groups reflecting the city's cosmopolitan makeup was ignored. Instead, the narrative established on June 30 proved to be simple and powerful: one occupying regime, supposedly made up of Jewish communists, had murdered the "real" residents, ethnic Ukrainians. German troops, individual members of the Nachtigall Battalion (a unit under the command of the Abwehr led by Roman Shukhevych and made up of Ukrainians),[11] local militia that included some OUN members, and other local residents then participated in a carnival of violence.[12] It was accompanied by anticommunist rituals; elsewhere, Ukrainians constructed victory arches to the recently-proclaimed National Ukrainian Revolution and its liberating forces, members of the OUN-B.[13] The city's Jews were humiliated, beaten, raped, and tortured and many were killed. Once the Jews who had exhumed the dead in L'viv prisons had arranged them neatly for all to see, they were shot. The corpses of murdered Jews in July 1941 were not arranged neatly, as testimonies and photographs reveal.

John-Paul Himka has eloquently described some of the horrors that happened around the Lonsky Prison on July 2:

> The experience at Lontskoho has been described in detail by Tamara Branitsky. What she saw when she arrived there was Jewish women, older men, and children standing in a corner under the wall. On the other side of the yard were mounds of dead people, and Jewish men were sorting them. They had to move them from one place to another. Inside the yard there were SS and Gestapo. She and her mother and sisters were kept there

for about an hour, although it seemed to them an eternity. Eventually her mother worked up the courage to approach an officer and ask in German what they intended to do with them. He responded: We will put you all under the wall and shoot you. However, later, high-ranking Gestapo officers came and told all the women and children to go home. As they went home, the people on the sidewalk continued to throw rocks at them. Her mother extended an arm to protect her sister—she was hit by a rock, and blood gushed from her arm. Eventually they made their way home. Matylda Wyszynska and her family also experienced Lontskoho. Her father was taken first. He was brought home a day and a half or two days later completely unconscious. He stank of corpses. He remained unconscious for a long time, nervous movements and screams being the main signs of life. She and her stepmother were also taken. They were saved by a Ukrainian militiaman at the scene who was the brother of a school friend—those with the power to do harm also have the power to save.

According to a Jewish source, a German officer put a stop to the mob violence at Lontskoho. A German non-commissioned officer tried to protect the Jewish labourers while the crowds on the rooftops demanded their death. The mob was quelled only when a German officer intervened and shouted with indignation: "We are not after all Bolsheviks."[14]

The laying out of the dead around L'viv's prisons, the museum today tells us, was the foundational act of a new Ukraine. On the Lonsky Memorial walls, only the NKVD victims' names appear. The documents that are spread over the walls are all NKVD files that contain the same names. The official website contains only one section under the subheading "Archive." It is dedicated to the June 1941 mass executions.[15] On the museum's website, the fact that Jews and Poles were also among the victims is noted, but only in passing. The story told here is that ethnic Ukrainians were killed by Soviet authorities and that the acts of violence committed within, particularly between June 22 and June 30, 1941, are the ones worth commemorating. The present-day museum establishes a powerful narrative that fixes important dates, perpetrators, and victims as foundational ones. Lonsky Museum therefore provides exculpatory evidence for the OUN and other Ukrainian nationalists: those killed by the NKVD could not have taken part in the pogroms that followed; therefore the victims honored here deserve to be viewed as victims, not victimizers. The victims of the pogrom, which was unleashed by the laying out of dead bodies on June 30, are not commemorated at Lonsky. Instead, the victims of NKVD violence in June 1941 are transformed inside the walls of the museum into martyrs: just as the notion of martyrdom was central to the creation of Judaism and Christianity as distinct entities,[16] so too is establishing the victimhood of the OUN dead of June 1941 central to the creation of contemporary Ukrainianness. In other words, for a modern Ukraine to exist as a distinct entity, it needs martyrs. They can be found in Lonsky Prison. The NKVD files with the names of the martyrs on them act as relics.

The ground around the prison was once saturated with blood. The cult of death promoted today in and around the building metaphorically uses this blood as the symbol of a new nation. Ukraine, the building cries out, was built in part on the bodies and blood of the people who died inside during those June days.

On June 8, 2015, Valentyn Nalyvaichenko, the head of the Security Service of Ukraine, dedicated a new memorial in the prison yard. His speech in many ways testifies to the first major role the Lonsky Prison performs:

> Occupation, aggression, torture, death. It was here in June 1941. We were not spared by the torturers, regardless of whether they were Nazis or Communists. Ukrainians, Poles, and Jews were not spared. The youngest person who died here in this dungeon in June 1941 was Witold Martsehovskyy, a young Pole. The greatest victims who suffered in these Ukrainian dungeons throughout the country and all over the Ukrainian lands were those who fought against enslavement and who led the Ukrainian liberation movement. Here and now, today, we understand who we are after this fight and who we are through the continuation of this struggle. Today this site preserves the faith of those who died, but most importantly it preserves the dignity and victory of every Ukrainian. Eighteen months ago, we Ukrainians—I recognize you personally!—were unarmed, unprotected, and with wooden sticks took up against Yanukovych's weapons. A year later, our patriotic volunteers, military officers of the SBU [Sluzhba Bezpeky Ukrayiny, Security Service of Ukraine] and the armed forces, and all Ukrainians continue to defend their homeland against the aggressors in present-day Moscow, who have planned to enslave Ukraine for a long time and are maliciously planning to destroy Ukraine. And because they failed (and will fail!), places such as this one should remain in our hearts![17]

It's not a subtle speech and requires little unpacking. The event took place on the very spot where the bodies of the dead were laid out in June 1941. The Lonsky Prison preserves the spirit of those who died in June 1941, all deemed to be Ukrainian patriots fighting for independence, and conjures up their ghosts as heroes to inspire present-day Ukrainians. The villains then and now—both the museum's exhibits and Nalyvaichenko's speech dissolve the distance between 1941 and 2015—came from Moscow.

Outside the museum entrance, just across the street, is another memorial (fig. 3.4). Its placement is not a coincidence, nor is it any subtler than

Figure 3.4. Monument to the Victims of Communist Crimes, L'viv. *Photograph by Stephen M. Norris*

Nalyvaichenko's speech. Designed by sculptor Petro Shtaier and architect Roman Syvenkyi, the Monument to the Victims of Communist Crimes was unveiled in 1997. The twisted, tortured body at the center of the monument is the stand-in for all those bodies uncovered in July 1941, the sacred national souls the museum commemorates.

MEMORY LAUNDERING AT LONSKY

The Lonsky Prison Museum has one focus on June 1941, but it also conveys a longer, even more contentious, history. In *Architectural Agents*, Wharton writes that buildings may be anthropomorphized when they help us understand amnesia. In many cases, buildings embody false amnesia, or "a perpetrator's manipulation of the history of an act in order to avoid taking responsibility for its commission."[18] One task for architectural historians, she concludes, is to uncover how a building tells both truths and lies in the way it remembers.[19] The Lonsky Prison does not disregard or erase truth; it just massages the truth in the stories told on its walls. In narrating a particular form of truth, the Lonsky Prison Museum serves as a site for memory laundering. It does so in at least two significant ways.

First, Lonsky transforms Stepan Bandera, members of the OUN (and more specifically, the OUN-B), and members of the UPA (Ukrains'ka povstans'ka armiia, the Ukrainian Insurgent Army formed by the OUN in 1942) into historical victims. Second, by making Bandera and his comrades victims, the museum stresses a contentious version of history, particularly in how it tells the story of the Holocaust. Both Per Anders Rudling and John-Paul Himka have termed this "Holocaust negationism," which is a useful concept, but I think the museum engages much more in what I want to suggest should be termed "memory laundering."[20] The Holocaust is not entirely ignored inside Lonsky; it is just narrated in a fashion that contains some truths and some falsehoods.

To see how the museum engages in this practice, we have to go backward and forward in time from 1941. On its website, the Lonsky Museum narrates a Foucauldian-like history of itself as a site that transitioned from a building meant to discipline soldiers to one used entirely for punishment.[21] Built in 1889–90 by Iurii Iankovskii on what was then Łąckiego street, the building initially served as a barracks for Habsburg gendarmes. The site's location on a hill overlooking the heart of what was then the city called Lemberg made it a suitable location for a building to house the city's protectors.[22] When Lemberg became part of the new Polish state after 1918 and the city was renamed Lwów—an era the museum refers to as "the era of Polish occupation"—the new authorities turned the building into a prison. In the 1920s and 1930s, the prison housed members of the Ukrainian Military Organization (UVO, led by Yevhen Konovalets') and the OUN.[23] When the Soviets occupied the city after the Nazi-Soviet Pact in 1939, the new authorities continued the practice of using the building for a prison and even renamed it "Prison #1 [Tiur'ma no. 1]." Between 1939 and 1941, the Lonsky Prison was home again to numerous members of the OUN as well as Polish nationals. The museum's website focuses on the OUN members and their trials, punishments, and executions that have a connection to the prison. It ends with a vivid narration of how Roman Shukhevych, the commander of the Nachtigall battalion, rushed to the prison as the German armies took the city, only to discover the corpses of the June 1941 NKVD murders, including that of his brother, Yuriy. The story told here is that the bodies of Yuriy and others were exhumed, displayed, and filmed, testifying to "the crimes of Soviet power." The people who were ordered to dig up the bodies, mostly Jews, are not mentioned, nor are their fates.[24]

After the bodies were displayed, the German occupiers again found the Lonsky site useful as a prison. The museum website narrates this period carefully, noting that Nazi policies "were not directed solely against the city's Jews, although they suffered the most because they made up the largest number of the city's residents." With these and other short qualifiers out of the way, the main story returns to the Ukrainians. The site declares that neither the Nachtigall Battalion nor the OUN-B members started the pogroms that immediately followed German occupation (historians who have studied these events, including John-Paul Himka and Tarik Cyril Amar, agree; nevertheless, individuals from these units did participate). Instead, criminals, Poles, and "other nationalities" took part. The main focus of the "German Occupation Period," not surprisingly, is the Ukrainians of L'viv and members of the OUN. The site declares that "The Lonsky Prison housed representatives of all nationalities of the city's population. In addition to being shot, they also died of hunger and abuse. Thus, in one week in December 1941 forty Ukrainians died in the jail." The heart of this history is how the Nazis recognized that Bandera's OUN was an "enemy to the occupying regime," complete with a reprinting of a November 25 order that stressed the need to arrest OUN members.[25] Lonsky under the Nazis was similar to Lonsky under the Soviets, a connection drawn again when the museum's website narrates the second Soviet occupational period.[26] Throughout time, in short, the building was a site where occupational powers punished, tortured, and killed Ukrainians who wanted independence.

Here's where the one mention of Bandera on the museum walls takes on particular significance. The document is from November 25, 1941, and highlights the break between Bandera's movement and the Nazis (see fig. 3.5). As it states, "the Bandera Movement is preparing a revolt in the Reichskommissariat which has as its ultimate aim the establishment of an independent Ukraine. All functionaries of the Bandera Movement must be arrested at once and, after thorough interrogation, are to be liquidated." By the time it was issued, Bandera and his two brothers, also active members of the OUN-B, were in German concentration camps.[27] The museum therefore tells a straightforward story of Stepan Bandera the eternal prisoner: he was held at Lonsky in 1936 (after being held in Polish prisons) and then was held in a German concentration camp for most of the war. The effect is to turn the building into a dispensing agent: Bandera and his followers are not held accountable for violence; instead, they are identified as prisoners, and therefore victims, of political violence. Lonsky thus establishes in brick and mortar what the Ukrainian Institute of National Memory and Ukrainian nationalists have advocated: namely, that Bandera, the OUN, and UPA have been subject to Soviet propaganda that has unfairly demonized them.[28]

The Lonsky Prison engages in what we might call "memory laundering." This activity is not unlike money laundering, which, as Peter Reuter and Edwin

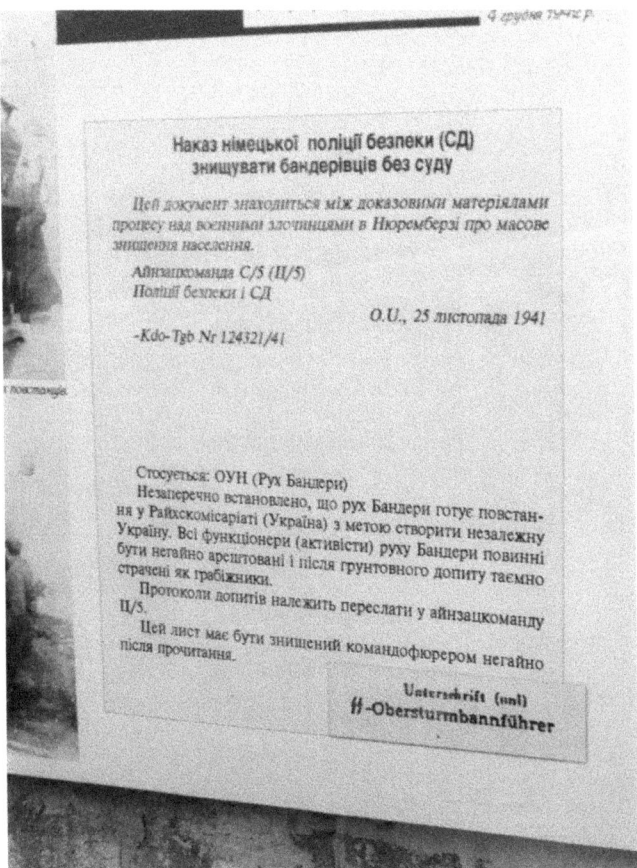

Figure 3.5. The November 25, 1941, order on Lonsky's walls. *Photograph by Stephen M. Norris*

Truman have noted, takes place in three stages. First is the placement of funds derived from illegal activity, followed by the layering of those funds by passing them through many institutions and jurisdictions to disguise their origins, then their integration into an economy where they appear to be legitimate.[29] Money laundering can take many forms, but one of the most common is "structuring," or "smurfing," in which illegal cash is broken into small parts and placed alongside legitimate money in order to disguise it.

With that basic framework in mind, we can begin to see how the Lonsky Prison engages in an analogous practice. Bandera is placed alongside the Ukrainians murdered in June 1941 by NKVD agents; the violent acts his followers committed in the months that followed are not mentioned and are therefore cleansed from

Figure 3.6. Memory laundering at work. *The Lonsky Museum brochure*

the record. Bandera, the OUN-B, and UPA are turned into legitimate victims of occupation and oppression. This memory laundering is clearest in one of the official pamphlets the Lonsky Museum publishes and distributes to visitors (see fig. 3.6). One of its pages lists five people who were imprisoned in the building. Bandera is first, followed by two other OUN-B members, Kateryna Zaryts'ka and Ivan Klymiv. They are followed by two famous Ukrainian dissidents, Viacheslav Chornovil, who was imprisoned at Lonsky in 1972, and Iryna Senyk, the former OUN member who became a poet and member of the Ukrainian Helsinki Watch Group. All five are identified as people who fought for Ukrainian independence and who were imprisoned at Lonsky for their efforts.

To integrate this memory into history, the Lonsky Museum focuses again on the one time Bandera was held within its walls. The imprisonment and trial of Bandera and other OUN members at Lonsky in 1936 therefore becomes the central episode in this memory laundering.

Bandera and eleven other OUN members had already been tried in Warsaw between November 1935 and January 1936. They were found guilty of various crimes, including the assassination of a Polish official. Bandera gained notoriety at that trial by refusing to speak Polish and answering questions only in Ukrainian. The trial also marked the first time OUN members performed a fascist salute in public: Vira Svientsits'ka, as she was taking the stand, turned toward her fellow defendants, raised her right arm, and declared "Slava Ukraini!" (glory to Ukraine).[30] All the defendants were found guilty and received life imprisonments; at the end of the verdict, Bandera shouted "Iron and blood will decide between us." His fellow OUN members responded with a shout of "Slava Ukraini!"[31]

A second trial, this time of twenty-three OUN members, including several already convicted in Warsaw, took place in L'viv in May and June 1936. The OUN defendants, Bandera among them, were housed in the Lonsky Prison. Bandera, testifying in Ukrainian, stated that he would not confess guilt "because all my revolutionary activities were the fulfillment of my duty," which he defined as "the preparation of a rebirth and the organization of an independent Ukrainian state."[32] After the second trial also ended in guilty verdicts, Bandera delivered a speech that Grzegorz Rossoliński-Liebe has characterized as one mixing "fanaticism, martyrdom, nationalism, fascism, and sentimentalism."[33] The OUN leader ended by stating, "the measure of our idea is not that we were prepared to sacrifice our lives, but that we were prepared to sacrifice lives of others."[34]

The memory laundering at Lonsky Museum today effectively retries Bandera and his comrades and finds them not guilty.[35] The OUN-B, the building declares, was involved in the fight for an independent Ukraine. Placing Bandera and his fellow nationalists alongside the lists of those murdered by the NKVD in June 1941 and later dissidents creates a genealogy of Ukrainian patriots who were persecuted throughout the violent twentieth century. The Lonsky Museum turns them into the founding fathers and mothers of the new, independent Ukraine. That Bandera and his fellow OUN-B members engaged in violent acts, particularly against Jews and Poles, does not matter; Bandera's declaration at his L'viv trial, while he was being held at Lonsky, acts as the final words on this subject.

Per Anders Rudling has pointed out that there's a sinister side to the way the museum remembers its past. On June 22, 2011, the L'viv city council placed posters created by the Center for the Study of the Liberation Movement all over the city. One of the images, Rudling writes, "is a famous photo of a woman who discovered a loved one: a son, a husband, or a father, among the many victims, killed by the NKVD before the Soviets retreated in panic." The posters equated Nazi crimes with communist crimes and in doing so, he argues, they "externalize the violence and reduce Ukrainians to victims without agency." But "the original photos actually depict three atrocities, acts of political violence committed by three totalitarian forces: the Soviets, the Germans, and Ukrainian Nationalists." On the original, dating from the June 1941 massacres at the prison, several Jewish residents of the city sit while militiamen from the OUN-B–organized militia issue instructions. The Jews in this photograph are the ones who were forced to exhume the dead bodies, lay them outside in the prison yard for all to see, and then await execution themselves. By selectively using these photographs, Rudling argues, the Lonsky Museum is "a prime example of postcommunist Holocaust negationism." "In its permanent exhibit," he writes, "we again encounter the photo of the traumatized woman, photoshopped to obfuscate the plight of the Jews at the hands of their tormentors from the OUN militia. The Jews, awaiting their death at the hands of the OUN militia are literally covered up with large target boards of Soviet crimes. A target board with an exact number of 1,681 depicts the number of NKVD victims at Lonts'kyi prison. There is no mentioning of the pogrom, or the role of the OUN in its execution."[36]

As this episode suggests, the memorial museum also acts as a clearinghouse of sorts for other acts of memory laundering. These efforts gained legitimacy under the presidency of Viktor Yushchenko (2005–10), who promoted the glorification of Ukrainian nationalists, particularly members of the OUN and UPA (the president also promoted commemorating the Holodomor, as Daria Mattingly's chapter notes). Yushchenko established the Ukrainian Institute of National Memory in 2006, named Roman Shukhevych a "Hero of Ukraine" later that year, and, in October, issued a directive to make October 12 a Day of Memory for the Victims of the Holodomor and Political Repressions. These political-memory policies provided the foundations for the museum: the directive served as the basis for the site's creation as a memorial museum.[37] Yushchenko's memory policies culminated, quite controversially, with his decision in 2010 to name Stepan Bandera a "Hero of Ukraine," a decision his successor, Viktor Yanukovych, rescinded. Yet in many ways Yushchenko's policies let the genie out of the bottle, never to return. The remembrance practices about 1941 that had developed underground during the Soviet era, practices that tended to view Bandera, Shukhevych, and other members of the OUN and UPA as pure heroes because they had fought against the Soviet Union and had been demonized in Soviet propaganda.[38] Yushchenko's decisions legitimized these beliefs and gave them renewed purpose.[39]

Today the Lonsky Museum regularly hosts events, book signings, and other activities that adhere to the history told within its walls and on its website. In March 2015, to pick a representative example, the museum hosted a book launch for Olesya Isayuk's new biography of Roman Shukhevych (who is also memorialized inside the museum). Billed as a "scientific-popular biography," Isayuk's work used NKVD, Polish, and Ukrainian archives and depicted the OUN commander not only as a fighter for Ukrainian liberation but also as a husband, father, businessman, and politician. Funded by the Center for Research on Liberation Movements and promoted in the newspaper *Ukrainian Pravda*'s "Historical Truth" section, the event perfectly encapsulates the process of memory laundering: Isayuk works as a researcher for both the Center for Liberation and the Lonsky Prison Museum.[40] In this way, the Lonsky memory laundering forms a key part of the nationwide efforts to produce a new, nationalist version of Ukrainian history. In fact, these efforts are intimately connected: the head of the Institute of National Memory created under Yushchenko, Volodymyr Viatrovych, previously worked as head of the Center for the Study of the Liberation Movement in L'viv. In the words of Jared McBride, "what unifies his [Viatrovych's] approach is a relentless drive to exculpate Ukrainians of any wrongdoing, no matter the facts."[41]

The Lonsky Museum, it is worth pointing out, has a significant address these days. It is no longer on Lonsky Street. Its address is now 1 Stepan Bandera Boulevard. At the other end of the boulevard stands a statue of Bandera erected in 2007. The museum's decision to heroize Bandera came just a few months before president Viktor Yushchenko declared him a "Hero of Ukraine" (later revoked by his successor, Viktor Yanukovych), effectively taking the memory laundering within Lonsky and making it a national affair.[42] Tarik Cyril Amar has rightly concluded that the Lonsky Prison, Memorial to the Victims of Communism, and Bandera statue form "an axis of national suffering and nationalist triumph."[43]

A BRIEF TOUR THROUGH AN ALTERNATIVE LONSKY

On its walls, the prison tells the stories of a few individuals. They include only OUN members, including well-known figures such as Shukhevych and less well-known figures such as Father Mykola Khmil'ovs'kii, a Ukrainian Greek Catholic priest who was imprisoned for four years in Lonsky (1950–54). The Prison Museum could also tell other stories. They might include the following ones. These stories might be best read as the displays that could have been on Lonsky's walls.

We could envision this parallel universe version of Lonsky by returning to the time right after the bodies were laid out in the prison yard. On July 6, 1941, Ukrainian militia members arrested around forty Jews and brought them to a L'viv prison. The captives were told to stand against a wall and wait for their executions. As the executions were carried out, a German officer in charge told the executioner that his work was done for the day. One of the men arrested but not shot that day in the prison yard was a thirty-two-year-old resident of the city named Simon Wiesenthal.[44] Wiesenthal, who was born in nearby Buczacz and who lived in what was then Lwów in 1941, of course survived the pogroms and Holocaust and became the world's most famous Nazi hunter.

Kazimierz Bartel was born on March 3, 1882, in Lemberg. A mathematician by training, Bartel was a professor at Lwów Polytechnic University for most of World War I. He was conscripted into the Austro-Hungarian Army near the war's end, returned to his native city, and served as a commander of railway troops during the battles that followed the creation of the Polish Republic. His successes led him to be named minister of the railway system and to be elected in 1922 to the Sejm (Polish parliament). He would eventually serve three times as prime minister after Józef Piłsudski's coup d'état in 1926. Bartel resigned initially from politics in 1930, returned to his post at Lwów Polytechnic, and became its rector. It was here, in 1939, where Bartel again served as head of the city's civic committee preparing for the German invasion. When the city fell to Soviet forces instead, Bartel traveled to Moscow, met with Soviet colleagues, and agreed to write scientific books (there is some lingering controversy over whether Bartel was approached about serving the Soviet state). When the Germans did invade in June 1941, Bartel was arrested on July 2 and taken to the Gestapo prison on Pełczyńska Street. He was transferred on July 21 to Lonsky Street and tortured. Karolina Lanckorońska, a professor of Renaissance art and culture at the same university who was also held in Lonsky, recalled that the Germans called Bartel a "Commie-Jew" and made him clean the boots of his captors. Five days after arriving at Lonsky, Bartel was taken just outside the city and shot.[45]

The famous Nazi hunter who survived the L'viv pogroms and the former prime minister of Poland who did not are just two examples of the people associated with Lonsky and what happened in 1941 that the building does not talk about today. There are others who could be brought into an alternate Lonsky Museum. Walking toward the museum on that 2011 summer day, I passed 12 Kopernyka Street. In 1941, it housed the apartment of Krystyna Chiger and her family. She was six when she watched her fellow Jewish citizens forcibly marched up her street on their way toward the Lonsky Prison in June 1941. She would write of that time:

> As a small child, from my window, I could see it was terrible. I was not supposed to watch, but I could not look away. With the help of the Ukrainians, I could see, the German soldiers were pulling the Jews out into the street and shooting them on the spot or taking them on the transport to the Piaski, the sand quarry northwest of town where Jews were executed. It was too soon for the establishment of the forced labor camp on Janowska Road, but already large numbers of Jews deemed unfit for work were being sent by transport to the concentration camp at Belzec.[46]

Her family managed to hide in the sewers of L'viv, aided by a Polish worker named Leopold Socha. Chiger would write about her story in her 2008 memoir, *The Girl in the Green Sweater*, which was adapted by Agnieszka Holland into an Academy Award–nominated film under the title *In Darkness*.[47]

One of the people who might have walked by her could have been Emanuel Schlechter. (The stories of L'viv's Jews are, for obviously tragic reasons, hard to be precise about.) Schlechter was born in the city in 1904 and served in its 1920 defense before moving to Poland and launching a career as one of the most popular songwriters of the era. His tunes often featured in hit films. Schlechter moved back to his home city in the late 1930s to work at the Lwów Teatr Miniatura. When the Nazis invaded, he, along with his wife and young son, were arrested. They ended up first in the L'viv ghetto and then at the Janowska Concentration Camp just outside the city. They died in 1942 or 1943.[48]

It's also possible that Chiger could have seen Leon Weliczker or a member of his family. Born in Stojanov to a fairly prosperous family (his father ran lumberyards), he moved to Lwów in 1933 when he was eight. The Weliczkers feared what would happen to them in 1939, when the Soviet regime first established power, but managed to survive the nationalization of their business. In his memoir, he would recount his family's experiences during the pogroms. He recalls, "At the beginning of August 1941, we heard that an order had been issued to the Ukrainian militia to arrest all the respectable and well-known Jews in Lvov and to drive them into the courthouse yard in Loketko Street. After being tortured terribly, most of the Jews were shot. The rest were placed in the courthouse jail only to be led out a few days later to the same fate."[49] Weliczker was sent to the Janowska camp, escaped, was recaptured, and was assigned to work in the "Death Brigade" that used bonfires and tools to destroy evidence of Nazi crimes in L'viv. He would survive this punishing work too. Weliczker would testify at both the Nuremberg and the Eichmann trials, noting at the latter one that he was the only member of his extended family that had survived the Holocaust. He would write his memoirs of this time in 1963, *The Road to Janowska*. In total, Weliczker (who would change his last name to Wells when he emigrated to the United States) lost seventy-six members of his family.[50]

To grasp the way the building can be narrated in radically different ways, one needs only to read the separate Ukrainian and Polish Wikipedia pages for the site. The former tells the story of how the prison primarily functioned as a punishment and execution center for Ukrainian nationalists. Bartel is mentioned in one sentence, but also singled out are Bandera, Mykola Lebed, Yaroslav Stets'ko, and Mykola Khmil'ovs'kii. The focus on June 1941 NKVD killings is in this entry. The bulk of the article explains the Memorial Museum and its focus on "the most tragic period in the history of the Lonsky Prison—the Soviet occupation."[51] The Polish version also explains the basic history of the site and notes that NKVD agents executed 924 prisoners there in June 1941, but singles out Juliusz Tadeusz Tarnawa-Malczewski, Jan Nalborczyk, and Rudolf Regner. The entry then tells about the Gestapo's use of the prison, including the executions of Bartel, before concluding with one sentence about how Lonsky served as a NKVD/MVD/KGB prison from 1944 to 1991.[52]

These are stories not of liberation movements for Ukraine, but of other people who lived in L'viv or found themselves there during the period the Lonsky Museum commemorates. These are competing stories, ones that contest the focus of 1941 in terms of victims, victimizers, and ethnicities.[53] These are stories of people who fought for Polish independence or for Ukrainian independence, or who just worked and lived in what was once a cosmopolitan city. These are stories that would capture the ways Ukrainians in L'viv could be both victims and victimizers, and of how the city caught its own "Jedwabne syndrome" in the summer of 1941.[54] These are stories that the building does not tell.

CONCLUSION: SLAVA UKRAINI!

In his influential study of post-Soviet Russian memory, Alexander Etkind argues that Russia has not yet come to terms with the millions who died during the Communist Era. He concludes that a consensus has not yet developed about the meanings of that period, that the Russian state has shown little concern with investigating the crimes of communism, and that, as a result, post-Soviet culture "has produced unusual, maybe even perverted, forms of memory."[55] Russia remains haunted by its recent past, he posits, because the dead have not been given a proper memorial. One aspect of what Etkind calls "warped mourning" is the predominance of what he calls "soft" memory over "hard." Soft memory consists of novels, texts, films, and the like, while hard "consists primarily of museums." In Russia and eastern Europe, Etkind argues, extending his focus outside Russia, novels, films, and debates about the past "vastly outpace and overshadow" monuments, museums, and memorials.[56] The result is that remembrance is always unstable, unfixed, constantly up for debate.

The Lonsky Prison Museum inverts this paradigm. The building is a "hard" memory site, but one that offers a highly contentious, highly controversial version of history.[57] Lonsky Prison captures a lot. The building evokes the ongoing politics of memory in Ukraine since 1991 and reveals how new cultures of remembrance have developed since the Soviet collapse.[58] In his study, Tarik Cyril Amar argues that the post-Soviet remaking of memorial sites in L'viv is not merely a reversal of Soviet-era memories but a complex reworking of the past. The years since 1991, he writes, represent "the first time in Lviv's postwar history when the city's population has been able to form a public sphere (or spheres) and openly and officially relate to its memory as a subject."[59] The second half of the twentieth century was one where official Soviet narratives of a "Golden September," when L'viv first joined the Soviet Union, and the "Great Fatherland War," where all Ukrainians fought to return to the Soviet Union, were the only ones tolerated in public. Now, Amar writes, Ukrainian nationalists are turning "the falsifications of Soviet propaganda into a rhetorical strategy."[60]

On my way out of the Lonsky Museum in 2011, I took a glance at the guest book. On its pages, the most popular responses left by visitors were the OUN-B's slogans of "Slava Ukraini!" followed by "Heroiam slava! [glory to the heroes]." One person responded with "Russkie vpered v chorty! [Russians go to hell!]" A visitor from Vienna wrote that he "now has a deeper understanding of Ukraine's history" and hoped "may freedom prevail!"

The Lonsky Prison does not house any prisoners anymore, but in its contentious rendering of the past, its captives are Mnemosyne, the personification of memory in Greek myths, and her daughter, Clio, the Muse of History.

NOTES

My thanks for the insightful feedback from participants and audience members at a panel on perpetrators and postcommunist memory held at the Ninth World Congress of the International Council for Central and East European Studies in Makuhari, Japan, on August 5, 2015, where I first presented a version of this chapter. I also want to thank John-Paul Himka for comments on a draft and for sending me his article on the museum. Emily Channell-Justice provided feedback on a later version of this chapter and helped steer me toward better Ukrainian transliteration. Finally, a special thank-you to Vitaly Chernetsky, who has taught me much about Ukraine and who took me to the Lonsky Museum in 2011.

1. Annabel Jane Wharton, *Architectural Agents: The Delusional, Abusive, Addictive Lives of Buildings* (Minneapolis: University of Minnesota Press, 2015), xiv.

2. Ibid., xviii.

3. "Misiia" (Mission), http://www.lonckoho.lviv.ua/muzej/misiya.

4. Here I am building on George Mosse's influential interpretation of how World War I established new patterns of remembrance (*Fallen Soldiers: Reshaping the Memory of the World Wars* [Oxford: Oxford University Press, 1990]). The Lonsky Museum presents the actual suffering of Ukraine during World War II: A 2004 study lists the total Ukrainian war deaths at 6,850,000 people, or 16.3 percent of the population. Of these, a full 5,200,000 were civilians, whereas military victims "only" constituted 1,650,000 (Vadim Erlikhman, *Poteri narodonaseleniia v XX veke: spravochnik* [Moscow: Russkaia panorama 2004], 23–35).

5. Wharton, *Architectural Agents*, 4.

6. Timothy Snyder, *Bloodlands: Europe between Hitler and Stalin* (New York City: Basic, 2010), xi.

7. For a comprehensive documentary history of the events, see Ksenya Kiebuzinski and Alexander Motyl, eds., *The Great West Ukrainian Prison Massacre of 1941: A Sourcebook* (Amsterdam: Amsterdam University Press, 2016). For a history of the city that places the events of 1941 in a larger framework, see Tarik Cyril Amar, *The Paradox of Ukrainian Lviv: A Borderland City between Stalinists, Nazis, and Nationalists* (Ithaca, NY: Cornell University Press, 2015). The events of 1941 are covered in ch. 3.

8. For an excellent analysis of the history and memory evoked (and ignored) at the museum, see John-Paul Himka, "The Lontsky Street Prison Memorial: An Example of Post-communist Holocaust Negationism," in *Perspectives on the Entangled History of Communism and Nazism: A Comnaz Analysis*, ed. Klas-Göran Karlsson, Johan Stenfeldt, and Ulf Zander (Lanham, MD: Lexington, 2015), 137–66. I thank Professor Himka for sending me his article and for comments on a draft of this chapter.

9. For the details of these events, see John-Paul Himka, "The Lviv Pogrom of 1941: The Germans, Ukrainian Nationalists, and the Carnival Crowd," *Canadian Slavonic Papers* 53, nos. 2-3-4 (June-September-December 2011): 209–43.

10. The Germans made a film of the events that is now available on the museum's site and on YouTube: https://www.youtube.com/watch?t=16&v=MBOaHtq1rqc.

11. These events are still the source of controversy in Ukraine and among historians of the period. For a relatively temperate example (the discourse often gets nasty, particularly in the comment sections of online newspaper articles and on blogs), see the reaction to John-Paul Himka's "Lviv Progrom of 1941" when it was published in Ukrainian by *Istorichna pravda*. Himka's article appeared on December 20, 2012: http://www.istpravda.com.ua/research/2012/12/20/93550/. The lengthiest critique was written by Serhy Riabenko, "Slidami 'L'vivs'kogo pogromu' Dzhona-Pola Khimki," *Istorichna Pravda*, February 20, 2013, http://www.istpravda.com.ua/articles/2013/02/20/112766/. Himka wrote a short response, "Shche kil'ka sliv pro l'vivs'kii pogrom," *Istorichna Pravda*, February 25, 2013, http://www.istpravda.com.ua/columns/2013/02/25/114048/.

12. Himka notes, "To some extent, the pogrom was a carnival." (Himka, "Lviv Pogrom of 1941," 212). He goes on to argue that although the OUN-B and its followers did not initiate the pogrom, "they provided its engine" (243).

13. The OUN, or Organization of Ukrainian Nationalists, was formed in 1929 and split in 1940 along generational lines. The older members continued to follow Andriy Melnyk (1890–1964); the younger generation turned toward the more active and more violent faction led by Stepan Bandera (1909–59). The two are distinguished as OUN-M and OUN-B.

14. Himka, "Lviv Pogrom of 1941," 218–19. For more on the subject of the OUN and the pogroms, see Per Anders Rudling, *The OUN, the UPA, and the Holocaust: A Study in the Manufacturing of Historical Myths*, Pittsburgh, PA: Carl Beck Papers in Russian and East European Studies, No. 2107 (2011).

15. "Masovi rozstrili 1941 [Mass shootings 1941]," http://www.lonckoho.lviv.ua/arhiv/masovi-rozstrily-1941.

16. See Daniel Boyarin, "Martyrdom and the Making of Christianity and Judaism," *Journal of Early Christian Studies* 6, no. 4 (1998), 581.

17. "Valentin Nalyvaychenko vidkriv pam'iatnii znak u 'Tiurmi na Lonts'kogo,'" http://www.lonckoho.lviv.ua/podiji/valentyn-nalyvajchenko-vidkryv-pamyatnyj-znak-u-tyurmi-na-lontskoho.html. Translations by Stephen M. Norris. For similar sentiments expressed in two other visits (by Canadian prime minister Stephen Harper and Ukrainian Canadian Congress president Paul Grod in 2010 and 2013, see "Memorial Service at Lonsky Street Prison," http://risu.org.ua/en/index/all_news/ukraine_and_world/ukrainians_outside_of_Ukraine/53445/, and "Kanads'kii prem'er rozumie ukrains'ku istoriiu krashche za Azarova," *Istorichna pravda*, October 26, 2010, http://www.istpravda.com.ua/short/2010/10/26/1374/. Harper is said to have signed the guestbook and "left his admiration for the Ukrainian struggle for freedom and independence" while lamenting that the "myth of communism" still exists and that the "crimes of communist regimes" are not well understood.

18. Wharton, *Architectural Agents*, 61.

19. Ibid.

20. See Himka, "Lontsky Street Prison." Himka writes that the museum "glorifies OUN without mentioning or admitting that the militia associated with OUN was deeply involved in murders and other atrocities against Jews on the very premises of the Lontsky St. prison and in the other Lviv prisons in July 1941." "Thus," he argues, "the museum is a place where Jewish memory is erased as well as the memory of crimes against Jews perpetrated by Ukrainian nationalists (138)." For an informative study on how the Ukrainian diaspora has also negated the Holocaust, see Grzegorz Rossoliński-Liebe, "Holocaust Amnesia: The Ukrainian Diaspora and the Genocide of the Jews," *New Cold War: News and Analysis of the Multipolar World*, September 20, 2016, https://www.newcoldwar.org/holocaust-amnesia-ukrainian-diaspora-genocide-jews/.

21. It's not hard to see the applicability of Foucault's influential 1975 study *Discipline and Punish* on how modern prisons are an expression of power and how they discipline both prisoners and civilians alike.

22. "Peredistoriia v'iaznitsi 'na Lonts'kogo,'" http://www.lonckoho.lviv.ua/istoriya/istoriya-vyaznytsi/peredistoriya-vyaznytsi-na-lontskoho.

23. This history, along with details of the prison itself and its organization taken from the Central State Historical Archive of L'viv, is traced on the Lonsky's site: "Period pol'skoi okupatsii, 1919–1939," http://www.lonckoho.lviv.ua/istoriya/istoriya-vyaznytsi/period-polskoji-okupatsiji-1919-1939-rr.

24. "Radianskii period, 1939–1941," http://www.lonckoho.lviv.ua/istoriya/istoriya-vyaznytsi/radyanskyj-period-1939-1941-rr.

25. "Nimets'ka okupatsiia, 1941–1944," http://www.lonckoho.lviv.ua/istoriya/istoriya-vyaznytsi/nimetska-okupatsiya-1941-1944.

26. "Radians'ka okupatsiia, 1944–1991," http://www.lonckoho.lviv.ua/istoriya/istoriya-vyaznytsi/radyanska-okupatsiya-1944-1991-rr.

27. The most thorough study of Bandera and his life can be found in Grzegorz Rossoliński-Liebe, *Stepan Bandera: The Life and Afterlife of a Ukrainian Nationalist: Fascism, Genocide, and Cult* (Stuttgart: ibidem, 2014). Bandera's wartime activities are covered in ch. 5 of that book.

28. See the "myths" listed by the organization in the wake of Ukrainian president Petro Poroshenko's 2014 designation of October 14 as the Day of the Defender of Ukraine Day, usefully translated into English at "Ukraine's Institute of National Memory Addresses-Mythsabout-UPA for the New Day of the Defender," *Euromaidan Press*, October 17, 2014, http://euromaidanpress.com/2014/10/17/ukraines-institute-of-national-memory-addresses-myths-about-upa-for-the-new-day-of-the-defender/. For an overview of the "Bandera debate" in contemporary Ukraine, see Eleonora Narvselius, "The 'Bandera Debate': The Contentious Legacy of World War II and Liberalization of Collective Memory in Western Ukraine," *Canadian Slavonic Studies* 54, nos. 3–4 (2012): 469–90.

29. Peter Reuter and Edwin Truman, *Chasing Dirty Money: The Fight against Money Laundering* (Washington, DC: Institute for International Economics, 2006), 3.

30. Rossoliński-Liebe, *Stepan Bandera*, 139.

31. Ibid., 151.

32. Ibid., 155.

33. Ibid., 158.

34. Ibid., 159.

35. The Lonsky Prison is not the only site that engages in memory laundering. I delivered an earlier version of this chapter at the Ninth World Congress of the International Council for Central and East European Studies in Makuhari, Japan, on August 5, 2015. Two days earlier, I visited the Yasukuni Shrine in Tokyo, which honors the nearly 2.5 million Japanese soldiers who died in wars between 1869 and 1947. Among the names are 1,068 designated as war criminals by the International

Military Tribunal for the Far East in 1946, 14 of whom are Class-A (they include Doihara Kenji, Hirota Kōki, Itagaki Seishirō, Kimura Heitarō, Matsui Iwane, Mutō Akira, and Tōjō Hideki). A head priest, Matsudaira Nagayoshi, secretly enshrined the fourteen in 1978, thus placing them alongside the countless other soldiers who died in Japanese wars: they are not distinguished from others enshrined at the site. Two excellent books in English cover these controversies at the shrine: Franziska Seraphim's *War Memory and Social Politics in Japan, 1945–2005* (Cambridge, MA: Harvard University Press, 2006), and Akiko Takenaka's *Yasukuni Shrine: History, Memory, and Japan's Unending Postwar* (Honolulu: University of Hawai`i Press, 2015). Takenaka's conclusion that the unending controversies over the shrine indicate that Japan experiences an "unending postwar" is particularly relevant for understanding the Lonsky Prison site's importance.

36. Per Anders Rudling, "Memories of Holodomor and National Socialism in Ukrainian Political Culture," in *Rekonstruktion des Nationalmythos? Frankreich, Deutschland und die Ukraine im Vergleich*, ed. Yves Bizuel (Göttingen, Ger.: Vandenhoek and Ruprecht, 2013), 248–49.

37. See Himka, "Lontsky Street Prison," 139.

38. These practices were also developed in the large Ukrainian diaspora in Canada, as John-Paul Himka and Per Anders Rudling have both noted in their works on the subject. See also Serhy Yekelchyk's excellent article, "National Heroes for a New Ukraine: Merging the Vocabularies of the Diaspora, Revolution, and Mass Culture," *Ab Imperio* 3 (December 2015): 97–123. Yekelchyk rightly notes that the Bandera celebrated today is the symbolic one (that is, the person who resisted the Soviet Union and Soviet myths), not the historical one (that is, the leader of a murderous faction of Ukrainian nationalists).

39. For a short overview of this subject, see Andrii Portnov, "Bandera Mythologies and Their Traps for Ukraine," *Open Democracy*, June 22, 2016, https://www.opendemocracy.net/od-russia/andrii-portnov/bandera-mythologies-and-their-traps-for-ukraine. For a longer version, see Rudling, *The OUN, the UPA, and the Holocaust: A Study in the Manufacturing of Historical Myths*, Pittsburgh, PA: The Carl Beck Papers in Russian and East European Studies No. 2107, 2011.

40. "Anons: U 'Tiurmi na Lonts'kogo'—prezentatsiia knizhki pro Romana Shukhevicha," *Ukrains'ka Pravda*, March 28, 2015, http://www.istpravda.com.ua/short/2015/03/28/148034/. The following month, the same publisher and same backers put out Mikola Posivnich's new biography of Stepan Bandera. The Lonsky Prison Museum hosted a discussion of it on the museum's website: "U 'tyurmi na Lonskoho'—prezentatsiya novoji biohrafiji ctepana bandery," April 5, 2015, http://www.lonckoho.lviv.ua/podiji/anonsy/u-tyurmi-na-lontskoho-prezentatsiya-novoji-biohrafiji-ctepana-bandery.html. For an insightful account about the controversies surrounding Shukhevich, the Nachtigall battalion, and the pogroms in L'viv, see John-Paul Himka, "Debates in Ukraine over Nationalist Involvement in the Holocaust, 2004–2008," *Nationalities Papers* 39, no. 3 (May 2001): 353–70.

41. Jared McBride, "How Ukraine's New Memory Commissar Is Controlling the Nation's Past," *Nation*, August 13, 2015, https://www.thenation.com/article/how-ukraines-new-memory-commissar-is-controlling-the-nations-past/. McBride notes that Viatrovych's decisions reflect the Soviet-era remembrance practices mentioned earlier: when faced with problematic facts found in documents, he tends to dismiss them as Soviet forgeries. Within Ukraine, as McBride writes, he is widely seen as a trusted, fresh young source. See Viatrovych's response to McBride's and Josh Cohen's criticisms in "Real and Fictional History in Ukraine's Archives," *Kyiv Post*, May 9, 2016, http://www.kyivpost.com/article/opinion/op-ed/volodymyr-viatrovych-real-and-fictional-history-in-ukraines-archives-413382.html. In it, Viatrovych defends his work, mostly by arguing (correctly) that Soviet officials always lumped Ukrainian nationalists in the Nazi camp and also downplayed the Holocaust.

42. For more, see Timothy Snyder, "A Fascist Hero in Democratic Ukraine," *New York Review of Books*, February 24, 2010, http://www.nybooks.com/daily/2010/02/24/a-fascist-hero-in-democratic-kiev/.

43. Tarik Cyril Amar, "Different but the Same or the Same but Different? Public Memory of the Second World War in Post-Soviet Lviv," *Journal of Modern European History* 9, no. 3 (2011): 390. Amar covers well the controversy surrounding the museum, including the open letter signed by sixty-five academics to protest its contentious rendering of the past, but his story ends in 2009 (when he wrote the article and when the museum was still unfinished). "Lonski," he correctly observed, "may easily turn into a site where only Ukrainian suffering will be remembered while other victims and Ukrainian perpetrators will be aggressively consigned to oblivion. This would be a particularly powerful signal, since Lonski has a comparatively well-known past as a place where victims come from different ethnic as well as political backgrounds" (393).

44. See Wiesenthal's memoir, *The Murderers among Us* (New York: McGraw-Hill, 1967). Wiesenthal's various memoirs and recollections have been subjects of debate, for he often contradicted himself about this time in his life and what he was doing in Lwów. (He states he studied there at the Polytechnic School, but no records have been found that prove his attendance.) Still, no one doubts he was in the city and observed the 1941 events. For more, see Tom Segev, *Simon Wiesenthal: The Life and Legends* (New York: Doubleday, 2010).

45. Lanckorońska was a Polish aristocrat who recounted Bartel's time at Lonsky in her memoir, *Wspomnienia wojenne 22 IX 1939—5 IV 1945* (Cracow: Znak, 2002). Lanckorońska would end up in Ravensbruck and would write about her time there: *Michelangelo in Ravensbruck: One Woman's War against the Nazis* (Boston: Da Capo, 2008).

46. Krystyna Chiger, *The Girl in the Green Sweater: A Life in the Holocaust's Shadow* (New York: St. Martin's, 2008, 29.

47. Chiger, *Girl in the Green Sweater*. Agnieszska Holland, *In Darkness* (Poland, Zebra Films, Sony Pictures Classics, 2012).

48. *Biblioteka piosenki*, s.v. "Schlechter, Emanuel," http://www.bibliotekapiosenki.pl/Schlechter_Emanuel.

49. Leon Wells, *The Janowska Road: Survival in a Nazi Death Camp* (2014 kindle edition), Location 963.

50. Leon Wells, *The Janowska Road: Survival in a Nazi Death Camp* (New York: Macmillan, 1963). Wells's biography is recounted in the book's introduction. For another example of the Jewish experience in L'viv, see David Kahane's "Oral History Interview," March 27, 1991 (accession number 1995.A.1272.28, RG number RG-50.120.0028), from the United States Holocaust Memorial Museum's online collection, http://collections.ushmm.org/search/catalog/irn502645.

51. "Tiurma na Lonts'kogo," *Wikipedia*, https://uk.wikipedia.org/wiki/%D0%A2%D1%8E%D1%80%D0%BC%D0%B0_%D0%BD%D0%B0_%D0%9B%D0%BE%D0%BD%D1%86%D1%8C%D0%BA%D0%BE%D0%B3%D0%BE.

52. "Muzeum Pamięci Narodowej 'Więzienie przy Łąckiego' we Lwowie," *Wikipedia*, https://pl.wikipedia.org/wiki/Muzeum_Pami%C4%99ci_Narodowej_%22Wi%C4%99zienie_przy_%C5%81%C4%85ckiego%22_we_Lwowie.

53. For more on the period between 1939 and 1941 in the city, including how Bartel, Welickzer, and others could be integrated into it, see Christoph Mick, "Lviv under Soviet Rule, 1939–1941," in *Stalin and Europe: Imitation and Domination, 1928–1953*, ed. Timothy Snyder and Ray Brandon (Oxford: Oxford University Press, 2014), 138–62.

54. That individuals or families could be both victims and victimizers is one of Jan Gross's major arguments in his work, *Neighbors*, which also put the July 10, 1941, pogrom in that Polish town under more scholarly scrutiny. The debate that followed the publication of Gross's book in Poland parallels many of the debates surrounding the June and July 1941 events in L'viv. See Gross, *Neighbors: The Destruction of the Jewish Community in Jedwabne, Poland* (Princeton, NJ: Princeton University Press, 2001) and Antony Polonsky and Joanna Milchlic, eds., *The Neighbors Respond* (Princeton, NJ: Princeton University Press, 2004). The "Jedwabne Syndrome" as applied to Ukraine in 1941 comes from Alexander Prusin, "A 'Zone of Violence': The Anti-Jewish Pogroms in Eastern Galicia in 1914–1915 and 1941," in *Shatterzone of Empires: Coexistence and Violence in the German, Habsburg, Russian, and Ottoman Borderlands*, ed. Omer Bartov and Eric Weitz (Bloomington: Indiana University Press, 2013), 362–77.

55. Alexander Etkind, *Warped Mourning: Stories of the Undead in the Land of the Unburied* (Stanford, CA: Stanford University Press, 2013), 245.

56. Ibid., 176–77.

57. A handful of scholars have explored the politics of memory in contemporary Ukraine, particularly in western Ukraine. Uilleam Blacker contextualizes how the experiences of Poles and Jews have disappeared from the present-day memoryscape of L'viv, including the Lonsky Prison, in his article, "Urban Commemoration and Literature in Post-Soviet L'viv: A Comparative Analysis with the Polish Experience,"

Nationalities Papers 42, no. 5 (2014): 637–54. Andriy Portnov provides a nice overview of the evolution of the arguments over how to remember the past in "Memory Wars in Post-Soviet Ukraine (1991–2010)," in *Memory and Theory in Eastern Europe*, ed. Uilleam Blacker, Alexander Etkind, and Julie Fedor (Basinstoke, UK: Palgrave Macmillan, 2013): 233–54. John-Paul Himka analyzes the cultural and historical contexts for why the Holocaust is still comparatively ignored in the region in his "Obstacles to the Integration of the Holocaust into Post-communist East European Historical Narratives," *Canadian Slavonic Papers* 50, nos. 3-4 (2008): 359–72, a topic he also studies in "The Reception of the Holocaust in Postcommunist Ukraine," in *Bringing the Dark Past to Light: The Reception of the Holocaust in Postcommunist Europe*, ed. John-Paul Himka and Joanna Michlic (Lincoln: University of Nebraska Press, 2013), 626–62. David Marples has written extensively on the remembrance of Bandera, the OUN, and other contentious aspects of Ukrainian history. His book, *Heroes and Villains: Creating National History in Contemporary Ukraine* (Budapest: Central European University Press, 2007), covers these issues.

58. For an excellent overview of this topic, see Volodymyr Kravchenko, "Fighting Soviet Myths: The Ukrainian Experience," in *The Future of the Past: New Perspectives on Ukrainian History*, ed. Serhii Plokhy (Cambridge, MA: HURI, 2016), 437–74.

59. Amar, "Different But the Same?," 376.

60. Ibid., 384.

STEPHEN M. NORRIS is Walter E. Havighurst Professor of Russian History and Director of the Havighurst Center for Russian and Post-Soviet Studies at Miami University (Ohio). He is author of two books on Russian cultural history, including *Blockbuster History in the New Russia: Movies, Memory, Patriotism* (2012), and editor of five books on Russian history and culture, including *Russia's People of Empire: Life Stories from Eurasia, 1500 to the Present* (with Willard Sunderland, 2012). He is currently writing a biography of the Soviet political caricaturist Boris Efimov.

Figure 4.1. Karlag Museum, founded 2001. http://karlagmuseum.kz/kz/ [for Karlag]. https://museum-alzhir.kz/en/ [for the Alzhir women's camp]. *Photograph by Steven Barnes*

FOUR

Remembering the Gulag in Post-Soviet Kazakhstan

STEVEN A. BARNES

The tiny village of Dolinka, Kazakhstan, some forty-five kilometers southwest of the city of Karaganda, is dotted by the typical ramshackle single-story dwellings found in small rural settlements all over the former Soviet Union.[1] Until just over a half century ago, Dolinka served as the capital of the infamous Karaganda Corrective Labor Camp (Karlag), an enormous camp complex that stretched hundreds of kilometers through Kazakhstan's steppe and held hundreds of thousands of prisoners as one of the largest and longest-lasting outposts of Stalin's notorious Gulag.[2] Like so many former Gulag outposts in Russia, Dolinka continues to serve as part of the post-Soviet Kazakhstani penal system.[3] Immediately upon entering the town, you pass high cement walls intended to obscure view of the notorious labor camp AK 159/6, from which reports of current torture and beating of inmates periodically emerge.[4] Driving further through the settlement, you pass several blocks of single-story hovels when a massive, city-block-long, two-story neoclassical building appears rather jarringly out of the steppe land. Some eighty years ago, prisoners constructed this building to serve as headquarters of the Karlag administration. The enormous structure—which housed only the central Karlag administration and was supplemented by supervisory and armed guard staff in the camps; many subdivisions spread throughout the northern Kazakh steppe—attests to the massive number of prisoners who suffered in this labor camp outpost. Abandoned and boarded up until recently, the building now gleams after some $800,000 was spent to transform it into the Museum of Memory of the Victims of Repression in the Dolinka Settlement (hereafter the Karlag Museum).[5] Officially founded in 2001, but not opened till May 2011, the Karlag Museum is probably the largest Gulag-related museum in the former Soviet Union.

Figure 4.2. A broken *shanyrak*. Photograph by Steven Barnes

Entering Karlag's former headquarters you immediately notice a broken *shanyrak*, the small framed circular opening at the center of a yurt's roof (fig. 4.2). The broken shanyrak symbolizes a victimized ethnic Kazakh population, for the shanyrak plays an important symbolic role in contemporary Kazakhstan as a shorthand image to evoke the nomadic culture of the Kazakh past. The official state emblem of Kazakhstan is a stylized shanyrak, and national holidays such as the spring equinox celebration of Nauryz see yurts erected along the major thoroughfares of Kazakhstani cities. The shanyrak, the legend goes, was the one piece of the yurt that would survive year after year and would be passed from one generation to the next. The destruction of the shanyrak thus visually represents a key ingredient in what I call the standard Kazakhstani narrative of Soviet repression—the Soviets' destruction of the tie between contemporary Kazakhs and their ancestors' culture, a tie that only an independent Kazakhstan

Figure 4.3. Arch of Sorrow. *Photograph by Steven Barnes*

has been able to reestablish. The broken shanyrak, so prominently placed in the entrance of the Karlag Museum, one of the most important sites of Kazakhstani public memory of Soviet repression, provides the first indication of what I will call the standard historical narrative of Soviet victimization and independent Kazakh rebirth. The shanyrak reminds us that this narrative is being shaped to a significant degree as one of particularly Kazakh (as opposed to Kazakhstani) victimization and rebirth. While non-Kazakh victims are certainly not ignored in the primary sites of Kazakhstani public memory of Soviet repression, the narrative as a whole takes on a distinctly Kazakh form in creating and reinforcing the standard historical narrative.[6]

Some twenty-five kilometers from the Kazakhstani capital city of Nur-Sultan, the Museum Memorial Complex of Victims of Political Repression and

Totalitarianism "ALZhIR" (hereafter the Alzhir Museum) sits on land once occupied by the famed Akmolinsk Camp for Wives of Traitors to the Motherland, a special Karlag subdivision that held the often prominent wives of the repressed at the height of Stalin's "Great Terror."[7] Walking across the museum grounds, you cross under the eighteen-meter Arch of Sorrow (see fig. 4.3). According to the museum's own description, the arch was designed to evoke both a helmet and a traditional Kazakh woman's headdress, the *ak zhaulik*, "symbolizing male strength and female innocence and purity." Further, the two colors of the arch, black and white, "represent accord and harmony between peoples, religions, cultures of different ethnic groups, and also the permanent existence of both good and bad in our life."[8] Thus, from the moment of arrival, the Alzhir Museum announces to its visitors this same narrative of victimization. Even when that narrative evokes the multicultural, multiconfessional character of the Kazakhstani population, it does so in a way that is coded as Kazakh.[9]

A close reading of the Karlag and Alzhir Museums reveals much about how Kazakhstan publicly remembers the history of Soviet repression and opens up questions about the extent to which this public memory is available to the Kazakhstani population and whether these museums represent any kind of coming to terms with the past in Kazakhstan. Many experts on the post-Soviet space have identified an open discussion and public coming to terms with the experience of Soviet repression as critical for ensuring that post-Soviet regimes respect democracy and human rights. Accordingly, the absence of active public memory of Soviet repression is given a prominent causal role in their failure to do so. As Anne Applebaum writes in her Pulitzer Prize winning *Gulag: A History*, "If the Russian people and the Russian elite remembered—viscerally, emotionally remembered—what Stalin did to the Chechens, they could not have invaded Chechnya in the 1990s, not once and not twice. To do so was the moral equivalent of postwar Germany invading western Poland. Very few Russians saw it that way—which is itself evidence of how little they know about their own history."[10] Surely most would recognize this as gross oversimplification, yet I rather suspect we have some sense that a public coming to terms with the Soviet past is a moral good that would have salutary effects in any post-Soviet independent state.

At first glance, Kazakhstan would seem exemplary when it comes to publicly acknowledging and remembering the history of Soviet repression. The center of Nur-Sultan houses a large monument readily visible on a hill in the city park that is devoted to the victims of the various forced labor camps in Kazakhstan. The current Chairman of the Security Council of Kazakhstan, the first and longtime president of post-Soviet Kazakhstan, and the last communist leader of the Kazakh Soviet Socialist Republic, Nursultan Nazarbayev, openly discusses the repression and destructiveness of the Soviet past. Two museums have received substantial government financial support, and Nazarbayev himself attended the opening of the Alzhir Museum in 2007. (Of course none of this can really tell us whether Kazakhstanis "viscerally, emotionally" remember this history, as called for by Applebaum, but at first glance, state support for what Alexander Etkind has called the "hardware" of memory has been substantial.)[11]

It seems to me that these efforts have established and reinforced a standard Kazakhstani Soviet repression narrative that with slight variations revolves around five main features repeated in various venues: the destruction of the Kazakh intelligentsia (particularly the suppression of Alash Orda), the massive famine that accompanied sedentarization/collectivization on the steppe, the vast expanse of Gulag incarcerated space in Kazakhstani territory including camps and places of exile, the environmental destruction from above-ground nuclear weapons testing in the nuclear polygon around Semipalatinsk, and finally the rebirth of the Kazakh nation and the transition from totalitarianism to democracy starting in 1991.[12]

Yet, despite all of this outpouring of public memory, Kazakhstan remains under the de facto rule of its last communist-era leader, essentially a dictator even if no longer officially the president, and finds itself far from the democracy it so often claims to be. Kazakhstan was rated as "not free" in 2020 by Freedom House with scores of 18 out of 60 for civil liberties and 5 out of 40 for political rights (where higher scores equate to more freedom.) The state allows no substantial opposition presence in the political system, and the electoral system repeatedly manufactured results in excess of 90 percent for its first and post-Soviet president, and even over 70 percent for his hand-chosen successor. Protests are often ruthlessly suppressed, as were the striking miners in Zhanaozen, who faced violent suppression of their 2013 protests. Even journalists attempting to cover the aftermath of the Zhanaozen events were arrested.[13] Rather obviously, then, remembering past repression and prevention of current repression do not necessarily go hand in hand. The relationship of historical memory to present politics is far more complicated than some might have us believe.

Nonetheless, perhaps public memory of the Gulag in Kazakhstan has something to teach us about public memory of Soviet repression, and about politics, society, and culture in today's Kazakhstan. Upon closer inspection, public memory of Soviet repression in Kazakhstan appears less central than what we might first think, and despite the enormous and laudable work of museum staff, the content of that public memory may not meet the goal of promoting respect for democracy and human rights. To probe the shape and limits of this memory, this chapter provides a close reading of the Karlag and Alzhir Museums, the two major Gulag museums in Kazakhstan, placing them in the broader context of public memory of Soviet repression in Kazakhstan and memories of traumatic, violent, and unjust historical events well beyond the former Soviet space.

The Karlag Museum occupies all three floors (two above ground and a basement) of the enormous Dolinka headquarters with no fewer than thirty halls and exhibitions. The museum combines traditional museum practice with today's oft-imitated experiential museum. Leaving behind the broken shanyrak in the entrance, the first floor features a series of exhibit rooms devoted to the standard Kazakhstani Soviet victimization narrative: the political repression of the Kazakh intelligentsia, the foundation of Karlag, its economic activities, repressed artists, women and children in Karlag, deportations of non-Kazakh ethnic groups to Kazakhstan, repressions of the post-Stalin years, and post-Soviet Kazakhstan as an independent state. These exhibit halls, in what I would call the traditional part of the Karlag Museum, are mostly dominated by a series of glass display cases holding historical photographs, artifacts, and text blocks explaining the history of Soviet repression in general and the Karlag labor camp in particular.

From the very outset, the text describing the Karlag camp emphasizes that it was "a typical formation of a colonial type with its center in Moscow. The administration of Karlag was subordinate only to the GULag People's Commissariat for Internal Affairs (Narodnyi Komissariat Vnutrennykh Del; NKVD) in Moscow. Republican and regional Party and Soviet organs had no influence on the actions of the camp leadership."[14] A nearby text block on the village of Dolinka reinforces the message, emphasizing that "the Administration of Karlag was subordinate only to the GULag NKVD in Moscow." Karlag is thereby removed from its local context with the assertion that local (i.e., Kazakh) authorities had no control over this outpost of Moscow's colonial subjugation of Kazakhstan. In a strict bureaucratic sense, the description is accurate; unlike many camps, the Karlag administration was subordinated directly to the Gulag bureaucracy in Moscow rather than to republic or local authorities. The assertion that republican and local bodies had "no influence" on the camp is an overstatement, however, for Gulag camps had wide interactions with their surrounding communities.[15] What is important, though, is the role played by this explanatory text: the Gulag is to be seen as an external imposition on an essentially passive population in Kazakhstan, so much so that even local party and Soviet officials have no authority in the camp universe.

Descending to the basement level, the museum turns toward the experiential. The Karlag Museum capitalizes on a long history of morbid mental imagery of Soviet secret police basements. Basements, like that of the notorious Lubyanka in Moscow or those now memorialized at the Museum of Genocide Victims in Lithuania, were places of imprisonment, torture, and all too often execution. Even though the tour guides admit that they have no particular information that individuals were ever held, interrogated, or tortured there, the conclusion implied in the decision to place the experiential exhibits in the basement of the Dolinka headquarters is clearly intentional.

The dark, dank corridor of the basement level, barely renovated with concrete floors, contrasts sharply with the first-floor corridor's inviting, red runner carpet stretching the length of the building and abundant natural and artificial light. Entering the basement is intended to evoke a feeling in the visitor of entering a different world, a different time. Here in the basement the walls are bare, broken up only by a series of doors on one side of the corridor, and no text blocks guide visitors along the corridor; they are invited to enter the unknown—to feel rather than think about the history they are confronting. Enter through any one of the doors along the corridor, and you enter an imagined prisoner's life world.

Mannequin prisoners, guards, bureaucrats, and interrogators occupy a punishment cell, male and female barracks, a torture chamber, an infirmary, a morgue, an office for photographing and fingerprinting prisoners, and even a scientific laboratory. Evoking the image of Gulag prisoners from Aleksandr Solzhenitsyn's *One Day in the Life of Ivan Denisovich* (along with the famous picture of Solzhenitsyn from *Gulag Archipelago* in which he is dressed in a camp prisoner uniform), the prisoner mannequins all wear number patches on their clothing.[16] Genuine period artifacts—bowls and spoons, prisoner mugshots and so on—are intermingled with the mannequins and other reconstructions, such as barrack bunks, to draw the visitor into a world simultaneously imaginary and real. Often it is impossible to tell the authentic artifact from the reconstruction.

Perhaps the basement room most readily evoking the Stalin era is the only one without a mannequin (fig. 4.4). A single bare bulb illuminates sparse furnishings pregnant with meaning. A water bucket and two small stools are the room's only furniture. One stool sits in the far corner, the other directly in the room's center. Lifting your gaze from the central stool, you notice that a pair of rusting manacles hangs from the ceiling. Other bits of steel and chain hang from the walls. A meter-long stick leans against a side wall, just beyond the water bucket. One end of the stick has been splattered with a vibrant red paint that suggests not eighty-year-old bloodstains but evidence of more recent prisoner beatings. Every wall is splattered with this "blood" in both the stick's vibrant shade and a much darker hue, simulating both recent torture activity and a long history of brutal prisoner beatings. A "bloody" handprint on the far wall evokes a prisoner driven to madness trying to somehow pass through the walls to escape the pain. Even the water bucket has "blood" running down its sides. The only hope for respite comes through a doorway to the morgue, where a "blood"-stained stretcher marks what seems to be the only possible escape from the building—death.

The torture chamber is undoubtedly morbid, but also surprisingly powerful. In leaving behind any connection to the real (none of the items in the room appears to be genuine period artifacts), the room feels somehow realer than any other. My tour guide explained that they had found no evidence that such torture ever occurred in the basement of the Dolinka headquarters, but she was at pains

Figure 4.4. Torture chamber. *Photograph by Steven Barnes*

to explain that such things happened, even if not in this particular space. The experiential museum basement raises difficult questions about the limits of the acceptable in a Gulag museum. Standing in the torture chamber, one cannot help but recall the furor raised in the early 2000s when Igor Shpektor, then mayor of the far north Russian Gulag city of Vorkuta, proposed offering tourists a Gulag adventure. As the *New York Times* described Shpektor's idea, "Then he spun an improbable vision of hard times and hard bunks, where tourists could eat turnip gruel and sleep in wooden barracks in a faux camp surrounded by barbed wire and guard towers, patrolled by soldiers and dogs. 'Americans can stay here,' he went on. 'We will give them a chance to escape. The guards will shoot them'— with paint balls, naturally, not bullets." The codirector of the local chapter of Memorial, Evgeniia Khaidorova, denounced the idea as "worse than sacrilege."

Although his vision was never realized, Shpektor at the time seemed undaunted, telling the *New York Times* that "it should look like the Stalin camps ... so that people today can understand what those prisoners went through." When asked whether the idea would offend some, he asserted that "people should see what should not be repeated again."[17]

I remember reading the article in the *New York Times* in 2005 and being appalled that such an "adventure" was even under consideration. Yet I do wonder what, if anything, makes the basement of the Karlag Museum that different? If the comparison with the Vorkuta mayor's proposal had not struck me during my visit to the museum, it certainly would have based on other activities at the Karlag Museum. Apparently, in May 2013, staff of the Karlag Museum toyed with a plan to allow guests "to become 'Stalin-era prisoners' for one night." The plan was abandoned only when local officials argued that it could conceivably "psychologically traumatize" the participants. Nonetheless, the museum hosted five hundred to a thousand visitors for a "Night in Karlag," a night-time tour of the museum complete with museum staff replacing the mannequins and acting out the experiential parts of the museum—in one room performing "a mock interrogation scene ..., [and in another portraying] an inmate ... hanging by his hands [in the manacles hanging from the ceiling in the torture chamber] while being mistreated by a guard." Visitors were offered unspecified "Gulag-type meals" to up the level of supposed realism.[18] On one hand, the event was a "success." As I will discuss further, obtaining substantial visitor traffic is a significant challenge for a museum in such a remote, hard-to-reach location. Furthermore, "A Night in Karlag" was covered by at least four Kazakhstani television stations and one international one.[19] Yet video of the event strikes one as absurd and unseemly, the power punch of the empty torture chamber absent with an actor hanging from the manacles, while a "guard" almost comically repeatedly demands of the prisoner, "Don't sleep." The patent unreality of the actors breaks the spell cast by the empty torture chamber.

Experiential museums such as the Karlag Museum have been sites of significant controversy, raising significant moral questions about acceptable limits in the portrayal of atrocity. The US Holocaust Memorial Museum faced harsh criticism for the experiential elements of its permanent exhibit, especially but not only for its funneling of visitors through the type of freight car that carried many Holocaust victims to the site of their mass execution.[20] Perhaps seeking to avoid similar controversies, the new National Museum of African American History and Culture in Washington, DC, has largely avoided any experiential component in its portrayal of the history of chattel slavery in the United States.[21] The Karlag Museum raises additional questions—not only about what is acceptable in a museum representation of atrocity history, but also what is acceptable on what could be considered "sacred ground" (even though I raise some questions later in this chapter over whether the Karlag administration building in fact qualifies as sacred ground). As critical as some are of the US Holocaust Memorial Museum, its experiential practices operate in Washington, DC, rather than on the grounds of Auschwitz. The Karlag Museum occupies the very space used by Soviet authorities to manage the operation of the Karlag labor camp. A great deal of emotionality is attached to sacred space, as Edward Linenthal has shown in writing about debates over proper use of battlefields, the footprint of the Alfred P. Murrah Federal Building (site of the Oklahoma City bombing), and Ground Zero in New York.[22]

The Karlag Museum's "A Night in Karlag" raised additional difficult questions with its use of actors to reenact an imagined version of Karlag's history. (I do not mean to suggest that events like those depicted during these reenactments did not happen. Rather, the scenes portrayed in the museum were stylized representations of events that likely happened in some place and in some form, but not necessarily in exactly the way shown or in the specific space in which the reenactments took place.) Reenactment brings in a wide range of comparative considerations and difficult questions of appropriateness. Historical reenactment has long been prominent among US Civil War enthusiasts. Yet critics have long stood opposed to such practices that glamorize war, turning its horrors into an entertaining weekend activity. Even more controversial is the yearly reenactment since 2005 of the 1946 lynching of four African Americans at Moore's Ford in rural Georgia. Controversy attends not only to the question of whether reenacting the event is acceptable, but also for its locus in a more recent and still unresolved history. Organizers claim that their purpose is to call attention to the history of racial violence in the United States and to encourage elderly local citizens who might have knowledge of the 1946 events to come forward in a case that has to this day never resulted in prosecution.[23]

Reenactment raises the tricky question of how to locate the boundary between the experiential museum that appropriately creates a visceral response from its visitors and the theme park that inappropriately commercializes and trivializes the history of violence and oppression. Colonial Williamsburg and similar "living history" heritage sites certainly blur the line with their constantly in-character actors moving about and interacting with visitors. Colonial Williamsburg, one of the most popular tourist destinations in Virginia, engages in a significant idealization of life in eighteenth-century Virginia. Yet it is difficult to combine an "authentic" portrayal of colonial Virginia, and its attendant ills like slavery, with the kind of idealized, family-friendly entertainment that has made the place so successful with tourists. In the late 1970s, a significant number of actors were added to portray slaves, but overt violence like brandings and lashings is not reenacted. In 1994 a reenacted slave auction at Colonial Williamsburg drew so much controversy that it has never been repeated. Does it change our attitude on such reenactments when we realize that lynchings were reenacted and audio-recorded in the United States in the 1890s not for protest but for commercial purposes, and as Mark Auslander describes, "to satisfy white public voyeuristic curiosity?"[24] Even today, can one view the lynching postcards of "Without Sanctuary" without feeling just a little complicit looking at objects produced precisely for a voyeuristic purpose? When I require students to view the photographs for a class on how states and societies cope with the aftermath of mass violence, to what extent am I complicit with perpetuating the gaze that itself was part of the humiliation of the lynching spectacle and the terrorization of racial minorities?[25]

I do not pretend to have a simple answer to these complex questions. I do want to note, however, that intellectually or viscerally, through language and image or in a more immersive and experiential fashion, remembering the past does not necessarily result in the reconciliation or healing we might seek.[26] Does visceral traumatization connect the viewer with the traumas of the past, or does it merely preserve and transmit that trauma into the present? The experiential museum and reenactment may, in the end, simply be too problematic for use in portraying the history of atrocity.

Leaving the Karlag Museum's basement, my tour guide led the way to the building's second floor, where the experiential side of the museum continued, but absent the heavy connotations of a secret police basement, in a decidedly lighter way. First, we entered a palatial office that was once occupied by the Karlag chief. A mannequin chief stands casually behind the desk, a hand in one pocket, gaze fixed out the window onto the expansive grounds of the Karlag headquarters. The office has been beautifully restored, and the museum resisted any urge to somehow turn the space into one of blood and nightmare.[27] The office is strikingly devoid of anything that might connect this particular bureaucrat with the dirty, brutal world of the forced labor camp.

The final stop on the Karlag Museum tour was in a pair of halls that re-created the Karlag library and the "Central Club Named after S. M. Kirov" that existed in the Dolinka settlement from the Stalin era until the 1990s. In the club, two mannequins occupy a stage that stands in front of several rows of chairs. A male mannequin is dressed in a suit and bowtie, playing an accordion. A female mannequin accompanies him onstage in a dress with a scarf draped over her head and shoulders. Her hands are crossed in front of her chest in a way that indicates she is singing. A red banner hangs over the stage reading "Glory to the Bolshevik-Leninists, veterans of the Party, war, and labor!" Nothing in the scene would indicate these mannequins are prisoners, until you notice a third mannequin peeking out from behind the curtain at the back of the stage. Walking around the stage, the mannequin comes into full view in his secret police uniform with a gun holster on his belt. Reports differ on whether these clubs were primarily intended for prisoners or for camp staff. It is likely that a club in Dolinka, given the sheer number of Karlag staff who worked in the village, was primarily intended for the entertainment of staff. The performers, however, at these clubs were typically drawn from among the prisoners (many of whom had been professional performers before their arrest.)

The library next door holds a large number of books. Stamps inside many book covers tell you that they were property of the Politotdel (Political Department) of Karlag, an indication that they were primarily for the use of Karlag staff rather than prisoners. Yet a table in the room holds a 1934 edition of the Karlag camp newspaper *Putevka*, a product of the "cultural-educational department" of the camp and thus a production for the prisoners. Among the other books, a copy of volume 16 of the 1934 edition of the *Bol'shaia sovetskaia entsiklopediia* (*Great Soviet Encyclopedia*) is opened to the title page. Five editors' names are blacked out, no doubt removed during the Great Terror of the latter half of the 1930s, when arrested and executed individuals became official nonpersons.

The inclusion of the library and club, along with paintings and other artwork completed by prisoners during their time in Karlag, offers some idea of the potential for such a big Gulag museum to tell the story in complex and interesting ways. Yet walking away from the Karlag Museum, it is the experiential elements of the museum that most stick with you.

Turning to the Alzhir Museum, we find ourselves seemingly on safer ground. Less experiential, the Alzhir Museum focuses on the cognitive and the artistic-symbolic (see fig. 4.5). It is a museum to be apprehended rather than felt, to be read rather than experienced. The Alzhir Museum predates the Karlag Museum by several years, opened in 2007 in conjunction with the tenth anniversary of the declaration of May 31 as the Day of Memory of Victims of Political Repression. A group of Kazakhstani architects, sculptors, and engineers completed the purposely built museum structure under the leadership of famed Kazakh architect and artist Saken Narynov. The architecture itself evokes the artistic-symbolic focus. The Alzhir Museum, staff seems almost overly prepared to explain, was officially founded on Nazarbayev's initiative. Then president Nazarbayev personally attended and spoke at the museum's opening event on May 31, 2007. The Alzhir Museum was built from nothing and is a substantial complex, and so state financial support for its construction must have been substantial.

The Alzhir Museum repeats the standard Kazakhstani Soviet repression narrative, which builds toward a conclusion with independent Kazakhstan triumphant. The official museum catalog asserts that the museum's foundation was

Figure 4.5. Alzhir Museum. *Photograph by Steven Barnes*

"an important event in the reestablishment of justice in relation to the innocent victims of totalitarianism as one of the most painful consequences of the Red dictatorship."[28] Nazarbayev, speaking at the opening, tried to define the meaning of the museum and the particular lessons from the history of Soviet repression that hold importance for contemporary Kazakhstan. It is not surprising that his reading of history justifies his own regime, and in a veiled way, its use of repression against political opponents.

> No promises of universal happiness can justify the suffering and death of innocent people. Neither prosperity nor harmony and progress can be imposed by violence and cruelty. This is the most important historical lesson that we have learned, and which we must always remember. This lesson is still relevant today. A society in which there is confrontation will never be happy. Therefore, we must protect the peace and harmony in our Kazakhstan....
> Today we say to all those who died and all those who survived those terrible years—your sacrifices were not in vain. You passed on to future Kazakhstani generations immunity to the virus of violence and extremism.[29]

Nazarbayev's reading of the Soviet past not only juxtaposes this dark past to today's supposed transition to democracy, but strikingly, his lessons from the history of Soviet repression provide the foundation for ongoing repression today. As Freedom House reports, "In December 2012, a court invoked laws against 'extremism' to ban the unregistered opposition party Algha and the People's Front, another opposition movement. Algha leader Vladimir Kozlov had been sentenced to seven and a half years in prison in October for his alleged role in the Zhanaozen violence. He was found guilty of heading an illegal group, inciting social hatred, and calling for the violent overthrow of the constitutional order."[30] The very repression of the striking miners in Zhanaozen could be justified in the name of "peace and harmony in our Kazakhstan." The suffering and death of innocent people is a tragedy whether in the name of "promises of universal happiness" or in the name of a society with no "confrontation." Many of my Kazakh friends praise Nazarbayev and his government for the avoidance of the types of ethnic clashes that have occurred in so many other former Soviet republics, yet they do not ask (or do not know) about the suffering that allows for this peace.

Although the museum is built on the site of Alzhir and therefore logically focuses to some extent on Alzhir, that is not and was never intended to be the sole focus. As the museum director writes in the catalog, "However, limiting the multilateral activities of the museum collective to the history of that camp and the fates of the women passing through that hell would not be completely correct. In fact, as the very name of the museum attests, the museum-memorial complex is irrefutable Proof not only of the consequences of political repression and totalitarianism, but also a Reminder of the unacceptability in the future of similar crimes against the human."[31] And, it is important to note, it is always tied back to specifically Kazakh concerns. Writes the director, "Our visitors, thus, become witnesses to the destruction of the Kazakhs as a nation, the suffering of thousands of innocent victims of the Dictatorship of the Soviets, beginning from the colonization of Kazakh lands by tsarist Russia. And in the depths of their soul, they will agree that nostalgia for the Communist past is blasphemy. They will with others pass through the torment to freedom, and they will sense in themselves the invaluable advantages of their Motherland—Independent Kazakhstan."[32]

This is not intended to indicate that non-Kazakh victims are completely forgotten in the museum, but the repression of Kazakhs is privileged. In his speech at the opening, Nazarbayev specifically highlighted a list of a dozen famous Kazakh cultural and scientific figures repressed in the Stalin years, "along with thousands of others fallen from repression."[33] Although these twelve Kazakhs are the only individuals named in his speech, it is important to note that Nazarbayev devoted several sentences of the short speech to the "thousands and thousands of people of various nationalities who died in these years," and he specifically called out the Germans, Poles, Koreans, Crimean Tatars, Turks, Greeks, Kalmyks, and "representatives of peoples from the northern Caucasus" who were deported to Kazakhstan in the Stalin years.[34]

The first floor of the museum is devoted primarily to topics other than Alzhir in a series of display cases (with an art installation in the middle of the circular room that is discussed a bit later). The first display case starts with the end of the Kazakhstani narrative of Soviet repression. It is a copy of President Nazarbayev's decree from April 14, 1993: "On the Rehabilitation of Victims of Mass Political Repressions." Thus, immediately, the "happy ending" of the narrative is announced, as "independent Kazakhstan" represents the end of repression and the rebirth of the Kazakh nation. The remainder of the first floor comes from the collection designated "The 'Alash' Collection and the Kazakh Intelligentsia." "Alash" refers to the short-lived Alash Orda political party that claimed to rule in the name of Kazakh autonomy during the years of the Russian Civil War. The Alzhir Museum writes Alash into their narrative as the anti-Bolshevik precursor of post-1991 independent Kazakhstan. Alash was, they claim, based on "general democratic, humanistic, and liberal principles." The museum does acknowledge that many Alash leaders worked in state and Soviet organs in the 1920s, but a careful delineation puts the repression of these "supporters of the liberal-democratic movement" at 1928, thus cleansing them of any connection with the Stalinist regime and the collectivization-sedentarization that proved so immensely destructive in Kazakhstan. Almost all of Alash, they write, was repressed and shot by the end of 1938.[35]

The remainder of the first floor focuses on a variety of important Kazakh cultural figures and the usually tragic fates that befell them in the 1930s. This pantheon of martyrs establishes a key element of the Kazakhstani narrative of Soviet repression—the Kazakhs as anti-Bolshevik, liberal, democratic victims of an evil regime. Yet the museum portrays Kazakhs, and especially Kazakh women, not only as victims but also as sympathetic toward the women who were imprisoned in Alzhir. The soft, shiny eyes of twenty women's faces rendered in various sizes in black and white watch your ascent along the semicircular staircase to the museum's second floor. You are leaving the male-dominated world of the Kazakh intelligentsia, they seem to say, and are about to enter our space, women's space. At the top of the staircase, you immediately notice a diorama behind glass of the environs of the camp, as it may have appeared at the moment of the first women's arrival to Alzhir. The tour guide tells you a story—clearly one of the museum's favorites. As the newly arrived Alzhir prisoners walked toward their camp under NKVD guard, they would come across a group of local Kazakh women who showed the guards their hostility to these "enemies of the people" by hurling what seemed to be rocks at the prisoners. Yet one of the prisoners, knocked to the ground, noticed that the "rocks" had a strange odor. Upon closer inspection, she discovered that the women were not hurling rocks, but *kurt* (sometimes *qurt*), a cheese made from drained sour milk that is formed into balls. Rather than indicating their hatred for these prisoners, the Kazakh women were showing their sympathy for the prisoners' plight, providing precious food to the hungry. Local kindness did not end there. The museum catalog states, "The local population ... was sympathetic to the imprisoned women. In the winter, they brought food to the women on sledges—fish, sour cream, bread. The women were very thankful to the locals, who understood that these women were only guilty of being the wives, sisters, and daughters of their husbands, brothers, and fathers."[36]

This sets the tone for much of the museum's portrayal of women generally, be they Alzhir prisoners or local Kazakh women. The Alzhir prisoners have long been a particularly moving story for those recounting the history of Soviet repression, both for the fact that they were women and for being something like double victims. Not only were they married to men who were mostly arrested and executed for invented crimes, but they were themselves arrested not even for made-up crimes but merely for being married to the wrong men. The image of the innocent, well-educated, empathetic female victim dominates memory of Alzhir. Drawing both on traditional notions of women's predominant role in the family, but also on the fact that these women were arrested precisely for playing their family role, portrayals of Alzhir prisoners often follow the same form used by Nazarbayev in his speech at the opening: "The memory of the women—the wives and daughters separated from their parents, the mothers and sisters of the repressed—will remain forever in our hearts."[37] In fact, not uncommonly, these women are referred to and refer to one another in their memoirs not as prisoners, but merely as "wives." This makes the important distinction between these women and the "criminals" and "prostitutes" in other labor camp divisions.

The remainder of the museum's second floor is devoted to the history of Alzhir. Display cases tell the stories of particular Alzhir prisoners through photographs, artifacts, official documents, and the like. The women spotlighted fall into two groups, the famous and the Kazakh.[38] Women who are part of the exhibit include Rakhil' Plisetskaia (actress and mother of the famed ballerina Maia Plisetskaia), Zinaida Tukhachevskaia (sister-in-law of the famed Soviet Marshal Mikhail Tukhachevskii), Galina Serebriakova (a writer and wife of Grigorii Sokol'nikov, People's Commissar of Finance), Natal'ia Sats (director of the Moscow Musical Theater for Children, which is now named after her), among others. Curiously, Serebriakova and Sats along with other famed imprisoned wives like Anna Larina Bukharina (wife of Nikolai Bukharin) have been claimed by the museum for the Alzhir story, even though they were never prisoners in this camp. In some cases like that of Larina, these claimed famous prisoners were arrested under the same NKVD order on arresting family members of traitors to the motherland but were held in one of the other Gulag camps set up for the purpose. In other cases like Sats and Serebriakova, they were arrested under other circumstances and were never at Alzhir.[39]

The display cases are notable for the fact that nearly every one of them includes at least one photograph or biography of a prisoner of Kazakh ethnicity—this despite that fact that the list of Alzhir prisoners by ethnicity indicates that Kazakh women only made up about 1 percent of the Alzhir prisoner population. Thus, although I never did a precise count of women portrayed in the museum, Kazakh women are overrepresented by around 15 to 25 times their actual portion of the prisoner population.[40] The museum has clearly made a conscious decision to expend great effort gathering and portraying the lives of specifically ethnic Kazakh women.

The rather dry display cases are broken up by re-creations of a prisoner barrack, a prisoner under interrogation, and a woman working in a garment factory.[41] On the surface, these displays seem quite similar to the rooms in the Karlag Museum basement. Mannequins and artifacts are used to re-create the look and feel of some aspect of prisoner lives. (The mannequins here also mistakenly have numbers on their uniforms.) Unlike those in the Karlag Museum, however, these are decidedly hands off to visitors. Rather than rooms, these are more accurately seen as recesses in the external wall of the museum and can be viewed only through bars or from behind a red rope line, keeping the visitor at a distance. The architecture of the museum dictates that none of these "rooms" has depth; the back of the scene is only several feet from the corridor in which the visitor stands as an outsider, not able to enter but only to peek in at Alzhir women's lives.

At the Alzhir Museum, depth and emotional response are not the preserve of the historical recreations but of the art installations and paintings around the grounds and inside the museum. Next to the diorama, the new arrival on the second floor notices what seems to be a prison cell (see fig. 4.6). Titled "Fetters," a grid of bars is broken up only by a prison door. Twenty disembodied hands reach out from a reflective black backdrop, alternately gripping or draped over the cell bars, seemingly reaching out from an abyss of emptiness and despair.

Dominating the central space and readily visible from every floor, a Saken Narynov sculpture hangs from the ceiling. In "Freedom and Unfreedom," two interconnected doughnut-shaped cages of gridded wire imprison fifteen white doves. Some beat their heads against the cage, seeking to reach freedom. Others have died in their failure to escape detention, while a lucky few have broken through to the outside of the cage.[42] Sitting below "Freedom and Unfreedom," directly in the center of the first floor, is "The Flower of Life." A tall black sculpted flower breaks through the stone floor. It is intended to represent the continuation of life amid the horrors and difficulties on display in the museum. Yet the decision

Figure 4.6. "Fetters" prison cell, Alzhir Museum. *Photograph by Steven Barnes*

to use a black flower, traditionally a symbol of death, undercuts this message to a degree. In the museum's initial days, the flower was fresh, real, and red.

Two other installations are worth specific mention, both outside the museum. When entering the grounds, after passing under the Arch of Sorrow, two seated figures mark the extreme left and right of the paved entrance walkway (fig. 4.7). These works of the sculptor Zhenis Moldabaev are titled "Struggle and Hope," a female figure who is supposed to represent the turn to poetry and beauty as a way to mentally escape from captivity, and "Despair and Helplessness," a male figure with downcast eyes to represent the loss of hope for an escape to freedom.[43] In winter, both figures, lightly dressed and covered in snow and frost, strongly evoke the prisoner suffering from the freezing cold.

The other installation surrounds the back and sides of the museum (see fig. 4.8). Reminiscent of the Vietnam Veterans Memorial in Washington, DC, the "Wall of Memory" is a series of black stone walls carved with the names of nearly eight thousand women who reportedly spent time in Alzhir (though also including a few of those famous women noted above who were never actually there).

The installation serves two functions similar to those of the Vietnam Memorial. First, it is an affecting reminder of the immense scale of those affected by the camp. Second, it serves as a site of mourning for those with relatives who suffered

Figure 4.7. *Despair and Helplessness* statue. *Photograph by Steven Barnes*

in the camp. Further, the site is a place for public mourning and memorial. Visiting delegations can lay flowers at the wall in a show of respect for the victims. Nazarbayev laid flowers at the wall during the opening ceremony.

Combined with other art pieces, the Alzhir Museum creates an emotional response in the visitor without recourse to the experiential practices of the Karlag Museum basement. It is on the whole a more cognitive experience, but through a series of effective art installations is still able to call forth a visceral response from its visitor. Its emotional impact is different—more serene and less frightful, calling its visitor not to put on the prisoner's shoes, but to silently contemplate and respectfully mourn.

I want to conclude this discussion with a few thoughts about the importance of place in understanding the limits of these post-Soviet Kazakhstani Gulag

Figure 4.8. Wall of Memory. *Photograph by Steven Barnes*

museums. The decision to place the two museums on actual locations used by the camps, while understandable, has placed the public memory of the Gulag in Kazakhstan decidedly on the periphery. Authenticity and sacred space have been chosen over accessibility and visibility. The privileging of authenticity of place leaves the two museums geographically displaced from the realm of everyday experience. The sites are rather conveniently out of the way and out of the day-to-day reality of the national narrative that can thus focus more on the supposed triumph represented by Kazakhstani independence and the supposed "transition from totalitarianism to democracy" rather than dwell on the black spots of the past. The Kazakhstani population does not have to confront the discomforting memories of the Soviet past, a past perhaps more complicated than the standard narrative might have it, in which Kazakhs are innocent victims of a perpetrator that seems no longer to exist.

In some respects, even the focus on authenticity of place is rather false. The decision to place the Karlag Museum in the headquarters building is easily understandable from a practical perspective. The museum was able to take over and rehabilitate this massive, preexisting building. It obviously also contains a certain logic in the realm of authenticity of place. You can actually stand in the real office of the chief of this massive forced labor camp. No doubt this can be affecting. I certainly felt an odd sense of connection with history, standing in this office where so many of the decisions that I wrote about in my first book were made. Yet this is not the same as standing on the hallowed ground of Auschwitz, at Ground Zero in New York City, or even on the ground over the various marked and unmarked Gulag graves one can find around the Kazakhstani steppe. The Karlag administration building is not the place where prisoners suffered and died; it is where the paper pushers pushed their papers. The building better represents Hannah Arendt's "banality of evil" than it represents the suffering of the system's victims. After all, the camp chief's office does not strike one as markedly different from the office of a university rector or the director of a steel mill, or perhaps even the office of the museum's director located in the same building. (I was never in the director's office at the Karlag Museum, and so I cannot say for certain, but my suspicion is that it would look similar if less spacious other than the absence of Stalin-era furnishings.) Here is one of the important reasons that the museum has created the experiential spaces in the basement, even in the absence of evidence that torture and executions actually took place in the confines of this particular building. One suspects, though, that a stronger explanatory factor is the trend of museums generally toward experiential exhibits.

Privileging authenticity of place creates other difficulties as well. It is quite difficult to get to either museum. No public transport serves either location. Even by private car it is no easy trip. Traveling to the Alzhir Museum, as I did daily over the course of two weeks in late winter 2013, required traversing roads under reconstruction that rather resembled driving through a battlefield scarred by potholes the size of bomb craters. The employee van that graciously brought me to the museum each day constantly swerved back and forth across the road at a snail's pace, trying to find a line by which travel was even possible through the mess. The twenty-five-kilometer trip regularly took an hour or more. The Karlag Museum is located even more remotely, though at least the roads were rather good. Nonetheless, being forty-five kilometers from the city of Karaganda, where most residents still do not have cars, presents a significant impediment to building a substantial patronage. During two weeks of daily research in the collections of the Alzhir Museum, I never once saw a visitor to the museum (though I do know that a group from Nazarbayev University visited the museum on one of the weekends when I was not working). Whenever I wanted to revisit a tour to a portion of the exhibit, I had to ask somebody to turn the lights on. I saw no other visitors during my single afternoon tour of the Karlag Museum. These are mass-consumable museums that are not being consumed by the masses.

By privileging the authentic Gulag location, the museums re-create the geographic isolation that was an integral part of the operation of the Gulag. Even as scholars have increasingly questioned Solzhenitsyn's metaphor of the Gulag as an archipelago, showing that the Gulag was more thoroughly integrated with local civilian populations than previously thought, the opening up of the geographic extremes of the Soviet Union was always an important part of the Gulag's work. Although many buildings were constructed by prisoners, one cannot really find such an "authentic" Gulag location within the cities of Nur-Sultan and Karaganda.

The result of all this is that the museums allow the Kazakhstani state to take the steps that it "should," acknowledging the history of Soviet repression and memorializing the victims, without actually allowing that past to impinge too heavily upon the triumphal narrative of independent Kazakhstan that dominates public spaces in the new capital city. This no doubt proves convenient, because too thorough a questioning of the Soviet past and the violations of human rights that were such a feature of communist rule might raise discomforting questions about Nazarbayev's own activities in the Communist Party from the 1960s until his rise as the Communist Party leader of Kazakhstan shortly before the Soviet collapse.

Furthermore, the inaccessibility of the museums limits the capacity of the populace to engage with and take advantage of the possibilities of using Gulag memory to break down essentialist identities and narratives in post-Soviet Kazakhstan. Thus, while the Gulag museums in Kazakhstan would seem to offer the opportunity to challenge essentialist identities that Alison Landsberg describes as "prosthetic memory," they ultimately fail to do so. Landsberg describes the importance of capitalism and the commodification of memory for making memory readily available to anyone willing to pay for its products, thus removing memory from belonging to any one particular group. The geographic displacement of these Gulag museums undercuts any notion of availability. Technically available to any in the population, the museums' locations limit the actual spread of that memory.

The inaccessibility of the museums, and of public memory of repression in Kazakhstan more generally, allows ethnic particularist elements of the national narrative to go largely unquestioned. The ethnic particularism of Kazakhstani public memory of Soviet repression both makes that memory politically acceptable and simultaneously limits its capacity to create any meaningful working through of the past. That is, on the one hand, it is easier to tell the story of Soviet repression in Kazakhstan because the particularist memory allows for a politically palatable narrative. The Kazakhs were victims of Soviet (read: Russian) repression, usually passive victims or active resisters.[44] They were certainly not to be read as perpetrators. Soviet repression was something "they" did to "us." The story can be given an uplifting conclusion that validates the current Kazakhstani regime—the triumph of Kazakhstani independence over Soviet repression. Yet this convenient narrative avoids other, harder questions. After all, Soviet repression is not so easily divided into a "they" who carried out evil deeds and a "we" who suffered yet persevered and ultimately triumphed. Rather, Soviet repression made such black-and-white distinctions highly problematic. Many were both victims and perpetrators in this system, actively denouncing their fellow citizens one minute and repressed under the accusations of others the next.[45] Anna Akhmatova, speaking of the complex moral universe of the post-Stalinist Soviet Union, when many returned from the camps, famously said, "Two Russias stare each other in the eyes: the ones that put them in prison and the ones that were put in prison."[46] Yet the moral world of Soviet repression was even more complicated than Akhmatova had it, for a great many Soviet people belonged on both sides of that equation.

With individuals as prominent as Nazarbayev himself who have a past as Communist Party functionaries, it is imperative that the narrative of the Soviet past be tightly controlled, lest these sorts of moral complications arise. Archival collections on the history of Karlag that were open at the beginning of the new millennium are now unavailable to scholars, an action that seems so at odds with the general thrust of the Kazakhstani government toward an open (if somewhat marginalized) discussion of the repressive Soviet past. Several published books, including my own, have been based on research conducted when these archival materials were available. Nobody in 2013 seemed able to definitively answer my questions about why the archive had been closed. Many people—people who have worked either as scholars or as museum staff on the history of Karlag—seemed not even to know that the Karlag archive had once been accessible, some even asserting that it had been confiscated and taken to Moscow in the Soviet era. I heard this even from people who had several books on their shelves that had used the archive, and the Karlag Museum even had a few documents from the collection in its displays. It is hard to tell which, if any, of the stories that I heard about the Karlag archive's closure is true and whether the archive will at some point in the future reopen to scholars. The significant state support for the Gulag museums discussed in this chapter, the presence in Nur-Sultan of a centrally located monument devoted to the Gulag in Kazakhstan, and the willingness of even Nazarbayev to discuss the topic openly make it rather curious that the archive has closed. But if one thinks more about control of the narrative of Gulag memory in post-Soviet Kazakhstan, it conceivably makes more sense. The many thousands of pages in the archive are susceptible to scholarly interpretation and contain unknown information. The museums and monuments can more readily control the narrative and are thus less potentially dangerous, especially if the museums are shunted off to geographically marginal spaces.

Perhaps, in the end, what the museums and monuments of Kazakhstan capture is the need for the narrative of Soviet repression in Kazakhstan to be standardized and, most important, controlled. Nonetheless, in spite of some limitations in their content and the rather definitive failure of Kazakhstan to become a truly democratic country that universally respects human rights, these museums make sure that the history of Soviet repression is not lost and make it at least potentially available to those who wish to use a narrative of the past to challenge the shortcomings of the present.

NOTES

Research and writing of this chapter were supported by a National Endowment for the Humanities Fellowship and the American Councils Research Scholar Program with funding from the US Department of State's Program for Research and Training on Eastern Europe and the Independent States of the Former Soviet Union (Title VIII). I want to thank the eminent scholar of memory studies and my George Mason colleague, Alison Landsberg, who allowed me to brainstorm ideas with her for how to think about these museums.

1. A note on terminology: throughout the chapter, I use the term *Kazakh* to refer specifically to the ethnic group, while I use the term *Kazakhstani* to refer to a resident of the country without ethnic designation. (Thus, ethnic Russian, Korean, and Kazakh citizens of Kazakhstan would all be "Kazakhstani," but only ethnic Kazakhs would be "Kazakh.") This follows the usage of the Kazakhstani president and other political and cultural figures, although they do sometimes mistakenly use the term *Kazakh* when context suggests they mean *Kazakhstani*.

2. The history of Karlag is the primary focus of my book, Steven A. Barnes, *Death and Redemption: The Gulag and the Shaping of Soviet Society* (Princeton, NJ: Princeton University Press, 2011).

3. On geographic continuity in the post-Soviet Russian penal system, see Judith Pallot, "The Topography of Incarceration: The Spatial Continuity of Penality and the Legacy of the Gulag in Twentieth- and Twenty-First Century Russia," *Laboratorium* 7, no. 1 (2015): 26–50.

4. When I first visited Dolinka in 2006, the cement walls were not present, and the watchtowers of the colony were readily visible. But the colony has given Kazakhstan's penal service something of a black eye in the intervening years, which likely led to the attempt to obscure it from view. On prisoner abuse at the Dolinka labor colony, see reports from Radio Free Europe/Radio Liberty, "Inmate Who Filmed 'Kazakh Prison Video' Found Hanged in Jail," July 23, 2010, http://www.rferl.org/content/Inmate_Who_Filmed_Kazakh_Prison_Video_Found_Hanged_In_Jail/2107712.html; Radio Free Europe/Radio Liberty, "Kazakh Prison Inmates Mutilate Themselves in Protest," June 4, 2010, http://www.rferl.org/content/Kazakh_Prison_Inmates_Mutilate_Themselves_In_Protest/2062062.html; and Radio Free Europe/Radio Liberty, "UN Official Says Kazakh Prisoners Tortured, Abused," May

14, 2009, http://www.rferl.org/content/UN_Official_Says_Kazakh_Prisoners_Tortured_Abused/1731791.html.

5. The figure comes from Zhanat Kundakbayeva and Didar Kassymova, "Remembering and Forgetting: The State Policy of Memorializing Stalin's Repression in Post-Soviet Kazakhstan," *Nationalities Papers* 44, no. 4 (2016): 611–27.

6. Here, I disagree with the interpretation of Kundakbayeva and Kassymova ("Remembering and Forgetting"), who argue that the general Kazakhstani politics of Soviet repression memory has managed to avoid the ethnicization that has occurred in other non-Russian post-Soviet states. I agree with their point that a focus on ethnic Kazakh suffering is a component of the Alzhir Museum, but they believe it is an exception to the general rule. I intend to show that this ethnicization of memory is readily apparent at the Karlag Museum as well. Although it is clearly not exclusivist, meaning attention is also devoted to the suffering of non-Kazakh ethnic groups in Kazakhstan, the two museums are clearly to be read as tales of Kazakh suffering and heroism.

7. The Russian acronym formed from this unofficial camp name equates to *ALZhIR* (*Akmolinsk lager' zhen Izmennikov rodiny*), which is also the Russian for both Algeria and Algiers. Akmolinsk is one of the names the city had prior to being renamed Astana when it became the Kazakhstani capital in the 1990s and Nur-Sultan in 2019 to honor Nursultan Nazarbayev when he stepped down from the presidency.

8. The description comes from the former online virtual museum, "Arch of Sorrow," *Internet Archive*, June 20, 2013, https://web.archive.org/web/20130620154441/http://alzhir-eng.ucoz.ru/photo/arch_of_sorrow/2-0-4. As with the text in the physical museum, the online museum was trilingual in Kazakh, Russian, and English. The English translation was, with only a few exceptions, extraordinarily well done. As a result, unless noted otherwise, I adopted the museum's English-language text, which I have checked in all cases against its Russian version. The museum's website has since been reconfigured, and I have not yet been able to locate the cited texts in the new version. As noted further on herein, some of the pages from the former website were no longer recoverable when this chapter was submitted. I have noted the dates on which I originally accessed the site. When possible, an Internet Archive version of the original site has been included. The new version of the website can be seen at http://museum-alzhir.kz/, accessed December 22, 2016.

9. Although my knowledge of the Kazakh language is limited, I was able to verify that the Kazakh version of the virtual tour contained this same sentence about different ethnic groups and religions. http://alzhir.ucoz.kz/photo/asiret_a_pasy/1-0-4, accessed October 24, 2013, is now unavailable and is not captured by the Internet Archive.

10. Anne Applebaum, *Gulag: A History* (New York: Doubleday, 2003), 572.

11. Alexander Etkind, "Post-Soviet Hauntology: Cultural Memory of the Soviet Terror," *Constellations* 16, no. 1 (2009): 182–200; and Etkind, *Warped Mourning: Stories of the Undead in the Land of the Unburied* (Stanford, CA: Stanford University Press, 2013). A broader treatment of monuments, memorials, and museums in

post-Soviet Kazakhstan can be found in Kundakbayeva and Kassymova, "Remembering and Forgetting."

12. Sometimes, though less prominently, the rebirth is traced back to the 1986 ethnic disturbances in Almaty, when Kazakhs faced repression for protesting the installation of an ethnic Russian as Communist Party leader of the Kazakh Soviet Socialist Republic. The very last display case of the Alzhir Museum has a few words about these events.

13. Freedom House, "Kazakhstan," 2020 freedom scores, accessed April 13, 2020, https://freedomhouse.org/country/kazakhstan/freedom-world/2020. For comparison's sake, Russia gets a 15 out of 60 and 5 out of 40 in the two categories, while Uzbekistan gets 8 out of 60 and 2 out of 40.

14. Although text blocks in the Karlag Museum are trilingual in Kazakh, Russian, and English (in that order), the museum's English translations are of low quality. As a result, all quotations from Karlag Museum text consist of my own translations from the Russian text.

15. On Karlag's place in the life of Karaganda region, see Barnes, *Death and Redemption*. For the interactions of other Gulag outposts with their surrounding communities, see Alan Barenberg, *Gulag Town, Company Town: Forced Labor and Its Legacy in Vorkuta* (New Haven, CT: Yale University Press, 2014); and Wilson Bell, "Was the Gulag an Archipelago? De-convoyed Prisoners and Porous Borders in the Camps of Western Siberia," *Russian Review* 72, no. 1 (2013): 116–41.

16. This is a historical inaccuracy. For all but a very few Karlag prisoners, these number patches would not have been worn. The number patches were introduced in new supremely harsh *katorga* camp subdivisions created in 1943. The number of prisoners in these katorga divisions never exceeded sixty thousand out of a total labor camp population of some 2 million. Karlag had only a small *katorga* subdivision, designed to hold prisoners designated for a *katorga* division but unable to work because of their status as invalids. Most prisoners who wore the number patches spent their camp terms in the so-called "special camps" (*osobye lageri*), the type of camp described in Solzhenitsyn's famous *One Day in the Life of Ivan Denisovich*. Several of these camps, including the one in which Solzhenitsyn himself spent time, existed in Kazakhstan, but Karlag was not one of them.

17. Steven Lee Myers, "Above the Arctic Circle, a Gulag Nightmare for Tourists?," *New York Times*, June 6, 2005, http://www.nytimes.com/2005/06/06/international/europe/06russia.html?_r=0. More recently, the tourism minister of the Sakha republic urged using former Gulag sites as a center for ecotourism in the republic. "Sakha Republic Hopes to Encourage Gulag Tourism," *Moscow Times*, March 28, 2014, https://www.themoscowtimes.com/2014/03/28/sakha-republic-hopes-to-encourage-gulag-tourism-a33426.

18. Yelena Weber and Antoine Blua, "In Kazakhstan, Spending Saturday Night in the Gulag," Radio Free Europe/Radio Liberty, May 20, 2013, http://www.rferl.org/content/kazakhstan-gulag-tour/24991694.html. It is unclear whether the fault belongs to the tour guide or the authors, but the article contains several

mistakes in its recounting of Karlag's history. The name of the Karlag chief is given as Otto Bin rather than the correct Otto Linin. Further, the article incorrectly asserts that under Linin was the only time when men and women lived together in Karlag.

19. See television news footage from Astana television, http://youtu.be/l8pDWQ322kU; Eurasia Channel 1, "The Lives of Arrestees is Recreated in the Karlag Museum," May 20, 2013, http://youtu.be/WPjYQo_XTQo (removed from YouTube as of December 22, 2016); Karaganda Channel 1, "A Night in the Museum of the Victims of Karlag," May 21, 2013, http://youtu.be/GWaJzQK4nEU; Telekanal 24KZ, "A Night in Karlag," May 20, 2013, http://youtu.be/GnAFGpK7Now; and RTVi, "A Night in Karlag," May 20, 2013, http://youtu.be/btzZyPn4jNs.

20. Edward Linenthal, *Preserving Memory: The Struggle to Create America's Holocaust Museum* (New York: Viking, 1995); Alison Landsberg, *Prosthetic Memory: The Transformation of American Remembrance in the Age of Mass Culture* (New York: Columbia University Press, 2004).

21. The only exception is a single small room that in an oblique fashion seeks to evoke slave ships, yet it does so in a symbolic fashion rather than by making any attempt at actual recreation of the slave ship experience.

22. Edward Linenthal, *Sacred Ground: Americans and Their Battlefields* (Urbana: University of Illinois Press, 1991); Linenthal, *The Unfinished Bombing: Oklahoma City in American Memory* (Oxford: Oxford University Press, 2001). On Ground Zero, Linenthal's comments have been ubiquitous in the public sphere. See, for example, his comments in Dinitia Smith, "Hallowed Ground Zero; Competing Plans Hope to Shape a Trade Center Memorial," *New York Times*, October 25, 2001, http://www.nytimes.com/2001/10/25/arts/hallowed-ground-zero-competing-plans-hope-to-shape-a-trade-center-memorial.html.

23. See Mark Auslander, "'Holding On to Those Who Can't Be Held': Reenacting a Lynching at Moore's Ford, Georgia," *Southern Spaces*, November 8, 2010, http://www.southernspaces.org/2010/holding-those-who-cant-be-held-reenacting-lynching-moores-ford-georgia.

24. Auslander, "Holding On."

25. If your curiosity must be satisfied, see http://withoutsanctuary.org/, accessed December 22, 2016.

26. This is decidedly the case with the reenactment of the Moore's Ford lynching, where local public opinion is decidedly split along racial lines about whether the activity encourages racial healing and reconciliation or "unintentionally feed[s] cycles of hatred and retribution" (Auslander, "Holding On").

27. During "A Night in Karlag," however, the office was used to reenact an interrogation scene, with the actor portraying the Karlag chief as a harsh and intimidating interrogator.

28. *Katalog kollektsii fonda muzeia "ALZhIR"* (Astana, Kazakhstan: Muzeino-memorial'nyi kompleks zhertv politicheskikh repressii i totalitarizma "ALZhIR," 2012), 4.

29. "Work Schedule of the Head of State," *Nomad*, May 31, 2007, http://www.nomad.su/?a=3-200706010335.

30. Freedom House, "Kazakhstan," 2013 freedom scores, http://www.freedomhouse.org/report/freedom-world/2013/kazakhstan, accessed December 22, 2016.

31. *Katalog kollektsii*, 4.

32. Ibid.

33. "Work Schedule," May 31, 2007.

34. "Work Schedule," May 31, 2007. Although their presence in the camps and especially at Alzhir is not left out of the museum, by focusing on those groups that were exiled to Kazakhstan because of their nationality, Nazarbayev leaves out any reference to Russians, Ukrainians, or Belarussians—thousands of whom would suffer in camps and in exile as alleged "kulaks."

35. *Katalog kollektsii*, 6.

36. *Katalog kollektsii*, 126.

37. "Work Schedule," May 31, 2007.

38. Sheila Fitzpatrick, in an account of her visit to Astana and the Alzhir Museum, also made note of the museum as a gallery of famous women ("Kazakhstan's City of Gold," *The Monthly*, October 2013, http://www.themonthly.com.au/issue/2013/october/1380549600/sheila-fitzpatrick/kazakhstan-s-city-gold).

39. The entries in the Alzhir Museum catalog make clear the true stories of these women and do not comment on why it chose to include them, even though they were never in this camp. See *Katalog kollektsii*, 135, 147.

40. Eighty-seven Kazakh women prisoners are listed out of a total of "more than 8,000" prisoners. On the total prisoner population, see "History of the Camp Alzhir," *Internet Archive*, May 11, 2013, https://web.archive.org/web/20130511102529/http://alzhir-ru.ucoz.ru/publ/muzej_quot_alzhir_quot/istorija_lagerja_quot_alzhir_quot/istorija_lagerja_quot_alzhir_quot/13-1-0-6. For the list of Kazakh women prisoners, see "Kazakhs," *Internet Archive*, June 17, 2013, https://web.archive.org/web/20130617045012/http://alzhir-ru.ucoz.ru/publ/muzej_quot_alzhir_quot/spisok_zhenshhin_uznic_lagerja_quot_alzhir_quot/kazashki/14-1-0-39.

41. The women at Alzhir designed, built, and operated a garment factory.

42. See the image at http://museum-alzhir.kz/images/media_alzhyr/IMG_2174.jpg, accessed December 22, 2016. The description comes from http://alzhir-ru.ucoz.ru/photo/svoboda_i_nevolya/2-0-49, accessed October 27, 2013, now unavailable, and not captured by the Internet Archive. For similar Narynov pieces without the doves, see http://www.ahmadyarts.com/artists/narynov, accessed December 22, 2016.

43. The descriptions come from http://alzhir-ru.ucoz.ru/photo/otchajanie_i_bessilie/1-0-20 and http://alzhir-ru.ucoz.ru/photo/borba_i_nadezhda/1-0-21. Both accessed October 27, 2013, now unavailable, and not captured by the Internet Archive.

44. On occasion, Kazakhs are presented not as victims but as resisters. See, for example, the painting in the Karlag Museum devoted to the 1929 "Tokyrau Rebellion," an uprising of one hundred largely unarmed Kazakhs against collectivization in the Aktogai district, or the Alzhir Museum's display case honoring the 1986 Almaty events as "the first nationalist-liberationist" action in the Soviet Union.

45. This dynamic is shown quite clearly in Wendy Goldman's *Inventing the Enemy: Denunciation and Terror in Stalin's Russia* (Cambridge: Cambridge University Press, 2011), and its consequences are explored in Vasily Grossman's novel written in the 1960s, *Everything Flows* (New York: New York Review of Books Classics, 2009). For more, see Etkind, *Warped Mourning*, 7–8.

46. See the entry on Anna Andreevna Akhmatova in Helen Rappoport, *Joseph Stalin: A Biographical Companion* (Santa Barbara, CA: ABC-CLIO, 1999), 3.

STEVEN A. BARNES is Associate Professor of Russian and European History at George Mason University. He is author of *Death and Redemption: The Gulag and the Shaping of Soviet Society* (2011) and the forthcoming *Gulag Wives: Women, Family, and Survival in Stalin's Terror*.

Figure 5.1. The Cheka House (Corner House), Riga, after renovation (2016), founded 1993 (Occupation Museum), 2014 (KGB House). http://okupacijasmuzejs.lv/. *Photograph by Katja Wezel*

FIVE

Riga's Cheka House
From a Soviet Place of Terror to a Latvian Site of Remembrance?

KATJA WEZEL

In 2014, the European Commission awarded the Latvian capital of Riga—together with the Swedish city Umeå—the title "European capital of culture." The European Commission grants this title each year to a different city with the aim to "highlight the richness and diversity of cultures in Europe" and, among other goals, to provide an "opportunity for regenerating cities."[1] As part of the award, the European Union provides one year of funding for special projects. One of the special projects funded during Riga's year of culture in 2014 was the opening of the KGB building or *Stūra Māja* (corner house) as a museum. From 1940 to 1941 and 1944 to 1991, the building on the corner of Freedom Street (Latv. *Brīvības iela*) housed the Soviet political police and state security in Riga and its primary prison. After its temporary use by the Latvian state police, upon the retreat of the KGB in 1991, the large five-story building stood empty for six years. On May 1, 2014, accurately timed for the twenty-fourth anniversary of the declaration of the restoration of Latvia's independence on May 4, 1990, the new museum opened its doors to the public.

Its location on Freedom Street was a prime reason for the inclusion of the building in the European Capital of Culture program. "Freedom Street" was one of six thematic lines in the proposal for the European Capital of Culture program. One of Riga's longest streets, stretching from the city center to the suburbs, it symbolizes the city's history in particular ways. Named after Tsar Alexander I during the Russian imperial period, it became Freedom Street when Latvia established its independence; its name changed to Lenin Street, Hitler Street, and again Lenin Street during and in the aftermath of World War II, until Latvians once again renamed it Freedom Street in 1991.

The museum features a general exhibition of the history of the building and its use by the Soviet political police and state security on the first floor. It serves as a subdivision of the Riga-based Occupation Museum, which covers the entire period of Latvia's history between 1940 and 1991, including the Nazi period.² In contrast to the Occupation Museum, the Cheka House focuses on the period of Soviet rule: This was the time when the building was used as a prison.³ Guided tours take visitors to the prison in the basement. The exhibition is sponsored by the Museum of the Occupation of Latvia, which receives support from the Latvian state and from the donations of the Latvian émigré community worldwide.⁴ The building itself belongs to the state and is rented by the Occupation Museum on an annual lease; the Cheka House employees work for the Occupation Museum. In 2014, special funding from the European Capital of Culture fund allowed not only for the necessary renovations to open the building as a museum but also for organizing five special thematic exhibitions on the fourth and fifth floor of the building.

For Latvians, the house at the corner of Freedom Street—the Stūra Māja—is a symbol of the atrocities committed during the Soviet era. Besides this, the building also symbolizes Latvia's history in the twentieth century, which Latvian historians have characterized as a "struggle for survival."⁵ Or, to use the words of the Latvian human-rights activist and dissident Gunārs Astra (1931–88), who spent several years in Soviet prisons and who is cited in the museum's exhibition,

> I believe these times will vanish
> like a horrible nightmare.
> This gives me the strength to stand here and breathe.
> Our nation has suffered a lot and has learned
> to survive and it will survive
> these dark times too.

The building's history and the focus of the museum's exhibition offer insight into Latvian memory politics. Starting with the history of the house itself, this chapter aims at exploring (a) the way in which this central Riga building has been turned into a Latvian site of remembrance, and (b) which characteristics this reveals about Latvia's memory politics in general. This chapter is primarily based on observations by the author—I visited the exhibition four times between 2014 and 2017—and the informative materials published by the museum, its website, sources on memory politics in Latvia in general, and interviews with the museum's exhibit coordinator, Aija Abene, and the two historians who were primarily responsible for the concept of the exhibition in 2014 and its subsequent expansion in 2016, Rihards Pētersons and Inese Dreimane.

Latvians use the term *Stūra Māja* when talking about the house and the museum. To foreign visitors, the museum advertises itself as "KGB building"

Figure 5.2. The house at the corner shortly after its completion in 1910.
Courtesy of Latvia's National Archive

or "KGB Museum." For this chapter, however, I am deliberately using the phrase *Cheka House* when referring to the museum. *Cheka* is the term most commonly used in the museum (and generally in Latvia) when referring to the Soviet political police and state security. Yet, as I will demonstrate, the term *Cheka* represents a conundrum that is also a showcase of Latvian memory politics.

THE BUILDING AND ITS PRE-SOVIET HISTORY

The Latvian architect Aleksandrs Vanags constructed the house at the corner of Stabu and Freedom Street (then: Alexander Street, named after Tsar Alexander I) in 1910 when Riga was still part of the Russian Empire. Its impressive architecture symbolizes the peak of the city's industrial development, when Riga had just become the port with the biggest sales volume in the Russian Empire, overtaking even Saint Petersburg and Odessa. The photograph in figure 5.2, which is also displayed in the first part of the Cheka House exhibition that tells the building's history, shows the building soon after its completion. The store on the ground floor, a flower shop, advertised in Russian, German, and Latvian—the three languages most spoken in Riga at that time. Before World War I, Riga was a multiethnic port city. Latvians made up the majority of the population, followed by Russians, Germans, Poles, Lithuanians, and Jews.

Architect Vanags had studied at Riga's Polytechnical Institute, the Russian Empire's first technical university and the forerunner of today's University of Latvia. Whereas the building's façade echoes the trend at that time, turning toward a neoclassical design, its interior—lobbies, staircases, and ceilings—feature art nouveau, the style that dominated Riga's architecture at the beginning of the twentieth century. For only a very short time, from 1910 to 1930, was the building used for the purpose it had been designed for: as an apartment building with stores on the ground floor and large, spacious apartments on the upper floors. In 1930, ownership of the house passed to the Latvian Ministry of Interior and, in 1940, the Soviet Ministry of Interior and the Soviet political police and state security became its owners.

Echoing Riga's turbulent history in the aftermath of World War I and the Russian Revolution, the house's architect, Aleksandrs Vanags, was killed in Riga's first brief period of Bolshevik rule (December 1918 to May 1919) during the Latvian Civil War. The architect's fate thus foreshadowed the later story of the building. As architect of some of the most outstanding buildings during Riga's industrial revolution, the Bolsheviks considered Vanags a member of the "bourgeois elite," and he shared the same fate as other affluent inhabitants of Riga, who became victims of the Red Terror.

THE CHEKA HOUSE AS A SYMBOL FOR LATVIAN SUFFERING

Upon entering the building from the corner entrance, one finds oneself in the hallway that once served as the main entrance during the Soviet period (see fig. 5.3). The interior still has a Soviet touch, having been only superficially renovated to make space for a ticket office and signs in three languages—Latvian, Russian, and English—that identify the political police that the building used to house as Cheka. Cheka is the abbreviation for *Chrezvychainaia Komissiia* (in English, Extraordinary Commission), which was the official name used for the Soviet political police between 1917 and 1922.

There is a second sign in the entrance hall with the abbreviations КГБ—VDK—KGB, the name of the Soviet state security from 1954 to 1991, and the one most commonly used outside Latvia; in Latvian, *Cheka* is the preferred term for the Soviet state security agency.[6] It is the term used throughout the exhibition, on the Latvian website, and by the tour guides when referring to the Soviet political police, despite that fact that during the first year of Soviet rule in Latvia, 1940–41, the organization's official name was already NKVD (Narodnyi Komissariat Vnutrennykh Del), in English, People's Commissariat for Internal Affairs.

Conceptualizing the exhibition of the Cheka House, the historians in charge decided to give the popular term *Cheka* preference over the historically "correct"

Figure 5.3. Entrance hall. *Photograph by Katja Wezel*

one.[7] On the exhibition walls inside the museum, the term *NKVD* is used, but only when referring to the official titles of NKVD officers. The exhibition also briefly lists the various names of the Soviet political police, but it provides no analysis of the renaming or accompanying changes within the structure and methods of Soviet state security.

This ahistorical use of the term *Cheka* stands out and is noteworthy even when comparing the exhibition to other museums portraying Soviet or communist rule in the Baltics and other parts of Eastern Europe. Whereas the word *Chekist* (referring either to an individual who worked for the secret service or more broadly as a derogative term) is still commonly used in Russia and elsewhere in the former Soviet Bloc, other museums of communism—such as the Museum of Genocide Victims in Vilnius[8]—tend to use the last official name, KGB, when referring to

Soviet state security. This raises the question, what caused the dominance of the term *Cheka* in Latvia?

It is likely that the term *Cheka* traveled with the thousands of refugees that were evacuated from the territory of today's Latvia to the interior of the Russian Empire during World War I and returned to Riga after the war. In comparison with other Baltic provinces, the number of refugees from Courland and from Riga, where workers followed the evacuation of their industries to the Russian mainland, was particularly high.[9] During and after the Russian Revolution, Latvian refugees gained firsthand experiences of the Cheka and its methods, before many of them returned to Latvia in the early 1920s.[10] Russian opponents of Bolshevik rule also found refuge in Latvia during and after the end of the Russian Civil War.[11] Between 1920 and 1930, the number of Russians living in Latvia more than doubled.[12] Many left their Russian homeland precisely because they were fleeing the prosecutions of the Cheka.

On the other hand, Latvian communists were among the most eager early supporters of the Bolsheviks. Several Latvians held high-ranking positions in the Cheka upon its creation under the leadership of Felix Dzerzhinsky. Two of Felix Dzerzhinsky's most trusted assistants in the political police were Latvian: Iakov Khristoforovich Peters (alias of Jēkabs Peterss) and Martin Ivanovich Latsis (alias of Jānis Sudrabs). Peters was second in command after Dzerzhinsky, and at the height of the Red Terror in 1918 both Peters and Latsis gained a reputation for cruelty and brutality.[13] A large number of these early Latvian supporters of the Bolshevik regime, including Peters and Latsis, later became victims of Stalin's purges in 1937 and 1938. With such entanglements between Latvian communists and the Cheka, it is not surprising that the term was absorbed by the Latvian language.

The involvements of Latvian communists with the young Bolshevik regime could provide most insight into why the term became so dominant in Latvia. But the history of communism, and the strong Latvian support for the communist idea in the early days of the Russian Revolution, is not discussed or portrayed in the Cheka House. Instead, the narrative of the museum and of the Soviet secret police starts with the first Soviet occupation, depicting the Cheka entirely as a foreign, outside force occupying Latvia together with regular Soviet troops. As the museum's website explains, "On June 17, 1940, regular Soviet armed forces entered Latvia together with specialized internal military that established the activities of the Cheka. The Cheka continued actively working in Latvia until 1991 and is responsible for deaths of thousands of Latvian citizens, as well as for physical and mental suffering."[14]

This description is wrong insofar as there was no Cheka between 1940 and 1991. The exhibition's use of the term *Cheka* for the whole period of the Soviet political police and secret service's dealings in Latvia, 1940–41 and 1944–91, is therefore ahistorical. It is also, though, a political statement, one that it needs to be analyzed in the framework of memory politics. Since the 1990s, Latvian memory politics has stressed that the entire Soviet era was characterized by ongoing severe human-rights violations.[15] Therefore, the lack of a distinction between the phases of Soviet rule, and the overall use of the term *Cheka*, which implies that nothing changed in the methods of the secret police even if it changed its name several times—from Cheka to GPU, to OGPU, to NKVD, and finally to KGB—is congruent with the Latvian narrative of Soviet history.

According to Rihards Pētersons, the main historian in charge of developing the exhibition's concept in 2014, there is yet another reason for the dominance of the term: *Cheka* echoes the victim's narrative. As Pētersons stressed, "Cheka is the term everybody knows."[16] For him it is *the* term that the people, who have lost relatives in the basement of the house at the corner or, in general, as a consequence of the Soviet crimes, will most likely associate with the building. In video interviews shown in a separate area of the ground-floor exhibition, survivors indeed refer to the terms *Cheka* and *Chekist* when speaking about their experiences.

The use of the term *Cheka* in the exhibition has further implications and consequences for the way the museum presents Latvia's history during the Soviet era. By using the locally preferred term *Cheka*, the exhibition underlines the specific Latvian suffering. Whereas the ground-floor exhibition mentions other museums of communism, such as the Hungarian "House of Terror" and the Lithuanian "Museum of Genocide Victims," the Cheka House does not explicitly compare Latvia's experience under Soviet rule with other communist dictatorships. No attempt is made to explain the idea of communism and how it took root in Russia *and* Latvia during the Russian Revolutions of 1905 and 1917. Instead, citing the *Black Book of Communism*, the ground-floor exhibition portrays communism as an ideology of terror that came to Latvia with the outside forces of (Russian-speaking) Soviet occupiers.[17]

This narrative contributes to a rather simplified version of history. The crimes committed by the Soviet political police are not contextualized as part of the history of the Soviet Union *and* Latvia. The lack of contextualization makes it difficult for the audience to understand the correlations between local communist perpetrators, actions of the Soviet power in Latvia, and their policies in other parts of the Soviet Union. This narrative also glosses over the fact that some of the perpetrators were ethnic Latvians: Although the names of Latvian perpetrators such as Alfons Noviks, who was head of the Soviet state security in Riga during the most gruesome Stalinist period in the 1940s and early 1950s, are mentioned, their biographies (and ethnicity) are not discussed.[18] Instead, the ground-floor exhibition gives a rather diffuse impression about the crimes of the Soviet regime without alluding to the collaboration of Latvians. The exhibition and the account of the tour guide during the basement tour imply that the human-rights violations committed by the Soviet political police continued with the same forcefulness during the *entire* period of Soviet rule in Latvia. The aim of the Cheka House museum is not to explain communism or how it took root in Latvia, but rather to evoke an emotional reaction and a feeling of compassion with the Latvian people and their suffering under Soviet rule.

TOURING THE FORMER PRISON AND THE CHEKA HOUSE EXHIBITION

The most interesting aspect of the Cheka House exhibition—and at the same time the part that is accessible only when booking a guided tour—is the basement and former prison. When the museum first opened in 2014, it initially offered the vast majority of tours to Latvian visitors. Currently, however, most Latvian visitors are high school students on field trips, who come for prebooked tours, whereas foreign visitors take 90 percent of the general tours available without prebooking.[19] Hence, the museum offers most guided tours in English. Russian- and German-language tours are available upon request when booked in advance. In a typical month, the museum has approximately three thousand visitors, most of whom not only visit the ground-floor exhibition but also take the tour through the prison.[20] In the summer months of July and August when most tourists visit Riga, numbers go up to six thousand visitors a month.[21] Since the prison tour takes approximately one and a half hours, the majority of visitors spent more than one and a half hours at the museum.

Touring the basement prison and observing the interrogation rooms, the thick prison wall doors, the sparse daylight and furniture, and the almost complete lack of sanitary appliances provides a glimpse into the harsh reality of the some of the most gruesome aspects of the Soviet era (see figs. 5.4 and 5.5). During the two tours that I personally participated in—one in July 2014 and another in May 2016—the picture was completed by the narrative of a tour guide, whose accounts were based mostly on witness testimonies. The narrative provided the tale of an overcrowded prison during the Stalin era: The larger cells had up to nine beds but could have up to twenty prisoners. At the peak of the Stalinist repressions, the forty-four prison cells thus held several hundred prisoners. The anecdotes of our tour guide primarily recalled testimonies of prisoners incarcerated in the early years of Soviet rule, in 1940–41 and during the late 1940s and early 1950s. The story emerging from the tour guide's explanations pictured the harsh life of prisoners exposed to constant sleep deprivation, extreme lack of nutrition, physical and emotional abuse, and torture.

Figure 5.4. Basement and former prison of the Cheka House. *Photograph by Katja Wezel*

Typically, the Cheka House was the first place of imprisonment. From it, prisoners could be sent to other prisons, be sent to the Siberian gulag prison camps, or be freed again. Evidence found after the Soviet political police quickly evacuated the building in late June 1941 indicates that at least 186 individuals were shot in the building during the first Soviet occupation.[22] In the Stalinist period, torture was widespread. The NKVD would imprison people simply because they knew someone about whom the political police hoped to gain information. Prisoners might be released again once torture had either revealed their secrets or demonstrated that they knew nothing.

Witness testimonies from the early days of the prison provide not only the main narrative of the tour guides. They also once more underline the overall message of the entire Soviet period as a time of widespread crimes against humanity.

Figure 5.5. Stele close-up from courtyard exhibition.
Photograph by Katja Wezel

Only when asked did our tour guide differentiate between the Stalin era and later, less repressive periods of Soviet rule.

Despite the widespread public interest in the topic, very little research has been done so far about the Cheka House, its perpetrators, and its victims. Rihards Pētersons, one of the historians in charge of developing the exhibition, explains that "Historians know very little [about the Cheka House]."[23] This is one reason the memories of the victims stand in the center of the exhibition: In-depth historical research only started in 2014 with the Government Commission for KGB Research, but the Cheka House was not its main focus.

The Cheka House is currently poorly funded and has few resources for research. The regular staff consists of an exhibit coordinator, six tour guides, and one historian. At the moment of writing, it remained unclear whether the Cheka

Figure 5.6. Courtyard exhibition, opened 2016.
Photograph by Katja Wezel

House would survive as a museum. To draw more attention to the importance of the site, which provides insight into the way the Soviet political police worked in Latvia, the museum organized a series of lectures in 2016, inviting experts working on the Soviet security organs. The aim was not only to educate the public what happened in the building during Soviet rule but also to gather more information about the history of the building from eyewitnesses.[24]

The intention to enrich the material collection and providing more information based on historical research is also visible in the museum's latest addition: In 2016, a new exhibition focusing on the victims of Soviet mass shootings in June 1941, prior to the arrival of Nazi troops, opened in the courtyard of the Cheka House (fig. 5.6). Historian Inese Dreimane gathered the vast majority of material for this exhibition. For the first time, the exhibition provides an overview of the range of individuals who were shot by the NKVD in late June 1941, right before the Soviet political police was forced to evacuate the building and retreat together with the Soviet army. (This exhibit parallels that in the Lonsky Street Prison Museum, the subject of Stephen Norris's chap. 3 in this volume.) In the form of white sepulchral steles, the exhibition gives the victims a face and an identity. The selection of victims presented here was largely based on the availability of photographs.[25]

The steles provide a picture of each victim and list the victim's name, year of birth, profession, and ethnicity and how the person was killed (usually by a shot in the back of the head). All victims presented in this courtyard exhibition were exhumed on July 4, 1941. After the occupation by German troops, Nazi authorities immediately used the evidence from the exhumed bodies to publicize the Soviet atrocities and portray themselves as the army that "liberated" Latvia from the "Bolshevik-Jewish" aggression. As a visitor of this courtyard exhibition, one can get a sense of what kind of people were targeted by the Soviet political police: victims were predominately male and belonged to all ethnic groups. The victims presented here were arrested in the final days of the first year of Soviet rule. NKVD officers shot them either at the Cheka House or at the Riga Central Prison before the arrival of German troops in Riga on July 1, 1941. Sometimes the exact date of arrest and their killing is known; in other cases, the sign provides only the approximate time of arrest.

The names on the steles include, for instance, Eduards Mārtiņš Rinks, born 1905, military instructor at the Marine Technical School and captain of the Latvian army, arrested June 23–26, 1941; Dmitrijs Iševskis, born 1894, Russian journalist, shot June 28, 1941; Vilis Alfrēds Pīkans, department head at the Vairogs factory, killed June 27, 1941; Jozefs (Jāzeps) Kagans, born 1894, Jew, director of an enterprise, arrested June 23, shot June 27, 1941; Fricis Brunenaus, born 1903, laborer at the Zunda sawmill, arrested June 23–28, 1941; Alfreds Hermanis Reinis, born 1909, German worker at the Paris Commune textile mill, arrested June 24, 1941. As even this very incomplete list shows, victims did not need to fulfill all prime criteria of a Soviet enemy of the people as "carrier of bourgeois nationalism." At the same time, it becomes clear that certain groups were more likely to become victims of the Soviet regime in 1941. Many victims identified by the biographical sketch had been members of the Latvian police, security, or armed forces prior to Soviet occupation, belonged to the German minority, or had bourgeois professions.[26]

This exhibition is particularly relevant because it sheds light on the events most affected by the propaganda war that Soviets and Nazis waged during World War II and that continued in its aftermath. In 1942, the Nazi administration commissioned the publication of a booklet, a collection of photographs and documents, with the title *The Year of Horror* (Latv. *Bagais Gads*)—sometimes also translated *The Horrible Year* or *The Year of Terror*.[27] The booklet also featured photographs taken at the Cheka House after its takeover by the Nazis. Because research on this topic was prohibited during the Soviet era, this Nazi propaganda booklet for a long time remained one of the only easily available sources of information about the crimes committed during the first year of Soviet rule. It was republished in Latvian and English in 1996 and is currently available on the internet.[28] The booklet's contents are highly problematic because it overemphasizes the involvement of Latvian Jews in the Soviet administration during 1940–41, underlining the Nazi claim of having liberated Latvia from "Bolshevik-Jewish oppression" or the "Jewish Chekists."[29] The booklet aims to make Jews responsible for the terror committed during the first year of Soviet rule and to justify the mass killings of Jews in the summer and fall of 1941, as well as the brutal ghettoization of the remaining Jewish population and their use for slave labor. The desired side-effect of the booklet was also to inhibit feelings of compassion among Latvians for their Jewish neighbors.

The ground-floor exhibition of the Cheka House reused photographs from the Nazi propaganda booklet. The term *Bagais Gads* is also used on the information walls of the ground-floor exhibition of the Cheka House—without quotation marks or an explanation about its use as a propaganda term by the Nazis. For Latvians both terms, *Cheka* and *Year of Horror*, belong together and are associated with the Soviet occupation. It remains one of the crucial tasks of Latvian pedagogy to free its historical narrative from the remnants of both Nazi and Soviet propaganda. It would therefore be desirable to give the courtyard exhibition a more central space and make it accessible without getting one's feet wet in the Cheka House courtyard. The courtyard exhibition adds a crucial layer of memory by providing the names, biographical data, and ethnic identity of various victims shot by the Soviet regime, supplementing the visitor's understanding of the multiplicity of the building's history.

THE CHEKA HOUSE: AN AUTHENTIC *LIEU DE MÉMOIRE*?

Museums at historical locations, especially at locations where crimes have been committed, always face the problem of serving two functions: education and commemoration. The function of educating Latvia's citizens about the dark sides of the Soviet history became already apparent during the independence movement in the late 1980s: In 1989, members of the anti-Soviet activist group Helsinki-86 staged protests in front of the building, stating "Helsinki-86 asks to declare the KGB a criminal organization," thereby pointing to the building's history as a crime scene and criticizing the ongoing communist rule in Latvia (see fig. 5.7).

Figure 5.7. Protest by the Group Helsinki-86 in front of the Cheka House (the KGB building); Photograph by Harijs Burmeistars. *Courtesy of Latvia's National Archive.* LNA LVKFFDA, 194008N.1

In 2003, financed largely by donations from the Latvian émigré organizations abroad, the Occupation Museum installed a commemorative plaque called "Black Threshold" (see fig. 5.8).[30] It commemorates the physical and emotional abuse of those who were tortured or died in the building. The dedication in English reads "During the Soviet occupation the state security agency /KGB/ imprisoned, tortured, killed and morally humiliated its victims in this building." Although the English translation uses the term *KGB*, the Latvian original gives the state security agency's name as Cheka. The Cheka House was thus already a place of commemoration before it became a museum.

The Cheka House is currently both a place of commemoration *and* a place of education. The pedagogical function of the museum, however, is frequently overshadowed by the commemorational aspect of the exhibition. According to Rihards Pētersons, who conceptualized the ground-floor exhibition for its opening in 2014, its aim is to see "the meaning of this building through the eyes of these people [the witnesses]."[31] Pētersons stresses the high value of these first-hand experiences, which, according to him, enhance the understanding of this time period and of the horror connected to it. In that framework, authenticity becomes a primary goal for the exhibition—and this goal is often reached better by memory than by history.

Figure 5.8. Memorial on the façade of the Corner House building. *Photograph by Katja Wezel*

As Pierre Nora pointed out in his study of the French *lieux de mémoire*, history and memory are not synonyms but in fact very often opposites.[32] Whereas memories are subjective recollections of events, history is the attempt to (re)construct the past by taking into account different perspectives and weighing them against each other. The Cheka House is a Latvian *lieu de mémoire* in which memory sometimes supersedes history. The result is that popular terms such as *Cheka* are to be regarded as correct because they are the ones that the victims used in their interviews. By virtue of being part of victims' recollection of events, the term becomes instantly genuine. As Nora explains, "Memory, being a phenomenon of emotion and magic, accommodates only those facts that suit it. It thrives on vague, telescoping reminiscences, on hazy general impressions or specific symbolic details. . . . History, being an intellectual, non-religious activity, calls for analysis and critical discourse. Memory situates remembrance in a sacred context."[33] It is exactly this "sacred context" that becomes obvious if one analyzes the conception behind the Cheka House exhibition. For many Latvians, the history of the Soviet occupation, and in particular the Soviet terror embodied in the crimes that happened in the Cheka House, has become sacred.

Analyzing Latvian popular history, a trend emerges that generally emphasizes the memories of eyewitnesses, which are regarded as more lively and trustworthy. This is, for instance, the concept behind the two-volume popular history of Latvia called *Mūsu Vēsture* (Eng. *Our History*). It states as its intention on its book cover: "Be warned: This is not a boring official history textbook that was written by power hungry and corrupt historians, whose main task is—as one could sometimes think—to write with God's help so that nobody will be harmed, who might once be in charge and on whom it might depend if one gets its piece of bread and butter. This is real, genuine, truthful and interesting history."[34] The authors of *Mūsu Vēsture* used only memoirs as their sources and no academic literature. They claim that this makes their "history book"—which should rather be called a "memory book"—more truthful. They present their stories as "magical," and as something that grasps your heart as "interesting" and "truthful."

As the late Tony Judt pointed out, suspicion of official interpretations is one of the legacies of communism in Eastern Europe.[35] Having been forced to read between the lines for decades and being used to trusting the neighbor's hearsay more than the newspaper, it is no surprise that memories are regarded as more trustworthy than official accounts of history. In Latvia, memories of Soviet victims in particular are handled as treasures that need to be protected. Recent Russian interventions, such as the annexation of Crimea and the destabilization of Eastern Ukraine, as well as Russian memory politics under Vladimir Putin, who once again has made it acceptable to glorify Stalin's empire, move the memories of Latvia's victims of Soviet terror even more into the realm of religion. In such a political climate, the memories of the victims of Soviet terror easily become the only trustworthy and authentic history.

CONCLUSION

Despite criticism, the Cheka House is an important exhibition that one hopes will be continued—and revised. Ideally, it should function both as a site of remembrance and a history museum, which explains to visitors the history of the building while providing detailed information about the Soviet political police and security service, as well as about human-rights violations in the context of the overall history of communism. As I have pointed out, it would be particularly crucial to reflect more broadly and critically on Latvia's history and on how its history has been affected by Nazi and Soviet propaganda. Only critical historical analysis can help avoiding the reuse of propaganda terms such as *Year of Horror*. Moreover, memories of Latvian victims need to be studied just like any other source. They should not be regarded as sacred and untouchable but should be integrated into a discussion that encourages public debate.

It is also necessary to become aware of the dangers of externalizing all perpetrators and crimes committed under Soviet rule. Doing so hinders the process of coming to an understanding about Latvia's Soviet history, which includes the Russian-speaking population and embraces their memories as well. So far, historical narratives within Latvia are still split along ethnic lines. The message of the Cheka House exhibition is currently, broadly speaking, one of the suffering of ethnic Latvians at the hands of Soviet (i.e., Russian-speaking) perpetrators. Such a narrative impedes a (potential) dialogue with Latvia's Russian minority—which in Riga makes up nearly 40 percent of the population. Since the ground-floor exhibition provides free-of-charge information in three languages—Latvian, English, and Russian—it is hard to assess how many Russian speakers visit the museum. The low demand for Russian-language tours through the prison basement is not sufficient evidence to suggest a general lack of interest in the topic (and the museum) among Russian speakers, especially because the younger generation of Latvia's Russian speakers has adequate language skills to attend a Latvian language tour. Still, making the exhibition more generally about the experience of communism could help to overcome barriers between Latvian and Russian speakers, especially if Latvia's long history of genuine engagement with the communist idea and aspects of Latvians' collaboration with the Soviet regime were portrayed as well.

NOTES

1. Creative Europe, European Commission, "European Capitals of Culture," accessed March 18, 2018, http://ec.europa.eu/culture/tools/actions/capitals-culture_en.htm.

2. There are several museums in Riga dedicated to the Nazi occupation and the history of the Holocaust in Latvia, the most important being the Riga Ghetto Museum, accessed March 18, 2018, http://www.rgm.lv/?lang=en, and the Žanis Lipke Memorial, which has a museum attached to it, accessed March 18, 2018, http://www.lipke.lv/en/museum/zanis-lipke-memorial.

3. The Nazis did not use the building as prison or for their security services. The Secret State Police (*Gestapo*) and the Security Service (*Sicherheitsdienst*) had their own "corner house" at a different location (Alexander Welscher and Norbert Beckmann-Dierkes, *Im dunklen Keller der Erinnerung* [Riga: Konrad Adenauer Stiftung, 2016], 131).

4. For the Occupation Museum, see their catalog: Valters Nollendorfs, ed., *Museum of the Occupation of Latvia: Latvia under the Rule of the Soviet Union and National Socialist Germany, 1940–1991* (Riga: Occupation Museum Foundation, 2002). See also Gundega Michel and Valters Nollendorfs, "Das Lettische Okkupationsmuseum, Riga," in *Der Kommunismus im Museum: Formen der Auseinandersetzung*

in Deutschland und Ostmitteleuropa, ed. Volkhard Knigge and Ulrich Mählert (Cologne: Böhlau, 2005), 117–29.

5. Daina Bleiere, Ilvars Butulis, Inesis Feldmanis, Aivars Stranga, and Antonius Zunda, *History of Latvia: The 20th Century* (Riga: Jurmava, 2006), 12.

6. See the website about the exhibition: Izstāde "Čekas Vēsture Latvijā" [Exhibition "The history of the Cheka in Latvia"], accessed March 18, 2018, http://okupacijasmuzejs.lv/lv/apmekle/izstade-cekas-vesture-latvija/.

7. Rihards Pētersons, interview by Katja Wezel, Riga, July 12, 2014.

8. See Neringa Klumbytė's article, chapter 1 in this volume.

9. Mark R. Haitle, *Riga at War, 1914–1919: War and Wartime Experience in a Multiethnic Metropolis* (Marburg, Ger.: Herder-Institut, 2014).

10. Inese Dreimane, interview by Katja Wezel, Riga, August 9, 2016.

11. See George F. Kennan's description of the rich cultural Russian life in Riga promoted by Russian émigrés in the late 1920s (*Memoirs 1925–1950* [Boston: Little, Brown, 1967]), 29–30.

12. For the census in 1920 and 1930, see Valsts Statistiskā Pārvalde, *Latvijas Statistiskā Gada Grāmata 1921* (Riga: Müllera spiestuve, 1922) and Valsts Statistiskā Pārvalde, *Treša Tautas Skaitīšana Latvijā 1930. Gadā* (Riga: Grāmatrūpnieks, 1930).

13. George Leggett, *The Cheka: Lenin's Political Police* (Oxford, UK: Clarendon, 1981), 266–68.

14. Translation from Latvian, see Latvian original at "Kas bija Čeka?" [What was the Cheka?], accessed March 18, 2018, http://okupacijasmuzejs.lv/lv/apmekle/izstade-cekas-vesture-latvija/kas-bija-ceka/.

15. See, among others, Saeima of the Republic of Latvia, "Declaration on the Occupation of Latvia," in *Policy of Occupation Powers in Latvia 1939—1991: A Collection of Documents*, ed. Elmārs Pelkaus (Riga: State Archives of Latvia, 1999), 564–65. For an in-depth discussion, see Katja Wezel, *Geschichte als Politikum: Lettland und die Aufarbeitung nach der Diktatur* (Berlin: Berliner Wissenschafts-Verlag, 2016), 147–48.

16. Pētersons interview.

17. Stéphane Courtois, Nicolas Werth, Jean-Louis Panné, Andrzej Packowski, Karel Bartošek, and Jean-Louis Margolin, *The Black Book of Communism: Crimes, Terror, Repression* (Cambridge, MA: Harvard University Press, 1999).

18. Alfons Noviks (1908–96) was people's commissar of Internal Affairs of the Latvian SSR (1940–41) and people's commissar (or minister) of State Security of the Latvian SSR (1944–52). For more details, see Wezel, *Geschichte als Politikum*, 132–33; Eva-Clarita and Vello Pettai, *Transitional and Retrospective Justice in the Baltic States* (Cambridge: Cambridge University Press, 2015), 65–66.

19. Aija Abene (KGB Building exhibit coordinator), email correspondence, March 12, 2018.

20. Aija Abene (KGB Building exhibit coordinator), interview by Katja Wezel, Riga, May 13, 2016.

21. Abene, email correspondence, March 12, 2018.

22. See the information booklet sold at the Cheka House: Museum of the Occupation of Latvia, *The KGB Building Exhibition* (Riga: OMB, 2016).

23. Pētersons interview.

24. Abene interview.

25. Inese Dreimane, interview by Katja Wezel, Riga, August 9, 2016. The other victims that have been identified are listed with their names.

26. The number of German victims is particularly high in view of the fact that most Baltic Germans had left Latvia in November 1939, prior to the Soviet occupation. Germans were clearly a prime target of arrest and shooting after the German attack on the Soviet Union, even if they had a working-class background.

27. Pauls Kovaļevskis, Oskars Norītis, and Miķelis Goppers, eds., *Bagais gads: Attēlu un dokumentu krājums par boļševiku laiku Latvijā* (Riga: Zelta Abele, 1942). See also Markus Lux, "'Das Jahr des Grauens': Die Auseinandersetzung mit der Vergangenheit in Lettland," *Zeitschrift für Geschichtswissenschaft* 47 (1999): 811.

28. "Latvia: Year of Horror," accessed April 8, 2020, http://www.jrbooksonline.com/PDF_Books/LatviaYearOfHorror.pdf.

29. Compare Kaspars Zellis, *Ilūziju un baiļu mašinērija: Propaganda nacistu okupētajā Latvijā; vara, mediji un sabiedrība (1941–1945)* (Riga: Mansards, 2012), 191–93 and 197–202.

30. See the website of the Riga monument agency: Rīgas pieminekļu aģentūra "Piemiņas zīme melnais slieksnis," March 11, 2018, http://www.rigaspieminekli.lv/?lapa=piemineklis&zanrs=1&rajons=3&id=73.

31. Pētersons interview.

32. Pierre Nora, "Introduction: Between Memory and History," in *Realms of Memory: The Construction of the French Past*, ed. Pierre Nora (New York: Columbia University Press, 1996), 3.

33. Ibid.

34. Lato Lapsa, Sandris Metuzāls, and Kristīne Jančevska, *Mūsu Vēsture, 1985–2005*, vol. 1 (Riga: Atena, 2008).

35. Tony Judt, "The Past Is Another Country: Myth and Memory in Post-war Europe," in *Memory and Power in Post-war Europe*, ed. Jan-Werner Müller (Cambridge: Cambridge University Press, 2004), 172.

KATJA WEZEL is Research Associate at the University of Göttingen, Germany. She completed her PhD in 2011 at the University of Heidelberg, Germany, with a thesis on memory conflicts in post-Soviet Latvia. Among her recent publications are "The Unfinished Business of Perestroika: Latvia's Memory Politics and Its Quest for Acknowledgement of Victimhood in Europe," *Nationalities Papers* 44, no. 4 (2016): 560–77, and *Geschichte als Politikum: Lettland und die Aufarbeitung nach der Diktatur* (2016).

Figure B.1. The objects of despair: interior to Holodomor Memorial Museum, Kyiv. *Wikimedia Commons*

B

HALL OF NATIONAL TRAGEDIES

The Polish poet Miron Białoszewski (1922–83), a participant in the Warsaw Uprising of 1944, wrote that it took him two decades before he could properly conceive of the best way to write about his experiences. "For twenty years I could not write about this. Although I wanted to very much. I talked. About the uprising. To so many people. All sorts of people. So many times. And all along I was thinking that I must describe the uprising, somehow or other *describe* it. And I didn't even know that those twenty years of talking—I have been talking about it for twenty years—because it is the greatest experience of my life, a closed experience—precisely this talking is the only device suited to escribing the uprising."[1] In the end, Białoszewski decided to write his memoir as a "rambling monologue," one that he hoped would capture the truth of that experience.[2] Before he finished, and while he was still in the talking phase, an American journalist visited him in Warsaw. The journalist, Joseph Alsop, described the poet's apartment as a place unlike any other in the world, for every piece of furniture had been "wounded at some time in the past" and the decorations also spoke of destruction and lost ideas. The English translator of Białoszewski's memoir calls the apartment "a museum of crippled objects."[3]

Hall A of this volume featured sites that evoke the entirety of the communist era, suggesting it should be understood as a period of occupation and trauma. This section has similar themes, but the two museums we will visit focus on particular events and narrates them as national tragedies. The Warsaw Uprising of 1944 forms the basis of contemporary Polish nationhood, one that taps into long-standing mythologies of Polish resistance to Russian domination. The Warsaw Uprising Museum provides a useful framework for understanding the Communist Era that followed (and for forgetting any aspects of conformity or collaboration): Poles resisted the Nazis and Soviets in 1944; after they were defeated and exhausted, the Red Army then imposed an occupation regime on the country.

In her work with surviving members of the uprising, Erica Tucker notes that many of her informants remember August 1944, just as Białoszewski had, as the most wonderful time in their lives; a time "with memories of a beautiful youth spent fighting for the return of Polish independence."[4] One participant summed up these feelings thusly: "So, listen, if there were horrible, terrible things, nightmarish problems with wounded who were beyond help, there was also a certain amount of laughter."[5] The uprising came to be remembered as a "sacred time," one to be preserved in memory during the Communist Era, particularly as the state insisted that 1944 was unjust.

In Kyiv, now capital of an independent Ukraine, another tragedy now serves as the foundational event for modern Ukrainian nationhood: the famine of 1932–33, known as the Holodomor. On November 28, 2006, the Verkhovna Rada of Ukraine decreed the law "On the Holodomor of 1932–33 in Ukraine." It recognized the event as a genocide and also sought to honor the victims' memory, respect those who survived, and realize the "moral duty to past and future generations of Ukrainians" through "the need to restore historical justice and affirm the unacceptability of manifestations of violence in society." The law also noted "that for decades the tragedy of the Holodomor of 1932–33 in Ukraine was officially denied by the authorities of the USSR."[6] Two years later, the Ukrainian government opened a massive memorial museum in central Kyiv dedicated to these notions.

The site provides a space to listen to the millions who died in the famine. Their voices had been silenced during the Soviet era: the government forbade use of the word *famine* to describe the horrors of 1932 and 1933, and the word was first used publicly only in 1987. Those who managed to survive the horrors can finally testify. Oleksandra Radchenko, a teacher, wrote in her diary on June 2, 1932, "how difficult it is to live, desperately difficult. In general the times are exceptional, unknown in history. All are suffering from malnutrition and famine, and generally from a half-indigent way of life. There is a terrible and oppressive indifference to everything."[7] A collective farmer named Mykola Reva wrote to Stalin in 1940 because he was, "it would seem, our friend, teacher, and father" and needed to know "the whole truth." The truth was "the dark reaction of the hungry year of 1933, when people ate tree bark, grass, and even their own children, when thousands of people died of starvation, and *all this before the eyes of the communists, who drove their cars across our bodies and impudently praised life*."[8]

The two sites analyzed in this hall, like those in the first one, aim to evoke emotions among visitors. They are not spaces associated with an occupying regime; instead, they are centrally located and draw attention to the event they remember as a formative one. The Uprising Museum and National Museum "Holodomor Victims Memorial" commemorate the dead and see those who died in 1944 or 1932–33 as martyrs for the nations that would be re-created after 1989. These are sites of glorification and victimization: in both examples, heroes fight against Soviet occupiers; victims die at the hands of those same occupiers. In both examples, the real history, the stories and memories of individuals, had been deliberately distorted or suppressed. Remembering them becomes a means of asserting rightful independence.

These two sites evince the legacies of the so-called Bloodlands, where, in Timothy Snyder's account, the Nazi and Soviet regimes murdered fourteen million people between 1933 and 1945. The first date marks the end of the Soviet famines, a "world of death."[9] Snyder explains why the narrative of the Holodomor served as a powerful undercurrent among survivors: "the basic facts of mass hunger and death, although sometimes reported in the European and American press, never took on the clarity of an undisputed event."[10] The Soviet state did much to erase stories of the famine, ensuring they would lay dormant and become aggrieved memories. The end date in Snyder's study just encompasses the 1944 uprising, which Stalin encouraged because it served his larger purposes (killing Germans), but Stalin did not help because it also served his larger purposes (preserving Red Army lives for the final push). In the end, as Snyder writes, the uprising did make further resistance against the Soviets more difficult. The events of 1944 therefore became "the beginning of the confrontation that was to come."[11] As the Red Army and Soviet government worked to establish an unpopular communist system, they also cleansed official remembrances of two events that ran counter to the narrative of liberation they imposed: Katyn and 1944.

The two museums studied here therefore seek to redress the suppression of historical truth under communism by memorializing horrific events. The Poland of today, the Warsaw Uprising Museum narrates, is a strong nation because Poles remembered the events of 1944 during the Communist Era. It reassembles the crippled objects once stored in places such as Białoszewski's apartment in order to arrange them into a narrative of heroic experience. Contemporary Ukraine, the memorial museum in Kyiv suggests, exists in part because Ukrainians remembered the horrors once inflicted upon them. The objects displayed and hung in the site testify to the exceptional, unknown experiences of Ukrainians.

NOTES

1. Quoted in Madeline Levine, Translator's Introduction to Miron Białoszewski, *A Memoir of the Warsaw Uprising* (New York: New York Review of Books, 2015), xii.
2. Ibid.
3. Ibid., x.

4. Erica Tucker, *Remembering Occupied Warsaw: Polish Narratives of World War II* (DeKalb: Northern Illinois University Press, 2011), 163.

5. Ibid., 182.

6. The law is reproduced in Bohdan Klid and Alexander Motyl, eds., *The Holodomor Reader: A Sourcebook on the Famine of 1932–1933 in Ukraine* (Alberta: Canadian Institute of Ukrainian Studies Press, 2012), 73–74.

7. Ibid., 182.

8. Ibid., 187.

9. Timothy Snyder, *Bloodlands: Europe between Hitler and Stalin* (New York: Basic, 2010), 48.

10. Ibid., 56.

11. Ibid., 310.

Figure 6.1. A Patriotic Sanctuary. Warsaw Uprising Museum, founded 2004. http://www.1944.pl/. *Roman Eugeniusz, Wikimedia Commons*

SIX

Sensing the Uprising
The Warsaw Uprising Museum and the Emotions of the Past

STEPHEN M. NORRIS

PROLOGUE

When he delivered his 1980 Nobel Prize in Literature acceptance speech, Czesław Miłosz paid tribute to poets who had preceded him who had also written in his native language. Miłosz made the case for understanding his works within a larger context: the "quest for reality" that poetry aimed for, particularly poetry that tried to anchor itself in "peculiar circumstances of time and place."[1] He spoke about the enduring existence in 1980 of "two Europes," a separation that invoked the Iron Curtain but one that went beyond that metaphor, for his Europe was one that had descended into "the heart of darkness of the Twentieth Century." Because of this journey, Miłosz said, his own search for what is real through his poetry and prose was a quest to separate reality from illusion. He went on to add that while he was a Polish poet, for that was his native language taught to him by his parents, he had grown up in Lithuania, a multicultural and multilingual place that had experienced the dark heart of the century up close. Because of the history experienced in the region, he noted (and in the printed version of his speech he capitalized *history*), it was hard for a poet to capture the reality on the ground. Instead, it was better to float above, to write as an exile like Dante. Even in this role, however, the poet's task was not an easy one, for the history of the century and of his other Europe was so tragic.

Miłosz wondered how to write about the Holocaust, despaired at the fact that many sought to deny it had happened, but also struggled with how to insert other horrific events into popular memory. He noted that at the time of his speech, the three Baltic republics did not appear on maps as independent states, a testament to how two dictators continued to haunt the two Europes. And he mentioned

Poland. He referred to friends who had been murdered in 1940 but whose tombs could not bear this date, declaring "it is absurd not to be able to write how they perished, though everybody in Poland knows the truth: they shared the fate of several thousand Polish officers disarmed and interned by the then-accomplices of Hitler, and they repose in a mass grave." And of course he referred to 1944, asking whether "the younger generations of the West, if they study history at all," should "hear about the 200,000 people killed in 1944 in Warsaw, a city sentenced to annihilation" by Hitler and Stalin.

Miłosz's speech was indeed about reality and illusion. It was about historical truth and propagandistic lies. It was also about memory and forgetting. In the end, he apologized for "laying bare a memory like a wound" and then mused that, in light of the awful historical reality he had already noted, it "is possible there is no other memory than the memory of wounds." Although he worried that memories buried within the "other Europe" could continue to cause pain, he hoped that poems, novels, and films from Poland, Hungary, and Czechoslovakia could also make memory "our force," protecting residents against official speeches and lies. He concluded with a paradox, how remembering the past century often revealed the "pull of despair, of impending doom" that brought nihilistic thoughts to the surface and yet how the same century that could produce these sentiments was also one full of "faith and hope." How, in other words, can a poet draw useful links between the past and future?

In 2001, another Polish poet, Wisława Szymborska, wrote a short, moving work, "The End and the Beginning." It too tackles themes Miłosz raised and it too speaks to the wounds memory causes.

> After every war
> someone has to clean up.
> Things won't
> straighten themselves up, after all.
>
> Someone has to push the rubble
> to the side of the road,
> so the corpse-filled wagons
> can pass.
>
> Someone has to get mired
> in scum and ashes,
> sofa springs,
> splintered glass,
> and bloody rags.
>
> Someone has to drag in a girder
> to prop up a wall.

Someone has to glaze a window,
rehang a door.

Photogenic it's not,
and takes years.
All the cameras have left
for another war.

We'll need the bridges back,
and new railway stations.
Sleeves will go ragged
from rolling them up.

Someone, broom in hand,
still recalls the way it was.
Someone else listens
and nods with unsevered head.
But already there are those nearby
starting to mill about
who will find it dull.

From out of the bushes
sometimes someone still unearths
rusted-out arguments
and carries them to the garbage pile.

Those who knew
what was going on here
must make way for
those who know little.
And less than little.
And finally as little as nothing.

In the grass that has overgrown
causes and effects,
someone must be stretched out
blade of grass in his mouth
gazing at the clouds.[2]

David Rieff has argued that in this work Szymborska articulates "the ethical imperative of forgetting so that life can go on—as it must." Otherwise, he adds, "we are left always with Miłosz's memory of wounds," for "the blood never dries.... The memory of a grudge endues."[3] It's this tripartite schema—whether dwelling in the recent past just dredges up painful memories designed to reopen wounds, or whether remembering the past can help to educate young people so that they can get over it in order to bring new hope, or whether it's just best to get on with life and to forget the past—that makes the year 1944 and memories of that year so powerful in Poland. No wonder Miłosz referred to it directly and Szymborska symbolically starts with its aftermath. Both spoke about the way 1944 had become an emotional memory for so many Poles. In a sense, Miłosz and Szymborska debated the parameters of remembrance itself: is it best to dwell on painful episodes, to remind people all the time about problematic pasts, as Miłosz mused, or is it better to get on with life and not to think too deeply about pain for fear it will affect the everyday, as Szymborska suggested? This basic question is one all postcommunist states have posed, but the Polish answer to it helps to explain why a museum that so openly appeals to emotions has acted as a battlefield of fights over memory's wounds.

MEMORY'S BATTLEFIELDS

Opened on the sixtieth anniversary of the event it commemorates, Warsaw's Uprising Museum (Muzeum Powstania Warszawskiego) seeks to assail visitors with the sights, sounds, tastes, moods, and feel of 1944. The history it tries to remember is one that formed a central component, perhaps even *the* central component, of Polish nationhood during the Communist Era. At the same time, the museum does more than just remember the past. Through its sensory experiences meant to foster an emotional attachment to 1944, the Uprising Museum and the events it regularly sponsors create new memories of the uprising for visitors who were not alive at the time. Reliving the past, or reliving a recreated past, ensures that the right sort of remembrance takes place in the present.

The Warsaw Uprising of 1944 forms part of what scholars have termed the "master narrative" of modern Polish nationhood, one centered on heroic resistance in Warsaw to oppressive systems. In the twentieth century, Polish uprisings resisted the Russian Empire, the Soviet state, the Nazi occupation, and the Soviet state (again). The uprising and its remembrance therefore fit within larger historical narratives: launched in August against the ongoing Nazi occupation, the Polish Home Army (Armia Krajowa, or AK) sought to throw off one occupier before the Soviet Red Army arrived. The AK hoped to legitimize the Polish government-in-exile as the one needed to reestablish an independent state after the war. They failed, though the AK and its supporters managed to resist for sixty-three days, fighting in intense urban conflict. The Red Army waited across the Vistula River and offered no support. After the Nazis defeated the AK, they leveled the city. Soviet forces therefore entered a ruined landscape and began the process of establishing a friendly government there.[4] As Timothy Snyder has summarized it, "no other European capital suffered such a fate: destroyed physically, and bereft of about half of its population."[5]

This brief history lesson cannot do justice to the ways that the uprising mattered in Polish remembrances during the Communist Era, but it does establish the basic factors that shaped it.[6] Memories of the uprising served as a way to delegitimize the Polish communist government as one imposed on an unwilling population. It tapped into and expanded on memories of previous uprisings dating back to the eighteenth-century partitions. Because of the contentious nature of the 1944 events and the way that the Polish communist government downplayed the uprising, most remembering had to take place surreptitiously. Marking the symbol of the AK on a wall, for example, became an act meant to keep the idea of the uprising alive. From the late 1940s until 1989, communist officials treated the uprising as an aggressive response to Soviet liberation in central Europe, denigrated the Home Army for launching it, denounced them for capitulating, and instead heroized the so-called People's Army (Armia Ludowa) for their assistance in liberating Poland.[7] Because the communist government eventually commemorated the 1943 Warsaw Ghetto Uprising and not the 1944 Warsaw Uprising, Warsaw remained a battlefield of sorts, one where memories, landscapes, and identities often competed with one another.[8] For some, the Ghetto Uprising overshadowed the more important Uprising of '44, further complicating Polish-Jewish relations after 1945.[9] Regardless, the myth of '44 only grew in stature throughout the four decades of communist rule and became a powerful way for many Poles to align themselves against the state and against Moscow: remembering '44, in other words, became an act of private resistance.

The culmination of these memory trends appeared almost immediately after June 1989, when the new Polish government began building memorials to the uprising and many Poles erected their own. The memory landscape of Warsaw since 1989 has been dominated by commemorating the victims of the Communist Era, with 1940 and 1944 as the foundational dates for these efforts. (The former date commemorates the deportations and executions of Poles after the 1939 Soviet occupation.) Building a centrally located museum to the uprising therefore served as a means of turning Communist Era practices on their heads.

Because of the way the Polish communist state downplayed the 1944 Uprising, the remembrance practices that developed before 1989 were also largely emotional in character. A sort of stealthy mythologization took place over the decades. The Solidarity Movement particularly capitalized on it and made 1944 a central part of its emotional appeals.[10] Lech Kaczyński, former Solidarity activist and the mayor of Warsaw from 2002 to 2005, was one of the driving forces behind the museum's creation. He declared that because the communist state had officially ignored the uprising, "all that remains is memory, amazement at the enormity of the committed crime, but first of all admiration for the insurgents' courage and generosity in offering their lives." Kaczyński went on to claim that "contemporary nations need such memory and the moral strength that comes from reliving their history." "The Warsaw Rising Museum," he asserted, "is being built so that this memory may remain with us forever."[11] Lech Wałęsa had also spoke about these memory practices a decade before, declaring in 1994 that the memory of the uprising, just like the insurgents and the city itself, had been "murdered," and that 1944 was "Poland's great tragedy," one that "still moves our hearts, disturbs our minds, returns as a fundamental question."[12] For Wałęsa, the Solidarity leader who became president, the memory of the Uprising had been internalized, made into an emotional source of remembrance: "the flame of the Rising remained in people's souls and hearts. It was passed on from generation to generation."[13]

The museum was built on these concepts. It was designed, Wałęsa noted at its opening, "to place considerable importance on conveying the atmosphere of the Rising and arousing the emotion of visitors."[14] The Warsaw Uprising Museum therefore may be best understood as a particular type of "sensory museology," to borrow a term from David Howes.[15] In a special issue of the journal *Senses and Society*, Howes reminds us that eighteenth-century museums once had a tactile function before becoming places of more passive spectatorship during the nineteenth century. A return to this approach has now become evident, with touch and smell becoming part of museum experiences, creating a sensation of intimacy. Howes and his collaborators see this recent trend as a counterbalance to the didactic instruction many traditional museums offer.

The Uprising Museum, however, is an example of a sensory museum meant to enhance didactic instruction. Museumgoers are invited to return to 1944, experience it through all their senses, and emerge with a renewed sense of patriotism. A visit to the museum, in short, attempts to dissolve the distance between 1944 and the present and to base contemporary patriotism on the emotions of the Uprising. In a sense, the museum declares victory in the memory battlefields that had taken place during the Communist Era and presents the 1944 uprising as the defining point of recent Polish history before and during communism: preserving the memory of it from the 1940s to the 1980s, in other words, helped to achieve victory in 1989.

SENSING THE PAST, FEELING HISTORICAL EMOTIONS: INSIDE THE WARSAW UPRISING MUSEUM

Located in a former streetcar power plant on Przyokopowa Street, the Uprising Museum, in the words of its architect Wojciech Obtułowicz, sought to "combine old and new." Paweł Kowal, the cofounder of the museum and later a politician in the Law and Order Party, has characterized the site as an emotional one above all. The exhibits, he writes, "evoke the emotions showing true people in their daily lives, their love, friendship, brotherhood in arms, death, hope and despair."[16] Emotions, he notes, are also evoked among visitors, for they are "inevitable when we return to the history of insurgent families, when we know all the names of dead mothers, fathers, cousins, uncles fighting in the Rising that can be read from the stone plaques on the Wall of Remembrance in the Freedom Park."[17] Finally, the museum attempts to work with the emotions of younger visitors, for "children experience their emotions differently."[18] To evoke emotions, Kowal argues, the museum was carefully built to "put visitors in a certain mood," to "facilitate an encounter with the mementos of history," and to provide "access to the mementos of history and the possibility for self-discovery."[19] One means of providing the moods that will in turn evoke the right emotional experience comes through music: Tomasz Stańko composed music specifically for the main halls and Joszko Broda arranged insurgent songs "in a modern way" for the Little Insurgents Room.[20] In the end, Kowal writes, the old power plant "became a kind of patriotic sanctuary."[21]

The central feature of this sanctuary, and the first spot that attempts to create the emotional atmosphere necessary for understanding the museum, is the Beating Heart (fig. 6.2). A massive steel monument that rises above all three levels of the exhibition space, the Beating Heart is inscribed with each day of the uprising interspersed with bullet holes. As the signs around it declare, the monument represents the "beating heart of fighting Warsaw," where the "voices of insurgent Warsaw are also enclosed." The heart symbolically pumps the lifeblood of patriotism and captures the ways Polish patriots kept the memory of 1944 alive in their own hearts. Every so often communiqués from the insurgent radio station are played around it along with popular songs and patriotic hymns. The official guidebooks declares, "You have to touch the Monument, place your ear to its surface—the sounds and melodies of the successive days of the Warsaw Rising reverberate in every bullet hole, conveying the atmosphere of those days."[22]

Once visitors have listened to the beating heart of the uprising, they can enhance their journey to the past by climbing into the reconstructed sewer tunnels within the museum. AK members developed an elaborate communication system through Warsaw's sewers in August 1944, making it possible, as signs state, "to maintain links between individual sites of combat, to transfer casualty replacements, to supply food and ammunition, and to evacuate insurgent units, civilians, and the wounded that were cut off by the enemy."[23] When the Nazis discovered what was going on, they began to destroy the sewers, brick up or put wire over entrances and exits, and drop gas into them (Andrzej Wajda later immortalized these events in his 1956 film *Kanał*). The museum's "Into the Sewers" exhibit allows visitors to climb into 1944 and experience the feeling of the insurgents. If the

Figure 6.2. The Beating Heart. *Photograph by Stephen M. Norris (2011)*

Beating Heart pumps the lifeblood of patriotism, the recreated sewers serve as the museum's veins. Once inside, guides urge you to maintain silence, grab onto the clothes of people in front of you, and turn off the lights in order to convey the claustrophobic atmosphere that AK insurgents experienced in 1944.

The museum employs a tactile approach in all its exhibits, not just the Beating Heart and the Into the Sewers. Throughout the exhibits, visitors can tear off calendar pages that provide information about the days just before and during the uprising, complete with the weather (it was 21°C on July 29) and details of AK activities (on July 29, insurgents were mining bridges to prepare for the uprising). When you enter the museum, your feet even feel changes: from the slick floors of the entrance, you walk onto recreated cobbled streets of old Warsaw. In the first exhibit hall, visitors can pick up 1940s telephones and listen to insurgents tell their stories of preparation and participation in the uprising (fig. 6.3). On the walls near the telephone booths, the words of Deputy Prime Minister Jan Stanisław Jankowski are inscribed: "We wanted to be free and to owe that freedom to nobody." "The whole complex truth about the five-year occupation of Poland and the two months of the Warsaw Rising," the official guidebook states, "is contained in this one sentence," for it represented "the last attempt to save Poland from Soviet enslavement."[24]

Figure 6.3. Listening to stories of the uprising. *Photograph by Stephen M. Norris (2011)*

In the section the Joy and Sorrow of the Insurgents, the museum attempts to convey the euphoric atmosphere that characterized the early days, as citizens were "intoxicated by the idea of freedom regained after five years of brutal occupation."[25] In these exhibition rooms, visitors can see the red-and-white armbands worn by insurgents, touch the guns and weapons used by them, and look at their photographs (see fig. 6.4). You are invited, in other words, to step into their shoes and place yourself in the uprising. The sorrow comes in the last rooms, dedicated to the Soviet entry and occupation and featuring documents and stories from the operations of the Soviet People's Commissariat for Internal Affairs and "SMERSH" (SMERt' SHpionam) that arrested Poles. It also comes in rooms dedicated to the dead of the uprising, particularly the 108 Blessed exhibit with the names of the priests and chaplains who died, officially "raised to the glory of the altars by Pope John Paul II" in 1999.[26] This part of the museum also contains a Place of Remembrance (fig. 6.5), which consists of replications of the hastily dug graves from Warsaw's courtyards: here "a hundred insurgents, killed during the fighting for Warsaw, are looking out at you. They are smiling, full of life—one of the finest generations in the history of Poland."[27] The rooms of the museum, in other words, ask you to travel back to 1944 and experience the emotional ups and downs of insurgents, from the euphoria of August to the misery of October.

Figure 6.4. Insurgent machine gun on display. *Photograph by Stephen M. Norris (2011)*

Figure 6.5. Sorrow: The Place of Remembrance. *Photograph by Stephen M. Norris (2011)*

Figure 6.6. The taste of the uprising: the museum's café. *Wikimedia Commons*

Visitors are reminded in numerous displays that the museum aims to "convey the atmosphere of the Uprising," a multisensory goal that even includes taste. The café inside the museum, where visitors can rest and take a break from the sewers, sights, and sounds of 1944, is not just any museum café (fig. 6.6). It contains coffee grinders and other utensils used at the time and features a "menu of insurgent Warsaw." The café also serves red wine from Fukier's restaurant in Old Town, chocolate scraps from Fuchs, bread from the Ursuline nuns, noodles with jam or tomato sauce from reserves of Sopłem, and "spit soup" with barley from the Haberbusch brewery in the city center. All Warsaw in 1944 therefore helps to sustain you, the virtual insurgent. The café design is modeled in part after the makeshift ones run by "Peżetki," women from the Pomoc Żołnierzowi (PZ; Soldier's Aid) who prepared meals and even entertained insurgents. "U Aktorek" café at the museum captures these PZ efforts and is also named after an actual place in the Łubieński Palace. Finally, it resembles in part the café from the era of German occupation known as "Pół Czarnej" (Half a Black Coffee) that operated on Kredytowa Street. Performers from that time "gaze out from photographs decorating the walls; press from the time of the occupation and Rising is available for reading" as you eat your pastries and other treats.[28]

These emotional appeals extend to all ages. Children can experience the Uprising in the Little Insurgent Room, where school-age visitors "can learn, in a way appropriate to their age, about the history and the values that guided the insurgents in 1944."[29] In this exhibit, children can play with period toys and games, participate in a recreated puppet show performed during the Uprising, help to build barricades, and reenact the Scouts' Field Postal Service. Complete with a copy of the famous 1983 Little Insurgent statue that stands near the Old Town Square, the room "wants to show that the reality of the fighting city was equally ruthless and perhaps even more frightening for the young than for adults."[30] These are lessons that can be taken home. The museum's gift shop sells a board game produced by Egmont and the museum that allows you to play as Scouts delivering messages to occupied Warsaw before the Nazis catch you.

As you leave, the last exhibit is titled "Soviet Terror" (fig. 6.7), one that explains how the new occupying regime attempted to crush the spirit of 1944 you have learned to embrace in your visit. Near this exhibit is a smaller one dedicated to Pope John Paul II. In it, you can watch his famous June 1979 Warsaw address from his first visit back to his homeland. The pope's words from that year—"Do not be afraid" and "Let your spirit come and renew the face of the earth"—visitors are informed, "gave the Poles unusual strength and faith" that created the Solidarity Movement a year later.[31] The pope also remembered the uprising in his address, declaring that "it is impossible to understand this city of Warsaw, the capital of Poland, that undertook its unequal struggle with the German invaders of 1944, the struggle in which it was abandoned by the allied powers, the struggle in which Warsaw had to surrender and was buried under its own ruins, if one does not remember that the same ruins also buried Christ Our Savior Bearing the Cross in front of the Holy Cross Church on Krakowskie Przedmieście Street."[32] One of the clearest examples of the Polish national myth as a "Christ of nations,"[33] the pope's homily, which airs on a continuous loop in this room, became the impetus for Poles to begin "to learn the true history of the Warsaw Rising and its leaders, a history that had been either concealed or falsified until then (the pope's 1979 address)."[34]

The museum battles throughout with Communist Era memory projects (or forgetting projects), hoping this time through its emotional invocations, culminating with the pope's, to achieve victory. In a mostly sympathetic review of this self-proclaimed "patriotic sanctuary," John Radzilowski noted that the Warsaw Uprising Museum "attempts to do at least three things which are not fully compatible: provide an educational forum on the Rising for the general public in Poland, especially young people; serve as a central commemorative site for the Rising and a forum for public and scholarly discussion of the event; and educate foreign visitors with limited knowledge of wartime Poland on the Rising and thus provide an avenue to understand the war as the central tragedy of modern Polish history."[35] The Museum of the Warsaw Uprising, he concludes, "thus functions as a kind of temple of memory in which the traditional educative function of the displays is subordinated to the need to recover and come to terms with one of

Figure 6.7. Soviet Terror: the last exhibit in the museum. *Photograph by Stephen M. Norris (2011)*

the most traumatic events in Polish history."[36] Coming to terms with a more nuanced, critical view of history is not as significant as the museum's function as a memorial to the dead and to murdered memories.

The sensory, mood-making engagement promoted by the museum does not stop within the walls of the building itself. The Uprising Museum and its staff have promoted a number of events, publications, and films that also attempt to recreate the sights, sounds, and atmosphere of August 1944. What follows are two examples of these efforts, which, much like the children's game available in the gift shop, are meant to export the emotions evoked in the museum to other audiences.

EXPORTING EMOTIONS: THE UPRISING IN COMICS

Story 1. A ruined Warsaw. Two Home Army soldiers, one a woman with close-cut blond hair, stealthily walk through the city. A wounded Nazi soldier discovers them and yells "Halt!" He points a machine gun at them. A look of recognition passes between the woman and the Nazi officer. He asks, "Marta?" He remembers her. They were lovers, but she was found out and had her hair shorn as punishment. The Nazi pauses. The woman, sensing his hesitation, pulls out a pistol and shoots him. As the officer, now on the ground, reaches for his weapon, the woman steps on his hand and shoots him again. The second Home Army soldier stammers, "He... he knew your name. Marta, did you know him? Who was he?" Turning away, Marta states "No one."

Story 2. The interior of a Catholic church. The litany of Our Lady of Mercy can be heard throughout, calling on the Virgin Mary to provide hope, mercy, and kindness. A Nazi soldier, unmoved by the words, sees a golden image of the Virgin hanging on the wall. He snatches it, bites it to make sure it is real, and shows it off to his two comrades. They laugh as he licks it before placing it in a pocket. At that moment the prayer calls for punishment to sinners. The floor of the church is littered with bodies of Poles who have been massacred by the Nazis. One is a blond-haired nurse lying face up in the middle of the bodies. She is not dead; she is the one praying. She slowly reaches for a gun and declares she will mete out punishments herself. She shoots the three Nazis, who drop to the floor. The nurse collapses and dies. One Nazi survives, grabs his chest where the bullet struck, and realizes that it lodged in the icon of Mary he took from the wall. He has survived.

These stories, while gripping, are not entirely factual ones. Instead, they appear in the comic book series Uprising 44 sponsored by the Uprising Museum, Polish *Post*, Klub Swiata Komiksu, *Gazeta Wyborcza*, and *Gildia.pl*.[37] Each year these partners hold a competition for comic artists to submit short works that relate to the museum's mission to promote the memory of the uprising. The winners are collected in an anthology: the two stories related above appeared in the 2010 edition. The first story, "W Miłości i na Wojnie" (In love and in war), by Janusz Ordon and Radek Smektała, received third place in the competition, and the second one, "Traf" (Luck), by Ernesto Gonzales and Grzegorz Janusz, took first prize. The museum's director, Jan Ołdakowski, noted that, at first, comics artists attempted to depict the uprising in more or less literal ways, but Luck stood out because it captured something more universal, about the "unobvious character of providence" in history.[38]

Comics, as Dieter De Bruyn has argued, have become an important medium for Polish historical memory in the 2000s. Individual titles or anthologies have dealt with Józef Piłsudski's Poland, the Nazi invasion, World War II, the Poznań revolt in 1956, and the Solidarity Movement. As De Bruyn rightly notes, these historical narratives are far from accidental, for they tend to focus on events that communist histories "distorted or silenced."[39] The comic competition aims to connect younger generations to the events of 1944 while reminding older readers of the uprising's sacrifices. De Bruyn focuses on whether these museum-sponsored anthologies represent a part of a hegemonic or counterhegemonic discourse on the meanings of 1944 and concludes they are mostly hegemonic, building on the notion that the uprising was a sacred, patriotic event. At the same time, the comics extend the sensory, emotional experiences promoted in the museum itself: throughout the anthologies, readers are invited to place themselves in the shoes of insurgents, experience the thoughts and emotions of 1944, and reflect on them. The Beating Heart pumps on the pages of comics too. It also beats throughout the films sponsored by the museum.

EXPERIENCING THE UPRISING ON SCREEN

"See the true Uprising." The tag line from the 2014 documentary film *Warsaw Uprising* sponsored by the museum, released in time for the seventieth anniversary of the event and the tenth anniversary of the museum's opening, attempts to transfer the sensory aspects of the building to celluloid. As the film's press kit boasts, six hours of authentic newsreels filmed in August 1944 by the Bureau of Information and Propaganda of the Polish Underground Army Headquarters make up the entirety of the eighty-seven-minute film. To make the film took "six months of work, a team of military, clothing, and architecture consultants, urban planners, Warsaw experts and historians, thousands of color editing consulting hours, 1200 shots, 1440 hours of colorizing and reconstruction, 112,000 selected frames, 648,000 minutes of film frames reconstruction, 22,971,520 megabytes of data," which are "only a few numbers that help appreciate the enormous effort and means dedicated to this Uprising project." Just as all of Warsaw participated in the efforts of August 1944, it seems, countless Varsovians pitched together to bring that month back to life on screen.

This resuscitation came about because of the museum. Jan Ołdakowski, the director, and Piotr Śliwowski, head of the History Department at the museum, conceived of the project and put the team together. The creators "wanted to show more than just the historical event; first, and above all, they wanted to show the people who were part of it." This desire was again one meant to evoke an emotional response: Milenia Fiedler, who worked as the artistic supervisor, commented that the film's use of narration, which attempted to sound like a dialogue between the cameramen of the time, hoped to produce a film in which "presence, emotions, and actions are recorded by the camera operator."[40]

The documentary consists of actual footage shot by AK cameramen (though colorized by the contemporary filmmakers), but dialogue was added to it that reflected the sort of memory battlefields just discussed. The director, Jan Komasa, made the decision to add the storyline and worked with three writers to develop it. The uprising is narrated by a US airman who has escaped from a German camp and two Polish cameramen. The American's role serves a didactic purpose: he "discovers" the heroism of Poles in '44 and hopes to promote it. The two Poles argue about what they are filming, the pretty girls they see through their lenses, and the heroism they capture. They also have to justify the fact that they are filming and not fighting. Eventually they enter the uprising and fight. The documentary is therefore clumsy and dramatic all at once: the authentic footage is moving; the dialogue often inelegant and contrived.

The press materials for the documentary consistently declared that "historical authenticity" and "historical accuracy" within it was overseen by "historians from the Warsaw Uprising Museum, experts in urban studies and architects, Warsaw specialists and consultants in weaponry and armaments cooperating with the Warsaw Uprising Museum."[41] If the museum legitimized the emotional remembrance of the uprising itself and made it official history, then the film, along with the comic series, legitimized the museum's sensory experience as the central component of contemporary Polish memory culture. Milena Fiedler characterized the film as one where the material was edited "not as an objective recording of reality but a subjective truth about the people who experienced this reality."[42] The official press kit put out by the museum took this notion a step further, for it stated that the film reduced the distance between the past and present, making the uprising real and therefore changing the past into the present.[43] This dissolution of time serves as the "project's exceptional educational and social value," for it means that in watching the film, "we stand face to face with the Uprising as close as never before."[44] Both the museum and its documentary film project thus allow contemporaries to refight the uprising every day. Within the museum's walls and in cinema halls, again to invoke the language of the press kit, "technology brings out truth," for the "reality of the Warsaw Uprising" consists of "feeling the great emotions experienced by the film's protagonists."[45] Ensuring this "historical accuracy of emotions (my term)," we are informed, "was a great challenge" that "caused the team many headaches and countless sleepless nights."[46] The film crew and museum staff, in other words, also dissolved the distance between past and present: their heroic efforts echoed those of the insurgents.

The heroism did not end with the documentary. Jan Komasa, the director, would also make a feature-length fictional film, *Miasto 44* (City 44). The museum opened on the sixtieth anniversary of the actual uprising; the film debuted in time for the seventieth. *Miasto 44* is a love story set amid the uprising, which is depicted as an event driven by young Poles. Stefan Zawadski, whose officer father died in 1939, lives with his mother, an actress, and his younger brother. He and his friends, including his childhood friend, Kama (Kamila), join the AK. Kama has long hoped that Stefan will fall in love with her. As he joins them, however, he falls in love instead with Ala (Alicja). Their squad of AK soldiers rescues a group of Jewish prisoners in their first engagement, one of whom joins the AK's ranks. Just before she is shot by a Nazi soldier, Stefan then saves Ala's life: the two kiss for the first time in a ridiculous slow-motion sequence where bullets dance around them. Stefan proves to be brave yet impetuous and is wounded in the very next sequence. He also watches his mother and brother executed by Nazis. While he is recovering in a hospital, the Nazis attack it and this time Ala saves his life. The two make their way through an increasingly bloody and destructive landscape, escape through the sewers, and rejoin their comrades. Stefan rejoins the unit while Ala tends to wounded Poles in a makeshift hospital. The two promise to find each other and state that their only goal is for each other to survive. While apart, though, Stefan has sex with Kamila in another ridiculous slow-motion sequence that features bombs dropping around them: Komasa, in an interview, declared that these two scenes were risky but that viewers "do not tolerate boredom and sometimes you need to bust up a scene in order to bring out the emotions."[47]

Stefan narrowly escapes death several more times; all his friends and comrades die, including Kamila (she is shot by a tank but manages to survive just long enough to tell Stefan she is sorry and that Ala is still alive). He arrives at the hospital where Ala was working only to discover a pile of corpses (in the preceding scene, a Nazi arrives and leers at Ala). He puts a gun in his mouth to commit suicide in front of another Nazi officer and the corpses but cannot do it. The officer spares his life, and Stefan stumbles across a city littered with the dead. He jumps into the Vistula and swims toward a sandbank in the middle where he first met Ala. He imagines she is there again and the two hold hands while they watch Warsaw ablaze. As the camera pans out, we see that Stefan sits alone. The cityscape transforms to the contemporary one.

One critic immediately noted the connections between the film's attempts to immerse viewers in the experiences of 1944 and the goals of the Warsaw Uprising Museum to do the same, commenting that *Miasto 44* lives up to the "emotions of the insurgents."[48] Małgorzata Dzieduszycka-Ziemilska, a retired government official and author, described her experience watching *Miasto 44* as a "painful" one that made it "not easy to write about."[49] The pain came because she "knew and loved so many of these people [in the film], some of whom I saw also in the other film, *Warsaw Uprising*." In the feature film, "we are engulfed in fire and blood, explosive noise, atrocities and horrific wounds." Much as he had for the documentary, Komasa is described as having performed heroic labor in making *Miasto 44*, which took eight years to make, and "involved collaboration with hundreds of his peers, along with war veterans, politicians, journalists, and countless numbers of Varsovians who kept their fingers crossed for him regardless of their position in the endless national discussion—debate, if you will—about monumental decisions made under extreme circumstances." The only site Dzieduszycka-Ziemilska can cite for this debate is, of course, the Uprising Museum, which she acknowledges is "often accused of taking the position of apologist for the Uprising" and "promoting an irrational patriotism that can only lead to more defeats." She defends the museum's position by referring to the documentary, which she describes as containing a power "without equal in film" because "we are transported to August 1944" and experience the hope, enthusiasm, idealism, courage, and hopelessness of that time.

These feelings, Dzieduszycka-Ziemilska argues, transfer to *Miasto 44*, which is "disturbingly faithful" in its depiction of the "emotions of 20-year olds [sic]" it focuses upon. In the end, she concludes the film suggests the uprising was doomed before it began because of the "idealistic and hopeful youth" who led it, Poles who were "trapped between their patriotic devotion to independence and cruel reality." At the same time, she notes that she left the film full of emotion: "sadness and anger at once enveloped me and left me empty."

The prominent film critic Tadeusz Sobolewski was also full of emotion after watching the film, but much more negative about it noting that the film debuted after the uprising had been turned into "a wave of mindless insurgent kitsch" that cater to emotions and melodrama.[50] The result was a "commercialized" film full of "hyper-realistic images" that only furthered the myth of '44 without analyzing it. *Miasto 44* is a film, both Sobolewski and Dzieduszycka-Ziemilska argue, about twenty-somethings then and for twenty-somethings now, creating a pop-culture kind of memory formation. In the end, Sobolewski writes, the film is about special effects, emotions, and shock. The "chain of emotions" created onscreen, he concludes, do not lead to any real historical understanding.[51] It is history turned into a game, a museum of trauma, a history of excess without metaphor or a search for real meaning.

Other critics disagreed, including Sobolewski's colleague, Jacek Szczerba, who responded to the former's critical stance.[52] Szczerba posited that the "emotional content" of *Miasto 44* is a positive aspect as long as one understands that emotions, more than deep critical thinking, *are* the message of the film. Komasa's film is "cruel" and contains atrocities on a par with Elem Klimov's *Come and See*. (Komasa would often invoke Klimov's film in interviews.) The understandable response to these scenes and to the love story that also develops onscreen, Szczerba concludes, is an emotional one. It is that response, he writes, that makes the film both a good one and one that can speak to contemporary audiences.

While critics and audiences debated the film's merits—Sobolewski's and Szczerba's reviews generated a number of online responses that mirrored their respective positions—*Miasto 44* nevertheless took the messages of the museum outside its walls and transferred them to the big screen. Both films did well at the box office: *Miasto 44* was overall the fourth-highest-grossing film in 2014 and second-highest-grossing Polish film (after *Bogowie*; it also beat out Hollywood films such as *The Wolf of Wall Street* and *Hunger Games*), and *Warsaw Uprising* was the seventh-highest-grossing Polish film (feature or documentary) of 2014 and nineteenth-highest overall (still beating out films such as *Guardians of the*

Galaxy).⁵³ Both films also furthered the goals of the museum to invite viewers to feel the uprising, to experience it viscerally and emotionally, and to therefore create new memories of 1944 in the present.

EMOTIONAL OVERLOAD?

The emotions evoked inside and outside the museum have not been pleasant ones for everyone. Maria Janion, the Polish scholar and feminist, has criticized the Warsaw Rising Museum for being just another "messianic apology of a hecatomb of blood" that allows "children to play at Warsaw insurgents." Janion, citing Benedict Anderson's theory of the imagined community and noting that nations are constructed, critiqued much of postcommunist Polish patriotic culture as a culture that views the nation as primordial. The museum, Janion lamented, did not "reveal the full complexity of this tragedy" and still was in need of taking an intellectual approach to Polish national myths rather than an emotional one.⁵⁴

Yet that might be precisely the point of the museum and its numerous projects: the comics and films are a small part of how the museum spreads its messages, which are all conveyed in the form of emotional appeals to immerse oneself in the spirit of 1944 in order to remember it today. Scientific work on how emotional appeals function might offer interesting insights into the museum's major efforts. One Swiss study on how emotional stimuli affect the brain concludes that people pay more attention to emotional appeals than to neutral ones and that "emotional attention" can shape memories, thoughts, and actions.⁵⁵ Sensory processing through the amygdala (the two almond-shaped groups of nuclei within the temporal lobes of the brain that process memory and emotional reactions) is enhanced by emotional appeals; our memories and perceptions can be influenced by "the affective significance of sensory events" and by emotional language.⁵⁶ The exhibits, events, lectures, films, concerts, comics, and other emotional appeals made by the museum help to connect Poles and others to the events of 1944, fostering virtual memories of that event among people who were not alive at that time.⁵⁷

The museum's efforts certainly have proven to be a success. In 2015, *Gazeta Wyborcza* reported that the site had enjoyed a record number of visitors in that year (630,000), including 100,000 who visited in August to time their experience with the anniversary of the event. The documentary film, the paper reported, had been seen by 1.8 million people in theaters and another 1.7 million watched a television program of insurgent songs produced by the museum. In its survey conducted among visitors, the museum enjoyed an 81 percent positive response for 2015.⁵⁸ Sensing the emotional past at the museum, it turns out, could also be one used to inspire contemporary defenders of the capital: Warsaw's police department held their 2015 oath-taking ceremony at the museum. In the press release for the event, Warsaw's police commissioner noted that the oath took place at a unique setting that is "special for every Pole," one where "the heroic and tragic struggle for freedom" that took place in 1944 might inspire tomorrow's policemen.[59]

EPILOGUE

The Uprising Museum ensures that 1944 has become the central date in modern Polish history and has set into place new memory practices that use that year as a means of downplaying the Holocaust and the 1943 Warsaw Ghetto Uprising. The museum also uses the memory wounds inflicted in 1944 to explain the Communist Era as an occupation. The emotions conveyed within its walls and promoted outside them have turned memories into history.

The museum's narrative and its activities have helped to lay the foundations for the current Law and Justice Party's outlook on Polish national history, which stresses Polish heroism and Polish victimization (the party's cofounder, Lech Kaczyński, was mayor of Warsaw when the museum opened and helped to provide both governmental and financial support for its creation). They are, as Jan Gross has written, rewriting Polish history through ahistorical means.[60] (Gross should know: he has specifically been targeted by the current regime.) Part of their revisions included battles over the planned World War II museum in Gdańsk. The museum, conceived at the time the Uprising Museum opened, aimed to tell a global history of the conflict and would feature thirty-seven thousand objects including, for example, US and Soviet tanks, documents from besieged Leningrad, and photographs of civilian bombing campaigns in Europe and Japan. The initial plan for this museum, as Timothy Snyder has written, would have gone beyond the national focus present in so many memorial sites. It would also have placed Polish experiences in larger contexts. Yet it would have by definition challenged the idealized version of the past promoted by Law and Justice and, by extension, the Uprising Museum, by dedicating space to the Holocaust and to local collaboration. The Gdańsk museum, in short, would have presented Poles as both victims and victimizers, as Gross did in his award-winning book, *Neighbors*: among the exhibits would be the keys from the Jews of Jedwabne taken by their Polish neighbors before they killed them.[61] Originally scheduled to open in January 2017, the museum opened amid controversy in March: the Polish government announced it wants the museum altered to focus more on the "Polish experience" in the war and threatened to cut off funding or close it if it does not.

When the anthropologist Erica Tucker returned to Warsaw in 2008 to reconnect with her informants who had provided the memories for her book on 1944 in memory, she asked them about the newly opened Uprising Museum. Most stated the site was not for them, but for the young. They also frequently echoed the words of one woman who, when asked what she liked best about the museum, simply replied, "just the fact that it exists."[62] The wounds of the past and of past memories that Miłosz referred to in his Nobel speech have in part been healed by creating an emotional site for young Poles. At the same time, one wonders whether the fact that the Uprising Museum exists is enough, for its existence brings up the very questions Miłosz and Szymborska raised in their poems. Tony Judt once warned that all our museums and memorials and obligatory school trips to them are not signs that we are ready to remember, but indications that we feel we have done our penance and can now begin to let go and forget, leaving the stones to remember for us.[63] The battle over memory's wounds inflicted in 1944 has been won in Poland. With this victory has come a relegation of more nuanced versions of the war and the Ghetto Uprising to the sidelines. The stones that remember the past in today's Warsaw are therefore fake ones: they are the recreated cobblestones under the feet of the Uprising Museum's visitors.

NOTES

1. Czesław Miłosz, "Nobel Lecture," December 8, 1980, http://www.nobelprize.org/nobel_prizes/literature/laureates/1980/milosz-lecture.html.

2. "The End and the Beginning," from *Miracle Fair* by Wislawa Szymborska, translated by Joanna Trzeciak. Copyright © 2001 by Joanna Trzeciak. Used by permission of W. W. Norton and Company, Inc.

3. David Rieff, *In Praise of Forgetting: Historical Memory and Its Ironies* (New Haven, CT: Yale University Press, 2016), 144.

4. For histories of the uprising, see Norman Davies, *Rising '44: The Battle for Warsaw* (New York: Penguin, 2004), and Włodzimierz Borodziej, *The Warsaw Uprising of 1944*, trans. Barbara Harshav (Madison: University of Wisconsin Press, 2006). For a history of the uprising that is placed within a longer scope of Poland during World War II, see Halik Kochanski, *The Eagle Unbowed: Poland and Poles in the Second World War* (Cambridge, MA: Harvard University Press, 2012).

5. Timothy Snyder, *Bloodlands: Europe between Hitler and Stalin* (New York: Basic, 2010), 308.

6. For more, see Erica Tucker, *Remembering Occupied Warsaw: Polish Narratives of World War II* (DeKalb: Northern Illinois University Press, 2011).

7. Tucker, *Remembering Occupied Warsaw*, 231.

8. See Sławomir Kapralski, "Battlefields of Memory: Landscape and Identity in Polish-Jewish Relations" *History and Memory* 13, no. 2 (Fall–Winter 2001): 35–58.

9. It is not surprising that there have been intense debates about the AK's relationship with Polish Jews and the Ghetto Uprising participants. For years, many

argued the AK was saturated with anti-Semitism, while other, more nationalistic, historians have defended the underground. Joshua Zimmerman's recent book makes a persuasive and comprehensive case that the AK, as an underground umbrella organization of more than three hundred thousand people, cannot be reduced to any one stereotype (Zimmerman, *The Polish Underground and the Jews, 1939–1945* [Cambridge: Cambridge University Press, 2015]).

10. Jacek Zygmunt Sawicki, *Bitwa o prawdę: historia zmagań o pamięć Powstania Warszawskiego 1944–1989* (Warsaw: DiG, 2005). For a memoir of the uprising that reads like an aural and visual account, see Miron Białoszewski, *A Memoir of the Warsaw Uprising*, trans. Madeline Levine (New York: New York Review of Books, 2014).

11. Quoted in Paweł Kowal and Paweł Ukielski, eds., *The Days of Freedom* (Warsaw: Warsaw Uprising Museum, 2009), 3.

12. Ibid., 19–20.

13. Ibid., 21.

14. Ibid., 38.

15. David Howes, "Introduction to Sensory Museology," *Senses and Society* 9, no. 3 (2014): 259–67.

16. Paweł Kowal, "How We Built the Museum," in *Guidebook to the Warsaw Rising Museum* (Warsaw: Muzeum Powstania Warszawskiego, 2007), 8.

17. Ibid.

18. Ibid., 10.

19. Ibid.

20. Ibid.

21. Ibid., 9.

22. *Guidebook to the Warsaw Rising Museum*, 61.

23. Ibid., 112.

24. Ibid., 51.

25. Ibid., 80.

26. Ibid., 128.

27. Ibid., 149.

28. Ibid., 119.

29. Ibid., 57.

30. Ibid.

31. Ibid., 180.

32. Ibid.

33. For more on Catholicism and modern Polishness, see Brian Porter-Szucs, *Faith and Fatherland: Catholicism, Modernity, and Poland* (New York: Oxford University Press, 2011).

34. *Guidebook to the Warsaw Rising Museum*, 180.

35. John Radzilowski, "Remembrance and Recovery: The Museum of the Warsaw Rising and the Memory of World War II in Post-communist Poland," *Public Historian* 31, no. 4 (Fall 2009): 150.

36. Ibid., 152.
37. *Powstanie '44: Powstanie '44 w komiksie Antologia prac konkursowych 2010; Morowe Panny* (Warsaw: Egmont Polska and Muzeum Powstania Warszawskiego, 2010), 7–13, 24–27.
38. Quoted in Alex Kłoś, "Powstanie znów w komiksie: Tym razem wygrał 'Traf,'" *Gazeta Wyborcza*, December 1, 2010, http://warszawa.wyborcza.pl/warszawa/1,34889, 8745888,Powstanie_znow_w_komiksie__Tym_razem_wygral__Traf_.html.
39. Dieter De Bruyn, "Patriotism of Tomorrow? The Commemoration and Popularization of the Warsaw Rising through Comics," *Slovo* 22, no. 2 (2010): 50–51.
40. Their statements appear on the film's official website, *Warsaw Rising*, http://warsawrising-thefilm.com/the-film/.
41. Jan Komasa, dir., *Warsaw Rising* (Poland, Alvernia Studios, 1944), http://warsawrising-thefilm.com/the-film/.
42. Official press kit for the film on the film's website: http://warsawrising-thefilm.com/the-film/.
43. Ibid., 4.
44. Ibid.
45. Ibid., 10.
46. Ibid.
47. Łuksz Knap, "Jan Komasa, reżyser 'Miasto 44': Wojna to wyrwane ręce i gałki oczne," *Gazeta.pl*, accessed February 5, 2020, https://weekend.gazeta.pl/weekend /1,152121,16742730,jan-komasa-rezyser-miasta-44-wojna-to-.wyrwane-rece-i-galki .html
48. Ibid.
49. Małgorzata Dzieduszycka-Ziemilska, "Tragedy as Art: Miasto 44," *Cosmopolitan Review* 6, no. 3 (Fall–Winter 2014), http://cosmopolitanreview.com/miasto-44/.
50. Tadeusz Sobolewski, "Sobolewski recenzuje 'Miasto 44': 'Doskonała imitacja wielkeigo kina,'" *Gazeta Wyborcza*, July 30, 2014, http://wyborcza.pl/1,75475 ,16404671,Sobolewski_recenzuje__Miasto_44____Doskonala_imitacja .html.
51. Sobolewski reached similar conclusions after watching the film at the National Stadium screening. See his "Przeżyj sobie powstanie," *Gazeta Wyborcza*, September 18, 2014, http://wyborcza.pl/piatekekstra/1,140705,16668256,Przezyj _sobie_powstanie___Miasto_44__wedlug_Sobolewskiego.html.
52. Jacek Szczerba, "Miasto 44 na plus," *Gazeta Wyborcza*, September 18, 2014, https://wyborcza.pl/piatekekstra/1,140705,16668269,_Miasto_44__na_plus .html.
53. "Polish Yearly Box Office," *IMDBPro*, Box Office Mojo, accessed February 5, 2020, http://www.boxofficemojo.com/intl/poland/yearly/.
54. Jarosiaw Kurski, "Moje herezje antynarodowe—rozmowa z Mari Janion," *Gazeta Wyborcza*, May 26, 2006, http://serwisy.gazeta.p1/kultura/i,34791,3374302 .html, accessed January 11, 2017.

55. Patrik Vuilleumier, "How Brains Beware: Neural Mechanisms of Emotional Attention," *Trends in Cognitive Sciences* 9, no. 12 (December 2005): 585–94.

56. Ibid., 585. For language, see Tony Buchanan, Kai Lutz, Shahram Mirzazade, Karsten Specht, N. Jon Shah, Karl Zilles, and Lutz Jäncke, ""Recognition of Emotional Prosody and Verbal Components of Spoken Language: An fMRI Study," *Cognitive Brain Research* 9 (2000): 227–38.

57. Susanna Trnka studied the emotional memories among many Czechs twenty years after 1989 and how all her subjects have "memories" of that event, including people who were children at the time. She concludes that emotional, affective, and sensory appeals have played the dominant role in shaping public memories of the Velvet Revolution. In a sense, the Warsaw Uprising Museum attempts to do the same. See Trnka, "When the World Went Color: Emotions, Senses, and Spaces in Contemporary Accounts of the Czech Velvet Revolution," *Emotions, Space, and Society* 5, no. 1 (2012): 45–51.

58. Tomasz Urzykowski, "Rekordowa frekwencja w Muzeum Powstania Warszawskiego," *Gazeta Wyborcza*, December 31, 2015, http://warszawa.wyborcza.pl/warszawa/1,34862,19414600,rekordowa-frekwencja-w-muzeum-powstania-warszawskiego.html.

59. "Ślubowanie w Muzeum Powstanie Warszawskiego," *Policja.pl*, December 8, 2015, http://www.policja.pl/pol/aktualnosci/119950,Slubowanie-w-Muzeum-Powstania-Warszawskiego.html.

60. Jan Gross, "Jaroslaw Kaczynski's Party Is Rewriting the History of Poland," *Financial Times*, March 13, 2016, https://www.ft.com/content/67532c78-e62d-11e5-a09b-1f8b0d268c39.

61. Timothy Snyder, "Poland vs. History," *New York Review of Books*, May 3, 2016, http://www.nybooks.com/daily/2016/05/03/poland-vs-history-museum-gdansk/. See also Jan Gross, *Neighbors: The Destruction of the Jewish Community in Jedwabne, Poland* (Princeton, NJ: Princeton University Press, 2001).

62. Tucker, *Remembering Occupied Warsaw*, 252.

63. Tony Judt, "The 'Problem of Evil' in Postwar Europe," *New York Review of Books*, February 14, 2008, http://www.nybooks.com/articles/2008/02/14/the-problem-of-evil-in-postwar-europe/.

STEPHEN M. NORRIS is Walter E. Havighurst Professor of Russian History and Director of the Havighurst Center for Russian and Post-Soviet Studies at Miami University (Ohio). He is author of two books on Russian cultural history, including *Blockbuster History in the New Russia: Movies, Memory, Patriotism* (2012), and editor of five books on Russian history and culture, including *Russia's People of Empire: Life Stories from Eurasia, 1500 to the Present* (with Willard Sunderland, 2012). He is currently writing a biography of the Soviet political caricaturist Boris Efimov.

Figure 7.1. Holodomor Victims Memorial. On the left: the domes of the Kyiv Pecherska Lavra complex and the Church of the Savior at Berestove. In the center: the Tower of Memory of the museum and the museum's exit in the slope underneath. The National Museum, founded 2008. http://memorialholodomor.org.ua/. *Wikimedia Commons*

SEVEN

Enforcing National Memory, Remembering Famine's Victims
The National Museum "Holodomor Victims Memorial"

DARIA MATTINGLY

INTRODUCTION

Preserving the memory of millions that starved to death and narrating their story is a difficult undertaking. The National Museum Holodomor Victims Memorial is the largest institution of its kind in Ukraine, dedicated to the victims of the 1932–33 famine, known as the Holodomor,[1] which claimed almost four million lives.[2] Like the majority of Ukrainian museums, it is state-run and reports to the Ministry of Culture. The Holodomor Victims Memorial Museum has become a national institution where foreign dignitaries are taken as part of the protocol of their visit to Ukraine, and therefore its message can have a great impact both inside and outside the country. According to the museum, in 2019 it welcomed 179,002 visitors.[3] Having acquired its current national status not long ago, it holds a monopoly in Ukraine over the institutionalized remembrance of the man-made famine in Ukraine. Therefore, the museum's importance in memory politics in today's Ukraine would be difficult to overestimate.

The creation of the memorial museum faced two deep and complicated underlying problems. First, it took fifty years before the establishment of the museum was considered. Second, even then it took seventeen years before anything was done. It was impossible to imagine a memorial to the victims during the fifty years of the famine's denial by the officials in Soviet Ukraine. It was not until 1987, when Ukrainian communist leader Volodymyr Shcherbytskyi acknowledged the famine in public during the celebration of the seventieth anniversary of Soviet rule in Ukraine,[4] that the museum could even be considered. In the following several years, a swath of crosses and makeshift memorials to the victims were erected across the country. The choice of the site and the construction of the central memorial took decades, however. One of its suggested locations in Kyiv witnessed an upscale housing complex built instead, and another suggested location was on a highway, hardly accessible by visitors on foot or by public transport. In the end, Viktor Yushchenko, then president of Ukraine, opened its memorial part in 2008 on the slope of a park in central Kyiv. Its museum section is still unfinished and is currently inside the memorial part. In July 2015 the memorial received its current name: the National Museum Holodomor Victims Memorial.

Shortly before the museum received its current name, Vyacheslav Kyrylenko, Ukraine's minister of culture at the time, appointed the current director of the museum and declared that one of the key aims of the new management was to ensure that all visitors to the museum recognize the Holodomor as a genocide of the Ukrainian people. His words defined the vector for the museum's narrative precisely: "This museum is responsible for enforcing the policy of national memory. And all its visitors must leave the museum with a clear understanding that the events of 1932–1933 were a deliberate destruction of the Ukrainian people."[5] This aim is further elaborated by the museum's development objective for 2015–20: "the museum strives to become a world-class institution and an influential agency in forming civil society in Ukraine. Through research, education, and cultural activity the museum will inform society about the act of genocide of the Ukrainian people and honour everybody who perished or was not born as a result of the tragedy. The museum will also help the consolidation and development of the Ukrainian nation, its historical consciousness and culture as well as accumulate regional and local history research of the Holodomor. All this will help to understand this tragedy better and to develop the necessary skills to prevent similar crimes taking place in the future."[6]

The history and the declared mission of the museum could serve as a vignette of the state's assessment of its past—dissemination of the knowledge about the famine, enforcing its interpretation of the past, and meeting public demand for remembrance. This chapter starts with a detailed description of the museum—its location and permanent exposition—and discusses new approaches the museum has adopted. It then continues to analyze the challenges the museum faces in its exposition and narrative. This structure allows me to assess the museum's role in preserving the memory of the Holodomor and popularizing the knowledge of this devastating famine.

DESCRIPTION OF THE MUSEUM

Location

The Holodomor was a man-made famine executed on a great scale that words alone cannot explain. Though the museum does not have extensive holdings, it provides a broader context to the understanding of the 1932–33 Famine by engaging with researchers and artists on the subject as well as by using the museum's installation to spread its message. The Holodomor occurred almost everywhere in prewar Soviet Ukraine. Although it did not claim victims in central Kyiv where the museum is located, it is not far from sites of the famine, and the city's population was directly and indirectly affected by the event. Many starving peasants came to the big cities in hope of finding food and died by the thousands.[7] The residents of major cities were mobilized to work in the villages during the harvest of 1933 and witnessed the devastated countryside. Mass graves exist in most villages, and unknown burial places lie in the fields, in the outskirts of the cities, and by the major train stations.[8]

The Holodomor Victims Memorial could not be attached to a central location or to some site that speaks for itself, like the famous memorials of Hiroshima, the Normandy beaches, Buchenwald, and Auschwitz. Neither are there sites specifically associated with the Holodomor perpetrators, like the House of the Wannsee Conference Memorial and Educational Site, the Topography of Terror and Wewelsburg District Museum with the Final Solution. But its location is important. Before the visitors exit onto a busy street of Kyiv full of life, in stark contradiction to the indoor exhibition, they have to walk through a park offering a far-reaching view of the left bank Kyiv over the wide and quietly flowing Dnipro River. Although most of the left bank is now built up, the valley still boasts some green. The view of the growing city across the river manifests life and walking through the park provides space for reflecting on the museum experience. The museum's significance also derives from its function as the commemorative center for the Holodomor in Ukraine every November, as well as other events it hosts or organizes throughout the year. The museum is abstract, but it creates a powerful meaning.

The memorial complex itself is deeply metaphorical beyond the symbolism imbued by its designers. The artist Andriy Haidamaka, the architect Yuriy Kovaliov, and sculptors Mykola Obeziuk and Petro Drozdovskyi tried to tell the story of the famine in the facade and sculptures in the nearby park.[9] Nested inside a hill in the Park of Glory (Park Slavy), its location is rather evocative of the complicated history of Ukraine. On one side, the museum borders the Soviet monument of Eternal Glory to the soldiers fallen during the Great Patriotic War,[10] while on the other side it borders the Orthodox Church of the Savior at Berestove. This church was a former residence of Kyivan Rus princes and hosts a tomb of the Monomakh dynasty, including that of Yuriy Dolgorukiy, who founded Moscow. The Red Army site and the Holodomor site each marks events that took millions of lives, and the church points to connections between Russian and Ukrainian histories. These two sites and the complicated histories they speak of also help us understand the narratives told within the nearby Holodomor Museum. Because the Holodomor is interpreted as the genocide of the Ukrainian people in the museum's vision, the Soviet Union, and Russia as its legal successor, are regarded as the oppressors that inflicted suffering on Ukraine. Hence, the position of the museum between the landmarks linking the Moscow and Soviet legacy could be read as symbolic as affirmation of a change in the memory politics in Ukraine.

Walking through the Museum

An alley leading to the museum from the street through the park starts with two stone angels—the solemn guardians of the souls of the victims. The alley is paved with black cobblestones, which symbolize the black fertile earth of the Ukrainian countryside and serve as a tilled soil of memory. These installations remind visitors that a devastating famine on the fertile Ukrainian soil is no accident. The poor harvest and excessive grain requisitions would certainly have caused starvation as it had in the past, but adding the confiscation of all foodstuffs, banning travel, and enacting other restrictive legislative provisions led to the famine of unprecedented scale. Some symbols might not be obvious to the onlooker, but others are telling. At the beginning of the path, one meets a life-size sculpture of a young, emaciated girl holding five ears of wheat (fig. 7.2). She embodies the famine's youngest and most vulnerable victims. This sculpture has become the starting point of the protocol visit of any international delegation to the museum, and flowers are laid by foreign governments' delegations there to respect the victims. The number of ears of wheat in her hands is not accidental—the law on the theft of socialistic property, passed in 1932 when starving peasants tried to take ears from the fields, was widely referred to as "The Law of Five Ears of Wheat." Had peasants or their children been caught for taking anything from the fields, they could be killed on the spot, beaten, or receive up to ten years in concentration camps. By the end of 1932, some forty-five hundred people had been executed under this law and more than a hundred thousand had received ten-year sentences in gulag labor camps.[11] The artist drew inspiration for this sculpture from his own memories of collecting wheat as a child during the famine of 1946–47.[12]

The alley finishes with a whitewashed, thirty-meter-high bell tower in a shape of a candle with an intricate gilded flame and steps down to the museum underneath the candle tower (fig. 7.3). The bell tower also features glass crosses of various sizes symbolizing the victims—larger crosses for the adult souls and smaller for the children. At the base of the tower are four black crosses with storks trying to fly away. The birds symbolize life and peace in Ukrainian folklore and, here in the museum, they are intended to represent the rebirth of Ukrainian people. Adorning the pathways leading to the museum are numerous domestic millstones. When found during the famine, local officials broke them to prevent peasants from milling grain at home. Here they also acquire a second meaning—they are milling through history. On the first Saturday in November, which is the official day of the Holodomor commemoration in Ukraine, almost all surfaces

Figure 7.2. Sculpture of the girl with five ears of wheat near the museum's entrance in the park. The museum's candle tower is in the background. *Photograph by Daria Mattingly*

around the entrance and the slopes of the hill on the museum's right are covered with candles brought by the public or distributed by the museum.

Inside the museum, which in one sense functions as a metaphorical tomb to the victims, a small room holds a collection of posters. These rotating, thematically organized images are exhibited for a short time along with an interactive audio screen explaining the posters in Ukrainian and in English. After the poster room, one continues into the Hall of Memory—a large, round room directly underneath the tower housing many volumes of the Book of Memory (a martyrologue with the names of the victims, survivor testimonies, and archival documents). Current exhibitions and permanent ethnographic collections lie around the room. The martyrologies in the hall, well lit up and available for reading, were compiled in 2007 by local teams of researchers and officials and published

Figure 7.3. Museum's tower, which symbolizes a candle in memory of the victims. *Photograph by Daria Mattingly*

in 2008.[13] The volumes are not complete, for data on the victims are missing in many villages. Some villages no longer remember their vanished pre-Holodomor populations, erased by the famine and the postfamine repressions; other villages disappeared altogether or were abandoned shortly after the tragedy. The process of recovering names is ongoing, and one can submit data at the museum.

In the middle of the Hall of Memory is a transparent enclosure filled with grain, around which one can light a candle in memory of the victims, as at the United States Holocaust Memorial Museum. The enclosure with wheat symbolizes the grain and food requisitions in 1932–33 that led to the deaths of millions. At the time, bread and other flour-based food constituted most of the peasant diet in Ukraine; bread was often referred to as "the head of everything."[14] Therefore, confiscation of grain meant drastic changes to the diet of most peasants in Ukraine.

Figure 7.4. The Bell of Memory at the exit of the museum overlooking the opposite bank of Dnipro River in Kyiv. *Photograph by Daria Mattingly*

This underground building has only one source of natural light, apart from the grain enclosure at the foundation of the tower in the hall, which enhances the impression of a tomb. At the end of the museum sequence, one leaves this dark, powerful place and faces a panoramic view over the river, for the exit is carved out of the hill's slope. Finally, visitors are reminded of the continued presence of the Holodomor: there is a bell they can ring in memory of the victims that is similar to the one at the Hiroshima memorial complex (fig. 7.4).

On both sides of the exit black granite slabs with the fourteen thousand names of the villages affected by the Holodomor testify to the crime scenes, to faraway places, some of which disappeared but most of which have since revived and gone back to a degree of normality. Along the paths are other slabs with engraved quotes by the survivors and witnesses, scholars, and public figures. The slabs are reminiscent of the so-called "black boards"—an extreme measure applied to the villages, collective farms, and even whole districts for not meeting grain procurement quotas in late 1932 and in 1933. These blacklisted places were refused all supplies and were often blockaded by the security services, militia, or the military. The mortality rate varied from one blacklisted village to another, in proportion to how strictly those measures were applied, the very blacklisting of a place meant fewer chances for survival for its inhabitants.

New Approaches

To present a story about an emotionally charged event is not easy. The task becomes even more overwhelming when the majority of the audience might struggle to identify with the everyday life of the victims. Ukrainians today are no longer raised in thatched cottages or accustomed to the rural lifestyle now that two-thirds of the population is urban. How will the gap in time and context between the museum's visitors and the victims, survivors, and participants of the Holodomor be bridged when the distance between firsthand experience and present and future visitors is only going to increase over time? By now, most visitors were born long after the Holodomor and, after a visit to the museum, they will understand that horrible things took place in the past, in many cases to their ancestors. This trauma will be removed from them further and further in time until it is presented as a historical fact in books and museums. Research shows that if children are not engaged during museum visits, they do not necessarily visit museums as adults, in particular, if the museum visits are put in place of their lectures on the subject in what school students refer to as "mausoleum-museums."[15] In other words, replacing classroom lectures with museum visits that fail to engage younger visitors will decrease their visits to the memorial as adults. Therefore, effectively engaging the younger generation is vital.

A possible route could be a psychological approach called "identification" by Jeffrey Ochsner, one that is already part of the Holocaust Museum experience, "where objects are conceptual as well as authentic—i.e. they communicate complex information, knowledge and understanding." The Holocaust Museum attempted a direct identification with the victims by issuing identity cards upon admission matched with gender and age of an actual victim or survivor, thus providing an individual story for the museum experience. One could argue about the effectiveness of the identity-card system, but it is often through a shared object or shared experience that the otherness of those nameless victims can be overcome, making a visitor feel and act as much like the victims as possible.[16] Although many of the existing techniques to bring the past to life would be ineffective for this museum (there are no smells, feels, or sounds of the Holodomor that one can recognize without previous experience of famine), there are artifacts that the museum's visitors can understand and associate with themselves regardless of the country or context from which they come. In such a way, visitors will be able to associate themselves with the victims and thus grasp the universal interpretation the museum hopes to transmit.

This approach was adopted by the museum in May 2016 in its temporary exhibition of elaborately embroidered shirts, called *vyshyvanky,* worn in rural Ukraine and exchanged for food during the famine. The highly publicized exhibition, entitled *"Vyshyvanka Worth of Life,"* featured authentic shirts from private and institutional collections and provided explanations of how these personal items were exchanged by the peasants during the famine.[17] Some survivor accounts tell of entire houses being exchanged for a loaf of bread.[18] The power of the shirts as artifacts came in part from their ordinariness and contemporariness. They are still fashionable and are worn today and therefore are easily readable as personal items. The similarity between the old shirts and the ones worn on the streets of contemporary Kyiv helped to foster the sense of the despair felt by the famine's victims. To help with this connection, the museum also screened a documentary on the *vyshyvanky* titled "National Heritage."

Another example of using artifacts that visitors can easily read was the exhibition *Masks of Holodomor* by Samara Pearce in February 2018. The collection of photographs of starvation by Alexander Wienerberger were displayed against the images taken today by his great-granddaughter Samara. The juxtaposition is startling and provides reminders of the famine that was taking place everywhere in Ukraine and implies state complicity in the events. Effective approaches of identification with the victims of the Holodomor through artifacts was adopted by the Chernihiv history museum in its exhibition on the Torgsin's activity in the province during the famine in the exhibit by Mykola Horokh.[19] Torgsin was a state network of stores in 1931–36 that redeemed gold, silver, and foreign currency from the Soviet population at considerably lower prices in exchange for foodstuffs. Personal jewelry such as rings, earrings, and crosses were displayed together with the artifacts from the Torgsin shops. Thus the most ordinary personal items in the museum can be the most powerful for overcoming the sense of otherness, particularly if they are put in the context of an understandable human struggle for survival.

The museum's adoption of new approaches such as identification through objects is not incidental. Its management has been changing the museum dramatically: it has become vocal and visible. Its staff members participate in international exchange programs, take part in television and other programs, and maintain a powerful presence on social media.[20] Their plans for the future are even more ambitious. The museum's current curator, Olesia Stasyuk, puts a lot of effort and enthusiasm into her daily work by organizing exhibitions, seminars, workshops, themed lectures, and other events. The museum's media work is superb and their ongoing projects like collecting data and family photographs of the victims are praiseworthy.

Overall, the museum meets the memory expectations of the overwhelming majority of Ukrainian and Russian visitors alike.[21] Many reviews left online and in the museum's guest books suggest that the museum's representation of the past is what the public expects to experience. Interaction between the museum and its visitors produces personal, lasting memories. An awareness of visitor expectations—whether finding long-lost relatives in the famine, lighting a candle to their memory, or learning about the famine itself, defines the museum. The dialogue between the museum and its visitors is not reduced to the visitor's book, it also tells how all museums could function.[22]

CHALLENGES

Symbolism

In its current presentation, the museum screens a number of reproduced historical photographs, reprints of archival documents, and documentaries on the walls of the Hall of Memory to sustain and validate the narrative of the man-made famine. A large number of farm tools are also on exhibit in the Hall of Memory. Unfortunately, there are no interpretative texts next to them to provide some explanation to the context in which objects were used or the reasons for selecting them for display, let alone attesting to whether they are authentic relics of the famine. History museums often employ period reconstructions to explain how the artifacts once fit into the lives of people at the time, and sometimes the lines between authenticity and reconstruction are intentionally blurred to make the viewers feel "what it was like." As we have mentioned, visitors might no longer be able to recognize these tools, nor would future generations. Recognizing the difficulty some of the audience might have in relating to the events of the Holodomor (few tourists, let alone contemporary Ukrainians, have experienced starvation or grain requisitions), chosen artifacts are not likely to help the viewers to relate to the victims.

Another segment of the museum's target audience possibly struggling to understand the farm tools would be foreign visitors. Powerful as it is, some of the museum's symbolism might not be easily grasped by most of its foreign audience without a guided tour to explain them, which is highly recommended in the reviews left online by the museum's visitors from abroad.[23] Some of the objects exhibited inside are explained or are self-explanatory—including the grain, the candles, and the bell of memory. The angels, crosses, and the sculpture of the emaciated girl are understood regardless of one's nationality, the reason behind the number of ears of wheat she is holding might be missed by most tourists unless they take special interest in Soviet history. Likewise, the black cobbles representing Ukrainian soil, manual milling stones that were rarely still used in other European countries in the 1930s, as well as most artifacts in the Hall of Memory might require additional explanation. The special significance of the storks for Ukrainians who grow up in the countryside might not be obvious to the foreign visitors either. This situation could be solved by the introduction of audio guides in several languages, already adopted in some Ukrainian museums[24] and planned by the National Museum Holodomor Victims Memorial in the near future.

Even more revealing are the comments by many foreign visitors who had not initially planned to visit the museum. In most cases, they discovered the museum on their way to a more famous landmark in Kyiv—the thousand-year-old Orthodox monastery and museum Kyiv Pecherska Lavra. At the memorial they open a previously unknown page of Ukraine's history, and all reviewers agree the museum does it well. To address this issue, the current management of the museum actively seeks to reach out wide and far. In April 2016 the announcement of the Arsenalna Station at Kyiv Metro (a rapid transit system) included mention of the museum. A closer look at the museum's activity reveals a daily string of events to boost its publicity: foreign delegations and school visits and exchanges with other institutions are covered in social media, its website, and the press.

The Perils of Ethnocentric Narrative

The museum's narrative was clearly defined by Ukraine's minister of culture in 2015 as the story of genocide against the Ukrainian people. The museum's mission includes the legitimation of this genocidal narrative as part of the nation-building process, one that identifies the aggressor and victim and offers a better understanding of the famine. The current interpretation of this narrative, however, might be regarded by some segments of the museum's audience as reductive, as based on reading along ethnic lines and on a clear dichotomy within the interpretation of the past. This reductive narrative and focusing on premodern Ukrainian village life could be observed in a close reading of the exhibition and the museum's website, in the events organized by the museum, and the publicity created by such events.

In accordance with the genocidal narrative, in its exhibition the museum interprets the famine as the result of Ukraine being subjected to the communist policies of Stalin and his close associates (see fig. 7.5). Had Ukrainians defended their own state after the revolution in 1917, the museum suggests, the famine would not have occurred. The assumption is that the Ukrainian state is the appropriate entity to convey the memory of the famine within a teleological narrative of victimhood and resistance in the struggle of the Ukrainian people for independence

Figure 7.5. The poster on perpetrators in the museum. The title at the top reads "Chief Organisers of Holodomor-Genocide" with photographs of Lazar Kaganovich and Viacheslav Molotov. The subtitle reads "Chief Executors of Holodomor-Genocide in Ukraine, Appointed by Stalin" with photographs of Stanislav Kosior, Vsevolod Balitskyi, Vlas Chubar, Pavlo Postyshev, Hryhoriy Petrovskyi, and Mendel Khataievich. *Photograph by Daria Mattingly*

and nation building. The famine belongs to the regime that targeted Ukrainian peasants: millions of victims were Ukrainians, they did not survive, did not have families. The current citizens of Ukraine are the offspring of the survivors. They are the grandchildren and great-grandchildren of those murdered or affected by the famine, deportations, and repressions.

Now that Ukraine is independent, the memory of the victims could be preserved and their experience retold. Furthermore, as the exhibition explains, Ukrainian peasants were not passive victims in the years preceding the famine—they actively resisted collectivization but their resistance was brutally suppressed. Under current circumstances, the tie between the victims and their descendants is not only personal and historical, but political: it bonds all Ukrainians to each other as survivors of a catastrophe who are still under threat in their country (in a sense reclaiming the victims as Ukrainian citizens in a fashion similar to the Lithuanian Museum of Genocide Victims; see chapter 1). Only the memory of the past tragedy, unity, and preserving the contemporary state can prevent history from repeating itself. Thus the museum acts as a central site for narrating the new history of Ukraine as a nation, an entity that has witnessed its citizens in their struggle for independence across the decades, and transforms the famine victims to citizens.

The museum refers to the present day in its story and does so through an interpretation of the past that seeks not only to legitimize but, to some degree, criticize the present. To adopt a Foucauldian analytic to read the museum as a text,[25] any museum can be regarded as a part of discursive formation that does not operate in a vacuum; it produces a narrative that is shaped by the rules of the existing discourse. How the museum responds to the present depends on the discourse prevalent in Ukrainian society today. This reading goes beyond the schematic narrative template of victimhood suggested by Wertsch, which is the case in other new museums in the former Soviet states, where Ukrainians in particular are portrayed as the victims of different states at different times.[26] From this point of view, the genocidal narrative reinforces the victimhood of the Ukrainian people, which might be reflective of how most members of Ukrainian society interpret the past.

The museum's victimhood narrative also identifies victims and aggressors along ethnic lines by explaining the current presence of certain ethnic minorities in Ukraine because of the actions of the Soviet regime. This is an approach that other museums of oppressive regimes have taken, but it is not the only one available. The founders of the Museum of Occupation of Latvia, for example, elected "to represent criminal regimes and individuals, not peoples, ethnic groups, or social classes, as being responsible for the crimes committed during the occupation periods."[27] For instance, in 2015 the Holodomor Museum launched an exhibition of the archival documents on the post-Holodomor resettlement of more than twenty thousand families from Russia and Belarus in the villages of south and east Ukraine devastated by the famine. According to the exhibition, the empty Ukrainian villages were repopulated with more than a hundred thousand Russian and Belarusian settlers who were provided with everything they required to start anew.[28] The exhibition aimed to explain the existence of a strong Russian-speaking community in the east and south Ukraine during the events of 2013–14, when the language and ethnic factors were used by some media to explain the violence.

Such a narrative, while somewhat popular with the public on social media, in fact contradicts the findings from decades of archival research by a respectable body of scholars and also was immediately refuted by many established historians of the Holodomor.[29] Although the figures on settlers coming from Russia and Belarus to Ukraine in late 1933 were true, the exhibition failed to include archival evidence on the number of those settlers who left the villages in the following six months and almost the same number of Ukrainian peasants brought to the same region from other parts of Ukraine. The message of the exhibition therefore was simple and clear: the current Russian population in the south and east Ukraine is the result of Soviet repopulating of the area in the years after the famine despite other scholars finding that the majority of the ethnic Russians settled in the region after World War II.[30] The message of the exhibition, not the conclusions of historians, was replicated by mass media and reposted in social networks that encouraged the development of negative attitudes and stereotypes of the Russian-speaking minority. Thus, the museum's narration of the genocide spilled over into interpretations of the current political crisis in Ukraine.

The ethnic narration leaves no room for non-Ukrainian victims of the Holodomor either, an omission that also does not help foster a better understanding of the 1932–33 Famine. There is no mention of the Polish, Russian, German, Czech, and Jewish populations' experiences of the famine, despite the availability of research on the subject. Although some minorities were underrepresented in the countryside, nevertheless there were victims among them too.[31] For instance, there is archival evidence on the death and starvation of the Jewish workers in small towns such as Tulchyn, Berdychiv, and Korosten during the famine. Moreover, there is a wide array of testimonies from all ethnic minorities and social groups. A legitimate historical narrative of the famine that enveloped the whole of Soviet Ukraine cannot rest solely upon the personal memories of one ethnic group. To quote Martin Sherwin, "Those who insist only on their own memories of the past are condemning the rest of us to avoid it."[32]

The ethnocentric reading of the famine is further illustrated by the collection of farm tools from Ukrainian Polissia and Slobozhanshchina and some from Hutsulshchyna that are part of the current exhibition. Though the Holodomor did not occur in the latter region, these authentic artifacts that are supposed to be representing the everyday life of Ukrainian peasants at the time and provide context for the narrative. And the exhibition gives no explanation next to the objects of how they were used. One has to have previous knowledge of the artifacts or be acquainted with the history of agriculture. Neither is there a clear connection drawn between these artifacts and any particular individual story. On the museum's website, the artifacts are interpreted as examples that illustrate how *Ukrainian* people "always were and remain extraordinary talented, hardworking and skilled.... [These artifacts] allow us to feel the energy of generations."[33] The use of the phrase "the extraordinariness of Ukrainians" implies that there were less talented or skilled non-Ukrainians.

This ethnocentric reading was also strongly present in the exhibition of the embroidered shirts, the *vyshyvanky*, which were described as the "genetic code of Ukrainian nation" and the "gene of Ukrainianness."[34] Ironically, this rhetoric is reminiscent of the Soviet grand narrative and Marxist notions of nation as an ethnic rather than political group. The Soviet approach in assessing ethnic groups is further reflected in the museum's reference to Crimean Tatars as "brotherly people."[35] Such a stratification of ethnic groups was the policy of the very regime the museum criticizes. One might ask about the authentic shirts the starving peasants exchanged for bread: who preserved them until they were purchased by the museum or collectors? The descendants of perpetrators on the ground? Were they ethnic Ukrainian too?

The museum fails to explain the perpetrators on the ground beyond the cliché of the Other, the secret police or the deviant element of Ukrainian village society. Although locating the aggressor at the top level is rather straightforward—Stalin and his functionaries in the Kremlin—this narrative nevertheless does not explain the Holodomor's mechanism on the ground. As a part of the Stalinist policies of transforming the peasant countryside into an industrialized state and establishing total control over its population with little regard for individual human life, the Holodomor was, like the Holocaust, a modern phenomenon. It would not have happened without a strong, disciplined state and thousands of people trained, motivated, conditioned, or compromised to participate.

The current narrative is disturbingly comforting: the Soviet Union has collapsed, the former Communists are presumably no longer in power, and we should therefore just remember the victims. Few words are devoted to the role of the rank-and-file perpetrators and other participants of the famine that claimed millions of lives: not just workers and communists from the cities but local teachers, railway workers, local officials, collective farmworkers, students, and even children as young as fifteen. In this narrative, they are reduced to the poor stratum of the village, communists from the cities and security services devoid of the agency that is placed with Stalin and his functionaries in the Kremlin. Description of the perpetrators is given on the posters and in the electronic chronicle inside the museum: communist leaders, fanatics, and state security representatives—that is, alien to the village. They organized the famine-genocide against the Ukrainians, took all grain for export, and kept the peasants under control. To this end, the museum creates a sense of belonging within a community and defines it in relation to outsiders.[36] At the same time, the existing narrative legitimates the discourse of anonymous perpetration on the middle and lower level. So does one leave the museum with a sense of justice when none of the rank-and-file perpetrators was put on trial since Ukraine became independent, or with a clear understanding of *how* this famine was possible on the ground? It's a question left open.

The absence of the rank-and-file perpetrators lies possibly in seeking to avoid controversy in the memorial devoted to the victims. Moreover, as with the Holocaust memorials in general, there is "a universal willingness to commemorate suffering experienced rather than suffering caused,"[37] so including local participation in the narrative could challenge its current premises and prove to be rather sensitive for public discussion. It might also stem from the persistent lack of a detailed and nuanced approach in this sort of assessment of the past, viewing it still in black and white while appealing to collective suffering. Politicians as well as the general public are still debating who should be designated official heroes and villains,[38] and as part of the dichotomy in this reductive reading of the past, the museum helps to identify victims in the former category. Yet explaining why people participated in the Holodomor by using the latest research on the perpetrators of mass violence, genocides, and crimes against humanity might offer exactly what the museum is trying to achieve; namely, a better understanding of how to prevent similar crimes in the future. Reducing the lower-rank perpetrators to the outcasts and outsiders is not supported by the latest research,[39] nor does it encourage further studies or a better understanding of the genocide.

A narrative about genocide does not have to be reductive, ethnocentric, or omissive. Its artifacts are not required to be authentic, but they can be conceptual and thought-provoking.[40] A state-sponsored narrative that presents the independent nation-state of Ukraine as the ultimate answer to the Holodomor-genocide can still include all ethnic groups and uphold human life as the highest value against totalitarian regimes. Genocidal and universalist narratives are not mutually exclusive, though when they are, the division corresponds to the social and intellectual environment in which they are disseminated.[41] Both narratives, Omer Bartov has argued, omit such aspects of the mass killings as political and socioeconomic conditions that acted as major factors in generating and perpetuating the killing of millions. Narratives tend to revolve around emotion and mourning, but they can also encourage questions and analysis.

Changes to the museum's narrative could address the universal meaning of the Holodomor, especially because doing so is consistent with its aims and objectives. It could encourage further questions: does the noninvolvement of other countries during the famine or their refusal to admit its genocidal nature imply a shared responsibility other governments ought to bear? If the Holodomor is one of the other mass murders in world history, then what purpose does the museum serve beyond the preservation of memory of this one episode? If the ethnic Ukrainians are the main focus of the exhibition, then the narrative should present the reasons for the international community to take interest in this Ukrainian catastrophe. The museum's narrative could be chronological and start with the events in Ukraine after 1917 to provide a broader context—that is, the establishment of the Soviet rule and its policies in the 1920s. At the same time, it could include other events in the Soviet Union: Stalin's take on the agriculture and on Ukraine in particular, the famines in other regions and the Stalinist methods of state-sanctioned violence, central control and prevention of contingency and the aftermath of the famine.

CONCLUDING REMARKS

Through its narrative and the exhibition, the museum tells the story of a tragedy that deeply affected Ukraine. The museum organizes various events in conjunction with other museums and institutions in Ukraine and abroad that specialize in history, genocides, totalitarian regimes, and human rights. It also hosts organized school visits and various events and has some of its material translated into English. The museum has launched programs aiming to find the locations of mass burials of Holodomor victims and produces a printed and online system to identify the victims. Its commemorative events of the famine and other tragic pages in the history of Ukraine are second to none. Its target audience, therefore, is mixed and diverse. Thus, the museum has to focus on how its various parts of its audience might require different points to be addressed.

The Holodomor Museum is successful in presenting the facts of the Holodomor, though it does not offer the possibility of a closer identification with the Holodomor victims. The perpetrators and the bystanders, like the victims, were human beings. Can their participation be explained (not excused) in the Holodomor? The fundamental moral dilemma for the museum would be to accept the fact that human beings of any race or nationality are capable of everything under certain circumstances. The famine was a catastrophe and its horror will be felt if visitors can understand how it was possible. The museum's narrative could also address the universal meaning of the Holodomor rather than err, especially in light of its own aims and objectives.

As with the sites on perpetrators of the Holocaust, the difficulty with explaining the mechanism of the Holodomor lies in conveying the actuality that the majority of perpetrators were ordinary men and women, as most perpetrators did not think of themselves as perpetrators, even after the war.[42] Perhaps the prime example of a perpetrators site in the case of the Holocaust is the House of the Wannsee Conference near Berlin,[43] where senior government officials of Nazi Germany and Schutzstaffel (SS) leaders met to discuss the Final Solution and its implementation on January 20, 1942. A possible equivalent in the Holodomor's history is the building of Kharkiv opera house, where a CP(b)U conference on grain procurement took place in July 1932. Of course, neither the meeting in Wannsee nor the conference in Kharkiv was a starting point of either catastrophe that was to unfold. The memorial near Berlin elaborates on the evidence showing the senior officials' knowledge (and tacit approval) of discrimination against the Jews. Many published collections of the archival documents on the Holodomor show similar, if not better, awareness of the already existing devastation and violence in the countryside by the republic's officials in 1932. Yet some district officials found the courage in July 1932 to criticize the quotas levied on them in Moscow in front of Molotov and Kaganovich. The event could exemplify alternatives for action the perpetrators on the ground could resort to, rather than explaining their compliance by fear of repression.

Identification with victims ultimately reassures the audience, somewhat ambitiously, of their ontological innocence. This reassurance is unwarranted, according to Ernst van Alphen, and unhelpful in education and preventing genocides and mass killing in the future. He suggests partial and temporary identification with the perpetrators to make "one aware of the ease with which one can slide into a measure of complicity."[44] Indeed, it seems that a careful analysis to understand the perpetrators, rather than their deeds, would explain to the audience how the Holodomor was possible.

The methods in the Wannsee Memorial focus on independent inquiry rather than the museum's interpretation of the events and its participants. The school classes research a specific theme and then deliver presentations on their findings—an approach different from a lecture on "how it really was." Moreover, the House of the Wannsee Conference offers seminars aimed at professional groups like the Bundeswehr or medics that teach how people of their profession responded to the inhumane policies of the Third Reich like mass shootings of the Jews and euthanasia programs.[45] Likewise, the soldiers of Zbroini Syly Ukrainy (Armed Forces of Ukraine) could learn how the soldiers of the armed forces at the time participated in the logistics of the famine—rounding up peasants, staging summary executions, guarding the supplies, and so on and consider the scope for action while not in time of war. The medics, in their turn, can examine how the cause of death was forged in the death certificates. As in chapter 1 of the current volume, the approach in the House of the Wannsee Memorial is to analyze one perpetrator group or various roles to establish how perpetrators behaved.

The pedagogical value of including ordinary people as perpetrators in the narrative comes from Adorno's adage that "the roots of perpetration lie with the persecutors, not the persecuted."[46] Including personal stories of field guards, chairmen of the farms, and collective farmers who proceeded with orders and led ordinary lives after the famine will individualize them; juxtaposing their stories with a number of victims in their respective villages would stress the magnitude of their actions. Such an approach will help to avoid reductiveness in explaining the motivation of the perpetrators and show how the famine was possible by drawing attention to perpetrators as members of the society, no matter how difficult it is to accept. Placing them within the context of other examples of mass killing could prevent dismissing them as deviant elements of Ukrainian society or as the Other. It is the evidence of ordinary people capable of starving their neighbors to death, albeit on someone else's orders, that might have a large impact and stimulate reflection.

Adopting such an approach might be a challenging task for the museum, for some of its recent exhibits lacked accuracy, which, in turn, compromises the efforts of the museum in pursuing its agenda. Apart from the discussed exhibition on Russians settlers in the districts devastated by the famine, in March 2016 the museum hosted a presentation on the latest archival discovery by Volodymyr Serhiychuk,[47] who claims the total number of victims in Ukraine was between seven and ten million. Though this claim was immediately refuted by demographers who dedicated years of research on the question,[48] the museum continues to maintain these unconfirmed figures. In 2016 and 2017, with Kyiv Shevchenko University, the museum organized two conferences that focused on the number of victims and its participants and issued a statement supporting the figures. Furthermore, the director of the museum personally contacted academic institutions abroad and strongly advised their researchers and teaching staff to use the "correct" figures of the Holodomor victims. In the news media, museum curator Stasyuk denounced the demographers as "immoral" for refuting the higher figures.[49]

The new figures also were used in the art installation 163: Art for the Memory by Rostyslav Bortnyk that took place at the museum in September 2016, which toured in other cities in Ukraine in 2017.[50] The number 163 is the number of grains in the five ears of wheat for which, according to Bortnyk, people were shot or sentenced to ten years in camps. The number of victims he used was provided by the museum and, according to the demographers, appears to be exaggerated.[51] The Institute of Demography at the National Academy of Sciences of Ukraine has repeatedly addressed the museum's ongoing use of unverified numbers of victims.[52]

Neither is spared from controversy is the construction of the actual museum next to the memorial, which started in 2019. Many researchers felt that the concept of the future museum should be developed at the Ukrainian Academy of Sciences by employing leading scholars on the subject from various disciplines. According to the critical body of scholars who initiated a letter addressed to the government of Ukraine, the project has instead been "monopolized" by the current management of the museum. The list of the signatories up to date included renowned historians and public figures in Ukraine and abroad.[53]

There are many important historical events in the living memory of Ukrainians, yet the Holodomor remains one of world-shaping significance and continues to figure most prominently in its political and cultural domain. It interests both scholars and the general public. By the time the museum part of the complex is completed, most the last survivors of the Holodomor will have long passed away. Its management might change as well, and so will its approach to the narrative and the exhibition. That being the case, both the interpretation and the representation of the Holodomor could be different. All visitors, whether scholars on the subject or the lay public, Ukrainians or non-Ukrainians, the offspring of the victims or of the participants, will be able to learn of the event only through archival documents or memoirs, films, or museums. The Holodomor will by then have become everyone's foreign country, and the museum's role in providing us with tools and resources to explore it will inevitably construct our memory and knowledge of it. This is an incredible task and an immense responsibility for the museum and, as its current narrative and exhibition suggest, the museum will take up this challenge.

NOTES

1. Throughout the article, I use the terms "the Holodomor" and the "1932–33 famine" interchangeably. The term *Holodomor* stresses the man-made character of the famine. The complexities of various interpretations of the term and the debate they have generated are beyond the scope of this article.

2. Estimations of the number of victims vary; most demographers and historians accept a number close to 4 million rather than a higher one. (Jacques Vallin, France Meslé, Serhiy Adamets, and Serhiy Pyrozhkov "Kryza 1930 rr," in *Smertnist ta prychyny smerti v Ukraiini u XX stolitti*, ed. France Meslé and Jacques Vallin (Kyiv: Vydavnychyi dim "Stylos," 2008), 37–65; Omelian Rudnytkyi, Nataliia Levchuk, Oleh Wolowyna, Pavlo Shevchuk, and Alla Kovbasiuk (Savchuk), "Demography of a Man-Made Human Catastrophe: The Case of Massive Famine in Ukraine 1932–1933," in *Demography and Social Economy* no. 2 (24) (2015): 53–80; Omelian Rudnytskyi, Nataliia Levchuk, Oleh Wolowyna, and Pavlo Shevchuk, "Famine Losses in Ukraine in 1932 to 1933 within the Context of the Soviet Union," in *Famines in European Economic History: The Last Great European Famines Reconsidered*, ed. Declan Curran, Lubomyr Luciuk, and Andrew Newby (London: Routledge, 2015), 192–223; Oleh Wolowyna, "Comments on the Demographic Consequences of the Holodomor," in *After the Holodomor: The Enduring Impact of the Famine on Ukraine*, ed. Andrea Graziosi, Lubomyr Hajda, and Halyna Hryn (Cambridge, MA: Harvard University Press for the Ukrainian Research Institute at Harvard University, 2013), 243–50; Stanislav Kulchytskyi, *Ukraine's Demographical Losses from Famine in 1932–1933 According to the General Census of*

the Population in 1937, paper presented to the conference Population of the USSR in the 1920s and 1930s in Light of Newly-Declassified Documentary Evidence, Toronto, January 1995; Sergei Maksudov, *Poteri naseleniia SSSR* (Benson, VT: Chalidze Publications, 1989), 159–69.

    3. Report on the museum's work in 2019 is at https://holodormuseum.org.ua/pdf-zvit/, accessed March 2, 2020.

    4. Liudmyla Grynevych, "Golod 1932–1933 u publichnii kulturi pamyati ta suspilnii svidomosti v Ukraiini," in *Problemy istorii Ukraiiny: fakty, sudzhennia, poshuky* no. 17 (2007), 391–92, citing Central State Archives of Public Organizations of Ukraine, Kyiv, collection 1, inventory 32, file 2859, 29–30; Radianska Ukraiina, 1990, February 7; Ruslan Pyrih, ed., *Golod 1932–1933 rokiv na Ukraiini: ochyma istorykiv, movoiu dokumentiv* (Kyiv: Politvydav Ukraiiny, 1990), 3–4.

    5. Ukraine Ministry of Culture, "Olesya Stasyuk Appointed New Director of National Museum "Memory of Victims of Famine in Ukraine," March 26, 2015, http://mincult.kmu.gov.ua/control/uk/publish/article?art_id=244921364&cat_id=244913751.

    6. Museum's Development Concept, accessed January 4, 2020, https://holodormuseum.org.ua/en/about-the-museum/pro-muzej/.

    7. Ruslan Pyrih, ed., *Holodomor 1932–1933 rokiv v Ukraini: Dokumenty i materialy* (Kyiv: Vydavnychyi dim Kyievo-Mohylianska akademia, 2007), 875–76.

    8. On preserving memory on site or remotely, see Timothy W. Ryback, "Evidence of Evil," *New Yorker*, November 15, 1993, 68–81; Steven Erlanger, "St. Petersburg Journal; The Russians Revisit Stalin's Never-Never Land," *New York Times*, June 1, 1994, A4, http://www.nytimes.com/1994/06/01/world/st-petersburg-journal-the-russians-revisit-stalin-s-never-never-land.html.

    9. The website of the museum, accessed April 1, 2020, https://holodormuseum.org.ua/istoriia-natsionalnoho-muzeiu-memorial-zhertv-holodomoru/.

    10. The term "Great Patriotic War" refers to the period in World War II between June 22, 1941, and May 9, 1945.

    11. Andrea Graziosi, *L'URSS di Lenin e Stalin: storia dell'Unione Sovietica, 1914–1945* (Bologna: Il Mulino, 2007), 333; Robert W. Davies and Stephen G. Wheatcroft, *The Years of Hunger: Soviet Agriculture, 1931–33* (London: Palgrave Macmillan, 2009), 166–68.

    12. A more detailed description of the memorial complex is at the National Institute of Memory of Ukraine, accessed on January 3, 2016, at https://archive.is/20121222080152/www.memory.gov.ua/ua/396.htm.

    13. *Knyga Pam'iati zhertv Holodomoru 1932–1933 rokiv v Ukraiini* (Kyiv: Oleny Teligy, 2008). Online volumes are at http://www.memory.gov.ua:8080/ua/publication/content/1522.htm, accessed February 7, 2020.

    14. Iryna Ignatenko, *Etnologiia dlia narodu: Sviata, tradytsiii, zvychaii, obriady, prykmety, viruvannia ukraintsiv* (Kyiv: Klub knyzhkovogo dozvillia, 2016).

15. Linda Norris, "Who Are Museums For?," *History News*, 65, no. 4 (Autumn 2010): 8.

16. Jeffrey K. Ochsner, "Understanding the Holocaust through the U.S. Holocaust Memorial Museum," *Journal of Architectural Education* 48, no. 4 (1995): 240–49.

17. See a video-report on the presentation on May 18, 2016, "Vyshyvanka Worth of Life," last accessed May 23, 2016, https://www.youtube.com/watch?v= 2D6r1LKQCac; "Exhibition 'Embroidery with Value in Life, Opened in the Holodomor Museum in Kiev," *Radio Svoboda*, May 18, 2016, http://www.radiosvoboda.org /content/news/27743219.html.

18. Dmytro Shupyk, Serhiy Bilan, and Vasyl Osheka, *Doroga do ridnogo domu (Istoriia sela Popivky Myrgorodskogo raionu Poltavskoii oblasti* (Poltava: PP Pravedniuk, 2013), 177.

19. More on the exhibition by Mykola Horokh in the video "Robbery, Soviet Style" at http://www.gorod.cn.ua/news/foto-i-video/69991-pograbuvannja-po -radjanskomu-video.html, accessed February 7, 2020; Stanislav Kopot, "'Robbery in the Soviet Union' at the Historical Museum," *Radio Svoboda*, February 2, 2016, http://newvv.net/culture/Culture/243781.html.

20. For instance, there are two webpages of the museum on one social network alone, both last accessed on April 1, 2016: https://www.facebook.com/Національний -музей-Меморіал-жертв-Голодомору-853746961369758/; https://www.facebook .com/pages/Holodomor-Famine-Museum-Kyiv-Ukraine/547255545309987.

21. Scanned visitors' books since 2009 are available upon request at memoholod@ ukr.net.

22. Susan A. Crane, "Memory, Distortion, and History in the Museum," *History and Theory* 36, no 4 (December 1997): 47.

23. The examples that follow are drawn from almost ninety-five reviews left by the museum's visitors at the online resource Tripadvisor, https://www.tripadvisor .co.uk/Attraction_Review-g294474-d3229223-Reviews-National_Museum_The _Memorial_in_Commemoration_of_Famines_Victims-Kiev.html, and Google Reviews, https://www.google.com/search?q=Google+Reviews+holodomor+museum &oq=Google+Reviews+holodomor+museum&aqs=chrome..69i57j69i64l2.4574j0j4 &sourceid=chrome&ie=UTF-8#lrd=0x40d4cfa14d864295:0x65795d704fb58089,1,,,. Both websites were last accessed on April 1, 2016.

24. For example, audio guides in English and other languages are used in the Ukrainian National Chernobyl Museum, 1 Khoreva St., Kyiv, Ukraine, http:// chornobylmuseum.kiev.ua/en/mainpage/, last accessed April 1, 2016.

25. Alexander C. Wright, "Myth, Rhetoric and Human Tragedy in Lithuanian Museums and Sites of Memory," *Acta Turistica* 25, no. 2 (December 2013): 191–209.

26. Elena Ivanova, "Changes in Collective Memory: The Schematic Narrative Template of Victimhood in Kharkiv Museums," *Journal of Museum Education* 28, no. 1 (Winter 2003): 18.

27. Laura A. Lenss, "Capturing the Next Shift: The Mapping of Meaning onto the Museum of the Occupation of Latvia," *Future Anterior* 3, no. 1 (Summer 2006): 53.

28. Anastasiia Zanuda and Svitlana Dorosh, "Rozkryttia arkhiviv: iak pislia Golodomoru na Donbas pereselialy rosiian," *BBC Ukrainian* online, June 2, 2015, http://www.bbc.com/ukrainian/society/2015/06/150522_holodomor_donbass_russia_az.

29. See Hennadiy Yefimenko, "Pereselennia ta deportatsii v postholodomorni roky (1933–1936): poraionnyi zriz," in *Problemy istorii Ukrainy: fakty, sudzhenniia, poshuky*, no. 22 (2013): 136–65.

30. On resettlement in the south and east provinces of the Ukrainian Soviet Socialistic Republic, see Central State Archives of Public Organizations of Ukraine, Kyiv, collection 1, inventory 20, file 6392. On postwar migration into the Ukrainian SSR, see Bohdan Krawchenko, *Social Change and National Consciousness in Twentieth-Century Ukraine* (Basingstoke: Palgrave Macmillan, 1985).

31. See Oleksandr Ivanov and Ihor Ivankov, "Demografichni vtraty etnichnykh nimtsiv USRR u roky holodomoru," in Volodymyr Lytvyn, ed., *Holod 1932–1933 rokiv v Ukraini: prychyny ta naslidky* (Kyiv: Naukova Dumka, 2003), 514–27; Vasyl Marochko, "Natsionalni menchyny v roky holodomoru," in Volodymyr Lytvyn, ed., *Holod 1932–1933 rokiv v Ukraiini: prychyny i naslidky*, 527–37.

32. Crane, "Memory, Distortion, and History," 44.

33. See description of the museum's exhibition, last accessed on April 1, 2020, https://holodomormuseum.org.ua/vystavka/holodomor-nyshchennia-identychnosti/.

34. Ibid.

35. Ibid.

36. Thomas Laqueur, "The Holocaust Museum," *Threepenny Review* no. 56 (Winter 1994): 32.

37. Sybil Milton, cited in Edward T. Linenthal, *Preserving Memory: The Struggle to Create America's Holocaust Museum* (New York: Viking, 1995), 199.

38. For debates on heroes and villains, see David R. Marples, *Heroes and Villains: Creating National History in Contemporary Ukraine* (Edmonton: University of Alberta, 2008); Clifford J. Levy, "Hero of Ukraine's Splits Nation, Inside and Out," *New York Times*, March 1, 2010, www.nytimes.com/2010/03/02/world/europe/02history.html.

39. On the subject of the rank-and-file perpetrators, see Valeriy Vasyliev, Nickolas Vert, and Serhii Kokin, *Partiyno-radians'ke kerivnytstvo Ukraiins'koii SSR pid chas Holodomoru 1932–1933: Vozhdi. Pratsivnyky. Actyvisty. Zbirnyk dokumentiv ta materialiv* (Kyiv: Instytut istorii Ukraiiny, 2013); Stepan Drovoziuk, "Sotsialno-psykhologichny portret silskogo 'aktyvista' 20–30-kh rr. v ukraiinskii istoriograpfii," in *Problemy istorii Ukrainy: fakty, sudzhennia, poshuky*, no. 9 (2003): 360–372; Olena Lysenko, "Typologia povedinky silskykh aktyvistiv u konteksti zdiisnennia sutsilnoi kolektyvizatsii silskogo gospodarstva v Ukraini (pochatok 1930-kh rr),"

in *Istoriia Ukraiiny: Malovidomi imena, podiii, fakty*, no. 36 (2010): 189–203; Tamara Demchenko, "Svidchennia pro Holodomor iak dzherelo vyvchennia fenomenu stalinskykh aktyvistiv," in *Problemy istorii Ukrainy: fakty, sudzhennia, poshuky*, no. 19, vol. 2 (2010): 71–81; Valeriy Vasylyev and Lynne Viola, *Kolektyvizatsiia i elianskyi opir na Ukraiini (lystopad 1929—mart 1930)* (Vinnytsia, Ukraine: Logos, 1997); Daria Mattingly, "Idle, Drunk and Good-for-Nothing. Cultural Memory of the Rank-and-File Perpetrators of the Holodomor," in ed. Małgorzata Głowacka-Grajper and Anna Wylegała, *The Burden of the Past: History, Memory, and Identity in Contemporary Ukraine* (Bloomington: Indiana University Press, 2020), 19–48.

40. Dominika Rank, "Na vidkryttia museiu Polin u Warshavi," *Ukraina Moderna*, December 4, 2014, http://uamoderna.com/blogy/dominika-rank/museum-polin-warsaw-1.

41. Omer Bartov, "Chambers of Horror," *Israel Studies* 2, no. 2 (Fall 1997): 82.

42. Caroline Pearce, "The Role of German Perpetrator Sites in Teaching and Confronting the Nazi Past," in *Memorialization in Germany since 1945*, ed. Bill Niven and Chloe Paver (Basingstoke, UK: Palgrave Macmillan, 2010), 169.

43. See the website of House of the Wannsee Conference: Memorial and Education Site: https://www.orte-der-erinnerung.de/en/institutions-2/#1501833877022-ff6b31c7-aee91df4-a69b

44. Ernst van Alphen, "Playing the Holocaust," in *Mirroring Evil*, ed. Norman L. Kleeblatt (New York: Jewish Museum and Rutgers University Press, 2002), 77.

45. Pearce, "Role of German Perpetrator Sites," 172.

46. Pearce, "Role of German Perpetrator Sites," 175.

47. More on the Volodymyr Serhiychuk's presentation at Yevheniia Tyukhtenko, "Istoryk nazvav novi tsyfry vtrat pid chas Holodomoru 1932–1933," *Radio Sbvoboda*, March 12, 2016, https://www.radiosvoboda.org/a/27605525.html.

48. A team of forty five historians, including a number from the Institute of the History of Ukraine (National Academy of Sciences), working on debunking the myths in the historiography of Ukraine (http://likbez.org.ua/authors-list); Nataliia Levchuk in discussion with Volodymyr Serhiichuk in the museum: "Novyi spor vokrug Golodomora: Video," *Novosti-N*, March 15, 2016, http://novosti-n.org/ukraine/read/119020.html.

49. "Institut Demografiyi spetsialno prymenshuie kilkist zhertv Holodomoru—istoryky sturbovani," *Gazeta.ua*, October 7, 2016, https://gazeta.ua/articles/history/_institut-demografiyi-specialno-primenshuye-kilkist-zhertv-golodomoru-istoriki-sturbovani/727569.

50. See the website dedicated to the exhibit, accessed September 1, 2017, http://163.com.ua/.

51. See the artist's comments in Nataliia Kushnirchuk, "Orihial'nu vistavku, prisvyachyenu zhyertvam Holodomoru privyezi u Ternopil," *INTB TV*, March 20, 2017, http://intb.te.ua/2017/03/оригінальну-виставку-присвячену-жер/.

52. Demographers' press conference on the number of victims appeared at "Demografi nazvali tochnye chislo vtrat nacyelyennya ukrajini pid chas Holodomoru v 1930-kh rokakh," *Unian.ua*, November 25, 2017, https://www.unian.ua/society/2259489-demografi-nazvali-tochne-chislo-vtrat-naselennya-ukrajini-pid-chas-golodomoru-v-1930-h-rokah.html.

53. "Naukovci prosyat' abi koncepciyu Muzeyu Holodomoru rozrobili v NAN," *Ukrinform.ua*, https://www.ukrinform.ua/rubric-society/2401594-naukovci-prosat-abi-koncepciu-muzeu-golodomoru-rozrobili-v-nan.html.

DARIA MATTINGLY is a Leverhulme Early Career Research Fellow at University of Cambridge, UK, where she also teaches Russian history. Her doctoral thesis explored the identifiable and memorial traces of the rank-and-file perpetrators of the Holodomor, while her current book project focuses on Jews in the 1932–33 famine.

Figure C.1. Cameras made in the GDR. Source: *Wikimedia Commons*

HALL OF EVERYDAY LIFE

Ivan Klima, the Czech writer and playwright, used to avoid any discussion of his membership in the Communist Party. He recounted that a BBC Radio editor once asked him to talk about it, prompting a momentary crisis. "For quite a long time now," Klima recollects, "I have considered the Communist Party, or, more precisely, the Communist movement, a criminal conspiracy against democracy. And it is not pleasant to remember that, even though it was for a short period, I had been a member of this party."[1] In the end, Klima attempted to wrestle with these facts and with the fact that he had lived throughout the communist era in Czechoslovakia. He decided to write his memoir. He gave it the title *My Crazy Century*.

The exhibits in the first two halls capture the prototypical memory sites that have sprouted in postcommunist societies. New nations have crafted new narratives out of the recent past, stories that by and large explain the Communist Era through emotional lenses of tragedy and trauma visited on locals by an occupying regime.

Yet the majority of citizens in the new states of Central and Eastern Europe who lived under communism did not live during the famines or the war. The lived experience of communism for them was one rooted in the 1960s, 1970s, and 1980s. As the governments and institutions of these new nations developed remembrance sites and historical narratives that focused on tragedy, another emotion began to surface in response: nostalgia. The half-century of communism in Eastern Europe may have been crazy, but it was also a time where people lived their everyday lives. In the reunified Germany in particular a number of small, private, unofficial museums sprang up that aimed to capture the everyday under communism. These museums attempted to connect both domestic and foreign visitors with happier feelings, those associated with the life of a vanished system.

In his outstanding study, Jonathan Bach argues that, after 1990, East Germany (formally the German Democratic Republic, or GDR) became "a present absence, invoked mostly to be disavowed."[2] As a result, the material objects of everyday life that had once formed part of life under the GDR appeared "dislocated, disembodied, and out of context,"[3] particularly as the German state crafted a narrative that primarily focused on suffering under communist East Germany. Bach's study examines "acts of appropriation," among them how many former East Germans built personal museums out of abandoned objects that were connected to memories and lived pasts. These everyday museums, which dot the map of the former GDR, "function as a form of antipolitics at a time when many ex-citizens of the former GDR confronted feelings of powerlessness"; their "tactile, interactive, and informal modes of representation are a form of appropriation that allows them to claim the important mantle of authenticity."[4] These memory sites see themselves as correctives to politicized museums that claim everything was bad in the GDR.

If the museums in the first two halls predominately captured memories that had been forgotten or suppressed under communism, the museums of the everyday capture what their creators feared was already forgotten after communism. In both Prague and Berlin, as you will read, two centrally located museums captured these trends in the form of sites meant to attract foreign tourists as much as former citizens feeling nostalgic for their former lives. The Museum of Communism and the DDR Museum build on the sentiments that created the private, small museums of communism elsewhere, but also created a new form of postcommunist nostalgic tourism. Inside, you are invited to enter a lost world, sit on communist-era couches in communist-era living rooms, touch objects. In doing so, as the creators of the Life under Communism Museum in Warsaw write (another recently founded example of this sort of museum), you can get in touch with the lives of your parents or, if you lived through the crazy half-century, you can remember the "light and the dark times."[5]

NOTES

1. Ivan Klima, *My Crazy Century*, translated by Craig Craves (New York: Grove, 2009), 1.
2. Jonathan Bach, *What Remains: Everyday Encounters with the Socialist Past in Germany* (New York: Columbia University Press, 2017), 1.
3. Ibid., 5.
4. Ibid., 48.
5. See their website: https://mzprl.pl/?lang=en/.

Figure 8.1. Entrance to the Museum of Communism (original location), Prague, founded 2001 (private museum). http://muzeumkomunismu.cz/.
Wikimedia Commons

EIGHT

The Czech Museum of Communism
What National Narrative for the Past?

MURIEL BLAIVE

In the aftermath of the 1989 Velvet Revolution, a political debate took place in the Czech Republic over the best way to deal with the country's recent history. Issues at stake included the purging of the former elites, the banning of the Communist Party, and the opening of the party and secret police archives. These issues have exposed a fault line within the Czech political sphere and the wider public. More than thirty years later, can an appeased narrative of the communist past unite these deeply divided communities? Is it realistic for a "neutral, authoritative, and trustworthy" vision to find its place in a museum of communism, for instance?[1]

In order to achieve minimal legitimacy, an institutionalized museum should be seen as apolitical. Sociological research shows that a museum is not seen as trustworthy by the public if it is not identified as presenting credible information.[2] People expect an exhibit to be backed by solid research rather than propaganda—by history rather than politics. Shaping a historical vision the public sees as objective takes time. Collected artifacts are not neutral; they tell the story of the people who owned, produced, or used them: "Museums are about people, and collections are merely manifestations of human desires."[3] They are always the outcome of a social "renegotiation of history."[4]

The Czech museal landscape points to the impediments preventing a social and academic renegotiation of communist history. Only one museum covers the communist period—although a project for a new, weirdly- named Museum of the Twentieth Century Memory is now also under way in Prague. The existing Museum of Communism is private and it is located in a touristic area in the center of Prague. Its premises (1500 square meters) are organized into three sections: The Dream, The Reality, and The Nightmare. As its website indicates, it covers politics, history, sports, economics, education, arts, propaganda, the People's

Militia and the Secret Police, censorship, the judiciary, coercive institutions, and labor camps.[5] The museum's most relevant feature, however, is that it is ignored by the Czech public and academic elites: it caters almost exclusively, albeit quite successfully, to tourists and foreign students. Why is this museum's reception so discriminative?

EAST VERSUS WEST: A CULTURAL MISUNDERSTANDING?

In their attitude to the communist past, the former East and the West are not equal. Amy Jane Barnes describes how Westerners appear to be fascinated by the legacy of communism. She writes that a "facet of the European tourist industry caters for an apparently significant tranche of consumers keen to experience communist culture first-hand, often with ironic intent. A company in Berlin offers Trabi-tours of the former eastern sector. Or how about a visit to a Soviet bunker in Lithuania? The fad is not solely restricted to Europe: tourists can hire Jiang Qing's limousine for a tour of Beijing. The deal includes: 'Russian caviar, French champagne and copies of the Little Red Book on the velvet upholstery.'"[6]

Western visitors enjoy this transgression in Prague, too. When it was still in its original premises (it has recently moved), the Museum of Communism obligingly boasted about its location: "The Museum is above McDonald's and open from 9 am to 9 pm (including holidays). V. I. Lenin must be turning in his grave."[7] Although Western tourists smile at the irony of the capitalist West commodifying the communist iconography,[8] many, probably most, Czechs are not amused. Czech media and the wider public have displayed little interest in the creation and launching of this museum. When they did, the McDonald's reference was brushed aside for an issue deemed more relevant: the museum was created by a *foreigner*, moreover, a foreigner who has never experienced communism firsthand, a US businessman named Glenn Spicker.[9]

The German weekly *Der Spiegel* ran a report on the museum's opening at the end of 2001 and made note of the Czech indifference. It also interviewed Glenn Spicker, who claimed to understand and respect the fact that Czechs had such a painful memory of repression that they were not interested in his project. Still, Spicker expressed with his customary sense of humor the hope that people would soon be lining up at his museum's door just as they used to line up for fruits and vegetables under communism.[10] In 2010 he explained that he had conceived the museum as a gift to the Czechs, at a time when he deemed perfectly understandable for people to turn their backs on this painful past and focus their energy on building the future: "I hire Czechs. This is a museum by Czechs for Czechs. Obviously, it's going to be for tourists, but it should be the Czech view."[11] The journalist who interviewed him remarked that there was a certain irony in an American teaching the Czech people about their communist history. It is as if Spicker's US origins principally denied him a narrational legitimacy on Czech history.[12] Spicker did concede that most of his Czech friends did not find it necessary to visit the museum because they had grown up under communism and thought they already knew everything,[13] as did most Czechs. But because he sees himself primarily as a businessman, the rejection did not disturb him. Although, or perhaps because, he has been living in the Czech Republic since 1991, the implicit and explicit reproach for his lack of national authenticity leaves him unmoved.

Spicker claims he had no strong ideological motive in mind when he opened the museum, short of respectfully paying tribute to the victims.[14] David Lowe and Tony Joel note that the museum specifies on its website that it should not serve as a "filter for contemporary political issues in the Czech Republic."[15] Spicker conceived of the museum as only one business venture among others, including jazz outlets and restaurants. The title of an article dedicated to the museum project crystalizes his lack of training in history: "Jazzy Caterer Cooks Up a Museum of Communism."[16] His, he claims, was only a personal interest in collecting communist artifacts ever since the early 1990s, until he had accumulated so many of them he was uncertain how best to use them. "One night, brainstorming with some pals and his girlfriend, they remarked upon the ironic fate of a couple of relics of communism: The ex-Klement Gottwald Museum is now a bank; the ex-V. I. Lenin Museum now houses the U.S. Information Service. Eureka! What Prague needed, they agreed, was its own Museum of Communism."[17] To help him in this new venture, he hired the services of Jan Kaplan, a Czech film director who has been living in the United Kingdom since 1968.[18] Although Kaplan has done more than a fair job with this museum, his living abroad distances him also from the Czech public.

The private ownership of this museum also raises the crucial question of state patronage in Europe. Just like the Jewish Museum in Prague, Spicker's enterprise does not benefit from public funds—and is therefore much more expensive to visit than a public museum. Spicker set the entrance fee at a level that would allow him to get a return on his four-million-crown investment. Originally set at 130 Czech crowns (now 290; about $6 raised to about $12.50 at 2020 exchange rates), the hefty price has greatly contributed to disqualifying the museum for being "non-Czech" on the domestic market. The absence of state subsidies thus creates its own negative stereotype and the bulk of the thirty-five thousand visitors per year are foreigners. Never mind that in the past they included Croatian journalist Slavenka Drakulić, who wrote, in her book on museums of communism across Europe, an amusing chapter on Spicker's outlet as told from a mouse's viewpoint.[19] These financial constraints have doomed the foreign-perceived museum from the start to earning meager public legitimacy.

Spicker studied political science in the United States and the United Kingdom, and so he is not uneducated,[20] but his grasp of history is intuitive rather than academic. Coming from Berlin, where he resided before Prague, he was one of the first individuals in the Czech Republic to sense the potential of nostalgia for communism in business ventures. Another one of his projects was café Propaganda. When he created and registered it in 2010 before filling it with communist artifacts, he learned that another Propaganda business already existed—but the latter purposely remained on an almost amateur level and did not bother to file with the business registry, thus holding no trademark rights to the name.

This original Propaganda bar had been created ten years previously, in 2000. It was very early for any openly nostalgic venture in the Czech Republic, but it was a small, purposely nontrendy joint exclusively oriented to a student clientele. Since Spicker's Propaganda was much bigger, involved live bands, and, in the words of the original student Propaganda's owner, was "meant for foreigners," she was unfazed by its opening and she did not even see it as competition.[21] She was right: although it was reasonably successful, when Spicker came up with a new idea, he closed down Propaganda and opened a fast-food burrito chain in its place. Meanwhile, the original Propaganda is still operating.

WHY IS THE MUSEUM OF COMMUNISM NOT FINDING ITS LOCAL PUBLIC?

Is the museum's intrinsic quality therefore in question? This section argues that such is not the case; the museum is reasonably well crafted and presented. Its failure to achieve public recognition has more to do with the Czech nation's complicated relationship to its communist past than with questionable historical content. Any museum's wider mission is to mediate between the object under study and the audience, as well as to reflect on the "role of the Other in the creation of the Self and national identities."[22] In that instance, the Other is the past communist Czechoslovakia, from which the Self (today's Czech state, presumably democratic) intensely wishes to distance itself. Just as Amy Jane Barnes sees Maoist China's representation in British museums as a study of Great Britain rather than of China, we may approach the Prague Museum of Communism and its reception as telling us more about the contemporary Czech Republic than about Czechoslovak communism. The real issue is the image of communism that contemporary Czechia wishes to deliver to itself and to the world. What are the "palimpsests upon which official social, political and cultural identities of Self and Other are constructed"?[23]

In the Czech Republic, just as in other Central European societies, communism was externalized after 1989 as a noxious ideology alien to the national culture. As I have argued elsewhere, the postcommunist Czech Republic has rebuilt its post-1989 identity on a democratic premise: the alleged "real" Czech culture, purportedly repressed by an illegitimate communist regime, is intrinsically democratic.[24] In post-1989 national historiographical production, the communist past has generally been represented as one that has no place in its legitimate history.[25] This vision largely fails to account for the fact that Czechoslovakia was in a very different situation in 1945 than its Central European neighbors, notably Poland, Hungary, and even what was to become East Germany. It was a genuine victor in World War II and treated as such by the Red Army, that is, with much more leniency than the other occupied countries. After liberating Czechoslovakia, the Red Army left on December 1, 1945.[26]

Czechoslovakia was also a country that leaned politically to the left. It was highly industrialized and boasted a large working class, politically organized by the Social Democratic Party, and after 1921 also by the Communist Party. Because of its particular history (the defeat of the Hussite movement and forced re-Catholicization of the country by Hapsburg Austria after 1620),[27] it was also not very religious. The Czechoslovak Communist Party was not an *ad hoc* political movement born in 1944 out of a clandestine fringe whose life depended on the Soviets, as was the case in Poland, Hungary, and East Germany, but a domestic force of significance. Numerous Czech intellectuals and artists—perhaps the majority—especially the younger generation who came of age in the aftermath of World War II, were communist sympathizers, if not card-carrying members. They were among the party's most vocal and visible proponents.[28] Let us not forget also that Czechoslovaks felt betrayed by the West when France and Great Britain supported Hitler's plan to incorporate the Sudetenland into Germany in 1938. The annexation resulted in the country's dismantlement.[29]

Indeed postwar, precommunist Czechoslovakia was a country that had freshly expelled its German minority, which had counted for no less than a third of the population in the Czech part of the country. The redistribution of the land, housing, and belongings of the departing Germans was orchestrated with fake generosity by the Czechoslovak Communist Party. As it controlled the local administration, it reaped the corresponding benefits in popularity.[30] Moreover, Czechoslovakia had put itself in the Soviet Union's debt: President Edvard Beneš saw it as his personal mission to convince Stalin to support the expulsion of the Sudeten Germans in 1943, perhaps at too high an eventual cost.[31] To be fair, after the Munich debacle, it was clear that only the Soviet Union could guarantee Czechoslovakia's safety in the postwar period, especially against an angry Sudeten German community now resettled across the border in Austria and Germany.

The Czechoslovak Communist Party did not even need to rig the postwar elections: it won 38 percent of the vote in the free elections of 1946 (30 percent in Slovakia, 43 percent in Bohemia), becoming by far the largest party in the country. The communist takeover needed no involvement of the Red Army and took place legally if also through threats after a clumsy political maneuver on the Democrats' part; on the contrary, two hundred thousand demonstrators came to show their support, and the freely elected Parliament almost unanimously voted in favor of the new government (none voted against; ten abstained). President Beneš signed the new government in.[32] By the end of 1948, the Czechoslovak Communist Party counted no fewer than 2.5 million members, twice as many members per capita as in Hungary and four times as many as in Poland. Half the eligible Czech population enrolled.[33]

Although terror and political repression also were used by the Czechoslovak regime in its Stalinist phase, communism doubtlessly retained stronger claims to legitimacy in Czechoslovakia than it had in other communist countries.[34] There was no 1956 in Czechoslovakia because there was no strong popular discontent;[35] the 1968 Prague Spring occurred with the massive support of the population and was interrupted only by the Warsaw Pact invasion. Even during the 1970s era of so-called normalization, the regime still enjoyed a measure of legitimacy grounded in a generous social-welfare policy and socialist pop culture.[36] Dissidents, in particular Václav Havel, were well known in the West but they remained marginal in Czechoslovakia. Charter 77 garnered approximately two thousand signatories from 1977 to 1989, as opposed to ten million members for the Polish trade union Solidarność in 1980, for instance.

It is impossible to understand the Czech Republic's dealing with the past after 1989 if we do not keep this specific history in mind—all the more so because the Czech (not the Slovak) exit strategy from communism took an unexpected shape, one that appeared paradoxical to many. After having been the most "communist" country of the bloc, the Czech Republic turned almost overnight into the most anticommunist country.

COMMUNISM AND ANTICOMMUNISM
ARE CLOSER THAN IT SEEMS

This unexpected twist is, in fact, linked to the legitimacy deficit of the dissident movement during the 1989 Velvet Revolution. The Czechoslovak population was doubtlessly weary of the communist regime in mid-November 1989. It did not want to stand aside after Poland and Hungary had held partially free elections and the Berlin Wall was already down. There was, however, no organized political opposition. The only individuals who could qualify as a credible alternative to the Communist apparatchiks were the dissidents, who were quite marginal in Czechoslovak society. They were neither well known nor very popular—after the

1948 and 1968 fiascos, Prague intellectuals did not enjoy a good reputation among the working class. The only argument on which they could build their political capital was that they were, and had been ever since 1968, critical of the regime: "The zealous protection of their status as 'opposition' during the round-table negotiations guaranteed that the dissidents would enter the new post-communist period as holders of the symbolic power to represent 'society' as its delegates."[37]

The dissidents were legitimately eager to secure communism's demise, as well as to maintain their monopoly over symbolic political capital. They "developed a discursive strategy involving a complete rejection of the Communist past such that anybody associated with it, even as a reformer or as a critic, was immediately suspect."[38] Václav Havel and his peers brandished the anticommunist narrative as the source of a newfound political legitimacy in November–December 1989. This strategy, which was born out of necessity, did not illustrate the fact that there were many anticommunists in the country but, on the contrary, that there were so few of them. No strong reform movement existed even within the Czechoslovak Communist Party. The dissidents (many of whom had been Communist Party members in the past) had to reinvent themselves along this anticommunist line because the party they were attempting to circumvent was still strong. In fact, it not only continued to exist but polled 15 to 20 percent of the vote for another two decades after 1989. The postcommunist Czech state project is in this sense an anticommunist power project of the intellectuals.[39]

How is this development concretely linked to the commemoration of the communist regime after 1989? The Czech dissidents' strategy "reclaimed history and memory as an act of resistance against communist power, which they described as a power to erase and forget."[40] The "injunction to remember" the communist repressive violence becomes, as Milan Kundera put it in his *Book of Laughter and Forgetting*, "the struggle of man against power."[41]

The postdissidents who created an anticommunist identity for themselves and for the country built a strong legislative apparatus: in 1991 and 1992 they adopted the so-called lustration laws,[42] the most radical of such measures in all postcommunist countries. These laws' aim was to prevent former communists from holding any important position in the new administration or in the economy. This radical measure is incidentally one of the main reasons that Slovakia, which knew almost no dissidents and felt no urge to radically break with a communist past that had overseen its industrialization and its growth as a federal republic, decided to break away from the Czech Republic.[43]

Two other pieces of legislation of the immediate postcommunist period are worth consideration: one is the 1990 Act on Judicial Rehabilitations,[44] which ordered the automatic rehabilitation and compensation of approximately two hundred thousand citizens who had been condemned on the basis of certain paragraphs of the communist criminal code.[45] These people, or their descendants, were notified of their rehabilitation by the courts without having to argue their case, which, in the absence of any epistemological reflection about what might have constituted a political offense under communism, leaves a number of questions about their level of anticommunist engagement. To give but one example, black marketeering was considered treason by the communist regime and was punishable by death, but how political was this crime?

The second piece of legislation to take into account is the 1993 Act on the Illegality of the Communist Regime and on the Resistance To It. It named the "Czechoslovak Communist Party, its leadership and its members" as collectively responsible for the system of government that "prevailed in the years 1948–1989, and mainly for the programmatic destruction of the traditional values of European civilization, the conscious tramping of human rights and freedoms, the moral and economic decay brought about by judicial crimes and terror."[46] This law is crucial to this chapter's topic, insofar as it prevented for many years the public expression of any type of nostalgia for the communist past. To say anything about the previous government that was not strictly anticommunist, especially in the frame of any public institution such as schools or a museum, became tantamount to supporting a "criminal regime." The 1993 law criminalized the communist past in a way unprecedented in postcommunist Europe.

The level of polarization within Czech society induced by these political measures slowed down the academic debates over the communist past for years to come. It also defined a level of political correctness stemming from memory's officially ascribed healing role that is still difficult to challenge today, at least in public institutions.[47] Neither historians (who work directly or indirectly for the state, be it through the Academy of Sciences, the Institute for the Study of Totalitarian Regimes, Charles University, or other regional universities) nor legislators have really questioned this interpretation of the communist past as one that is foreign to the country's cultural traditions. On the contrary, the one-dimensional criminalization of the communist past was reinforced in 2000. Articles 303–5 of the Czech criminal code forbade the support of a movement that "promulgates racial, ethnic, religious," or—and that is a Czech addition—"class hate." In addition, "A person who publicly denies, casts doubt on, advocates or attempts to justify the Nazi, Communist or other genocide or other crimes against humanity committed by the Nazis and Communists is liable to imprisonment for a term of six months to three years."[48]

Moreover, any commemoration of the past is redefined as a necessarily emotional reminder of the suffering caused by the communist regime. There again, the politically correct display of emotion involved in any mention of the communist past goes against a museum's mission. As mentioned above, a museum is supposed to be apolitical, impartial, and value neutral, in other words non-judgmental, a state that can be achieved only through emotional distance.[49] This ideal is clearly not attainable yet as the Czech Republic is still dominated by partisan debate concerning the communist past.

COMMUNISM: THE ANTICOMMUNISTS' BEST ENEMY

In this context, we need to identify communism not as the Other but as the Other Within (Pearce) in Czech society. Barnes sees the Other Within as corresponding to the Orientalist Other in Saidian discourse: it is a "counterpoint to European rationality and/or a subversive commentary upon 'normal' culture."[50] If so, we understand why any collection of objects pertaining to this Other Within will be deemed "improper, transgressive and irrational":[51] it represents everything that Czech state institutions wish to reject. In order to account for the Czech domestic participation in the advent of communism, the official narrative has to be one of victimization—only terror and the Soviet involvement can explain why a previously democratic society would surrender to a totalitarian regime.

Methodologically speaking, this means that any historical approach adopting the "totalitarian narrative" has to be top-down and political, exclusively focused on power, repression, and violence, as well as on palpable events: the 1948 communist takeover, the 1968 Warsaw Pact invasion, the 1989 Velvet Revolution. The reassuring structure of these "events" is specific to this type of memory; by "overcoming trauma," it is "meant to cure society and protect it from itself, from its tendency to repeat abnormal and dangerous patterns of behavior."[52] A bottom-up approach in terms of everyday life, on the other hand, is anathema.

The conventional, totalitarian approach also gives priority and precedence to direct witnesses: only people who have actually been there in person and seen what was to be seen with their own eyes, it is widely believed, including by Czech historians, can know the "historical truth" about communism. Such a stance takes little account of postwar methodological innovations. Starting from the 1950s, Western historiography developed sophisticated methodologies to deal with live witnesses. At least since Hannah Arendt questioned the wisdom of refocusing the Eichmann trial in Jerusalem (1961) on the witnesses and specifically on the victims' tale of suffering rather than on Eichmann himself and his crimes,[53] Holocaust studies have reflected on their interaction with memory studies and approached the witness and witness testimony with great caution. So too their traumas, their words, and their silences, their embodiment and their affects, as well as the "complex relationship between enunciation, listening and truth."[54] Marianne Hirsch and Leo Spitzer warn for instance, on the basis of Holocaust memory, that a "hyperbolic emphasis on trauma and the breakdown of speech has risked occluding the wealth of knowledge and information transmitted by thousands of witnesses who have been eager to testify to the victimization and persecution they have suffered." Indeed, one of the possible uses of witness testimony is "linked to a troubling idiom of uniqueness and exceptionalism, potentially supporting nationalist and identity politics."[55]

Moreover, we know that memory is unreliable in that it is perpetually recreated: every time we tell a tale, we reinvent the story to fit our new present.[56] We remember the last time we remembered an event rather than the event itself. Far from working like a video camera, our memory "rewrites the past with current information, updating recollections with new experiences."[57] To entrust witnesses with establishing the historical truth is thus a perilous endeavor.

These caveats were rarely taken into account by mainstream historiography when dealing with communist memory in the Czech case, as in most other postcommunist countries. A simplistic narrative of communist history opposing the good people to the bad communists and secret police collaborators largely succeeded in quashing methodological innovations even in the academic sphere, from 1989 until the museum of communism's opening in 2001, and partly even into the 2010s. Although Czech nationalism and medieval studies are internationally acclaimed, contemporary history has long remained at the level of nineteenth-century positivism: the document still often serves as historical proof without adequate contextualization. Social, everyday, and oral history have long remained marginal, for they are suspected of a leftist view that would minimize the extent of the communist terror.[58] One of the main goals of the anticommunist memory politics, which was little challenged by academic history, has been to settle accounts with the past: as Gil Eyal shows, restitution, persecution, and screening exerted a symbolic influence on society. The message drawing a sharp line between past and present and "sacrificing a 'scapegoat' for society's sins," helped the postcommunist present to settle and a majority of citizens to "put the past behind them."[59]

THE PROBLEMATIC WESTERN COMMODIFICATION OF COMMUNIST-ERA ARTIFACTS

In this context the Western "communist kitsch" approach is tantamount to insulting the nation. The Museum of Communism failed to experience contemporary success at the time of its appearance in 2001 because, on the surface, it is quintessentially Western in its amused commodification of communist era artifacts. To all appearances, it empties the iconography of communism of its original meaning to replace it with Western consumerism; what is even more unforgivable, it gives its presentation a perceived "veneer of cool."[60] Communism is for Western

Figure 8.2. Socialist heroes and socialist realism. *Photograph by Muriel Blaive*

Figure 8.3. Work and consumption. *Photograph by Muriel Blaive*

visitors just frightening enough that "owning, displaying and wearing objects which pertain to communism are not exactly taboo," but "just dangerously rebellious enough to produce an enjoyable emotional frisson."[61]

Spicker's museum is, however, not only "cool" but simultaneously a retro museum of the communist times. It is not informed by the anticommunist political statement considered obligatory at the time of its opening for any endeavor dealing

Figure 8.4. Punishment and persecution. *Photograph by Muriel Blaive*

Figure 8.5. Leisure. *Photograph by Muriel Blaive*

with the communist past. It is object-centered rather than victim-centered. Insofar as museums significantly contribute to creating personal and shared identities,[62] it offers an identity that the Czech state has not wished to embrace (yet), a history that the country does not feel proud of.[63] It is, in fact, a museum that was ahead of its times; in particular, it has been a pioneer in its intuitive introduction of everyday life under communism, which it calls "daily life."

Figure 8.6. Talking about the past. *Photograph by Muriel Blaive*

Exhibits of everyday life under communism are highly successful in other capital cities; for instance, in Berlin at the museum of the Kulturbrauerei dedicated to life in the German Democratic Republic (Deutsche Demokratische Republik; DDR),[64] at the DDR Museum[65] or even at the Palace of Tears at the former border crossing of Friedrichstrasse,[66] because they convincingly recreate and embody the former East German nation, be it in a pleasantly nostalgic atmosphere or as a tragic reminiscence.[67] In the Czech Republic, the history of everyday life was long branded as revisionist by historians and is seen as an insult to the victims by the public.

THE BELATED BIRTH OF THE RETRO MOVEMENT

Alternatively, filmmakers, writers, and journalists (as well as nonhistorian social scientists (anthropologists, sociologists), architects, designers, and artists) do not feel bound by the anticommunist state narrative. They had already started to question the political status quo by the end of the 1990s. Although the historical milieu was getting increasingly conservative in the 2000s in proportion to the political power derived from the control of the state narrative, art and design students have recreated the world of everyday life under communism on several occasions.

One exhibit took place in 2007 and was entitled *The Husák 3+1: Housing Culture in the 1970s*. Created by Lada Hubatová-Vacková's students in Design and New Media History and Theory, it exhibited from October 3 to 22, 2007, a "typical" socialist flat of the 1970s. Czech Press Agency ČTK reported favorably on the exhibit.[68] Another temporary exhibit explicitly entitled "Everyday Life under Communism" opened at the Dancing House in Prague in 2016—an exhibit aiming at a touristic public with a whopping entrance price, that also achieved little success with the wider public.[69] Nevertheless, it contributed to reversing an anti–everyday life definition of political correctness about the communist past, a new trend that will doubtlessly strengthen in the coming years. Its curator, Nikola Lörinczová, a young Czech filmmaker who has a passion for retro artifacts, in an interview even pronounced the forbidden word *nostalgia*: "There is no doubt that the exhibition will be most interesting for older people and people who experienced this period and who will doubtlessly experience strong feelings of nostalgia over things that were once part of their life. On the other hand, young people should get something out of it as well because it will give them some insight into how people lived, how things worked and the environment that surrounded us."[70]

If nostalgia was and remained taboo, a serious retro movement appeared by the end of the 2000s and is now finally giving way to a similar fad for communist-era brands that the Czech Republic's neighbors have long experienced.[71] Not always convinced by the virtues of a postcommunist democracy that proved remarkably corrupt during the past three decades, the Czech population has been increasingly indulging in this new vision of the communist past that is now, at least in pop culture, not altogether negative.

In contrast with academic historians, Czech journalists have also proven receptive to innovative renditions of the communist past. Already in 2009, a prestigious exhibit at the Victoria and Albert Museum in London, *Cold War Modern*,[72] put on display a number of artists from the 1950s and 1960s Czechoslovak regime, notably a famous propaganda poster *Build the Nation, You Shall Strengthen Peace* (Buduj vlast, posílíš mír) from artist Vojtěch Němeček. Far from being offended at Czechoslovakia being remembered in the West today for its communist propaganda prowess, Czech Press Agency (ČTK) held and widely reproduced throughout the media an interview with cocurator David Crowley. The tone of the questions and of the article suggests that the journalists might have actually been flattered at Czechoslovakia taking its place in today's Cold War history: "The Cold War was fought not only in politics and through military exercises, but also on the battlefield of consumer manufacture and design. This is the premise of an exhibit at the Victoria and Albert Museum in London that presents to the public 300 artifacts from the years 1945 to 1970. Many of them come from the former Czechoslovakia."[73]

The curators' intent was not criticized but, on the contrary, fully endorsed: "The exhibit contrasts the outspoken propaganda with the pure lines of the objects serving for daily consumption, as well as with the artistic works documenting those times. That is how the Vojtěch Němeček poster *Build the Nation, You Shall Strengthen Peace* found its way into the famous London museum, as well as first-rate glass works from Stanislav Libenský, collages from Jiří Kolář and a model of the transmission tower and hotel Ještěd, which, according to the curators, belongs to the underrated treasures of Czechoslovak architecture."[74] David Crowley's pragmatic, depoliticized approach, was well received: "'We tried to show how objects were used as a propaganda tool of socialist modernity. But we simultaneously wanted to underline that in the East there were many talented people and we wanted to refute the common misperception of grayness and shortages attached to the communist countries,' said curator Crowley."[75]

A NEW PARADIGM?

Can we contemplate the possibility that a form of national pride, taken away by forced enlistment in fighting the Cold War on behalf of its losers, has been awaiting restoration in Central Europe? Could it be that a new Cold War memory is being born, one that will unify the former east and the former west in a common, proxy Cold War memory? Is this new Cold War memory progressively replacing the memory of the communist times?

Amy Jane Barnes proposes an analysis of the post-1989 development that aptly describes Glenn Spicker's enterprise: while postcommunist countries were turning their backs on their communist history, Western collectors saw the potential of the discarded communist artifacts. "The emasculation of the symbolic power in this appropriation, assimilation and recycling of communist aesthetics for the creation of new icons of ironic consumerism seems to reaffirm our perceived political and cultural superiority," she writes.[76] If so, the Czech reaction to Cold War Modern might indeed document an underlying social desire to establish a memory of communism on a par with the Western Cold War memory.

This potential upcoming victory of the Western memory of the Cold War (rather than the Eastern memory of communism) is not entirely spontaneous or organic. Another icon of the Western Cold War, James Bond, was imported into the Czech Republic in a perhaps unexpected form: a commercial for Coke Zero, "Unlock the 007 in You," that was released in 2012 jointly with the James Bond film *Skyfall*.[77] As argued elsewhere,[78] this commercial, which starts at café Slavia where Václav Havel and his dissident friends famously met, can be read as an endeavor to reunite the James Bond pomp (Western memory of the Cold War) with Havel's "power of the powerless" phrase (Eastern memory of the communist period). "Unlock the 007 in You" downplays James Bond to an amusing, everyday life, level: the quaint anti-hero tries to snatch the villain's girlfriend to share a Coke Zero with her. His limited material means (notably, in the funniest scene, a moped in place of the famed Aston Martin) seem to underline Havel's message that everyone can rise against the regime by just speaking the truth at one's own modest level—everyone can "unlock their inner James Bond" and become a hero.

Yet this proxy Cold War memory did not originate from the former Eastern Europe: on the contrary, just as the Cold War concept itself it was a Western invention. The commercial indeed originated in a Europe-wide campaign directed by Publicis. The Parisian Publicis agency won the contest, specifically French copywriter Antonin Jacquot. His motivations in writing the script of "Unlock the 007 in You" had nothing to do with reuniting the Western and the Eastern memories of the Cold War. The spot was shot in Prague rather than Paris because it was cheaper; it was shot at café Slavia because the author searched for a quintessential European-looking building that a Europe-wide public could identify with; the downplay of the James Bond pomp was part of the Publicis commission and reflects the new James Bond orientation of the past few films. In recent years, the Western hero has become increasingly modest, turning his back on the ever-increasing gadget sophistication of the previous decades—the aim is for younger generations, who are not familiar with the 1970s James Bond films, to identify more easily with the hero.[79]

What are we to make of this unwitting merging of Eastern and Western memories of the Cold War or communist period? We might be witnessing the birth of a new form of cultural colonialism. As Amy Jane Barnes underlines it, "The act of possessing, manipulating and assimilating the visual culture of a 'defeated' or passed ideology would seem to operate on much the same psychological level as the theft and destruction of culturally significant objects from palaces and museums as an act of conquest." These "trophies of war" become "symbolic of the defeated regime."[80] Barnes's analysis does explain the positive reaction to the exhibit *Cold War Modern* in the Czech Republic as a way to acquire, manipulate, and subvert the original artifacts so as to reinvest them with a new meaning and gain control over them.[81] In Pierre Bourdieu's terms, we might be spectators to a transfer of symbolic capital, that is, "the prestige, legitimacy and influence" held by an authoritative individual or institution.[82]

CONCLUSION: POLITICS AND KITSCH, POLITICS OF KITSCH

For the tenth anniversary of the Museum of Communism in 2012, Czech Public Radio organized a visit by the leader of the Communist Youth, Zdeněk Milata, together with Glenn Spicker and the museum's (Czech) co-owner, Jana Čepičková.[83] The journalist neutrally described the museum's purpose as being to "explain to tourists what communism was about." But when this improbable delegation entered the reconstructed secret police interrogation room, the communist representative started to shout: "And where is the list of all the victims killed by foreign agents or of border guards who died while accomplishing their duty?" while pulling it out of his bag. The thirty-year old museum co-owner Jana Čepičková answered, "I will give you the list of people executed [by the Communists] and it will certainly be longer."

The journalist then describes how the Communist Party representative was offended at the reconstructed grocery store, which was mostly empty so as to illustrate the shortage of goods under communism. And he concluded the article by recounting that Glenn Spicker was excitedly awaiting the end of communism in Cuba to open a Museum of Communism there—before Milata interrupted him with a rant, claiming that the US regime might well fall before the Cuban one, as the healthcare is free there and the regime solider than was previously assumed.

The dialogue leaves little doubt about the controversial character of any representation of communist history in the Czech public space. If we are to believe Sheila Watson, the educated and affluent part of a museum audience always privileges a sense of "impersonal heritage," whereas the wider public prefers a narrative presented in terms of "personal past," that is, "a sense of the past that is experienced in personal terms, of which the best example are personal memories and family histories."[84] She quotes Bourdieu as suggesting that learning leads to an aesthetic distancing, a disposition that rejects personal involvement. Conversely, a working-class popular aesthetic encourages participation and excitement.[85]

In this particular Czech constellation, neither has been possible. Because communist history has been politicized, no aesthetic distancing has been possible on the part of the political and academic elites: the communist past means more than ever personal involvement, to be used and abused in current politics. And because the narrative on the communist past has been confiscated by the anticommunist state discourse, the "working class" can also hardly express its memory of, let alone nostalgia for, communism. Participation and excitement are still subversive.

There is yet no symbolic space available in Czech culture to allow for a museal representation of communism that would hope to achieve minimal national recognition. The vision of communism in the Czech Republic is rooted in an essentialist myth centered on the alienation of communism from the dominant culture. The urgency in creating an anticommunist national identity that the country could be proud of took precedence over a more genuine, grassroots, popular rendering of the past—now increasingly known as the retro attitude. In other words, the right-wing, conservative, top-down narrative of the communist past still has the upper hand, while Glenn Spicker's approach is informed by a left-wing, bottom up, intuitive grasping of the communist past—while simultaneously hiding behind a superficial, Western, commodification of it. Spicker's endeavor serves to reveal the conflicting characteristics of the current Czech state and societal attitudes in dealing with the communist past, torn as they are between a duty of memory, a moral injunction to condemn the past regime, a distaste for commodification, a temptation to westernize its memory of the communist past, and a nostalgia that is finding new channels to express itself.

NOTES

This article is published as part of the research project Rulers and Ruled in Poland and Czechoslovakia (1945–1968): Practical and Methodological Challenges in the Historicization of Complex Relationship" supported by the Grant Academy of the Czech Republic number 16–26104S. Many thanks to Shawn Clybor for his critical remarks on the text.

1. Simon Knell, *National Galleries: The Art of Making Nations* (London: Routledge, 2016), 4, cited by Amy Jane Barnes, *Museum Representations of Maoist China: From Cultural Revolution to Commie Kitsch* (Farnham, UK: Ashgate, 2014), 1.

2. Fiona Cameron, "Moral Lessons and Reforming Agendas: History Museums, Science Museums, Contentious Topics and Contemporary Societies," in *Museum Revolutions: How Museums Change and Are Changed*, ed. Simon J. Knell, Suzanne McLeod, and Sheila Watson (London: Routledge, 2007), 331.

3. Simon J. Knell, Suzanne McLeod, and Sheila Watson, Introduction to Knell et al., *Museum Revolutions*, xix.

4. Ibid., xxii.

5. See Muzeum komunismu (website), accessed September 3, 2018, http://muzeumkomunismu.cz/about/.

6. Barnes, *Museum Representations*, 171.

7. See its presentation on the museum's website, http://muzeumkomunismu.cz/about/. The presentation reminds one of the image of Lenin's statue being taken away by helicopter in reunified Berlin, as shown in the film *Goodbye, Lenin!*, with Lenin's arm grotesquely raised in an empty threat and pointing at what is now the void. This was yet again a depiction of formerly communist Europe that was in fact the work of a Western European German filmmaker, Wolfgang Becker. See the scene on YouTube in the film's trailer, accessed December 28, 2016, https://www.youtube.com/watch?v=u5hzmwGW4Ac.

8. Barnes, *Museum Representations*, 171.

9. See, for instance, the webpage of a famous television show, *Krásné ztráty* (Beautiful losses), that featured a Glenn Spicker interview in 2011, accessed January 10, 2017, http://www.ceskatelevize.cz/porady/1096002521-krasny-ztraty/211562250500021/. See also Miroslav Krupička, "Glenn Spicker: The American Who Brought Bagels to the Czech Republic," *Český rozhlas*, January 15, 2015, http://www.radio.cz/en/section/panorama/glenn-spicker-the-american-who-brought-bagels-to-the-czech-republic.

10. "Ostalgie auf Tschechisch," *Der Spiegel*, December 29, 2001, http://www.spiegel.de/reise/staedte/museen-ostalgie-auf-tschechisch-a-174808.html.

11. Anna Storm, "An Interview with Glenn Spicker, Owner of the New High-End Mexican Restaurant Agave," *Prague TV*, April 6, 2015, http://prague.tv/en/s72/Directory/c203-Dining/n2473-An-Interview-with-Glenn-Spicker-owner-of-the-new-high-end-Mexican-restaurant.

12. A Czech (and more generally central European) form of "castle mentality" (Shawn Clybor) has been noticed and analyzed by numerous scholars. See, for instance, Andrea Orzoff, *Battle for the Castle: The Myth of Czechoslovakia in Europe, 1914–1948* (Oxford: Oxford University Press, 2009); Derek Sayer, *The Coasts of Bohemia: A Czech History* (Princeton, NJ: Princeton University Press, 1998); Jeremy King, *Budweisers into Czechs and Germans: A Local History of Bohemian Politics 1948–1948* (Princeton, NJ: Princeton University Press, 2002); Mary Heimann, *Czechoslovakia: The State That Failed* (New Haven, CT: Yale University Press, 2009).

13. Suchi Rudra, "Interview: Glenn Spicker," *Expats.cz*, March 4, 2010. http://www.expats.cz/prague/article/interviews/glenn-spicker-interview/.

14. "In a grim reconstruction of an StB [secret police] interrogation cell, the blunt statistics of the communist era are recorded: 178 executions, 257,000 prison sentences for political offences, 200,000 paid police spies and 500,000 party members expelled during the purges that followed the Soviet-led crushing of the Prague Spring in 1968" (Nick Holdsworth, "Prague Recalls Dark Days of Communism," *Telegraph*, January 12, 2002, http://www.telegraph.co.uk/travel/723100/Prague-recalls-dark-days-of-communism.html). These statistics are in fact slightly exaggerated, but they do document the museum's desire not to belittle Czech suffering under communism.

15. David Lowe and Tony Joel, *Remembering the Cold War: Global Contest and National Stories* (New York: Routledge, 2013), 86.

16. Alan Levy, "Bagels and Marx with Little Glen," *Prague Post*, November 21, 2001, http://www.praguepost.cz/archivescontent/34265-bagels-and-marx-with-little-glenn.html.

17. Ibid.

18. See, for instance, Jan Kaplan and Krystyna Kosarzewska, *Prague: The Turbulent Century* (Cologne, Ger.: Könemann, 1997).

19. Slavenka Drakulić, *A Guided Tour through the Museum of Communism: Fables from a Mouse, a Parrot, a Bear, a Cat, a Mole, a Pig, a Dog, and a Raven* (New York: Penguin, 2011).

20. See the Wikipedia entry for the museum, accessed January 14, 2017, https://en.wikipedia.org/wiki/Museum_of_Communism,_Czech_Republic.

21. Zuzana Drtilová, "Propaganda na každém pražském rohu: Kavárny se hádají o název" [Propaganda at every corner of Prague: cafés are battling for a name], *iDnes.cz*, August 10, 2010, http://praha.idnes.cz/propaganda-na-kazdem-prazskem-rohu-kavarny-se-hadaji-o-nazev-plm-/praha-zpravy.aspx?c=A100810_1430791_praha-zpravy_ab.

22. Barnes, *Museum Representations*, 2. For a discussion on the importance of the Other in defining the Self, see Timothy Ingold, *Key Debates in Anthropology* (London: Routledge, 1996), 239, quoted by Barnes, *Museum Representations*, 8.

23. Amy Jane Barnes, "Displaying the Communist Other: Perspectives on the Exhibition and Interpretation of Communist Visual Culture," in *The Thing about Museums: Objects and Experience, Representation and Contestation*, ed. Sandra Dudley, Amy Jane Barnes, Jennifer Binnie, Julia Petrov, and Jennifer Walklate (London: Routledge, 2012), 316.

24. Muriel Blaive, "National Narratives of Czech Identity from the Nineteenth Century to the Present," in *Geschichtsbuch Mitteleuropa: Vom Fin de Siècle bis zur Gegenwart*, ed. Anton Pelinka, Karin Bischof, Walter Fend, Karin Stögner, and Thomas Köhler (Vienna: New Academic Press, 2016), 161–89.

25. This phenomenon was analyzed by Pavel Kolář and Michal Kopeček, "A Difficult Quest for New Paradigms: Czech Historiography after 1989," in *Narratives Unbound: Historical Studies in Post-communist Eastern Europe*, ed. Sorin Antohi, Balázs Trencsényi, and Péter Apor (Budapest: CEU, 2007), 173–248. See also Pavel Kolář and Michal Pullmann, *Co byla normalizace? Studie o pozdním socialismu* [What was normalization? Studies on late socialism] (Prague: Lidové noviny/ÚSTR, 2017).

26. See Muriel Blaive, *Une déstalinisation manquée: Tchécoslovaquie 1956* (Brussels: Complexe, 2005), 157–75.

27. See Nancy Wingfield, *Flag Wars and Stone Stains: How the Bohemian Lands Became Czech* (Cambridge, MA: Harvard University Press, 2007).

28. See Shawn Clybor, "Laughter and Hatred Are Neighbors: Adolf Hoffmeister and E. F. Burian in Stalinist Czechoslovakia, 1948–1956," *East European Politics and Societies* 26, no. 3 (2012): 589–615.

29. See Martin Brown, *Dealing with Democrats: The British Foreign Office and the Czechoslovak Émigrés in Great Britain, 1939 to 1945* (Frankfurt: Peter Lang, 2006).

30. Muriel Blaive, *Une déstalinisation manquée*, 141–46.

31. Vojtěch Mastný, *Russia's Road to the Cold War: Diplomacy, Warfare, and the Politics of Communism, 1941–1945* (New York: Columbia University Press, 1979).

32. Muriel Blaive, *Une déstalinisation manquée*, 149–56.

33. Ibid.

34. Several high-profile figures whom we associate with victims of the regime in the Stalinist era (Karel Teige or Adolf Hoffmeister, for instance) were clamoring at the time to be involved in the new regime, not to dismantle or escape it. See Shawn Clybor, "Socialist (Sur)Realism: Karel Teige, Ladislav Štoll and the Politics of Communist Culture in Czechoslovakia," in *History of Communism in Europe*, vol. 2, *Avatars of Intellectuals under Communism*, ed. Dalia Báthory (Bucharest, Rom.: Institute for the Investigation of Communist Crimes, 2011), 143–67.

35. Muriel Blaive, 'Perceptions of Society in Czechoslovak Secret Police Archives: How a 'Czechoslovak 1956' Was Thwarted," in *Perceptions of Society in Communist Europe: Regimes Archives and Popular Opinion*, ed. Muriel Blaive (London: Bloomsbury, 2018), 101–22. For an excellent sociology of the Czechoslovak Communist Party, see

Michel Christian, *Camarades ou apparatchiks? Les communistes en RDA et en Tchécoslovaquie, 1945–1989* (Paris, PUF, 2016).

36. Paulina Bren, *The Greengrocer and His TV: The Culture of Communism after the 1968 Prague Spring* (Ithaca, NY: Cornell University Press, 2010).

37. Gil Eyal, "The Making and Breaking of the Czechoslovak Political Field," in *Pierre Bourdieu and Democratic Politics*, ed. Loïc Wacquant (Cambridge, UK: Polity Press, 2005), 160.

38. Ibid., 159.

39. Gil Eyal, Ivan Szelényi, and Eleanor Townsley, *Making Capitalism without Capitalists: Class Formation and Elite Struggle in Post-communist Central Europe* (London: Verso, 1998), 160.

40. Gil Eyal, "Identity and Trauma: Two Forms of the Will to Memory," *History and Memory* 16, no. 1 (April 2004): 19–20.

41. Ibid., 20.

42. Act No. 451/1991, Establishing Additional Conditions for the Execution of Some Functions in State Bodies and Organizations of the Czech and Slovak Federal Republic, Czech Republic and Slovak Republic (so-called big lustration law), October 4, 1991, http://www.proyectos.cchs.csic.es/transitionaljustice/sites/default/files/maps/info/lustration-mechanisms/czech_lustration_law_1991.pdf, and Act No. 279/1992, on Some Additional Prerequisites for the Execution of Some Functions Occupied by Appointed or Nominated Servicemen of the Police of the Czech Republic and the Prison Service of the Czech Republic (so-called small lustration law), April 28, 1992, http://www.proyectos.cchs.csic.es/transitionaljustice/sites/default/files/maps/info/lustration-mechanisms/czech_republic_279_1992.pdf.

43. See Gil Eyal, *The Origins of Postcommunist Elites: From Prague Spring to the Breakup of Czechoslovakia* (Minneapolis: University of Minnesota Press, 2003). See also Gil Eyal, "Identity and Trauma," 5–36, in which he analyzes the specific forms of memory of communism that dominated the Czech Republic on one side and Slovakia on the other: maintaining identity by embedding intellectuals in the nation for the former, in order to heal through truth and overcome trauma, positioning intellectuals as transcendent pastors of civil society for the latter.

44. Act 119/1990, on Judicial Rehabilitations, April 23, 1990, http://www.proyectos.cchs.csic.es/transitionaljustice/sites/default/files/maps/info/personal-rehabilitation/czech_judicial_rehabilitation_1990.pdf.

45. Because the rehabilitations were issued by each individual court that condemned specific individuals, no single composite figure has been officially computed yet. The indeterminacy has led to much speculation about how many people might have been rehabilitated; the more anticommunist the source, the higher the figure. The numbers vary from two hundred thousand to two hundred sixty thousand, the former being much more credible.

46. See full text here: Act 198/1993, July 9, 1993, http://www.proyectos.cchs.csic.es/transitionaljustice/sites/default/files/maps/info/other-legislation/czech-republic-/czech_rep_illegality_communist_regime_1993.pdf.

47. Eyal, "Identity and Trauma," 37.
48. Czech Penal Code, accessed January 10, 2017, http://www.en.nkp.cz/services/penal-code. See also Laure Neumayer, "Integrating the Central European Past into a Common Narrative: The Mobilizations around the 'Crimes of Communism' in the European Parliament," *Journal of Contemporary European Studies* 23, no. 3 (2015): 344–63.
49. Cameron, "Moral Lessons," 332.
50. Barnes, "Displaying the Communist Other," 316–17.
51. Susan Pearce, *On Collecting: An Investigation into Collecting in the European Tradition* (London: Routledge, 2013), cited by Barnes, "Displaying the Communist Other," 317.
52. Eyal, "Identity and Trauma," 10–12.
53. Marianne Hirsch and Leo Spitzer, "The Witness in the Archive: Holocaust Studies/Memory Studies," *Memory Studies* 2, no. 2 (2009): 152.
54. Ibid.
55. Ibid.
56. Heather Saul, "Your Memory Rewrites the Past and Edits It with New Experiences, Study Finds," *Independent*, February 5, 2014, http://www.independent.co.uk/news/science/your-memory-rewrites-the-past-and-edits-it-with-new-experiences-study-finds-9109559.html. For the original study, see Donna J. Bridge and Joel L. Voss, "Hippocampal Binding of Novel Information with Dominant Memory Traces Can Support Both Memory Stability and Change," *Journal of Neuroscience* 34, no. 6 (February 5, 2014): 2203–13.
57. Saul, "Your Memory Rewrites."
58. As notable exceptions, we can cite the work of Michal Pullmann and his colleagues at the Institute for Economic and Social History (ÚHSD) at Charles University in Prague. (A few of Pullamnn's students are now working at the Institute for the Study of Totalitarian Regimes, which should contribute to modifying the latter's hitherto conservative approach in the coming years.) We could also mention Miroslav Vaněk (since 2017 director of the Institute of Contemporary History), Adéla Gjuričová, Petr Roubal, Martin Franc, and Michal Kopeček, also at the Institute of Contemporary History of the Academy of Sciences.
59. Eyal, "Identity and Trauma," 24. This situation has been improving in recent years.
60. Barnes, *Museum Representations*, 178.
61. Barnes, "Displaying the Communist Other," 317.
62. Watson, "History Museums, Community Identities and a Sense of Place," in Knell et al., *Museum Revolutions*, 160.
63. See, on the contrary, the example of the fishing industry in Yarmouth, England, and the *ad hoc* creation of a new local identity as an example of a successful renegotiation of history in Watson, "History Museums," 169–70.
64. See its website, accessed January 10, 2017: http://www.hdg.de/museum-in-der-kulturbrauerei/.

65. See the DDR Museum website, accessed January 10, 2017: http://www.ddr-museum.de/en.

66. See its website, accessed January 10, 2017: http://www.museumsportal-berlin.de/en/museums/tranenpalast/.

67. For a reflection on the intimate relationship between museums and the nation, see Knell, *National Galleries*.

68. "Husákovo 3+1: Podívejte se, jak jsme žili za socialismu" [Husák 3+1: Look how we lived under socialism], *iDNES* magazine, October 10, 2007, http://bydleni.idnes.cz/husakovo-3-1-podivejte-se-jak-jsme-zili-za-socialismu-fhr-/dum_osobnosti.aspx?c=A071009_160805_dum_stavime_web.

69. Sydney Spier, "Exhibition: Retro 70s and 80s at the Dancing House Gallery," *Prague.tv*, June 23, 2016, http://prague.tv/en/s72/Directory/c206-Art-and-Culture/n6264-Exhibition-Retro-70s-and-80s-at-the-Dancing-House-Gallery.

70. Daniela Lazarová, "Retro Exhibition Highlights Communist-Era Lifestyle," *Radio Praha*, June 16, 2016, http://www.radio.cz/en/section/panorama/retro-exhibition-highlights-communist-era-lifestyle.

71. See Veronika Pehe, *Velvet Retro. Postsocialist Nostalgia and the Politics of Heroism in Czech Popular Culture* (New York: Berghahn, 2020).

72. Jane Pavitt and David Crowley, eds., *Cold War Modern: Design 1945–1970* (London: V and A, 2008).

73. ČTK (Czech press agency), "Londýnská výstava odhaluje roli designu za studené války" (A London exhibit examines the role of design under the Cold War), *Týden.cz*, September 28, 2008, http://www.tyden.cz/rubriky/kultura/umeni/londynska-vystava-odhaluje-roli-designu-za-studene-valky_82641.html.

74. Ibid.

75. Ibid.

76. Barnes, *Museum Representations*, 171–72.

77. See "Unlock the 007 in You—New Coke Zero Commercial," YouTube, accessed April 8, 2020, https://www.youtube.com/watch?v=gUIFL8iVQRE.

78. Muriel Blaive, "'The Cold War? I Have It at Home with My Family': Memories of the 1948–1989 Period beyond the Iron Curtain," in *The Cold War: Historiography, Memory, Representation*, ed. Konrad Jarausch, Christian Ostermann, and Andreas Etges (Munich: de Gruyter, 2017), 201–23.

79. Telephone interview of Antonin Jacquot led by Muriel Blaive on October 20, 2016. With many thanks to Rémi Diligent (Havas Czech Republic).

80. Barnes, *Museum Representations*, 172.

81. Ibid., 173.

82. Benjamin Forest and Juliet Johnson, "Unraveling the Threads of History: Soviet-Era Monuments and Post-Soviet National Identity," *Annals of the Association of American Geographers*, 92, no. 3 (2002): 525.

83. Ľubomír Smatana, "Muzeum komunismu? Jenom byznys, tvrdí šéf Mladých komunistů" [The museum of communism? It's only a business venture, claims the head of the Young Communists], *Český rozhlas*, November 16, 2012, http://www

.rozhlas.cz/zpravy/historie/_zprava/muzeum-komunismu-jenom-byznys-tvrdi-sef-mladych-komunistu--1137637.
84. Watson, "History Museums," 161–62.
85. Ibid.

MURIEL BLAIVE is currently Researcher at the Institute for the Study of Totalitarian Regimes in Prague after being adviser to the Director for Research and Methodology at the same institute from 2014 to 2018. In 2018–2019 she was EURIAS Senior Fellow at the Institute for Human Sciences (IWM) in Vienna. She is a sociopolitical historian of postwar, communist, and postcommunist central Europe, in particular of Czechoslovakia and the Czech Republic. Her most recent publications include the volume that she edited, *Perceptions of Society in Communist Europe: Regime Archives and Popular Opinion* (2018).

Figure 9.1. DDR Museum, Berlin, founded 2006 (private museum). http://www.ddr-museum.de/de. *Wikimedia Commons*

NINE

Stasiland or Spreewald Pickles?
The Battle over the GDR in Berlin's DDR Museum

STEPHEN M. NORRIS

On the occasion of the sixtieth anniversary of the end of World War II, the highly influential magazine *Der Spiegel* put out a special edition entitled "The Germans: Sixty Years after the War." The editors attempted to take stock of the "burdens of the past," which, as they noted, had not gone away after 1989 and the subsequent reunification. Instead, the burdens had just become clearer. Among the numerous articles devoted to that most German of activities, captured best by the fact that the language has a word for "coming to terms with the past," *Vergangenheitsbewältigung*, were editorials by Michael Jürgs and Angela Elis on the subject of "Ossies and Wessies." In his self-described diatribe, Jürgs, a former editor of the equally influential *Stern*, despaired that former East Germans, or Ossies, had ruined reunification, drunk as they were on a special form of nostalgia (ostalgie) for a former dictatorship. In his understanding, Ossies were ungrateful for the freedom Wessies had given them. Opinion polls that revealed how former citizens of the German Democratic Republic (GDR) were disenchanted and depressed told Jürgs that Ossies "enjoy the role of victim so much" that they do not want to give it up.[1] In her riposte, Elis suggested it was Wessies such as Jürgs who enjoyed playing the victim. Rather than being frightened of newfound freedom, Elis wrote, Ossies had actually fought for it in 1989 and had not been given it from birth as Wessies had. "The fact is," she concluded, "although Whiner Wessie does not deserve the Better Ossie, he could still learn a lot from him" if only, she noted, "he weren't so afraid of reunification."[2]

Although more than a little tongue-in-cheek—the two would coauthor a book entitled *Typisch Ossi, typisch Wessi* the following year—the exchange illustrated a basic divide in German memory culture about the former GDR that has persisted since the fall of the Berlin Wall. In one collection dedicated to the subject,

David Clarke and Ute Wölfel noted the "fundamental lack of consensus about what the GDR was and what it should mean to Germans today."[3] For some, the East German experience should primarily be remembered as a dictatorship, one symbolized best by its notorious secret service, the Stasi, or as a "Stasiland," to use the term popularized by Anna Funder.[4] For others, the GDR should best be remembered at the level of the everyday, one in which state surveillance certainly played a part, but one that competed for attention with bands such as the Pudhys and brands such as the Trabant. Jürgs and Elias were taking part in this debate, which essentially asked whether a focus on the everyday, or the history of everyday life (in German, *Alltagsgeschichte*), helped to capture the GDR experience properly or trivialize it.

These differences played out in the "Wessie versus Ossie" debate cited above. Yet even this divide might be too neat: for Ossies who experienced the Stasi's tortures firsthand, it defined their GDR; while Wessies could also feel a sense of nostalgia for the more mundane aspects of the world that once was the GDR. The division of memory culture, then, was as much mental as geographic. It helps to form what scholars have termed "a battleground of memory," one with multiple fronts and a multitude of combatants.[5]

It is a conflict fought in two movies that gained international attention: Wolfgang Becker's 2003 *Good Bye, Lenin!* represents the quintessence of ostalgie (at least as it was popularly understood: it's a complex film that ruminates on past experience and change), and Florian Henckel von Donnersmarck's 2006 *The Lives of Others* represents the glum image of the Stasi-dominated GDR many feel should be remembered most (at least in the eyes of many critics; it too is a complex examination of conformity and resistance in the GDR).[6] Naturally, both filmmakers saw their films as correctives to popular views: Becker's to a 1990s, Wessie-dominated, vision of East Germany, and von Donnersmarck's to the ostalgic vision offered in, well, *Good Bye, Lenin!*

These battles and debates—including the cinematic versions—are also at the heart of three museums in Berlin, each in a not-so-friendly dialogue with each other (much like Jürgs and Elis). In this museum conflict, the Wessie-von Donnersmarck vision delivered the first blow, and the Ossie-Becker vision counterpunched. Opened in 1994 on the site of the former Stasi prison, the *Gedenkstätte Berlin-Hohenschönhausen* [Berlin-Hohenschönhausen Memorial], as its tourist pamphlet proclaims, "embodies like no other the 44-year-old history of political persecution in the Soviet Occupation Zone and the German Democratic Republic." In addition to the Memorial Museum, the former Stasi headquarters also became a museum after reunification: first occupied and run by former prisoners who had been interrogated in its halls, the Stasi Museum reached an agreement in 2010 with the German government to turn it into a jointly run, state-funded space. Partly in response to these Stasi-centric museums and more broadly in response to the increasing perception that the history of the GDR should be remembered not solely as a repressive one, the DDR Museum opened in 2006 (in German, DDR = Deutsche Demokratische Republik; the English version is German Democratic Republic). Located in the heart of Berlin near Museum Island, the museum bills itself as a "hands-on experience of history," one that brings visitors closer to the "real" GDR than the one presented elsewhere. Together, the three museums help explain, as Chloe Paver has written, the "clear division between museums documenting the inhumanity and criminality of the East German state and museums documenting so-called 'everyday life.'"[7] They also act as ongoing sites of memory staking out claims to the best way to remember the GDR: should it be conceptualized above all as a Stasiland or a place where the Stasi and Spreewald Pickles coexisted?

FILM BATTLES: LENIN VERSUS THE STASI

Perhaps the best way to introduce the dialectic between the Stasi Museum and the DDR Museum is to emphasize the contrasts between 2003's *Good Bye, Lenin!* and 2006's *Lives of Others*. The two films had wide releases, enjoyed massive media coverage (as well as coverage from academics), and managed to achieve worldwide acclaim. In many ways, the two films served as shorthand for ongoing debates about Ossies and Wessies, ostalgie and Stasiland. Becker's and von Donnersmarck's movies also, as we will see, frequently served as reference points when debating the creation of the DDR Museum. Just as it's impossible to evaluate the DDR Museum without taking into account the earlier Stasi Museum, it is similarly impossible to evaluate either museum without turning to the two films.

Becker's *Good Bye, Lenin!* appeared not long after Leander Haussmann's 1999 comedy about life in the 1970s in East Berlin, *Sonnenallee*. That movie cast life for teenagers in the GDR as similar to that elsewhere: the protagonist, Michael, listens to music, pines after a girl, and hangs out with friends. Politics interferes at times (the girl Michael likes is already seeing a West Berliner; a friend is shot by a border guard but survives thanks to the Rolling Stones album that helps to deflect the shot) but does not dominate life. Critics suggested that the film glorified life in the GDR. One review in *Der Spiegel* particularly suggested that the ostalgie present in *Sonnenallee* proclaimed that "what we had in the GDR was also nice," deflecting attention from how things were really not so nice, turning the film into an "East German version puberty-comedy" version of *The Last Waltz* and *American Graffiti*.[8]

Becker's film was therefore slotted into this sort of interpretation. The story of Alex Kerner and his family, *Good Bye, Lenin!* is set at the time of the Berlin Wall's fall. Alex's mother, Christiane, is a diehard supporter of the regime, particularly because she has raised her two children after her husband abandoned the family. The mother has a heart attack when she sees Alex arrested for participating in an antigovernment demonstration and falls into a coma. While in that state, her beloved state collapses. Her doctors tell Alex and his sister, Ariane, that they should ease the mother into the new circumstances, and so they contrive to set up an elaborate ruse meant to convince their mother that the GDR survives. Comedic and sometimes touching moments ensue. The film was largely interpreted then and since as a quintessential example of ostalgie, but it offered just as much meditation on the inevitability of change, the way to cope with it (even through nostalgia, which in part acknowledges the past is past), and some of the hopefulness of *die Wende* (the "turn-around," used to refer to the Fall of the Wall in 1989 and reunification the following year). For all its complexities, many tended to remember the film through the search for Spreewald Pickles that Alex and Ariane carried out in order to give their mother authentic GDR food. In this vision, the search for pickles became a search to recover the GDR that was lost and, by extension, an attempt to hide from the realities of the Stasi, the oppressive government, and the police that arrested Alex. Ostalgie thus became not so much a reflective nostalgia meant to cope with change, but a restorative nostalgia attempting to bring back an imagined golden age, including its pickles.[9]

Even the most perceptive critics tended to wonder about whether *Good Bye, Lenin!* helped come to terms with the GDR past or trivialized it. Writing about the boom in "ostalgie shows," including television programs that resulted from Becker's film, Matthias Lohre characterized them as the "DDR Reloaded." Although he noted that the film did not divide East Germans into "good dissidents and evil Stasi people," he still noted that the film's turn from black-and-white to shades of gray led him to fear that the more repressive aspects of the East German dictatorship were being trivialized.[10] Such fears characterized reviews of the film. Most of the critics were positive about how the movie captured the mood of the reunification era but were less positive about the interpretations the film made about that event. One report in *Der Spiegel*, "Welcome Back, Lenin!," noted that some entrepreneurs wanted to capitalize on *Good Bye, Lenin!*'s popularity and build a DDR theme park.[11]

The Lives of Others therefore acted as and was interpreted by many to be a corrective to this ostalgic vision. Set in 1984 and therefore deliberately conjuring up Orwell, *The Lives of Others* tells the story of a Stasi agent, Gerd Wiesler, who is assigned to surveil an East German playwright, Georg Dreyman, and his girlfriend, the actress Christa-Maria Sieland. Wiesler initially is told by his superior, Grubitz, that Dreyman is suspected of antiregime politics and illegal publishing. He (and the viewer) soon learns that the Minister of Culture, Bruno

Hempf, has been blackmailing Sieland into sleeping with him and wants Dreyman out of the way. What follows is a window into the ways Stasi surveillance worked: Dreyman slowly becomes more and more disillusioned with the regime (he does not know he is being watched), thus becoming more like the figure the state paints him as. Wiesler too becomes disillusioned and increasingly empathizes with Dreyman and Sieland. As the Stasi agent grows in sympathy, Sieland feels increasingly trapped. She eventually steps in front of a truck, committing suicide. When Stasi agents search Dreyman's apartment and find nothing because Wieland has filed false reports (he uses his initials and number, HGW XX/7 to do so), the playwright remains free. The Stasi agent, however, is demoted to a filing job. Only after 1989 does Dreyman learn that he was under surveillance and, thanks to the newly opened files available at the Stasi Museum, that agent "HGW XX/7" had covered for him in his reports (interestingly, the director of the Berlin-Hohenschönhausen Memorial, Hubertus Knabe, initially refused to let von Donnersmarck's film on location because he did not like the idea of a movie with a Stasi officer as a hero of sorts). Dreyman dedicates his newest work to the agent; Wiesler purchases the book as the film ends.

Von Donnersmarck stated that his desire to make a film about the Stasi's hold over the GDR resulted in part from childhood memories of visiting relatives in the East and the fear that crossing the border generated.[12] In another interview with *Spiegel*, his interviewer asked about *Good Bye, Lenin!* Von Donnersmarck responded,

> Over the last few years, East German films have presented a very weird view of the GDR. German cinema has tended to portray the GDR as this funny place with quirky weird characters, which no one takes seriously. The menacing aspects of the state, such as the Stasi or the border troops, are just portrayed as amusing. That is really very different to what I experienced at the time. I remember an atmosphere of great fear, and of great mistrust. You have to tell the whole story of the GDR by showing the terror, as well as people's good sides and the beautiful aspects of the country.[13]

Much as Becker's film generated intense discussions about ostalgie, von Donnersmarck's initiated what the German press dubbed a "Stasi-debatte."[14] At stake was the central question about how best to remember the GDR: as a Stasiland or for its Spreewald pickles?

The literature on ostalgie is enormous,[15] and the number of scholarly studies of the two films equally large. The divide over memory is echoed in the literature too: for the most part, scholars analyzed the nostalgia in Becker's film sympathetically, and most scholarly studies of Donnersmarck's criticized the "inauthentic" history he narrated.[16] The two exist as an unintentionally planned pair, and reviews of *Das Leben der Anderen* frequently assumed you had already seen Becker's movie and understood it as the apex of ostalgie. In his review for *Der Spiegel*, Reinhard Mohr gave it the title "*Stasi ohne Spreewaldgurke* [The Stasi without Spreewald Pickles]," a clear reference to *Goodbye, Lenin!* and the quest to find GDR pickles.[17] "After *Sonnenallee, Good Bye, Lenin!, NVA,* and *Der rote Kakadu,*" Mohr writes, "*Das Leben der Anderen* is the first German feature film that seriously covers the core of the GDR, which collapsed in 1989, but which consisted of the systematic harassment and oppression of its citizens in the name of 'state security,' without trabi-nostalgia, Spreewald-Pickle-Romanticism, and other folkloristic hullabaloo [*Klamauk*]."[18] Writing for the *Süddeutsche Zeitung*, Rainer Gansera used almost identical language, commenting that von Donnersmarck's film "made an impression about how the GDR dictatorship felt in the Orwellian year of 1984, without Ostalgie, Spreewald pickle folklore, or Trabi jokes."[19] Instead, the critic concludes, the director has placed "a portrait gallery of the cynical rulers, the careerists and followers, and the transformation of Wiesler at the heart of his film."[20] Echoing these words, Andreas Kilb from the *Frankfurter Allgemeine*, after noting the "cheerfulness" of the GDR in Becker's vision, declared that "only with *The Lives of Others* does the inner working of the Stasi become the center of a feature film."[21] In an otherwise nuanced review of the film, Matthias Ehlert mused that *The Lives of Others* might be understood on one level as "a kind of historical supplement to *Good Bye, Lenin!*."[22]

These comparisons contained repetitive themes: all thought the best way to understand *The Lives of Others* was through remembering the GDR presented onscreen in *Good Bye, Lenin!* (or, more accurately, the perceived ostalgic vision of the GDR in that film); all found von Donnersmarck's film more historically accurate. Even those reviewers who did not judge *Lives* to be better for its more "realistically" rendered GDR still referred to Becker's movie. Evelyn Finger, writing in *Die Zeit*, declared that *Lives of Others* is the "best post-Wende film about the GDR" because it is "as political as *Sonnenallee*, as philosophical as *Good Bye, Lenin!*, and as sarcastic as *Berlin is in Germany*."[23] The film is significant, therefore, in that numerous critics and commentators believed that it represented the start of a new era of remembrance practices about the GDR, one that left ostalgie behind to focus on the oppressive mechanism of the GDR dictatorship.

HANDS ON A GDR HARD BODY

If the opening salvo in the cinematic memory battle over the GDR was fired by "ostalgic" films such as Becker's, the opening shot in the museum battle was taken by the Stasi. The Berlin-Hohenschönhausen Memorial, or Stasi Prison Museum, opened in 1994 and is housed in the very building that served as the Stasi's main prison. Like the Museum of Occupations in Lithuania, the Lonsky Prison in L'viv, or the Gulag Museums in Kazakhstan, the Stasi Prison uses its ominous history and its ominous architecture to "embody like no other the 44-year history of political persecution in the Soviet Occupation Zone and the German Democratic Republic," as its pamphlet states. Built as a soup kitchen during the Nazi era, the Soviet occupation force used it as a prison, one where "living conditions were catastrophic (again in the words of the pamphlet handed out to visitors)." Prisoners helped to construct some of the most abysmal aspects of the site, including the so-called "U-Boot" cells in the basement, now part of the museum. After the creation of the Stasi in 1951, the site served again as a prison. Memorial plaques narrate the stories of the people held inside its cells, including participants in the 1953 Uprising, political opponents, dissidents, and ordinary citizens. The overall narrative conveyed in the museum is one von Donnersmarck took up in his film (which was shot at the site after its director initially opposed it): the Stasi was everywhere and this place served as the primary site to inflict cruelty.

The broader conflicts and seemingly insurmountable divide between remembering the GDR through these sorts of "trauma sites" or through nostalgic sites led to the so-called "Sabrow Commission," a government-appointed body of experts assigned in 2005 to mapping out a strategy for the future of German remembrance (and, naturally, the future of government resources earmarked for remembrance). Named after its chair, the historian Martin Sabrow, the commission published its report in May 2006, recommending that a "more balanced landscape of memory [*Erinnerungslandschaft*]" be created.[24] The report criticized "the trivialization of the GDR" in local museums that had sprung up dedicated to everyday life and called instead for a national museum to deal with the subject.[25] At the same time, Sabrow later advocated an inclusion of the everyday in state-sponsored GDR memory sites, arguing that "the everyday is not the opposite of dictatorial rule but its complement."[26] One of the first and loudest critics of the report was Hubertus Knabe, the director of the Stasi Museum, who complained that a state-sponsored GDR museum would take visitors away from his and also decried the very idea of a museum of the everyday, characterizing the approach as one that presented the GDR as a "social experiment on a grand scale instead of an inhuman dictatorship."[27] Knabe was joined by many German politicians, and plans for a state-sponsored museum were abandoned by the new Christian Democratic Union–Social Democratic Party coalition government that greeted the report (the commission was sponsored by the Social Democratic-Green coalition).

As Silke Arnold-de Simine has perceptively argued, the report's critics automatically assumed that any focus on the everyday would leave out surveillance in favor of trivialization and sentimentalism.[28] She situates this assumption within broader historical arguments stemming from the so-called *Historikerstreit* and the criticisms of *Alltagsgeschichte* of the 1980s. The GDR memory battle certainly can be understood as a continuation of these debates, which fought over how to remember the Nazi past, but in many ways the landscape greeting the Sabrow report was already churned up with opinions about the Stasi Museum, ostalgie films, and reunification. In a sense, the divergence of opinions over how to remember the GDR was the logical result of divided historical memories produced between 1945 and 1989 and the intense discussions of *Vergangenheitsbewältigung* in Germany since 1990. To a certain degree, these competing processes were bound to run into conflict with each other.

When two entrepreneurs decided to open a privately funded, centrally located museum of the everyday in Berlin, they were in part responding to the failure to implement the Sabrow report. From the get-go, the organizers of the DDR Museum also had to respond to the Stasi Prison Museum's claims on memory. Robert Rückel's opening statement in the official guidebook to the museum reads "before the opening . . . one question kept coming up in interviews; I was asked my opinion regarding some colleagues' statements, who consider the display of everyday life in the GDR a belittlement of a dictatorship."[29] Noting the debate that broke out, one that coalesced around the Stasiland/ostalgie axis, Rückel responded, "the GDR was a dictatorship—that is unquestionable—and in a dictatorship the state shapes life much stronger than in a democracy." At the same time, "in a dictatorship the people laugh, play, love, and undermine the regulations on a small scale. This is the history of everyday life and it is a part of GDR history."[30] After trumpeting the museum's initial successes in luring visitors along with the 2008 study that showed more and more Germans are forgetting the GDR past, Rücker argues that his museum helps with *Vergangenheitsbewältigung* by "show[ing] all aspects of the GDR in an objective way."[31] Head of research Stefan Wolle reached similar conclusions in his introduction, noting that although the state infiltrated life in many ways, East Germans still lived ordinary lives. "The GDR," he writes, "was more than just an artificial product of ideology and power—for millions of people it was their life."[32]

Simine has noted that the museum is far from traditional in many respects, not least because it does not aim to collect objects for research and preservation purposes, but to "furnish a master narrative."[33] By touching, climbing on, and smelling objects, visitors access knowledge "almost by osmosis."[34] One of the most conspicuous objects housed in the museum, and one of the objects visitors are encouraged to touch, sit in, and climb into, is a Trabant (see fig. 9.2). White, small, and beguiling, the Trabi of the DDR Museum perfectly encapsulates the larger arguments about remembrance of the GDR. When the East German state still existed, the mass-produced car, to use the words of Daphne Berdahl,

Figure 9.2. Oh, Trabi, Oh! DDR Museum. *Wikimedia Commons*

"occupied a critical place in and represented an important aspect of everyday life in a socialist 'economy of shortages.'"[35] Simultaneously prized and hated by East Germans, who waited up to fifteen years to obtain one, but mostly mocked by West Germans, who liked to joke about them in comparison to sleek models such as Porsche, Mercedes, and Audi (one favorite: "how do you double the value of a Trabi? Fill it up with gas"), the Trabant served as "a key symbol of socialist inefficiency, industrial backwardness, and inferiority."[36] After the Wall's fall and the end of the car's production, however, the Trabi became an object of longing. Ostalgie films helped to fuel these feelings—one early film was called *Go, Trabi, Go!*—helping to turn the car into its "ultimate object," one that former GDR residents could look at to "reclaim a devalued self."[37]

The museum Trabi evokes these forces. Visitors can open its doors, climb in its front seat, smell its interiors, pop the trunk. A correspondent for the *Berliner Kurier* visited and proclaimed the Trabi "the favorite of all visitors" but entitled the piece "Oh, Trabi, Oh! Why Does Everyone Want to Pet It?"[38] In doing so, is one coming closer to an understanding of life in a participatory dictatorship? Or enjoying a car hated as much as loved at the expense of thinking about the more oppressive aspects of that system?

Figure 9.3. Jump into the Trabi time machine! Trabi simulator, DDR Museum. *Wikimedia Commons*

The DDR Museum has upped the ante in terms of answering these questions: a new "Trabi Simulator" is available at the museum, where you climb into a sky-blue car and transport yourself back to the past (fig. 9.3):

> The Trabant was not the only car on East German roads, but no other model was invested with such loyalty and love. Known universally as the Trabi, or Trabbi, ownership of this doughty little vehicle promised a measure of freedom in an unfree country. Those hoping to acquire one faced a long wait.
> **JUMP IN! STRAP YOURSELF IN AND EXPERIENCE AN AUTHENTIC DRIVING EXPERIENCE**
> Take the unique opportunity to enjoy an authentic Trabi experience in our Trabi simulator. Rev up the engine and rattle through a simulated Berlin high-rise tower block estate: a proper journey back in time! Our simulator projects a realistic 3D reproduction of a Berlin housing development onto the front windshield of our original Trabant P 601. Visitors can drive explore the development: pass shops, apartments, and parking spaces and watch out for 114 other Trabis in the original colors "papyrus white," "glacier blue," or "beaver brown" while listening to the original sounds of the Trabant P 601.

Figure 9.4. Pieces of personal memory, part I. GDR living room, DDR Museum. *Photograph by Stephen M. Norris*

The journey through 60,000 square meters of the housing development, the squealing of the pedals and the somewhat shaky carriage make for a highly authentic experience.

If you have trouble starting the car, a pair of ladies' tights could be useful . . . a perfectly workable replacement for an old-fashioned fan belt.[39]

Although the Trabi represents the largest object, other exhibits encourage similar journeys to the past. The GDR living room and kitchen also seek to transport visitors (fig. 9.4). Inside, you can sit on an East German couch, watch East German television, open East German cabinets and drawers, grasp East German utensils, operate East German appliances. On its blog, the DDR Museum features four rooms: a children's bedroom, a living room, and a kitchen. Collectively they are the primary spaces of everyday life and the primary sites of memory around which the museum builds its mission. "Don't be shy, feel free to open drawers and cupboards, look inside, and let the contents surprise you" when entering the bedroom, Melanie Alperstaedt encourages in her blog post.[40] This is a place "many readers will probably remember" and, because of this, "the kindergarten (another room in the museum replicates a GDR schoolroom) and the children's room are probably the most emotionally touching parts of our exhibition," for one might feel "melancholy" for one's past.[41] The living room, while less emotional, evokes familiarity, comfort, and sameness, for the ubiquitous furniture and other items might be termed "GDR-ordinary."[42] The kitchen likewise brings the same ordinariness, full as it is of items bought from the Kaufhalle. Inside its recreated space, one can lay one's hands on utensils and appliances and learn about "to what extent gender equality actually existed in the DDR."[43] The German-language website features other hands-on sites to remember: the garage and how it captures "private life in the GDR,"[44] a kindergarten room full of items that evoke "living history,"[45] a screen in the children's room that allows you to browse old GDR children's books.[46] The site therefore makes virtual what the museum promises as real when you visit: its brochure explains that "history comes alive," that "the DDR Museum offers a hands-on experience of everyday life in the state that has vanished," and that "exhibits are to be handled."

One visitor concurred on the museum's blog:

> I like the exhibition very much, because it is so entertaining and interactive. In each corner, you can do something: Sit down in a Trabi, open a closet or trying on some cloth.
>
> What I like the most is the living room. But not always! I like it the most, when I am alone and I am sitting on the sofa, watching GDR tv without anybody else in the room. Just me and the atmosphere of a GDR living room. Then it feels like time travel.
>
> For me, it is easy to experience this special feeling, because I can come to the museum before it opens or after it is closed. But if you visit the museum as a normal guest: If you come in the evening, and if you be lucky, you can sit down on the sofa as I like it and you will feel like being in your own living room in these times![47]

Rooms and cars represent the best objects for virtual time travel in the DDR Museum, but the bulk of the exhibits consist of a collection of objects arranged in seventeen thematic areas ranging from fashion to state security. The Stasi is not absent from the space: visitors can pull out drawers to see the ways agents dressed or test out a listening device (fig. 9.5). As the museum's official website declares, "It's not just about reading and looking; many of the exhibits require our guests to open doors, pull out drawers, press buttons and pull levers in order to access information, pictures, films and objects." Combining the themes that run the gamut of the GDR's history allows the organizers to claim that "Eschewing nostalgia, we enable you to immerse yourself in the world of Real Existing Socialism. A wealth of exhibits give in-depth insight into the realities of everyday life in a long-defunct system. Coming of age and going to school; full employment and queuing for food; Stasi surveillance and the Berlin Wall. There's a living room

Figure 9.5. Pieces of personal memory, part III. Stasi uniforms, DDR Museum. *Photograph by Stephen M. Norris*

with the original GDR smell. In the wardrobe a blue FGY (Free German Youth) shirt hangs next to the "latest" Dederon fashion. Apparent normality—but the room is bugged by the Stasi.[48]

The number of objects available to see and touch is massive, making any single visit to the museum impressionistic: you get a flavor for the varieties of life in the GDR. My photographs from 2009 reveal that I was struck by the objects related to the Puhdys (full confession: I listened to their compilation album *Zwanzig Hits aus Dreissig Jahren* extensively while writing this article), the displays of East German border guard uniforms, a drawer that contained examples of the steroids used by GDR athletes, the kitchen utensils, Katerina Witt, an authentic GDR toilet (fig. 9.6), and the football signed by members of the GDR team that beat their West German rivals at the 1974 World Cup. To a certain degree, the museum's promise to transport you back to the past and to experience it as a foreign country worked: I watched East German television, spied on colleagues, tested out kitchen products, replayed football matches, and smelled my first Trabi.

> The Trabi in our exhibition still smells of the GDR. Take your place at the wheel, rev up the engine and rocket off through the simulated world of an

Figure 9.6. Pieces of personal memory, part II. GDR Toilet, DDR Museum. *Photograph by Stephen M. Norris*

East German housing estate. The simulated sights and sounds of the original make for an authentic experience.

There is even more to discover in the DDR Museum: a television in an authentic reproduction of a GDR living room shows original television programs. Rummage through the original "Carat" living room cupboard and smell the odor of the spice rack in the reproduction kitchen. We have even placed an original GDR pressure cooker on the stove. Sit in our authentic GDR cinema chairs and watch original cinema newsreels; replay the 1974 soccer game "East Germany vs. West Germany" on the football table; or learn to dance the Lipsi. . . .

Large-format propaganda photographs obscure the realities which the East German government sought to hide from its citizens: the privileges of the "more equal" Party elite, opposition movements and the realities of life in prison. Take a seat in a ministerial Volvo or learn about the nascent opposition movement. The reconstruction of a Stasi interrogation allows you to take the place of a suspect, listening to the tape recording of an interrogation by placing your elbows on the desk and your hands on your ears.[49]

Stefan Wolle, the head of research and a well-respected scholar of the GDR, has described the objects as "pieces of memory [Erinnerungsstücke]" that represent broken pieces of a mirror.[50] Part of the problem of these everyday objects as pieces of memory is that the state itself viewed the everyday as a site of intervention. East Germans, like other communist citizens, certainly found ways to carve out private lives, develop interests and hobbies, and even resist or complain about the system. Objects of "the everyday" displayed in a new museum, particularly consumerist products made by the state in its command economy, thus could be at risk of trivializing a dictatorial regime if not contextualized or represented properly.[51] The trick is in overcoming this burden, in "challenging the ground rules" of state-supported GDR memory museums such as the Stasi Headquarters,[52] while also complementing them in the way Sabrow called for. Does the hands-on approach to history that the DDR Museum promotes work in this fashion? Certainly Wolle and Rückel think so.

If the DDR Museum acted as an alternative or a complement to the Stasi Prison Memorial and Museum, its private funding and revisionist approach led to a battle over another GDR museum site in Berlin. Housed in the former headquarters of the agency, the Stasi Museum, as its website proclaims, reveals how "The rulers created a system of power based on force, threats, rewards and privilege. Individuals were taught to conform, comply and, whenever possible, participate. The SED [Sozialistische Einheitspartei Deutschlands], with unrestrained access to almost all areas of life—the churches remained an exception—was able to comprehensively control the population and to reward and reprimand as needed."[53] Featuring objects worn by Stasi agents and used by them, the focus throughout is on the people who worked for the agency and the methods they used to surveil the population. The ominous highlight is the carefully preserved office suite of Erich Mielke, the last head of the Stasi, complete with his actual furniture. Founded right after the 1990 occupation of the site by Jörg Drieselmann and fellow demonstrators, the museum operated mostly under the control of the occupiers, all of whom were former Stasi prisoners. In 2010, after two decades of preserving the site, the occupiers' organization, named "Astak" (for anti-Stalinist action), was asked by the German government to vacate the site so that the state could take it over, renovate it, and run is as a museum. Astak fought back, insisting that everything they had preserved remain so that the former Stasi headquarters did not become "another slick, modern museum."[54] Moreover, the museum had proven its worth because, as one *Spiegel* article noted, it had been used as a shooting location in *The Lives of Others*.⁵⁵ For his part, Helge Heidemeyer, who heads the department of education and research at the Stasi archives and whom the German government assigned to renovate the Stasi Museum, feared that private museums such as the Checkpoint Charlie site and the DDR Museum, combined with private enterprises such as the popular Trabi tours, threatened to turn the capital into an "East German theme park for tourists."⁵⁶ In the end, a compromise was reached. Astak still maintains the museum with government money and a new permanent exhibition set up through Astak and the Stasi Archives opened in 2015. Mielke's office, used as a location in *The Lives of Others*, remains preserved.

CIRCULAR DEBATES?

The arguments over the DDR Museum unfolded in a way not too dissimilar from the one between Jürgs and Elis. In its international edition, *Der Spiegel* noted that the new space "caps a trend of 'Ostalgie' that went mainstream in 2003 with the sentimental international hit film 'Good Bye, Lenin,'" describing Becker's movie as one that "was one of the first to gloss over the dark side of Communism to look at how most people led their day-to-day lives."⁵⁷ The report quotes both Peter Kenzelmann, an ethnologist and original founder of the museum, and Robert Rückel and their vision, one that combines some of the "darker elements of communist life" with more "mundane" objects of everyday life. At the same time, the interpretative element of the *Spiegel* article comes from the museum's critics, including Rudolf Trabold, a spokesman for the German Historical Museum, who states that "there's really no need for this museum," explaining that "the focus is too narrow," placing it "on the level of 'Goodbye Lenin'—it's filled with consumer goods from the DDR but there is no context. It's sort of like saying, 'Oh, wasn't it all nice?'"⁵⁸ The article concludes that the museum is "riding on the tail-end of a wave of Ostalgie" introduced by Becker's film, which presented "a side of East German life that many are more keen to remember than the Stasi chapter." "In recent months," the report continues, "Germans have been taking a more sober look at East German history," one where "recent films like 'Das Leben der Anderen' (*The Lives of Others*) have depicted the DDR as it really was for many: a terrifying police state that monitored and persecuted tens of thousands of its citizens."⁵⁹

A year after this report, *Der Spiegel* covered the "Ostalgie boom" (*Ostalgie boomt*) that the DDR Museum had helped to generate. Citing a study conducted by the Free University of Berlin that concluded that German schoolchildren know less and less about the GDR and the division of Germany than they should, the report connected the DDR Museum's appeal to a recently opened exhibition on everyday life in the GDR housed within the Berlin Carre in Alexanderplatz.

The brainchild of Maik Schwolow, the exhibit does not "tell a political story," but preserves memories and life. The director of the Stasi Memorial, Hubertus Knabe, criticized what he saw as the lack of reflection in either the DDR Museum or Schwolow's exhibition, declaring "I find it problematic to take the everyday life of the GDR out of its political context."[60]

Taking a broader (and more scholarly) view, professor of German literature Katrin Kohl has conceptualized the memory of the GDR in the two decades since its collapse as one framed by temporal and physical boundaries (Wessies versus Ossies to a certain degree, but also defined by those who lived in the GDR, those who lived outside, and those born since). Moreover, because of the nature of reunification and subsequent dominance of Federal Republic of Germany memories, the GDR became "an illegitimate site for positive memories. The only accepted interpretation was of the GDR as 'Stasiland,' that memorable label invented by Anna Funder to identify the state with its surveillance network."[61] This initial view, Kohl argues, helped to fuel the ostalgie sentiment, simultaneously furthering the sense that the GDR continues to be a "mental reality," one best understood through powerful metaphors.[62] These metaphoric constructions come from "history" projects such as 2009's television presentation and book *Meine DDR* and fiction such as Werner Bräunig's 2007 *Rummelplatz*. Museums have also shaped (or solidified) this mental (after)life, one in which "the establishment of the DDR Museum in 2006 marked a change of perspective on the GDR: instead of documenting the horrors of 'Stasiland,' it gives an insight into the 'Alltag eines vergangenen Staates [everyday life of a former state].'"[63] The museum, Kohl concludes, turns the GDR into "an object of anthropological study with the entertainment value of a theme park."[64] It legitimizes ostalgie just as the Stasi Museum legitimizes the notion of the GDR as a Stasiland (just as *Good Bye, Lenin!* and *Lives of Others* did, respectively).

The DDR Museum and its Stasi counterparts have therefore formed important bulwarks in the battlefield over memory. As Anna Saunders and Debbie Pinfold have argued, museums in general are "traditionally sites where reliable, objective information is conveyed to the general public" and therefore "tend to be perceived as more authoritative than literary fiction about a historical period."[65] But the creation of "memorial museums" in Germany adds a different layer, they suggest, for they "ask the visitor not simply to learn about the past, but to enter into an emotional relationship with it."[66] These emotional attachments further memory divisions (Saunders and Pinfold name Becker's and von Donnersmarck's films as part of the way emotional attachments to the past get made): the Stasi Museum and Stasi Prison Museum both use former inmates as guides in order to bring visitors into their experiences, whereas the DDR Museum is built in part on the fun of enjoying the hands-on approach.

One might therefore conclude that the memory battlefield will never reach a truce and its divisions may never be breached. Wolfgang Emmerich, writing in 2009, posited that the divisions in contemporary German society over GDR memory are the direct result of two distinct cultural memories produced in the two Germanys after 1945. Rather pessimistically, Emmerich concludes that the alienation between East and West will continue for the foreseeable future and will take three generations to overcome.[67] Monika Deutz-Schroeder and Klaus Schroeder, who conducted the 2007 Free University survey, similarly argue that the ostalgic version of GDR history distorts the past and impedes true democracy.[68]

This basic dichotomy of opinion, one reflected onto contemporary German memory cultures, might best be understood as a "people's paradox," to use the phrase employed by Mary Fulbrook. In her comprehensive history of the GDR, Fulbrook offers a useful way to evaluate the GDR and, by extension, how best to remember it. She begins by noting the popular perception of the East German system at the time of its collapse, a perception fueled by images of drab, gray buildings, drab, gray people, and life in a drab, gray, oppressive state. The East German people, this view held, were watched over, walled in, contained in wires, and surveilled through the Stasi. Yet, as Fulbrook writes, once scholars, journalists, and others wrote of the GDR in these terms, "protesting voices began to be raised." "Faced with accounts of repression, complicity and collusion," she notes, "former citizens of the GDR claimed that their own memories and experiences told them otherwise."[69] This view was one of happy childhoods, normal life, work, family, and play. Fulbrook's account encapsulates this "fundamental paradox" and "massive disjuncture" between "analyses of the dictatorial political system of the defunct GDR, on the one hand, and the experiences, perceptions, and memories of many of those who lived through it, on the other."[70] Like all good histories written by good historians, Fulbrook's history of the GDR can be understood as one that emphasizes both repressive and normal aspects.

The GDR was thus "a very different kind of dictatorship" than the Nazi one, mostly because it lacked the popular enthusiasm of the former and was "imposed from above and from without" on a "defeated, demoralized, disoriented" population.[71] At the same time, it lasted for forty years and managed to create a society that learned to "play by its rules and were even committed to some of its ideals."[72] The Wall was necessary for the GDR to survive, Fulbrook argues (and therefore the state "lacked intrinsic legitimacy"), but the "vast majority of East Germans were caught up in a system in which they had to participate; and by virtue of their participation, they were themselves changed."[73] "This was a system that was more like a honeycomb full of criss-crossing little cells than a simple homogeneous pot of 'the people' with a repressive lid, the 'regime,' clamped down on it to keep the contents from boiling over."[74] Like all histories, in other words, the GDR's was complex and needs to be treated as such.

The DDR Museum's layout, as well as its general approach to remembering the past, works as the sort of honeycomb imagined by Fulbrook. It also attempts to conceptualize the GDR's history as a complex, multifaceted one. The divisions one hears so often in Germany today, whether in the media or from scholars, may not be unbridgeable after all, particularly if, like Peter Thompson, we view the Stasi-ostalgie divide as one representing "the conjoined twins of really existing socialism."[75] Or we could embrace what Silke Arnold-de Simine has characterized as the "increasingly diversifying" landscape of GDR remembrance in Germany.[76] The DDR Museum is part of a bigger whole, one that includes the Stasi Museum and the Stasi Prison Museum, but also the Checkpoint Charlie Museum, the Berlin Wall Memorial, the Museum at Bernauer Strasse, and a host of other plaques, memorials, and memory sites. And that's just in Berlin: memory sites dot the German landscape, including numerous other privately run museums of everyday life in the GDR. Jonathan Bach has posited that these museums "play an active role in making the GDR everyday available for representation through material culture" and, in so doing, play a vital role in how Germans are working through their communist past.[77]

Perhaps the best way to conclude would be to give the last word to Robert Rückel, the DDR Museum's director: "Museums and other organizations dealing with the 'coming to terms with the past,'" he writes, "have the responsibility to show all aspects of the GDR in an objective way. Only when the apparent or real positive sides are set against the undoubted horrible facts, will it be possible to objectively convey the character of the GDR."[78] Or we can simply note that Jörg Drieselmann, a former prisoner of the Stasi who occupied its headquarters and still maintains the Stasi Museum, also sits on the advisory board of the DDR Museum. It seems we can watch both *Good Bye, Lenin!* and *Lives of Others*, look at Stasiland, and eat our Spreewald pickles too.

NOTES

1. Michael Jürgs, "Frightened of Freedom, Ossies?," *Der Spiegel* special international edition: "The Germans: Sixty Years after the War," April 2005, 148.

2. Angela Elis, "Frightened of Reunification, Wessies?," *Der Spiegel* special international edition: "The Germans: Sixty Years after the War," April 2005, 151.

3. David Clarke and Ute Wölfel, "Remembering the German Democratic Republic in a United Germany," in *Remembering the German Democratic Republic: Divided Memory in a United Germany*, ed. Clarke and Wölfel (New York: Palgrave Macmillan, 2011), 4. In the introduction to their edited volume on remembering the GDR, Anna Saunders and Debbie Pinfold open with a similar dichotomy: on January 14, 2012, the former Stasi headquarters reopened after renovations; that same day, a group of former GDR cabaret singers held a concert that featured popular hits from East

Germany. Saunders and Pinfold conclude that the two events tell us all we need to know "about the continued relevance of GDR remembrance in united Germany" (*Remembering and Rethinking the GDR: Multiple Perspectives and Plural Authenticities* [New York: Palgrave Macmillan, 2013], 2).

4. Even in this instance, as Sara Jones has argued, individual memories about the Stasi and how to remember it publicly constitute "contested heritage" and a "memory dispute" (Jones, *The Media of Testimony: Remembering the East German Stasi in the Berlin Republic* [New York: Palgrave Macmillan, 2014]). See also Anna Funder, *Stasiland: Stories from Behind the Berlin Wall* (New York: HarperCollins, 2002).

5. Saunders and Pinfold, *Remembering and Rethinking the GDR*, 4. Mary Fulbrook has usefully divided this debate over history and memory of the GDR into sites that deal with *Verklärung* (idealization) and those that deal with *Erklärung* (explanation), offering another analytical lens. See her "Histories and Memories: *Verklärung* or *Erklärung*?" in Clarke and Wölfel, *Remembering the German Democratic Republic*, 91–101.

6. Jan-Wermer Müller has stated that German critics of GDR remembrance sites claim former East Germans "have been allowed to impose a very soft image of the dictatorship, more *Goodbye Lenin* than *The Lives of Others*." See his "Germany's Two Processes of 'Coming to Terms with the Past'" in *Remembrance, History, and Justice: Coming to Terms with Traumatic Pasts in Democratic Societies*, ed. Vladimir Tismaneanu and Bogdan Iacob (Budapest: Central European University Press, 2015), 215.

7. Chloe Paver, "Colour and Time in Museums of East German Everyday Life," in Saunders and Pinfold, *Remembering and Rethinking the GDR*, 132.

8. Marianne Wellershoff, "Musik der Freiheit" *Der Spiegel*, October 4, 1999, http://www.spiegel.de/kultur/kino/sonnenallee-musik-der-freiheit-a-45232.html.

9. Svetlana Boym, *The Future of Nostalgia* (New York: Basic, 2001). For an intriguing example of how former East German citizens reacted to the film and sought to combat its inauthentic aspects (in their views), see Jana Hensel, "Die SPD gründet eine Generation 89—und keiner will dazugehören," *Spiegel*, October 30, 2003: http://www.spiegel.de/politik/deutschland/ostalgiegipfel-die-spd-gruendet-eine-generation-89-und-keiner-will-dazugehoeren-a-271910.html.

10. Matthias Lohre, "DDR Reloaded," *Der Spiegel*, August 7, 2003, http://www.spiegel.de/kultur/gesellschaft/erinnerungskultur-ddr-reloaded-a-260109.html.

11. "Welcome Back, Lenin!," *Der Spiegel*, February 27, 2003, http://www.spiegel.de/wirtschaft/ostalgie-freizeitpark-welcome-back-lenin-a-238037.html.

12. See Diane Carson, "Learning from History in *The Lives of Others*: An Interview with Writer/Director Florian Henckel von Donnersmarck," *Journal of Film and Video* 62, nos. 1–2 (2010), 13.

13. "'I Remember an Atmosphere of Fear,'" *Spiegel Online*, May 12, 2006, http://www.spiegel.de/international/cinematic-confrontation-with-east-germany-s-stasi-i-remember-an-atmosphere-of-great-fear-a-415625.html.

14. Edith Siepmann, "Alles verlogen, Flierl muss weg!," *Der Spiegel*, May 4, 2006, http://www.spiegel.de/kultur/gesellschaft/stasi-debatte-alles-verlogen-flierl-muss-weg-a-409920.html.

15. See Hans-Günter Eschke, "Nostalgie-Ostalgie? Kritische Bemerkungen zu einer ideologischen Betrachtungsweise der Wirklichkeit," *Aufklärung und Kritik* 1 (1997): 116–32; Daphne Berdahl, "(N)Ostalgie for the Present: Memory, Longing, and East German Things," *Ethnos* 64, no. 2 (1999): 192–211; Martin Blum, "Remaking the East German Past: Ostalgie, Identity, and Material Culture," *Journal of Popular Culture* 34, no. 3 (2000): 229–53; Dominic Boyer, "Ostalgie and the Politics of the Future in Eastern Germany," *Public Culture* 18, no. 2 (2006): 361–81; and Paul Cooke, *Representing East Germany since Reunification: From Colonization to Nostalgia* (New York: Berg, 2005). To my mind, Daphne Berdahl's account of the phenomenon is the most convincing. She argues that ostalgie "both contests and affirms a new order" (the reunified Germany). On the one hand, nostalgia for things from the GDR helps to challenge the dominant discourse of the new Germany (largely one driven by Wessies) that East Germany was backward and oppressive all at once; on the other hand, nostalgia for old objects and the consumer boom for these objects is a form of acknowledging that the GDR has passed into history. See Berdahl, "(N)Ostalgie for the Present," 48–59.

16. On *Good Bye, Lenin!*, Roger Hillman analyzed it as an example of counterfactual history, or history in the subjunctive; Jennifer Kapczynski sees it as a contradictory commentary on ostalgie itself, but one that ultimately gives in to its nostalgic visions; Oana Godeanu-Kenworthy likewise sees it as caught in a self-laid trap, one between visions of commodity and of simulacrum; Joseph Jozwiak and Elisabeth Mermann interpret the film as a product of the very historical moment that gave rise to ostalgic feelings even while it moves in part beyond it. See Roger Hillman, "Goodbye, Lenin (2003): History in the Subjunctive," *Rethinking History* 10, no. 2 (June 2006): 221–37; Jennifer Kapczynski, "Negotiating Nostalgia: The GDR Past in *Berlin Is in Germany* and *Good Bye, Lenin!*," *Germanic Review* (2007): 78–100; Oana Godeanu-Kenworthy, "Deconstructing Ostalgia: The National Past between Commodity and Simulacrum in Wolfgang Becker's *Good Bye Lenin!* (2003)," *Journal of European Studies* 41, no. 2 (2011): 161–77; Joseph Jozwiak and Elisabeth Mermann, "'The Wall in Our Minds?': Colonization, Integration, and Nostalgia," *Journal of Popular Culture* 39, no. 5 (2006): 780–95. On *The Lives of Others*: Thomas Lindenberger argues that it is a film in the style of exploitation films and therefore ought to be called "Stasisploitation," one that presents inauthentic elements of the past as lived history; Daniela Berghahn views it as a fairy tale of sorts that offers an ahistorical redemption for the dictatorship; Owen Evans sees it as offering a contradictory yet effective message about the recent past and what he terms "an authenticity of affect"; finally, Cheryl Dueck dissects the argument in Germany that posited the film as humanizing the Stasi, making their actions seem legitimate (and she found it unsatisfying). See Thomas Lindenberger, "Stasisploitation: Why Not? The Scriptwriter's Historical Creativity in 'The Lives of Others'" *German Studies Review* 31, no. 3 (2008): 557–66; Daniela Berghahn, "Remembering the Stasi in a Fairy Tale of Redemption: Florian Henckel Von Donnersmarck's *Das Leben der Anderen*," *Oxford German Studies* 38, no. 3 (2009): 321–33; Owen Evans, "Redeeming the Demon? The Legacy of the Stasi

in *Das Leben der Anderen,*" *Memory Studies* 3, no. 2 (2010): 164–77; Cheryl Dueck, "The Humanization of the Stasi in *Das Leben der Anderen,*" *German Studies Review* 31, no. 3 (2008): 599–609. Finally, Nick Hodgin has examined the relationship between *Heimat*, memory, and nostalgia in films about the GDR made since 1989 in his *Screening the East: Heimat, Memory, and Nostalgia in German Film since 1989* (New York: Berghahn, 2011). Hodgin particularly singles out Becker's and von Donnersmarck's films (along with Oliver Hirschbiegel's *Downfall*) as movies that restored German cinema's reputation abroad in the 2000s, mostly because of their "perceived cultural influence."

17. Reinhard Mohr, "Stasi ohne Spreewaldgurke," *Der Spiegel*, March 15, 2006, http://www.spiegel.de/kultur/kino/das-leben-der-anderen-stasi-ohne-spreewaldgurke-a-406092.html.

18. Ibid.

19. Rainer Gansera, "In der Lauge der Angst," *Süddeutsche Zeitung*, May 19, 2010, http://www.sueddeutsche.de/kultur/film-das-leben-der-anderen-in-der-lauge-der-angst-1.894518.

20. Ibid.

21. Andreas Kilb, "Verschwörung der Hörer," *Frankfurter Allgemeine*, March 21, 2006, http://www.faz.net/aktuell/feuilleton/kino/kino-verschwoerung-der-hoerer-1306894.html. Similar comparisons appear in Mariam Lau's "Schluss mit lustig," *Die Welt*, March 22, 2006, https://www.welt.de/print-welt/article205515/Schluss-mit-lustig.html; and Anke Westphal's "Keine Sensation," *Berliner Zeitung*, March 22, 2006, http://www.berliner-zeitung.de/keine-sensation--der-film--das-leben-der-anderen--von-florian-henckel-von-donnersmarck-unsere-liebe-stasi-15501262. In the former, Lau argues that films such as *Good Bye, Lenin!* made the GDR seem funny and *The Lives of Others* meant "realism is gradually penetrating" into German cinema. In the latter, Westphal posits that, unlike ostalgie films such as Becker's, Donnersmarck's movie shows how ideology penetrated private life in the GDR. In what has to be one of the more interesting scholarly examinations of the film (and further proof of its impact), Diana Diamond, a psychology professor at City College of New York, argues that Wiesler's transformation captures what psychologists call "embodied simulation," which can lead to greater empathy and behavioral change. See her "Empathy and Identification in von Donnersmarck's *The Lives of Others,*" *Journal of the American Psychoanalytic Association* 56, no. 3 (2008): 811–32.

22. Matthias Ehlert, "Der Freund auf meinen Dach," *Die Welt*, February 12, 2006, https://www.welt.de/print-wams/article138605/Der-Freund-auf-meinem-Dach.html.

23. Evelyn Finger, "Die Bekehrung," *Die Zeit*, March 23, 2006, http://www.zeit.de/2006/13/Leben_der_anderen.

24. Silke Arnold-de Simine, *Mediating Memory in the Museum: Trauma, Empathy, Nostalgia* (New York: Palgrave Macmillan, 2013), 161. For the report in its entirety, see Martin Sabrow, ed., *Wohin treibt die DDR-Erinnerung? Dokumentation einer Debatte* (Göttingen, Ger.: Vandenhoeck and Ruprecht, 2007).

25. Simine, *Mediating Memory*, 161.

26. Quoted in Jonathan Bach, "Collecting Communism: Private Museums of Everyday Life under Socialism in the Former East Germany," *German Politics and Society* 33, no. 1-2 (Spring–Summer 2015), 136.

27. Simine, *Mediating Memory*, 161.

28. Ibid., 162. Simine also makes the interesting argument that GDR museums focusing on the everyday has gendered connotations, for the items on display in them tend to be ones associated with women, the female realm, home, childhood, and family. Among the objects she singles out is the "Schwalbe" scooter, which was used by working women in the GDR and became a "cult object" because of its use in *Good Bye, Lenin!* (164). Bach concurs with this assessment in "Collecting Communism."

29. Robert Rückel, "A Warm Welcome" (Stasi Prison Museum guidebook), 4.

30. Ibid.

31. Ibid., 5.

32. Stefan Wolle, "The Human Being Is at the Centre of Attention" (introduction to Stasi Prison Museum guidebook), 9.

33. Simine, *Mediating Memory*, 179.

34. Ibid.

35. Daphne Berdahl, *On the Social Life of Postsocialism: Memory, Consumption, Germany* (Bloomington: Indiana University Press, 2009), 61.

36. Ibid., 62.

37. Ibid., 65. For more on the Trabant's GDR history, see Eli Rubin, "The Trabant: Consumption, Eigen-Sinn, and Movement," *History Workshop Journal* 68, no. 1 (2009): 27–44.

38. "Oh, Trabi, Oh! Warum wollen alle diesen Trabant tätscheln?," *Berliner Kurier*, April 3, 2013, http://www.berliner-kurier.de/berlin/kiez---stadt/oh--trabi--oh--warum-wollen-alle-diesen-trabant-taetscheln--4438850.

39. DDR Museum, "A Hands-on Experience of History," http://www.ddr-museum.de/en/exhibition/highlights/trabi.html.

40. DDR Museum, "Children's Bedroom, Part 1" (blog), accessed February 24, 2020, http://www.ddr-museum.de/en/blog/exhibition-news/the-childrenrsquos-bedroom-part-1-memories-bruce-springsteen-and-a-space-ship.

41. Ibid.

42. DDR Museum, "The Living Room: A First Impression" (blog), accessed February 24, 2020, http://www.ddr-museum.de/en/blog/exhibition-news/the-living-room-part-1-a-first-impression.

43. DDR Museum, "The Kitchen, Part 3: The Perspective of the Curator" (blog), accessed February 24, 2020, http://www.ddr-museum.de/en/blog/exhibition-news/the-kitchen-part-three-the-perspective-of-the-curator.

44. DDR Museum, "The Garage in Our Exhibition: Part 1, the Idea" (blog), accessed February 24, 2020, http://www.ddr-museum.de/de/blog/ausstellungsnews/die-garage-in-unserer-ausstellung---teil-1-die-idee.

45. DDR Museum, "Keeping Memories Alive: QR Codes with Object Photos in the 'Kindergarten'" (blog), accessed February 24, 2020, http://www.ddr-museum.de

/de/blog/ausstellungsnews/erinnerungen-wach-halten-qr-codes-mit-objektfotos-im-ausstellungsbereich-kindergarten.

46. DDR Museum, "The Children's Room: Part 4, View of the Past" (blog), accessed February 24, 2020, http://www.ddr-museum.de/de/blog/ausstellungsnews/das-kinderzimmer---teil-4-ausblick-in-die-vergangenheit.

47. DDR Museum, "My Favorite Exhibit" (blog), accessed February 24, 2020, http://www.ddr-museum.de/en/blog/museum-news/my-favorite-exhibit.

48. *DDR Museum* (website), accessed February 24, 2020, http://www.ddr-museum.de/en.

49. DDR Museum, "A Hands-on Experience of History," accessed February 24, 2020, http://www.ddr-museum.de/en/exhibition.

50. Quoted in Simine, *Mediating Memory*, 180.

51. A point made by Bach in his "Collecting Communism."

52. Ibid., 140.

53. *Stasi Museum* (website), http://www.stasimuseum.de/en/enausstellung.htm.

54. Wiebke Hollersen, "Fighting over the Past," *Der Spiegel*, June 3, 2010, http://www.spiegel.de/international/germany/fighting-over-the-past-former-stasi-headquarters-provide-headache-for-berlin-a-698267.html.

55. Ibid.

56. Ibid.

57. Susan Stone, "Museum Offers 'Ostalgic' Look at East Germany," *Spiegel Online*, July 20, 2006, http://www.spiegel.de/international/ddr-living-museum-offers-ostalgic-look-at-east-germany-a-427579.html.

58. Ibid.

59. Ibid.

60. Nadine Schimroszik, "Ostalgie boomt," *Spiegel Online*, November 26, 2007, http://www.spiegel.de/reise/staedte/ddr-museum-in-berlin-ostalgie-boomt-a-519677.html. Knabe also characterized ostalgie as "the sauce of glorification poured over the GDR past" (Jones, *Media of Testimony*, 12).

61. Katrin Kohl, "Conceptualizing the GDR—20 Years After," *Oxford German Studies* 38, no. 3 (2009): 266.

62. Ibid., 267.

63. Ibid., 270.

64. Ibid.

65. Saunders and Pinfold, *Remembering and Rethinking the GDR*, 5.

66. Ibid.

67. Wolfgang Emmerich, "Cultural Memory East v. West: Is What Belongs Together, Really Growing Together?," *Oxford German Studies* 38, no. 3 (2009): 242–53.

68. Quoted in Jones, *Media of Testimony*, 13.

69. Mary Fulbrook, *The People's State: East German Society from Hitler to Honecker* (New Haven, CT: Yale University Press, 2005), 1.

70. Ibid., 2.

71. Ibid., 291.
72. Ibid.
73. Ibid., 292.
74. Ibid.
75. Peter Thompson, "'Die unheimliche Heimat': The GDR and the Dialectics of Home," *Oxford German Studies* 38, no. 3 (2009): 283.
76. Simine, *Mediating Memory*, 165.
77. Bach, "Collecting Communism," 136.
78. Rückel, "Warm Welcome," 5.

STEPHEN M. NORRIS is Walter E. Havighurst Professor of Russian History and Director of the Havighurst Center for Russian and Post-Soviet Studies at Miami University (Ohio). He is author of two books on Russian cultural history, including *Blockbuster History in the New Russia: Movies, Memory, Patriotism* (2012), and editor of five books on Russian history and culture, including *Russia's People of Empire: Life Stories from Eurasia, 1500 to the Present* (with Willard Sunderland, 2012). He is currently writing a biography of the Soviet political caricaturist Boris Efimov.

Figure D.1. A Soviet Time Machine? Museum of Soviet Arcade Games, St. Petersburg. *Wikimedia Commons*

D

HALL OF RUSSIAN MEMORY

The first two halls in our museum established narratives of suffering, listed the names of victims, and built pantheons to commemorate tragic events in order to remember the recent past. These remembrance practices, whether implicit or explicit, held the Soviet Union and its successor state, Russia, as the chief victimizer. In the counterexamples, those focusing on the everyday, the questions of Soviet occupation did not matter as much (if at all).

Contemporary Russian museums, while analogous in seeking to establish new narratives, identify victims, and commemorate new heroes that differed from hegemonic Soviet ones, obviously could not start with blaming the Soviet Union or Russia. Nor could nostalgic tourism sites focus on the same everyday, the same material objects and goods, in the way German and Czech museums could. At the same time, as Tony Judt aptly notes in his history of postwar Europe, the Russians "had memories of their own." These memories did not differ as greatly from the Soviet narratives as the memories held elsewhere in the Soviet Bloc. "World War Two," Judt writes, "*was* a 'Great Patriotic War'; Soviet soldiers and civilians *were*, in absolute numbers, its greatest victims; the Red Army *did* liberate vast swathes of eastern Europe from the horrors of German rule; and the defeat of Hitler *was* a source of unalloyed satisfaction and relief for most Soviet citizens—and others besides."[1] The memories that developed in Russia during communism, in other words, were not quite as aggrieved as elsewhere in the former bloc. Russian museums of communism therefore deserve their own hall, but it should be a wing within the same museum as those containing the Hall of Genocide, Occupation, and Terror, the Hall of National Tragedies, and the Hall of Everyday Life.

In the most comprehensive attempt to understand postcommunist Russia memory published to date, Alexander Etkind suggests that the lack of recognition of Communist Era trauma has created a "society of ghosts" in contemporary Russia. The undead of communism, he provocatively argues, haunt present-day Russia, waiting to be acknowledged and then buried. Etkind terms this situation "warped mourning," one in which post-Soviet Russia overlooks the violence and trauma of the Stalin period. The "undead," he claims, return in "soft" memory outlets and not "hard" ones: in Etkind's view, too many unsettled arguments have dominated remembrance practices at the expense of settled debates about the meanings of the past. "In Russia and eastern Europe," he writes, "novels, films, and debates about the past vastly outpace and overshadow monuments, memorials, and museums."[2] Monuments and museums, however, are like "crystals that settle in a solution of memory, provided that this solution is strong and stable."[3] What are needed, at least in this understanding, are museums of communism.

Russia now has them, as the three entries in the exhibit hall illustrate, but they do not reflect a solution of memory. Rather, the State Museum of Gulag History, the Butovskii Shooting Range, and the Museum of Soviet Arcade Games capture how Russian remembrance after communism has captured multivalent memories. The first two sites have relatively long histories themselves, both emerging out of nonstate attempts to remember Soviet trauma. Both have now been accepted (in some views, coopted) by the state. The third, a place to play Soviet era arcade games, also sprung from grassroots efforts. Taken together, the three offer tentative steps toward understanding the trauma of the Stalin era and how to approach the everyday habits of Soviet citizens. The focus is on victims in the first two (and narrowly defined ones, as the two chapters elaborate) and both present problematic interpretations, yet they acknowledge the dead. In the third museum, tourists can play games they once played under communism or learn to play games their parents played. Perhaps Russian memory after communism is not so warped after all.

NOTES

1. Tony Judt, *Postwar: A History of Europe since 1945* (New York: Penguin, 2006), 825.
2. Alexander Etkind, *Warped Mourning: Stories of the Undead in the Land of the Unburied* (Stanford, CA: Stanford University Press, 2013), 176.
3. Ibid.

Figure 10.1. Gulag Museum, Moscow, founded 2004 (Petrovka location), 2015 (current location). http://www.gmig.ru/. *Photograph by Jeffrey Hardy*

TEN

Commemorating and Forgetting Soviet Repression: Moscow's State Museum of GULAG History

JEFFREY HARDY

The new State Museum of GULAG History opened its doors to the public in late 2015, nearly a quarter of a century after the fall of the Soviet Union.[1] It occupies a beautifully reconstructed though somewhat austere brick building just outside Moscow's Garden Ring Road, three kilometers due north from Red Square. The museum defines its mission as teaching about and memorializing Soviet repression. This is certainly no easy feat, particularly in today's climate of revitalized Russian nationalism that promotes a generally heroic picture of the Soviet Union and of its most infamous leader, Joseph Stalin. Complicating its aim further is the museum's organizational status: it was founded by a victim of Stalinism, it is managed by Russian academics and museum professionals, and it is owned and funded by the state. This diversity of interests makes the State Museum of GULAG History a fascinating case study of memory construction in contemporary Russia.

Soviet history is littered with episodes that bear the hallmarks of, if not genocide, then certainly mass trauma: violence, a sense of helplessness, and a sense of betrayal.[2] The issue of coming to terms with the traumatic past were first raised publicly by Nikita Khrushchev in his famous secret speech of 1956 and were then renewed by both state and nonstate actors in the heyday of Mikhail Gorbachev's *glasnost'* campaign.[3] Since the collapse of the Soviet Union in 1991, politicians, former dissidents, academics, and others throughout the post-Soviet space have debated how, or even whether, to commemorate the victims of the Soviet experiment in the public space. In the Russian Federation, the legal inheritor of the Soviet legacy, conversation over how to memorialize these traumatic events has been especially heated, with conflict typically occurring between human-rights organizations devoted to keeping the memory of trauma alive and a strong state that is fiercely nationalistic and that at least partially identifies with its Soviet predecessor.[4]

Organizations such as Memorial, Vozvrashchenie, the Sakharov Center, and more recently the Last Address Project have been active since the late 1980s in publishing memoirs and lists of victims and in creating public monuments and museums to commemorate the victims of Soviet repression. Although they may at times quibble over the details of particular memory sites, they are united in the desire for more and more prominent commemoration.[5] As Jenny Edkins points out, survivors of mass trauma events in a variety of contexts in recent decades have sought public places to mourn. But monuments are not just about mourning. They also present "a way of resistance" to the state that persecuted them, a perpetual reminder of the state's past crimes.[6] This combination of mourning and resistance is certainly present in the post-Soviet Russian case.

Such pressure for public commemoration has greatly complicated memory politics for the state. The state has certainly been involved in some commemoration of Soviet atrocities. Gorbachev, Boris Yeltsin, and Vladimir Putin have all followed Khrushchev's lead in publicly denouncing Stalin's crimes. Yet there has also been resistance, particularly when it comes to monuments and museums. The Russian state is far from unique in attempting to frame past trauma in a way conducive to a unifying nationalist narrative, which is the typical and expected response from posttrauma political actors. Beyond this, however, Edkins finds that, in commemorating past atrocities, states typically offer victims and survivors "sympathy and pity in return for the surrender of any political voice."[7] Official commemoration, thus, is designed to help the nation move forward in unity, to prevent the crimes of the past from influencing the politics of the future.

Scholars have also weighed in on this debate, primarily to argue that Russia's monuments and museums devoted to Soviet repression are insufficient for proper memorialization, and that this has grave social and political consequences. As Alexander Etkind, writing of the lack of such a monument in Vologda and more broadly of the absence of a significant national memorial in Russia, remarks, "There is nothing more conspicuous than an absent monument."[8] Etkind argues that, by neglecting the creation of "hard memory"—by which he means memorials and museums as opposed to the "soft memory" of literature and artistic works—contemporary Russian culture remains short-sighted and therefore warped.[9] Moreover, the Russian state, by taking a half-hearted approach to memorializing Soviet victims, is signaling that the transformation from Soviet to post-Soviet politics is incomplete.[10] Such conclusions are founded on Alexander and Margaret Mitscherlich's groundbreaking observation that Germans' unwillingness to confront their Nazi past in the decades after World War II led to a damaged collective psyche.[11] This "collective denial of the past" in Germany was eventually replaced with a sense of *Vergangenheitsbewältigung* (translatable as "coming to terms with the past"), accompanied by a series of public monuments and museums dedicated to exploring the Holocaust. This process has not been without controversy, but the hope of scholars such as Etkind is that a similar process in Russia will produce a healthier social psychology and a humbler and more self-aware state.

What with the intense negotiations over monuments and "memorial museums" dedicated to historical traumas in Germany, Rwanda, South Africa, and South America, not to mention the United States and its complicated memory politics surrounding slavery and the destruction of Native Americans, it is no surprise that Russia has been similarly vexed by such issues.[12] Who to commemorate, how to commemorate, and whom, if anyone, to blame are the central questions posed by any memorial project, and the purpose of this chapter is to examine these questions, along with the tension between the state and civil society, through the lens of the State Museum of GULAG History.[13] This museum presents a fascinating case study of negotiated commemoration in post-Soviet Russia. Led by a talented and energetic young director, it in many positive ways documents the crimes of the past, evokes an emotional response, presses visitors to ponder how knowing about the past can help direct the future, and engages the broader community outside normal museum hours. In other ways, however, the museum falls short, in part as a result of compromises made to please its constituencies. Its narrative is sometimes muddled, it lacks a central shrine for mourning, it does not define what is meant by the term *Gulag*, it fails to assign blame beyond Stalin and his top henchmen, and it neglects large categories of Soviet victims. Ultimately, the museum tells a story that is palatable to both the state and the human-rights organizations, and this is perhaps its greatest success and failure.

A BRIEF SURVEY OF GULAG MUSEUMS AND MONUMENTS IN THE RUSSIAN FEDERATION

The first monument to victims of the Gulag was already erected in Moscow before the fall of the Soviet Union when the Moscow City Council, under pressure from nascent human-rights organizations, ordered a stone to be brought from the Solovetsky Islands and placed at Lubyanka Square on October 30, 1990.[14] The location in front of KGB headquarters was certainly significant, as was the stone's origins: The Solovetsky Islands were the site of the infamous Solovetsky Special-Purpose Camp, the 1920s-era correctional-labor experiment that paved the way for the creation of the Gulag in 1930.[15] The date too held special meaning. On October 30, 1974, Soviet dissidents first celebrated a Day of Political Prisoners, with several Gulag inmates beginning a hunger strike to commemorate (as they saw it) the shedding of innocent blood by Soviet authorities. In 1991, amid the power struggle between Boris Yeltsin and Mikhail Gorbachev, this date was declared by the former an official Day of Remembrance of the Victims of Political Repressions.

Since the Solovetsky Stone was erected in Moscow, a number of other monuments and museums have been established in Russia, both by the state and by various human-rights organizations. A similar stone from the Solovetsky Islands was eventually placed in Saint Petersburg, with a plaque simply stating "To the Prisoners of the Gulag."[16] Other monuments also dot the Petersburg cityscape. On the Solovetsky Islands themselves a small but impressively rich museum dedicated to the Gulag occupies a former barrack from that era, and a nearby Alley of Remembrance boasts several monuments commemorating those who died there.[17] In Magadan, the infamous "Capital of the Gulag," the monumental Mask of Sorrows designed by famed sculptor Ernst Neizvestnyi was dedicated in 1996.[18] Also in Magadan, the state-run regional museum has long had a large exhibition devoted to the Gulag, and, on the famous Kolyma Highway, a small private museum operates in the town of Yagodnoe. Noril'sk since just before the fall of the Soviet Union has featured a number of Gulag monuments at the site of a mass grave on territory that since 1995 has been known as Golgotha, after the biblical place of suffering and death. A few prison museums run by state agencies can be found, such as Tomsk's Memorial Museum located in the former People's Commissariat for Internal Affairs (Narodnyi Komissariat Vnutrennykh Del; NKVD) prison.[19] Other monuments and exhibitions dot the map of Russia, many of them placed and operated by local chapters of the Memorial Society. The majority of these, however, are small, offering the viewer little information on their meaning.[20]

As these varied museums and monuments demonstrate, both the Russian state and civil society have played an active role in memory construction related to the Gulag. At times, however, conflict has emerged between the two, as illustrated by Perm-36, by far the largest and most influential museum and monument to the victims of the Gulag (until the opening of the new Museum of GULAG History, at least).[21] Officially called the Memorial Complex of Political Repression, the museum opened in 1994 on the site of a former corrective-labor colony within the vast Gulag system. Boasting more than 370 square meters of exhibit space and tens of thousands of visitors each year (despite its remote location), it uniquely presented to visitors an intact camp-style place of confinement. But Perm-36 was not just any Gulag site, most of which had been left to ruin or converted to other uses after Khrushchev's dramatic transformation of the Soviet penal system; from 1972 to 1988 it was the primary place of detention for those convicted of treason, anti-Soviet propaganda, espionage, and other antistate crimes.[22] As such, much of the museum was devoted to exploring the life and suffering of the Soviet Union's political prisoners in the era of the dissidents.[23]

Yet this all changed in 2014. From 1994 to 2014, the museum had been run by the local chapter of the Memorial Society, but in 2012–13 the organization increasingly came under attack by state authorities, who charged it with accepting foreign money and promoting a "fascist" (and thereby anti-Russian) historical narrative.[24] In 2014 the Perm Province government successfully sued and took ownership of the museum, temporarily closing it before reopening it with a new slate of exhibits. The new exhibits emphasized not so much the suffering of political prisoners, but rather the cultural life of common criminals and guards alike and the contribution they made to the war effort of the 1940s.[25] The Gulag is thus depicted within the powerful narrative of national suffering during wartime, of sacrifice for a greater good.[26] As Lev Gudkov, a prominent public intellectual and director of a well-known nongovernmental public-polling organization, the Levada Center, explains, "the Cult of Victory not only removed responsibility from the state, it retrospectively justified the entire Stalinist regime. Victory justified and 'explained' the Terror and the necessity of absolute force in preparing for the coming war."[27] The debate over how the Gulag should be remembered, at Perm-36 at least, is thus a struggle waged by Putin's semiauthoritarian regime on the one side and Russia's democratic opposition on the other. Although the latter strove to tell a grim story of repression and suffering, the authorities now in charge of the museum frame the Gulag as an indispensable (albeit at times unsavory) part of the growing might and power of the Soviet Union. It was a place, in other words, where the guilty atoned for their sins while helping to industrialize the country in its defense against fascism and the West.

THE GULAG MUSEUM ON PETROVKA STREET

This tension between the state and civil society was also present, albeit in less direct form, at Moscow's original Museum of GULAG History. Although the Solovetsky Stone was established in Moscow even before the collapse of the Soviet Union, the capital city for more than a decade after lacked a Gulag museum. This changed when prominent Soviet-era dissident and former Gulag inmate Anton Vladimirovich Antonov-Ovseenko successfully lobbied the Moscow city government under Mayor Yuri Luzhkov to found the State Museum of GULAG History on July 31, 2001.[28] Its doors on Petrovka Street in downtown Moscow opened to the public on May 18, 2004, after three years of preparation, with funding coming primarily from the Moscow city government.[29] In the first years of its existence, the museum was poorly attended, and original plans for three thousand square meters of exhibition space in the city-owned building were abandoned,

Figure 10.2. Petrovka Street Museum entrance. *Photograph by Jeffrey Hardy*

leaving just the original three hundred square meters. As Antonov-Ovseenko lamented in 2007, the museum and its subject are "of little interest for the new generation. They are interested in television and the Internet, while the older generation is tortured by daily life—how their pensions are not enough to live on.[30] Compounding this was the complete lack of public relations conducted for the museum by the city or federal government; the state seemed content to let the museum exist but did little to promote it (or to heat it in the winter).[31] By 2009 the situation had not improved, with only approximately thirty people per day visiting the museum.[32]

Visitors to the Petrovka Street museum discovered an eclectic collection of artifacts and experiences in a poorly arranged space. The entrance to the museum was easily overlooked among the upscale hotels, shops, and restaurants on this high-end street just north of the Bolshoi Theater, perhaps helping to explain its low visitation numbers despite its central location (fig. 10.2). After finding the passageway leading to the inner courtyard of the building, an extended passageway of barbed wire and guard towers led to the door, with poster-sized photographs of several prominent victims of Stalin's terror adorning the exterior façade. Once inside, visitors could wander a few small rooms of exhibitions by themselves or be led around by a guide dressed as a prison guard, with translation into other languages typically not available.[33] Prominently featured were a few rooms devoted to experiential displays, with life-size wax figures of Gulag authorities and inmates. The goal was clearly to place guests inside an interrogation room, barrack, or punishment cell, to help them feel at least some of the claustrophobic oppression experienced by those labeled enemies of the state in Soviet times. Other displays included the personal effects of inmates, documents from the Gulag archives, snippets from memoirs, and a map depicting the location of the Gulag system's primary corrective-labor camps. Although the staff was always eager to help visitors understand the history of the Gulag, or at least the fate of prominent Bolsheviks and cultural figures repressed during the Great Terror, ultimately the museum gave the feeling of being unfinished and of being too small to represent the enormity of the Gulag's place in Soviet history.

Because of the museum's location just a few blocks from Red Square, city officials soon after its opening began to consider moving it to a less central site.[34] In 2011 the move was announced, with the city promising to help fund the full three thousand square meters of space called for in the original plans in exchange for vacating the Petrovka Street building.[35] An old, four-story building on Pervyi Samotechnyi Pereulok just outside the Garden Ring in north-central Moscow was chosen (the new site is only about two kilometers from the previous location), and renovation work commenced. After four years of preparation and publicity, including a widely publicized 2014 tour of the building by Sergei Sobianin, mayor of Moscow, the new city-funded and city-owned museum opened on October 30, 2015, the official Day of Remembrance of the Victims of Political Repressions. Although neither Putin nor Sobianin attended the grand opening (the deputy mayor of Moscow led the official delegation), it was widely covered in the Russian press.[36] Twenty-five years after the dedication of the Solovetsky Stone, a new state-sponsored monument to the Gulag had been established.

EXHIBITING THE GULAG

The new Museum of GULAG History at Pervyi Samotechnyi Pereulok stands in a fairly secluded residential neighborhood not far from the infamous Butyrka Prison. Signs in both Russian and English direct visitors (who manage to at least find the general area) to its location, which otherwise might remain hidden. Once there, however, the four-story building is quite striking; while obviously old, with two-toned brick patterns adorning its facade, evidence of a recent and expensive remodel abounds: industrial modernist paneling on the sides of the building, new windows and doors, and a modern and raised roof. The second- and third-floor windows are covered with nicely-finished boards (the shabby-sounding "boarded up"

Figure 10.3. First exhibition room with cell doors. *Photograph by Jeffrey Hardy*

does not quite fit the distinctly modernist impression), leading the observer to conclude that this is no ordinary building. But without the prominent signs in Russian and English on either side of the central entryway, one would not likely guess that this was a memorial museum. There is no sense of commemoration or remembrance here—no barbed wire, no monument, no pictures of victims. Further investigation reveals that this building has no ties to Soviet-era repression.

The entry to the museum replicates the clean, industrial look of the exterior, blending steel beams and polished concrete flooring with rough-cut brick. After purchasing tickets and leaving their coats and bags in lockers (and perhaps patronizing a small café), visitors are directed to the start of the exhibits on the second floor. The heavy steel door leading into the first exhibition room (fig. 10.3) helps create a sense of passage from one world into another with the intense darkness of the room, a stark contrast to the well-lit stairwell, really cementing this feeling. The visitor immediately becomes aware that the museum is actively creating a somber mood, something that is further reinforced by the whispered and reverential voices of black-clad staff members who patrol the exhibit space.

The first room of the Museum of GULAG History is devoted to prisons, which in the Soviet Union were most commonly used for pretrial detention and investigation, although some inmates served in prison after their sentencing. Of particular interest to the museum curators are prison cells themselves. Rectangular white outlines on the floor demarcate the actual size of communal cells in the Soviet Union's best-known prisons: Butyrka, Vladimir Central, Matrosskaia Tishina, and Kresty. Two metal bedframes help give perspective to the space, and a caption on the wall explains how cells were persistently overcrowded in the Soviet era. While the seemingly large communal cells drawn on the floor actually work against this idea of claustrophobia, the main exhibit in the room, a mock cell constructed with various doors from prisons from around the Soviet Union, is more effective. This cell represents the smallest of the four presented at just seven square meters, and visitors are encouraged to go inside, paying attention to the peephole and food slot in each door. The desired effect, according to the electronic exhibit guide, is to create "a metaphorical 'space of imprisonment,' in which you can literally 'in your skin' feel the suffocating atmosphere of imprisonment." Indeed, while no cell ever looked like this, with ten doors serving as walls, the visitor is able to sense the history and significance of the doors, representing the boundary between freedom and unfreedom.

The first exhibition room of the museum also presents the first of what will be many video presentations. On the far wall from the entrance a projection displays a homemade video of a recent walk-through of the remains of an "illegal" prison of the Soviet era, in the Chaunskii Corrective-Labor Camp of the Chukotka region in the far northeast. According to the accompanying sign, investigating prosecutors in 1954 (immediately after Stalin's death) determined that the prison, then holding 212 inmates, had not been authorized by any legal body in the Soviet Union. It was the site of illegal repression, in other words. That such illegalities were part and parcel of Stalinist repression generally is driven home by the inclusion of a decaying wooden door from this very prison in the cell made of doors.

After ascending a set of stairs, the visitor is presented with a balcony room overlooking the prison display that is devoted to the Great Terror. The first exhibit here is a montage of propaganda posters, which date from 1918 to 1938, depicting the watchful Soviet security forces and their various enemies. The central focus of the room, however, is a series of displays related directly to 1937–38. An interactive electronic exhibit with twenty slides educates on a variety of details, such as repression in the army, repressed nationalities, NKVD employees, methods of investigation, and locations of burials. The central set of displays, however, focuses squarely on the several hundred thousand executions carried out during these years. A large poster demonstrates how many execution lists were signed by each member of the Politburo, with Stalin's signature appearing on 357 (surpassed only by Viacheslav Molotov's 372). But the crux of the execution exhibit is composed of three screens set against a dark background. The middle one displays a long list of alphabetized names moving slowly up the screen, victims of the Great Terror. The screen on the right, meanwhile, displays actual execution orders and the one on the left shows pictures of individual victims along with their names, basic biographical information, dates of arrest, and dates of execution. Although there is a keypad on the central display to allow visitors to search for a particular name, as soon as that name appears it slowly moves up the screen along with the rest of the names, suggesting that any one individual is still just one of several hundred thousand victims.

Opposite these screens is a bench, inviting visitors to sit and watch the names scroll by and the faces and execution orders to appear, one by one. Meanwhile, targeted speakers broadcast a series of prolonged and low musical notes, provided both by instrument and by a men's choir, with the notes often played at discordant intervals. Occasional higher-pitched metallic notes further contribute to the uncomfortable audio effect. Additional background noise is provided by the triumphal sounds of show-trial propaganda films that are being shown on a large screen to the viewer's left. The volume on these films is louder than the background noises, but in the many pauses in the films the visitor again hears the underlying sounds of men softly singing, crying out, as it were, from the dead. These audio devices, along with the darkness pervasive in this and in all rooms of the museum, create a decidedly disquieting atmosphere for contemplating the seemingly endless list of victims.

After passing by the propaganda films, the visitor descends a stairway into the main exhibition hall of the museum (fig. 10.4), pausing on the way to admire a series of brightly lit display cases, shimmering in the darkness. Further investigation reveals them to contain various Gulag artifacts from regional museums. These to some extent document daily life in the camps: a handmade chess set, objects produced in Gulag workshops, eating utensils, coins, letters, and clothes (see fig. 10.5).

At the end stands a large map showing the location of Gulag camps, together with their maximum actual inmate population. On the floor next to the displays is a timeline etched into the wooden floor, laying out twenty-six important moments in the rise and fall of repression in the Soviet Union. Above the lit displays, meanwhile, stands an enormous white screen. Though typically empty and silent, a video projector can be activated to show rare video footage of prisoners laboring and more recent clips depicting the remnants of remote camps on the barren hills of the Kolyma region. As opposed to the quiet bass notes being sung and played in the previous room, loud and varied choral voices accompany this short video display, yet the frequent dissonant notes remain constant. With both video and audio filling the entire hall, visitors are interrupted from whatever they are reading or viewing, forced to confront this audiovisual representation of the enormity of the Gulag.

Figure 10.4. Main exhibition hall. *Photograph by Jeffrey Hardy*

Figure 10.5. Artifacts of daily life. *Photograph by Jeffrey Hardy*

In two rooms overlooking this main hall are exhibits devoted to, in turn, "reforging" and production. *Reforging* is a quintessentially Soviet term that refers to the process of turning convicts into educated, cultured, hardworking, and law-abiding citizens, and the camps of the Gulag were in theory supposed to privilege this task above all others.[37] The chief method through which reforging was to occur was labor, which conveniently coincided with the primary motivation behind sending inmates to large camps devoted to mining, railroad construction, canal construction, factory construction, and city construction.[38] (These are the museum's five categories of central economic tasks performed by the Gulag. Absent, perhaps for lack of space, are logging and agriculture, which also occupied substantial numbers of Gulag inmates.) The displays in these two rooms are largely informational, with relatively few pictures or artifacts accompanying a number of posters and interactive displays. And the posters themselves in these rooms adopt a detached, matter-of-fact tone, only rarely employing such phrases as "ruthless exploitation." Clearly the point of these rooms is to present an objective, scholarly account of these two aspects of Gulag life. Although the sheer volume of information is a bit overwhelming, it is thoroughly researched and provides those interested in more than a quick walk-through a wealth of knowledge drawn from now-declassified archival material. Beyond this, the most interesting feature in these rooms is a video projection of lengthy excerpts from eight Soviet "documentary" films from the 1920s and 1930s that show highly idealized pictures of life and labor at Solovki, the Belomor Canal, Kolyma and at other Gulag camps.[39]

Below the production and reforging exhibits, in two small side rooms off the main hall, are video exhibits called *The USSR and Soviet Society: From Arrest to a Labor Camp* and *My Gulag: The Living Book of Memory*. The first provides a starkly unsettling environment, with two large video projections facing each other and benches between them for visitors to sit and watch. The volume on each is roughly the same, but the content is starkly different: one shows a series of 1930s-era Soviet propaganda videos detailing how joyful life was in the Soviet Union and the other displays a Gulag survivors discussing their own decidedly unhappy experiences in the same decade. As the placard describing the room makes clear, "the visitor can decide for himself the angle of view and compare what can be seen." The intended effect, which is successfully realized, is that visitors cannot focus on one screen without hearing the other. One cannot watch the optimistic portrayals of the 1930s without hearing the voices of people whose lives were torn apart in those years. Likewise, one cannot listen to the accounts of arrest and imprisonment without hearing triumphal music and the voices of happy young people on the quest to build socialism.

The second side room, *My Gulag*, is less discordant but no less unsettling. In one corner, a large video display shows survivors talking about their experience in the prisons and corrective-labor camps of the Gulag. In the other corner stands a display that is meant to look like an illuminated book opened to a particular page. Two projectors from above show a small video of a former inmate on the left-hand page and his or her biography on the other page. A targeted speaker from above provides the narration without seriously interfering with the video on the other side of the room. The videos recount testimony collected from dozens of survivors, and guests could theoretically sit for hours without seeing the same film twice. An accompanying placard frames the survivors in a heroic light: "The heroes of the 'My Gulag' project have the courage not only to keep a memory of the tragic pages of their biography, but they also consider it their duty to share this memory."

After visiting the four side rooms, visitors pass by the map of the Gulag at the far end of the main hall and enter the penultimate room of the museum. This focuses primarily on the Doctors' Plot and Stalin's death. In the middle of the room is a large pentagonal display, with very detailed explanatory posters on four exterior sides telling the story of how Jewish doctors came under attack by Stalin's regime in the early 1950s. The fifth side of the pentagon is open to an interior room, inside which the four walls contain video displays of grieving people paying their last respects at the viewing of Stalin's corpse. Visitors are thus immersed in the experience of Stalin's funeral. Looking back through the opening in the fifth wall, visitors see a video display of former Gulag inmates and ordinary Muscovites relating how they experienced Stalin's death. Although many ordinary citizens grieved for their deceased leader, former inmates remember celebrating, but also being worried that the situation in the Gulag could get worse.

Also in this penultimate room is a display of around a dozen famous Gulag inmates, complete with copies of (or at least photocopied selections from) their memoirs. Guests are thus given the chance to inspect their written testimonies. An interactive electronic display of the memoirists reinforces this exhibit, providing their picture, biographical information, and choice quotations from their writing that defines what the Gulag was or how to make sense of it. One of them, from Varlam Shalamov's *Kolyma Tales*, reads: "A man is not lost immediately. A man loses strength, and with it his morale. For the camp is the triumph of physical strength as a moral category.... I consider and have always considered that violence against another's will is the most awful crime against mankind." Another, from Evgeniia Fedorova's *Na ostrovakh GULAGa*, ponders who is to blame for these crimes, the NKVD, the inmates themselves, or perhaps even fate. It concludes with the condemnatory, yet simultaneously exculpatory line: "You are all guilty! For this was the Stalinist era."

A final staircase back up to the third story leads visitors to the ninth and last room, which is devoted to release and rehabilitation. Informational posters and a streaming video tell of the difficult reintegration into society that released inmates faced. A series of wooden placards gives biographical details for some of

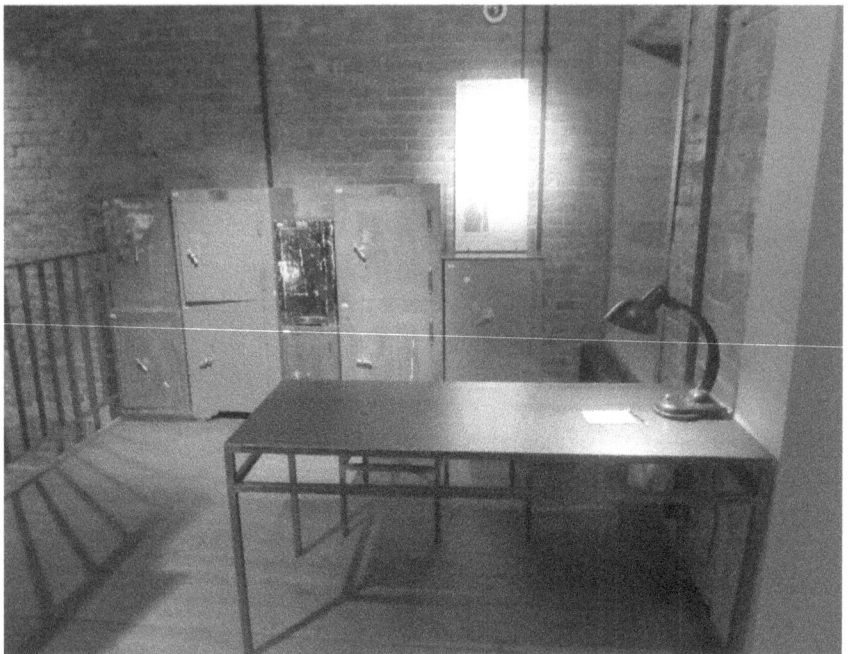

Figure 10.6. Safes symbolizing secrecy. *Photograph by Jeffrey Hardy*

the scientists and specialists who had been imprisoned. And a display on secrecy (complete with a period desk and safes (see fig. 10.6) that feel somewhat out of place) tells of how information about the Gulag was withheld from Soviet citizens.

At the end of the room are two final displays. The first is a compilation of newsfeeds from contemporary Russia that deal with the Gulag and how it is memorialized. Here one finds journalists, church officials, and even Vladimir Putin talking about the horrors of Soviet repression and the need to never forget the painful lessons of the past. Finally, as the visitor leaves, she is confronted with two open-ended statements and a question painted in bold letters on the wall: "This won't be repeated if I . . .; To understand the past one must . . .; What must be done today so that the past is not repeated tomorrow?" With this bridge between the past, present, and future established, the walk-through ends. Two flights of stairs lead back to the café, cloakroom, and exit.

INTERPRETING THE GULAG

According to its official website as of the time of this writing in 2016, the Museum of GULAG History "belongs to the category of museums of remembrance, at the root of each of which lie painful events that are difficult to comprehend."⁴⁰ In many ways, the museum fulfills this purpose of memorializing the atrocities of the Soviet era. The beautifully renovated building and high-quality displays suggest that the museum and its government sponsor spared no expense in commemorating the past. Copious information about the Gulag is presented in a variety of formats, most prominently interactive electronic displays, videos, posters, and artifacts. Witness testimony in video form is particularly valuable in telling the story of repression and, as Edkins terms it, "challeng[ing] structures of power and authority."⁴¹ The videos help to build empathy and "give back the faces" to repressed individuals.⁴² The interplay of darkness and light, together with the effective manipulation of sound, create moods that are at times uncomfortable, but at other times reverential. The balance between the two conflicting emotions is carefully managed and appropriate for the subject matter and the aims of the museum.⁴³ It is clear the curators took seriously their charge to create a "secular sacredness" in which to mourn the dead.⁴⁴

The museum is also to be commended for its community outreach. As the Moscow city government declared upon its opening, the museum "will become a modern cultural and scientific center, devoted to research, discussion, and public demonstration of the epoch of Stalinist repression."⁴⁵ Led by a young and active director, Roman Vladimirovich Romanov, the museum is vigorously fulfilling this mission. It regularly hosts discussions on a variety of human-rights-related topics; it holds movie screenings and poetry readings in the evenings; it organizes a volunteer force to aid victims of Stalinist repression and perform other civic duties; it hosts tours, seminars, and master classes for teenage students; and it publicizes its activities through various forms of traditional media and social media.⁴⁶ It also boasts a library and archive, organizes scientific expeditions to former Gulag sites, and performs ongoing oral history work devoted to interviewing surviving Gulag prisoners.⁴⁷ The museum clearly is more than just a building and a few exhibits. Through the efforts of its director, staff, and volunteers, its outreach and influence extend broadly into the community.

On the matter of audience, it is telling that all the museum's displays are in both Russian and English. The translations are not always perfect and the English, grammatically speaking, should have been checked by a native speaker, but the meaning typically is clear. Even many of the videos have English subtitles provided. Clearly the museum is oriented in part toward educating foreigners about Soviet history and demonstrating the degree to which Russia has come to terms with its bloody past. As for Russians, the target audiences appear to be students, intellectuals, and family members of victims. School groups are often led on curated tours through the museum, with emphasis placed on the terror inflicted on innocent victims. Intellectuals are treated to a wealth of information presented from the perspective of both the regime and the victims. Family members of victims, meanwhile, are provided sitting areas both in the main hall and in the My Gulag room to reflect and to mourn.

Conspicuously absent for a museum that strives to be a memorial museum, however, is a focal shrine dedicated to those who perished. Such shrines are common at similar museums. The US Holocaust Memorial Museum, for instance, has the Hall of Remembrance, complete with memorial flame and hexagonal skylight.[48] The Historical Museum of Yad Vashem similarly has a Hall of Remembrance with eternal flame, and also a Hall of Names, a large domed room on which photographs of victims are displayed.[49] These typically minimalist or abstract displays in large rooms at the end of memorial museums are an attempt to cope with the fundamentally "unrepresentability" of extremely traumatic events.[50] Perhaps the building at Pervyi Samotechnyi Pereulok was deemed not large enough or proportionally incorrect for such a shrine, or maybe the director wanted to keep the museum more educational, with a focused narrative. Either way, it is a significant omission for a museum tasked with memorializing "painful events that are difficult to comprehend."

Another interesting choice made by the museum director was to eschew the experiential displays of the museum's predecessor. There are no bloody wax figures and no staff members dressed as guards. And there is certainly nothing similar to, for instance, the Warsaw Uprising Museum or Karlag Museum discussed in this volume or the Middle Passage display of the International Slavery Museum at Liverpool, gruesome and multisensory experiences designed "to mark, or even scar, the subjectivities of its spectators."[51] The Museum of GULAG History is designed to be informational and commemorative, not experiential. Evocative (and often gory) works of art, such as the paintings of famed Gulag artist Nikolai Getman or the sketches of Danzig Baldaev are also missing. One experiences to some extent the suffocating space of a prison cell and sees a pair of handcuffs and a few grave markers, but these are the only physical reminders of the suffering inherent in prisoners' Gulag experience. Certainly the decision to avoid becoming "a morbid theme park" resembling the torture museums now found across Europe is commendable.[52] Still, one is struck by the fact that the chart providing the stark mortality rates of the 1930s and 1940s are literally tucked away in one of the rooms. The unknowing visitor, therefore, could pass through the museum thinking that the only mortal victims of Stalinism were those executed in the Terror and that the Gulag was only a place of mass confinement, not one of intense suffering and death.

One persistent problem of the museum is that seemingly out-of-place artifacts and displays are found in several of the rooms. For instance, the narrative of the first room centers on the prison, the first step in any inmate's journey, but a large wall shows a blueprint for a corrective-labor camp and another provides information on the Solovetsky Special-Purpose Camp. Most of the several artifacts on display also come from camps rather than prisons, and even the video of the prison at the Chaunskii Corrective-Labor Camp is out of place, it being more an elaborate punishment barrack for camp inmates rather than a true prison. Similarly, the room devoted to reforging has a large display about the Belomor Canal, constructed using Gulag labor. Although the canal construction is famous as an example of reforging in action (at least the book *Belomor* written by Maxim Gorky and others made such a case), the display here is about the canal itself rather than the songs, theater troupes, newspapers, labor incentives, and other methods of reforging. Two large wooden display cases with informational cards and a few artifacts in the same room likewise having nothing to do with reforging. In such instances, the driving narrative of each room and of the museum as a whole is muddled.

Another critique is that the typical visitor (one without hours to spend watching the excellent *My Gulag* videos, that is) discovers relatively little about everyday life in the Gulag generally. There are actually few artifacts in the museum as a whole, and those there are, are generally presented without explanation or context. The various items displayed in the main hall are typical. Clothes, toys, uniform numbers, miniature sculptures, eyeglasses, and other items invite questions but provide no answers. Did inmates wear these clothes or were they produced in camp workshops? Did eyeglasses connote special significance in the camp hierarchy? Did all inmates wear numbers or were they reserved for special prisoners? In addition to such unanswered questions, there is no presentation of a typical day for a Gulag inmate, and the room on production remains focused on the large projects completed (or not) by prisoners, rather than the effect of labor on the inmates themselves. Important context on everyday life is also missing from the exhibit on the illegal prison at the Chaunskii Corrective-Labor Camp, which makes no mention of the fact that this camp, like many others, was populated in the late Stalin era by rival gangs engaged in the infamous "bitches' war," with the administration often taking one side or the other. Indeed, there is nothing in the museum about the thieves-in-law gang network and its rivals, the rich variety of criminal songs and tattoos, and everything else associated with the criminal underworld that to a greater or lesser extent ruled the camps of the Gulag. Crucially, this means that the visitor cannot properly understand the point of the illegal prison, nor is he exposed to some of the most important facets of camp life.

An important conceptual issue related to the Museum of GULAG History that bears mention is that the museum never explicitly addresses what is actually meant by the term *Gulag*. The omission is highly problematic for an institution with that term in its title. For a memorial museum to serve its intended ends, after all, the atrocity warranting memorialization must be defined in some way. Strictly speaking, the Gulag was a system of corrective-labor camps and colonies that existed from 1930 until 1960, when it was decentralized and placed under control of each of the fifteen republic ministries of internal affairs (although a centralized penal administration would be re-created several years later under Leonid Brezhnev). This strict definition is problematic for several reasons: there were penal institutions in the Soviet Union, including camps, before the creation of the Gulag; there were penal institutions, such as prisons, that did not fall under the Gulag's jurisdiction, and there were certainly penal institutions after the abolition of the central Gulag administration. Moreover, there were various other institutions of repression in the Soviet Union: special settlements, exile, and, of course, execution, among others. And how to characterize investigatory work and pretrial detention performed by the secret and regular police forces? Does this also fall under the Gulag rubric?

Scholars have certainly differed in how they have defined the Gulag, depending largely on the story they are telling.[53] The Museum of GULAG History, unfortunately, fails to perform this foundational task. Some rooms hold to the narrower concept of the Gulag as a system of judicial incarceration but others seem to broaden the definition to include all forms of repression. Yet the chronological parameters of the museum, roughly 1917 to 1958, suggest a definition of the Gulag that includes only the Lenin and Stalin eras, with the Khrushchev era representing only the dismantling of the Gulag. And since Lenin himself never really appears in the museum, and the amount of material dealing with the 1917–23 period is very sparse, the museum patron is left with the impression that *Gulag* means Stalinist repression.

This implicit definition can even be further narrowed when one considers the victims that are featured in the museum. Almost without exception they are political figures, academics, scientists, artists, and other intellectuals convicted according to Article 58 of the Criminal Code of the Russian Soviet Federated Socialist Republic, which dealt with counterrevolutionary crimes such as espionage, treason, and spreading anti-Soviet propaganda. They are often referred to as political prisoners, although that term is problematic in a country where everything was interpreted through a political lens. National groups, the army, party officials, and kulaks occupy a very small place in the museum, and common criminals are almost wholly missing. Since political prisoners never constituted more than half of all inmates, this choice calls for (yet never receives) an explanation. The Gulag, then, seems to be defined not as the extensive penal system that it actually was, but as all forms of Stalinist repression against innocent political and intellectual elites. In fact, the official Moscow city government announcement of the opening of the museum confirms that "the Museum of GULAG History is the only state museum that is wholly devoted to the history of political repression in the USSR."[54]

This at once narrow (in terms of chronology and victims) and broad (in terms of its scope of repression) definition is apparent in most rooms of the museum, which prominently display political prisoners of the Stalin era. The placard for a prison door from Saratov in the first room, for instance, explains that the biologist Nikolai Vavilov died in that prison. The last two rooms likewise devote significant space to the biographies and writings of scientists and intellectuals. Defining the term *Gulag* as political repression is brought into sharpest relief by the *Doctors' Plot* display. For the Gulag as a place of confinement, the *Doctors' Plot* is completely insignificant. Hundreds of people, including a number of prominent Jewish doctors, were arrested in the last year of Stalin's life in what Soviet media declared to be a vast anti-Soviet conspiracy, but when Stalin died they had not yet been convicted and sent to the camps. After Stalin's death, the charges were quickly dropped and they were released.[55] Most historians of the Soviet penal system, therefore, would not consider devoting so much space (including a large display case with period medical instruments that have nothing to do with repression at all) to this episode. Yet if the Gulag is interpreted to mean Stalinist repression against intellectuals generally, then perhaps constructing an elaborate display to this last wave of arrests makes some sense.

This observation also holds true for the room on the Great Terror, which focuses not on how the Terror affected the camps and inmates of the Gulag, or even how the Terror resulted in a dramatic expansion of the Gulag, but on how Politburo members personally sentenced people to execution. Again, the focus here is on repression generally rather than incarceration, and repression against political figures and intellectuals in particular. As one of the posters explains, the Great Terror was launched in order "to destroy all possibility of political opposition, and to cut off any attempts at nonconformist thought." Thus, although there is a display of Order No. 00447, which primarily targeted broad layers of society, the room and the museum as a whole do little to enlighten the visitor about the breadth of Soviet repression.[56]

Leaving ordinary Soviet citizens out of Gulag memorialization raises serious concerns about how the past is being constructed and who deserves commemoration. Certainly many of the nonpolitical prisoners incarcerated in the Gulag were guilty of no crime other than being labeled class enemies or members of potentially hostile national groups.[57] (On this note, it bears mentioning that national groups from the newly annexed western borderlands are wholly omitted from the Gulag narrative, even as they played a significant role in Gulag life in the 1940s and early 1950s.) Another large group of prisoners fell victim to anticrime sweeps in which police were known to round up whomever they could find to fill quotas.[58]

Inmates from a third group were found guilty of small crimes such as petty theft yet were given draconian sentences.[59] In a stark contrast to the Butovskii Shooting Range memorial complex treated by Julie Fedor and Tomas Sniegon in this volume, to bring forth a final example of an excluded group, religious prisoners are completely written out of the narrative presented in the Museum of GULAG History.[60] Political prisoners, in other words, did not have a monopoly on the undue repression that Stalin's paranoid regime meted out. As Susana Draper demonstrates, this issue is not unique to the Museum of GULAG History or to Soviet commemoration generally. Monuments and museums in South America likewise privilege the experience of political prisoners at the expense of their nonpolitical counterparts.[61] Most memorial museums, in fact, leave out some victims in favor of others.[62] Such similarities, however, do not exculpate the Museum of GULAG History for ignoring the majority of Soviet victims.

And it is not just ordinary Soviet citizens who are omitted from the narrative; the dissidents of the post-Stalin era, also victims of political repression, are similarly neglected. The final room of the museum seems to suggest that the political prisoners were all released in the 1950s and that repression ceased. In fact, thousands of "antistate" prisoners remained after Khrushchev's release programs had concluded, and a small but steady stream of new convictions ensured that this category of inmates would never disappear. Held primarily at the Dubravnyi Corrective-Labor Camp in the 1960s and then the Perm-36 Corrective-Labor Colony in the 1970s and 1980s (as well as in punitive psychiatric wards), they proclaimed their innocence until the fall of the Soviet Union. Others, such as Andrei Sakharov and Andrei Amalrik, were forced into internal or external exile, but their stories too are not presented in the museum.

Though highly problematic, this focus on political repression under Stalin serves the interests of both the state and civil society, who have joined forces to produce the museum. Human-rights campaigners in Russia have long been more interested in state-run repression against intellectuals and political nonconformists than against ordinary citizens. The focus is not surprising, for most Russian human-rights organizations, including the original Museum of GULAG History, were founded by former political prisoners themselves. For them, the museum serves the purpose of memorializing their own suffering and the suffering of their friends and family, even as it denies the same to others.

As for the state, as many scholars have noted, state actors "typically strive to shape representations of the past in their present interests."[63] For the Russian state in this particular context, focusing almost exclusively on Stalin-era political prisoners means that its past transgressions can be neatly compartmentalized. These mistakes, however egregious, can then be frankly acknowledged and atoned for, with blame placed squarely on the shoulders of just a few individuals. In the end, the state emerges penitently triumphal over its bloody past. This interpretation confirms what Soviet and post-Soviet rulers from Khrushchev onward have maintained, declaring most of Stalin's political victims innocent while stating or implying that the dissidents were actually guilty of anti-Soviet propaganda and agitation. Therefore, there is no need to memorialize Andrei Sinyavsky, Yuli Daniel, and Aleksandr Ginzburg, among many others, not to mention post-Soviet figures like Anna Politkovskaya, Sergei Magnitsky, and Mikhail Khodorkovsky. Indeed, this is the problem of memorializing the dissidents: whereas it is somewhat possible to draw a line at Stalin's death and speak of an end to repression, if one acknowledges post-Stalin political victims, then the connection to the present is too sharp. With human-rights organizations such as the Sakharov Center and Memorial recently running into trouble with Russian authorities for their opposition to the Putin regime, the Museum of GULAG History appears to be cornered into this compromise because of its reliance on city funding.

If the focus on Stalin-era political repression rather than the Gulag as a whole unites the interests of state and civil society, the stark absence of perpetrators in the museum seems an uneasy compromise between the two. As has been noted in relation to other memorial museums, issues of motive and blame are particularly vexing. Some museums present the names of low-level offenders, others assign blame more to structural forces at play.[64] At the Museum of GULAG History, Stalin and a few of his lieutenants are assigned clear blame for the Great Terror and Doctors' Plot, but missing from all but the *My Gulag* video memoirs are the interrogators, guards, and camp bosses with whom Gulag inmates interacted every day. The museum thus appears to subscribe to Evgeniia Fedorova's quotation cited earlier, placing blame simply on the fact that "this was the Stalinist era." In this manner, high-level intentionalism is blended with a low-level structuralism to produce a narrative in which only a select few are guilty. On the one hand, this can be seen as a victory for the state, which would prefer a narrative in which the Russian people and even most state officials are essentially blameless for Soviet atrocities. On the other hand, the new exhibits at Perm-36 demonstrate that a wholly state-run museum would be tempted to portray guards in a sympathetic light. Most of them, after all, were not there willingly, and they endured their own struggles and hardships, including the execution of a number of camp officials during the Great Terror. In excluding them from the Museum of GULAG History, their suffering and their guilt are both silenced.[65]

CONCLUSIONS

The 2015 redevelopment of Moscow's Museum of GULAG History is a significant step forward in the memorialization of those who suffered and died under

Soviet rule. The shift from the small and eclectic museum at Petrovka Street to the professional and narrative-driven museum at Pervyi Samotechnyi Pereulok exemplifies the progression from short-term intergenerational memory to long-term transgenerational memory that Aleida Assmann describes. Anton Vladimirovich Antonov-Ovseenko's "heterogeneous and fuzzy bottom-up memory" in the museum's first iteration has been transformed into "a much more explicit, homogeneous, and institutionalized top-down memory."[66] Although officially associated with the Moscow city government rather than the Russian federal government, the museum is clearly sanctioned and supported by the top levels of the Russian state. The museum in its expanded and better-funded form can therefore rightly be viewed as the first major national museum devoted to the Gulag and to Soviet repression.

Alexander Etkind is certainly correct to note that "states do not eagerly erect monuments that memorialize their guilt," and so it is not surprising that this museum was not completed until a quarter century after the fall of the Soviet Union.[67] Located not far from Moscow's center, the museum offers "hard memory" evidence that the Russian state understands at least to some extent the necessity of such memorialization. As a public statement signed by Prime Minister Dmitry Medvedev declared in 2015, "Russia cannot fully become a government based on the rule of law ... without commemorating many millions of its citizens who became victims of political repressions."[68] Certainly Putin's efforts to rehabilitate Stalin's legacy and repress human-rights organizations in Russia casts some doubt on the sincerity of such statements. Still, the new museum, funded by the state, does not at all exhibit the "salvation memory" found in places such as Peru's police museums, which unabashedly declares the repression of tens of thousands of Peruvians necessary to save the country from the Shining Path insurgency.[69] Rather, the Museum of GULAG History stands as a tangible monument to the murderous misdeeds of the Soviet state.

If, as Marshall Sahlins claims, "an event becomes such as it is interpreted," then the Museum of GULAG History is certainly a flawed memorial.[70] It does many things well, but ultimately it feels incomplete to the point of being misleading. Caught between competing pressures, it largely exhibits the repression of political and intellectual elites under Stalin, a compromise narrative palatable to both the state and civil society, rather than a more comprehensive treatment of the Soviet Gulag (whether interpreted narrowly or broadly). Like other memorial museums, it serves "to both remember and forget," with many categories of people and experiences left out of the museum's memorialization.[71] To be fair, the issues that the Museum of GULAG History grapples with, at times unsuccessfully, are not easy to resolve in the limited space of the museum building and with the limited attention span of its visitors. As Paul Williams finds in his survey of memorial museums, "the issue of who should be remembered... can be as vexed as that of who to blame."[72] Even taking into account its constraints, however, the Museum of GULAG History fails to satisfactorily engage these questions.

It must be noted that the new Museum of GULAG History is still young and there are already changes in the works that will render parts of this chapter obsolete. The artifacts displayed in lit cases in the main exhibition hall will at some point be returned to the regional museums to which they belong, and another temporary display or perhaps a permanent display will be created. There are also plans to construct in the near future a memorial garden in the courtyard behind the building, which would provide additional space for contemplation and mourning. The director certainly appears open to modifications based on expert feedback, even hosting a roundtable discussion in March 2016 at which historians, journalists, and museum experts explored the ways in which the Gulag should be portrayed in the museum setting. Even if the problems and tensions brought forth in this chapter are left unaddressed, however, the museum as currently constituted is a clear step toward the creation of a more complete public memory of the Soviet era.

A further step toward the memorialization of the Soviet Union's bloody past, it should be noted by way of epilogue, is also in the works. The Museum of GULAG History has been recently involved in helping to select the design and in fundraising for a new monument dedicated to victims of political repression in Russia. Called the "Wall of Grief," it is slated for installation at the intersection of the Garden Ring and Academician Sakharov Avenue, a major artery named for the physicist-turned-dissident Andrei Sakharov that connects the Garden Ring to Komsomolskaya Square (home of three major railway stations). The monument will depict partially discernible human figures embedded in a large wall—six meters high and thirty-five meters long—that architect Georgii Vartanovich Frangulian hopes will convey the "magnitude of the tragedy." That such a massive monument is being built on Putin's order at a major intersection in central Moscow is further testament to Russia's willingness to remember and commemorate the victims of communist repression. And the words of the monument's architect place the past, and hence the monument itself, squarely within the broader ongoing debate about the Soviet legacy: "I did not believe that there would ever be a chance to construct such a monument, but it absolutely should exist in a state where repression destroyed almost the entire future of the country and deprived it of the opportunity to be wonderful and bright, prevented it from developing properly."[73] Such evocative language and the monument itself stand in stark contrast to how the Stalin era is typically portrayed by political elites in Russia today and in textbooks used by Russian schoolchildren. Thus, even as the contemporary Russian state continues down a path of state-sponsored repression supported by an ultranationalist ideology that lauds the Stalin era as one of economic and military victories, it is also allowing and even engaging in unprecedented memory construction that commemorates at least some of the atrocities of the Soviet state.

NOTES

1. The term *Gulag* is an acronym that stands for the Main Administration of Camps (*Glavnoe Upravlenie Lagerei*), the bureaucratic institution that managed the Soviet Union's penal apparatus. In common usage *Gulag* also refers to the extensive network of labor camps and colonies. In Russian, this acronym is sometimes represented in full caps, as seen here in the name of the museum.

2. Jenny Edkins, *Trauma and the Memory of Politics* (Cambridge: Cambridge University Press, 2003), 4; Duncan Bell, "Introduction: Memory, Trauma and World Politics," in *Memory, Trauma and World Politics: Reflections on the Relationship between Past and Present*, ed. Duncan Bell (Houndmills, UK: Palgrave Macmillan, 2006), 8. On the genocide question, see Norman Naimark, *Stalin's Genocides* (Princeton, NJ: Princeton University Press, 2010), and the varied responses to it in Mark Kramer, "Perspective on Norman Naimark's *Stalin's Genocides*," *Journal of Cold War Studies* 14, no. 2 (Summer 2012): 149–89.

3. One might note that even as Nikita Khrushchev decried Stalin's crimes and eventually moved Stalin's body out of the Lenin Mausoleum, he did not create a monument to the victims of Stalinism. For the Soviets, the evils of Stalinism were to be briefly addressed but then forgotten. See Polly Jones, *Myth, Memory, and Trauma: Rethinking the Stalinist Past in the Soviet Union, 1953–70* (New Haven, CT: Yale University Press, 2013).

4. See, for instance, post-Soviet Russia's construction of World War II monuments, as depicted in Nataliya Danilova, *The Politics of War Commemoration in the UK and Russia* (Houndmills, UK: Palgrave Macmillan, 2015), 146–207. In this, the Russian case is not unusual. As Duncan Bell explains, "memory is capable of being yoked to state power, in the name of nationalism, or employed in opposition, as a challenge to the dominant narratives." Bell, "Introduction," 15.

5. Particularly heated are debates over how to characterize the regime, with most favoring as a label either totalitarian or Stalinist. See, for instance, Stephen Kotkin, "Terror, Rehabilitation, and Historical Memory: An Interview with Dmitrii Iurasov," *Russian Review* 51, no. 2 (April 1992): 243.

6. Edkins, *Trauma and the Memory of Politics*, 8.

7. Ibid., 9. See also Danilova, *Politics of War Commemoration*, 8; and Rachel Ibreck, "The Politics of Mourning: Survivor Contributions to Memorials in Post-Genocide Rwanda," *Memory Studies* 3, no. 4 (October 2010): 330–32.

8. Alexander Etkind, *Warped Mourning: Stories of the Undead in the Land of the Unburied* (Palo Alto, CA: Stanford University Press, 2013), 175.

9. Etkind, *Warped Mourning*, 176–77.

10. Etkind, *Warped Mourning*, 183.

11. Alexander and Margaret Mitscherlich, *The Inability to Mourn: Principles of Collective Behavior*, trans. Beverley R. Placzek (New York: Grove, 1975), 28. "Collective amnesia" after periods of trauma is certainly not unique to the Germans. See, for instance, the experience of France after the defeat of 1870 and after the fall of the Vichy regime in Peter Burke, "Afterthought on Afterlives," in *Afterlife of Events: Perspectives of Mnemohistory*, ed. Marek Tamm (Houndmills, UK: Palgrave Macmillan, 2015), 268–69. Also influential for Etkind is Jacques Derrida, who proposes that the past continues to haunt the present. See Jacques Derrida, *Specters of Marx: The State of Debt, the Work of Mourning, and the New International*, trans. Peggy Kamuf (London: Routledge, 1994).

12. Paul Williams, *Memorial Museums: The Global Rush to Commemorate Atrocities* (Oxford: Berg, 2007).

13. By using the term "civil society" in this chapter, I am alluding to human-rights organizations such as Memorial and the Sakharov Center. There is considerable discussion about whether Russia has a true civil society, but these organizations characterize themselves as such and at root they exist in order to help defend Russian citizens against state overreach. For the purposes of this chapter, this is sufficient justification for using the term, even if the standing of these organizations is weak in comparison with their Western European counterparts. For recent scholarship dealing with Russian civil society, particularly as it relates to the law and policing, see, among others, Alexander N. Domrin, "Ten Years Later: Society, 'Civil Society,' and the Russian State," *Russian Review* 62, no. 2 (April 2003): 193–211; Brian D. Taylor, "Law Enforcement and Civil Society in Russia," *Europe-Asia Studies* 58, no. 2 (March 2006): 193–213; Graeme B. Robertson, "Managing Society: Protest, Civil Society, and Regime in Putin's Russia," *Slavic Review* 68, no. 3 (Fall 2009): 528–47; and Julie Hemment, "Nashi, Youth Voluntarism, and Potemkin NGOs: Making Sense of Civil Society in Post-Soviet Russia," *Slavic Review* 71, no. 2 (Summer 2012): 234–60.

14. Etkind, *Warped Mourning*, 185.

15. Aleksandr Solzhenitsyn characterized it as the mother of the Gulag from which "the Archipelago . . . began its malignant advance through the nation." Aleksandr Solzhenitsyn, *The Gulag Archipelago, 1918–1956: An Experiment in Literary Investigation III–IV*, trans. Thomas P. Whitney (New York: Harper and Row, 1975), 57, 74.

16. Etkind, *Warped Mourning*, 185.

17. Etkind, *Warped Mourning*, 191–92; Neil MacFarquhar, "A Tug of War over Gulag History in Russia's North," *New York Times*, August 31, 2015.

18. Etkind, *Warped Mourning*, 186–88.

19. Other notable prison museums at Lubyanka, Butyrka Prison, and Vladimir Central are open only by special arrangement and thus have little public visibility.

20. One census compiled in 2007 counted 1,140 monuments and plaques devoted to Soviet repression across the post-Soviet space, though far from all of them are devoted to the Gulag specifically. Etkind, *Warped Mourning*, 186, 189.

21. Alexander Etkind is curiously dismissive of this significant museum, perhaps because it does not fit his narrative of missing monuments. Etkind, *Warped Mourning*, 191.

22. For more on the downsizing and transformation of the Gulag system after Stalin's death, see Jeffrey S. Hardy, *The Gulag after Stalin: Redefining Punishment in Khrushchev's Soviet Union, 1953–1964* (Ithaca, NY: Cornell University Press, 2016).

23. Elena Bobrova, "Soviet-Era Gulag Museum NGO Perm-36 Announces Closure," *Russia beyond the Headlines*, March 6, 2015, http://rbth.com/society/2015/03/06/soviet-era_gulag_museum_ngo_perm-36_announces_closure_44297.html. Cached versions of this and all internet sources are in possession of the author.

24. Bobrova, "Soviet-Era Gulag Museum"; Ola Cichowlas, "The Kremlin Is Trying to Erase the Memory of the Gulag," *New Republic Online*, June 23, 2014, https://newrepublic.com/article/118306/kremlin-trying-erase-memories-gulag; and "Gulag Museum Inspected for Extremism," *Moscow Times*, August 26, 2014, https://www.themoscowtimes.com/2014/08/26/gulag-museum-inspected-for-extremism-a38752.

25. Mikhail Danilovich and Robert Coalson, "Revamped Perm-36 Museum Emphasizes Gulag's 'Contribution to Victory,'" *RFE/RL Online*, July 25, 2015, http://www.rferl.org/content/russia-perm-gulag-museum-takeover-contribution-to-victory/27152188.html.

26. As Edkins explains, "as long as memories are organized in a framework of nations and states there will always be attempts to recount even genocides and famines as triumphs and their victims as having sacrificed their lives for future generations." Edkins, *Trauma and the Memory of Politics*, 117.

27. Lev Gudkov, "Proslavlenie pobedy—sposob kollektivnogo samoutverzhdeniia," *Lenta.ru*, May 7, 2016, https://lenta.ru/articles/2016/05/07/9may/.

28. See Order No. 702-PP of the government of Moscow, issued July 31, 2001, https://www.mos.ru/authority/documents/doc/19457220.

29. As with Perm-36, this museum is also omitted without explanation from Alexander Etkind's survey of memorial and museums devoted to Soviet repression, bringing into question some of his conclusions. Etkind, *Warped Mourning*, 184–95.

30. "A Little House of Horrors on Ulitsa Petrovka," *Moscow Times*, March 20, 2007.

31. Liudmila Lunina, "Mesto lisheniia nesvobody," *Ogonek* no. 15 (April 18, 2016): 32. http://www.kommersant.ru/doc/2961547.

32. Miriam Elder, "Russia's Stalin Revival," *Global Post*, May 30, 2010, http://www.globalpost.com/dispatch/russia/090910/josef-stalin-gulag-museum.

33. The editor of this volume, Stephen Norris, recalls volunteering to translate for a group of Australian tourists when he visited the museum. His reward for this service was a personal visit with the founder, Antonov-Ovseenko.

34. "Little House of Horrors."

35. "Kul'turnyi tsentr pamiati zhertv politicheskikh repressii sozdadut v Moskve," *RIA Novosti*, November 3, 2011, http://ria.ru/culture/20111103/479342643.html.

36. "Muzei istorii GULAGa otkrylsia v Moskve v novom zdanii," *TASS*, October 30, 2015, http://tass.ru/obschestvo/2393856.

37. For more on reforging, see the contemporary propaganda account and the scholarly treatment of the Belomor Canal: Maxim Gorky, Leopol'd Auerbach, and Semen Firin, eds., *Belomor: An Account of the Construction of the New Canal between the White Sea and the Baltic Sea* (New York: Harrison Smith and Robert Haas, 1935); Julie Draskoczy, *Belomor: Criminality and Creativity in Stalin's Gulag* (Brighton, MA: Academic Studies, 2014).

38. The best explication of labor as reforging and all the problems associated therewith is Steve Barnes, *Death and Redemption* (Princeton, NJ: Princeton University Press, 2011).

39. The film excerpts shown are from *Kontsentratsionnyi lager* (Koskinokomitet, 1918); A. Cherkasov, *Solovetskie lageria osobogo naznacheniia* (Sovkino, 1927–28); A. Lemberg, *Belomorsko-Baltiiskii vodnyi put'* (1932); T. D'iakonova, *Belomorsko-Baltiiskii Kanal im. Stalina* (1933); *Kolyma* (Soiuzkinokhronika, 1934); E. Volk, *Shturm ukhty* (Leningradskaia Soiuzkinokhronika, 1935); R. Gikov, *Moskva-Volga* (Soiuzkinokhronika, 1937); and S. Savenko, *Na stroike vtorykh putei* (1937–38).

40. "O muzee," *Muzei istorii GULAGa*, formerly available at http://www.gmig.ru. The website has since been restructured and this page, along with the mission statement, has been replaced.

41. Edkins, *Trauma and the Memory of Politics*, 5.

42. Williams, *Memorial Museums*, 33.

43. Other, similar museums sometimes struggle with this balance. On the Hector Pieterson Museum in Soweto, for instance, Lynn Meskell writes that "one is made uncomfortable at all possible opportunities within the museum and its environs, rusting iron, dripping water, confined spaces, uncomfortable seating, all designed to inflect visceral horror through phenomenological means." Meskell, "Trauma Culture," 171, quoted in Bell, *Memory, Trauma and World Politics*.

44. Williams, *Memorial Museums*, 40; Avril Alba, *The Holocaust Memorial Museum: Sacred Secular Space* (Houndmills, UK: Palgrave Macmillan, 2015), 7.

45. "Muzei istorii GULAGa otkrylsia dlia posetitelei," Moscow City Website, November 2, 2015, https://www.mos.ru/news/article/2732073.

46. A Russian journalist, for instance, visited the museum after seeing an announcement for a move night. Lunina, "Mesto lisheniia nesvobody."

47. A rotating selection of these are available on the museum website and on a 'Moi GULAG' channel on YouTube.

48. Alba, *Holocaust Memorial Museum*, 76.

49. Alba, *Holocaust Memorial Museum*, 122.

50. Silke, *Mediating Memory in the Museum*, 203.

51. Arnold-de Simine Silke, *Mediating Memory in the Museum: Trauma, Empathy, Nostalgia* (Houndmills, UK: Palgrave Macmillan, 2013), 107; Alison Landsberg, *Prosthetic Memory: The Transformation of American Remembrance in the Age of Mass Culture* (New York: Columbia University Press, 2004), 101.

52. Williams, *Memorial Museums*, 102.

53. To take just three examples, although Galina Ivanova writes of the Gulag broadly as an economic and social phenomenon that transcended Soviet society, Steven Barnes characterizes it somewhat more narrowly as "the entire Soviet forced labor detention system," and Viktor Berdinskikh restricts the term to the camps and colonies controlled by the Gulag administration. Galina Ivanova, *Labor Camp Socialism: The Gulag in the Soviet Totalitarian System*, trans. Carol Flath [London: Routledge, 2000], xx; Barnes, *Death and Redemption*, 1; and Viktor Berdinskikh, *Istoriia odnogo lageriia* [Moscow: Agraf, 2001], 5–6.

54. "Muzei istorii GULAGa."

55. For more on this, see Jonathan Brent and Vladimir P. Naumov, *Stalin's Last Crime: The Plot against the Jewish Doctors, 1948–1953* (New York: HarperCollins, 2001).

56. For more on Order No. 00447, see J. Arch Getty and Oleg V. Naumov, *The Road to Terror: Stalin and the Self-Destruction of the Bolsheviks* (New Haven, CT: Yale University Press, 1999), 468–80.

57. Among others, see Alexander Nekrich, *The Punished Peoples* (New York: W. W. Norton, 1981); Lynne Viola, *The Unknown Gulag: The Lost World of Stalin's Special Settlements* (Oxford: Oxford University Press, 2007).

58. On this, see Paul Hagenloh, *Stalin's Police: Public Order and Mass Repression in the USSR, 1926–1941* (Baltimore, MD: Johns Hopkins University Press, 2009).

59. Peter H. Solomon Jr., *Soviet Criminal Justice under Stalin* (Cambridge: Cambridge University Press, 1996).

60. Religion is prominent in other post-Soviet memorials and museums in Russia. Danilova, *Politics of War Commemoration*, 152.

61. Susana Draper, "Against Depolitization: Prison-Museums, Escape Memories, and the Place of Rights," *Memory Studies* 8, no. 1 (2015): 62–74.

62. Alba, *Holocaust Memorial Museum*, 71; Ibreck, "Politics of Mourning," 330.

63. Ibreck, "Politics of Mourning," 332.

64. Williams, *Memorial Museums*, 134–36.

65. On the issue of perpetrators in Gulag literature and history, see Cynthia Hooper, "Bosses in Captivity? On the Limitations of Gulag Memoir," *Kritika* 14, no. 1 (Winter 2013): 117–42.

66. Aleida Assmann, "Transformations between History and Memory," *Social Research* 75, no. 1 (Spring 2008): 56.

67. Etkind, *Warped Mourning*, 182.

68. Ivan Nechepurenko, "New Policy on Commemorating Victims of Repression at Odds with Actions," *Moscow Times*, August 19, 2015.

69. Cynthia Milton, "Curating Memories of Armed State Actors in Peru's Era of Transitional Justice," *Memory Studies* 8, no. 3 (2015): 364.

70. Marshall Sahlins, *Islands of History* (Chicago: University of Chicago Press, 1985), xiv.

71. Lynn Meskell, "Trauma Culture: Remembering and Forgetting in the New South Africa," in Bell, *Memory, Trauma and World Politics*, 170.

72. Williams, *Memorial Museums*, 139.

73. Kseniia Knorre-Dmitrieva, "V Moskve poiavitsia 'Stena skorbi,'" *Novaya Gazeta*, October 1, 2015, http://www.novayagazeta.ru/arts/70179.html.

JEFFREY HARDY completed his graduate work at Princeton University in 2011 and is currently Associate Professor of History at Brigham Young University. His research centers on the Soviet Gulag, and his first book, *The Gulag after Stalin*, was published by Cornell University Press in 2016. He is currently working on a book-length project investigating religious belief and practice in the Gulag.

Figure 11.1. Entrance sign to the Butovo Poligon, founded 2002 (Research-Education Center run by the Russian Orthodox Church). http://www.martyr.ru/.
Wikimedia Commons

ELEVEN

The Butovskii Shooting Range
History of an Unfinished Museum

JULIE FEDOR
TOMAS SNIEGON

The Butovskii shooting range (Butovskii poligon) on the southern outskirts of Moscow is one of the most important known sites of memory of Soviet state terror. The vast majority of such sites in Russia remain unknown, undocumented, or both, especially those around Moscow, despite or perhaps precisely because of its importance as the nerve center of Soviet power, where the most crucial decisions were made and implemented.[1] The Butovskii poligon is one of only five confirmed Stalin-era mass grave sites in Moscow and the Moscow region. It represents a small but rare island of knowledge; thanks to a set of unusual historical circumstances, it has been possible to identify 20,761 individuals who were executed and buried there in mass graves between August 8, 1937, and October 19, 1938;[2] it is still possible—and even probable—that the actual number could be significantly higher.[3] The victims include representatives of around sixty nationalities and many faiths, as well as atheists, but Butovskii is a particularly important site of Russian Orthodox memory—940 of the known victims were priests and laity of the Russian Orthodox Church and 332 of them have been canonized as martyrs in the twenty-first century.[4]

The site's uniqueness and its proximity to Moscow might lead one to expect it to be more prominent and more developed as a site of memory. On major religious holidays, the site receives a reasonably large number of visitors, but it is largely quiet for the rest of the year: a peaceful and green place, covered with wildflowers and apple trees.[5] Like most other sites of Soviet terror in Russia, there is no museum attached to the site, which has largely been neglected by the federal government.[6] For those occasional writers and artists who have reflected on the site, it stands as a symbol of the fundamental and drastic incompleteness of the process of mourning the victims of state terror in Russia—the conceptual artist

Irina Nakhova has imagined a bus stop on the route leading to the site as a kind of purgatory;[7] for others, the site serves, perhaps above all else, as a symbol of the impunity of the perpetrators and of the ongoing ethical blindness of Russian society today.[8]

In this chapter, we examine the history of the (incomplete) struggle to create a memorial museum at the Butovskii poligon. The processes of memorialization and musealization of atrocity sites and mass grave sites are always complex,[9] but the case of Butovo—as of Russia more broadly—stands out as a particularly fraught and ultimately unresolved example. After more than twenty-five years of debate and campaigning on the issue, plans to create a memorial museum at the site remain unrealized. The Butovo Memorial Research-Education Center (founded 2002) lists the creation of a museum of the memory of the victims as its primary aim, yet very little progress has been made on this front. Little or no material support has been provided for the project by the state, and the energies of the site's custodians have frequently been expended by fighting off competing claims to the site from commercial developers, and also by residents of the former KGB dacha settlement neighboring the site.[10] Theoretically, the Butovskii poligon enjoys the state's legal protection as an official "historical monument of regional significance"; in practice, it remains vulnerable and relies on ad hoc gestures of powerful individuals such as the patriarch of the Russian Orthodox Church and high-ranking politicians.

Developments in the last five years, however, and especially since the government's adoption of the "State Policy Concept on Immortalizing the Memory of the Victims of Political Repressions" in August 2015, suggest that the impasse may soon be broken through a kind of compromise solution.[11] The museum project now seems to have gained high-level support. It would appear that the Presidential Council for the Development of Civil Society and Human Rights has lent its support to plans to create a federal museum at the site, and that funding for it may finally be forthcoming. Instead of a museum for all the victims buried here, however, the site is now being spoken of as the "Russian Golgotha" museum focused exclusively on victims of religious repressions.[12] The solution is framed as an inclusive one and one that reveals not just the religious meaning of the site but also its patriotic meaning. We view the solution as marking a convergence of state and church memory politics, a convergence that dovetails with the state's growing emphasis on traditional values as a cornerstone of Russian national identity. The developments are reflected in recent efforts to transform the concept of the secular museum, developing in its place a model of the "Christian museum" or "church museum" with a special relationship to the state (including the right to lay claim to state budgetary funds). This emerging memorial museum model is in sharp contrast to the majority of new memorial museums at atrocity sites that have appeared globally in the past two decades within the human-rights paradigm.[13]

We begin by looking at the history of the competing attempts to frame, define, and claim ownership of the site since its discovery in the early 1990s, tracing out the process in which it came under the custodianship of the Church. We then examine the state's changing relationship to the site, including the most recent shift toward supporting construction of a federal museum there as part of the new state memory politics that have marked the Medvedev interlude and Putin's current presidential term. What kind of museum will it be? Who will create and run it? Who will be remembered there, and how? What kind of story will the museum tell about the events it memorializes?

A SACRED SITE: THE BUTOVSKII POLIGON AS A SITE OF ORTHODOX MARTYRDOM

At the most basic level, the Butovskii poligon's post-Soviet history is the story of the Russian Orthodox Church's gradual acquisition and definition of the site as an Orthodox sacred site.[14] According to some accounts, the acquisition happened partly by default, when both the state authorities and secular civil society organizations such as Memorial allegedly refused to take responsibility for the site in the mid-1990s. Since an active community of descendants of Orthodox victims had taken shape by this point, they stepped into the breach and took the initiative. This is how the story is told by Archpriest Kirill Kaleda, dean of the church of the Russian Holy New Martyrs and Confessors at Butovo and grandson of a victim buried at the site (see fig. 11.2). According to Kaleda, in late 1994, after details on the Orthodox clergy and laity buried at the site came to light, Patriarch Aleksii approached the FSK (from 1995, the FSB) requesting that a plot of land be provided for construction of a church at the site.[15] Kirill Kaleda recounts the developments as follows:

> In response ... the Moscow Regional Administration proposed that not only the entire territory of the Butovskii burial site, but also the territory of the burial site at Kommunarka,[16] be transferred to the Church. It turned out that as early as in the late '80s–early '90s the KGB leadership had made several approaches to the Regional Administration with requests to transfer the territories in question to some other organization. The leadership of the Moscow region, realizing what these objects were, simply didn't know who would be able to take up their custodianship.

The proposal was unexpected, but on reflection the patriarch gave it his blessing.[17]

Figure 11.2. Inside the church. *Photograph by Tomas Sniegon*

In another interview, Kaleda also mentioned financial considerations as playing a role here:

> In the 1990s the execution sites proved unneeded by anybody: the authorities didn't know what to do with them.... The Butovskii poligon was supposed to be transferred [from the FSB] to the Moscow regional authorities. But the Moscow regional authorities had no desire to increase the burden on their budget. Simultaneously, a public religious organization had emerged—a group of active laity who built a church [at the site in 1994–96]. At the same time, the FSB staff realized that this place couldn't become a park for strolls, that someone would have to invest effort and money in maintaining the poligon.[18]

The federal television channel *REN-TV* echoed Kaleda's narrative, reporting in 2002 that "The idea to carry out improvement [*blagoustroistvo*] of this site [in this case, the nearby Kommunarka site] and to create monuments here arose ten years ago. But nobody apart from the Russian Orthodox Church declared any desire to take over [*osvoit'*] the territory."[19] In other words, through its apathy, secular civil society had forfeited the right to any claim to the site.

Elsewhere Kirill Kaleda does acknowledge that the transfer of the site to the Church created "tension among the secular public," but he claims that both the Moscow city and Moscow regional governments, as well as Memorial and the Association of Victims of Political Repressions, "refused... to take responsibility for these graves" and only the Church was prepared to take on the role of "preserving and memorializing" the site.[20]

Secular memory activists take a different view on the events and dispute the notion that the site was unwanted and unclaimed. On this issue, Memorial Society founding member Lev Razgon, for example, commented, "The Orthodox

Church's behavior... leaves something to be desired. After all, they took away for a church parish the land of the Butovskii poligon, where there had been plans to build a memorial complex in memory of the more than twenty thousand Soviet people shot there. Some need memory, but others need real estate [*zemel'naia sobstvennost'*].[21] In other words, the Church had appropriated and monopolized the site, effectively preventing the construction of secular memorials there; moreover, the Church's actions were financially motivated.

In general, the narrative of secular civil society's indifference to the sites of memory of victims of terror is difficult to square with the history of secular memory activism during the period. It was at this time that the giant Mask of Sorrow monument was built in Magadan to commemorate suffering of the Gulag victims there.[22] In Moscow, the newly established Sakharov Center hosted the country's most comprehensive exhibition on the history of Soviet state terror in 1996.

Mikhail Mindlin, one of the main activists who had fought hardest to identify and document the graves at the site, tells the story of the Church's acquisition as follows:

> We requested that a federal memorial complex be opened at Butovo, and that prior to this the territory be temporarily handed over to the Moscow Patriarchate, which intended to build a church in memory of the martyrs. And suddenly, a resolution from the administration of the Moscow region's Leninskii district: all territory and also the adjoining land was to be handed over not temporarily, but in perpetuity [*navechno*] to the Russian Orthodox Church. No place was left for a memorial. But after all the executed people of forty-nine nationalities are buried there! Sometimes it seems as though some bosses [*nachal'niki*] erect monuments not to the dead, but to themselves."[23]

This version of events would seem to highlight the emerging state-church alliance, such that local politicians stood to benefit from fostering good relations with the Church. Meanwhile, the Russian leadership under the president Boris Yeltsin was establishing closer contact with the Russian Orthodox Church after Yeltsin's violent conflict with the Parliament in 1993. In 1994, Yeltsin and Patriarch Aleksii II reached an agreement that the state would cover most of the costs of reconstruction of the Cathedral of Christ the Savior in Moscow that the church had been allowed to rebuild in 1990. Moscow mayor Yuri Luzhkov was also involved in this $300 million deal that ended with the opening of the cathedral in 2000.[24]

Kaleda has also justified the Church's acquisition of the site on the grounds that only the Church proved capable of preventing commercial development of the site. In the mid-1990s the site narrowly escaped what would have ultimately meant its demise, after construction of residential housing for a new microdistrict began along the perimeter of the site. Construction was prevented at the eleventh hour (the basement floor of one of the buildings reportedly still remains in place) after, on request, the patriarch intervened and asked Luzhkov to stop the construction.[25] Kaleda has claimed that, in this way, "the church effectively saved the Butovskii poligon" and that this is why the decision was made to transfer the whole site to the parish of the Church of Russian New Martyrs and Confessors.[26] In this account, the Memorial Society appears as well-intentioned but ultimately weak and ineffectual, and on these grounds, again, an unfitting custodian for the site.

The Church assumed custodianship of the site in 1995.[27] Construction of a small wooden church was completed at the gravesite in 1996 and was consecrated as the Cathedral of Russian New Martyrs and Confessors, becoming the first Russian church devoted to the new martyrs (fig. 11.3).[28] At first, Catholic, Muslim, and Jewish clergymen attended memorial services at Butovo, but they soon stopped coming, discouraged by the exclusively Orthodox orientation.[29] Later, a much larger stone church was built at the site (completed in 2007; see fig. 11.4). Since May 2000, the patriarch has conducted as annual open-air service at the site at Easter. The site is now well established as one of the main sites associated with the Church's new martyrs of the twentieth century. It is one of a small number of sites now labeled the "Russian Golgotha," a title reserved for places of the highest religious importance, such as Ganina Yama near Yekaterinburg, where the remains of Nicholas II and his family were discovered in the 1970s, and the Solovetsky Monastery. The Butovo site's status as a leading site of martyrdom was reinforced in particular by ceremonies in 2007, in which the twelve-meter-high wooden Solovetsky Cross was brought by boat from the Solovetsky Islands and erected near the new stone church at Butovo, thereby establishing a symbolic connection between the two sites of Russian martyrdom.[30] Several weeks later, on October 30, President Putin visited the site to attend a religious service conducted by Patriarch Aleksii II.[31] These events marked the definitive elevation of the Orthodox mode of remembering the Soviet terror to hegemonic status, in preference to the secular, human-rights-focused version offered by the Memorial Society.[32] The same day, the Orthodox Church issued a statement proclaiming that the crimes of the Communist Era should be commemorated with prayers and not political meetings. According to this approach, in keeping with Christian tradition, the "proper form of memorialization" is observed when "people without any meetings and demonstrations go to the places of execution or other places of memory and take part in collective prayer."[33]

A key milestone in the history of the campaign to musealize the site was the creation of the Memorial Research-Education Center Butovo in 2002. According to the center's website, it was created "at the initiative of parishioners of the church and relatives of the victims and with the blessing of His Holiness Patriarch Aleksii II, with the aim of coordinating the efforts of state, religious, and public

Figure 11.3. The wooden church. *Photograph by Tomas Sniegon*

Figure 11.4. Church of the New Martyrs and Confessors. *Photograph by Tomas Sniegon*

organizations in the creation of a memorial complex at the Butovskii poligon."[34] As the quote exemplifies, the Church's de facto monopoly of the site is often framed in terms of pluralism and inclusivity, and suggestions that the Church is well placed to act as a kind of intermediary able to transcend worldly divisions and to bring state and civil society together.[35] In practice, the Church's privileged status and increasingly close relationship with the state means that the two structures cannot always be neatly separated.[36]

According to the center's director Igor' Gar'kavyi, in 2002 the church made a deliberate decision not to seek a formal partnership with the state in managing the site.[37] The preference was to create an autonomous noncommercial center that would be better equipped to resist both sudden political changes in the country and efforts to impose a "politically correct" universalized memory of the Gulag. Its noncommercial status would enable the Church to ensure that the predominantly Russian context of the site of memory was clearly marked.[38] In theory, the center coordinates the commemorative efforts of state, religious, and public organizations;[39] in fact, its autonomy meant that the church obtained the power to decide what and who would be commemorated in Butovo, and how.

The center has conducted an immense amount of work collecting and organizing data on the victims. It has also begun collecting items for a museum, a selection of which are on display in a glass case in the main church at the site. But the primary aim of creating a museum of in memory of the victims at the site, described on the center's website as its "main task,"[40] remains elusive: no museum has materialized.[41]

There have, however, been ongoing discussions about plans for a future museum and the shape it might take. The plans have changed over time as focus has narrowed from the original plan for a museum to all victims to one devoted exclusively to the victims of antireligious repressions, or, according to some reports, only to Orthodox victims. Over time, as we shall see later in this chapter, the memorial museum project has become increasingly identified with and subsumed under the Orthodox new martyrdom discourse, which has now become the dominant lens through which the Soviet past is viewed in Russian public life.

THE STATE'S RELATIONSHIP WITH BUTOVSKII POLIGON: MOSCOW CITY AND MOSCOW REGIONAL AUTHORITIES

As to the state's involvement with the site as well, events have apparently been driven primarily by ad hoc actions undertaken by particular powerful individuals. It was thanks to Moscow mayor Yuri Luzhkov's direct intervention, for example, that the site's road and transport infrastructure were improved and a connecting bus route to Moscow was created in 1998.[42] Most often such actions have been carried out at the behest of the patriarch. For example, according to the former governor of the Moscow region, Boris Gromov, the Moscow regional administration's 2001 decision to pass a resolution declaring the site a historical monument of local significance was made at the request of the patriarch.[43] Later, it was Gromov who seems to have played a key role in the works undertaken at the site in 2005 with a view to tidying it up and putting the graves in order, again with the blessing of the patriarch.[44]

The main frame used by the state authorities for the site has been the frame of "heritage [*nasledie*]"; the site's right to state protection is based on its legal definition as an "object of cultural heritage (monument of history and culture)."[45]

Russian federal law specifies three categories of cultural heritage objects: federal ("possessing historical-architectural, artistic, scholarly, and memorial value, with special significance for the history and culture of the Russian Federation"); regional (with special significance for a subject of the Russian Federation); and local (municipal) (with special significance for a particular municipal formation).[46] Upon being granted this status, the land in question is placed on an official register and becomes subject to state protection and to various restrictions on the types of activities that may be conducted there.

There have been several stages in the process of defining the site as a heritage site that enjoys the legal protection of the state. The first step was to establish proof that the mass graves at the site existed. The correct legal procedure in such cases is to open a criminal case, triggering investigation and exhumation of the site by the procuracy. Despite official procedure, the path taken was to conduct a small informal dig at the site, in 1997, in order to obtain the *corpus delicti* required in order to attain official status for the site as a protected heritage site, but in such a way as to avoid opening a criminal investigation or conducting a full-scale excavation of the site. The law was deliberately broken on the grounds that the site contained holy relics that must not be disturbed. As Kirill Kaleda put it, "We didn't want the remains to be disturbed, all the more so since in many cases these are relics. And we dared to carry out these digs simply having received the blessing of His Holiness Patriarch Aleksii."[47]

The failure to carry out a comprehensive excavation of the site or to exhume and rebury the victims is not unusual in the Russian context.[48] Although in recent decades there has been a growing consensus globally on the need to exhume and identify victims of state terror in pursuit of human rights and transitional justice,[49] Russia is one of several cases that represent exceptions.[50] In the case of the five confirmed mass graves in Moscow and Moscow region, "not a single one ... has been studied, reburial of the remains of the deceased has not taken place."[51]

The church's position on the issue of exhumation and reburial seems somewhat peculiar. On the one hand, as Bitutckii points out, "the tenets of Orthodoxy ... dictate that an unmarked pit may not be considered a proper place of burial for an Orthodox Christian, and that any remains within one require reinterment with all due ceremony, which in turn requires exhumation."[52] Yet often, in the case of Butovo as well, we find Orthodox clergy opposing exhumation and reburial.[53] Yakov Krotov has been especially scathing on this issue and sees the failure to excavate the Butovo site as reflecting a fundamental contempt for the victims. He writes that the Butovo site is "an excellent symbol of the whole of contemporary Russia. A lifeless gloss on the surface, while unwanted people are crushed [*skomkany*] and dumped somewhere out of sight. They are of no interest, and are needed only as a prop for lies."[54] Krotov also says, "What's the basis for the Orthodox veneration of relics? It is respect for the body. If the bodies of the people tortured in this meat grinder are still lying there in a heap, can we really say that this is a memorial? This is not a memorial, this is a dump, with a glamorous pimple [i.e., the stone church] next door."[55]

Under the 2001 resolution declaring it a site "of local significance," the Butovo site received some degree of legal protection. Its borders were defined and it was divided into zones with various degrees of protection and levels of regulation. Subsequently, in autumn 2005, work was carried out at the site, funded by the city of Moscow and Moscow regional authorities, which included marking the thirteen confirmed burial pits with grave mounds, planting greenery, and building walking paths across the site.

In 2008, the site's status was upgraded from a "historical monument of local significance" to one of "regional significance," again by order of the Moscow regional government. Consequently, it comes under the purview of the Moscow Regional Ministry of Culture. Its status means that economic and other activities are strictly regulated (at least in theory) on the site's territory, which is officially defined as a "site of memory [*pamiatnoe mesto*], where mass executions and burials of victims of political repressions occurred in the 1930s–50s." It is specified that any work at the site is to be "oriented toward activization of the historical-memorial and natural-landscape potential of the monument." In the surrounding territory, too, there are height restrictions in place on any new buildings, and in general, there is a ban on "any violations—in the planning, location, type or nature of buildings and facilities [*blagoustroistvo*]—in the structural-functional, compositional, architectural relationship of the traditional open spaces, the appearance [*oblik*] of the monument's surrounds, its emotional perception [*yego emotsional'nogo vospriatiia*]."[56] The state's intervention thus consists of an attempt to set the limits of what is acceptable in the space; it was ordered, for example, that any "dissonant objects—sheds [*saraev*], utility structures, basements of incomplete houses"—be removed. Within the protected zone, it is permitted to grow plants and trees, to tidy up the territory, to repair old buildings, and so on; but it is expressly forbidden to pollute the soil, fill in the ponds, or dump any objects in the pond and stream.[57]

Even after the 2008 resolution, however, the site has periodically come under threat from developers. In 2011, for example, the Galaxy Group construction company was investigated by the Moscow Regional Ministry for Culture after the company began laying underground communications across the memorial's territory.[58] These and other episodes seem to have arisen in part out of confusion about the precise boundaries of the site. The Butovo Memorial Center staff and local clergy have complained that room apparently is left for creative interpretations of the building restrictions on the part of would-be developers.[59]

At one level, the failure to create a museum at Butovo is the result of a simple lack of funds. In part, the lack reflects the incomplete nature of the relevant legislation. Federal law stipulates that burial sites of this kind must be restored and preserved, and yet it does not provide for any mechanisms to fund such work.[60] The problem is compounded by an ongoing lack of clarity about the level of state agencies responsible for the site: federal, regional, or local,[61] and the precise nature of the involvement of the Russian Orthodox Church and civil society organizations. For example, because part of the territory of the Butovo site now belongs to the Church, its right to claim state budget funds has frequently been called into question.[62]

The annual cost of the basic upkeep of the site, incurred by the parish of New Martyrs, is around three million rubles annually. As Kseniia Luchenko writes, this "makes it impossible to finance additional projects, including those linked to memorial work."[63] Kirill Kaleda has repeatedly complained about the fact that no funds have been allocated despite the fact that the site has been declared a monument of regional historical significance.[64] Again, the funding that has been provided has been on an ad hoc basis, which has meant taking advantage of opportunities that have risen at times when the site has received high-level attention. For example, in 2005, the Moscow regional and Moscow city authorities each contributed twenty million rubles toward putting the grave sites in order.[65] The funding apparently resulted from the patriarch's attention to the site and his annual visits as of 2000, which, according to Kirill Kaleda, led to a "cardinal change" in the attitude of the Moscow regional and city authorities.[66] Luchenko writes that "Sponsors or additional budgetary money are sometimes found at one-off events: every year ahead of the patriarch's visit the road is repaired; recently a bell tower was built."[67] The Moscow city government also provides buses to transport up to six hundred descendants of victims to the site each year at Radonitsa, the second Tuesday of Easter, when family graves are visited.[68] Most recently, one anonymous sponsor for the long-discussed "Garden of Memory" project at the site apparently withdrew after the beginning of the war in Ukraine in 2014.[69]

Lack of funds—itself reflecting in part a deeper lack of political will—is a major reason for the failure to date to realize any of the memorial museum projects floated in connection to the site. As we shall see later in this chapter, however, recent legislative changes may mean that state funds will materialize in the near future. There is also an ongoing campaign to raise funds for the museum through private donations.[70]

THE STATE'S RELATIONSHIP TO THE BUTOVSKII POLIGON: THE FEDERAL LEVEL

Memory Politics in Putin's Russia

In the late 1980s and early 1990s, discoveries and excavations of the mass graves of victims of Soviet state terror received a great deal of attention. As Irina Paperno noted in 2001, many held high expectations at first that the processes of exhuming and mourning the victims would stimulate change, but such hopes were not fulfilled—in place of catharsis, clarity, or closure, the processes more often brought only more confusion and chaos, as the numerous difficulties thrown up by the graves themselves were revealed (for example, on reaching a consensus and telling a coherent story about the graves; or on drawing a clear line between the murderers and the victims).[71]

There has been less discussion—either in Russian public life or in memory studies literature—on the fate of these sites in the Putin era. At one level, lack of attention to the topic arguably reflects the ways in which the Putin regime has successfully neutralized the old Gorbachev-era oppositional democratic discourses on the history and memory of Soviet state terror, in part by appropriating elements of these discourses, transforming and reconstituting them in the process, while simultaneously discrediting their sources. This has taken place in the context of an ongoing quest for a new master narrative of the Soviet past, and of the history of Soviet terror in particular, the quest for a "usable past" with which Russia might operate both at home and abroad. Putin's 2007 visit to the Butovo site marked the beginning of a series of attempts to formulate a new official position on the Soviet terror. In contrast to the preceding years of ambiguity and ambivalence punctuated by occasional tentative attempts to defend Stalin's record, in recent years Putin and the ruling United Russia party have made various moves toward institutionalizing and canonizing the notion of the history of the Soviet terror as a catastrophe to be mourned. If, as recently as in 2007, Putin was sponsoring a history textbook that notoriously described Stalin as an "efficient manager," by summer 2009 he was announcing that Solzhenitsyn's *Gulag Archipelago* was to become a compulsory part of the secondary school (year 11) curriculum, something that Putin himself described as an "emblematic event."[72]

The Medvedev Interlude

The beginning of the Dmitry Medvedev presidency raised hopes that a federal memorial museum for the victims of state terror might finally be a real possibility. Expectations were focused in particular on a project aimed at creating a national memorial museum complex at Kovalevskii Forest near Saint Petersburg, the site of another mass grave that was uncovered by Memorial Society activists in 2001.

In summer 2009, the Petersburg Memorial Research Center submitted a major proposal to Medvedev on the project.[73] Medvedev approved the initiative and instructed the relevant ministries to develop the proposal, which also received support from Saint Petersburg city government and the Russian Orthodox Church.[74] On October 30, 2009, Medvedev gave a speech marking the Day of Memory of Victims of Political Repressions, in which he called for the creation of "museum-memorial centers to pass on the memory of the past from generation to generation."[75] In a statement that received a great deal of media attention, he said that he was "convinced that the memory of national tragedies is just as sacred as the memory of victories."[76]

At the time, it seemed to many as though the time was ripe for the advent of a new type of memorial museum in Russia. Theretofore, Russia had largely been untouched by what Williams has called the "global rush to commemorate atrocities" associated with the rise of the memorial museum; some Soviet memorial museums were devoted to wartime atrocities against civilians, such as the Khatyn' complex in Belarus, but they were executed within the paradigm of the Soviet myth of the Great Victory in the war.

The Kovalevskii Forest project was conceived as a departure from the conventional Russian model of the memorial museum as a museum "devoted to an outstanding person or an important historical event and created at the site linked to the ... individual or event in question."[77] Its designers declared that it would be unique in Russia in combining memorial and museum components, as "a site of memory of a new type, synthesizing both elements, essential for comprehensive work with the Russian national historical trauma: state terror directed against the country's citizens."[78] In lobbying for such a project, activists from the Memorial Society and other supporters of the idea of a federal museum frequently made reference to international practice regarding memorial museums. "Taking into account the experience of creating sites of memory in Russia and abroad, it was decided that in the Russia-wide museum-memorial complex not only would testimonies of the epoch of repressions and destroyed lives be presented, but mechanisms would also be proposed for making sense of the tragedy, thereby creating prospects for overcoming it. In other words, the complex will combine both memorial elements (preservation of the memory of the victims) and museum elements (related to cognition and understanding)."[79]

Consequently, a plan for a memory park combined with a museum-memorial complex was prepared by the Memorial Society in Saint Petersburg in 2010.[80] That plan, however, has not been realized and the destiny of the site of memory remains unclear; on November 6, 2015, the Ministry of Justice declared the Memorial Society in Saint Petersburg a foreign agent, claiming that the organization acted in a foreign name against Russian interests.[81]

Recent Developments: The Fedotov Working Group on Historical Memory

Overall, the shift toward an official anti-Soviet or anti-Stalinist memory politics over the past decade has remained formal, declaratory, and subject to strict limitations. The shift would appear to be above all else a strategic move aimed in part at avoiding the reputational costs of fighting memory wars with Russia's neighbors and sending a signal about contemporary Russia's antiauthoritarian credentials, but couched so as to simultaneously avoid assuming responsibility for the crimes of the Soviet regime. Rather than denying others' claims to victimhood, Russia should embrace its position as the "biggest victim" of all and should take regional leadership in devising memory policies on this issue, thereby gaining symbolic capital and boosting the country's international prestige.[82] One of the proponents of such a position, international relations expert and influential lobbyist Sergei Karaganov, went so far as to argue, in a programmatic article published in the official newspaper *Rossiiskaya gazeta* in July 2010, that Russia must "find within herself the strength to admit that the whole of Russia is one big Katyn, strewn with the mostly nameless graves of millions of the regime's victims."[83]

Later, Karaganov would go on to coauthor, together with leading figures from the Memorial Society, a comprehensive draft proposal, "On Immortalizing the Memory of the Victims of the Totalitarian Regime and on National Reconciliation." The document was presented to President Medvedev by its authors, the Working Group on Historical Memory under the Presidential Council for the Development of Civil Society and Human Rights, in February 2011.[84] It was framed as a policy aimed at the modernization of Russian social consciousness,[85] and also at "national reconciliation."[86]

One of the key recommendations made by the working group was that the lack of monuments at the federal level needed to be addressed. It noted that among the hundreds of monuments to victims of Soviet state terror throughout the country, almost none of them involved the federal authorities, and that many such initiatives had stalled in the 1990s. The group's proposal stated that a minimum of two national museum-memorial complexes should be created in Moscow and Saint Petersburg. It also made a number of recommendations on the need for the "active participation of the federal state power" in "uncovering, preserving, putting in order, and, where possible, memorializing sites of mass graves." The FSB, the Interior Ministry and Rosarkhiv should be tasked with conducting a targeted search for archival documentation on such sites; further, that a federal law should be prepared with a view to granting a special legal status to memorial cemeteries of victims of terror, and it should be analogous to the status of memorial military cemeteries.[87]

This initiative has so far yielded little concrete action on federal museums,[88] though there have been periodic announcements of plans on this front. For example, in January 2013 it was announced that Perm-36 was to be declared a model museum and that two "national centers of memory of the victims of political repressions" were to be created on the basis of this model, one at the Butovskii poligon and the other at an as-yet-undetermined site near Saint Petersburg.[89] But it is hard to see what progress there has been. Mikhail Fedotov reportedly complained to Putin in summer 2014 that implementation of the federal memory policy had been "sabotaged" by individual bureaucrats (though he also noted that, thankfully, there were individual regional leaders who understood the importance of this work and were prepared to fund it; though Kaleda seems to say on this point that the lack of clear funding mechanisms meant that when regional leaders allocated funds to this purpose, they later faced difficulties from the parliamentary chamber of accounts).[90] In summer 2014, Fedotov announced plans to create a major chain of museums, to be headed by the Museum of GULAG History, that would include museums at Kommunarka and Butovo and the Solovetsky stone (see chap. 10, by Jeffrey Hardy, on the story of the GULAG Museum).[91] During the same meeting, Fedotov reportedly asked Putin for an amendment to the existing law, "On the Rehabilitation of Victims of Political Repressions"; that it should be renamed the "On the Rehabilitation and Commemoration of Victims" so that it might then be amended to allow the allocation of funds to preserve and maintain mass gravesites.[92]

Subsequently the plan for a "targeted federal program" was downgraded to a "state policy concept," which was eventually adopted by the government in August 2015.[93] The concept's opening section frames the issue in terms of "efficiency," "innovation," economic development, and "human capital," all of which are linked to "construction of a national identity." Such aims as the establishment of the rule of law and respect for human rights are presented as secondary aims flowing out of the primary aims. Other secondary aims listed are "the strengthening of [Russia's] positive image abroad" and "the formation of active patriotism."[94]

A traditionalist discourse is also used here to frame the need for remembrance of victims of political repressions. The document speaks of "Russia's tragic experience ... after the October events of 1917, which is characterized by a rupture of traditions, loss of continuity of cultural experience, destruction of intergenerational connections."[95]

In the list of tragedies Russia has suffered, religion-based repressions are in first place:

> Apart from the colossal losses sustained during the period of the Civil and Great Patriotic Wars, Russia experienced a whole series of other tragedies, including:
>
> - persecutions against representatives of religious confessions;
> - postrevolutionary emigration of the most educated part of the population, sustained discrimination against those representatives of the prerevolutionary elite who chose to remain in Russia;

- collectivization, bringing numerous victims among the deported and dekulakized, and also the destruction of the individual peasant household economy, which had been the foundation of the country's economy for the course of centuries;
- famine, linked to forced collectivization, and claiming the lives of millions of people;
- mass repressions, in the course of which millions of people were deprived of life, became prisoners of the GULAG, were deprived of property and subjected to deportation.[96]

This emphasis on religious repressions is reflected in the shift toward speaking of the future museum at the Butovskii poligon as a museum devoted to victims of religious repressions, rather than victims of terror more broadly. By May 2016, for example, Fedotov was referring to the future museum as the "Russian Golgotha" museum.[97]

The legislative amendments proposed by Fedotov to Putin in summer 2014 were duly passed in March 2016. Article 18-1 now stipulates that state authorities at all levels from federal through to local have the right "to undertake measures for the commemoration of victims of political repressions and to support the activities of organizations and citizens aimed at commemorating the victims of political repressions, in particular with regard to the discovery [*vyiavlenie*] and improvement [*blagoustroistvo*] of burial sites of the victims, discovery [*vyiavlenie*] of archival documents on the history of the political repressions, and the creation and supplementation of museum expositions."[98]

Two other legislative amendments were made simultaneously. The law "On Noncommercial Organizations" was amended to include "commemoration of victims of political repressions" as an activity that could legally be funded by "organs of state power and organs of local self-government" (see Article 31-1).[99] New text was also added to the law "On Objects of Cultural Heritage (Monuments of History and Culture) of the Peoples of the Russian Federation," setting out the procedure for registering burial sites of victims of mass repressions.[100] The Regnum news agency summarized these changes as follows: "The right of organs of state power and the municipalities to carry out measures for commemoration of victims of repressions, and also to support relevant activities of organizations and citizens, is being strengthened. Such organizations could now 'count on the state's financial support.'"[101]

And yet: this move was accompanied by a renewed assault on the Memorial Society. On the very same day that *RIA Novosti* reported on these events under the headline "NKOs [noncommercial organizations] Commemorating Victims of Repressions Will Be Able to Count on State Support in the RF [Russian

Federation],"[102] it also reported that "Yekaterinburg 'Memorial,' recognized as a foreign agent," had been "fined 300 thousand rubles."[103]

In general, civil society memory activists such as the Memorial Society have periodically been subjected to intense state pressure.[104] The pressure has not been applied consistently; in 2013, for example, Memorial's "Necropolis of Terror" project, headed by Irina Flige, received a presidential grant to support its work.[105] But the general trend is strongly in the direction of greater repression. The interregional nongovernmental Memorial Rights Defense Center and the International Historical-Educational Charity and Rights Defense Society Memorial were officially declared to be foreign agents in July 2014 and October 2016, respectively, decisions that the Memorial Society is fighting in the courts. The Memorial Society is gradually being squeezed by fines imposed for its failure to declare its foreign agent status.[106] Meanwhile, the state has effectively handed over custodianship of the Soviet past and responsibility for commemorating and mourning the victims of Soviet state terror to the Russian Orthodox Church.

THE RISE OF THE "CHRISTIAN MUSEUM"?

What, then, do we know about the future museum at Butovo, and how it will frame the mass graves and narrate their victims' stories? It is clear that the primary focus will be the Orthodox new martyrs buried at the site. One of the main frames used for these martyrs to date has been the Great Patriotic War frame. During the patriarch's seminar at Butovo in 2015, for example, the patriarch merged victims of terror and victims of the war, claiming that, "from the religious point of view, life given up for the Motherland . . . and the feat of the new martyrs are combined in a great sacrifice to God, brought for the salvation of our Fatherland."[107] The patriarch went so far as to declare that "This is a kind of shared feat, and perhaps, without the one there would not have been the other. Had the new martyrs and confessors renounced their faith, Christ, the Church, had they joined the ranks of the blasphemers, then, perhaps the people too would not have had sufficient spiritual strength to resist the enemy.[108] Here, then, the terror appears as a kind of miraculous event that made victory possible. This narrative effectively dispenses with any need to investigate or interrogate the history any further.

A further indication of the kind of narrative such a museum might offer is given by a 2002 teacher's guide designed for use with secondary-school students in conjunction with an excursion to the site. Here the Butovskii poligon is imagined as a place of joy and peace, transformed by the presence of the martyrs.[109] It also seems that the emphasis will likely be placed on the lessons to be derived from the martyrs' lives, rather than understanding how and why they were killed. Thus, the Butovo Memorial Center's mission statement includes restoring historical

Figure 11.5. Memorial cross. *Photograph by Tomas Sniegon*

justice "by means of the maximum possible preservation for future generations of the spiritual, scholarly, and aesthetic values created by the people who perished during the years of the mass repressions."[110]

The case of the Butovo museum also reflects broader developments taking place in the Russian museum sphere. The modern Western museum is generally viewed as a secular institution that developed in part as a substitute for the sacred sites of the past,[111] but in contemporary Russia, a struggle to redefine the role of the museum as an institution is currently underway. In tandem with calls for museums to play a greater role in the "spiritual-moral, and patriotic education of young people, and ... preservation of national identity and strengthening the unity of Russian society,"[112] the Russian Orthodox Church has been lobbying for a greater role in the museum sphere, predicating its claim on the special relationship between church and state in Russia.[113] Specifically, there have been moves toward creating a new category of museums, sometimes referred to as "nonstate Christian-oriented museums."[114] It looks likely that the Butovskii poligon museum will be positioned within this newly emergent category. In December 2014, Kirill Kaleda took part in the conference The Christian Museum in the Contemporary World, aimed at redefining the institution of the museum. The conference was described by one participant as marking "the birth of a new cultural phenomenon of our time: Christian museums of Russia" and "an important and extraordinary event that may have serious consequences for the development of the Christian culture of contemporary Russia."[115] In its concluding document, the conference called on the patriarch to give his blessing to the creation of an alliance of Christian museums and to note the key role played by the Russian Orthodox Church in heritage conservation.[116]

The origins of this development can be traced back to May 2010 when the Commission for Interaction between the Russian Orthodox Church and the museum community was created under the patriarch's Council for Culture. Its aims are "creation of a system of church-state expertise and control over the conservation, restoration, and use of monuments of church art."[117] The commission was created in the context of an ongoing conflict between the Russian Orthodox Church and the museum community in Russia,[118] as the Church has moved to appropriate various sites and objects that the Church claims were being neglected by their secular custodians.[119] The Church's initiative in this vein has sparked debates over the role of Church and state in the museum sphere and over the function of the contemporary museum as an institution more broadly. In September 2016 the patriarch met with leading representatives of the Russian museum community and expressed his view on the fundamental affinity of mission shared by museums and the Church: "The museum educates, elevating the human soul, and in this the Church and the museum are close to one another.

We preserve tradition, we preserve the moral paradigm of humanity." He saw no tension or contradiction here: "today we live in a state where, by God's grace, there is no danger of the church renouncing her inherent obligations, and there is no coercion of the museum community to support one or another ideology."[120]

Other actors in this sphere have highlighted the specificity of the Christian museum: "Despite the fact that all museums have functions in common (collection, research, education, etc.), a **fundamental** difference between the Christian and the secular museum lies **in the aims pursued by them**. In the secular museum, exhibits are perceived as objects of cultural-historical or artistic, aesthetic value. In the Christian museum, on the other hand, the spiritual content of sacred objects is placed in the foreground" (emphasis in original).[121] Igor' Gar'kavyi sees the church building at the site and the museum project as "deeply interlinked."[122] In its research, the Butovo Memorial Center has devoted a great deal of attention to exploring various Russian traditions of memorializing the dead, such as the practice of building churches "on the blood" as a means of transforming places of violence and grief into sacred sites. The center also runs research projects aimed specifically at studying alternative Russian traditions related to mass graves of the "victims of social catastrophes."[123] Such projects seem to be aimed at least in part at finding historical precedents with a view to justifying the particular route that has been taken—that is, minimal exhumation and no reburial of victims.

The Church has also clashed with the Memorial Society over another mass grave site: the Levashovskoe cemetery site, in December 2012. In this case, the church was looking for a place to build a chapel at the site, and hence a plot of land at the site without graves had to be found.[124] The Ingriia search detachment was brought in to check the selected site for graves; there were some media claims that they fudged the search work, so as to clear the way for construction of the chapel.[125] The Saint Petersburg branch of the Memorial Society opposed the construction of the chapel and called into question "the precision of the check that had been carried out for the absence of graves at the proposed construction site." They also said that the public had been misled about the scale of the proposed construction, which would in fact dominate the site. In an official statement, the Memorial Society noted that "Levashovskoe memorial cemetery is not an Orthodox cemetery, where such construction would be entirely natural, but a memorial complex, which must be preserved in its existing form."[126]

In the case of Butovo, Igor' Gar'kavyi claims to be opposed to waging any "memory competition" at the site whereby only "some groups are remembered while others are forgotten."[127] Kirill Kaleda agrees: "It is important that the memorial be shared: we are consciously not taking the path of establishing monuments to separate groups of victims, for example, Latvians, Ukrainians, Lithuanians, Finns, or metallurgists, or concrete victims, as is often done at similar sites, for example at Levashovo. From the very beginning our community decided that the Lord had laid them down together, then let them be together—after all, they share a common grave."[128]

Statements of this kind seem disingenuous. The Memorial Society's position is not to divide victims on national or ethnic grounds; on the contrary, the society has consistently emphasized that "it is of fundamental importance that a dialogue of national memories emerge out of this diversity [of victims]. The memory of Soviet terror is the shared memory of *narodov* [of different nations and ethnicities]. This memory does not divide but unites, because it contains not only shared responsibility for these events, but also the memory of joint resistance to the killing machine, and the memory of international solidarity and human mutual assistance."[129]

According to Mikhail Fedotov, the Presidential Council for the Development of Civil Society and Human Rights has "reached an understanding" that in order to create a museum at the site, "it will be necessary to combine the efforts of the Russian Orthodox Church, the Moscow regional government, and the federal authorities." The statement was published under the headline "Rights Defenders: ROC [Russian Orthodox Church] Must Help Transform the Butovskii Poligon into a Museum."[130] In other words, the subtext seems to be that the Church's financial assistance is required in order to make the museum project happen. It may be that recognition of this fact helps to explain the apparent recent shift in how the future museum has been defined. Fedotov's latest statements on the future museum describe it as devoted exclusively to repressions on religious grounds.[131]

CONCLUSION

At a meeting with Putin in December 2016, Mikhail Fedotov asked the president to save a date in his diary: on October 30, 2017, the Wall of Grief memorial was to be officially unveiled at the Butovskii poligon.[132] The prospect of an actual bricks-and-mortar museum at the site, however, still seems unclear.

One set of buildings proposed as a site—the nearby set of buildings that were used by the state security organs in the 1940s–50s apparently as warehouses and a garage[133]—stands empty and neglected. The site previously belonged to the FSB; reportedly, the FSB was willing to give it up for the creation of a museum, but legally a transfer direct from the FSB to the Russian Orthodox Church was not possible. Instead the site was transferred to the Federal Agency for State Property Management (Rosimushchestvo), where it was designated for commercial purposes. Rosimushchestvo later passed it to a daughter structure. An offer was made at one point to allow the Church use of the buildings for a monthly payment of four hundred thousand rubles; the offer was rejected by Fedotov's council.

In 2014 the patriarch asked Medvedev to return the buildings to the federal treasury so that they might then be transferred directly to the Church without any financial obligations attached.[134] Fedotov has publicly indicated his support for this proposal with a view to creating a national museum at the site.[135] Should the transfer eventuate, the Butovo Center will have, as Gar'kavyi put it, "a huge exhibition space . . . a thousand square meters of exhibition space. And if we succeed in doing this, then at the Butovskii poligon—the central site for honoring the new martyrs—there will be created a churchwide museum of memory of the new martyrs. . . . This will be our Russia-wide center of veneration of the new martyrs.[136] A separate initiative is also underway to have the site listed as a UNESCO world heritage site.[137]

Meanwhile, as in other cases, the memory of Butovo has been migrating to the online sphere. The "Calendar of Memory" website (http://sinodik.ru/) is built around a database of Butovo victims that has been painstakingly constructed by volunteers. At the website, clicking on a date brings up quite a lot of detail about the victims shot on that date.[138]

High-sounding policies notwithstanding, the Putin government's general neglect of the mass graves and other atrocity sites that dot the country's landscape has been very conspicuous. It is very rare for such sites to be granted federal status and protection.[139] We find here a lack of state-sponsored monuments, memorials, and museums—what Alexander Etkind has called the hardware of cultural memory, reflecting a crystallization of memory that is made possible only once the minimal conditions for a basic consensus on the past have been met.[140] At one level, the state's reluctance to engage with this issue reflects the ongoing ambiguities about defining a new post-Soviet Russian identity; hence the difficulty in creating museums—institutions where identity is defined and displayed.[141]

For many reasons, the sites of mass graves and atrocities present particular challenges for musealization. Jay Winter has observed that battlefield sites are "halfway between cemeteries and museums."[142] Mass graves of the victims of state terror present an even more charged and complex combination of features. The challenges associated with the memorialization and muzealization of such sites are linked to the fact that, as Ferrandiz and Robben point out, mass graves are themselves a "technology of terror" whose effects are long-lasting: "The deliberate commingling of human remains in unmarked graves bewilders survivors and heightens the disorder, anxiety, and division of the citizenry. As a sophisticated technology of terror, these types of graves aim to erase the memory of violence, and at the same time consolidate regimes of fear that might last for decades.[143]

Svetlana Malysheva notes that in the Soviet case, the practice of burying the executed in mass graves was a tool for stigmatizing the victims.[144] Any future museum at Butovo must also engage with these aspects of the site's history.

Yet before musealization can occur at an atrocity site, the dead must be laid to rest. Dying and mourning are social acts.[145] In Butovo's case, these acts have not been completed, which is also an important factor impeding the creation of a museum at the site.

The development of Butovo as a site of memory of the gulag clearly illustrates how the post-Soviet Russian state has deliberately given up its effort to develop a new coherent postcommunist narrative of the Stalinist terror that could include Butovo as one of its central places. At the same time, state authorities have preferred to hand over responsibility to the Russian Orthodox Church rather than to a liberally oriented organization or society that could use the site to promote respect for human rights and liberal values in Russia. Once the Orthodox Church had shaped the former killing field according to its own values and goals, the state and the Church started to collaborate more closely, exploiting their relationship in order to attack their opponents and strengthen their positions. The main goal was not to focus on victims and mourn all of them regardless their origin, but to praise first of all those who belonged to the Orthodox Church and give their suffering a deeper—religious and patriotic—meaning, exemplified by the government's current push to use the gulag memory in order to develop "active patriotism" (deiatel'nyi patriotizm) "in partnership with religious and other public associations" in order to "strengthen the moral health of Russian society."[146] Thus, the collaboration gives the church leaders a more or less free hand to modify the form of the site of memory at Butovo according to their own ideological and political goals and substantially weaken pluralistic discussion about the crimes of the Soviet regime. It also enables a common national mobilization against external "enemies of Russian national and spiritual values" at the cost of self-reflection.

Kirill Kaleda argues that the achievements that have been made at the site represent "a vivid demonstration of the fruitfulness of the united efforts of the Church, society, and state in the cause of preserving and multiplying our cultural heritage."[147] Arguably, however, the site's history rather reflects the symbiosis of Church and state, the Church's de facto privileged position, and the ongoing slow crushing of secular civil society in Russia.

NOTES

1. On current efforts aimed at improving documentation, see Olga Lebedeva, "Topography of Terror: Mapping Sites of Soviet Repressions in Moscow," *Journal of Soviet and Post-Soviet Politics and Society* 2, no. 2 (2016): 221–28. Saint Petersburg is also underdocumented relative to its importance; as of February 2011, only one such site had obtained official status: the Levashovo Memorial Cemetery (which acquired official status in 1989). But even here, reportedly "state participation in the creation of

this site of memory is of a nominal nature" and most of the work was done by civil society and victims' families (Anastasiia Leonova, "Kovalevskii les," *Uroki istorii XX vek*, February 10, 2011, http://urokiistorii.ru/memory/place/1339). In July 1989 it was officially recognized by the Leningrad city soviet's executive committee as a "memorial cemetery" (Lev Shlosberg, "Levashovskoe Yevangelie ot naroda," *Pskovskaya guberniia*, September 26, 2012, http://gubernia.pskovregion.org/number _609/03.php. In late 2015 the site was also officially recognized as a "object of cultural heritage of regional significance" ("V Peterburge Levashovskoe kladbishche priznano pamiatnikom kul'tury," *Radio Svoboda*, January 2, 2016, http://www.svoboda.org/a/27464446.html; Aleksandra Mikhailova, "Levashovskoe kladbishche priznano pamiatnikom," *S uvazheniem k pamiati* no. 1 (January 2016), http://www.funeralassociation.ru/ru/newspaper/archives/8916/8905/?PHPSESSID =e8a29a50d25378039d2beddcce71e044.

2. This makes the site exceptionally well documented, comparatively speaking, in the post-Soviet context. Even though no archival documents specifying a site of burial have been found, it has been possible to establish beyond reasonable doubt, by piecing together the available evidence in conjunction with eyewitness testimony from former Chekists, that the identified victims were buried at Butovo (Arsenii Roginskii, "Posleslovie k spiskam zakhoronennykh v 'Kommunarke,'" *Kommunarka*, accessed November 26, 2016, http://www.memo.ru/memory/communarka/).

3. L. A. Golovkova, K. F. Lyubimova, L. I. Gromova, A. S. Nikitina, *Butovskii polygon: Kniga pamiati zhertv politicheskikh repressii* (Moscow: Alzo, 2007), 5–6.

4. The Levashovskoe Memorial Cemetery is another important such site, where almost 2,500 Orthodox clergy and laity are believed to be buried (of an estimated forty-seven thousand buried at the site in total). Even though the estimated number of victims at Levashovo is much higher than at Butovo, Butovo is by far the more prominent Orthodox site of memory.

5. A journalist writing in 1998 lamented the fact that "nobody knows that one can visit Butovo, where there was an NKVD execution ground, and pay respects to the ashes of thousands of those innocently killed here, and honor the memory of one's kin" (Tat'iana Sergeeva, "Poka zameten sled . . . ," *Moskovskaya pravda*, no. 30 [1641], February 17, 1998). According to the director of the Butovo Memorial Center Igor' Gar'kavyi, the annual number of visitors to the site is roughly thirty thousand (Igor' Gar'kavyi, interview by Tomas Sniegon, Butovo, April 9, 2014). A more recent estimate, however, cites only about ten thousand visitors annually, which could indicate a declining trend since 2014 ("Protoierei Kirill Kaleda: 'Organizatsiia tserkovnogo muzeia—eto ochen' sereznoe napravlenie," *Revizor.ru*, February 15, 2018, http://www.rewizor.ru/interviews/kirill-kaleda-butovskiy-poligon-mesto-massovyh-kazney-i-zahoroneniy-jertv-stalinskih-repressiy/). Precise figures, or data on where these visitors come from, are unavailable because the site is accessed without tickets or formal procedures. The majority of visits take place on religious holidays, especially Radonitsa, when the Moscow city government provides a number of free

buses to bring victims' descendants to a service at the site (Aleksandr Volkov, "Protoierei Kirill Kaleda: 'Blagodaria tomu, chto na Butovskom poligone sovershaetsia Beskrovnaya Zhertva, zdes' proiskhodit izmenenie dukhovnoi obstanovki," *Official site of Moscow Patriarchate of Russian Orthodox Church*, February 11, 2007, http://www.patriarchia.ru/db/text/194486.html). Special services are also held on February 7, the saints' day for the Russian new martyrs and confessors.

6. Local museums are a different story; Memorial's "Virtual Gulag" currently features 127 museums dealing with the theme of terror and the Gulag; the "Virtual Gulag" was indeed created as an attempt to compensate for the lack of a national Gulag museum and to bring together the various museum projects and initiatives spread across the former Soviet Union; see the virtual Gulag Museum, accessed February 26, 2020, http://www.gulagmuseum.org/showObject.do?object=3315723&language=1. On postsocialist museums, see Zuzanna Bogumił, Joanna Wawrzyniak, Tim Buchen, Christian Ganzer, and Maria Senina, eds., *The Enemy on Display: The Second World War in East European Museums* (Berghahn, 2015); Julie Fedor, "War Museums and Memory Wars in Contemporary Poland," in *A Companion to Heritage Studies*, ed. William Logan, Mairead Nic Craith, and Ullrich Kockel (Wiley 2015); Cristina Vatulescu, "Prisons into Museums: Fashioning a Post-communist Place of Memory," in *Rites of Place: Public Commemoration in Russia and Eastern Europe*, ed. Julie Buckler and Emily D. Johnson (Evanston, IL: Northwestern University Press, 2013), 315–35; Oksana Sarkisova and Peter Apor, eds., *Past for the Eyes: East European Representations of Communism in Cinema and Museums after 1989* (Budapest: Central European University Press, 2007).

7. "Khudozhnik Irina Nakhova," *Radio Blago*, October 19, 2016, http://www.radioblago.ru/vremyakultury/irina-nahova. For other works dealing with the Butovskii poligon theme, see also the installation "Archeology at Butovo" by Dar'ia Krotova, http://www.iragui.com/ru/Artists/Works/55, and the prize-winning documentary film *Ya k vam travoiu prorastu . . .* (dir. Aleksei Kolesnikov, 2005).

8. See Slava Sergeev's story about a group of friends who decide to visit the site after a night out drinking: Slava Sergeev, "Gnev," *Znamia* 1 (2016).

9. For further discussion, see Paul Williams, *Memorial Museums: The Global Rush to Commemorate Atrocities* (Oxford, UK: Berg, 2007).

10. On this former KGB dacha settlement as a site of memory, see Fedor (unpublished manuscript).

11. "Kontseptsiia gosudarstvennoi politiki po uvekovecheniiu pamiati zhertv politicheskikh repressii," August 15, 2015, http://president-sovet.ru/documents/read/393/#doc-1.

12. "Gruppa po uvekovecheniiu pamiati zhertv repressii posetila Butovskii poligon," *RIA Novosti*, May 26, 2016, https://ria.ru/society/20160526/1439693311.html.

13. On which, see Silke Arnold-de Simine, *Mediating Memory in the Museum: Trauma, Empathy, Nostalgia* (London: Palgrave Macmillan, 2013) (for this point, see p. 76); and Williams, *Memorial Museums*. See also Tomas Sniegon, "Dying in the

Soviet Gulag for Future Glory of Mother Russia? Making 'Patriotic' Sense of the Gulag in Present-Day Russia," in *Cultural and Political Imaginaries in Putin's Russia*, ed. Niklas Bernsand and Barbara Törnquist-Plewa (Leiden: Brill, 2018), 105–40.

14. For the most detailed overview of the site's history, including the story of the discovery of the graves and the long search for archival documents and witness testimony confirming the history of the executions and burials at the site, see L. A. Golovkova, K. F. Lyubimova, L. I. Gromova, and A. S. Nikitina, *Butovskii poligon*. See also Igor' V. Gar'kavyi and Lidia. A. Golovkova, "Butovskii poligon v proshlom i nastoiashchem," *Kalendar' pamiati*, accessed February 26, 2020, http://sinodik.ru/poligon/; and Nérard François-Xavier, "The Butovo Shooting Range," *SciencesPo*, Februart 27, 2009, http://www.sciencespo.fr/mass-violence-war-massacre-resistance/fr/document/butovo-shooting-range.

15. Previously, in 1993, a memorial plaque had been erected at the site on the initiative of the Group for Commemoration of Victims of Political Repressions attached to the Moscow city administration and headed by Mikhail Mindlin, a key figure in the campaign to retrieve and disseminate knowledge about the site; see further Mikhail Sitnikov, "Poliana nad kotlovanom smerti," *Russkaia mysl'*, December 25, 1997.

16. On the Kommunarka site, see further L. A. Golovkova, *Spetsob"ekt NKVD "Kommunarka": 1937–1941* (Moscow: Be-Art-Grupp, 2009). The history of the Kommunarka site (about ten kilometers from Butovo) has been quite different from that of Botovo. See, for example, a 1998 article comparing the two sites and lamenting the fact that Kommunarka did not even have a memorial plaque, despite the fact that in November 1991 Luzhkov had issued instructions for one to be emplaced; "Six years have already passed . . . but the burial site . . . remains closed for access by relatives and all those wishing to honor the memory of the people who perished innocently and were buried there"; the article calls for creation of an initiative group to accelerate creation of a memorial at the Kommunarka site (Valentin Gordin, "Stalin: vsekh podozritel'nykh unichtozhit'," *Vecherniaya Moskva*, no. 274, December 7, 1998). See also Georgii Tselms, "Prestupnye tainy bezymiannykh mogil," *Novye izvestiia* no. 126, July 21, 2001. The profile of the victims buried at Kommunarka is also very different. The site was handed over to the Russian Orthodox Church in 1999 and now houses the Sviato-Yekaterininskii male monastery.

17. Kirill Kaleda, cited in V. V. Vedernikov, "Tserkov' i kul'tura: vzaimodeistvie ili konfrontatsii?," *Istoricheskaia ekspertiza* no. 4 (2015): 162–64, http://istorex.ru/page/tserkov_i_kultura_vzaimodeystvie_ili_konfrontatsiya.

18. Cited in Kseniia Luchenko, "Butovskii poligon," *Pravmir*, October 30, 2015, https://www.pravmir.ru/butovskij-poligon/.

19. "Unikal'nyi sluchai v rossiiskoi istorii stroitel'stva khramov," *REN-TV*, July 24, 2002. This broadcast is about the plans to open a monastery at Kommunarka. It cites Bishop Tikhon Vidnovskii: "Over sixty nationalities are buried here, for the Russian Orthodox Church there's no problem in this. And here at this site, there will be prayers for all the dead."

20. Kirill Kaleda, cited in Vedernikov, "Tserkov' i kul'tura."

21. Cited in Otto Latsis, "Lev Razgon: 'Ya napivaius' kazhdyi god piatogo marta,'" *Novye izvestiia*, no. 60, April 1, 1998. He went on: "I don't wish to demean [*preumen'shit' zaslugi*] the many officials who do a great deal for the preservation of memory, but they do this on their personal initiative out of a variety of reasons: some have relatives who perished, some have more intelligence and conscience. But the state as such is indifferent to this."

22. The fifteen-meter-high *Maska Skorbi* statue, by the famous Russian sculptor Ernst Neizvestny, was unveiled in June 1996.

23. Quoted in Otto Latsis, "Pamiat' naroda i derzhavnyi skleroz," *Novye izvestiia*, October 24, 1997.

24. Leslie L. McGann, "The Russian Orthodox Church under Patriarch Aleksii II and the Russian State: An Unholy Alliance?," *Demokratizatsiya*, 7, no. 1 (1999): 12–27.

25. Luchenko, "Butovskii poligon."

26. Ibid. This is despite the fact that, for example, the Memorial Society was also involved in the campaign to stop the construction at the site in the mid-1990s. The argument is that the Memorial Society's efforts were ineffective, and that it was only the patriarch who proved able to save the site; see Luchenko, "Butovskii poligon."

27. The full site is not owned outright by the church; some of it is church property, some is rented by the church, and some has been granted to the church for rent-free use; see Luchenko, "Butovskii poligon."

28. Anastasiia Denisova, "Chego my ne znaem o mestakh massovogo zakhoroneniia?," *Foma*, February 6, 2016, http://foma.ru/butovo-fakti.html (accessed January 17, 2017; site has since been updated).

29. David Satter, *It Was a Long Time Ago, and It Never Happened Anyway* (New Haven, CT: Yale University Press, 2012), 69.

30. See further Veronica Dorman, "From the Solovki to Butovo: How the Russian Orthodox Church Appropriates the Memory of the Repressions," *Laboratorium* 2, no. 3 (2010): 431–36; and Karin Hyldal Christensen, *The Making of the New Martyrs of Russia: Soviet Repression in Orthodox Memory* (New York: Routledge, 2017).

31. The Butovskii poligon also formed part of the setting for the historic reconciliation between the Russian Orthodox Church (Moscow Patriarchate) and the Russian Orthodox Church Abroad the same year.

32. On the competing secular and Orthodox modes of remembering the Soviet past, see further, for example, Zuzanna Bogumił and Dominique Moran, "Sacred or Secular? 'Memorial,' the Russian Orthodox Church, and the Contested Commemoration of Soviet Repressions," *Europe-Asia Studies* 67, no. 9 (November 2015): 1416–44; Zuzanna Bogumił, "Stone, Cross and Mask: Searching for Language of Commemoration of the Gulag in the Russian Federation," *Polish Sociological Review* 177 (2012): 71–90; Alexander Etkind, "Vremia sravnivat' kamni: postrevolyutsionnaya kul'tura politicheskoi skorbi v sovremennoi Rossii," *Ab Imperio* 2 (2004): 33–76; Julie Fedor, "Setting the Soviet Past in Stone: The Iconography of the New Martyrs

of the Russian Orthodox Church," *Australian Slavonic and East European Studies* 28, nos. 1–2 (2014): 121–53; Kathy Rousselet, "The Russian Orthodox Church and Reconciliation with the Soviet Past," in *History, Memory and Politics in Central and Eastern Europe: Memory Games*, ed. Georges Mink and Laure Neumayer (New York: Palgrave Macmillan, 2013), 39–53.

33. Satter, *Long Time Ago*, 74.

34. "O proekte: Istoriia proekta," accessed November 23, 2016, *Kalendar' pamiati*, http://p8.inetstar.ru/?q=static&id=2.

35. Incidentally, Russian law distinguishes between public [*obshchestvennye*] and religious associations, both of which "enjoy the right to assist [*sodeistvovat'*] the organs of state power and local self-government in the use, popularization, and state protection of objects of cultural heritage" (Federal'nyi zakon ot 250602002 N 73-FZ [red. ot 03.07.2016, s izm. ot 19.12.2016], "Ob ob'ektakh kul'turnogo naslediia..." Article 8 [22.10.2014 version]).

36. See further Katarzyna Jarzyńska, "The Russian Orthodox Church as Part of the State and Society," *Russian Politics and Law* 52, no. 3 (May–June 2014): 87–97.

37. Igor' Gar'kavyi, interview by Tomas Sniegon, Butovo, October 13, 2016.

38. Ibid. See also "Protoierei Kirill Kaleda: 'Organizatsiia tserkovnogo muzeia— eto ochen' ser'eznoe napravlenie," *Revizor.ru*, February 15, 2018.

39. "Memorial'nii Tsentr Butovo," *Butovo Training Ground—Russian Calvary*, http://www.martyr.ru/index.php?option=com_content&view=article&id=156&Itemid=20.

40. The center's website currently lists five key projects. The first listed is the museum; the other four are creating the database of victims buried at Butovo; researching the "ethno-confessional traditions associated with mass grave sites of victims of social catastrophes" (that is, searching for new forms appropriate to the mix and diversity of victims buried at the site and the nature of the violent death in question—here the Orthodox practice of building churches "on the Blood" is discussed); creating the "Russian Orthodoxy in the Twentieth Century" oral history archive; and creating the internet portal "The Russian Church in the Soviet Period: Memories and Testimonies," http://www.martyr.ru/index.php?option=com_content&view=article&id=156&Itemid=20.

41. But note that in December 2016 it was reported that a charity concert was held in "the new building of the Museum of the Memory of Victims" at the Butovskii poligon: "Blagotvoritel'nyi muzykal'nyi kontsert pamiati sviashchennomuchenika mitropolita Serafima (Chichagova)," December 29, 2016, http://www.martyr.ru/index.php?option=com_content&view=article&id=1122:2016-12-29-17-42-25&catid=4:commonnews&Itemid=1.

42. Luchenko, "Butovskii poligon"; and Gar'kavyi and Golovkova, "Butovskii poligon."

43. Cited in Nikolai Lobodiuk, "Butovskii poligon: Ne do kontsa prochitannaya tragediia," *Blagovest info*, October 14, 2008, http://www.blagovest-info.ru/index.php?ss=2&s=7&id=23325.

44. Members of the Moscow City Government's Permanent Interdepartmental Commission for Restoring the Rights of Rehabilitated Victims of Political Repressions were involved in this work, which was carried out in accordance with a plan drawn up by "Tsentrlesproekt" that had been blessed by the patriarch, approved by the Moscow Regional Ministry of Culture, and discussed at a public meeting, according to Kirill Kaleda, cited in Vedernikov, "Tserkov' i kul'tura." The patriarch also personally thanked Luzhkov and other officials for helping to make possible the first open-air service at the site in May 2000; see the patriarch's open letter, published in *Petrovka* 38, no. 29, July 26, 2000.

45. The relevant federal law is the law "On Objects of Cultural Heritage (Monuments of History and Culture) of the Peoples of the Russian Federation," last updated June 25, 2002, Federal'nyi zakon, "Ob ob'ektakh kul'turnogo naslediia (pamiatnikakh istorii i kul'tury) narodov Rossiiskoi Federatsii," ot 25.06.2002 N 73-FZ (posledniaya redaktsiia), Article 4, http://www.consultant.ru/document/cons_doc_LAW_37318/. As Jonathan Webber points out in his discussion of Auschwitz as a heritage site, the application of the term *heritage* to atrocity sites represents an unusual use of the term (Webber, "The Kingdom of Death as a Heritage Site: Making Sense of Auschwitz," in *A Companion to Heritage Studies*, ed. William Logan, Mairead Nic Craith, and Ullrich Kockel [Chichester, West Sussex: Wiley Blackwell, 2015], 117).

46. "On Objects of Cultural Heritage."

47. Cited in Volkov, "Protoierei Kirill Kaleda." Catherine Merridale interviewed the archaeologist and ethnographer Sergei Alekseyev, who was involved in work at the site, and she writes that "He and his associates decided long ago that Butovo's victims should lie in peace, however orderless their remains"; she notes that the decision here was to build churches rather than to dig (Catherine Merridale, *Night of Stone: Death and Memory in Russia* [London: Granta, 2000], 383. Since the martyrs buried at the site have been canonized, no exhumation can take place without permission from the church hierarchy, which was a factor complicating later digs at the site in 2001–5; see the account by one participant of these digs, Mikhail Frolov, "Butovskii poligon: arkheologiia rasstrelov," *Samizdat*, November 30, 2007 (edited February 17, 2009), http://samlib.ru/f/frolow_m_w/butovo.shtml.

48. It should be noted that in the cases of graves containing Jewish victims, such as those at Jedwabne and elsewhere in Poland, the remains have not been exhumed for different reasons (out of respect for Jewish religious practice).

49. See Francisco Ferrandiz and Antonius C. G. M. Robben, "Introduction: The Ethnography of Exhumations," in *Necropolitics: Mass Graves and Exhumations in the Age of Human Rights*, ed. Francisco Ferrandix and Antonius C. G. M. Robben (Philadelphia: University of Pennsylvania Press, 2015), 1–38.

50. On the Russian case, see further Elisabeth Anstett and Jean-Marc Dreyfus, "Introduction: Why Exhume? Why Identify?," in *Human Remains and Identification: Mass Violence, Genocide, and the "Forensic Turn,"* ed. Elisabeth Anstett and Jean-Marc Dreyfus (Manchester, UK: Manchester University Press, 2015), 3–4.

51. Memorial Society entry for "Moscow," "Mesta massovykh zakhoronenii i pamiatniki zhertvam politicheskikh repressii," accessed November 26, 2016, http://old.memo.ru/memory/martirol/pomniki.htm#_VPID_16.

52. Viacheslav Bitiutckii, "State Secrets and Concealed Bodies: Exhumations of Soviet-Era Victims in Contemporary Russia," in Anstett and Dreyfus, eds., *Human Remains*, 109. On the concern with proper burial as a central tenet of Orthodox Christianity, see further Karen Petrone, "Moscow's First World War Memorial," in Buckler and Johnson, eds., *Rites of Place*, 248.

53. See also Karel C. Berkhoff's account of the case of the Bykivnia site in Ukraine in the late 1980s. Berkhoff writes that when the issue of exhumation came up, "A representative of the Communist Party . . . smiled and declared it unnecessary, even *immoral*: 'We should not disturb the bones of those who perished—it's not Christian. All the more so because there was already an exhumation in December 1987. What's left to prove if we now know the main thing—who exterminated those people. No necrophilia, please!'" (Karel C. Berkhoff, "Bykivnia: How Grave Robbers, Activists, and Foreigners Ended Official Silence about Stalin's Mass Graves near Kiev," in Anstett and Dreyfus, eds., *Human Remains*, 70). At the Katyn site, too, in the mid-1990s, the local clergy cautioned not to disturb the dead by exhuming their remains (Alexander Etkind, Rory Finnin, Uilleam Blacker, Julie Fedor, Simon Lewis, Maria Mälksoo, and Matilda Mroz, *Remembering Katyn* [Cambridge, UK: Polity, 2012], 123).

54. Yakov Krotov, "Gde dolzhny byt' skelety" (*Biblioteka Yakova Krotova*, n.d.), http://krotov.info/spravki/mine/2_life/11_kladbische.htm (URL no longer active).

55. "Gibel' Muamara Kaddafi," October 31, 2011, http://krotov.info/library/17_r/radio_svoboda/20111029.htm.

56. "Around DNT Butovo," accessed March 1, 2020, http://dnt-butovo.info/karty_i_shemy/dnt_butovo_v_granicah_ohrannoj_zony_pamyatnika_istorii_butovskij_poligon/.

57. Ibid.

58. See "Zhil'e stroiat na poligone," *Metro* (Moscow), no. 131, December 8, 2011; and Margarita Sumarokova, "Zhilye doma sobralis' vozvodit' na mogilakh Butovskogo poligona," *Izvestiia* (Moscow edition), no. 230, December 8, 2011.

59. On November 11, 2015, additional changes were made to the Moscow regional government's resolution, with a view to further tightening control over construction and defining the borders (Pravitel'stvo Moskovskoi oblasti, "Postanovlenie 11.11.2015 g. no. 1047/41, O vnesenii izmenenii v postanovlenie Pravitel'stvo Moskovskoi oblasti ot 09.08.2011 no. 259/28 'Ob ob'iavlenii pamiatnogo mesta 'Butovskii poligon' v Leninskom raione pamiatnikom istorii regional'nogo znacheniia i utverzhdenii granits yego territorii i zon okhrany."

60. Artem Levchenko, "Protoierei Kirill Kaleda: Sozdanie tsentra pamiati zhertv stalinskikh repressii—vazhnaya, no trudnaya zadacha," *Pravoslavie i mir*, August 4, 2014, http://www.pravmir.ru/protoierey-kirill-kaleda-sozdanie-tsentra

-pamyati-zhertv-stalinskih-repressiy-vazhnaya-no-trudnaya-zadacha/. The point is also made by Aleksandr Daniel', cited in Leonova, "Kovalevskii les."

61. Again, see Daniel' on this, cited in Leonova, "Kovalevskii les."

62. See Kirill Kaleda's comments on this, cited in Levchenko, "Protoierei Kirill Kaleda."

63. Luchenko, "Butovskii poligon."

64. See, for example, Volkov, "Protoierei Kirill Kaleda," or "Protoierei Kirill Kaleda: 'Organizatsiia tserkovnogo muzeia—eto ochen' ser'eznoe napravlenie." *Revizor.ru*, February 15, 2018.

65. Volkov, "Protoierei Kirill Kaleda." See also then Moscow regional governor Boris Gromov's comments on joint efforts by Moscow city and Moscow regional authorities during this period in the Butovo site, cited in Nikolai Lobodiuk, "Piat' let bez prava peredyshki," *Moskovskii komsomolets*, no. 23762, December 29, 2004.

66. Volkov, "Protoierei Kirill Kaleda."

67. Luchenko, "Butovskii poligon."

68. Volkov, "Protoierei Kirill Kaleda."

69. According to Kirill Kaleda, cited in Levchenko, "Protoierei Kirill Kaleda."

70. See comments by Anatolii Mordashev, head of the Butovskii poligon pilgrimage-excursion service, cited in Denisova, "Chego my ne znaem?" Mordashev says that the museum will be housed in the former NKVD *komendatura* building at the site, which, he says, burned down in the mid-1990s but is currently being rebuilt to correspond with old photographs.

71. Irina Paperno, "Exhuming the Bodies of Soviet Terror," *Representations* 75, no. 1 (Summer 2001): 89–118. On the hopes that the discovery of the mass graves might enable Russia to "draw a line between our awful past and our present," see Tselms, "Prestupnye tainy."

72. Putin was referring to the launch of the new version of *Gulag Archipelago*, adapted for schoolchildren at Putin's request, included in the school literature curriculum, and launched in late October 2010. Putin noted that this coincided with the eve of October 30, the Day of Memory of the Victims of Political Repressions, and hailed it as an "emblematic event," describing the book as essential for Russian self-understanding (*RIA Novosti*, October 26, 2010). The decision to add it to the curriculum was made in summer 2009, partly, as Putin put it, as a tribute to Solzhenitsyn in the lead-up to the first anniversary of his death (*grani.ru*, September 9, 2009). On the evolution of Putin's relationship with Solzhenitsyn, see Robert Horvath, "Apologist of Putinism? Solzhenitsyn, the Oligarchs, and the Specter of Orange Revolution," *Russian Review* 70, no. 2 (April 2011): 300–18.

73. Leonova, "Kovalevskii les."

74. Ibid.

75. A detailed set of documents was put together in response to this proposal that such a memorial museum be built at Kovalevskii Forest (*Ioffe Foundation* [website], accessed March 1, 2020, http://iofe.center/node/26). The documents make frequent

reference to international examples of such memorial museums, for example, Auschwitz and Yad Vashem. It is noted here, for example, that "The international experience dictates the most appropriate [adekvatnuiu] form of reinforcing such tragedies in national memory: namely, the museum-memorial complex, like the 'Yad Vashem' Memorial in Israel and a whole series of analogous complexes in many foreign countries" (see letter from Irina Flige and Ruslan Lin'kov to Medvedev, 2). It calls for the creation of "a museum-memorial center of a new type, the first 21st century landscape museum in Russia" ("K Kontseptsii muzeino-memorial'nogo kompleksa 'Kovalevskii les,'" 1). It was proposed that it should include a "Zona kul'tovykh sooruzhenii" to be developed according to the wishes of religious communities such as the Russian Orthodox Church. The key concept was for "a special landscape environment: a Park of Memory" (2). It was underlined as crucial that it should be "an object of exclusively federal subordination" (2). But it looks as though the Russian Federation Ministry for Culture proposed that, because of the experience with the Butovskii poligon, the museum should be regional (see Busygin to Medvedev, December 9, 2009). It should have the legal status of a "state museum-sanctuary" [muzei-zapovednik]. The proposal included, among other interesting documents, a letter from the metropolitan of Saint Petersburg and Ladozhskii supporting it. Many of these documents emphasize that, as a letter to Medvedev from the Saint Petersburg Jewish community puts it, such a complex could play a role like Yad Vashem in fostering "consolidation of memory" in Russia.

76. Leonova, "Kovalevskii les."

77. Another defining feature of the Russian memorial museum is its location "at the site linked to the . . . individual or event in question" and its focus on "revealing and interpreting this link." The requirement that, in order to qualify as a *memorial'nyi muzei*, a museum must be built at a memorial site and must include genuine objects was formalized in 1967 in the *Polozhenie* on Memorial Museums of the System of the Ministry of Culture; "Memorial'nye muzei," accessed January 18, 2017, *Rossiiskaya muzeinaya entsiklopediia*, http://www.museum.ru/rme/sci_mem.asp.

78. Leonova, "Kovalevskii les."

79. Ibid. One of the authors of the project, Aleksandr Daniel', said the authors had made close study of projects in the Baltic states in particular. He also said that this project would be "a synthesis of strategies of memory in post-Soviet space and in this sense . . . a new phenomenon."

80. Kovalevskii Forest Memorial cemetery, accessed February 28, 2020, http://www.mapofmemory.org/47-01, and "K razrabotke kontseptsii MMK 'Kovalevskii les,'" *Cogita.ru*, last modified November 30, 2010, http://www.cogita.ru/pamyat/muzeino-memorialnyi-kompleks-kovalevskii-les/k-razrabotke-koncepcii-mmk-abkovalevskii-lesbb.

81. "Glava 'Memoriala' nazval udarom vnesenie chlenskoi organizatsii v reestr 'inoagentov,'" *TASS*, November 6, 2015, http://tass.ru/politika/2413929.

82. See further the comments by one of the architects of this policy, Mikhail Fedotov: "Sovetnik Medvedeva: pust' sovetskaya simvolika sokhraniaetsia, kak napominanie," *Delfi.lt*, June 12, 2011, http://ru.delfi.lt/news/politics/sovetnik-medvedeva-pust-sovetskaya-simvolika-sohranyaetsya-kak-napominanie.d?id=46523647. Fedotov argues here that "Russia is the biggest victim of the totalitarian regime."

83. Sergei Karaganov, "Russkaya Katyn'," *Rossiiskaya gazeta*, no. 5239, July 22, 2010, https://rg.ru/2010/07/22/istoriya.html.

84. "Predlozheniia ob uchrezhdenii obshchenatsional'noi gosudarstvenno-obshchestvennoi programmy 'Ob uvekovechenii pamiati zhertv totalitarnogo rezhima i o natsional'nom primirenii,'" Soviet under the President of the Russian Federation, old.president-sovet.ru/structure/group_5/materials/proposals_at_a_meeting_in_ekb/.

85. Although most of the concrete measures proposed in the document were drafted by the Memorial Society, their ideological packaging would appear to have been provided by Karaganov, to judge from the text, and from the fact that this division of labor was used in presenting the program to Medvedev, with Karaganov presenting the ideological sections, and Memorial head Roginskii handling the concrete measures. Karaganov has also mentioned that there were "clashes" with the Memorial Society in the course of drafting the document.

86. Leonova, "Kovalevskii les."

87. "Prilozhenie No. 1: Uvekovechenie pamiati zhertv totalitarnogo rezhima," http://old.president-sovet.ru/structure/group_5/materials/proposals_at_a_meeting_in_ekb/appendix_1.html.

88. But it has resulted in the new monument in Moscow, "Wall of Grief", by Georgii Frangulian, unveiled on October 30, 2017. http://kremlin.ru/events/president/news/55948 For debates over what position civil society should take toward the monument, see Vera Vasil'eva, "Moscow: diskussiia o pamiatnike zhertvam politicheskikh repressii," *Prava cheloveka v Rossii*, March 18, 2015, http://www.hro.org/node/21755.

89. Igor' Karnaukhov, "'Perm'-36' poluchit natsional'nyi status," *Rossiiskaya gazeta*, January 21, 2013, https://rg.ru/2013/01/21/reg-pfo/perm36.html. Kovalevskii Forest is one of the sites that has been proposed for a possible future national memorial museum; see "IMTs Kovalevskii Forest," *Ioffe Foundation*, accessed February 29, 2020, http://iofe.center/node/26.

90. According to Kaleda, cited in Levchenko, "Protoierei Kirill Kaleda."

91. Ibid.

92. Ibid.

93. "Kontseptsiia gosudarstvennoi politiki." Unusually, and curiously, the text of the concept is also provided in German on the official website. In February 2016, Putin signed an order creating an interdepartmental working group to coordinate the activities aimed at realizing the state concept on memory politics. The group

is headed by Mikhail Fedotov and includes deputy justice minister Alu Alkhanov ("Sozdana rabochaya gruppa, kotoraya budet zanimat'sia uvekovecheniem pamiati zhertv repressii," *RIA Novosti*, February 15, 2016).

94. "Kontseptsiia gosudarstvennoi politiki."

95. Ibid.

96. Ibid.

97. "Gruppa po uvekovecheniiu pamiati."

98. "O vnesenii izmenenii v otdel'nye zakonodatel'nye akty Rossiiskoi Federatsii v sviazi s uvekovecheniem pamiati zhertv politicheskikh repressii," Federal Laws of the Russian Federation, approved March 2, 2016, http://pravo.gov.ru/proxy/ips/?docbody=&prevDoc=102012774&backlink=1&&nd=102391508.

99. "Federal'nyi Zakon o Nekommercheskikh Organizatsiiakh," Federal Laws of the Russian Federation, approved December 8, 1995, http://pravo.gov.ru/proxy/ips/?docbody=&prevDoc=102391508&backlink=1&&nd=102039064.

100. "O vnesenii izmenenii."

101. "GD zakrepila pravo po uvekovecheniiu pamiati zhertv politicheskikh repressii," Regnum News Agency, February 26, 2016.

102. "Uvekovechivaiushchie pamiat' zhertv repressii NKO smogut rasschityvat' na gospodderzhku v RF—zakon," *RIA Novosti*, February 26, 2016.

103. "Yekaterinburgskii 'Memorial', priznannyi inostrannym agentom, oshtrafovan na 300 tys rublei," *RIA Novosti*, February 26, 2016.

104. On the related case of pressure exerted against the Perm'-36 Gulag museum, see further chapter 10 on the GULAG Museum by Jeff Hardy, in this volume.

105. Kseniia Kirillova, "Proverka pamiati," *S uvazheniem k pamiati* 2 (78) (February 2015), http://www.funeralassociation.ru/ru/newspaper/archives/7815/7804/. The project has produced the interactive "Map of Memory: Necropolis of the Terror and the Gulag": http://mapofmemory.org/. From 2015, the project has been transferred to the Ioffe Foundation, which, as of 2015, has taken over some of the Memorial Society's activities (http://iofe.center/).

106. See further "Russia: Governments vs. Rights Groups," *Human Rights Watch*, January 17, 2017, https://www.hrw.org/russia-government-against-rights-groups-battle-chronicle.

107. "Propoved' Sviateishego Patriarkha Kirilla po okonchanii Liturgii na Butovskom poligone," Moscow Patriarchate official site, May 16, 2015, http://www.patriarchia.ru/db/text/4081981.html.

108. Ibid.

109. See teacher's guide for a secondary-school class on Butovo in 2002, designed to be used in conjunction with an excursion to the site: Viacheslav Artamonov, "Butovo—raiskaya zemlia: Konspekt uroka dlia srednikh klassov," *Voskresnaya shkola* no. 4, January 26, 2002.

110. "O proekte: Istoriia proekta," *Kalendar' pamiati*, accessed January 17, 2017, http://sinodik.ru/?q=static&id=2.

111. Stephanie Shosh Rotem, *Constructing Memory: Architectural Narratives of Holocaust Museums* (New York: Peter Lang, 2013), 15. In the Russian case, the first secular museums appeared under Peter the Great; churches before that time can be seen as "proto-museums," fulfilling functions such as the preservation of relics and artworks, and churches sometimes were built to memorialize important events ("Memorial'nye muzei," *Rossiiskaya muzeinaya entsiklopediia*, accessed January 18, 2017, http://www.museum.ru/rme/sci_mem.asp). As Karen Petrone points out, before the eighteenth century, churches were also the only form of war memorials built in Russia (Karen Petrone, "Moscow's First World War Memorial," 245).

112. "Proekt Kontseptsii razvitiia muzeinogo dela v Rossiiskoi Federatsii na period do 2030 goda," 6. The document defines the museum as "a cultural institution guaranteeing the strengthening of society's spiritual-moral foundation and unity, education of patriotism, and conservation and inclusion into the world cultural circulation of the rich cultural-historical heritage of the peoples of Russia," ibid., 7. See also Ministerstvo Kul'tury Rossiiskoi Federatsii, "Gosudarstvennyi doklad o sostoianii kul'tury v Rossiiskoi Federatsii v 2014 godu," accessed December 24, 2016, http://mkrf.ru/upload/mkrf/mkdocs2015/%D0%B3%D0%BE%D1%81%D0%B4%D0%BE%D0%BA%D0%BB%D0%B0%D0%B4_%D0%B2%D0%BE%D1%81%D1%81D0%B8%D1%8F%20%D0%93%D0%94%20%D0%B8%20%D0%A1%D0%A4%20%D0%A4%D0%98%D0%9D%D0%90%D0%9B.pdf.

113. For example, the deputy director of a new Church museum created at Novodevich'e Monastery in 2010 says that it "positions itself as an Orthodox scholarly-educational institution, preserving memorial and historical relics linked to Russian statehood and Orthodoxy" (Aleksii Kulikov, "Tserkovnyi muzei Moskovskoi Yeparkhii RF i yego rol' v sokhranenii kul'turnogo naslediia," presentation to the scholarly-practical conference Khristianskii muzei v sovremennom mire, December 16, 2014, Moscow, http://acmus.ru/news/stati/cerkovniy_muzey_moskovskoy_eparhii_rpc_i_ego_rol_v_sohranenii_kulturnogo_naslediya/index.php).

114. Gennadii Belovolov, "Eto byl pervyi forum khristianskikh muzeev Rossii," *Russkaya narodnaya* liniia, December 24, 2014, http://ruskline.ru/news_rl/2014/12/24/eto_byl_pervyj_forum_hristianskih_muzeev_rossii/.

115. Ibid.

116. Ibid.

117. According to Vladimir Legoida, chair of the synodal Information Section of the Russian Orthodox Church, cited in "Komissiia po vzaimodeistviiu RPTs i muzeinogo soobshchestva sozdana v Rossii," *ITAR-TASS*, http://dalisr.narod.ru/inews/artnews_5630.html.

118. The conflict is also a result of the Church's campaign against exhibitions deemed to be blasphemous.

119. During the late Soviet period, the same accusation was leveled against the church by the state to justify the latter's custodianship of such sites; see Sanami Takahashi, "Church or Museum? The Role of State Museums in

Conserving Church Buildings, 1965–1985," *Journal of Church and State* 51, no. 3 (2009): 510.

120. "Sostoialas' vstrecha Sviateishego Patriarkha Kirilla s rukovoditeliami krupneishikh muzeev Rossii," *Official website of Russian Orthodox Church (Moscow Patriarchate)*, September 15, 2016, http://www.patriarchia.ru/db/text/4615343.html.

121. Igor' Mikhailov, "Khristianskie muzei v sfere sozdaniia kross-muzeinykh kommunikatsii," presentation to the scholarly-practical conference "Khristianskii muzei v sovremennom mire," December 16, 2014, Moscow, http://acmus.ru/ahm/materiali/doklad_hristianskie_muzei_v__sfere_sozdaniya_kross_muzeynih_kommunikaciy/index.php.

122. Gar'kavyi, "Pamiat' o mestakh skorbi," 39. By his account, "musealization of the Butovskii poligon began in 1995 when the territory . . . was transferred to the Russian Orthodox Church" ("Pravoslavnaya obshchestvennost' prosit ostanovit' zastroiku Butovskogo poligona," www.pravoslavie.ru, February 8, 2015, http://www.pravoslavie.ru/77116.html).

123. See Vedernikov, "Tserkov' i kul'tura"; and Igor' Gar'kavyi, "Pamiat' o mestakh skorbi," *Pokrov* 1 (2011): 38. The latter, for example, discusses the history of the church's special role in remembrance practices linked to anonymous mass graves and the graves of other categories of people buried without the usual rites. The example of World War I is frequently cited in this connection as a forgotten precedent that may have useful lessons for the current situation.

124. "Na Levashovskom kladbishche poiavitsia chasovnia," *Rosbalt—Peterburg*, December 16, 2012.

125. Natal'ia Sivokhina, "Na Farforovskoe prishli poiskoviki," *cogita.ru*, February 21, 2013, http://www.cogita.ru/pamyat/kultura-pamyati/na-farforovskoe-prishli-poiskoviki; "V 'Levashovskoi pustoshi' poiavitsia chasovnia dlia pominoveniia repressirovannykh leningradtsev," *tv100.ru*, December 19, 2012.

126. "'Memorial' protiv stroitel'stva v Levashovskoi pustoshi," *cogita.ru* (Saint Petersburg), December 15, 2012.

127. Gar'kavyi, cited in "Na Butovskom poligone postroiat 'Sad pamiati,'" *Rublev*, August 7, 2015, http://rublev.com/novosti/na-butovskom-poligone-postrojat-sad-pamjati.

128. Cited in Dar'ia Barinova, "Mogila dlia 20 tysiach chelovek: kak pomnit' o kazhdom?," Russian Orthodox church, Moscow City Eparchiate official website, October 30, 2016, http://moseparh.ru/mogila-dlya-20-tysyach-chelovek-kak-pomnit-o-kazhdom.html.

129. "Memorial'noye kladbishche Sandormokh," *Ioffe Foundation*, accessed February 29, 2020, http://iofe.center/sandormokh.

130. "Pravozashchitniki: prevratit' Butovskii poligon v muzei dolzhna pomoch' RPTs," *AUIPIK (Agentstvo po upravleniiu i ispol'zovaniiu pamiatnikov istorii i kul'tury)*, November 11, 2014, http://auipik.ru/pravozashhitniki-prevratit-butovskij-poligon-v-muzej-dolzhna-pomoch-rpc/.

131. See "Gruppa po uvekovecheniiu pamiati."

132. "Prezident Rossii provel zasedanie Soveta po razvitiiu grazhdanskogo obshchestva i pravam cheloveka," *Official website of the RF Presidential Council for the Development of Civil Society and Human Rights*, December 8, 2016, http://president-sovet.ru/presscenter/news/read/3623/. In the end, a granite wall engraved with the names of the known victims, listed according to the date on which they were murdered, was unveiled in Butovo on September 27, 2017, without Vladimir Putin's participation.

133. In August 2016, Igor' Gar'kavyi, said that the possibility of transferring these buildings to the Church was currently being discussed "at a very high level" (Igor' Gar'kavyi, interview by Yevgenii Belokhvostikov in "'Butovskii poligon daet opyt perezhivaniia pobedy nad smert'iu,'" Penza diocese website, August 20, 2016, http://xn----7sbbracknn1actjpi5e2ih.xn--p1ai/?p=90080.a. These buildings are something of a puzzle; it seems that little is known about their history. On Yandex maps, the site is labeled "KGB Archive"; we are grateful to Stephen Wheatcroft for discovering this during a visit to the site with Julie Fedor in May 2015. According to Igor' Gar'kavyi, on maps from the late 1950s, it is labeled simply "Archive" (authors' personal correspondence with Igor' Gar'kavyi, August 26, 2016).

134. The account given here paraphrases the report "V SPCh obsuzhdali sozdanie muzeia politicheskikh repressii protiv veruiushchikh," *Prava cheloveka v Rossii*, November 11, 2014, accessed November 24, 2016, http://hro.org/node/20599.

135. "Sviashchennik Kirill Kaleda rasskazal o stroike na Butovskom poligone i sozdanii muzei istorii politicheskikh repressii protiv tserkvi," *Official website of the RF Presidential Council for Development of Civil Society and Human Rights*, January 26, 2015, http://president-sovet.ru/presscenter/news/read/2177/.

136. Gar'kavyi interview by Belokhvostikov.

137. See the presentation "Traumatic Heritage of the 20th Century as World Heritage," delivered by Sakharov Center historian Natalia Samover in June 2017 as part of the symposium Cultural Heritage: A Platform for Dialogue, Yaroslavl', June 30, 2017, http://www.sakharov-center.ru/blogs/main/all/nauchny-simpozium-kulturnoe-nasledie-ploschadka-dlya-dialoga/. Natalia Samover notes in it that in 2014 Russia nominated two Great Patriotic War sites (Mamaev kurgan and the Stalingrad Memorial Complex) as candidates for World Heritage listing. A working group under the Presidential Council for the Development of Civil Society and Human Rights is proposing that the Butovskii poligon, together with the Moscow Canal (built by Dmitlag prisoners in the 1930s), the Levashovskoe memorial cemetery, and the Perm-36 museum, also be nominated for listing. The proposal was submitted to the Russian Ministry of Culture, where it has apparently stalled for lack of political will.

138. See further Oleg Khlebnikov, "Ekskursia po budushchemu muzeu: i pamiatniku zhertvam repressii byt'! Nesmotria na vozmozhnyi sabotazh chinovnikov," *Novaya gazeta*, April 16, 2015, https://www.novayagazeta.ru/articles/2015/04/17/63854-ekskursiya-po-buduschemu-muzeyu. See also the online

project run by Anatolii Mordashev, head of the Butovskii poligon's pilgrimage-excursion service; the website features an interactive map of Russian sites of Orthodox martyrdom: www.martyrmap.ru/.

139. The Katyn site is one exception. See further Etkind et al., *Remembering Katyn*, 115.

140. Alexander Etkind, *Warped Mourning: Stories of the Undead in the Land of the Unburied* (Stanford, CA: Stanford University Press, 2013), 176–77.

141. Sharon Macdonald notes that "the museum is an institution of recognition and identity par excellence. It selects certain cultural products for official safekeeping, for posterity and public display—a process which recognizes and affirms some identities, and omits to recognize and affirm others" (Macdonald, "Expanding Museum Studies: An Introduction," in *Companion to Museum Studies*, ed. Sharon Macdonald (Hoboken, NJ: Wiley, 2008), 4.

142. Jay Winter, "Museums and the Representation of War," *Museum and Society* 10, no. 3 (2012): 159. Some of those involved in looking after the Butovo site have argued that as a cemetery, a major museum there would be out of place; see the comment by FSB Colonel M. Ye. Kirillin, an official who was involved in the rehabilitation process: "I think that there's no need to erect any pompous and expensive constructions at Butovo. Let's not forget that this is first and foremost a cemetery.... I could envisage some kind of small museum near the Butovskii poligon, where one could obtain information about Butovo and see a memory book with the names and photographs of the people executed here. Perhaps this is my subjective opinion as a person who has been very involved with this site, but Butovo as it is now makes the strongest impression: this plank fence with barbed wire, this field, overgrown with wild grass mixed with flowers, the memorial plaque and the church in the distance—these things tell the visitor more than concrete or marble monuments" ("Zakonoproekt o protivodeistvii stalinizmu vnesen v GD: pravitel'stvo protiv," Regnum News Agency, March 25, 2016).

143. Ferrandiz and Robben, "Introduction," 1.

144. Svetlana Malysheva, "'Bratskie mogily' i 'vrazheskie mogil'niki': simvolicheskoe oznachivanie massovykh zakhoronenii v Sovetskoi Rossii/SSSR 1920-kh-1940-kh godov," *Soviet and Post-Soviet Review* (2016): 11. Malysheva notes that the mass grave was destigmatized during World War II, when it became both unavoidable and commonplace.

145. As Istvan Rev puts it, death "is not (just) a biological but a social and cultural fact and idea. Faced with the drama of death, we have no choice but to turn to the repertoire of available practices in order to turn the biological into an artificially slowed-down social process" (Rev, *Retroactive Justice: Prehistory of Post-Communism* [Stanford, CA: Stanford University Press, 2005], 10).

146. "Kontseptsiia gosudarstvennoi politiki."

147. Kirill Kaleda, cited in Vedernikov, "Tserkov' i kul'tura."

JULIE FEDOR is Senior Lecturer in Modern European History in the School of Historical and Philosophical Studies at the University of Melbourne. She holds a PhD in history from King's College, University of Cambridge, and is author of *Russia and the Cult of State Security* (2011) and coauthor of *Remembering Katyn* (2012). She is currently completing work on a book about militarism and memory in Putin's Russia.

TOMAS SNIEGON is a historian and Associate Professor in European Studies at the University of Lund, Sweden. His research focuses on the memory of traumatic events of the twentieth century in central and eastern European historical cultures and on the development of Soviet forms of communism in Europe during the Cold War. He is currently working on the project "Making Sense of the 'Good': Soviet Communist Dictatorship through Stalin's error, Khrushchev's Reforms, and Brezhnev's Period of Stagnation; A Historical Narrative by the Former KGB Chairman Vladimir Semichastny," based on analysis of his own extensive interviews with Vladimir Semichastny and financed by Riksbankens Jubileumsfond, the Swedish Foundation for Humanities and Social Sciences.

Figure 12.1. Museum of Soviet Arcade Games, Moscow, founded 2007 (private museum). http://www.15kop.ru/. *Photograph by Roman Abramov*

TWELVE

The Museum of Soviet Arcade Games
Nostalgia for a Socialist Childhood

ROMAN ABRAMOV

The contemporary world remains captivated by what Simon Reynolds has dubbed "retromania," displaying a vigorous appetite for commodified versions of nostalgia.[1] It is through nostalgia that various subcultures and the commercial industries of fashion and entertainment meet, sparking a constant search for the lost meanings of the life of the past, as well as inspiration for new commercial projects that employ the objects, images, and stories of the recent past. The bittersweet delight of the 1950s, 1960s, 1970s, and now even the 1980s and 1990s, has inspired the creation of new television series, led to the rebirth of interior design styles, and generated a renaissance of various gadgets, including cars. It is on these grounds that a participatory culture has developed, emerging from the work of leading enthusiasts, a group that largely consists of amateurs engaged in research activities such as the collection of key pieces, the establishment of private museums, and the reconstruction of and commercializing of the past. It is the recent history of a particular country that determines differences in the nature of retromania and in establishing the characteristics of a particular style of "old school." In Western countries, the phenomenon is primarily a result of postwar economic growth and the emergence of a mass consumer society, all of which produced an environment rich in material objects and cultural products.

In the postcolonial world, nostalgia has a contradictory nature. On the one hand, it is reminiscent of the era of colonial exploitation and, on the other hand, it makes references to local manifestations of a refined European lifestyle and elegant architecture. In the countries of the former Communist Bloc, the social memory of socialism has also taken on complex forms, largely as a result of the ambiguous ways the Communist Era is perceived in these countries. In many formerly socialist countries, it is common for the communist period to be interpreted as an era of historical tragedy and disaster. In that context, positive memories of the period are viewed as an undesirable deviation from the norm. Although there can be no doubt about the authoritarian nature of the political regimes in these countries from the 1940s to the 1980s, it is important to note that important social changes also occurred during the communist period because of rising living standards, better education, and new opportunities for upward social mobility. Therefore, the material artifacts of socialism (such as cars, clothing, toys, furniture, residential buildings) have also become the subject of a good-natured irony, reminding the older generation of their childhood and adolescence, submerging them back into a strange world of ideology, allowing them to come face-to-face with the everyday socialism of their youth. In the countries of the former Soviet bloc there are several kinds of museums dedicated to topics from the period of "real socialism" as diverse as oppression under the Soviet occupation displayed in the Terror Háza in Budapest and nostalgia for objects from the German Democratic Republic in Berlin, Leipzig, and Dresden museums.

One key sign of interest in this period can be found in the emergence of so-called folk museums on the socialist way of life.[2] Such museums weave together the cultural elements of nostalgia and its commercial motives and provide a form of entertainment. From 2006 to 2016, more than twenty-five such museums were founded in Russia, mainly specializing in the collection and exhibition of household items, interior design, and clothes from the period of "actually existing" or "developed" socialism, the era from the 1960s to the 1980s. Their exhibits often resemble a junk shop, which is unsurprising when the organizers of these museums are often amateur enthusiasts and traders who have identified Soviet nostalgia as an area ripe for commodification. This chapter sheds light on the special features of one particularly interesting folk museum, the Museum of Soviet Arcade Machines, which was founded in 2007 by a group of engineers from Moscow with a passion for Soviet gadgets. Currently, the museum is thriving and has opened an additional branch in Saint Petersburg. The museum is not merely a storeroom of nostalgia for the childhood in the late Soviet period; it is also a profitable commercial enterprise, a hip café, and an entertainment center for children and their parents.

ARCADE MACHINES: A SOCIAL AND SOVIET HISTORY

Scholars have paid little attention to the era of arcade machines that preceded the current generation of video games, which have heralded the dawn of postmodern virtual reality. It is in this regard is that Nick Dyer-Witheford and Greig de Peuter's influential book, *Games of Empire: Global Capitalism and Video Games*, is particularly revealing.[3] It emphasizes how a new generation has grown up with electronic video games and home video game consoles, which stands in stark contrast to previous generations, who generally paid little mind to arcade machines. It is worth pointing out that the first video games (particularly those of Atari) became entangled in a growing discourse that related their products to social problems and even moral panic. The discourse included accusations that the attachments children and adolescents felt to these games could lead to increases in aggression and could even result in crime.[4] Later, the proliferation of games on the Nintendo console platform led scholars to examine video games as part of a growing commodification of children's and adolescent's lives corresponding to innovations in the toy industry.[5] The 1990s witnessed a lengthy and active discussion among psychologists, sociologists, and anthropologists about the extent to which video games (and later computer games) were culpable in increasing violent and misogynistic tendencies among teenage boys hooked on violent video games, particularly first-person "shoot 'em' up" games such as *Doom*.[6]

By the beginning of the twenty-first century, a whole generation had grown up with the first video games and game consoles. As that age cohort entered adulthood, it must be underlined, no substantial growth in violence or misogyny was detected among them. Therefore, analysis of video games has gradually shifted in focus from the sociopsychological aspects of violence to the aesthetic and even the literary components of video games as part of the entertainment industry. The shift has occurred thanks to the efforts of entire subcultures of critics, historians, and video-game lovers, many of whom became analysts and archivists in the subject.[7] Thanks to their efforts, the image of video games has changed. The old image of video gaming as a low-grade, shabby form of electronic entertainment fit for only one use and popular among "loser" adolescents and adults has changed considerably.

The new image of video games is one of a rich and meaningful world with its own history rather than that of a world of lonely, isolated gamers. The current vision sees it as a source of cooperation and interaction. In the academic context, the analytical study of video games has also undergone a thematic enrichment. Now the subject is placed within the broader context of the transformation of modern culture alongside evolving technological progress. The change is also part of a gradual awareness of the growing role of the video-game industry as a new reality in media and culture. At the same time, new groups of researchers have emerged who employ narratology to analyze video games, examining them as texts with narratives. Alongside the narratologists, another group of scholars argue that video games should be primarily understood as a type of sport, especially because of the central role of sport-related features in them such as competition, structured rules, goals, and strategies.[8]

The history of gaming in the Soviet Union allows us to take slightly different approaches. Except for bets on the racetrack and certain cash raffles and official forms of the state lottery, gambling was banned in the Soviet Union. That is not to say people in the Soviet Union had no outlets to exercise their passion for gambling; the practice of playing card games for money involved not only criminal elements but ordinary citizens. Chess players would often play in parks for money, and pensioners would set up their own bingo games, making small cash bets. Some types of underground card games involving cash bets were common among teenagers. Meanwhile, the state offered a variety of avenues to legally expend one's gambling energies, such as the active development of arcade machines in parks during the first half of the 1970s. In 1971 an international exhibition called "Attraction-71" was held in Gorky Park, Moscow. The exhibition lasted just under two months and gave visitors the chance to see a variety of new arcade machines from different countries, including state-of-the-art US and Japanese models. Noticing the strong interest visitors showed in the exhibition, the Soviet government decided to purchase the exhibition samples and, using them as models, to develop their own line of arcade machines to be installed in parks and theaters. The contract for this work was given to Soviet defense enterprises and, three years later, the first industrial designs for Soviet arcade machines were completed, which would produce the models that became commonplace for millions of children throughout the last fifteen years of the Soviet Union.

In most cases, Soviet arcade machines were installed in the enclosed pavilions of city parks and the halls of some larger cinemas. In the context of the Soviet era, recreational parks were an important tool in the reorganization of urban spaces. This usage fit well with the state's ideological objectives and met the aim of providing leisure activities to citizens.[9] In the first decades of Soviet rule, the recreational parks embodied the Soviet idea of a socialist *kulturnost'* and sought to create a new life for the people of the Soviet Union.[10]

In the parks, which often occupy large areas with gardens and walkways, traditional park attractions such as the carousel, swings, bandstand pavilions, and refreshment stands still stood. They sat side by side with specially themed libraries and lecture halls for public education, as well as visual propaganda such as plaster sculptures of workers, Soviet athletes, and farmers. Also included were attractions designed to support military-patriotic education, including towers for parachute jumping, shooting ranges, and weight-lifting areas. After World War II, and from the 1960s to the 1980s in particular, the recreational functions of such parks became more important than their ideological components. An emerging Soviet consumer society demanded an increasing variety of leisure activities in their parks, and the demand was met by new discoteques, rides, and arcade machines, and at the same time military simulators and statues of muscular workers began to disappear from view.

Arcade machines became an important step in the evolution of recreational parks' function during the Soviet era; they came to embody the most advanced entertainment technology available at the time. With brightly painted cartoon pop art on the outside and complex electronic contents on the inside, these machines essentially existed as an element of Western mass culture within the landscape of late socialism. Furthermore, for many Soviet children and adolescents of the 1970s and 1980s, the machines served as their first introduction to the world of computer technology. Quite sophisticated devices for their time with their algorithmic operations, the machines offered an immersion into remote analogue virtual reality.

In the second half of the 1980s, during the height of Mikhail Gorbachev's reforms, schools and colleges began to offer computer classes that could teach young people the basics of computer science and cybernetics. The educational effort coincided with the mass production of Soviet-designed personal computers for the first time, the majority of which were unlicensed counterfeit copies of US and Japanese models. Personal computers began to be actively used in Soviet design bureaus and research institutes, often for the purpose of playing games. One of best-known classic computer games, Tetris, was invented by a Soviet programmer, Yevgeny Veselov, in 1985. It soon began to spread informally among programmers in both the Soviet Union and the Socialist Bloc as a whole. It was only later that the game burst out of the Communist Bloc and conquered the world.

Thus, Soviet children in the late 1980s became familiar with the world of computer games. Some games were available in schools equipped with computers, others could be found in the workplaces of Soviet engineers and programmers, who would sometimes take their children to work with them. It was against this background that the popularity of the Soviet arcade machines began to fall. In the 1990s, the decline was accelerated by the growth in the number of computers in the population, the proliferation of compact handheld consoles (mainly cheap Chinese copies of Nintendo's Game Boy), and gaming consoles for "Dandy" video games (an unofficial clone of the third-generation games console Famicom). The dissolution of the Soviet Union brought with it the collapse of the state's management of national parks and recreation, and many of the factories that produced Soviet arcade machines went bankrupt as well. In the absence of any body that could help maintain the Soviet arcade-machine industry, their presence gradually faded, with much of the equipment was converted to scrap metal. In place of the arcade halls, private computer clubs and internet cafes emerged, and much of the post-Soviet youth would end up passing their free time in them. It was only the explosion in mass nostalgia for the late Soviet Union and Soviet childhood, which began from 2004 to 2006, that rekindled interest in Soviet arcade machines.

Studies of postcommunist nostalgia in former socialist countries have demonstrated how the history of the Soviet myth continues to develop in post-Soviet space. The development can sometimes manifest itself as a negative myth about an awful past, a terrible example of "how not to live" that present and future generations must reject (see the other chapters in this section for examples). Equally, it is possible for the Soviet past to be presented as a positive myth of a golden age that, to the regret of many, has now departed forever. But not all aspects of the Soviet have enjoyed the same levels of popularity in public discourse. As it happens, it is the period spanning the 1960s to the first half of the 1980s that, employing Aleida Assmann's terminology, best reflects the "living collective memory" of a large part of post-Soviet societies.[11] There are a number of reasons for this. First, it was a period when private forces went on the offensive, disturbing the Soviet collective propped up by comprehensive surveillance and hegemonic ideological discourse. As the steel jaws of the Soviet regime gradually loosened, the last efforts to suppress resistance, as in the case of Czechoslovakia in 1968, did not do anything to halt the main pressure behind the collapse of the Soviet camp; the irresistible urge felt by households to organize their own "little stories," which would be performed in their own separate generic apartments, decorated with rugs of their choosing and Soviet status symbols such as varnished fitted cupboards with interior glass shelves.

The first discussions of nostalgic reminiscences of the late Soviet era emerged between 1996 and 1998. In the first instance, the discussions arose from the increasing popularity of the neo-Soviet consumer brands such as Zhiguli beer or Druzhba processed cheese.[12] Nostalgia was also linked to the release of television shows in which pop stars performed covers of songs from the Soviet period. This method of using Soviet imagery corresponds well with the commercial forms exploiting nostalgia described by the US philosopher Frederic Jameson in the conditions of what he saw as postindustrial capitalism.[13] Perhaps the most important factor at work in the Russian version of post-Soviet nostalgia is the strong enthusiasm for the period of stagnation [*zastoi*], which is historically considered to be from 1964 to 1985. For constructing meanings, however, it would appear that the "long seventies" are more central in the perceptions of *zastoi*. The 1970s was, after all, the decade when Soviet society gained maturity and appeared to be part of a permanent and immutable structure. Recent poll results, conducted by the Levada Center in Moscow, show that the Soviet leaders Brezhnev (56%) and Lenin (55%) scored highest on the question of who was Russia's best ruler in the twentieth century. Stalin, another figure whose historical role is the focus of heated discussions, comes in just behind the father of the Russian revolution (Lenin) and the provider of Soviet stability (Brezhnev) with half the respondents (50%) viewing him in a positive light. It is worth noting, however, that the percentage of respondents with negative views of Stalin (38%) was higher than the percentage for Lenin (28%) or Brezhnev (29%).[14]

Since the mid-2000s, post-Soviet nostalgia has become a truly remarkable social and cultural phenomenon sweeping through Russia's glossy magazines and internet. The material world of the Soviet is no longer quite as commonly viewed in terms of the gloomy and miserable, such as awkwardly designed everyday items of poor quality or lines for consumer goods in short supply. More and more people have come to see the Soviet as a means of escaping the dominance of European styles in interior design. It is also a vehicle for reveling in a former unique style, which can be witnessed when people hit the streets garbed in 1950s style crepe dresses with a Soviet-era FED camera in a leather case. In fashion magazines and on the internet, reviews of secondhand clothing shops and flea markets began to multiply, providing vital advice to those keen on supplementing their collection of Soviet vintage items. It is rather surprising that the desire for Soviet styles has had a great impact on the generation born largely just before or after the fall of the Soviet Union. For this generation, some of whom have now become office workers and part of a new urban intelligentsia, the Soviet world appears strange and attractive at the same time. Thus, people who were children or adolescents in the final years of the Soviet era have now become the key drivers in the popular museification of the late Soviet period.

THE MUSEUM OF SOVIET ARCADE MACHINES: THE HISTORY OF THE COLLECTION

One interesting manifestation of nostalgia for the late Soviet era can be found in the Museum of Soviet Arcade Machines in Moscow. This museum was founded in early 2007 by three young engineers from Moscow Polytechnic University, which, in the Stalin era, had strong ties to industrialization and the Soviet automotive industry. The founders of the museum explained their reasons for opening it as part of their nostalgic daydreaming about the late Soviet past, even though they themselves only caught the last years of the Soviet period as very small schoolchildren:

> I think this was a typical dream for a Soviet schoolboy, to have your own Battleship arcade machine. It is from this dream, which first appeared twenty-five years ago, that our museum originated. In the beginning, all my friend Alexander and I wanted to do was just find this arcade machine and bring it home with us. We started calling all the parks and clubs in town. And in Tagansky Park they told us, 'We have that machine. It is lying in our rubbish heap.' We arrived and took it away with us. We repaired it and put into the garage. Then we started looking for other machines and found Sniper, Basketball, Hockey, Crane.... Soon, we had so many they wouldn't fit in our two garages (the machines had already been forced out onto the street by this time.)[15]

When the garage-space phase of the project came to its conclusion and a significant period of collecting and repairing the machines was complete, the friends started to think about how to create a space from their Soviet childhood. The choice of arcade machines and toys from the 1970s and 1980s was one, they believed, that would draw in people of all ages. According to the French social scientist and one of the founders of memory studies Maurice Halbwachs, childhood plays a foundational role in the formation of collective memory, because the memories of our childhood resemble stereotypical marks that are imprinted on the scrolls of our memory.[16]

The personal experience of nostalgia usually revolves around certain childhood memories from an age of innocence; a time when life felt anchored in the family and human relations characteristic of childhood but was yet to be encumbered by the legal and bureaucratic difficulties of adult life. Although it would seem that this rather rosy version would depict childhood as lacking serious existential challenges, in reality children's lives have their share of problems and stresses.[17]

> With our Museum of Soviet Arcade Machines, we are striving to make a certain kind of museum of childhood. My dream is to have a museum in which various aspects of childhood are collected, such as toys, furniture, clothing, some related items, and food. We want to make a place that is interesting to come with one's children. The site, which acts as a time machine, say, for example, a father who has come with his child to our museum will, after a short time, also become a child, if only for an hour or two.[18]

It is around the period 2008–10 that, in various regions of Russia, a variety of private museums began to appear that were dedicated to reproducing the material world of the late Soviet period. Typically featuring a haphazard arrangement of Soviet toys, household items, radios, televisions, bicycles, and even automobiles, such museums combine commercial and nostalgic objectives. The Museum of Soviet Arcade Games was one of the first such projects to appear in the post-Soviet Space.

The Polytechnic University where the museum's founders worked and studied assisted them by providing them with the space, offering them use of an abandoned Cold War–era bomb shelter, which was located in the basement of a student dormitory. Similar bomb shelters existed in almost every factory or office in the Soviet Union and in later computer games and the emerging subculture of urban exploration, the bomb shelters were physical embodiments of a militaristic Soviet style. After the collapse of the Soviet Union, bomb shelters were either turned into commercial warehouses or simply abandoned. It was such an abandoned space that the founders of the Museum of Soviet Arcade Machines were

Figure 12.2. Games at the museum. *Photograph by Roman Abramov*

able to utilize in 2006: "We identified the bomb shelter as a good site. There was mold everywhere. Before we moved in, the place hadn't been used in ten years, we had to repair everything completely, paint the walls, and throw out the garbage they had accumulated [in them]."[19] As a result of their efforts, Russia's only museum of Soviet arcade machines came into being on the university campus in April 2007, where it simultaneously served as a basement student club and café. At first, the bottom floor of the museum held some of the most popular slot machines from the 1970s and 1980s: Battleship, Magistral, Safari, Fighter, and Tankodrom (fig. 12.2). At first, access by external visitors to the museum was restricted, and tours occurred not more than once a week. After three years, however, the museum founders identified the project's potential to generate a profit and decided to move to another, more spacious building, where the museum would be able to operate publicly on a permanent and full-time basis.

The move occurred during a period when nostalgia for the late Soviet period was palpably on the rise, a phenomenon not only attracting former Soviet schoolchildren and the older generation, but also younger people. It was also a period of greater interest in modernist Soviet architecture and a time when Moscow's first hipsters began enthusiastically hunting through flea markets for Soviet FED cameras, old-school household items, and furniture from the late Soviet period. At the same time, a variety of amateur museums of the Soviet past emerged alongside the Museum of Soviet Arcade Machines. The Museum of Soviet Arcade Machines, however, was one of the first and most prominent, for journalists offered extensive coverage of the museum and its organizers' activities throughout its existence.[20] From 2010 to 2014 the museum has changed its location several times, gradually gravitating toward Moscow's tourist center, ending up in spacious premises on a recently renovated pedestrian street in the district of Kuznetsky Most Metro station. Besides the Moscow branch, two more museums were opened as part of an expansion, one on Nevsky Prospect in Saint Petersburg (opened in 2013), the other in Kazan, the capital of Tatarstan (2014). In the latter case, the project suffered from commercial failure because, in the opinion of the museum's founders, locals were not very interested in Soviet Arcade machines. The failure could have another cause; namely, the city had already had its own "Soviet Lifestyle Museum" for ten years. Organized by the local intellectual and photographer Rustem Valiahmetova, the museum became one of the most popular attractions in Kazan. Thus, the theme of Soviet nostalgia was to a large extent covered by the preexisting museum and a new one was simply oversupply of demand.

It is worth giving special attention to how the creators of the museum located the Soviet arcade machines for their exhibits. In Soviet times, the installation and maintenance of arcade machines was overseen by a special organization called *Soyuzattraktsion*, which had branches in many cities. After the collapse of the Soviet Union, its centralized system for managing parks and other attractions disappeared. As a result, many of these machines were in poor working condition, for repair components were no longer supplied and the growing presence of computers throughout society undermined any incentive to retain that type of entertainment. The end product was that most Soviet arcade machines were handed over to scrapyards, where some lived on in warehouses and landfills. The museum founders conducted major survey work to find and restore Soviet arcade machines. They found their first models in Tagansky Park in Moscow: "We went to look in Tagansky Park and it turned out there were a few broken machines just lying there and doing nothing. We loaded them up and drove to them his grandfather's garage. We started looking for parts and found more and more of these broken metal hulks."[21] It was that the search expanded beyond Moscow to Russia's more remote regions, including the Urals: "We have arcade machines that came from very far away; we found some in very strange locations. For example, there is a story about the Dyatlov Pass, a spot where a group of Soviet tourists died in mysterious circumstances, a really tragic story. And some of our machines were brought in from one village, which is 120 kilometers from the pass. This was in the Northern Urals, a very difficult place to reach, but we found out about these machines, bought them, and brought them to Moscow."[22]

Often, the pair had to organize their searches in hard-to-reach and much-neglected spaces, which in Soviet times functioned as centers of recreation for children and teenagers, especially in the case of summer camps, where many of the arcade machines were installed. Thus, these engineers-turned-museum curators found themselves dragged into what is known as "urban exploration": the exploration of abandoned urban spaces and ruins. As A. Stackhanov puts it, "We went through abandoned camps, dilapidated village cinemas. We would end up finding machines in around one in ten of the places we went to. Every abandoned building had its own host watchman, who would not give us anything for free. Even if someone had left something in a garage or school basement for thirty years, they still did not want to part with it just like that."[23]

Sometimes in these parks and cinemas an exchange of old, broken arcade machines could be arranged in return for new entertainment such as a billiard table with a set of billiard balls and cue sticks. According to the founders of the museum, throughout the 1990s and 2000s, many slot machines had been dropped off at nonferrous metal scrapyards. The reason was that the machines contained sophisticated equipment with expensive nonferrous metal components that, when recovered in a scrapyard, provided appreciable financial return to raiders scavenging the remains of Soviet arcade machines. In addition, Soviet arcade machines are constructed of heavy metal parts and weigh in excess of 100 kg (220 lbs.). The design choice can be explained by the fact that they were produced by the Soviet military-industrial complex, where enterprises designed their products on the model of weapons, where the weight and cost of components were not critical deterrents to designers.

As has been mentioned, most of the museum arcade machines were in poor condition and in serious need of repair when found. Currently, spare parts and accessories for them are no longer manufactured and, therefore, the museum's creators are forced to retain three to four copies of a single model in order to provide backup components or "donor organs" for the working models.

Rummaging through factory archives can occasionally unearth diagrams and other documentation for the arcade machines. But, in general, very little technical information is still available, which creates additional difficulties in restoring the models for exhibit. Because new machine parts are no longer available and no industrial centers exist to reproduce them, the only source of spare parts is other copies of the machines standing in the museum hall or warehouse. In most cases, three or four idle models need to be kept on standby to support the operation of one working arcade machine: "The arcade machines break down almost every day. Almost any museum employee can fix minor damage. Visitors are often surprised when they see delicate young girls holding screwdrivers and other tools over a disassembled machine. We have a mechanic for the more serious breakdowns. If he cannot solve the problem, the machine is sent into the category of inoperative models."[24]

Thus, the activities involved in creating the Museum of Soviet Arcade Machines combine the art of collecting, engineering work, and skill in museum curation, as well as business know-how.

The Museum of Soviet Arcade Machines has generated a certain affective ideology, which combines the materialized and emotional experience of actually playing the game on the old Soviet machines with the player's own memories of and associations with the late Soviet period. The majority of the museum's visitors either were children or had not yet been born in the 1970s and 1980s. Thus, for them the experience is primarily both a mystification of the past and an opportunity for historical nostalgia. Since its founding, the Museum of Soviet Arcade Machines has held popular lectures on the anthropology of video games, establishing a relatively stable community of those interested in the history and development of the first arcade and computer games.

NOSTALGIA, MATERIALITY, AND HYPERREALITY IN THE MUSEUM OF SOVIET ARCADE MACHINES

At present, behind the storefront of the Museum of Soviet Arcade Machines, we find a successful commercial enterprise at work, with two offices in the central streets of Russia's two main metropolises, one near Kuznetsky Most in Moscow,[25] the other on Nevsky Prospect in Saint Petersburg. These spaces do not look like traditional museums; instead, they combine the aesthetic elements of a video-game arcade hall, a gift shop, and a hip Brooklyn café. The Moscow branch is clearly influenced by the concepts behind "new urbanism" as described by David Brooks,[26] which shifts the focus to the creation of new pedestrian zones, transforming the Russian capital into the shopwindow showcase of bourgeois and bohemian consumption. Visitors entering the museum are confronted by a reception desk decorated with abstract patterns and staffed by two welcoming museum employees. In the depths of the establishment, a café/burger joint is visible, with tables of a brutal design with thick boards fixed to hardy metal frames, all very much in the mold of Brooklyn's fashionable hip restaurants.

Having paid 450 rubles (about $7) on entry, each visitor receives a ticket and a handful of Soviet coins each with the value of fifteen kopeks (fig. 12.3). The coins are used as credits in order to play the Soviet arcade machines: the coin box of the arcade was, after all, calibrated to accept a currency no longer in circulation. Nowadays, computer game historians are more interested in the first generation of electromechanical machines, largely because they demonstrate how cybernetics at the time was employed in an attempt to achieve a realistic experience. Developers' efforts to visualize real actions and simulate physical movements depended on a limited arsenal of rather poor tools and capabilities.[27] The fusion of technical design, software engineering, and ergonomic and sociocultural

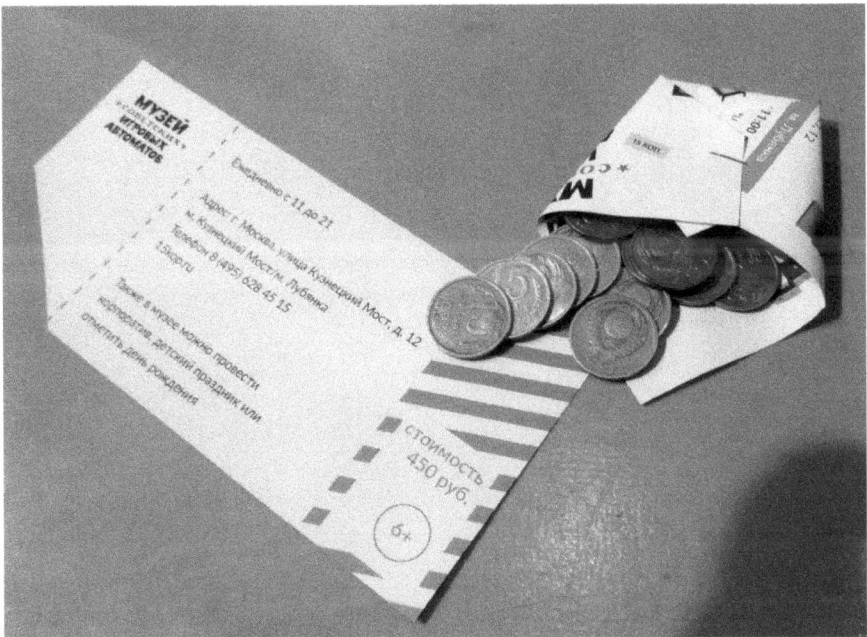

Figure 12.3. Soviet coins. *Photograph by Roman Abramov*

aspects in first-generation arcade machines often had their creators playing the role of jugglers or magicians, forced to employ primitive means to conjure up the sensation of reality.

As Charles Bernstein has noted, electromechanical arcade machines stand in sharp contrast to online games and home video-game consoles insofar as they have a different genetic lineage; they are the heirs of the older casino slot machines, which worked on the principle of raking in the maximal number of coins in the minimal amount of time from players, finding a way to compel them to return to the game time and time again.[28] That is the reason arcade machine games are divided into sections of small time intervals lasting two or three minutes, with skillful players winning extra bonus time rewards of not more than a minute. In this respect, Soviet arcade halls were the antecedents of the later post-Soviet casinos and served the function of extracting considerable sums from the pockets of the last generation of Soviet parents with Soviet Pioneer children who desperately wanted another attempt at their favorite arcade game. The strictly divided linear time segments, which operated along Fordist and behaviorist lines, tied in with the central need to keep feeding arcade machines with more coins, manipulating players to behave like biological reflex machines, providing little space for strategic decisions and prioritizing reaction time. Thus, what determined the development potential for learning arcade games was not the depths of one's intelligence

Figure 12.4. Prizes. *Photograph by Roman Abramov*

and creative energies but, rather, reflexes, reaction time, and physiology. These characteristics reflect the philosophy of arcade game creators, who wanted their games to be easy to learn but all but impossible to master skillfully.[29]

A citizen of today's Russia is far from accustomed to seeing Soviet coins with a denomination of 15 kopeks.[30] Only those over forty years of age will recall that these were the coins used when visiting arcades in the late Soviet period. After receiving the kopeks, one can begin the journey into the world of Soviet nostalgia via the Soviet arcade-game industry. I conducted participant observations of the museum's daytime work on a Thursday at the start of October 2016. During this time, the main visitors to the museum were either children 10–12 years old with their parents, who occupied the arcade machine hall, or students and other young people, who were mainly concentrated in the café/burger zone. My attention was soon drawn to the children and adolescents, who played these old-fashioned, shabby, and, at times, malfunctioning Soviet arcade machines with a surprising degree of passion and interest. The scene reminded me of a park from my own childhood, which held a one-story pavilion of arcade machines that, in the summer, would be filled with scenes of parents lining up with their children, who dreamed of playing their favorite games (fig. 12.4). Of course, it was my visit to the Museum of Soviet Arcade Machines that set off this nostalgic connection with my own childhood memories; my consciousness and my body reunited to remember forgotten sensations connected to physical interactions with this complex electromechanical equipment.

I was, however, surprised to find today's children so taken in by these archaic electromechanical aliens from the past. After all, these days almost every student has access to advanced computer games, whether on tablets and smartphones or computers, any of which far exceeds the capacity of primitive 1970s Soviet games to provide high-quality immersion in a virtual reality world. Nevertheless, the children put their smartphones to one side and enthusiastically played old games such as Battleship, Torpedo Attack, Dogfight, Drag Race, Sniper, Highway, Tankodrom, and the other games available at the museum (fig. 12.5). When possible, the children formed alternating teams of those who played and those who watched on the sidelines. It is worth noting that these children and adolescents were all born and raised in the post-Soviet era and lacked any personal, living memory of the time. All their knowledge is secondhand, learned from older relatives, television, or books. Therefore, it is hard to claim that their interest for these games reflects any longing for the Soviet period. The lure of these electromechanical arcade machines must lie elsewhere; perhaps we are observing a curiosity about a gradually vanishing material and physical version of leisure, in an era when this leisure form has departed into the space of computer networks and virtual reality in which every detail, such as the dirt on tank tracks, can be reproduced in a sterile if realistic manner. Here, in the world of the Soviet arcade game, we find a place for simple physical tricks manifested in the handiwork of the player who, like a magician in a live circus performing unpretentious miracles with rabbits and cylinders, offers a show for an audience in a manner familiar to previous generations. As is the case of magicians with their mirrors and disappearing objects, all those present share the realization that these material wonders result from the skilled manipulations of a joystick and buttons, but, for a moment at least, we believe in the miracle.

Thus, it is possible to view these Soviet arcade machines as devices that facilitate the transition from the epoch of mechanics to that of electronics. Despite having grown up in the world of online entertainment, 3D cinema, and laser shows, today's children and adolescents are actually attracted by the naivety and crudity on display in arcade machine portrayals of the reality of air battles or forest hunting through cheap devices such as hidden lights, optical illusions, and cardboard profiles of animals, airplanes, and ships.

It is worth recalling some of the work of Jean Baudrillard, who wrote in an era when electromechanical arcade machines were at the peak of their popularity. In his books *The System of Objects* (2005) and *Symbolic Exchange and Death* (1993) the French philosopher outlined the contours of a new world of hyperreality, where

Figure 12.5. Games at the museum. *Photograph by Roman Abramov*

the "natural substance of objects" would be replaced by "synthetic substances" on the basis of the universal counterfeit style of the world, which can be seen in the wide use of artificial materials in modernist interior design or the use of automation in production.[31] Modern computer games fundamentally reshape our relations with reality, creating the illusion of hyperreality and simulations of the highest order that are separated from the mechanics of the real world. Baudrillard's vision of a simulacrum of immersion into the world in many ways was captured by the film *The Matrix*, written by the Wachowski brothers, which also featured a rejection of corporality in the usual sense of the word. The electromechanical arcade machines of the 1960s and 1970s did not, however, involve a complete separation from the reference points of reality. Rather, their technical imperfections and the need to handle material mechanics such as joysticks and buttons, as well as the schematic manner in which the sea battles or hunting were presented, could be regarded as representing Baudrillard's simulacra of the first order. These simulacra, although not offering a break with the authenticity of the surrounding reality, did still outline the first trails of a surreal new "unreal" world, even if this world was soon brought crashing back down to reality after a short period of time (2–3 minutes), with the end of another round of game levels. From today's perspective, the Soviet slot machines can be perceived as the embodiment of a certain kind of cybernetic steampunk, where the mechanical interface of electronic devices has yet to be supplanted by the touch-screen tablet and high-quality graphics of computers and smartphones but survives as a necessary backup in a virtual world (fig. 12.6). Currently, this process of displacement continues apace, which we can see in the efforts of laptop manufacturers

Figure 12.6. "A good shot." *Photograph by Roman Abramov*

to replace the mechanical elements of the keyboard with touch screens. Soviet arcade machines then, offer a rather distinct if dead-end pathway in the evolution of electronic devices, one where mechanics plays an equal role to cybernetics.

Almost immediately in the aftermath of launching their actual Museum of Soviet Arcade Machines, the founders set out to make an online version, including a computer emulation of the most popular Soviet arcade machines, which can be played on a personal computers. According to Alexander Stakhannov, in order to organize the online version of the museum, they turned to one of Russia's best-known and most prestigious art designers, Artemy Lebedev, offering payment by means of installing some Soviet arcade machines in the office of his design bureau in Moscow.[32] In exchange, one of Lebedev's employees was tasked with the development of the museum site and creating an online simulation of the arcade games. It should be underlined that this online emulation is no substitute for the real use of the Soviet slot machines; the tactile sensations of rubberized submarine periscopes or the holding of a mechanical joystick to manipulate a fighter in the sky are central to experiencing the magic of the arcade game.

Upon purchasing a ticket and receiving their fifteen kopek credits, visitors are warned that, because of the mere age of the arcades, not all features may operate correctly and unexpected breakdowns can occur. Indeed, the hinges of the periscopes and steering devices are worn out, and sharp turns in steering are not always adequately reflected in the motion of the icons on the screen. Perhaps the antiquated and dilapidated state of the arcade machines is an additional signal reinforcing the sense the machines belong to a past reality rather than to a virtual one. Just as is the case with antiques, these machines act as repositories into which the spirit of the past can be concentrated, sending the user on a journey into the past, even if the visitor is a youngster with no lived experience of the Soviet Union. This is part of the appeal of these out-of-date contraptions; they bear on them traces of a past age and they are devices that have been repeatedly handled by thousands of the people from the past, all of which provides the game with an additional sense of immersion into the past. The arcade machines have physical implements that are both toylike and realistic, such as hunting guns, hard plastic wheels, racing cars with metal pedals for accelerators, and black-rubber submarine periscopes. All these material features make the game seem more real and natural, and, if anything, the regular malfunctions of the old and worn-out arcade machines only add additional charm and naturalness to the game play. After all, riding an old tank, car, fighter jet, or submarine was hardly an activity devoid of errors and malfunctions. In other words, the generation of the internet searches for and finds materiality in these games from another era.

PINBALL, 1973 BY HARUKI MURAKAMI: NOSTALGIC REMINISCENCES ABOUT ARCADE MACHINES

The popular Japanese writer Haruki Murakami has actively worked on the theme of nostalgia, which arises from the characters of his novels who often recall their own turbulent student youth, although his characters have not crossed the threshold of forty. In his novels *Pinball, 1973* (1980), *Norwegian Wood* (1987), *South of the Border, West of the Sun* (1992), Murakami emphasizes the ephemerality of the passing of time, the painful inaccessibility of even the recent past, and the trauma caused by rapid changes in surrounding circumstances and technologies. These feelings bring with them an existential break within one's own identity, and Murakami's writings seek to explore the nature of the rupture. The main body of his work focuses on tracing the difficult transition from the heady hopes and social progress of the turbulent 1960s to the gray stagnation of the 1970s and the cynicism characterizing the 1980s. It was in this era that Japan went through various stages of rapid economic growth and conquered a range of leading positions in global markets for goods and services. Murakami, however, sheds light on an aspect hidden behind the prosperity; the inner emptiness of Japan's sixties generation and the New Left, which occupied campuses in 1968–69 and held postwar rallies, only to end up as grist for the mill of the Japanese corporate machine, surrendering and serving as obedient white-collar workers, traditionally letting loose only on drunken Fridays in karaoke bars. Those who did not fit through the strict selection filters of Japanese corporate employers ended up as people who were "surplus to requirements" and left with a limited choices: either to become intellectual freelancers living on the periphery of the economic miracle, or to move toward religious or left-wing radicalism, pathways that are well described in the novels. Thus, Haruki Murakami's characters have much in common with the "superfluous man" of Russian literary classics in the nineteenth century, where intellectuals prove too deeply reflective for careers in religion, political terrorism, or the civil service and are well aware of how a social and cultural environment can change very quickly in a period of five years or so. For the heroes of Murakami's novels, nostalgia is not a form of trivial escapism but a means of coping with the present and one's place in the current moment, with the recent past employed as a litmus test.

The nostalgic poetry of arcade machines can be found in the novel *Pinball, 1973*, where the main character breaks away from his youthful illusions formed in the 1960s.[33] Living through the strange events of 1973, during which he, among other things, sets out on a search for his beloved Rocket arcade machine, which he spent his days and nights playing as a student. Although the Japanese *pachinko* pinball culture is a far cry from the world of Soviet arcade machines, in both environments it is possible to identify a common allure and charm connected to electromechanical machines. This is all the more so in the case of Murakami's novel, for the hero sought out a machine that was originally made for the US entertainment market and was not intended as a substitute for the "one-armed bandit."

The hero's efforts to find the pinball machine are organized with the assistance of an expert who is a real devotee of the pinball industry. His searches are conducted in a manner that is strikingly similar to that carried out by the founders of the Museum of Soviet Arcade Machines, for, in both cases, the equipment is often discovered gathering dust in scrap-metal collection points:

> There are several possibilities. Most often, machines are sold for scrap. The turnover is very rapid. A machine depreciates in three years, so it makes more sense to get a new one than it does to pay for repairs. Not to mention the role that fashion plays. So they're scrapped.... The second possibility is that someone might have picked it up second-hand. Old models that are still usable frequently end up in small bars, where they spend their last days being pawed by drunks and amateurs. The third possibility is that a collector might have picked it up. That's very rare, though. Eighty percent of the time they go for scrap.[34]

Another important coincidence the novel has with the history of the Soviet arcade machines is the story of the machine's design and construction. In the novel's case, we have Japanese companies that, after World War II, became skilled in the development of gaming machines. In the Soviet Union, the military-industrial complex was asked by the central government to commission the development of arcade machines on the basis of existing foreign models, and in Murakami's story the Japanese companies were ones that had lost military orders in the first postwar years:

> The firm Gilbert and Sands came late to the world of pinball. From the Second World War right through the Korean War, their primary business was manufacturing bomb-delivery systems, but when the fighting stopped they took the opportunity to embark on a new path, what we call the peace industries.... Their first pinball machine was completed in 1952. Not a bad job, either. It was very durable and cheap. But it didn't spark people's interest. To quote the review in Billboard magazine, it had all the sex appeal of a Soviet Women's Corps government-issue brassiere. Still, from a business point of view it was a success. The machine was exported to Mexico, then to other Central American nations. Countries short on specialized technical know-how. They were happy to get sturdy machines.[35]

Murakami's hero is led into the world of arcade machines by his eager guide and finally finds the machine of his desire among a collection belonging to an eccentric enthusiast, who had bought up a range of abandoned arcade machines from a scrap-metal yard. They depart to a Tokyo suburb to play another round on the legendary Rocket, which sits in an old hangar among seventy-seven other pinball machines. Upon coming into contact with the arcade machine, a wave of cathartic nostalgia descends on Murakami's hero, reminding him of his carefree days and wild nights as a student. As is the case with the Soviet arcade game Battle at Sea, the hero of the story does not simply see the Rocket pinball machine as a primitive set of electromechanical components with a rudimentary picture of the sky at night; in fact it is an enormous manifestation and realization of his own past, an opportunity to dive back into a lost world:

> The three-flipper Spaceship was waiting for me at the end of the line.... I stood before her, gazing with fondness at her familiar board. The blue of her cosmos, so deep and dark it looked like poured ink. The tiny white stars. And the planets: Saturn, Mars, Venus.... A pure white spaceship floated in the foreground. Lights burned in its windows, inviting you to imagine the happy family moments being shared inside. Shooting stars arched across the night sky. The field was just as I remembered. The same dark blue. The targets were pure white, like teeth flashing through smiling lips. The ten

lemon-yellow bonus lights, stacked to resemble stars, pulsing up and down. Saturn and Mars, the two kick-out holes, and Venus, the rotating target—taken together, the epitome of peace and tranquillity.[36]

Before visiting the Museum of Soviet Arcade Machines, I had never imagined that the past could be manifested in such a direct and physical manner; this materiality was expressed in the mechanics of turning a toy periscope and the tactile sensation of controlling the levers of a tank. Following in the footsteps of Murakami's hero, I embarked on a journey in time, to a period separated from me by more than three decades, returning me to a time when I, together with my parents, visited the park in my provincial city and "hung out" in the arcade hall, exchanging coin after coin for tokens. I remembered that I had always played badly back then, I never had fast reflexes, but I played with enthusiasm all the same, while my parents sat and watched how the machines emptied their pockets of all their fifteen-kopek coins. So it was that the Museum of Soviet Arcade Machines propelled me back to the memories of my childhood.

The role of the legendary pinball machine in the Murakami novel is, however, rather different; it acts as a moment when the now more mature hero of the novel finally closes the door on his youth. His meeting with the pinball machine, in this sense, resembles an appointment with a psychoanalyst or a Harold Garfinkel experiment, where the challenging questions of his life are answered in random order by a machine that imitates the reaction of a psychologist.

NOTES

This article was prepared as part of the Academic Fund Program at the National Research University Higher School of Economics (HSE) in 2017–18 (grant No. 17-01-0058) and by the Russian Academic Excellence Project "5-100." Additional information about this research can be found in Roman Abramov, "Nostal'gicheskie affekty i kommodifikaciya sovetskogo: na primere Muzeya sovetskih igrovyh avtomatov," INTERakciya. INTERv'yu. INTERpretaciya 1 (2018): 25–38.

1. Simon Reynolds, *Retromania: Pop Culture's Addiction to Its Own Past* (London: Faber and Faber, 2011).

2. Roman Abramov, "Muzeefikatsiia sovetskogo: Istoricheskaia pravda ili nostal'giia?," *Chelovek* 5 (2013): 99–111.

3. Nick Witheford and Greig de Peuter, *Games of Empire: Global Capitalism and Video Games* (Minneapolis: University of Minnesota Press, 2009).

4. Joseph R. Dominick, "Videogames, Television Violence, and Aggression in Teenagers," *Journal of Communication* 34 (1984): 136–47.

5. Marsha Kinder, *Playing with Power in Movies, Television, and Video Games: From Muppet Babies to Teenage Mutant Ninja Turtles* (Berkeley: University of California Press, 1991).

6. See Dave Grossman and Gloria Degaetano, *Stop Teaching Our Kids to Kill: A Call to Action against TV, Movie and Video Game Violence* (New York: Harmony, 1999); Eugene Provenzo, *Video Kids: Making Sense of Nintendo* (Cambridge, MA: Harvard University Press, 1991); Nel Alloway and Piter Gilbert, "Video Game Culture: Playing with Masculinity, Violence and Pleasure," in *Wired Up: Young People and the Electronic Media*, ed. Sue Howard, 95–114 (London: UCL, 1998); and Mary Flanagan, "Hyperbodies, Hyperknowledge: Women in Games, Women in Cyberpunk, and Strategies of Resistance," in *Reload: Rethinking Women + Cyberculture*, ed. Mary Flanagan and Austin Booth (Cambridge, MA: MIT Press, 2002), 424–54.

7. See Leonard Herman, *Phoenix: The Fall and Rise of Videogames* (Springfield, NJ: Rolenta, 1997); and Jessie Cameron Herz, *Joystick Nation: How Videogames Ate Our Quarters, Won Our Hearts, and Rewired Our Minds* (Boston: Little, Brown, 1997).

8. Espen Aarseth, "Computer Game Studies, Year One," *Game Studies* 1 (July 1, 2001), www.gamestudies.org/0101/editorial.html; and Noah Wardrip-Fruin and Pat Harrigan, eds., *First Person: New Media as Story, Performance, and Game* (Cambridge, MA: MIT Press, 2004).

9. Katharina Kucher, *Der Gorki-Park: Freizeitkultur im Stalinismus 1928–1941* (Cologne, Ger.: Böhlau, 2007).

10. Vadim Volkov, "The Concept of *Kul'turnost'*: Notes on the Stalinist Civilizing Process," in *Stalinism: New Directions*, ed. Sheila Fitzpatrick, 210–30 (London: Routledge, 1999).

11. Aleida Assmann, *Der lange Schatten der Vergangenheit: Erinnerungskultur und Geschichtspolitik* (Munich: C. H. Beck, 2006).

12. Irina Kaspe, "'S"est' proshloe': ideologiia i povsednevnost' gastronomicheskoi nostal'gii," in *Puti Rossii: kul'tura-obshchestvo-chelovek; materialy mezhdunarodnogo simpoziuma*, ed. Alexander Nikulin (Moscow: Logos, 2008), 205–18.

13. Frederic Jameson, "Nostalgia for the Present," *South Atlantic Quarterly* 2 (88) (1989): 517–37.

14. Maksim Ivanov, "Grazhdane Rossii progolosovali za Leonida Brezhneva," *Kommersant* 85, no. 3 (2013), www.kommersant.ru/doc/2194078.

15. Interview with Alexander Stakhanov, Director of the Museum of Soviet Slot Machines (Interv'yu s Aleksandrom Stahanovym, direktorom, "Muzeya sovetskih igrovyh avtomatov," 2013, https://games.mail.ru/pc/articles/feat/intervju_s_odnim_iz_osnovatelej_vystavki_sovetskih_igrovyh_avtomatov_aleksandrom_stahanovym_by_crazy_mega_man_list_ru/).

16. Maurice Halbwachs, "The Social Frameworks of Memory," in *On Collective Memory*, ed. Maurice Halbwachs (Chicago: University of Chicago Press, 1992), 41–43.

17. Millie Creighton, "Anthropology of Nostalgia," in *International Encyclopedia of the Social and Behavioral Sciences* (London: Elsevier, 2001): 10744–46.

18. Vasil'kov Egor, "My hotim, chtoby vzroslye lyudi igrali ...," August 6, 2009, http://www.chaskor.ru/p.php?id=9091.

19. Ibid, A. Stachkanov.

20. Roman Abramov, "Muzeefikatsiia sovetskogo: mezhdu barakholkoi i vintazhnym salonom," *Muzei* 6 (2013): 4–8.

21. Svetlana Vitkovskaya, "Muzei sovietskikh igrovikh avtomatov: kak prodat' nostalgiyu," Secret firmi, April 23, 2015, www.secretmag.ru/business/trade-secret/soviet-avtomat.htm.

22. Interview with Alexander Stakhanov, Director of the Museum of Soviet Slot Machines (Interv'yu s Aleksandrom Stahanovym, direktorom, "Muzeya sovetskih igrovyh avtomatov," 2013, https://games.mail.ru/pc/articles/feat/intervju_s_odnim_iz_osnovatelej_vystavki_sovetskih_igrovyh_avtomatov_aleksandrom_stahanovym_by_crazy_mega_man_list_ru/).

23. "Muzei sovietskikh."

24. Vitali Kovalchuk, "Prizovaya igra: kak ustroen muzej sovetskih igrovyh avtomatov" [Bonus game: How the museum of Soviet slot machines works], April 13, 2016, https://biz360.ru/materials/prizovaya-igra-kak-ustroen-muzey-sovetskikh-igrovykh-avtomatov/.

25. In the autumn of 2019, the Moscow office of the museum moved to the Exhibition of Achievements of National Economy (VDNH).

26. David Brooks, *Bobos in Paradise: The New Upper Class and How They Got There* (New York: Simon and Schuster, 2000).

27. Mark Wolf, "Abstraction in the Video Game," in *The Video Game Theory Reader*, ed. Wolf and Bernard Perron (London: Routledge, 2003), 47–67.

28. Charles Bernstein, "Play It Again, Pac-Man," *Postmodern Culture* 2, no. 1 (September 1991), http://pmc.iath.virginia.edu/text-only/issue.991/pop-cult.991.

29. David Murphy, "Hacking Public Memory: Understanding the Multiple Arcade Machine Emulator," *Games and Culture* 8, no. 1 (2013): 43–53.

30. Fifteen kopeks entitled a player to around two minutes of uninterrupted play on an arcade machine. It was a considerable sum for the time; in comparison, three kopeks would buy a glass of lemonade, twenty kopeks would cover a serving of ice cream or a loaf of bread. If one was to pass one hour in a Soviet arcade hall, it would cost around 3–4 rubles at a time when the average salary of a Soviet engineer was around 28 rubles a week.

31. Jean Baudrillard, *Symbolic Exchange and Death* (London: Sage, 1993).

32. Egor Vasil'kov, "My hotim, chtoby vzroslye lyudi igrali...," Muzej sovetskih igrovyh avtomatov v moskovskom bomboubezhishche" [We want adults to play...," Museum of Soviet slot machines in the Moscow bomb shelter], August 6, 2009, http://www.chaskor.ru/p.php?id=9091.

33. Haruki Murakami, *Pinball, 1973*, trans. Ted Goossen (New York: Vintage, 2015).

34. Ibid., 98.

35. Ibid., 93.

36. Ibid., 117–18.

ROMAN ABRAMOV is Dr.Sci in Sociology and Professor at the National Research University Higher School of Economics (NRU HSE) in Moscow. He is author of numerous articles on post-Soviet nostalgia and memory, including most recently "The Museification of the Soviet Past in Russia: Unfinished, Ambiguous and Contradictory" (in the *Journal of Soviet and Post-Soviet Politics and Society*) and "The Donbass As the Space of Socialist Enthusiasm, Memory and Trauma: Cinema and Literature Images" (in *Laboratorium: Russian Review of Social Research*).

Figure E.1. Memorabilia on sale in the Stalin Museum, Gori, 2015.
Wikimedia Commons

ROTATING EXHIBITS

Tony Judt has written that "Memory is inherently contentious and partisan: one man's acknowledgement is another's omission." Memory, he concludes, "is a poor guide to the past."[1] The exhibits and halls we have visited certainly advance Judt's point. Memory may be a poor guide to the past, but it is an illustrative guide to the present and to the immediate future.

Central and Eastern Europe experienced the postwar era as one during which historical memories had to be buried deep within individuals, not spoken out loud. Communist governments held monopolies on the past and established dominant narratives about it. Since 1989, however, the region "has been built upon a compensatory surplus of memory."[2] New museums and new memory sites have overturned their Communist Era counterparts. As we have seen, these new sites have brought aggrieved memories to the public sphere and brought much-needed attention to the traumas of the twentieth century. At the same time, these new sites have introduced problematic narratives of their own.

Acknowledging the past, particularly the traumatic past, is a necessary condition for the health of any society. For a truly healthy system, this acknowledgment needs to be as nuanced and inclusive as possible in order to prevent the growth and spread of a new strain of aggrieved memories. This, our last exhibit hall, allows us to think about how two museums have dealt with changing memories and shifting interpretations of the past: it has been three decades since the collapse of communism in the region, and these museums have adapted to changes in the memory landscape that have occurred since the original museums were built. They might best be understood as analogous to the rotating exhibit halls common in most museums: not permanent, but ever shifting in order to keep up with demand. In a sense, memory acts the same way.

NOTES

1. Tony Judt, *Postwar: A History of Europe Since 1945* (New York: Penguin, 2005), 829.
2. Ibid.

Figure 13.1. Joseph Stalin State Museum, Gori, founded 1957, updated 2009. https://www.facebook.com/stalinismuseumi/. *Photograph courtesy of Peter Kabachnik*

THIRTEEN

A Museum of a Museum?
Fused and Parallel Historical Narratives in the
Joseph Stalin State Museum

KATRINE BENDTSEN GOTFREDSEN

REASSESSMENTS OF THE PAST

As elsewhere in the former Soviet Union, Georgian independence in 1991 was accompanied by a political reassessment of the past. In the years that followed, both the distant national history and the more immediate Soviet past were continuously interpreted, employed, and (re-)represented in order to create new political identities, and envisioned future political developments as well.[1] In the wake of the 2003 Rose Revolution that brought Mikhail Saakashvili and his United National Movement (UNM) to power, the political future envisioned was one of modernization, democratization, and commitment to "Western values"—a vision that built heavily on a clear distancing from the Soviet past and its political regime.[2] The representation of the Soviet state as a colonial occupier and oppressor of Georgian national sentiments and freedom was promoted in a number of government initiatives and practices pertaining to cultural institutions, public space, and state events. One prominent example was the opening of the Museum of Soviet Occupation, a permanent exhibition of the National Museum in Tbilisi on the Georgian Independence day of May 26, 2006.[3] The museum is dedicated to the period of Soviet rule in Georgia between 1921 and 1991 and displays archival documents, photographs, and video footage, along with a number of other artifacts, explicating and evoking the repressive nature of the Soviet regime and the resistance, and eventual victory, of the Georgian nationalist movement.

This chapter takes its point of departure from another Georgian museum dedicated to Soviet history, namely the Joseph Stalin State Museum in the provincial town Gori—the birth town to Joseph Stalin. The museum is situated at one end of Gori's main central boulevard, Stalin Avenue, and the complex consists of a main building, a marble palazzo in Stalinist Gothic style, Stalin's wooden birth house protected by a mausoleum-like building with columns, and Stalin's personal railway carriage. The construction of the main building began in 1951, supposedly intended as a local history museum. By 1956, however, when the building was finished, it was clear that it was to become a memorial to Stalin, who died in 1953. In Soviet times, even after Nikita Khrushchev's Secret Speech that denounced Stalin's "cult of personality," the museum was an important venue for school excursions arriving from all over the country, as well as a main attraction for visitors to Georgia from other Soviet republics, along with tourists and study groups from outside the Soviet Union. The museum was closed for a short period around independence, but today it remains one of the main—if not the only—tourist attractions of Gori. Notwithstanding their attitudes toward Stalin as a historical figure, most locals stress the importance of the museum as a kind of trademark for their town and often note that Gori does not have much else to offer to outsiders other than its historical link with Stalin.[4]

As noted by Ivan Karp and Steven Lavine, "every museum exhibition . . . inevitably draws on the cultural assumptions and resources of the people who make it. Decisions are made to emphasize one element and downplay others, to assert some truths and to ignore others."[5] The main part of the present-day exhibition in the Stalin Museum was established in 1979 and, since then, only a few changes have taken place. Hence, reflecting the particular historical and political context of its creation, the present-day exhibition still displays elements and "truths" corresponding to its original construction for educational and ideological purposes within the Georgian Soviet Socialist Republic. In the context of the post–Rose Revolution Georgian nation-state, however, the displayed historical truths about the successful building of socialism, and the important part played by Stalin in that effort, were no longer officially seen that way. Therefore, the Stalin Museum constituted a somewhat problematic entity for the UNM authorities: on the one hand, it was a piece of local history held in high esteem by many locals—if not for its interior, then for the building's monumental presence in the town center and its surrounding park, which is a popular spot for walks and socializing. On the other hand, even if the museum was a popular tourist attraction, its celebrative tone and potential for acting as a Stalinist shrine was in stark contrast to the official attitude of the government toward Stalin and the Soviet regime and, furthermore, was highly problematic for Georgia's international image.

This image problem was amply illustrated in October 2007 when President Saakashvili, in connection with an official state visit to Denmark, was giving a lecture on Georgia's democratic and economic developments at the Danish Foreign Policy Society. After the lecture, a journalist from the audience posed the question of whether Georgia could ever succeed in becoming a progressive

European-minded state when the country still hosted a museum dedicated to honoring and glorifying Stalin. The president expressed his appreciation of the paradox and assured the journalist that the Stalin Museum was currently undergoing alterations and was to be turned into a "museum of a museum." The original museum would be turned into the object of exhibition and provided with analysis and metanarratives stressing its propagandist and deceitful representations. In the summer of 2010, I set out to ethnographically explore this process of reframing the museum, and the present chapter builds on data obtained from four months of spending most of my days in the museum observing and discussing the exhibition and daily work routines with employees and museum visitors. In what follows, I address the Stalin Museum as a productive, condensed site for analyzing how Soviet history, and in particular Stalin as a figure within it, was redefined and retold within a state-sponsored context so as to fit new political realities and visions of the post–Rose Revolution authorities.

In my analysis, I follow Michael Ames in assuming that "Representation is a political act. Sponsorship is a political act. Curation is a political act. Working in a museum is a political act."[6] In this assumption, I draw on two interrelated lines of thought within museum theory. First, one that emphasizes the museum as a site for representing particular versions of truth and "good" within the modern nation-state: a vehicle of control, for exercising and consolidating power through the ranking and classification of objects and people.[7] The proposition being that the Rose Revolution authorities had an interest in reclassifying and reordering the objects in the museum in order to have it reflect their understanding of the historical truth about the contemporary Georgian nation-state. Second, I draw on a line of thought that emphasizes that the power (intentionally or unintentionally) exercised through the construction of museum exhibits is not necessarily uncontested or undebated—neither within the museum, among staff, nor when encountered by museum visitors. In this sense, the museum is an arena for dialogue, negotiation, and contestation about the true nature of its subject matter.[8] In other words, the politics going on in a museum is not simply a matter of authorities exercising power to define truth and good but is also about staff and visitors responding to and negotiating its truth claims.

In the following sections, I will explore what happens to the political aspects of museum practice when the "true" history is viewed simultaneously through the eyes of the Soviet state and the contemporary Georgian nation-state. I will first describe the so-called Repression Room that was added to the museum exhibition in 2009 in an effort to update the ideological message sent by the museum. I will then go on to give a more thorough description of the main exhibition in order to compare its form and content with that of the Repression Room. Comparing the two parts of the exhibition amply illustrates the rather peculiar midway position the museum holds between past and present political ideology. Drawing on the literature, we would expect the Joseph Stalin *State* Museum to represent its subject matter, a piece of national history, according to the truths accepted in official state discourse. In practice, however, the museum largely represents a reading of (national) history crafted by the Soviet authorities in the context of the Georgian Soviet Socialist Republic—an entity that was by post–Rose Revolution authorities denounced as the very antithesis of the Georgian nation. Although the Repression Room fuses historical periods in an effort to illustrate a continuity between Soviet, Stalinist, and contemporary Russian political practices, the main exhibition displays two parallel historical narratives and provides a potential for separating Stalin as a national figure from the Soviet regime. Hence, I will argue that, as a result of its particular midway position between two states, and the practices and attitudes of its employees, the Stalin Museum displays ambiguity and room for interpretation rather than truth and certainty about the area of history it seeks to objectively and univocally represent.

THE REPRESSION ROOM

The Repression Room, as it is known among the employees, was added to the Stalin Museum's exhibition in 2009. According to the museum director of the time, Robert Maglakelidze, the creation of the room was part of an effort to alter the exhibition in order to tally with current official attitudes toward Stalin. I had participated in numerous guided tours of the museum and discussed the exhibition with guides and curators daily for weeks before I realized the room existed. The room is located in a corner of the museum's entrance hall. The door in the relatively dark corner being closed, with no signs to indicate its presence, I had not really given it any thought. Actually, I had not noticed it at all. About a month into my daily visit to the museum, however, I was taken there as part of a guided tour.

The room is dark and actually resembles more a narrow hallway than a room for exhibition. The right-hand wall is draped in red satin cloth, covered with triangles of ordinary notebook paper with handwriting in Georgian. What is written on the triangles, I was told, are the names and home regions of some of the Georgians sent to the gulag camps during the repression of the 1930s. On the wall is also a print, with portrait photographs, of some of the main Communist Party leaders from the October Revolution and the Soviet Union's first years. Most of the men portrayed were accused of conspiring against Stalin and the Communist Party and were sentenced and executed in the Moscow trials between 1936 and 1938. At the far end of the room stands an old wooden desk. On its right, a hallstand with an old Soviet military uniform, and, above it, red velvet

Figure 13.2. Door in the Repression Room. *Photograph courtesy of Peter Kabachnik*

flags with Soviet symbols and an image of Vladimir Ilyich Lenin. On the desk rest old notebooks and protocols with names and pictures of people with empty faces. Looking around the corner from the desk, one sees pieces of old-fashioned, yet colorful, clothing hanging from the ceiling. Together the setup seems clearly meant to connote the process of sending people off to the Siberian and Central Asian prison camps.

In the back corner, behind a half wall, is a small exhibition of professional photographs. They show the remains of a bombed apartment block. A woman lying in the street surrounded by rubble, screaming and covered in dust. Russian tanks rolling through the streets of Gori. The photographs are copies of some of the best-known press photographs to have traveled the world during and after the August 2008 war between Russia and Georgia.[9] Next to the photographs is a glass wall with an imitation of an old, dark prison cell behind it, known as the torture chamber (see fig. 13.2). The latter possibly intended to take the viewer back in time to the terror of the 1930s, or, as happened to me, into a collapsed space in time in which the purges of the 1930s, state terror in general, and the war with Russia in 2008 all merge. The room thus seemed to be a fusion of two time periods. In this respect, it is interesting to note the particular kind of temporal and representative collapse through which photographs of the material and human destruction caused by the Russian invasion and bombardment of 2008 is thought capable of acting as a support for a critique of the Stalinist terror. And, perhaps, vice versa: how the purges of the 1930s are thought to have explanatory power in relation to the suffering caused by the Russian invasion of Georgia in 2008.

The Repression Room in the Stalin Museum can be seen as a miniature, low-budget version of the Museum of Soviet Occupation in Tbilisi. Today, in the first hall of the latter exhibition, images and texts of the Bolshevik invasion are accompanied by a video projected on the wall showing Russian military parades, the Russian invasion of Georgia in 2008, and a public demonstration in Tbilisi with people waving the Georgian flag and banners with the words "Stop Russia." Here too, then, we are invited into a space, where documents and artifacts illustrative of Soviet repression are fused with images of present-day Russian militarism. In this approach, both exhibitions bear a similarity to the Tashkent Museum in Memory of the Victims of Repression analyzed by Sergei Abashin.[10] In his analysis, Abashin illuminates one of several efforts undertaken by Uzbek authorities to represent a version of history that supports a particular vision of the past and future of the Uzbek nation. As with the Repression Room and the Museum of Soviet Occupation, Abashin argues that the main ideological subtext of the exhibition in the Tashkent Museum in Memory of the Victims of Repression, and several similar state-sponsored museums in the former Soviet space (see the chapters by Neringa Klumbytė, Katja Wetzel, and Lorraine Weekes in this volume), is that of delegitimizing the Soviet past and delineating a political distance from Russia, which is regarded as the successor to the Soviet Union. In doing so, he continues, such exhibitions convey "A dichotomous picture in which there are only two historical actors—the one who suffers and the other who inflicts suffering.... The first actor is equated with the "nation"... and the second with the "empire" (or the "totalitarian regime"). Any kind of inner complexity or contradiction in the concepts "nation" and "empire" is excluded in principle, because it would destroy the opposition and void the meaning of the exhibit."[11]

Abashin demonstrates the point by analyzing the Tashkent exhibition within which, he argues, the Russian tsarist empire and the Soviet regime are fused into one actor, with one incessant political purpose: that of repressing the Central Asian peoples. In several ways, the Museum of Soviet Occupation and the Repression Room in the Stalin Museum can be seen as examples of the same ideological exercise, albeit with the exception that they fuse the early Soviet regime with the Russian state of 2008.

In light of Saakashvili's statement in 2007 and the general developments in the country after the Rose Revolution, I engaged with the Stalin Museum in the expectation of seeing the entire museum being recast along the lines of the Museum of Soviet Occupation and the Repression Room. I wanted to follow the internal processes and discussions among curators and other staff when re-creating the exhibition to make it fit a new ideological subtext. As it turned out, however, the main exhibition was not under reconstruction, and there was not much (explicit) talk of ideological subtexts going on among the staff. As mentioned earlier, I was not brought to the Repression Room till weeks after my arrival at the museum, and it was far from all visitors who were brought there by the museum guides at all. In that respect, the room forms a case example of an ideological recasting of a suffering national past but it remains an add-on to the larger exhibition in the grand upstairs halls of the museum. It is these halls I will now turn to.

A VISIT TO THE MAIN EXHIBITION

Even if (a subject I will return to later) a few additions and alterations have taken place in the recent years, the main exhibition still stands largely as it was created in 1979. The original subtext of this exhibition is thus not so much one of illustrating Georgian suffering at the hands of imperial power (be it tsarist Russia or the Soviet state) as one of the defeat of the tsarist empire and the successful building of a Soviet Socialist State of, and for, the people, with Joseph Stalin as the key figure. As we shall see in what follows, the first impression that meets the visitor in the upstairs exhibition is still that of a celebration of Stalin and the grandeur of the Soviet state.

Obviously, no two visits to the museum are the same, and no two visitors will have the exact same experience. Still, this section of my chapter is an attempt to synthesize the main features of the exhibition and the subjects discussed by the guides as they take visitors through the exhibition halls. It is based on notes and recordings from my daily participation in guided tours of the museum exhibition with English-, German-, Russian-, and Georgian-speaking guides, as well as a comparison of my observations to the guides' reading notes. Rather than minutely going through all the details of the exhibition, I will (in much the same way as the guides) primarily describe and refer to the items and stories that would most often receive extra attention and discussion—from visitors and guides alike.

Arriving as a visitor at the museum, you are stopped by a uniformed guard at the entrance. He rings a bell, and you are asked to wait a short while in the entrance hall (fig. 13.3). Right in front is a marble staircase with a red carpet leading to a life-size statue of Stalin. As the bell rings, one of the young museum managers will appear from the hallway opposite the guards' table.[12] She will welcome you (tentatively in either Georgian, Russian, or English depending on your appearance) and then explain the ticket prices, and ask you whether you wish to be accompanied by a Russian-, Georgian-, English-, German-, or French-speaking guide. It is actually possible to see the exhibition without a guide and be charged a lower ticket price, but most foreign visitors are advised to take a guide to ensure they fully experience all the details of the exhibition—not least because most of the items are still accompanied only by written comments in Georgian and Russian. Having chosen your preferred language, you are once again asked to wait a short while. The manager will disappear back into the hallway and look for the next guide in line to give a tour. After a few minutes, your guide will appear, introduce herself, and ask you to accompany her upstairs.

The first floor consists of six exhibition halls. Once you have shown your ticket and had it stamped by the guard at the entrance door, you enter the first hall and the guide begins her talk. Her opening line will draw attention to the fact that Stalin is portrayed differently by different states and people. Some will call him a dictator, a tyrant, or a great leader. No matter what the characterization, however, he is to this day acknowledged as an important and remarkable person of the twentieth century. The museum, she continues, addresses the phenomenon of Stalin from three points of view: first, his personal history—his family history, and his path from growing up as a poor boy in a Georgian provincial town to becoming the leader of one of the greatest states of the time. Second, Stalin as a politician, tactician, and military strategist. And third, as a psychological phenomenon with the ability to exercise great power and influence over individuals as well as the masses.[13] As a conclusion to this introduction, most guides will then quote Stalin's words to Viacheslav Mikhailovich Molotov in 1943: "I know

Figure 13.3. Entrance hall. *Photograph courtesy of Peter Kabachnik*

that after my death a pile of rubbish will be heaped on my grave, but the wind of history will sooner or later sweep it away without mercy."

The first hall is devoted to Stalin's youth and his revolutionary activities before the October Revolution. Among the exhibited items are photographs of Stalin's parents, Stalin as a young boy in the Gori church choir, Stalin as a teenager with his fellow students at the Tbilisi Ecclesiastical Seminary, a print of Stalin's first poem to be published in 1895 by the famous national writer Ilia Chavchavadze, Stalin's first police photograph after being arrested by the gendarmerie for revolutionary activities in 1897, and a map showing his six exiles in Siberia and the routes by which he fled five of these six exiles. Passing the photographs, the storyline of the guide takes you through Stalin's poor childhood in Gori, his flair for singing Georgian polyphonic church hymns and writing poetry, and his abilities as a student, which enabled him to enter the ecclesiastical seminary in Tbilisi in spite of his poor background. It was most likely this background, combined with the strict disciplinary regime of the seminary, that initially sparked his interest in revolutionary literature and eventually got him expelled. His expulsion led to his life as an underground revolutionary around the turn of the century and paved his way into the Communist Party and the Central Committee, of which he was elected general secretary in 1922.

On the wall is a photograph of the first government of the Soviets, the Public Commissars Council, including Stalin, who was the People's Commissar for National Affairs. Next to the photograph is a photocopied picture of Lev Trotsky, who was then the People's Commissar for International Affairs but who had been erased from the original. Also on display is a copy of a letter from Lenin addressed to the congress, in which he argues for the dismissal of Stalin as the general secretary of the Central Committee on the grounds that he was too rude and lacked tolerance, loyalty, and politeness. The photograph of Trotsky and the letter from Lenin to the congress have both been added to the exhibition recently. The reason for this was to nuance the exhibition, and show how certain historical facts were silenced or left out of the original exhibition and Soviet history making in general. Besides these two additions, the overall subtext of the hall seem to be one of a poor but hardworking and intelligent boy, who manages to enter higher education and, later, become a skilled and important revolutionary for the socialist cause. There is, however, a parallel story to be found that finds resonance in Georgian nationality rather than Soviet ideology: Stalin's singing in the church choir and his particular talent for the special Georgian polyphonic songs. His writing of romantic poetry, which was acknowledged by Ilia Chavchavadze, perceived to be one of the nation's founding fathers. And Stalin's childhood dream of becoming a Russian Orthodox priest. In other settings and situations, Orthodox Christianity, the polyphonic hymns, Chavchavadze and Georgian-language poetry, are all repeatedly and proudly invoked as symbols of specific features of Georgian national identity.[14]

The second hall mainly shows the period of industrialization up until World War II and is dominated by large posters and enlarged front pages of newspapers showing images of the great successes of the Soviet Union: Stalin kissing the pilot who first managed to cross the Atlantic; a smiling woman driving the first Soviet tractor; and the hero of socialist labor, Alexey Stakhanov (see fig. 13.4). These images of Soviet modernization and progress often receive limited attention from the guides. Instead, your attention is drawn to another recent addition to the exhibition: photocopied prints with portrait photographs of Trotsky, Lev Kamenev, Grigory Zinoviev, Nikolai Bukharin, Aleksey Rykov, Genrikh Yagoda, Nikolai Yeshov, Lavrentiy Beria, and Khrushchev. These were some of the men that carried out the repression of the 1930s, the guide informs you—a dark period in which millions of people were purged and died for political reasons. With the exception of Beria and Khrushchev, who both survived Stalin, the men portrayed were themselves punished and killed in the late 1930s. This addition to the exhibition forms a break with Soviet history making. First, it presents the harshness of the Soviet state and its agents by acknowledging that the purges and repression happened, but, in doing so, it also provides a metacommentary about Soviet manipulation of the truth. Although not new to the exhibition, another item is rarely missed in this hall: a copy of an official form for the elections in 1931 in which Stalin declares himself to be Georgian by nationality. This information is often given with a touch of pride. Contrary to the image of Stalin's reign as repressive of nationalities or of Stalin having denounced his Georgian origins and become Russian, the declaration is pointed to as an illustration that Stalin was proud of his Georgian nationality, that one of the most powerful men of the twentieth century did, in fact, acknowledge that he was a Georgian—from Gori.

The third hall is devoted mainly to World War II, or the "Great Patriotic War." Besides maps showing the shifting fronts, there are numerous photographs and articles on the war and the Soviet progress against Nazism. In what is termed the religious corner by the guides, documents show Lenin's order from 1919 banning religion. Pointing to a document bearing Stalin's signature, the guide explains that Stalin never agreed on the ban and, in 1939, began the rehabilitation of religious leaders. The prayers and moral support of the Orthodox Church and its material assistance to the forces played a great role in the victory in the war. In this hall is also the family corner, with photographs of Stalin's family members. Pointing to a photograph of his oldest son, Iakob, who was imprisoned in the Sachsenhausen concentration camp during World War II, the guide cites Stalin's comment when he was allegedly offered his son in exchange for a German

Figure 13.4. Second exhibition hall. *Photograph courtesy of Peter Kabachnik*

Figure 13.5. Fourth exhibition hall. *Photograph courtesy of Peter Kabachnik*

Figure 13.6. The Mourning Hall. *Photograph courtesy of Peter Kabachnik*

marshal: "War is war for everybody. Every Red Army soldier is my son. I will not exchange a soldier for a field marshal."

The fourth hall is dedicated to the years following World War II and Stalin's later political and diplomatic achievements (see fig. 13.5). It shows pictures of Stalin with Franklin D. Roosevelt and Winston Churchill at the Yalta Conference in 1945, Stalin at Potsdam in 1945, and Stalin making his last official speech at the Nineteenth Party Congress in 1952. The tour through Stalin's life is at an end, and the guide tells you that Stalin died in 1953—officially from a cerebral hemorrhage caused by high blood pressure. He was laid next to Lenin in his mausoleum on the Red Square in Moscow. In 1956, Khrushchev, first secretary of the Communist Party, delivered a speech at the Twentieth Party Congress in which he denounced Stalin and his cult of personality, and, finally, in 1961 Stalin was removed from the mausoleum and buried under the Kremlin walls. The fifth hall, also known as the mourning hall, is dark and the floor is covered with a thick red carpet (fig. 13.6). In the middle of the circular room, on a pedestal, the sixth copy of Stalin's death mask, taken shortly after he died, is on display. On the wall is a canvas showing Stalin in the coffin.

The final hall consists of a model of Stalin's office in the Kremlin, various personal effects and presents received from foreign leaders and representatives during Stalin's years in power. Having passed through the sixth hall, the guide will take you to see the house in front of the museum where Stalin was born and, finally, his personal railway carriage. These last steps of the tour involve more real objects and are, perhaps for that reason, not accompanied by much talk from the guide.

SOVIET, RUSSIAN, NATIONAL, LOCAL?

The Repression Room and the upstairs exhibition are constructed not just in different time periods and within different overall political contexts but also base on different strategies of display. In a discussion of the construction of ethnographic museums, G. B. Dahl and Ronald Stade draw on Barbara Kirschenblatt-Gimblett and make a distinction between *in situ* and *in-context* strategies of display, in order to discuss the various ways museums communicate through exhibitions.[15] In this definition in situ strategies create an illusion of continuity and "a presence beyond a presence"—in which detachment and rupture with the authentic environment has not taken place—and treat the exhibited objects as metonymic and mimetic: as standing in a one-to-one relationship with a reality outside the museum, and hence largely speaking for themselves. In contrast, in-context strategies provide a background and theoretical framing to the exhibited objects and place them in context through diagrams, charts, lectures, grand narratives, and so forth.

According to Kirschenblatt-Gimblett, the former run the risk of "undermining scientific seriousness" in favor of "theatrical spectacle," and the latter "exert strong cognitive control over the objects."[16]

In the case of the Stalin Museum, these two categories of strategy both seem to apply to a certain extent. The Repression Room bears a similarity to the in situ category because of its somewhat theatrical setting and the mimicking of letters and protocols and the torture chamber, all meant to draw the visitor into the everyday sites of the repression period. The addition of the photographs from the 2008 war create a particular temporal version of a "presence beyond presence." As a whole, the room imitates one snapshot situation in which Soviet repression and Russian aggression are fused by suspending, or collapsing, the wider context and historical passing of time. Following Abashin, the room and its "ideological subtext" correspond very well to the post–Rose Revolution political context and the official attitude to the powers represented.[17]

The upstairs exhibition, on the other hand, bears strong similarity to the in-context strategy. In it, objects are accompanied by charts, writings, and lectures, and there are two grand intertwined narratives driving the exhibition forward from hall to hall. One narrative is that of the successful defeat of the tsarist empire and the subsequent formation of a strong, modern, and victorious Soviet state. Intertwined with this is the narrative of the life, personality, and political successes of Stalin as it unfolded alongside the formation of the Soviet Union. Both these narratives and their relation to the exhibited objects, each in their own way, correspond to the political contexts of their creation. *Contexts*, I would argue, because one narrative corresponds with the ideology of the late Soviet state and its official writing of history, and the other corresponds with the particular place of the Georgian Soviet Socialist Republic within the Soviet Union, Stalin being a *national*, or even a *local*, having accomplished great political successes on the world scene. The "strong cognitive control" provided by the original framing of the upstairs displays is, in other words, based on two grand narratives. One, I would argue, is the official history of the Soviet state as told in the 1970s. The other is, at least partly, that of a powerful Georgian national. The latter may be seen as an illustration of how, after his death, and in the wake of Khrushchev's 1956 denouncement of his personality cult, revering Stalin became a symbol of patriotism and dissidence within the Soviet state.[18] The original exhibition, in this sense, encompassed the possibility of a double reading.

The first time I entered the upstairs exhibition, the array of documents, photographs, and posters gave me a feeling of stepping into another time and place. As illustrated in my narrative, however, for the majority of the tours I participated in, focus was placed on Stalin as a person, his personal history, personal characteristics, and powerful position in world politics rather than the actual political practices that took place during his reign. Now and then, there would be an add-on drawing attention to newly added objects in the exhibition. In the director's words, objects added in order to give a more balanced exhibition, not hiding the truth as it was practiced when the exhibition was first created. But as I have tried to demonstrate in this chapter, even if the additions to the exhibition are acknowledged by the guides, they are not necessarily directly associated with Stalin as much as with the Soviet regime and other powerful personae within it. In other words, *one* of the two grand narratives underlying the exhibition has been modified, and much of the positive and propaganda-like praising of the Soviet state has been toned down and critically juxtaposed with political repression, and the current need to add to the old truths. The second grand narrative, that of Stalin as a Georgian from Gori with a fascinating, powerful, and successful history and personality, has been kept intact in spite of the additions.

In the exhibition, we are told of a complex figure that holds the potential to be both Soviet and national, ruthless and religious, powerful and poetic. The fusion of Stalin with the Soviet Era and contemporary Russia, which forms the explicit subtext of the Repression Room, is not a given in the upstairs exhibition. Introducing objects and comments critical of the Soviet state and its creation may not, by default, include a critical reading of Stalin as a person. This, I would argue, because of the strategy of display combined with the dual context—Soviet and national-local—for the exhibit's creation. The extent to which Stalin is read critically then, depends on the attitude of the visitor and the framing provided by the guide's talk.

PROFESSIONALISM, OBJECTIVITY, AND LINGERING AMBIVALENCE

It should be clear from the description of the exhibition in this chapter that an interpretation of the political context for its creation is an important metatext if it is to send a politically correct message today. Many of the foreign visitors I talked to commented on the lack of critical distance and assessment of Stalin's deeds, and in newspaper features, guidebooks, and travel forums covering Gori, the museum is most often described as a slightly kitschy and disturbing shrine to Stalin, and the guides and employees as determined Stalinists.[19]

On my first day in the museum, I talked to Emma, a rather bashful and quiet woman in her fifties who has been working as a guide in the museum since the early 1980s. A little way into our conversation, she pauses. "Can I ask you something?" she probes. "If you are an anthropologist, then why is this place of interest to you?" Emma's question reflected a perplexity that I was to meet time and again during the months I spent in the museum. What was it that I was doing there if I insisted that I was not writing yet another biography of Stalin? As it turned out, it was difficult to explain to the director, guides, and curators of the museum that I was actually interested in their differing ways of representing Stalin and Soviet history. That I was looking for (what I understood to be) the micropolitical negotiations of truth and falsehood, right and wrong, good and bad, used by the employees when talking about the historical events and figures exhibited in the museum. My perspective quite simply conflicted with ideals of professionalism and objectivity in the staff's daily work.

Reflecting the UNM government discourse on modern progress, the museum director, Robert Maglakelidze, repeatedly described himself as an agent of modern change in the museum over the past years. This, he explained, had happened in close cooperation with the Ministry of Culture, an institution that was, as he put it, "always with us." The ministry received regular reports from the museum and helped out with the ideological work as well as organizational affairs. Assisted by the ministry, Robert had introduced professional management procedures according to "international museum standards," he explained. The museum now had a financial monitoring system. Every ticket sold was registered according to category, and the museum kept monthly statistics of the numbers and nationalities of visitors. The guides and managers took part in training courses offered by the Georgian Committee of the International Council of Museums. All these initiatives were aimed at ensuring a higher level of professionalism and objectivity. The introduction of "professional museum practice" and the close cooperation with the Ministry of Culture had also resulted in certain additions to the original exhibition, since, as Robert explained, "When I came here, this was a museum to a communist dictator. The tour started with the words 'Stalin, a great leader, was born here.' The truth was hidden behind those words. The museum must tell the truth in order to be interesting to tourists. That's why the first thing we did was to make changes to the exhibition." In other words, within this framework, the museum is a professional working place aimed at pleasing its customers and dedicated to offering an unbiased and neutral exhibition that shows the facts and leaves it to the visitors to form their own opinions about Stalin. Even though the director said the ministry was assisting with ideological work, it soon became clear to me that Robert and his employees alike ultimately viewed themselves as experts laying out historical facts, not interpreting them. What was being told in the museum was not subjective stories, or memories, but objective history. I became aware that for me to suggest that something akin to historical manipulation was going on in the museum seemed rather insulting to my interlocutors' professional standing.[20]

When discussing his efforts to recast the museum in recent years, Robert insisted that the museum was an important trademark for Gori and Georgia and *the* key museum of the Stalin period—but it necessarily had to tell the truth as it was known today. It should show visitors how "pompous and disgusting the Soviet era was." It would have three main purposes: to show the Soviet system under Stalin's leadership, to show the crimes committed during the repressions, and to show the house, personal effects, and personal carriage of a historical man. The museum in short, should be unique and the best of its kind and use its distinctiveness to attract tourists. The key word to accomplishing the museum's goal was professionalism and respect for the visitor, he continued. "We receive a lot of visitors who hate Stalin. We also have visitors who adore him. And people who know nothing about Stalin also visit our museum. All these three categories of visitors must be happy when they leave the museum. Through a professional management and organization of the museum, we will satisfy everyone."

The director's ideal of professional museum practice and objectivity was reflected in an emphasis on facts and professionalism in the everyday work of the guides and curators. There seemed to be a dominant perception that the linkage between history, facts, and the exhibited objects was immutable and that what they were laying out for the visitor was in principle a given, as long as one did not distort the facts. When I asked the guides their personal opinions about Stalin, I sensed that I was perceived as being overly direct. The majority would avoid the question by saying that Stalin was a complicated person with both good and bad sides and it was not up to them to make final judgments about his character. The official, or open, conclusion to a direct question seemed to be that Stalin was an important figure of the twentieth century and that their task was to guide people through the facts of the exhibition and encourage them make up their own minds.

When comparing this approach of the guides with visitors' impressions, it became obvious that the neutrality counting as professionalism on the part of the employees was actually quite often interpreted by visitors as selective and manipulative. Considering the layout of the main exhibition and the ideological context for its creation, the guides' refusing to make judgments or provide interpretations of the facts was often seen by visitors as a lack of willingness to employ a critical gaze. Paradoxically, however, I would suggest that the ambiguity one meets in the representation of Stalin and the Soviet period was partly created by staff trying to adhere to (rather than contest) the government and museum management's initiatives to improve objectivity, professionalism, and an unbiased service for visitors.

This said, when talking *around* the subject of personal attitudes and judgment, it was clear that employees themselves had very different, but also ambivalent, attitudes toward Stalin. I would often be talking to someone about what was understood to be negative aspects of Stalin's character and political reign: the famine of the 1920s, the repression, the gulag, or his ruthless and uncompromising character. Then suddenly they would change their angle and compare Stalin to Davit the Builder and Queen Tamar—both strong rulers of the Kingdom of Georgia in the "Golden Age" of the eleventh to thirteenth centuries. They had also killed political enemies and built the nation using ruthless methods, but today everyone knows that such were the times, and they are both praised as Orthodox saints. Similarly, a discussion of the hardships of the Orthodox Church during Soviet times and its revival after independence could often end with a comment that Stalin had been a great believer, or a talk about relatives who were exiled or imprisoned in the 1930s would end with a puzzled comment that these same people or some of their closest kin had still loved Stalin and had mourned his death deeply.[21] Such conversations displayed an uneasy ambivalence toward Stalin that partly contrasted with the ideals of objectivism and professionalism espoused by the director, and even more so, the official attitude of the authorities. If not directly outspoken, however, these subtle reflections did not necessarily conflict with *one* of the two underlying narratives of the main exhibition of the museum.

THE LIMITS OF AUTHORITY

I started this chapter by drawing attention to the rather paradoxical position of the Stalin Museum in relation to theories stressing museums as vehicles of authoritative truth-making. On the one hand, it is a state museum representing a historical figure under the sponsorship of the post–Rose Revolution Georgian state. Consequently, it is to be expected that the museum exhibition would reflect the historical truths accepted in official state discourse: truths in which Stalin is seen as a tyrant and a dictator, and a symbol of the communist suppression of people in general and the Georgian nation in particular. On the other hand, most of the museum's exhibition was constructed under the sponsorship of the late Soviet state and, as a result, the exhibit in itself represents the very historical truths that Saakashvili's government sought to denounce. It is against this backdrop that I have explored the practices and rationales through which the "political acts" of representation and negotiation played out in the museum during my fieldwork.[22]

The analyses of the exhibition and the ideals of a neutral outlaying of facts among the guides suggest that the tension between two state narratives causes the museum to represent an ambiguous rather than univocal political figure and history. Behind the new historical truths articulated by the authorities, alternative readings of Stalin still linger. Through the addition of "compromising" material to the original exhibition, the museum director, curators, and guides have drawn attention to inaccuracies and masked truths in the Soviet representation of its own history. Such compromising facts do not necessarily, however, compromise a parallel story told throughout the exhibition: one that views Stalin as a Georgian national displaying Georgian virtues that are also highly valued in independent Georgia. It is these virtues, among other factors, that cause certain ambivalences toward Stalin on the part of the staff. In other words, the parallel narratives in the original exhibition and the fact that the additions to the exhibition are only explicitly addressing one of them—that of the Soviet state—makes it possible to interpret Stalin as being both Soviet and national, ruthless and religious, powerful and poetic, and so on.

These insights do not in themselves counter the literature that stresses museums as important sites within modern states for representing particular authoritative versions of historical causality, truth, and moral and ideological good.[23] With the Stalin Museum, however, I have argued that we have encountered an empirical anomaly: two states are at work, two truths run parallel. The national aspects and virtues displayed in the original exhibit have a marked continuity with present ideas of Georgian national characteristics and virtues. The seeds for a national and local, rather than Soviet, reading of Stalin's life were laid out in the original exhibit. In light of the power of nationalist ideology and national symbols in contemporary Georgia,[24] I would argue that this reading has been much more counterintuitive to question, with the additions to the exhibition, than the legitimacy of the Soviet state. Hence, only one of the two grand narratives of the life of Stalin has been successfully reformulated by the changes made to the museum exhibition. The Soviet state is largely delegitimized along the lines of government discourse, and a new truth is being told. But the qualities of "Stalin the person" linger ambiguously between two interpretations: one aligning him with the virtues of Georgian nationality and pride, and another aligning him with the (now) delegitimized Soviet system.

It seems plausible to expect that the Stalin Museum is not the only museum displaying and struggling with this kind of duality that creates a potential for representing ambiguity rather than unilateral truths. Paradoxically then, the very strength of museums as authoritative presenters of a particular ideological truth and identity at a specific moment in time may also be what challenges the construction of other truths and identities under new historical circumstances. This is, perhaps, particularly so if we think of the many low-profile regional museums with limited funds and abilities to construct entirely new exhibitions when political circumstances change.

CODA

Turning the Stalin Museum into a museum of a museum proved itself difficult. Quite possibly reflecting this fact, in April 2012, the Georgian Ministry of Culture announced that it would make a completely new exhibition and turn the museum into an account of the Stalinist repressions. Over the summer of 2012, one would see a banner at the entrance to the museum reading "This museum is a falsification of history. It is a typical example of Soviet propaganda and it attempts to legitimize the bloodiest regime in history." But the announced new exhibition never materialized. In October 2012 Saakashvili's UNM was, to the surprise of many, defeated in the parliamentary elections by the Georgian Dream Coalition led by Bidzina Ivanishvili. The project of a new exhibition in the museum was laid to rest. Whether this reflected a pro-Russian stance of the Georgian Dream Coalition, as some UNM members and supporters would have it, or it simply reflected new priorities of a new government in office, is up for discussion. Nevertheless, the fact remains that in the summer of 2015 when I visited the museum to see how the place had developed since my fieldwork, it seemed as if nothing had changed. As one of the curators, who has been working in the museum for twenty-five years, drily noted when I asked her about the effects of recent political changes on her work: "You know, throughout time we were opened and closed several times and governments have used us for their political battles. But really, the place remains the same."

NOTES

This chapter elaborates and expands on my previous work published in "Evasive Politics: Paradoxes of History, Nation and Everyday Communication in the Republic of Georgia" (University of Copenhagen, 2013). All photographs courtesy of Peter Kabachnik.

1. See, for example, Irakli Chkonia, "Timeless Identity versus Another Final Modernity: Identity Master Myth and Social Change in Georgia," in *Developing Cultures: Case Studies*, ed. Lawrence E. Harrison and Peter L. Berger (New York: Routledge, 2006), 349–67; Barbara Christophe, "When Is a Nation? Comparing Lithuania and Georgia," *Geopolitics* 7, no. 2 (2002): 147–72; Mathijs Pelkmans, *Defending the Border: Identity, Religion, and Modernity in the Republic of Georgia* (Ithaca, NY: Cornell University Press, 2006); Ronald Grigor Suny, *The Making of the Georgian Nation*, 2nd ed. (Bloomington: Indiana University Press, 1994); and Jonathan Wheatley, *Georgia from National Awakening to Rose Revolution: Delayed Transition in the Former Soviet Union* (Aldershot, UK: Ashgate, 2005).

2. Katrine B. Gotfredsen, "Void Pasts and Marginal Presents: On Nostalgia and Obsolete Futures in the Republic of Georgia," *Slavic Review* 73, no. 2 (2014): 246–64; see also Paul Manning, "Rose-Colored Glasses? Color Revolutions and Cartoon Chaos in Postsocialist Georgia," *Cultural Anthropology* 22, no. 2 (2007); Francoise J. Companjen, "Georgia," in *The Colour Revolutions in the Former Soviet Republics: Successes and Failures*, ed. Donnacha Ó Beacháin and Abel Polese (London: Routledge,

2010), 13–29; and Stephen Jones, *Georgia. A Political History since Independence* (London: I. B.Tauris, 2013).

3. Other examples include the removal of Soviet Era monuments such as the World War II Memorial in Kutaisi and the Stalin Monument in Gori, the passing of the "Liberty Charter" in Parliament in May 2011 (a charter restricting the public display of Soviet (and Nazi) symbols and establishing a state commission to assess the prevalence of monuments, street names, inscriptions, and so forth, containing communist (or fascist) ideology and propaganda, and the introduction of the public holiday "Soviet Occupation Day" on February 25 to commemorate the invasion of the Red Army in 1921.

4. It is a general stereotype in Georgia (and beyond) that the people of Gori love Stalin and are very proud of having a special link with one of the main political figures of the twentieth century. A 2013 report from the Carnegie Endowment for International Peace, in fact, shows that as many as 45 percent of Georgians in general have a positive attitude toward Stalin (see Thomas de Waal, Maria Lipman, Lev Gudkov, and Lasha Bakradze, *The Stalin Puzzle: Deciphering Post-Soviet Public Opinion*, Carnegie Endowment for International Peace, 2013, https://carnegieeurope .eu/2013/03/01/stalin-puzzle-deciphering-post-soviet-public-opinion-pub-51075), and so portraying it as an issue pertaining only to Gori is hardly sufficient. I shall return to what I would term a rather general ambivalence toward Stalin later.

5. Ivan Karp and Steven Lavine, "Introduction: Museums and Multiculturalism," in *Exhibiting Cultures: The Poetics and Politics of Museum Display*, ed. Ivan Karp and Steven Lavine (Washington, DC: Smithsonian Institution Press, 1991), 1.

6. Michael M. Ames, "Biculturalism in Exhibitions," *Museum Anthropology* 15, no. 2 (1991): 13.

7. See, for example, Sergei Abashin, "*Mustakillik* and Remembrance of the Imperial Past: Passing through the Halls of the Tashkent Museum in Memory of the Victims of Repression," *Russian Politics and Law* 48, no. 5 (2010): 78–91; Benedict R. Anderson, *Imagined Communities: Reflections on the Origin and Spread of Nationalism* (London: Verso, 1991); Carol Duncan, "Art Museums and the Ritual of Citizenship," in *Exhibiting Cultures: The Poetics and Politics of Museum Display*, ed. Ivan Karp and Steven Lavine (Washington, DC: Smithsonian Institution Press, 1991), 88–103; and Donald Horne, *The Great Museum: The Re-presentation of History* (London: Pluto, 1984).

8. See, for example, G. B. Dahl and Ronald Stade, "Anthropology, Museums, and Contemporary Cultural Processes: An Introduction," *Ethnos* 65, no. 2 (2000): 157–71; Eric Gable and Richard Handler, "Public History, Private Memory: Notes from the Ethnography of Colonial Williamsburg, Virginia, USA," *Ethnos* 65, no. 2 (2000): 237–52; Richard Handler, "An Anthropological Definition of the Museum and Its Purpose," *Museum Anthropology* 17, no. 1 (1993): 33–36; and Karp and Lavine, "Introduction."

9. The war was the culmination of years of tension and occasional violent clashes in South Ossetia—a territory that is *de jure* part of Georgia but that declared

independence in the early 1990s and is today *de facto* independent with support from Russia. Reacting to intelligence reporting of a Russian military build-up close to the northern border of the region, to clashes between Georgian and Ossetian forces, and attacks on Georgian villages in the region, on August 7, 2008, the Georgian military launched an operation toward the South Ossetian capital, Tskhinvali, in order to "restore constitutional order." Fighting went on in South Ossetia for three days, and Russian forces reached Tskhinvali on August 8 in support of the South Ossetian side. On August 8, Russian forces started bombing military targets in and around Gori. Throughout the bombardment, which lasted for five days, several civilian locations, including apartment buildings and a school, were hit, and on August 12 a Russian cluster bomb hit the town's central square, killing and injuring a number of civilians. On August 11, Georgian ground troops were forced to retreat, and Russian forces began to advance into Georgia proper. Gori, situated approximately 25 km from Tskhinvali, was under Russian occupation until August 22.

10. Abashin, *"Mustakillik."*

11. Ibid., 80.

12. The category of manager is slightly misleading. In reality, it means that you meet the visitors and help them to buy tickets and organize a guide. Some of the managers, six at that time, have responsibilities such as "information," "educational service," "visitor service," and "excursion service," but in the interviews I conducted they did not seem to know what those responsibilities entailed in practice besides meeting the visitors in the museum entrance hall.

13. Recent biographers of Stalin have stressed the importance of Stalin-the-person for historical developments (as opposed to more structural approaches), as well the influence of Stalin's early years and sociocultural background on his psychological character and the kind of political figure he would later become. Examples of this trend have been Simon Sebag Montefiore, *Stalin, the Court of the Red Tsar* (New York: Alfred A. Knopf, 2004); Robert Service, *Stalin: A Biography* (Cambridge, MA: Belknap, 2005); Simon Sebag Montefiore, *Young Stalin* (New York: Alfred A. Knopf, 2007); Stephen Kotkin, *Stalin*, vol. 1, *Paradoxes of Power, 1878–1928* (New York: Penguin, 2014); and Alfred J. Rieber, *Stalin and the Struggle for Supremacy in Eurasia* (Cambridge: Cambridge University Press, 2015). As we shall see later in this chapter, in connecting the Stalin-the-person to Stalin-the-politician the museum exhibition also draws attention to Stalin's childhood and national and cultural background, albeit, for the most part, with different emphasis and implied moral conclusions. What a number of recent biographies have in common with the museum exhibition, however, is their attention to the multifaceted nature of Stalin as a person and the importance of his personality in his political reign and historical events.

14. See, for example, Pelkmans, *Defending the Border*; Peter Nasmyth, *Georgia: In the Mountains of Poetry* (New York: Routledge, 2006); and Katrine B. Gotfredsen, *Evasive Politics: Paradoxes of History, Nation and Everyday Communication in the Republic of Georgia* (PhD diss., Department of Anthropology, University of Copenhagen, 2013).

15. Dahl and Stade, "Anthropology, Museums, and Contemporary Cultural Processes."

16. Ibid., 162–64.

17. Abashin, *"Mustakillik,"* 80.

18. See, for example, Gia Nodia, "Georgia's Long Farewell to Stalin," *Radio Free Europe/Radio Liberty*, July 1, 2010, www.rferl.org/content/Georgias_Long_Farewell _To_Stalin_/2088243.html; Sergei Arutinov, "Introduction: Russian Culture in the 20th Century," in *Russian Culture*, ed. John Rickman, Geoffrey Gorer, and Margaret Mead (New York: Berghahn, 2001), vii–xx; and Suny, *Making of the Georgian Nation*, 302–3.

19. For examples of this trend, see, for example, Andrew North, "Georgia's Stalin Museum Gives Soviet Version of Dictator's Life Story," *Guardian*, August 4, 2015, https://www.theguardian.com/world/2015/aug/04/georgia-stalin-museum-soviet -version-dictators-life-story, as well as online entries about the Stalin Museum on Lonely Planet: "Stalin Museum," accessed August 4, 2017, https://www.lonelyplanet .com/georgia/gori/attractions/stalin-museum/a/poi-sig/502622/359316; and on Tripadvisor, "Gori: Stalin Museum," accessed August 4, 2017, https://www.tripadvisor .com/Travel-g317094-d1128827/Gori:Georgia:Stalin.Museum.html.

20. See, for example, Gable and Handler, "Public History, Private Memory"; and Handler, "Anthropological Definition." In "Public History, Private Memory," Gable and Handler show how the position of a historical museum becomes paradoxical in the sense than it (in times of consumerism and an experience economy) advertises itself equally as a place where people can make individual memories and at the same time for legitimacy purposes must claim to show properly researched historical facts. In this sense, this point may be seen within a wider context of professionalism, (market) competition, and consumerism, strongly advocated and hailed by the UNM government.

21. In concluding his analysis of the establishment of Stalin's authority as a national father of the Soviet Union, and its continuation after his death, John Schoeberlein poses a critique of the idea held by many, particularly Western, observers that if only people knew what had *really* happened during his reign, they would reject Stalinist authority (John S. Schoeberlein, "Doubtful Death Fathers and Musical Corpses: What to Do with the Dead Stalin, Lenin, and Tsar Nicholas?," in *Death of the Father, an Anthropology of the End in Political Authority*, ed. John Borneman [New York: Berghahn, 2004], 218–19). My preceding analysis supports Schoeberlein's argument that this is a simplification of the multiplicity of, often ambivalent, feelings that people are capable of having toward (national) father figures. (See also John Borneman, introduction to *Death of the Father*.)

22. See Ames, "Biculturalism in Exhibitions," 13.

23. Abashin, *"Mustakillik"*; Anderson, *Imagined Communities*; Duncan, "Art Museums"; Horne, *Great Museum*.

24. See, for example, Martin Demant Frederiksen, *Young Men, Time, and Boredom in the Republic of Georgia* (Philadelphia: Temple University Press, 2013); Gotfredsen, "Void Pasts and Marginal Presents"; Tamta Khalvashi, "Peripheral Affects: Shame, Publics and Performance on the Margins of the Republic of Georgia" (PhD diss., University of Copenhagen, 2015); Paul Manning, "The City of Balconies: Elite Politics and the Changing Semiotics of the Post-socialist Cityscape," in *City Culture and City Planning in Tbilisi: Where Europe and Asia Meet*, ed. Kristof Van Assche, Joseph Salukvadze, and Nick Shavishvili (Lewiston NY: Edwin Mellen, 2009), 71–102.

KATRINE BENDTSEN GOTFREDSEN holds a PhD in anthropology from the University of Copenhagen and is Senior Lecturer in Caucasus Studies at the Department for Global Political Studies, Malmö University. She has done extensive fieldwork in the Republic of Georgia, focusing in particular on local experiences of, and responses to, social and political transformation. Works include the journal articles "Void Pasts and Marginal Presents: On Nostalgia and Obsolete Futures in the Republic of Georgia" (*Slavic Review*, 2014) and "Enemies of the People: Theorizing Dispossession and Mirroring Conspiracy in the Republic of Georgia" (*Focaal*, 2016), and she coauthored (with Martin Demant Frederiksen) the monograph *Georgian Portraits: Essays on the Afterlives of a Revolution* (2017).

Figure 14.1. Vabamu Museum of Occupations and Freedom, Tallinn, founded 2003 (closed for renovations in 2018). https://www.vabamu.ee/. *Photograph by A. Lorraine Weekes*

FOURTEEN

Between Occupations and Freedoms
Memory, Narrative, and Practice at Vabamu in Tallinn, Estonia

A. LORRAINE WEEKES

INTRODUCTION

Between 1940 and 1991, the Republic of Estonia was occupied three times: by the Soviet Union in 1940, by Nazi Germany in 1941, and then again by the Soviet Union in 1944, this time for nearly fifty years (1944–91). In 2003, a dozen years after Estonia regained its independence from the Soviet Union, the Museum of Occupations opened in Tallinn, Estonia's capital, with the mission of researching and commemorating Estonians' experiences under these occupations. The museum sits near the city center, a few hundred meters from the central Freedom Square and a short walk from the Estonian parliament building and Stenbock House, the seat of the government of Estonia. It's not out of the way. Nevertheless, most of the Museum of Occupations' approximately twenty thousand annual visitors have historically been foreign tourists; in recent years, only about two thousand Estonians a year have found their way to the airy modernist museum.

One afternoon in mid-February 2016, the museum closed its doors for a press conference. A small stage was set up in front of one of its angular glass walls and a few dozen people sat before the stage in neat rows of white folding chairs. Merilin Piipuu, the museum's director, sat stage right. Stage left was museum board member Sten Tamkivi, a well-known Estonian entrepreneur with deep ties to Silicon Valley. Sandwiched between them in his signature bow tie was Estonian president Toomas Hendrik Ilves. Behind the trio, concrete suitcases scattered throughout the museum's external courtyard were visible through the glass wall. They were part of the sculptural piece *100 suitcases* (*100 kohvrit*) by Estonian artists Kaido Ole and Marko Mäetamm, which commemorates the Estonians who were forced to leave their homeland before and during the occupations.

Tamkivi opened the press conference with the observation that occupation, the museum's focal point, can be best understood as the absence of freedom. An enthusiastic, but vague, allusion to exciting changes on the museum's horizon followed. It was time, he said, for a "new chapter" in the history of the museum, time to launch the museum anew as a "thought world start-up," a civic society equivalent of the young and agile start-up firms of the private sector. Tamkivi turned to President Ilves for his perspective. How would the president characterize the relationship between the Museum of Occupations and the notion of "freedom"? After echoing Tamkivi's characterization of occupation as a dearth of freedom, Ilves elaborated on what he saw as the best way to safeguard against future intrusions on freedom: "We know what the lack of freedom means: it means everything that we have seen here for the last thirteen years." The president gestured around him and panned the museum with his gaze. "But the most important blow against the absence of freedom doesn't come by only focusing on this deficit. It comes from showing what an Estonian can do if he is given his freedom." To illustrate the point, Ilves pointed to country's nineteenth century past: "This has been a repetitive motif throughout Estonian history. If you look at the 1880s when the Baltic Germans [who held many Estonians in serfdom until the mid-1800s] came back twenty years after they'd left, they were in amazement, saying 'look at what these country simpletons (*maa Mätsid*) have done. Look!'" Estonia's achievements in the twenty-five years since the fall of the Soviet Union, especially in comparison with those of the other states that gained independence at the same time, the president suggested, merited similar attention and laudation.

After about twenty minutes of back-and-forth with the president, Tamkivi turned to director Piipuu and asked him to tell about the museum's new chapter. As Piipuu spoke, the facts, figures, and concrete plans behind the press conference and the somewhat abstract introductory expositions of freedom became clearer: the museum would double its exhibition space and broaden its focus. It would tell the story of Estonia's occupations but also share the stories of those who died during the Holocaust, were deported to Siberia, or exiled in the West. Moreover, it would tell the story of Estonia's embrace of freedom in the years since 1991; the underlying goal was to become not just an exhibition space but also a gathering place where Estonians, especially youths, could come to contemplate and debate the meaning of freedom. To reflect its new and broadened focus, the museum would change its name from the Museum of Occupations to the Museum of Freedom. Presumably riffing off the success Estonia's modern art museum had had with the nickname "KuMu" (a portmanteau of *kunst*, the Estonian word for art, and *muuseum*, the Estonian word for museum), the Museum of Freedom would go by the appellate "Vabamu," which was an analogous mash-up of *vabadus*, the Estonian word for freedom, and *muuseum*.

The public response to the announcement was swift and highly critical. People were angry and upset. Rhetoric flew. Do any of the museum's board members know what it feels like to "bury" a departed infant by dropping its body through the floorboards of a Siberia-bound cattle car? asked Mart Helme of Estonia's far right Conservative People's Party of Estonia.[1] Why don't they just make it about occupation and freedom and brotherhood and equality and call it the "Free-ItyMu" (*Vabasusmu*) or "OccuFrEqMu" (*Okvavõvemu*)?, suggested Jaak Jõerüüt sardonically.[2] Other criticisms were less vicious but no less negative about the proposed changes. The museum's exponents were quick to fight back, championing their plans through opinion pieces and interviews throughout Estonian media.[3] A discussion series on "how to remember" was jointly sponsored by the Museum of Occupations and Estonian public broadcasting and brought together academics, politicians, journalists, and other civic-sector thought leaders to discuss questions such as "What does resistance during occupation mean and where is its boundary?" and "Has twenty-five years been enough time to recover from occupations?"

Preliminary details about the planned rebuilding and a few mock-ups of future Vabamu exhibit spaces were made available online. Because the museum's opening was more than a year away, however, and detailed plans about what artifacts, histories and narratives Vabamu would feature (or exclude) were not initially made public, much of the debate about Vabamu was speculative and centered on fairly abstract concerns: the imperative to never forget the horrors Estonians endured during the Soviet occupation; the dangers of allowing postmodern moral relativism to attenuate the condemnation of historical injustice; the importance of national myths that celebrate Estonian agency, not just Estonian suffering. After providing a brief contextualizing discussion of the Museum of Occupations' founding and historical foci, I turn to this conflict surrounding Vabamu and tease out the key terms and themes of the controversy. I show that the hostility of the public response is a result of the fact that Vabamu was perceived as an affront to the memory of Estonian suffering and victimization that has, since the first national awakening in the nineteenth century, played a central role in how many Estonians understand Estonianness.

Running through, and growing out of, these existential discussions about Estonian national identity and collective memory are a series of much more particular disagreements about the appropriate purpose, function, and constituency of a museum of communism in twenty-first-century Estonia. Collectively, these debates about by whom, for whom, and in what manner the Soviet occupation should be museologized call our attention to the ways in which the controversy implicates normative questions about the form, function, and role of museums like Vabamu. At stake are not only the museum's name and thematic scope, but also the role the museum as an institution should play in the post-Soviet Estonian context. By using the controversy about Vabamu as a site for examining this nexus of past and pragmatics, of memory and museum operations, I hope not only to add to the already ample literature on post-Soviet memory culture in postcommunist Europe,[4] but also to provide a critical reflection on these competing normative assertions about the prerogatives and responsibilities of a museum in the post-Soviet, and arguably postcolonial, Estonian context.[5]

THE MUSEUM OF OCCUPATIONS

The Kistler-Ritso Foundation was established in 1998 by Estonian émigré Olga Kistler-Ritso. In its "Goals and Objectives" document—still available on the Museum of Occupations' website—the foundation described the museum it aimed to establish as a place where "the developmental processes during the period 1940–1991 can be studied and where relevant materials, both objects and documents, can be collected and exhibited." Five years later, in summer 2003, the Museum of Occupations opened its doors to the public. At its June 23 opening ceremony, Kistler-Ritso and Estonian member of parliament Tunne Kelam emphasized that one of the museum's animating missions was ensuring that the horrors of occupation were "never again!" repeated in Estonia. Scholars writing in a wide variety of contexts have shown how the heritage of genocide and atrocity is harnessed to ward off the repetition of history.[6] The Museum of Occupations' founders clearly hoped the testimonials, steely prison doors, and yellowed newspaper clippings they assembled and curated at the foot of Toompea Hill would serve a similar prophylactic effect.

As of this writing in fall 2016, the Museum of Occupations remains open to visitors. Though the museum routinely hosts temporary exhibits, much of its exhibit space has been left virtually unchanged since the museum opened its doors in summer 2003. The museum's first floor is a single light-filled room with high ceilings; glass cases filled with the museum's permanent exhibit line about a third of the room's perimeter (fig. 14.2). The cases' contents are presented with minimal interpretative text: military uniforms, firearms, housewares, handcuffs, and old telephones sit on glass shelves with small Estonian-language placards. The artifacts are organized chronologically and divided into seven temporal periods (fig. 14.3). Above each section of display, a monitor plays documentary footage about the period; the films feature narration of images and video reels as well as interviews, mostly with Estonian political elites and academics. They are in Estonian, but viewers can choose to watch them with English or Russian dubbing.

Scholars analyzing the permanent ground-floor exhibition of the Museum of Occupations have emphasized the ways in which it reinforces the binary between

Figure 14.2. First floor of the museum. *Photograph by A. Lorraine Weekes*

Figure 14.3. Museum artifacts. *Photograph by A. Lorraine Weekes*

blameless Estonian victims and the violent and barbaric savagery of the occupiers: Meike Wulf's discussion of the museum is subtitled "A Claim for Victimhood" and Jörg Hackman and Marko Lehti characterize the dominant purpose of the museum as "to present the Estonian nation as a victim of the Second World War and to legitimize its position with regard to domestic as well as foreign visitors."[7] Though the descriptive plaques that accompany the exhibition's displays eschew extensive substantive interpretation, the hours of documentary films that play above the display cases unequivocally present the Soviets as "brutal murderers who left the country burning everything in their way [in 1941], tortured and killed their prisoners and finally returned with a vengeance."[8] Estonians, by contrast, are presented either as helpless victims of Soviet violence or as soldiers forced by the savagery of the 1940–41 Soviet occupation to collaborate with the Germans in order to defend their homeland. As several scholars have noted, though the museum deals with both the Nazi and the Soviet occupations, its treatment of the latter overshadows its engagement with the former.[9] The museum is almost completely silent on the more than a dozen Nazi concentration camps that were located in Estonia[10] and the Estonians who guarded them.[11]

Numerous authors have documented the central role museums can play in consolidating, articulating, and producing key elements of community identity, be it at the local, national, or transnational scale. As Nelson Graburn reminds us, museums are not just "storehouses of humanity's heritage." To the contrary, they are, to quote Lorena Rivera-Orraca, simultaneously "inscribed in and inscribers of collective and individual memory, identity, and practices."[12] In emphasizing Estonians' historical victimization at the hands of the Soviets, the Museum of Occupations both reflects and solidifies the prominent position of victimhood and suffering in Estonian national identity narratives.

Narratives of victimization and suffering at the hands of foreigners have played a central role in Estonian national identity formation since at least the 1860s, when the centuries of Baltic German rule in Estonia were first mythologized as "700 years of [Estonian] slavery."[13] This formulation featured prominently in the nationalist movements of the late nineteenth and early twentieth centuries, and I have encountered it on several occasions during my fieldwork, not infrequently with "and fifty years of occupation" appended. Narratives of victimization and national suffering are also one of the dominant interpretive frameworks through which Estonia's twentieth-century history of occupation is understood: Karsten Brüggemann and Andres Kasekamp assert that, in in Estonia, "the politics of memory created a 'real' history that was based upon a common understanding of collective victimhood under Soviet rule" and Siobhan Kattago likewise notes that ethnic Estonians' memories of World War II and the Soviet period foreground "victimhood, occupation, deportation and national suffering at the hands of two dictatorships."[14] The emphasis on the persecution and subjection of the Estonian nation at the hands of outsiders is typical of post-Soviet postcoloniality, which is less focused on the resistance and agency of the colonized in the face of subjugation than are South Asian postcolonial studies.[15] Serguei Oushakine writes that "the paradigm of resistance is not the main driving force for post-Soviet postcoloniality. Instead, studies of the colonialist past are predominantly done to demonstrate the brutality of the colonizer."[16]

The centrality of victimization and suffering in national identity narratives is not unique to the post-Soviet context.[17] Aleida Assmann describes a turn away from histories that foreground conquest and heroics toward a "victim memory" that emphasizes suffering and trauma, and G. J. Ashworth maintains that violence is a "leitmotif that runs through many heritage resources" and helps to substantiate a "heritage of victimization," which can in turn promote national solidarity and the vilification of the excluded wrongdoers.[18] Heritage-based claims to victimhood, David Lowenthal adds, can be instrumental not only in fostering pride and internal unity, but also in achieving external recognition for groups' suffering and survival.[19]

VABAMU

While the word *occupations* may be missing from the short form of the museum's new name, there is every reason to believe that Estonia's history during the 1940–91 period will remain a central part of Vabamu's substantive focus. The discussion of Vabamu on the Museum of Occupations' website stresses that occupations will be one of Vabamu's key themes (along with resistance, restoration, and freedom) and that the museum will remain committed to documenting and describing Estonia's history of occupations. In nearly every interview she gives about Vabamu, the museum's director Merilin Piipuu emphasizes that the square footage dedicated to representing the period of occupations will actually increase in the new museum. Likewise, Sylvia Thompson, the president of the Kistler-Ritso Foundation board, stressed Vabamu's continuous engagement with the subject of Estonia's twentieth-century occupations in an early 2016 speech. In February 2016 Thompson, along with Kistler-Ritso Foundation board member Mike Keller, received Estonian state decorations for their support of the museum. In her acceptance speech, Thompson confirmed that "the stories of real people who lived in that terrible time of occupations: those whose lives were tragically lost, and those who survived; those who were deported to Siberia, those who fled West, and those who stayed" would remain "at the heart of Vabamu."[20]

Later in the same speech, however, Thompson offered an implicit defense of the plans to broaden the museum's thematic scope: "Estonia is remarkable not for its victimhood—sadly, there are far too many victims of evil in this world. Estonia is unique for its non-violent 'singing revolution' and its quick ascent to one of the most successful democracies in the world today.... These are things we can be proud to show the world."[21] Her words, along with those of other Vabamu exponents, suggest that though the museum's substantive engagement with the 1940–91 period of Estonian history will persist, the current Museum of Occupations' unwavering emphasis on Estonian victimization and suffering will be phased out. Writing in a newspaper editorial, Piipuu explicitly challenged the hegemonic role of victimhood narratives in representations of Estonia's recent past. Citing historian James Mark and ethnologist Tiiu Jaago, she asserted that "the stance of victimhood is not an objective description of what suffering individuals have lived through but a mode of self-representation that individuals use to make sense of what is happening around them."[22] A few months before the official announcement of the changes at Vabamu (and the resulting backlash), Piipuu gave an interview to *Estonian World*, an English-language blog targeted at the Estonian diaspora. In it she explained that "we do not just want to provide this narrative of suffering and victimisation, but give more hope to people and talk about freedom and how Estonian people got their freedom and what their recovery process was." She then offered an applied example of what this more multivocal treatment of Estonia's history of occupation might look like: "at the moment you can probably see only the most horrible stories [in the Museum of Occupations], but I have just met this woman who was in Siberia when she was a small child until she was six years old. She was saying how it was a really great time, how they played around and she was the head of her school class and what a great time she had—and that is what she remembers and we should tell this story as well."[23] Vabamu may continue to feature stories and artifacts from the period of occupations, but all signs suggest that its discursive framing of those materials will be much less prescriptive and suffering-centric than that of the Museum of Occupations.

Alongside the museum's less dogmatic approach to the topic of occupations will be a new thematic attention to questions related to liberty in contemporary Estonian society and a more pronounced emphasis on public engagement and outreach. "We hope that this building will become a space where we can have opinion festivals all year round," explained Piipuu, referring to the annual summer opinion festival that brings together Estonian politicians, thought leaders, artists, and the general public for a weekend of discussions and debates about issues of social concern and interest. When I interviewed Kistler-Ritso Foundation board member Sten Tamkivi in early 2016, he elaborated on the rationale for the museum's thematic expansion by drawing heavily on seasonal metaphors, explaining that Estonia had experienced "fifty years of winter" (occupation) and then a short spring in which the country managed to achieve reindependence without bloodshed. After more than two decades of a "generally nice warm summer," Tamkivi said, the relevance of the Museum of Occupations to contemporary Estonian society was not as clear as it once was:

> Now there has been 25 years of summer.... And we have this museum in downtown Tallinn that is still called "Winter." ... So, sure, we should never forget the winter, we should talk about the winter, we should try to understand why it happened and prohibit it from ever happening again. These are all the things that the museum does and will be doing. But we should be sharing the stories of how do you get out of that mess? Like how do you actually open up? How do you do these things after you get the chance? And those stories are not being told today, which I think is a gap.

Tamkivi pointed to the heated discussions in Estonian society about marriage equality and refugee resettlement as examples of controversies that could be productively considered through the analytic of liberty. By "putting liberty front and center," Tamkivi explained, Vabamu would provide a space where people could come together and consider not just what it means to be occupied, but also what it means, and what it takes, to build and maintain a free society.

THE BACKLASH AGAINST VABAMU

After the announcement that the Museum of Occupations would become Vabamu, one of the most immediate and sustained flashpoints of controversy was the planned name change, and especially the proposed shorthand Vabamu. For many of Vabamu's critics the nickname's hip sound and truncated form smacked of distasteful flippancy. Jaak Jõerüüt observed that semantically it is impossible to make either heads or tails of the word as it lacks clear meaning.[24] Estonian Canadian anticommunism activist Marcus Kolga suggested the name "conjures up images of unicorns, butterflies and little fluffy clouds."[25] As someone who speaks Estonian as a second language, it was hard for me to evaluate these allegations intuitively, but my interlocutors (mainly tech-savvy professionals and bureaucrats in their twenties and thirties) confirmed that the neologism's meaning is not clear on its face. One interlocutor strongly agreed the word has a casual and friendly "feel" to it, observing that it "sounds more like internet shorthand than a real name, you know like, 'pix from Vabamu, #suffering' on Twitter or something."

The issue was not just the name but the fact that *Vabamu* would be replacing and displacing the "Museum of Occupations," a name that plainly evidences Estonia's historical victimization at the hands of various foreign regimes. Helle Solnask, Deputy Chairman of the Estonian Heritage Society implied the name change amounted to hiding the horror of occupation behind a made-up word.[26] In a television interview broadcast on the Estonian public broadcasting channel, Leo Õispuu, the chairman of the Estonian Memento Union, suggested that if the museum's board was intent on renaming the museum, then they should consider "The Museum of Communist Crimes,"[27] suggesting that, at least for Õispuu, a suitable name was one that directly referred to the injuries suffered by Estonia and Estonians under Soviet rule, if not under the rule of the Nazis.

For Vabamu's proponents, critics' fixation on attacking the name *Vabamu* came at the expense of engagement with the actual changes planned at the museum and evidenced the hollowness of their critiques. In an interview with Radio 2 host Eeva Esse, Piipuu lamented that the public had focused on quarreling over the proposed name change at the expense of considering the central role occupations would continue to play as one of the museum's thematic foci. There were also substantive defenses of *Vabamu*. Sylvia Thompson explained that the name was preferable to the old one in part because the English the word *occupation* primarily refers to a line of work or vocation.[28] During the same interview, Kistler-Ritso Foundation board member Michael Keller tried to fend off the accusation that *Vabamu* was too abstract by pointing to the success of *MoMa* (the nickname used by the Museum of Modern Art in New York) and Estonia's modern art museum KuMu.[29]

At least two of Vabamu's opponents cited the Latin maxim *nomen est omen*— the name is a sign—in explaining their hostility to the museum's new moniker.[30] For these authors, the change from "Museum of Occupations" to "Vabamu" was problematic not just in and of itself, but also as a harbinger and symbol of the larger re-imagining of the museum. In an opinion piece distributed by Estonia's national public broadcaster, Rain Kooli observed that resounding in the name "Museum of Occupations" was "every lashing our ancestors have ever endured, every bloody suppressed uprising, every humiliation and every sneer."[31] The museum's name, Kooli asserted, is "symbiotically tied to nothing less than the entirety of our existence."[32] Thus, the debate surrounding the name change was so heated in part because wrapped up in it were much less concrete contestations about Estonian national identity and collective memory, or, to borrow Kooli's turn of phrase, "nothing less than the entirety of Estonian existence." The assurances offered by museum exponents, for example, that they'll actually increase the square footage dedicated to the occupation period and will have a whole room that looks like the inside of the railcars used in deportations, did little to assuage the fears of objectors who perceived Estonian national identity to be under attack.

The life histories of former dissidents such as Enn Tarto, who spent more than a dozen years in Soviet gulags, intersect with Estonian national history in profound ways, and those dissidents' opposition to Vabamu is undoubtedly informed by their personal experiences of violence, suffering, and barbarity at the hands of the Soviets. For many of Vabamu's critics, however, their perception of the museum as antagonistic to Estonian national memory and identity is likely informed as much by the central role that narratives of suffering and victimhood have historically played in the "authorized heritage discourses" of Estonian national identity as it is by their personal experiences of deprivation, suffering, or violence under occupation.[33] In Estonia, as elsewhere, "the cult of past martyrdoms and the awareness of contemporary dangers to national honor, sovereignty, and/or security are ... intertwined in a dynamic, ever-changing relationship."[34] One extension of this relationship is that suggestions by Vabamu's proponents that Estonia's national victimization is not unparalleled, should not be privileged to the total exclusion of personal histories that express individual happiness under occupation, and should be considered alongside post-Soviet Estonia's achievements is perceived as not just wrong, but also dangerous. The same self-reflexive and multivocal approaches to the past that Vabamu's proponents boast will enable Estonian youth to meaningfully engage with and learn from Estonia's history of occupation are perceived by Vabamu's critics as imperiling the significance and memory of that past. Helle Solnask's allegation that the museum's name change and reconceptualization threaten to "diminish the occupation era in Estonia" and Mart Helme's assertion that it "is our duty to remind our nation, its allies, and the rest of the world that we have been occupied and that suffering has been inflicted on us" are representative of such perceptions.[35]

Many of Vabamu's critics' arguments about the importance of recognizing victims, remembering atrocities, and condemning their perpetrators are reminiscent of those found in memory politics contestations in other parts of the world.[36] Running through critics' concerns about the dangers of forgetting the past and repeating history, however, were also two fairly Estonia-specific critiques of the proposed changes. First, several authors asserted that Vabamu grew out of a shortsighted excitement about Estonia's growing status as a leader in technology and e-governance. In their effort to celebrate Estonia's successes in the years since reindependence, these critics alleged, the museum's board was allowing the story of Estonia as an e-government leader and place of "freedom of entrepreneurship" to displace the more foundational account of Estonian survival and suffering. Second, some of Vabamu's critics argued that the museum's diminished emphasis on Estonian suffering and victimhood would not only attenuate its condemnation of communist atrocities but also play into the revisionist history of Putin's Russia. Before turning to some of the specific and applied contestations that grew out of the controversy surrounding Vabamu, I want to unpack both these interpretations and, in doing so, highlight the ways in which the controversy surrounding Vabamu is shaped by Estonia's historically particular relationship with both technological innovation and Russian representational regimes.

For some of Vabamu's critics, the unwelcome aspects of the museum's conceptualization are clearly linked to the ascendancy of the "e-Estonia" nation-building project, which they see as emphasizing Estonian innovation and technological futurism at the expense of engaging with and properly recognizing the past. In the years since its 1991 independence from the Soviet Union, and especially in the last decade, Estonia has established itself as a leader in e-governance and technological innovation. Estonian banks introduced electronic banking in 1996 and a few years later, a national electronic identity card was introduced. Estonians can vote, pay taxes, and check their health records online, and promoting Estonia's reputation as a leader in all things "e" has become an important part of the country's nation-branding efforts.

Responding to Sten Tamkivi's comments about Vabamu as a "start-up" of sorts, Jaak Jõerüüt asserted that "with all respect to those who work in the IT and start-up world, the notion of a 'thought world start-up' in this context is comically absurd."[37] Others saw the entire project, not just its framing as a start-up, as tied to "e-Estonia." In his provocatively titled opinion piece "Welcome to the e-Occupation Museum," Marcus Kolga argues that the Museum of Occupations is a casualty of the drive to frame Estonia as a technological leader: "e-Estonia's appetite to remember the evils of Nazi and Soviet terror has soured as the country marches toward the blinding shimmer of a start-up powered e-future."[38] Kolga's piece ran on Estonia's public news as well as on the blog of his media site UpNorth. Accompanying the piece on the UpNorth blog was an image of a smiling cartoon communist standing next to Vabamu; a large "Skype" logo has been tagged onto the side of the museum (fig. 14.4). Skype is an internet voice and video chat software that was developed by Estonian programmers in the early 2000s and remains a prominent symbol of Estonian national pride. In his commentary on the museum's planned changes, Markus Järvi similarly used Skype as shorthand for alluding to the narrative of Estonia as a leader in all things "e." Järvi suggests that for the "Vabamu crowd," remembering the deprivation and suffering of Estonians deported and murdered under communism is "totally *out*," and then mimicked the stance of the "Vabamu-ers" he was criticizing: "Come on, forget that suffering already! We are already in NATO and the American soldier boys want to die on our behalf so we can keep drinking coffee shop lattes and developing Skype."[39] Here, "drinking lattes" and "developing Skype" are symbols of vapid consumerism and an ahistorical celebration of Estonia's technological prowess. In Järvi's account, Vabamu is thus linked to the encroachment of new narrative of Estonia as a technological leader into an older and more central reading of Estonian identity.

The smiling communist giving a thumbs-up sign next to the Skype-branded Vabamu in the image illustrating Kolga's editorial alludes to another accusation

Figure 14.4. "Welcome to the e-occupation museum." *Used with permission*

lobbed at Vabamu by its critics: the rebranding of the Museum of Occupations as "Vabamu" helps rehabilitate Soviet crimes and plays into the Kremlin's delusional and dangerous assertion that Estonia's participation in the Soviet Union was voluntary. Russia's foreign ministry has previously criticized the Museum of Occupations for equating Nazism and communism and presenting the Soviet period as exclusively and unequivocally an unwelcome and illegal occupation.[40] Further, in the years since the Museum of Occupations opened, symbols of Soviet power, even those like Joseph Stalin that were once denounced for their connection to the communist atrocities, have come to play an important role in the contemporary national image of an increasingly bellicose and unpredictable Russia.[41] In this context, Vabamu's turn away from an exclusive and eponymic focus on occupations is perceived as not just political, but also geopolitical: a concession to a Russian representational regime that denies, or at the very least questions, the sovereignty and suffering of the Estonian people.

When former political prisoner and Estonian reindependence activist Enn Tarto, whose activism and political persecution under the Soviets are well documented in the Museum of Occupations, spoke out against the proposed changes on the national news, he suggested that the change would serve Russian political interests and noted that he had "heard many a communist shout that there was no occupation at all."[42] In this account, an unwavering and uncompromising commitment to articulating and disseminating a unified, strident, and consistent national narrative of illegal occupation is important in part because of the purchase and persistence of alternative versions of the past. The impenitent representational regime of Putin's Russia leaves little room for Estonian multivocality or self-reflexivity about collaboration. In his discussion of Vabamu, Marcus Kolga alleged that "Vladimir Putin and his legion of crypto-Soviet propagandists are no doubt licking their lips: the Estonians themselves are completing their work for them" and then provided an litany of the ways in which Putin has worked to deny the occupation of Estonia and embolden alternative readings of the Soviet past.[43] In these repeated gestures toward Putin and Russia, Vabamu's critics are concerned with how the refashioning of the museum would register in an international landscape where symbols and narratives from the Soviet past are relied on to rally support for a contemporary regime that denies the sovereignty of other post-Soviet states like Ukraine and Georgia. Collectively, their criticisms illustrate Assmann's argument that memory politics and heritage regimes operate at not just the national but also the transnational level.[44]

QUESTIONS OF MUSEUM PURPOSE, FUNCTION, AND PRACTICE

The debate surrounding the Museum of Occupations' rebranding involves not only questions about what it means to be Estonian but also questions about what the purpose, function, and intended audience of a museum that documents Estonia's painful past should be. In the rest of this chapter, I briefly highlight three sites of contention where issues of museum practice, management, and operations are implicated in the controversy surrounding Vabamu. The debates about by whom, for whom, and in what manner a contemporary Estonian museum of communism and occupations should operate illustrate the intersection of narrative and practice. They call our attention to the ways in which the controversy surrounding the substantive framing of Estonians' national identities and occupations' constitutive role in those identities is made manifest in, and indeed is partially coterminous with, fundamental questions about what the role of a museum of occupations in post-Soviet Estonia should be.

A Museum by Whom?

Olga Kistler-Ritso passed away in 2013 and her daughter Sylvia Thompson, a US citizen of Estonian descent, now presides over the Kistler-Ritso Foundation's board. Like many other private museums operating in Estonia, it receives some public support ($131,377 in 2014). The responsibility for its funding and management, however, falls on the board of the nonprofit Kistler-Ritso Foundation. When grilled about the proposed changes by members of the Estonian Parliament during a government briefing on March 16, 2016, Estonia's minister of culture Indrek Saar—whose ministry oversees public museums in Estonia—stressed that it is not the government's place to regulate museums owned and operated by private parties. During an interview with the Baltic News Service, museum director Piipuu similarly emphasized that because the museum is not a state institution, its board has the final say about its name and direction.[45]

Although even Vabamu's fiercest critics recognized the legal right of the private Kistler-Ritso Foundation to manage the museum in whatever manner it wishes, they often did so in a manner that called into question the equity and moral legitimacy of this absolute legal prerogative. "Whether it's a state museum or a privately operated museum," Ivo Visak observed, "a museum inevitably engages those on whose historical landscape it operates."[46] In other words, the museum might belong to the Kistler-Ritso Foundation, but the subject matter it represents and the stories it tells belongs to all Estonians who lived through the occupations.

Beyond just highlighting the public's stake in the museum's work and activities, some critics questioned the board's composition and the qualifications of its membership and president. For example, after pointing out the sewage-related jokes that arise from the similarity between Vabamu and *valamu* (the Estonian word for sink) and suggesting that those involved in the renaming had spent too much time abroad to have a good ear for the Estonian language, Mart Soidro notes that the ill-advised name change is unimpeachable legally speaking (*juriidiliselt on kõik korrektne*) because "Olga Kistler-Ritso invested 2.3 million Euros in the museum and after her death, decision-making power went to her daughter" and as a result "control over what happens to the museum now rests with a lady who lives across the pond."[47] Similar criticisms abounded. Betty Ester-Väljaots praised Olga Kistler-Ritso for not trying to "teach the home Estonians how they must talk about their past," implying Sylvia Thompson should learn from her mother's example. Õispuu described the museum's board as composed of businessmen or sponsors and Kolga complained that the dissidents and academics most closely linked, personally and professionally, to the period of the occupations had been expelled from the museum's board.[48] Thompson grew up as part of the Estonian diaspora in the United States and the board's Estonian members presumably spent some portion of their adolescence or early adulthood living in occupied Estonia. Unlike the museum's first director, Heikki Ahonen, however, none of the current board members are renowned as anti-Soviet political dissidents or victims of political persecution. Undergirding Ester-Väljaots, Õispuu, and Kolga's complaints then is the assertion that the expertise and qualifications necessary for representing and museologizing Estonia's history of occupation are not just professional, as in Kistler-Ritso board member Sten Tamkivi's background in business or board member Ott Sarapuu's experience with museum design, but personal: suffering and loss under the occupying regimes.

A Museum for Whom?

Years before the planned changes, one historian and former dissident involved in the conceptualization and the planning of the Museum of Occupations explained to Meike Wulf that the museum is "like a monument or a tombstone for the many people who have not returned." For those who returned, or never left Estonia, but lived through Estonia's occupations, the museum would, he continued, "be something to make them feel a little proud; that something like this is built for them."⁴⁹ The idea that the museum's primary beneficiaries are those who died during the occupations, who need a place to be memorialized, and those who suffered during the occupations, who need a place to reflect, is echoed in Igor Gräzin's assertion that the Museum of Occupations should not become "Vabamu" because it is Estonia's "only big memorial to the people who fell victim to the occupations.... We don't have anything else like it. It is a place where those who were repressed by the Soviets can come and reflect on their own fates and those of their fallen compatriots, knowing that their suffering and martyrdom are not forgotten."⁵⁰ Similar conceptions of the museum's core constituency are evident in Ivo Visak's assertion that the Museum of Occupations has become a "monument to the period it draws its name from" and Tunne Kelam's warning that it is degrading to the occupations' victims to strip their suffering of its prominent position in Estonian civic society.⁵¹

Vabamu's critics often privilege the suffering subject who has been victimized by the occupations as the museum's primary intended beneficiary, but the museum's exponents often explain the necessity of the proposed changes through reference to the needs of a very different demographic: Estonian youths who have no personal recollection of or experience with occupation whatsoever. In an op-ed written for Estonian Public Broadcasting after the museum changed its name, Piipuu argued that the museum would continue to remember the occupations but would do so by connecting them to freedom. This refashioning was necessary, she continued, because the museum needed to reach younger generations, "to make them understand the price we paid for the freedom that today is often taken for granted."⁵² Indrek Saar and Sylvia Thompson have both similarly appealed to the need to reframe and recontextualize the artifacts and stories presented in the museum for the benefit of those young people who have no personal memory of life in Soviet Estonia. The logic by which Vabamu's target audience is constructed is thus the mirror opposite of that undergirding descriptions of the museum as a monument or "something to make [those who suffered] feel a little proud." Estonian youths and schoolchildren are Vabamu's primary constituents not because of their memory or suffering, but because of their lack of it.

Museologization versus Memorialization

Inseparable from the question of the museum's target audience is that of the museum's fundamental nature and purpose. In an interview with Estonia's public television ETV, Piipuu alleged that Vabamu's critics had mistaken the museum for a monument. Estonia needed memorials for the victims of communism, but as a "contemporary, modern museum," Vabamu shouldn't be one. In other words, accessible programming that drew in and engaged guests on a variety of themes related to liberty was an appropriate modus operandi for Vabamu because it was a museum for visitors, not a monument for victims. Piipuu's contention points us to the ways in which the question of the museum's target audience is intricately intertwined with that of its mission and day-to-day functionality. What should the museum do and what types of activities and interactions with the past should it facilitate? At stake, then, in the conversations about Vabamu are not just issues of by and for whom a museum of occupations should be operated, but also issues of what a museum of occupations is and should do.

One evening while reading through opinion pieces about Vabamu in preparation for writing this chapter, I toggled over to Gmail for an e-mail break. Waiting in my inbox was a bulletin-board message about a Stanford campus lecture that was coming up on November 7, 2016, "From the Narrative of Suffering to the Value of Freedom," by Merilin Piipuu. I would still be in Tallinn, but at a lunchtime hour, one of the key players in the controversy surrounding the Museum of Occupations would be addressing what it means to "rebuild a museum within the memory landscape of a former Soviet Union republic" on my home institution's campus. Piipuu's biography was featured on the event website, and the first sentence caught my eye: "As the Managing Director of the Museum of Occupations in Tallinn, Estonia, Merilin Piipuu's main task is to turn the museum into a must-see destination for the people of Estonia as well as for the visitors of the country." The idea that the museum's poor visitation numbers necessitate the museum's revamping runs through many of proponents' defenses of the museum's refashioning, but the biography's use of the phrase "must-see destination" made clear for me, in a way that the appeals to the museum's low visitation had not, the ways in which the museum imagined by Vabamu's proponents was a fundamentally different type of institution than the Museum of Occupations. Although the latter presumes to be a museum one *must see* by virtue of its gravitas and the moral imperative to remember the crimes of the past, the former hopes to be a "must-see" destination by virtue of its attractions, activities, and community outreach. Vabamu endeavors to, at the very least, supplement the moral imperative of "must see" with the vibrancy and contemporary relevance implicit in "must-see."

Writing in defense of the Museum of Occupations and against Vabamu, Igor Gräzin explicitly attacked the idea that a museum's visitor metrics are a suitable measure of its merit or worth:

> The Vabamu supporters reveal their deep misunderstanding of culture, memory, and the nation in their assertion that as a result of its sad name the museum has few visitors. We should ask then, does the fact that fewer

than a thousand people have read *Kalevipoeg* [the Estonian national epic] mean that we should stop printing it and build a casino in the place of the Kreutzwald museum [a museum commemorating Kalevipoeg's compiler Friedrich Reinhold Kreutzwald]? The Museum of Occupations' value is not found in how many people visit it, but in the fact that it exists.[53]

Gräzin rejects not just the use of visitation numbers as a heuristic measure of museum success, but also the crowd-pleasing public engagement he fears the new museum will use to attract guests. If the museum becomes a place for political dialogue or a center for "hipster guitar playing and poetry readings," he reasons, it will cease to be a "sacred space for commemoration." Gräzin is not alone in the concern that focusing on community outreach will detract from the museum's putative main mission of documenting Estonia's painful past. Soidro preemptively ridicules Vabamu for warehousing the most atrocious artifacts of occupation, for example, the shackles and blood-stained clothing of political prisoners, so that mainstream thought leaders and citizen activists can have a "warm place where they can squat among themselves and organize festivals."[54] In this reading, the museum board's well-intentioned plans to remake the museum as a hub where youths come to learn about the Estonian past and contemplate its relevance to the present are reframed as a threat to the sanctity of national suffering. At issue are national narratives, yes, but also the practices and modes of embodied engagement with the past that Vabamu will facilitate through its programming. Gräzin rejects Vabamu's move away from a rigid narrative of Estonian suffering, but he also recognizes that this move is not just discursive, it is embodied in the hypothesized squatting of festival-goers and the feared displacement of victims and former political dissidents in favor of citizen activists and "mainstream thought leaders."

CONCLUSION

The spring 2016 announcement that the Museum of Occupations would become the Museum of Freedoms and that its historically singular focus on the occupations would be augmented (or diluted) by an engagement with the themes of resistance, restoration, and freedom generated an outcry that reverberated through Estonian public media for weeks. Though the museum's board and its critics are united by the conviction that it is important to continue talking about, researching, and museologizing the occupations, they disagree about how, by whom, and for whom this undertaking should be carried out. The museum's board and staff see expanding the museum's scope and connecting its collections to issues of contemporary social relevance as a way to engage a generation that has no personal memories of occupation. For Vabamu's critics, the same efforts represent an affront to those who do have personal memories of the occupation and the suffering it engendered. Since victimization and suffering at the hands of the Nazis and Soviets, but especially the Soviets, are an important of how many Estonians understand their national history and make sense of what it means to be Estonian, the museum's plans to deemphasize those aspects of the occupations by presenting them alongside stories that speak about resistance, restoration, and freedom were perceived by many as both misguided and dangerous. Some of the explanations offered for this belief were relatively specific to the Estonian context, for example, the contention that the proposed changes are linked to a misplaced enthusiasm about "e-Estonia" or will play into Russian neo-imperialism.

Implicated in the disagreement about how contemporary Estonian memory culture should relate to and conceptualize the occupations were several more pragmatic and functional disagreements about by whom, for whom, and to what end a museum of occupations should operate. These contestations call our attention to the fact that though the "memory politics" surrounding Vabamu are about discourse and narrative, they grow out of competing ideas about the role a museum like Vabamu ought to play in a postcommunist society. The reconceptualization of the Museum of Occupations as Vabamu can thus be read as a shift away from the model of a museum as an authoritative collection-based site managed by and consecrated for those who suffered under communism toward a model of the museum as a civic society organization or, to borrow James Clifford's formulation, a "contact zone," in which the museum's "organizing structure as a collection becomes an ongoing historical, political, moral relationship––a power-charged set of exchanges, of push and pull."[55]

In his introductory remarks at the press conference announcing the Museum of Occupations' transformation and rebranding, President Ilves suggested that freedom was being able to act and speak according to one's own will. During the question-and-answer session that followed the press conference, Mari-Ann Kelam—a member of the Estonian Parliament born in a German displaced persons' camp and raised in the United States—challenged his definition. Freedom, she asserted isn't "just about doing what you want, there's an important other side to it: responsibility." Living in Estonia, she continued, meant not just enjoying the liberties that come with life in a peaceful and democratic country but also shouldering the responsibility of working to make society better. The reconceptualization of the Museum of Occupations as Vabamu, Kelam feared, would hurt the museum's ability to educate visitors about this Janus face of freedom, about the duties that come along with liberty.

Kelam's linkage of freedom and responsibility resonates with the treatment of freedom offered by former Estonian president Lennart Meri at the opening of the Museum of Occupations in June 2003. The museum, Meri asserted "is no house of hatred, for it is our house of victory, our house of freedom. It makes us shoulder a heavy burden of responsibility, for it is our duty to protect our people and to defend Europe from the mistakes that have already exacted such a high cost." In both instances, freedom is not merely the sum of various liberal democratic rights, but rather a precondition for collective agency and responsibility.

Though some of Vabamu's critics were undoubtedly opportunistic in stoking the controversy surrounding the museum for personal political gain, many of the opinion pieces commenting on or decrying the change at the museum have, like Mari-Ann Kelam's comment, thoughtfully, if at times polemically, engaged with the question of what it means to be free of occupation without forgetting or dismissing the horrors and suffering it brought. In one way or another, many of the issues and debates connected to the reconceptualization of the Museum of Occupations touch on or intersect with the very questions Vabamu aspires to provoke dialogue about: How is a private organization's freedom of speech functionally circumscribed by the moral and political claims of other social actors? What type of engagement with the communist past will best ensure its horrors are never again repeated in Estonia? Without even opening its doors, Vabamu has emerged a site of discussion about the meaning and limits of occupation and freedom in post-Soviet Estonia.

NOTES

1. Mart Helme, "Okupatsiooni rehabiliteerimine ehk orwelliku maailma orjade vabariik," *Uued Uudised* (blog), April 14, 2016, https://uueduudised.ee/arvamus/mart-helme-okupatsiooni-rehabiliteerimine-ehk-orwelliku-maailma-orjade-vabarii/.

2. Jaak Jõerüüt, "Idee toppida vabadus ühte muuseumisse ja hakata seda seal arendama on absurdne," *Postimees: Arvamus*, April 4, 2016, https://arvamus.postimees.ee/3642085/jaak-joeruut-idee-toppida-vabadus-uhte-muuseumisse-ja-hakata-seda-seal-arendama-on-absurdne.

3. See Külli-Riin Tigasson, "'Vabamu' kõlab nagu 'kumu'!," *Eesti Ekspress*, April 20, 2016, Commentary, http://www.delfi.ee/a/74272035; Merilin Piipuu, "Remembering the Occupations Will Remain at the Heart of the Museum," *ERR, Estonian Public Broadcasting*, February 25, 2016, Opinion, http://news.err.ee/v/opinion/5c1c822f-a829-4b22-8577-658b5276e304/merilin-piipuu-remembering-the-occupations-will-remain-at-the-heart-of-the-museum; and Piipuu, "Okupatsioonidest Vabaduseni," *Õhtuleht*, March 7, 2016, http://m.ohtuleht.ee/721556/okupatsioonide-muuseumi-tegevdirektor-okupatsioonidest-vabaduseni.

4. See Tony Judt, "The Past Is Another Country: Myth and Memory in Postwar Europe," *Theoria* 87 (June 1996): 36–69; Jan-Werner Müller, ed., *Memory and Power in Post-war Europe: Studies in the Presence of the Past* (Cambridge: Cambridge University Press, 2002); Alexander Etkind, "Post-Soviet Hauntology: Cultural Memory of the Soviet Terror," *Constellations* 16, no. 1 (2009): 182–200; Aleida Assmann, "Europe:

A Community of Memory," *German Historical Institute Bulletin*, no. 40 (2007): 11–25; Meike Wulf, *Shadowlands: Memory and History in Post-Soviet Estonia* (New York: Berghahn, 2016).

5. Epp Annus, "The Problem of Soviet Colonialism in the Baltics," *Journal of Baltic Studies* 43, no. 1 (2012): 21–45; David Chioni Moore, "Is the *Post-* in *Postcolonial* the *Post-* in *Post-Soviet*? Toward a Global Postcolonial Critique," *Publications of the Modern Language Association* 116, no. 1 (2001): 111–28; Violeta Kelertas, *Baltic Postcolonialism* (Amsterdam: Rodopi, 2006); Piret Peiker, "Estonian Nationalism through the Postcolonial Lens," *Journal of Baltic Studies* 47, no. 1 (2016): 113–32.

6. See, for example, Nayanika Mookherjee, "'Never Again': Aesthetics of 'Genocidal' Cosmopolitanism and the Bangladesh Liberation War Museum," *Journal of the Royal Anthropological Institute* 17 (May 2011): S71–91; Laurie Beth Clark, "Never Again and Its Discontents," *Performance Research* 16, no. 1 (2011): 68–79; and Brandon Hamber, "Conflict Museums, Nostalgia, and Dreaming of Never Again," *Peace and Conflict: Journal of Peace Psychology* 18, no. 3 (2012): 268–81.

7. Meike Wulf, "The Struggle for Official Recognition of 'Displaced' Group Memories in Post-Soviet Estonia," in *Past in the Making: Historical Revisionism in Central Europe after 1989*, ed. Michal Kopecek (Budapest: Central European University Press, 2013), 217–41; Jörg Hackmann and Marko Lehti, "Myth of Victimhood and Cult of Authenticity: Sacralizing the Nation in Estonia and Poland," in *Rethinking the Space for Religion: New Actors in Central and Southeast Europe on Religion, Authenticity and Belonging*, ed. Catharina Raudvere, Krzysztof Stala, and Trine Stauning Willert (Lund, Sweden: Nordic Academic Press), 151.

8. Aro Velmet, "Occupied Identities: National Narratives in Baltic Museums of Occupations," *Journal of Baltic Studies* 42, no. 2 (2011): 202.

9. Paul Oliver Stocker, *Trauma, Memory and Victimhood: Estonia and the Holocaust, 1998–2012*, PhD diss., West Virginia University, 2013; Velmet, "Occupied Identities."

10. The camp at Klooga is mentioned, but it is called a labor camp and the museum spotlights someone saying that people housed there were able to leave to visit nearby villages (Velmet, "Occupied Identities," 197).

11. Meelis Maripuu, "Eesti Juutide Holokaust Ja Eestlased," *Vikerkaar* 8, no. 9 (2001): 135–47.

12. See Flora E. S. Kaplan, *Museums and the Making of "Ourselves": The Role of Objects in National Identity* (Leicester, UK: Leicester University Press, 1996); Fiona McLean, "Museums and the Construction of National Identity: A Review," *International Journal of Heritage Studies* 3, no. 4 (1998): 244–52; J. M. Fladmark, *Heritage and Museums: Shaping National Identity* (Routledge, 2015). Nelson Graburn, "A Quest for Identity," in *Museums and Their Communities*, ed. Sheila Watson (London: Routledge, 2007), 129. Lorena Rivera Orraca, "Are Museums Sites of Memory?" *New School Psychology Bulletin* 6, no. 2 (2009): 32 (emphasis in original).

13. Toomas Hiio, "Soviet Military Preparations in Estonia during the Year before Barbarossa," in *Northern European Overture to War 1939–1941: From Memel to*

Barbarossa, ed. Michael H. Clemmesen and Marcus S. Faulkner (Leiden: Brill, 2013), 407.

14. Karsten Brüggemann and Andres Kasekamp, "The Politics of History and the 'War of Monuments' in Estonia," *Nationalities Papers* 36, no. 3 (2008): 426; Siobhan Kattago, "Commemorating Liberation and Occupation: War Memorials along the Road to Narva," *Journal of Baltic Studies* 39, no. 4 (2008): 432.

15. Serguei Oushakine, "Postcolonial Estrangements: Claiming a Space between Stalin and Hitler," in *Rites of Place: Public Commemoration in Russia and Eastern Europe* (Evanston, IL: Northwestern University Press, 2013): 287.

16. Ibid.

17. See Maja Musi, "The International Heritage Doctrine and the Management of Heritage in Sarajevo, Bosnia and Herzegovina: The Case of the Commission to Preserve National Monuments," *International Journal of Heritage Studies* 20, no. 1 (2014): 54–71; Trudy Govier, *Victims and Victimhood* (Peterborough, Ontario: Broadview, 2014), 56–67; and Sara McDowell, "Time Elapsed: Untangling Commemorative Temporalities after Conflict and Tragedy," *Journal of War and Culture Studies* 6, no. 3 (2013): 185–200.

18. Aleida Assmann, *Der lange Schatten der Vergangenheit: Erinnerungskultur und Geschichtspolitik* (Munich: C. H. Beck, 2006), 76–78; G. J. Ashworth, "The Memorialization of Violence and Tragedy: Human Trauma as Heritage," in *The Ashgate Research Companion to Heritage and Identity*, ed. Brian J. Graham and Peter Howard (Burlington, VT: Ashgate, 2008), 231.

19. David Lowenthal, *The Heritage Crusade and the Spoils of History* (Cambridge: Cambridge University Press, 1998), 75.

20. "Sylvia Thompson Order of the Cross of Terra Mariana Award Acceptance Speech," February 27, 2016.

21. Ibid.

22. Piipuu, "Okupatsioonidest Vabaduseni."

23. Helen Wright, "Hope and Freedom: Remembering Estonia's Occupations," *Estonian World* (blog), September 24, 2015, http://estonianworld.com/life/hope-and-freedom-remembering-estonias-occupations/.

24. Jõerüüt, "Idee toppida vabadus ühte muuseumisse."

25. Marcus Kolga, "Welcome to the e-Occupation Museum," *ERR, Estonian Public Broadcasting*, February 22, 2016, Opinion, http://news.err.ee/v/opinion/323cddeb-fffb-4d9b-966f-26c64d870f34/marcus-kolga-welcome-to-the-e-occupation-museum.

26. Helle Solnask, "Miks pälvis Okupatsioonide muuseum karuteene medali?," *Õhtuleht*, April 20, 2016, Opinion, http://www.ohtuleht.ee/728661/kusimus-miks-palvis-okupatsioonide-muuseum-karuteene-medali.

27. Maria-Ann Rohemäe, "Kommunismiohvrid taunivad Okupatsioonide muuseumi uut nime." *ERR, Estonian Public Broadcasting*, March 27, 2016, http://uudised.err.ee/v/eesti/10055fee-0fb4-4880-ba08-01d0dfc23e92/kommunismiohvrid-taunivad-okupatsioonide-muuseumi-uut-nime.

28. Tigasson, "'Vabamu' kõlab nagu 'kumu'!"

29. Ibid.

30. Igor Gräzin, "Okupatsioonimuuseumi fantoom," *Õhtuleht*, March 14, 2016, Arvamus, http://www.ohtuleht.ee/722596/igor-grazin-okupatsioonimuuseumi-fantoom; Jõerüüt, "Idee toppida vabadus ühte muuseumisse."

31. Rain Kooli, "Okupatsioonist vabad või vabadusega okupeeritud?," *Uudised*, April 11, 2016, http://uudised.err.ee/v/arvamus/ca2a1893-1258-4791-b215-f9771b7c9d7a/rain-kooli-okupatsioonist-vabad-voi-vabadusega-okupeeritud.

32. Ibid.

33. Laurajane Smith, *The Uses of Heritage* (New York: Routledge, 2006), 29–34.

34. Aviel Roshwald, *The Endurance of Nationalism: Ancient Roots and Modern Dilemmas* (Cambridge: Cambridge University Press, 2006), 122.

35. Solnask,"Miks pälvis Okupatsioonide muuseum karuteene medali?"; Helme, "Okupatsiooni rehabiliteerimine ehk orwelliku maailma orjade vabariik."

36. James Joseph Orr, *The Victim As Hero: Ideologies of Peace and National Identity in Postwar Japan* (Honolulu: University of Hawaii Press, 2001); Ross MacDonald and Monica C. Bernardo, "The Politics of Victimhood: Historical Memory and Peace in Spain and the Basque Region," *Journal of International Affairs* 60, no. 1 (2006): 173–96; Laura Jeffery, "Victims and Patrons: Strategic Alliances and the Anti-politics of Victimhood among Displaced Chagossians and Their Supporters," *History and Anthropology* 17, no. 4 (2006): 297–312.

37. Jõerüüt, "Idee toppida vabadus ühte muuseumisse."

38. Kolga, "Welcome to the E-Occupation Museum."

39. Markus Järvi, "Meie reliikvia on Vabamu?," *Objektiiv* (blog), April 7, 2016, http://objektiiv.ee/meie-reliikvia-on-vabamu/.

40. Michael Tarm, "The Gift: Olga Ritso and Estonia's New Occupation Museum," *City Paper: The Baltic States*, March 14, 2004, http://www.balticsworldwide.com/occupation%20_%20museum%20_%20tallinn.htm; James Mark, "Containing Fascism : History in Post-communist Baltic Occupation and Genocide Museums," in *Past for the Eyes: East European Representations of Communism in Cinema and Museums after 1989*, ed. Oksana Sarkisova and Péter Apor (Budapest: Central European University Press, 2008), 360.

41. Dina Khapaeva, "Triumphant Memory of the Perpetrators: Putin's Politics of Re-Stalinization," in "Between Nationalism, Authoritarianism, and Fascism in Russia: Exploring Vladimir Putin's Regime," ed. Taras Kuzio, special issue, *Communist and Post-communist Studies* 49, no. 1 (2016): 61–73; see also Thomas Sherlock, "Russian Politics and the Soviet Past: Reassessing Stalin and Stalinism under Vladimir Putin," in "Between Nationalism, Authoritarianism, and Fascism in Russia: Exploring Vladimir Putin's Regime," ed. Taras Kuzio, special issue, *Communist and Post-communist Studies* 49, no. 1 (2016): 45–59.

42. Quoted in Mirko Ojakivi, "Enn Tarto on okupatsioonide muuseumi nimemuutmise vastu," *ERR, Estonian Public Broadcasting*, February 21, 2016,

http://uudised.err.ee/v/eesti/d8d9b804-b657-40ec-8d26-3152c9cf0e55
/enn-tarto-on-okupatsioonide-muuseumi-nimemuutmise-vastu.

43. Kolga, "Welcome to the e-Occupation Museum."

44. Aleida Assmann, "Transnational Memories," *European Review* 22, no. 4 (2014): 546–56; Aleida Assmann and Sebastian Conrad, introduction to *Memory in a Global Age: Discourses, Practices and Trajectories*, ed. Assmann and Conrad (New York: Palgrave Macmillan, 2010), 1–16.

45. Baltic News Service, "Direktor: Poliitika ei tohiks mõjutada okupatsioonimuuseumi nime," *Postimees*, March 10, 2016, http://www.postimees.ee/3613503
/direktor-poliitika-ei-tohiks-mojutada-okupatsioonimuuseumi-nime.

46. Ivo Visak, "'Okupatsioonide' asendamine 'vabamu' mõistega on häirivalt kafkalik," *Postimees: Arvamus*, March 28, 2016, https://arvamus.postimees.ee/3633883
/ivo-visak-okupatsioonide-asendamine-vabamu-moistega-on-hairivalt-kafkalik.

47. Mart Soidro, "Hundid söönud, lambad murtud?," *Meie Maa*, March 1, 2016, Opinion, https://www.meiemaa.ee/index.php?content=artiklid&sub=2&artid=69022.

48. Rohemäe, "Kommunismiohvrid taunivad Okupatsioonide muuseumi uut nime"; Kolga, "Welcome to the e-Occupation Museum."

49. Meike Wulf, "Politics of History in Estonia: Changing Memory Regimes 1987–2009," *History of Communism in Europe* no. 1 (2010), 250.

50. Gräzin, "Okupatsioonimuuseumi fantoom."

51. Visak, "'Okupatsioonide' asendamine 'vabamu' mõistega on häirivalt kafkalik"; Tunne Kelam, "Okupatsioonide muuseumist ei peaks saama paik, kuhu noored lähevad mõnusalt aega veetma," *Postimees: Arvamus*, https://arvamus.postimees
.ee/3597669/tunne-kelam-okupatsioonide-muuseumist-ei-peaks-saama-paik-kuhu
-noored-lahevad-monusalt-aega-veetma.

52. Piipuu, "Remembering the Occupations."

53. Gräzin, "Okupatsioonimuuseumi fantoom."

54. Soidro, "Hundid Söönud, Lambad Murtud?"

55. James Clifford, "Museums as Contact Zones," in *Routes: Travel and Translation in the Late Twentieth Century*, ed. James Clifford (Cambridge, MA: Harvard University Press. 1997), 192–93.

A. LORRAINE WEEKES received her PhD in the Department of Anthropology at Stanford University. Her research ethnographically examines Estonian e-government and its effects on the pursuit and enactment of citizenship, nationalism, and state sovereignty.

INDEX

Abashin, Sergei, 380–81, 389
Abene, Aija, 138
Act on Judicial Rehabilitations (1990), 225
Act on the Illegality of the Communist Regime and on the Resistance To It (1993), 226
affect, affective ideology, 7, 27–29, 36–38, 124, 127, 181, 186n57, 227, 265n16, 356
Ahonen, Heikki, 415
Akhmatova, Anna, 129
Alash Orda, 111, 121
Aleksii II, Patriarch, 307, 309, 310, 313
Alexander I, 137, 139
Alphen, Ernst van, 206
Alzhir Museum (Museum Memorial Complex of Victims of Political Repression and Totalitarianism 'ALZhIR'), 110–11, 118–27, 131n6, 134n34, 135n44
Amalrik, Andrei, 294
Amar, Tarik Cyril, 88, 93, 97, 102n43
ambiguity in museums, 37, 60, 316, 326, 345, 378, 392–94
Ames, Michael, 377
Anderson, Benedict, 181
anticommunism, anticommunist, 48–51, 53–55, 69, 70, 83, 224–27, 229, 231, 235, 409
Antonov-Ovseenko, Anton Vladimirovich, 279–80, 296
Anušauskas, Arvydas, 36
Applebaum, Anne, 52–53, 110–11

Arendt, Hannah, 127, 227
Arnold-de Simine, Silke, 251–52, 263
Arrow Cross, 55–56, 59–62, 66
Ashworth, G. J., 407
Assmann, Aleida, 296, 350, 407, 414
Association of Victims of Political Repressions, 308
Astra, Gunārs, 138
archives, 10, 25, 93, 219, 260, 281, 289, 355
artifacts, 3, 7, 8, 27, 79, 112–13, 122, 123, 196–99, 202–3, 204, 219, 221, 222, 228–34, 280, 283–85, 286, 289–91, 297, 346, 375, 380, 403–5, 408, 416, 418
artwork, 118, 121, 123–25, 207, 231, 290, 323, 339n11, 349, 401, 402, 410
"Astak" (organization), 259–60
Atari, 347
"Attraction-71" exhibition, 348
August War (Russo-Georgian War, 2008), 380, 397
Auschwitz, 116, 127, 191, 333n45, 336n75

Bach, Jonathan, 216, 263
Bagais gads (see Year of Horror)
Bakūnas, Algirdas, 23, 38n1
Baldaev, Danzig, 290
Bandera, Stepan, 15, 79, 82, 87–93, 96, 99n13, 101n38
Barnes, Amy Jane, 220, 222, 227, 233, 234
Bartel, Kazimierz, 94, 96

425

Battleship Arcade game, USSR, 351, 353, 359
Baudrillard, Jean, 359–60
Becker, Wolfgang, 246, 247, 249–50, 260, 261
Belomor Canal, 286, 291
Beneš, Edvard, 223, 224
Berdahl, Daphne, 252–53, 265n15
Beria, Lavrentiy, 29, 385
Berlin (*see* DDR Museum, Berlin)
Berlin-Hohenschönhausen Memorial, 246, 249, 250–51
Berlin Wall, 224, 245, 247, 248, 253, 257, 262, 263
Bernstein, Charles, 357
Besançon, Alain, 52–53, 54
Białoszewski, Miron, 157–59
Bielecki, Czesław, 55
Bitutckii, Viacheslav, 313
"black boards," 196
Bloodlands (*see also* Timothy Snyder), 82, 159
Book of Memory, Kyiv, 193
Bortnyk, Rostyslav, 207
Bourdieu, Pierre, 234, 235
Branitsky, Tamara, 83–84
Brezhnev, Leonid, 292, 350
Brīvības iela (*see* Freedom Street)
Brooks, David, 356
Brüggemann, Karsten, 406
Brygidki Prison (L'viv), 83
Brzezinski, Zbigniew, 54, 74n30
Bukharin, Nikolai, 122, 385
Bukarina, Anna Larina, 122
Bukovsky, Vladimir, 53, 55
Butovskii Shooting Range (Butovo Memorial Research-Education Center), 272, 294, 305–43
Butyrka Prison, 281, 283, 299

Central Lenin Museum, Moscow, 2–4, 5, 6, 7, 9
Čepaitienė, Rasa, 27–28
Cepickova, Jana, 234–35
Charter 77, 224
Chavchavadze, Ilia, 384–85
Checkpoint Charlie, 260, 263
cheka (*Chrezvychainaia Komissiia*, Soviet political police), 139–40, 141–43
Cheka House (Corner House), Riga, 20, 137–55

Chiger, Krystyna, 94–95
children, childhood, 4, 8, 34–37, 43n54, 56, 69–70, 83–84, 95, 112, 169, 173–74, 175, 181, 192, 196, 203, 248, 249, 255–56, 260, 262, 297, 345–46, 347, 348–49, 351–59, 365, 384, 408, 416
Chornovil, Viacheslav, 90–91
Chukotka, 283, 291
Church of the Russian Holy New Martyrs and Confessors, 307, 310
civil society, 190, 239n43, 276–79, 294, 295, 296, 299n13, 306, 307–9, 311, 315, 318, 321, 325, 327, 402
Clifford, James, 419
Cold War, 47, 48, 232, 233–34, 352
comics, 175–77, 181
commodification (of communist past), 7, 128, 228–34, 235–36, 346–47
computers and computer science in the USSR, 349
Corner House, Riga (*see* Cheka House)
Courtois, Stéphane, 53, 55, 59
Crane, Susan, 5
crimes against humanity, 42n45, 69, 145, 204, 226
critics, criticism, 11, 12, 15n45, 20, 26, 39n10, 53–54, 55, 58–59, 61–62, 69–70, 115–16, 152, 175, 179–80, 181, 201, 203, 207, 232, 246–50, 251, 260–61, 347, 392, 403, 409–16, 418–20
Crowley, David, 232–33
Czech Republic, Czechoslovakia (*see* Museum of Communism, Prague)
Czechoslovak Communist Party, 223–26

Dahl, G. B., 388
"Dandy" video games, 349
Daniel', Aleksandr, 336n79
Daniel, Yuli, 295
Day of Mourning and Hope, Lithuania, 24, 34, 38nn3–4
Day of Occupation and Genocide, Lithuania, 23, 24, 26, 38n3
"death tourism," 21
De Bruyn, Dieter, 176
de Peuter, Greig, 346
democratization, 130, 223, 316, 375, 419–20

deportations, deportees, 24, 25, 26–28, 30, 34–37, 41n24, 43nn47–48, 43n51, 50, 59, 61, 66, 112, 121, 167, 200, 320, 402, 406–7, 410, 412
Dianina, Katia, 5
dissidents, 27, 28, 53, 55, 91, 138, 224–25, 233, 248, 251, 275, 277–79, 294–95, 297, 410, 415, 418
Day of Remembrance of the Victims of Political Prisoners, 277–78, 281
DDR (see GDR)
DDR Museum, Berlin, 216, 231, 245–69
Doctors' Plot, 287, 293, 295
Dolinka, 107, 112, 113, 117–18, 130n4
"double victimization" (also "double genocide") narrative, 9–10, 19, 26, 39n10, 61
Dovlatov, Sergei, 1, 5, 7, 12
Drakulić, Slavenka, 7–8, 9, 221
Draper, Susana, 294
Dreimane, Inese, 138, 147
Drieselmann, Jörg, 259, 263
Druzhba cheese, 350
Dubravnyi Corrective-Labor Camp, 294
Dyer-Witheford, Nick, 346
Dzerzhinsky, Felix, 142
Dzieduszycka-Ziemilska, Małgorzata, 179–80

"e-Estonia," 412, 419
East Germany (see GDR)
Edkins, Jenny, 276, 289, 300n26
Eichmann Trial (1961), 95, 227
Elis, Angela, 245–46, 260
Ester-Väljaots, Betty, 415
ethnocentric narratives, problems of, 199–204
Etkind, Alexander, 11, 96, 111, 272, 276–77, 296, 300n21, 300n29, 326
European Commission, 137
European Union (EU), 47–49, 69, 137
everyday life, 11–12, 35, 67, 126, 166, 196, 202, 215–16, 227, 228, 230–32, 233, 246–47, 251–53, 255–56, 259–61, 263, 267n28, 271–72, 291, 346, 351
Eyal, Gil, 228, 239n43

famine (see Ukrainian famine, 1932–33; Holodomor)
FED camera, USSR, 351, 353
Fedorova, Evgeniia, 287, 295

Fedotov, Mikhail, 319, 320, 325, 326, 337n82, 338n93
Fiedler, Milena, 177, 178
Fighter arcade game, 353, 361, 362
Flige, Irina, 321
folk museums on the socialist way of life, Russia, 346
Foucault, Michel, 87, 100n21, 201
freedom, 15, 24, 25, 33, 37, 56, 80, 97, 111, 120, 123–24, 170–71, 182, 226, 245, 254, 283, 375, 402–3, 407–8, 416, 417, 418–20
Freedom Street, Riga, 137–39
FSB, Federal Security Service, 307, 308, 318, 325
Fulbrook, Mary, 262–63, 264n5
Funder, Anna, 246, 261

gangs (Gulag), 291
Ganina Yama, Yekaterinburg, 310
Gar'kavyi, Igor', 312, 324, 326, 341n133
GDR (German Democratic Republic, see also DDR Museum), 6, 74, 216, 231, 245–63, 265n15, 266n21, 267n28
genocide (see also "double victimization"; Holodomor), 9, 11, 20, 23, 24, 25–27, 36, 39n10, 53, 158, 190, 191, 199, 202–6, 226, 275, 298n2, 271, 404
Georgia, Georgian Soviet Socialist Republic (see Joseph Stalin State Museum, Gori)
Gestapo, 25, 28–29, 41n30, 80, 83–84, 94, 96, 153n3
Getman, Nikolai, 290
Goliash, Grygorii, 80
Good Bye, Lenin! (2003 film), 246, 247–50, 260, 261, 263, 265n16, 266n21, 267n28
Gorbachev, Mikhail, 6, 275–76, 278, 316, 349
Gori, 1, 12, 375–76, 380, 384, 385, 390, 391, 396n4
Gorky, Maxim, 291
Gorky Park, Moscow, 348
Graburn, Nelson, 406
Gräzin, Igor, 416, 417–18
Great Patriotic War (see World War II)
Gromov, Boris, 312, 335n65
Gross, Jan, 103n54, 182
Grybauskaitė, Dalia, 23–24
Gudkov, Lev, 279
Great Terror, 110, 118, 281, 283–84, 290, 293, 295

guided tour, tour guides, 4, 7–8, 80, 113, 117, 121, 132n18, 138, 144, 146, 198, 281, 283, 364, 378, 382, 384–85, 388, 390, 392
Gulag, 27–30, 34, 36, 60, 66, 107–35, 145, 192, 251, 272, 275–303, 309, 312, 316, 319, 320, 327, 329n6, 378, 392, 410

Hackman, Jörg, 406
Halbwachs, Maurice, 352
Hall of Memory, Kyiv, 193–94, 198–99
Havel, Vaclav, 224, 225, 233–34
Hein, Hilde, 64
Helme, Mart, 403, 411
Helsinki-86, 149–50
Hilberg, Raul, 52
Himka, John-Paul, 82–83, 87, 88, 99n20, 104n57
Hiroshima, 191, 195
Hirsch, Marianne, 227
Hitler, Adolf, 137, 164, 223, 271
Holocaust, 11, 14n36, 26–27, 28, 29, 47–48, 49, 50, 52, 54, 55, 56, 59–60, 65, 67, 69–70, 87, 94, 95, 115, 163, 182, 203–4, 205, 227, 277, 402
Holocaust denial, Holocaust negationism, 50, 87, 92, 182
Holocaust Museum (*see* United States Holocaust Memorial Museum)
Holodomor, 92, 189–213
Horokh, Mykola, 197, 210n19
House of Terror, Budapest, 20, 47–77, 143
Howes, David, and "sensory museology," 168
Hubatova-Vackova, Lada, 231–32
Hung, Chang-Tai, 5
Hungarian Revolution (1956), 49–51, 60, 63, 67, 224
Hungary (*see* House of Terror)

ideology, 5, 7, 27–28, 34, 36–38, 54, 56, 62, 63, 143, 221–22, 234, 252, 266n21, 298, 324, 327, 337n85, 346, 348, 350, 356, 376–78, 380–81, 384, 389, 391, 392, 394, 396n6
Ihász, István, 58, 64
Ilves, Toomas Hendrik, 401–2, 419
Institute of Demography at the National Academy of Science of Ukraine, 207
Institute of National Memory, Ukraine, 10, 15n45, 88, 92, 93

Institute of National Remembrance (IPN), Poland, 10
International Slavery Museum (Liverpool), 290

Jaago, Tiiu, 408
James Bond, 233–34
Jameson, Frederic, 350
Janion, Maria, 181
Jankowski, Jan Stanisław, 170
Janowska Concentration Camp, 95–96
Jedwabne, "Jedwabne syndrome," 96, 182, 333n48
Jews, 9, 13n28, 14n36, 19, 26, 36, 50, 59, 60, 61, 62, 67, 73, 83–85, 87–88, 92, 94–95, 99n20, 103n57, 139, 148, 149, 167, 178, 182, 183n9, 202, 206, 287, 293, 310, 333n48
Jõerüüt, Jaak, 403, 409, 412
John Paul II, Pope, 171, 174
Jolles, Adam, 6
Joseph Stalin State Museum, Gori (*see also* Stalin, Joseph), 374–99
Judt, Tony, 8, 14n36, 19, 53, 152, 183, 271, 371
Junes, Tom, 10
Jürgs, Michael, 245–46, 260

Kádár, János, 49, 59
Kaganovich, Lazar, 200, 206
Kalanta, Romas, 27
Kaleda, Archpriest Kirill, 307, 308, 313, 315, 323, 324, 327, 337n90
Kalvaitis, Vladas, 24
Kaplan, Jan, 221
Karaganda, 38n1, 107, 127–28
Karaganov, Sergei, 318, 337n85
Karlag, Karlag Museum (official name: Museum of Memory of Victims of Repression in the Dolinka Settlement), 20, 106, 107–18, 123, 125, 126, 127, 129, 131n6, 132nn14–16, 133n18, 290
Karp, Ivan, 376
Kasekamp, Andres, 406
Kattago, Siobhan, 406
Katyn, 30, 159, 164, 318, 334n53, 342n139
Kazakh famine, 1932–33, 111
Kazakhstan, 11, 20, 107–30, 130n1, 251
Kaczyński, Lech, 167–68, 182
Kelam, Mari-Ann, 419, 420

Kelam, Tunne, 404, 416
Kertész, Imre, 56
KGB (*Komitet Gosudarstvennoy Bezopasnosti*), 20, 25, 28, 29, 34, 36, 96, 137–39, 140–41, 143, 149, 150, 277, 306, 307
KGB Museum Latvia (*see* Cheka House)
Khatyn', 317
Khazanov, Anatoly, 5
Khmil'ovs'kii, Father Mykola, 93–94, 96
Khodorkovsky, Mikhail, 295
Khrushchev, Nikita, 6, 63, 275, 276, 278, 292, 294, 295, 298n3, 376, 385, 388, 389
Kirschenblatt-Gimblett, Barbara, 388–89
Kistler-Ritso, Olga, Kistler-Ritso Foundation, 404, 407, 408–9, 410, 414–15
Klement Gottwald Museum, Prague, 221
Klima, Ivan, 215
Klymiv, Ivan, 90–91
Knabe, Hubertus, 249, 251, 261
Kohl, Katrin, 261
Kolar, Jiri, 233
Kolga, Marcus, 409, 412–14, 415
Kolyma, 278, 284, 286, 287
Komasa, Jan, 177, 178–80
Kommunarka burial site, 307, 308, 319, 330n16, 330n19
Kooli, Rain, 410
kopek, 3, 356–58, 361, 365, 367n30
Kovács, Ákos, 64
Kovács, Attila Ferenczfy, 56, 58, 64
Kovalevskii Forest, 316–17, 328n1, 335n75
Kowal, Paweł, 168–69
Kresty Prison, 283
Krotov, Yakov, 313
KuMu, Tallinn, 402, 410
Kyrylenko, Vyacheslav, 190
Kundera, Milan, 225
kurt (cheese), 122
Kyzymovych, Maria, 80
Kyiv, 1, 158–59, 188, 189–207
Kyivan Rus', 191

Landsberg, Alison, 128
Lanzmann, Claude, 70
Last Address Project, 276
Latsis, Martin Ivanovich, 142
Lavine, Steven, 376
Law and Justice Party, Poland, 9–10, 182

"Law of Five Ears of Wheat," the, 192
Lebedev, Artemy, 361
legitimacy, 5, 28, 37, 48–49, 55, 59, 63, 69–70, 91, 92, 219, 221, 224, 225, 234, 262, 394, 415
Lehti, Marko, 406
Lenin Museum, Moscow (*see* Central Lenin Museum)
Lenin Museum, Prague, 221
Lenin, Vladimir, 2–4, 6, 220, 236n7, 292, 350, 380, 384, 385, 388
Levada Center, Moscow, 279, 350
Levashovskoe cemetery, 324, 327n1, 328n4, 341n137
Libensky, Stanislav, 233
liberation, 20, 27, 29, 33, 36–37, 49, 51, 85, 92, 93, 96, 159, 167
libraries, 117, 118, 289, 348
Linenthal, Edward, 116
Lives of Others (2006 film), 246, 247–50, 260, 261, 263, 264n6, 265n16, 266n21
Lonsky Prison Museum (National Memorial-Museum to the Victims of Occupying Regimes), L'viv, 20, 78, 79–104, 148, 251
Lörinczova, Nikola, 232
Lowenthal, David, 407
Lubyanka Prison, 112, 277, 299
Luchenko, Kseniia, 315
Luzhkov, Yuri, 279, 309–10, 312, 330n16, 333n44
L'viv, 1, 11, 20, 78, 79–97, 251

Macdonald, Sharon, 6–7, 342n141
Magadan, 278, 309
Magistral arcade game, 353
Maglakelidze, Robert, 391–92
Magnitsky, Sergei, 295
Malysheva, Svetlana, 326
maps, 3, 33, 163, 216, 278, 281, 284, 287, 341n133, 342n138, 384, 385
Mark, James, 408
Mask of Sorrow, Magadan, 278, 309
mass graves, 191, 305, 313, 316, 319–20, 326, 328n2, 334n53, 340n123
Matrix, The (film), 360
Matrosskaia Tishina Prison, 283
McBride, Jared, 10, 13n28, 15n44, 93, 102n41
Medvedev, Dmitry, 296, 307, 316–18, 326, 336n75, 337n85

Memorial Society, 276, 278–79, 295, 307, 308, 310, 316–18, 320–21, 324–25, 331n26, 337n85, 338n105
memoirs, 11, 28, 95–96, 102n44, 122, 152, 208, 276, 281, 286–87, 289, 295
memory, 6–7, 8, 14n36, 24, 37, 49, 51, 58, 69, 72n3, 80, 82, 149, 158, 163–66, 169, 174, 181, 198, 208, 220, 228, 261, 287, 296, 345, 350, 352, 359, 371–72, 403, 407, 410–11, 416, 417–18; Holocaust and, 47–48, 49, 52, 54, 55, 59, 65, 70; *lieux de memoire* (sites of memory), 1, 58, 60, 151, 255, 305, 310, 314, 317, 327; "memory laundering," 86–93, 100n35; "pieces of memory," 255–59; politics of, 4, 9–11, 15n45, 16n51, 27, 47–48, 54–55, 58–59, 70, 103n57, 138–39, 143, 152, 167–68, 174, 177–78, 180, 182–83, 189–90, 192, 201, 204, 216, 225–28, 233–36, 245–47, 249, 250–52, 262–63, 276, 277, 306–7, 308–9, 312, 316–19, 321, 324, 337n93, 403–4, 406, 411, 414, 419; "prosthetic memory," 128; Russian (*see also* Etkind, Alexander), 12, 96–97, 272, 275–76, 278, 305–6, 316–19, 326; Stalinism and, 109–11, 118, 122, 126, 128–29, 131n6, 189, 194–95, 199, 200, 297–98, 305–6, 309, 324–25; "storehouses of memory," 5
Meri, Lennart, 419–20
Miasto 44 (*City 44*, 2014 film), 178–81
Mielke, Erich, 259–60
Milata, Zdenek, 234–35
Miłosz, Czesław, 163–66, 183
Mindlin, Mikhail, 309, 330n15
Mink, András, 63
Mitscherlich, Alexander and Margaret, 276
Moldabaev, Zhenis, 124
Molotov, Viacheslav, 200, 206, 283, 382
Monument to the Victims of Communist Crimes, L'viv, 86
Moscow, 2–5, 6, 12, 19, 29, 37, 42n40, 85, 94, 112, 122, 129, 167, 191, 192, 206, 275, 277–82, 289, 292–93, 296–97, 305, 307–9, 312–15, 318, 325, 328n5, 330n15, 333n44, 334n59, 335n65, 341n137, 346, 348, 350, 351, 353, 354, 356, 361, 378, 388
Moscow Regional Ministry of Culture, 314
Murakami, Haruki, 362–65
Museum at Bernauer Strasse, Berlin, 263
Museum in Memory of the Victims of Repression, Tashkent, 380–81

Museum of Communism, Prague, 7–8, 216, 219–42, 271
Museum of Gulag History, Moscow, 272, 275–303, 319
Museum of Memory of Victims of Repression in the Dolinka Settlement (*see* Karlag)
Museum of Modern Art, New York, 410
Museum of the Occupation of Latvia, Riga, 138
Museum of Occupations and Freedom Fights, Vilnius (former Museum of Genocide Victims), 18, 20, 23–45, 60, 112, 141, 143
Museum of Revolution, Moscow, 2, 4, 5, 6, 7, 9
Museum of the Second World War, Gdansk, 182
Museum of Soviet Arcade Games, Moscow, 272, 345–68
Museum of Soviet Occupation, Tbilisi, 375
music, 23, 24, 64, 95, 169, 181, 247, 284, 286, 289, 291, 350, 384

Nachtigall Battalion, 83, 87, 88, 101n40
Nagy, Imre, 49, 50
Nakhova, Irina, 306
Nalyvaichenko, Valentyn, 85–86
Narynov, Saken, 118, 123
National Museum Holodomor Victims Memorial, the, 189–213
NATO, 34, 49, 412
Nazarbayev, Nursultan, 110–11, 118–19, 120–21, 122, 125, 127, 128, 129, 134n34
Neizvestnyi, Ernst, 278
Nemecek, Vojtech, 232–33
new museography, 64–65
Nikžentaitis, Alvydas, 27
Nintendo, 347, 349
NKVD (People's Commissariat of Internal Affairs), 24, 25, 28, 29, 33, 36, 43n51, 80–81, 83–85, 87, 89, 91, 92, 93, 96, 112, 121, 122, 140–41, 143, 145, 148, 278, 283, 287, 328n5
Nolte, Ernst, 53
Nora, Pierre, 151
Noril'sk, 278
nostalgia (*see also* ostalgie), 12, 120, 215–16, 222, 226, 232, 235–36, 245–46, 248, 249–50, 256, 265n15, 345–46, 349–54, 356, 358, 362–64

Noviks, Alfons, 143, 154n18
Nur-Sultan, 117, 118, 136, 137
Nuremberg Trials, "missed Nuremberg" concept, 52–53, 54, 68, 69, 95

objectivity, 5, 61, 64–65, 252, 261, 263, 286, 378, 390–93, 408
Obtułowicz, Wojciech, 168
October Revolution, 4–5, 6, 319, 378, 384
Õispuu, Leo, 410, 415
Ołdakowski, Jan, 176, 177
Orbán, Viktor, 50–51, 52, 56, 58
Organization of Ukrainian Nationalists (OUN), 80, 83, 84, 87–88, 91–93, 97, 99nn12–13, 99n20
Orthodox Church (*see* Russian Orthodox Church)
Orwell, George, 10, 248, 250
Ossie, 245–46, 247, 261
ostalgie, 245–50, 252, 253, 260–61, 263, 265nn15–16, 266n21
Oushakine, Serguei, 407

Padvaiskas, Ričardas, 29
Paperno, Irina, 316
paradoxes, 38, 164, 224, 262, 377, 392, 393, 398n20
partisans, 25, 27, 29–33, 34, 36–37, 38n2
Paver, Chloe, 247
Pearce, Samara, 197
Penny III, H. Glenn, 5–6
People's Commissariat of Internal Affairs (*see* NKVD)
Perm-36, 278–79, 294–95, 319, 341n137
perpetrators, 50, 54, 61, 65, 68–69, 84, 86–87, 126, 128–29, 143, 146, 153, 191, 200, 203–7, 295, 306, 411
Peters, Iakov Khristoforovich (also Jēkabs Peterss), 142
Pētersons, Rihards, 138, 143, 146, 150
Piipuu, Merilin, 401, 402, 407–8, 410, 414, 416–17
Piłsudski, Józef, 94, 176
Pinball, 1973 (Murakami novel), 362, 363–65
Plisetskaia, Maia, 122
Plisetskaia, Rakhil', 122
Poland, 9–10, 11, 15n45, 25, 54, 94, 95, 110, 159, 163–83, 223, 224

Polish Home Army (Armia Krajowa, AK), 166, 167, 169–70, 175, 177, 178, 183–84n9
political prisoners, 20, 24, 25, 26–28, 31, 36, 37, 71n3, 277–78, 279, 292–95, 413, 418
Polonsky, Antony, 9
postcolonialism, 11, 345, 404, 407
Prague (*see* Museum of Communism, Prague)
Prague Declaration (2008), 26
Prague Spring (1968), 224
Presidential Council for the Development of Civil Society and Human Rights (Russian Federation), 306, 325
prisons, prisoners, 10, 20, 24–25, 26–31, 33–34, 35, 36, 37, 38n1, 63, 67, 79–104, 107, 113, 115, 117–18, 120, 121–24, 125, 127–28, 129, 132n16, 137–38, 144–49, 150, 153, 153n3, 178, 237n14, 246, 250–51, 252, 259, 261, 263, 278–79, 281, 282–83, 286, 289, 290–94, 320, 341n137, 380, 385, 393, 404, 406, 413, 418
propaganda, 2, 66, 74n30, 80, 88, 93, 97, 148–49, 152, 177, 219, 222, 232–33, 258, 278, 283–84, 286–87, 295, 301n37, 348, 390, 395, 396n3
psychiatric prisons, 294
Pudhys (band), 246
Putin, Vladimir, 37, 152, 276, 279, 281, 288, 295, 296, 297, 307, 310, 316, 319, 320, 325, 326, 335n72, 337n93, 341n132, 411, 413–14

Radnóti, Sándor, 58
Radzilowski, John, 174–75
Rainer, János, 51
Razgon, Lev, 308
Red Army, 19, 60–61, 158–59, 166, 191, 223–24, 271, 388, 396n3
reforging, 286, 291
rehabilitation, 121, 126, 225–26, 239n45, 287, 319, 333n44, 342n142, 385, 413
religion, 26, 28, 30, 33, 67, 83, 110, 151, 152, 223, 226, 288, 294, 305–6, 308, 310, 312, 319–20, 321, 325, 327, 328n5, 332n35, 336n75, 363, 385, 390, 394
Rényi, András, 58
representation, 28, 48, 54, 55, 59, 61, 62–65, 67, 70–71, 115–16, 198, 208, 216, 222, 235, 263, 284, 294, 375, 377, 392–93, 408

repressions, 49, 59, 92, 107–12, 118–22, 128–30, 131n6, 132n12, 144, 194, 200, 206, 220, 224, 227, 262, 275–76, 278–79, 281–84, 288–89, 292–98, 306, 308, 312, 314, 317, 319–21, 323, 325, 377–81, 385, 388–90, 392, 395
resistance, 11, 25, 27–30, 31, 33–34, 35–36, 37, 49, 66, 80, 128, 157–58, 159, 166, 167, 199, 200, 225, 246, 259, 276, 321, 325, 350, 375, 403, 407, 418, 419
retro, 229, 231–35, 345
revisionism, revisionist, 27, 47–48, 52–55, 70, 231, 259, 411
Reynolds, Simon, 345
Rieff, David, 165
Rivera-Orraca, Lorena, 406
Roginskii, Arsenii, 337n85
Romanov, Roman Vladimirovich, 289
Rose Revolution (2003), 375–78, 381, 389, 393
Rossoliński-Liebe, Grzegorz, 91
Rückel, Robert, 252, 259, 260, 263
Rudling, Per Anders, 87, 92
Russian Golgotha, 306, 310, 320
Russian Orthodox Church, 191, 305–10, 312, 315, 317, 321, 323–25, 327, 336n75, 385, 393
Russo-Georgian War (*see* August War)

Saakashvili, Mikhail, 375, 376, 381, 393, 395
Saar, Indrek, 414, 416
Sabrow Commission, 251–52, 259
Sadūnaitė, Nijolė, 37, 44n64
Safari arcade game, 353
Saint Petersburg, Russia, 139, 278, 316–17, 318–19, 324, 346, 354, 356
Sahlins, Marshall, 296
Sąjūdis, 27, 30
Sakharov, Andrei, 294, 297
Sakharov Center, 276, 295, 299n13, 309
Sats, Natal'ia, 122–23
Schlechter, Emanuel, 95
Schmidt, Mária, 52–53, 56, 61, 62, 65
Schwolow, Maik, 261
Senyk, Iryna, 90–91
Serebriakova, Galina, 122–23
Serhiychuk, Volodymyr, 207
Shalamov, Varlam, 287
Shcherbytskyi, Volodymyr, 189
Shukhevych, Roman, 83, 87, 92–93
Siberia, 28, 34–36, 145, 380, 384, 402–3, 407, 408

"singing revolution," 408
Sinyavsky, Andrei, 295
Skype, 412
"Slava Ukraini!", 91, 97
Śliwowski, Piotr, 177
Slovakia, 224, 225, 239n43
SMERSH (SMERt' SHpionam, Soviet People's Commissariat for Internal Affairs), 171
Snyder, Timothy, 82, 159, 166, 182
Sobianin, Sergei, 281
Sobolewski, Tadeusz, 180, 185n51
Soidro, Mart, 415, 418
Sokol'nikov, Grigorii, 122
Solidarity Movement (Solidarność), 167–68, 174, 176, 224
Solnask, Helle, 409–10, 411
Solovetsky Islands, 277–78, 286, 291, 310
Solovetsky Stone, 278, 279, 281, 319
Solzhenitsyn, Alexander, *Gulag Archipelago*, 113, 128, 316, 335n72
Sonnenallee (1999 film), 247, 250
sovereignty, 27, 28, 33, 36–38, 51, 60, 61, 411, 413–14
Soviet Lifestyle Museum, Kazan, 354
Soyuzattraktsion, 354
Spicker, Glenn, 220–22, 229, 233, 234–35
Spiegel, Der (German magazine), 220, 245, 247, 248, 249, 250, 259, 260
Spitzer, Leo, 227
Spreewald pickles, 247, 248, 249–50, 263
Stade, Ronald, 388
stagnation (*zastoi*), 350, 362
Stakhannov, Alexander, 361
Stalin, Joseph, Stalinism, 6, 9, 12, 80, 107, 110, 112, 113, 115, 117, 120–21, 127, 129, 142, 143, 144, 145, 146, 152, 158–59, 164, 199, 200, 203, 205, 223, 224, 272, 275–76, 277, 279, 280, 283, 287, 289, 290, 292–95, 297–98, 298n3, 305, 316, 327, 350, 351, 374–95, 396n4, 397n13, 413
Stalin Museum (*see* Joseph Stalin State Museum, Gori)
Stasi Museum, Berlin, 60, 246–47, 249, 251–52, 259–60, 261, 263
Stasi Prison Museum (*see* Berlin-Hohenschönhausen Memorial)
Stasyuk, Olesia, 197–98, 207
State History Museum, Moscow, 2, 5
State Museum of GULAG History (*see* Museum of Gulag History)

State Policy Concept of Immortalizing the Memory of the Victims of Political Repressions, 306, 319
Stola, Dariusz, 10
Stūra Māja (*see* Cheka House)
Sudetenland, 223
Sudrabs, Jānis (*see* Latsis, Martin Ivanovich)
suffering, 7, 9, 11, 19, 20–21, 23, 26–29, 34–36, 37–38, 41n25, 47–48, 51, 54, 56, 58, 60, 80, 93, 102n43, 119–20, 124, 127, 131n6, 140–44, 153, 158, 192, 204, 216, 226–27, 271, 278–79, 290, 294–95, 309, 327, 380, 381, 403, 406–8, 409, 410–13, 415–16, 418–20
Szczerba, Jacek, 180
Szymborska, Wisława, 164–65, 166, 183

Tagansky Park, Moscow, 351, 354
Tallinn, 1, 12, 400, 401–20
Tamkivi, Sten, 401–2, 408–9, 412, 415
Tankodrom arcade game, 353, 359
Tarto, Enn, 410, 413
terror, political (*see also* House of Terror Museum), 11, 20, 25–26, 27, 29, 30–31, 34, 36, 37, 56, 59–60, 62–63, 67, 110, 117, 118, 140, 142, 143, 149, 151–52, 174–75, 224, 226, 227, 228, 249, 279, 280–81, 283–84, 289, 290, 293, 295, 305, 309–10, 313, 316, 317, 318, 320–21, 325, 326–27, 363, 380, 412
testimony, testimonies (*see also* witness), 14n35, 63, 83, 144–45, 193, 202, 227–28, 287, 289, 317, 328n2, 330n14, 404
Tetris, 349
Thompson, Sylvia, 407–8, 410, 414–15, 416
Tomsk, 278
Torbakov, Igor, 10–11
Torpedo attack arcade game, 359
torture, 20, 24–25, 27–31, 33, 37, 58, 66, 80, 83, 85, 86, 88, 94–95, 107, 112–15, 127, 144–45, 150, 246, 280, 290, 314, 380, 389, 406
tourism, tourists, 21, 70, 114, 116, 144, 198–99, 216, 219–20, 232, 234, 246, 260, 271, 272, 354, 376, 391–92, 401
Trabant (Trabi), 220, 246, 250, 252–56, 257–58, 260
Trabold, Rudolph, 260
Trotsky, Lev, 6, 384, 385
truth, 24, 49, 54, 58–59, 65, 82, 87, 152, 157–58, 159, 164, 170, 178, 227–28, 234, 376–78, 385, 390–92, 393–94

Tucker, Erica, 158, 182–83
Tukhachevskaia, Zinaida, 122
Tukhachevskii, Mikhail, 122
Tumarkin, Nina, 4

Ukrainian famine, 1932–33 (*see also* Holodomor), 158–59, 189–92, 194, 196–207, 208n1, 215, 320
Ukrainian Insurgent Army (UPA), 87, 88, 91–93
Ukrainian Military Organization (UVO), 87
Ungváry, Krisztián, 61
Union of Soviet Socialist Republics (also Soviet Union, USSR), 1–2, 6, 25, 27–28, 31, 34, 66, 93, 97, 107, 128–29, 143, 158, 192, 203, 205, 223, 271, 275, 277, 278–79, 282–84, 286, 292–94, 296, 297, 348, 349, 351, 352, 354, 362, 364, 375–76, 378, 381, 385, 389, 401, 402, 412, 413, 417
United States Holocaust Memorial Museum (USHMM), 67, 115–16, 194, 196, 290

Vabamu Museum of Occupations and Freedom, Tallinn (formerly Museum of Occupations), 401–24
Valiahmetova, Rustem, 354
Vanagas, Ramanauskas, 29
Vanags, Aleksandrs, 139–40
Vavilov, Nikolai, 293
VDK (*see* KGB)
Velvet Revolution (1989), 186n57, 219, 224, 227
Verdery, Katherine, 36–37
Vergangenheitsbewältigung ("coming to terms with the past"), 245, 252, 277
Verkhovna Rada, 158
Veselov, Yevgeny, 349
Viatrovych, Volodymyr, 10, 93, 102n41
victims, victimhood, 8–10, 12, 19–20, 23, 25, 26–27, 29, 30, 36–38, 47, 51–56, 58–61, 63, 65, 67–70, 80, 82, 84–86, 87–88, 91–92, 96, 102n43, 103n54, 108–9, 110, 112, 115, 119–22, 125–27, 128–29, 135n44, 140, 142–43, 146–49, 150–52, 155n26, 158–59, 167, 182, 189, 191–208, 221, 227–28, 230–31, 235, 245, 271–72, 275–77, 278, 280, 282, 284, 289–90, 292–97, 305–6, 307, 309, 310, 312–15, 316–21, 324–27, 328n2, 328n4, 330n16, 332n40, 333n47, 341n132, 380, 403, 406–9, 411, 415–18, 419

video displays, 65, 67, 143, 283, 284, 286–87, 289, 291, 295, 375, 380, 404
video games, 346–47, 349, 356; gaming in the USSR, 348
Vilnius (*see also* Museum of Occupations and Freedom Fights), 11, 20, 22, 23, 25, 29, 141
Visak, Ivo, 415, 416
visitors, 1, 5, 12, 20–21, 27, 29–34, 37, 62–65, 66–67, 70–71, 79–80, 82, 91, 97, 110, 113, 115–16, 120, 123, 125, 127, 138, 144, 148–49, 152, 158, 166–74, 181, 183, 189–90, 191, 192, 195–99, 205, 208, 215, 220, 221, 229, 247, 251–56, 261, 277–78, 280–84, 286–88, 290–91, 293, 296, 305, 328n5, 342n142, 348, 353, 355–56, 358, 361–62, 376–77, 381–82, 389–92, 397n12, 401, 406, 417, 419
Vladimir Central Prison, 283, 299n19
von Donnersmarck, Florian Henckel, 246–47, 249–50, 251, 261, 266n21
Vozvrashchenie, 276
vyshyvanky (embroidered shirts), 197, 203

Wajda, Andrzej, 30, 169
Wałęsa, Lech, 168
Wallenberg, Raoul, 70
Wall of Grief (Moscow), 297, 325
Wannsee Conference Memorial and Education Site, 191, 205, 206
Warsaw Ghetto Uprising (1943), 167, 182
Warsaw Pact invasion (1968), 224, 227
Warsaw Uprising (2014 documentary film), 177–79, 180–81
Warsaw Uprising Museum, 157, 159, 166–83, 290

Watson, Sheila, 235
wax figures, 58, 281, 290
Weliczker, Leon, 95–96
Wende, die, 248, 250
Wessie, 245–46, 247, 261
Wharton, Annabel Jane, 79, 82, 86–87
Wiesenthal, Simon, 94, 102n44
Williams, Paul, 20, 296
Winter, Jay, 326
witness, witnesses (*see also* testimony), 37, 63, 83, 120, 144, 145, 147, 150, 152, 191, 195, 227–28, 289, 328n4, 330n14
Wolle, Stefan, 252, 259
World War I, 94, 98n4, 139, 140, 142, 340n123
World War II, 4, 8, 10, 14n36, 15n45, 27–28, 31, 33, 36, 37, 59, 61, 80, 82, 88, 97, 137, 148, 166, 174, 176, 179, 182, 183, 191, 202, 205, 206, 215, 223, 245, 271, 276, 279, 298n4, 317, 319, 321, 348, 364, 385, 388, 406
Wulf, Meike, 406, 416

Yad Vashem, 67, 290, 336n75
Yagodnoe, 278
Yanukovych, Viktor, 85, 93
Year of Horror (Latvia), 149, 152
Yeltsin, Boris, 276, 278, 309
Yushchenko, Viktor, 92–93, 190

Zabuzhko, Oksana, 8
Zamarstyniv Street Prison (L'viv), 83
Zaryts'ka, Kateryna, 90–91
Žemaitis, Jonas, 30, 33
Zhanaozen, 111, 120
Zhiguli beer, 350

Lightning Source UK Ltd.
Milton Keynes UK
UKHW012136241020
372022UK00010B/436